The SAGE
Handbook *of*
Grounded
Theory

D1284010

The SAGE Handbook *of*
Grounded Theory

Edited by
Antony Bryant
Kathy Charmaz

Los Angeles | London | New Delhi
Singapore | Washington DC

First published in hardback 2007
First published in paperback 2010

SAGE Publications Ltd
1 Oliver's Yard
55 City Road
London EC1Y 1SP

SAGE Publications India Pvt Ltd
B 1/I 1 Mohan Cooperative Industrial Area
Mathura Road, Post Bag 7
New Delhi 110 044

SAGE Publications Inc.
2455 Teller Road
Thousand Oaks
California 91320

SAGE Publications Asia-Pacific Pte Ltd
33 Pekin Street #02-01
Far East Square
Singapore 048763

Library of Congress Control Number 2007920610

British Library Cataloguing in Publication data

A catalogue record for this book is available from the British Library

ISBN 978-1-4129-2346-0
ISBN 978-1-84920-478-1(pb)

Typeset by Cepha Imaging Pvt. Ltd., Bangalore, India
Printed in Great Britain by CPI Antony Rowe, Chippenham, Wiltshire
Printed on paper from sustainable resources

*'The mind is not a vessel to be filled,
but a fire to be ignited.' – Plutarch*

*This Handbook is dedicated to Barney G. Glaser
and to the memory of Anselm L. Strauss*

Contents

Notes on Contributors

Antony Bryant is currently Professor of Informatics at Leeds Metropolitan University, Leeds, UK. As an undergraduate he studied Social & Political Sciences at Cambridge, and completed a PhD at The London School of Economics. He later completed a Masters in Computing, followed by several years working as a Systems Analyst for a commercial software developer. In 1985 he joined Leeds Polytechnic (which later became Leeds Metropolitan University) as a lecturer in the School of Mathematics & Computing; and in 1988 he became BT Reader in Software Engineering, which involved leading a research team developing mathematical verification methods for software. In 1994 he was appointed Professor of Informatics at LeedsMet.

Apart from work with BT, he has worked on government IT projects, and collaborated with major commercial companies on a variety of ventures. He has developed and taught a wide range of post-graduate courses in South Africa, Malaysia, and China. He is currently ASEM Professor at the University of Malaya, and Visiting Professor at the University of Amsterdam.

His current activities include a research project on the role of the chief information officer, and the ways in which alternative organizational models (such as that used in open-source software development) might be used in community contexts as a model for collaboration and social innovation.

His recent publications include *Thinking Informatically: A New Understanding of Information, Communication & Technology* (Edwin Mellen, 2006), and editor and co-author of a series of articles in *Theory, Culture & Society* focusing on the work of Zygmunt Bauman and Gustav Metzger: 'Liquid Arts,' TCS 2007.

He is in the process of establishing *The Centre for Social Innovation* at LeedsMet, which will involve several public sector projects and seek to find ways of encouraging collaboration between public, private, and voluntary sector organizations.

Kathy Charmaz is Professor of Sociology and Coordinator of the Faculty Writing Program at Sonoma State University. She teaches in the areas of sociological theory, social psychology, qualitative methods, health and illness, and gerontology. As Coordinator of the Faculty Writing Program, she assists faculty in writing for publication and leads three faculty seminars on professional writing. In addition to writing numerous chapters and articles, she has written or co-edited six books including *Good Days, Bad Days: The Self in Chronic Illness and Time*, which won awards from the Pacific Sociological Association and the Society for the Study of Symbolic Interaction. Her book, *Constructing Grounded Theory: A Practical Guide Through Qualitative Analysis*, was published in 2006 by SAGE. Dr. Charmaz has served as the president of the Pacific Sociological Association, Vice-President of the Society for the Study of Symbolic Interaction, editor of *Symbolic Interaction*, and chair of the Medical Sociology Section of the American Sociological Association. She received the 2006 George Herbert Mead award for lifetime achievement from the Society for the Study of Symbolic Interaction.

Adele E. Clarke did her undergraduate work at Barnard College, a master's in sociology at New York University, her PhD at UC San Francisco with Anselm Strauss, and a postdoc in organizations at Stanford with Richard Scott. She is currently Professor of Sociology and History of Health Sciences at the University of California, San Francisco. She has taught the qualitative research methods sequence of courses there since 1990, and published on qualitative research in German and English. Her work on situational analysis includes an article in *Symbolic Interaction* (2003) and her book *Situational Analysis: Grounded Theory After the Postmodern Turn* (SAGE, 2005) which won the 2006 Charles Horton Cooley Award of the Society for the Study of Symbolic Interaction. Her paper on 'Feminisms, Grounded Theory and Situational Analysis' recently appeared in *The Handbook of Feminist Research: Theory and Praxis* (SAGE, 2006).

Dr. Clarke's research has centered on studies of science, technology, and medicine with special emphasis on common medical technologies that affect most women's health such as contraception, the Pap smear, and RU486. Her major work has been on the formation of the American reproductive sciences in biology, medicine, and agriculture including *Disciplining Reproduction: American Life Scientists and the 'Problem of Sex'* (University of California Press, 1998) which won the Eileen Basker Memorial Prize given by the Society for Medical Anthropology, and the Ludwig Fleck Award of the Society for Social Studies of Science. She also co-edited a volume focused on scientific practice titled *The Right Tools for the Job: At Work in Twentieth Century Life Sciences* (Princeton University Press, 1992; Synthelabo Press in French/Paris, 1996). In women's health, Clarke has co-edited *Women's Health: Complexities and Diversities* (Ohio State University Press, 1997) and *Revisioning Women, Health and Healing: Cultural, Feminist and Technoscience Perspectives* (Routledge Press, 1999).

Clarke's current project is focused on biomedicalization—the expansion of biomedicine into increasing areas of life (human and nonhuman) through implementing technoscientific innovations. With colleagues, she has published two papers, one in *Sciences Sociales et Sante* (2000, in French) and the other in the *American Sociological Review* (2003). Their edited volume of case studies,

Biomedicalization: Technoscience and Transformations of Health and Illness in the USA, is under contract with Duke University Press. Her next project will center around global health.

Eleanor Krassen Covan, PhD, is Director of Gerontology and Professor of Gerontology and Sociology in the Department of Health and Applied Human Sciences, University of North Carolina at Wilmington. Her areas of specialization include Gerontology, Applied research and qualitative evaluation methods, Life history review, Women's health, and Impact of disaster on the elderly.

As Director of Gerontology Programs she has been responsible for extending the university agenda with regard to teaching, research, and service in gerontology, and she works to expand gerontology service-learning opportunities.

She is Editor-in-Chief for *Health Care for Women International*, the Journal of the International Council on Women's Health Issues (ICOWHI). She has been a Fellow for The North Carolina Institute on Aging, University of North Carolina, Chapel Hill; NC Fellow, Association for Gerontology in Higher Education; and Board Member for the International Congress on Women's Health Issues.

Her recent publications include 2006 'Revisiting Caresharing and the Strategy of Hiding Frailty in a Florida Retirement Community.' *Grounded Theory Review*, 5: 2/3; 2005 'Meaning of Aging in Women's Lives,' in *Journal of Women and Aging*, 17: 3/4; 'Using Service-learning to Teach Research Methods to Gerontology Students,' in *Educational Gerontology*, 27: 7: 623–627; 'Revisiting the Relationship Between Elder Modelers and Their Protégés,' *Sociological Perspectives*, 43(4): S7–S20.

She has received awards from, among others, Sloan Foundation and Ford Foundation to support the development of Professional Master's Degrees in Gerontology Implementation and Planning

John W. Creswell, PhD, is the Clifton Institute Professor and has been Professor of Educational Psychology at the University of Nebraska–Lincoln since 1978. He specializes in research methods and writes, teaches, and conducts research on mixed methods research, qualitative research, and research designs. At the University of Nebraska, he co-directs the Office of Qualitative and Mixed Methods Research, a service and research unit that provides methodological support for proposal development and funded projects. In addition, he has been Adjunct Professor of Family Medicine at the University of Michigan Health System (2001–2005) and serves as a consultant on many family medicine and Department of Veterans Affairs large-scale funded projects.

He was recently appointed as Co-editor of the new SAGE Publications journal, the *Journal of Mixed Methods Research*. He has authored 10 books, and his bestselling books *Research Design: Qualitative, Quantitative, and Mixed Methods* (SAGE, 2003) and *Qualitative Inquiry: Choosing Among Five Traditions* (SAGE, 2007) have been translated into multiple languages and are widely used internationally.

Norman K. Denzin, Distinguished Professor of Communications, Research Professor of Communications, Cinema Studies, Sociology, Criticism and Interpretive Theory at the University of Chicago at Urbana-Champaign. He received his PhD from the University of Iowa in 1966. He is the author, co-author, or co-editor of over 50 books and 200 professional articles and chapters. He is the past President of The Midwest Sociological Society, and the Society for the Study of Symbolic Interaction. He is founding President of the International Association of Qualitative Inquiry (2005–), and Director of the International Center of Qualitative Inquiry (2005–). He is past editor of *The Sociological Quarterly*, founding co-editor of *Qualitative Inquiry*, and founding editor of *Cultural Studies—Critical Methodologies*, and *Studies in Symbolic Interaction: A Research Annual*.

His recent books include: co-editor: *Handbook of Qualitative Research*, 3/e (SAGE, 2005); *Flags in the Window: Politics and Identity in Post 9/11 America* (Lang, 2007); co-editor, *Globalizing Empire, Globalizing Dissent: Cultural Studies after 9/11* (Paradigm, 2007); co-editor, *Qualitative Inquiry and the Conservative Challenge* (Left Coast Press, 2006).

Ian Dey is an Honorary Fellow in the School of Social and Political Studies at the University of Edinburgh. His research has included work on young people and employment, development issues, family policy, and fertility. He has written several books, including *Qualitative Data Analysis: A User Friendly Guide* (Routledge) and *Grounding Grounded Theory: Guidelines for Qualitative Inquiry* (Academic Press). He is currently leading a research project sponsored by the Scottish Executive/ESRC into Fertility Variations in Scotland: Attitudes and Interactions.

Bob Dick, independent scholar and consultant. In the distant past Bob Dick was in turn shop assistant, electrician, draftsperson, recruitment officer, and industrial psychologist. He then accidentally stumbled first into a university course and then into an academic appointment. For most of the past 35 years he has been a practitioner and academic. He now divides his work time between independent scholarship, occasional academic work, and consultancy work in community and organizational change.

He has an adjunct appointment at Southern Cross University, where he maintains a substantial web site of action research resources. There, he also supervises action research PhDs and conducts an on line course in action research.

In both his scholarship and his consultancy Bob uses concepts and processes from action research, action learning, and community and organization development to help people improve their work, learning, and life. As he does so, he uses action research to improve his own practice. In his consultancy work he is more a generalist than a specialist, though action learning and applications of complexity theory have been recent emphases.

Surrounded by a large collection of books—change processes and qualitative research methods are well represented—he lives in Brisbane's leafy western suburbs. He shares his home with the love of his life, Camilla, in a house frequently overrun with grandchildren. He reads widely, mostly non-fiction, but spiced with an occasional piece of science fiction.

Carrie Friese is a doctoral candidate in sociology in the Department of Social & Behavioral Sciences, University of California, San Francisco. Her research to date has focused on the development and utilization of assisted reproductive technologies in the arenas of biomedicine and conservation of endangered species. Drawing on symbolic interactionism, grounded theory, and situational analysis, she traces how somatic cell nuclear transfer (or 'cloning') has traveled to endangered species preservation practices in the USA and the meanings this has for conservation and biomedicine. Her dissertation represents a sociological approach to considering the kinds of consequences reproductive techniques such as cloning have for humans, animals, and their relations. She has also co-authored articles that explore women's experiences of aging, infertility, and assisted reproductive technologies.

Dr. Barry Gibson is a senior lecturer in Medical Sociology in the School of Clinical Dentistry at the University of Sheffield. He studied at the University of Ulster where he achieved first class Honours in Sociology in 1992. He then went on to do a Masters in Paediatric and Preventive Dentistry by research at the Queen's University of Belfast in 1993 and completed his PhD at the Queen's University of Belfast in 1997. His PhD was a grounded theory study on the subject of infection control in dentistry. After this he worked as a Post-Graduate Research Fellow in King's College Dental School for a year before being appointed to a Lecturing post in Sociology and Informatics as Applied to Dentistry at Guy's, King's and St Thomas' Dental Institute in 1999. He then moved to the University of Sheffield in 2003 where he was appointed as a Lecturer in Medical Sociology. He is interested in the origins and practice of grounded theory as it was originally proposed. As a result he is a keen supporter of developments that led to the establishment of the *Grounded Theory Review* as a place for the publication of peer reviewed forms of classical grounded theory. He frequently provides advice to a wide range of students who are conducting grounded theory studies and he is interested in contributing to future developments of the method. To this end his substantive research interests include opening up the social systems theory of Niklas Luhmann. This work has culminated in an empirical study on changes in the meaning of oral health related quality of life that combined the theory of social systems with the grounded theory method. The connections between these two very disparate approaches have been thematized in further work looking at the connection between systems theory and grounded theory. Dr. Gibson has also published on identity, drug use, and oral health along with numerous papers on applied social science in the oral health related research context. At the University of Sheffield he has been instrumental in urging the establishment of the Childhood and Youth Oral health group where a number of PhD students are currently working on applications of the new sociology of childhood to applied oral health related research.

Barney G. Glaser received his BA degree at Stanford University in 1952. He studied contemporary literature for a year at the Sorbonne, University of Paris, and spent 2 years in the US Army, one of which was in Freiburg, Germany. Here, he became fluent in German and also studied literature at the University of Freiburg during off hours.

Dr. Glaser received his PhD from Columbia University in 1961, following which he joined Anselm Strauss at the University of California, San Francisco. He and Strauss collaborated in doing the dying in hospitals study and in teaching methods and analysis to PhD and DNS students.

Glaser's dissertation was published as a book, *Organizational Scientists: Their Professional Careers* (Bobbs-Merrill, 1964). In 1968, he published *Organizational Careers: A Sourcebook for Theory* (Aldine, 1968). His work with Anselm Strauss resulted in the 1965 publication of *Awareness of Dying* (Aldine) and was immediately a resounding success. Based on the tremendous interest in the study of the dying, Glaser and Strauss were asked to write *The Discovery of Grounded Theory* (1967) to show how the research had been done. This was another big success and as the seminal guide to grounded theory methodology is still in demand 40 years later. Glaser and Strauss followed the publication of *Discovery* with two more books on dying: *Time for Dying* (1968) and *Anguish* (1970) followed by *Status Passage* (1971) and *Chronic Illness and the Quality of Life* (1975).

For the past 30 years, Dr. Glaser has written extensively on classic grounded theory producing a further 13 books. His works are read throughout the world. Most are now published by Sociology Press (www.sociologypress.com). In addition to his books, Glaser has written countless articles and has become the source of guidance and inspiration for a global network of researchers seeking to study the methodology and undertake classic grounded theory research. To respond to the need and demand for methodological guidance, Glaser continues to offer annual grounded theory troubleshooting seminars that attract both novice and experienced researchers from around the world.

In recognition of his contribution to the research community, Dr. Glaser received an honorary doctorate from Stockholm University, Sweden in 1998.

Denise O'Neil Green received her PhD in public policy and postsecondary education from the University of Michigan, Ann Arbor. She received her Bachelor of Arts in behavioral sciences from the University of Chicago in 1985 and her Master's of Public Affairs in domestic policy from the Woodrow Wilson School of Public and International Affairs at Princeton University in 1987. She is currently an Assistant Professor in the Educational Psychology Department at the University of Nebraska–Lincoln and Senior Research Associate of the Office of Qualitative and Mixed Methods Research.

As a qualitative methodologist, Green's research expertise focuses on the development and implementation of qualitative research designs that aid social science and education researchers, policymakers, and administrators in understanding the complexities associated with diversity issues and diverse populations in the public policy, higher education, and K-12 education arenas. In particular, her research examines methods, practices, and strategies employed in qualitative studies that explore phenomena associated with racially and ethnically diverse populations. She teaches introductory and advanced qualitative courses, including diversity and qualitative methods, grounded theory, and qualitative approaches in education, which aid students from an array of disciplines, such as nursing, educational administration, counseling psychology, higher education, and family science.

To date, Green's publications have focused on diversity, affirmative action policy, and institutional engagement. Using a variety of qualitative approaches, her research examines salient dimensions that are important to higher education's successful engagement in the policy arena, as educational leaders promote the importance of diversity, educational excellence, and inclusive campus climates. Her research has been published in *Educational Policy*, *Urban Education*, *National Association of Student Affairs Professional Journal*, *Higher Education for the Public Good: Emerging Voices from a National Movement*, *New Directions for Community Colleges: Academic Pathways to and from the Community College*, and the *Journal of College Student Development*. Green has presented papers at national conferences, including the American Educational Research Association, the International Congress of Qualitative Inquiry, the Association for the Study of Higher Education, and the Association for Institutional Research. Green also offers workshops on diversity and qualitative methods.

Sharlene Nagy Hesse-Biber is Professor of Sociology at Boston College. She is co-founder and director of the Women's Studies Program at Boston College.

She is co-editor of: *Feminist Research Practice: A Primer* (SAGE, 2007); *Emergent Methods in Social Research* (SAGE, 2006); *Feminist Perspectives on Social Research* (Oxford, 2004); *Approaches to Qualitative Research* (Oxford, 2004); *Women in Catholic Higher Education: Border Work, Living Experiences and Social Justice* (Lexington, 2003); and *Feminist Approaches to Theory and Methodology* (Oxford, 1999).

She is coauthor of *The Practice of Qualitative Research* (SAGE, 2006); *Working Women in America: Split Dreams* (Oxford, 2005).

She is editor of *The Handbook of Feminist Research* (SAGE, 2007).

She is the author of *Am I Thin Enough Yet?* (1996) and *The Cult of Thinness*, 2nd Ed. (Oxford, 2007). Her forthcoming books with Guilford Publications are: *The Handbook of Emergent Methods* (co-edited) and *Mixed Methods for Qualitative Researchers*. Both books will be published in 2008.

She has written numerous articles in the fields of body image, qualitative methods, and computer approaches to qualitative data analysis. She is co-developer of HyperRESEARCH (for MAC/WINDOWS) (www.researchware.com), a computer software program for qualitative data analysis, and Hyper-Transcribe (MAC/WINDOWS), a stand-alone transcription software tool for transcribing digitized audio and video files.

Bruno Hildenbrand, Dr. rer. soc., studied sociology, psychology and political sciences at Constance University, Germany, where he learned qualitative research methods from Aaron V. Cicourel and Anselm L. Strauss who both were advisors in a research project led by Thomas Luckmann and Richard Grathoff. He is a Professor of Sociology at the Institute of Sociology, Friedrich Schiller University, Jena, Germany. Former appointments include the Universities of Constance, Marburg, and Frankfurt. His professional interests include socialization theory, professionalization theory, psychiatric sociology, rural sociology, qualitative research methods, especially case reconstructing research, and family therapy. He was an editor of the journal *System Familie* and is an advisory editor of the journals *Family Process, Sozialer Sinn, and Psychotherapie und Sozialwissenschaft*. His books include *Alltag und Krankheit—Ethnographie einer Familie* (Everyday Life and Illness—Ethnography of a Family), *Alltag als Therapie* (Everyday Life as Therapy), *Systemische Therapie als Begegnung* (Systemic Therapy as Encounter), Spanish edition: La terapia sistémica como encuentro (co-authored by Rosmarie Welter-Enderlin), *Landwirtschaftliche Familien in der Krise* (Farm Families in Crisis) (co-authored by Karl Friedrich Bohler), *Die Stadt der Zukunft—Leben im prekären Wohnquartier* (The City of the Future—Living in Precarious Neighbourhoods) (co-authored by Christa Berger and Irene Somm), *Fallrekonstruktive Familienforschung* (Case Reconstructing Family Research), *Einführung in die Genogrammarbeit* (Introduction to Genogram Work). Together with Charles B. Hennon he is editor of the special issue 'Farm Family Responses to Changing Agricultural Conditions: The Actor's Point of View' of the *Journal of Comparative Family Studies*, Vol. XXXVI, No. 3, 2005. His current research deals with the transformation of child welfare systems in East and West Germany (German Research Council's Special Research Area 580 at the Universities of Halle and Jena, Germany) as well as with biographies of young adults who grew up in a foster family, and he works on the issue of reintegration into the labor market of drug addicts by improving information and communication technologies.

Judith A. Holton is Editor-in-Chief of *The Grounded Theory Review*, an international peer-reviewed journal published by Sociology Press. She has collaborated with Dr. Barney Glaser in a number of seminars and publications including co-editing, with Dr. Glaser, *The Grounded Theory Seminar Reader* (Sociology Press, 2007). She holds a Master of Arts in Leadership and Training (Royal Roads University, Canada) and a PhD in Management Studies (University of Northampton, UK). Her research interests include the role of the informal organization in the knowledge workplace, grounded theory research methodology, team performance, and learning and innovation in organizations. In addition to her work as an organizational consultant, Dr. Holton is currently Chair, Research and Innovation, at Holland College, Charlottetown, PE, Canada.

Jane C. Hood received her PhD in sociology from the University of Michigan in 1983 and is currently an Associate Professor of Sociology at the University of New Mexico where she has taught since 1985. In addition to courses on gender and family, she teaches both undergraduate methods and a graduate seminar on qualitative data analysis. Publications include *Becoming a Two-Job Family* (Praeger, 1983) and *Men, Work, and Family* (1993). Over the past decade, Professor Hood has hosted several workshops on grounded theory and sampling in qualitative research. Her most recent article on this topic is 'Teaching Against the Text: The Case of Qualitative Methods' (*Teaching Sociology*, July 2006).

Margaret H. Kearney, PhD, RN, FAAN, is the Independence Foundation Professor and PhD Programs Director at the University of Rochester School of Nursing, in Rochester, NY, USA. A graduate of the PhD program in Nursing at the University of California, San Francisco, she studied with Anselm Strauss and Adele Clarke, originators and innovators of the grounded theory approach to qualitative inquiry, and with Patricia Benner, central proponent of hermeneutic phenomenology as a method for nursing research. This early exposure helped her appreciate distinctions and similarities in epistemology and resulting technique across qualitative traditions. Kearney's own work began with grounded theory studies of pregnant and parenting cocaine users and has since included a series of qualitative studies of women's efforts to change their health behaviors within complex social contexts, ranging from illicit drug use and violent relationships to weight management after childbirth and dietary change in later life. Maggie's current interest is approaches to qualitative analysis and synthesis. She has focused on the grounded theory tradition and contributed to clinical applications of grounded formal theory. Example articles include 'Ready to wear: Discovering grounded formal theory' (1998) and 'Levels and applications of qualitative research evidence' (2001). With an undergraduate degree in nursing from Columbia University and a graduate degree in women's health nursing from Boston College, Dr. Kearney has a strong clinical background in maternal-child nursing and women's health and is Associate Editor of the *Journal of Obstetric, Gynecologic, and Neonatal Nursing.* Author of over 40 articles, 2 books (*Understanding Women's Recovery from Illness and Trauma*, SAGE, 1999, and *Perinatal Impact of Alcohol, Tobacco, and other Substance Use*, March of

Dimes, 1999, 2nd edition forthcoming), and 4 book chapters, she is an active consultant in qualitative methods at universities and on research grants across the US. She is committed to teaching qualitative methods and is sought out for courses and lectures in a variety of venues.

Prof. Dr. Udo Kelle holds a chair for Social Research Methods at the Philipps-University of Marburg.

Udo Kelle, Dr. Phil, is a Professor for Social Research Methods at the Philipps, University of Marburg. He received his training in psychology (Diplom-Psychologe) at the University of Bremen and in sociology (PhD) at the Graduiertenkolleg der DFG (Graduate School of the German National Science Foundation) at the University of Bremen. Before becoming Professor in Marburg he was a researcher at the Special Collaborative Centre 186 of the German National Science Foundation in Bremen and as a Lecturer in Social Research Methods at the University of Vechta.

He was a Visiting Fellow at the University of Surrey, at Syracuse University in New York, at the Institute for Advanced Studies in Vienna and at the University of Minnesota. His research interests cover the fields of the methodology of social sciences, especially qualitative methods and their epistemological underpinnings and the integration of qualitative and quantitative methods, the sociology of the life cycle, and the sociology of ageing. He has written and edited seven books and 54 articles mainly in the field of social research methodology:

Kelle, Udo; Kluge, Susann (2007) *Vom Einzelfall zum Typus. Fallvergleich und Fallkontrastierung in der qualitativen Sozialforschung*. Wiesbaden: Verlag für Sozialwissenschaften (2nd edition, first edition 1999).

Kelle, Udo (2006) Combining Qualitative and Quantitative Methods in Research Practice—Purposes and Advantages. In Gürtler, Leo; Huber, Günter L. (Eds.). Special Guest Issue on Mixed Methods. *Qualitative Research in Psychology*, Vol. 3(4), pp. 293–311.

Kelle, Udo (Ed.) (1995) *Computer-aided Qualitative Data Analysis. Theories, Methods and Practice*. London: SAGE.

Lora Bex Lempert, PhD, MS, is a Professor in Sociology and the former Director of Women's Studies at the University of Michigan, Dearborn. She is also an Affiliated Research Scientist at the Institute for Research on Women and Gender at University of Michigan, Ann Arbor. She received her doctoral degree from the University of California, San Francisco. In 2002 and again in 2005 Dr. Lempert was a Fulbright Scholar posted to the Women's and Gender Studies Programme at the University of the Western Cape in Cape Town, South Africa. The central focus of her research and teaching interests in the USA involves the intersections of race, class, and gender as they affect interpersonal violence within families. She is the co-sponsor of the National Lifers of America Chapter 1014 at a local women's correctional facility. She is the lead instructor on a series of college level courses offered at the facility.

Her publications include: Cross Race, Cross Culture, Cross National, Cross Class, But Same Gender: Musings on Research in South Africa. *NWSA Journal.* August 2007. With Synnov Skorge; Silent No More, We're Hanging Out Our Dirty Laundry: The South Africa Clothesline Project. *Women in Action* 3 (2002).

Karen Locke, PhD, is W. Brooks George Professor of Business Administration at the College of William and Mary's school of business. She joined the faculty there in 1989 after earning her PhD in organizational behavior from Case Western Reserve University. Dr. Locke's work focuses on developing a sociology of knowledge in organizational studies and on the use of qualitative research for the investigation of organizational phenomena. She has authored *Grounded Theory In Management Research* and co-authored *Composing Qualitative Research* (now in its second edition): both published by SAGE. She has also authored numerous articles that appear in the discipline of management and organization studies. Her current work continues her interest in the processes of qualitative researching and focuses on exploring and explicating their creative and imaginative dimensions. Dr. Locke also serves as an associate action editor for *Organizational Research Methods* and is a member of the editorial board for *Academy of Management Journal.*

Günter Mey, PhD, is the Managing Director of the Berlin Institute for Qualitative Research. He organizes 'The Annual Berlin Meeting on Qualitative Research' and related events. Together with Katja Mruck, he conducts workshops for different institutions/research centers on interviewing, grounded theory methodology, etc.

He is by training a psychologist and was for a number of years assistant professor for Developmental Science/Psychology at the Technische Universität Berlin, where he conducted research on identity, cultural, psychology, and childhood.

He is the editor of *Forum Qualitative Sozialforschung/Forum: Qualitative Social Research (FQS)* and involved in other qualitative journals. His publications include many articles on open access publishing and on qualitative methods (f.c. on 'Qualitative Research in Germany,' with Katja Mruck, published in International Sociology, 2007) and various books, among them 'Children, Cities, and Psychological Theories: Developing Relationships' (with Dietmar Görlitz, Hans Joachim Harloff, and Jaan Valsiner, 1998), the first German handbook on qualitative methods in developmental psychology (2005), and the 'Grounded Theory Reader' (2007, together with Katja Mruck).

For further information see: http://www.institut.qualitative-forschung.de or the personal website: http://www.mey.qualitative-forschung.de.

Janice M. Morse is a professor and the Barnes Presidential Endowed Chair at the College of Nursing, University of Utah. She was previously a professor, Faculty and Nursing, and the Founder, Director, and Scientific Director of the

International Institute for Qualitative Methodology at the University of Alberta, Canada, and professor, at The Pennsylvania State University. With doctorates in both nursing and anthropology, she conducts research funded by NIH and CIHR, into suffering and comforting, as well as developing qualitative research methods. She is editor of the journal *Qualitative Health Research* (SAGE), an interdisciplinary journal published 10 times per year addressing qualitative methods and health. She is the recipient of many awards, including the Episteme Award (Sigma Theta Tau), and of more than 300 articles and 14 books on qualitative inquiry.

Katja Mruck, PhD, is the director of the Berlin Institute for Qualitative Research and the main editor of the online journal Forum Qualitative Sozialforschung/ Forum: Qualitative Social Research (FQS). She has conducted research on youth unemployment and public health and was a research associate for qualitative methods and evaluation at the Freie Universität Berlin for many years. Currently, she is involved in various projects on qualitative research and open access publishing, funded by the Deutsche Forschungsgemeinschaft. Among her publications are two FQS issues on 'Subjectivity and Replexivity in Qualitative Research' (co-edited with Franz Breuer and Wolff-Michael Roth) and a 'Grounded Theory Reader' (co-edited with Günter Mey).

For further information see: http://www.qualitative-research.net/fqs/ or http://www.institut.qualitative-forschung.de

Virginia Olesen, Professor of Sociology (Emerita), Department of Social and Behavioral Sciences, School of Nursing, University of California, San Francisco, has published major reviews of feminist qualitative research and continues to explore such vexing issues as skepticism, reflexivity, and researcher-participant co-creation of data. With Ellen Lewin, Sheryl Ruzek, and Adele Clarke, she pioneered feminist social science studies of women's health, leading to co-edited volumes, *Women, Health and Healing* (Lewin and Olesen); *Women's Health, Complexities and Differences* (Ruzek, Olesen, Clarke); *Revisioning Women, Health and Healing, Feminist, Cultural and Technoscience Perspectives* (Clarke and Olesen). She is keenly interested in the analysis of emotions in rationalizing health care systems and the implications thereof for humane work settings and care of the ill. Her most recent collaborative work has been as a team member in an interdisciplinary group (nurses, anthropologists, sociologists, physicians, social workers) examining issues around the health of women prisoners.

Vicki L. Plano Clark (PhD, University of Nebraska–Lincoln) is Co-Director of the Office of Qualitative and Mixed Methods Research, a service and research unit that provides methodological support for proposal development and funded projects at the University of Nebraska–Lincoln. She is also a Research Assistant Professor in the Quantitative, Qualitative, and Psychometric Methods program housed in the University of Nebraska–Lincoln's Department of Educational Psychology.

She teaches research methods courses, including foundations of educational research and mixed methods research, and serves as managing editor for the *Journal of Mixed Methods Research*. She specializes in mixed methods research designs and qualitative research and her research interests include the procedural issues that arise when implementing different designs as well as disciplinary contexts for conducting research. She has studied how mixed methods research is applied and accepted within different disciplines. She has authored and co-authored over 25 articles, chapters, and student manuals, including the book *Designing and Conducting Mixed Methods Research* (SAGE, 2007, with John W. Creswell) and a *Student Study Guide to Accompany Creswell's Educational Research* (Pearson Education, 2002, 2005). Her writings include numerous methodological discussions about as well as empirical studies using qualitative and mixed methods approaches in the areas of science education, family research, counseling psychology, and family medicine. She served as Laboratory Manager in the University of Nebraska–Lincoln Department of Physics and Astronomy (1993–2005), working with the Research in Physics Education Group, and has been a principal investigator on three National Science Foundation projects.

Jo Reichertz, currently Professor of Communication Science, University of Essen.

He studied Mathematics, Sociology and Communication Science at the Universities of Bonn, Essen and Hagen. He gained his doctorate in 1986, and his postdoctoral lecturing qualification (*Habilitation*) in 1991; both from the University of Hagen. Since 1992 he has been a Professor at the University of Essen. His research interests include sociology of knowledge, sociology of culture, sociology of religion, sociology of communication, sociology of law, Police Work, Qualitative Research, Hermeneutics.

His publications cover topics in the areas of the methodology of social scientific hermeneutics, manifestations of religiosity in the modern era, logic of police work (murder investigations), social forms of self-representation, sociology of the media, logic of research, pragmatism, abduction.

Recent books include: Reichertz, Jo (2000): *Die Frohe Botschaft des Fernsehens. Kultursoziologische Untersuchung medialer Diesseitsreligion.* Konstanz: Universitäts Verlag Konstanz; Reichertz, Jo & Nathalie Ivanyi (2002). *Liebe (wie) im Fernsehen. Eine wissenssoziologische Studie.* Opladen; Reichertz, Jo (2003). *Die Bedeutung der Abduktion in der Sozialforschung.* Opladen; Reichertz, Jo (2007). *Verstehen ist nicht das Problem.* VS Verlag: Wiesbaden.

Ronald J. Shope is Research Associate Professor at the University of Nebraska, Lincoln. He teaches distance classes in research methods including foundations of educational research, qualitative research and survey research and mixed methods research. In addition he is a research associate in the Office of Qualitative and Mixed Methods Research at the University of Nebraska, Lincoln and is the qualitative consultant in the Nebraska Evaluation and Research Center (NEAR). He also is Professor of Communication and Research and is the Director of Assessment and Institutional Research at Grace University in Omaha. In addition he is a research associate in the Office of Qualitative and Mixed Methods Research at the University of Nebraska, Lincoln. He holds a PhD in Speech Communication from the Pennsylvania State University (1995). Dr. Shope specializes in Grounded Theory and Case Study designs and has worked on mixed methods research projects. In addition, Dr. Shope has co-authored conference papers dealing with technology in teacher education and mixed methods research in mass communication. He has also authored instructor materials for several textbooks and has conducted workshops with John Creswell on qualitative and mixed methods research in the USA, Canada and Australia

Susan Leigh Star ('Leigh') is Senior Scholar at the Center for Science, Technology and Society, Santa Clara University. She is President of the Society for the Social Study of Science (4S), 2005–2007. She was formerly Professor of Communication at the University of California, San Diego. She has been writing in the fields of science studies, information science, and feminist theory for many years. Her contributions include *Sorting Things Out: Classification and Its Consequences* (MIT, 1999, co-authored with Geoffrey Bowker) and volume editor for science and technology, *Womens Studies International Encyclopedia* (Routledge, 2001). She is currently writing a monograph for MIT Press entitled *Boundary Objects and the Poetics of Infrastructure*. This book joins her experiences in information and computer science with observations and theory as a sociologist/anthropologist. She uses qualitative social science to analyze the social and moral orders inscribed into infrastructures of all sorts. With Martha Lampland, she is co-editing a volume of essays on standardization and its human faces. She holds degrees from Harvard University (BA) and from the University of California, San Francisco (PhD). At UCSF, as a graduate student, she studied with both Anselm Strauss and Barney Glaser. Her future research interests concern the material culture of psychiatry and psychiatric research, and the relationship between human suffering and both low and high technologies in that venue.

Phyllis Noerager Stern, DNS, LLD (hon), RN, FAAN, Professor and Glenn W. Irwin Research Scholar at Indiana University Purdue University at Indianapolis, Indiana studied with Barney G. Glaser and Anselm Strauss while pursuing her doctoral degree at the University of California, San Francisco in the 1970s. Over the ensuing decades, she has been engaged in doing grounded theory, and publishing both research and methodological articles and book chapters. In 1994, she coined the terms *Straussian* and *Glaserian* to label the two schools of grounded theory analysis. Phyllis is known for her mentoring ability; as editor of the scientific journal, *Health Care for Women International* from 1984–2001, she launched numerous first-time authors. In 1984, she organized the *International Council on Women's Health Issues* in Nova Scotia, Canada, and held the position of Council General until 2002. This organization through its biannual congresses enhanced the social and political position of women in Egypt, Botswana, New Zealand, Korea, Australia, and Thailand. Phyllis has held faculty positions at California State University Hayward, University of California, San Francisco, Northwestern State University at Shreveport, Louisiana, and Dalhousie University, Halifax, Nova Scotia.

Jörg Strübing currently teaches sociology at the University of Tübingen, Germany. In 1984 he received his diploma in social assistance, in 1987 his MA in Sociology with the University of Kassel (Germany). Between 1988 and 1993, he worked as a research fellow at the Center for Higher Education Research and as a lecturer at the faculty of sociology at the University of Kassel where in 1992 he received his sociological doctorate. He then worked as an assistant professor for empirical social research at both the Free University and the University of Technology of Berlin. In 1998, he was a visiting scholar at the University of Illinois at Urbana-Champaign. His habilitation in 2003 with the Free University of Berlin was followed by an appointment as a guest professor for international comparative sociology with the University of Göttingen, Germany. In 2004 he went from Berlin and Göttingen to the University of Tübingen where in 2007 he was appointed an adjunct professorship in sociology.

Among his latest books is an introduction to the life, work and theoretical achievements of Anselm Strauss (2006), a book on the methodological and science theoretical background of Grounded Theory (2004), a monograph on the pragmatist approach to the study of science and technology (2005), and an edited volume on classical texts on the methodology of interpretative social research (2004; together with Bernt Schnettler).

Professor Strübing is a board member of the section for Methods of qualitative social research within the Deutsche Gesellschaft für Soziologie (DFG) and Chair of the German Gesellschaft für Wissenschafts- und Technikforschung (GWTF e.V.). He divides his research interests between qualitative methods and methodology, interactionist social theory, and the study of science and technology issues.

Iddo Tavory is a graduate student in the department of Sociology at UCLA. He completed his Master's in Tel Aviv University Israel. Based on his Master's research he has edited and contributed to a book on the Sociology of New Age Communities in Israel, *Dancing in a Thorn-Field: The New Age in Israel* (2007). Currently, he is involved in ethnographic fieldwork in a Jewish Ultra-Orthodox community in Los Angeles.

Stefan Timmermans, PhD (University of Illinois, 1995) is professor of sociology at UCLA. He is author of *Sudden Death and the Myth of CPR* (Temple, 1999) and *Postmortem: How Medical Examiners Explain Suspicious Deaths* (Chicago, 2006, winner 2006 Freidson Award). He is co-author with Marc Berg of *The Gold Standard: The Challenge of Evidence Based Medicine and Standardization in Health Care* (Temple, 2003, winner 2005 Merton Award). His research interests include science studies, medical technologies, death and dying, and ethnography.

Cathy Urquhart is a senior lecturer in Information Systems at the Department of Information Systems and Operations Management at the University of the Auckland, New Zealand. Before coming to New Zealand in 2001, she worked at the Universities of Tasmania, Melbourne, and the Sunshine Coast in Australia. She was named as one of Australia's outstanding teachers of computing in the Australian *Campus Review* in November 1996. She has a strong interest in qualitative data analysis, especially the use of grounded theory in information systems, publishing on this subject in *Qualitative Research in IS: Issues and Trends* (edited by Eileen Trauth). She is an Associate Editor for *MIS Quarterly*, the primary information systems journal. She is on the editorial board of the *International Journal for Learning and Change*. She won the award for *Outstanding Paper* for *Information Technology and People* in 2000. She has a PhD in Information Systems from the University of Tasmania. Her other major research interest is the impact of IT on developing countries and the link between IT and poverty reduction.

Carolyn Wiener is Adjunct Professor in the Department of Social and Behavioral Sciences at the University of California, San Francisco (UCSF). She is a graduate of the Department of Social and Behavioral Sciences at UCSF, where she received her doctorate in sociology in 1978, having learned grounded theory, under the tutelage of the method founders, Anselm Strauss and Barney Glaser. Her research focuses on chronic illness, organization in health care institutions, the evolving medical technology scene, and health policy. As a student, she worked with Anselm Strauss and colleagues on the first qualitative study conducted in the USA on the care and management of pain and discomforts of hospitalized patients.

   After completing her PhD, she accepted the position of assistant research sociologist at UCSF, where she commenced work on a 4-year project with Strauss and colleagues, Shizuko Fagerhaugh and Barbara Suczek, on a study of the care of patients on medical machinery and the sociological and organizational aspects of technologized treatment. This study yielded two books and ten papers. She has collaborated with other UCSF School of Nursing faculty on research projects: on the treatment of acute illness in nursing homes (with Jeanie Kayser-Jones); on sleep-activity disruption in Alzheimer's (with Glenna Dowling); and on coping and self-care of cancer families (with Marylin Dodd), resulting in numerous co-authored articles.

Most recently, Dr. Wiener completed a study examining quality management and redesign efforts in hospitals and the interplay among agencies and hospitals around the issue of accountability. The book that stems from this study, *The Elusive Quest*, challenges the appropriateness of applying management techniques inherited from industry to hospitals, the feasibility of standardizing care through practice guidelines, and the concept that hospital performance should be quantitatively measured. The book has led to numerous speaking engagements, notably a keynote lecture, entitled 'Holding American Hospitals Accountable,' at the University of Nottingham international lecture series on Critiquing Health Improvement.

Dr. Wiener has taught Qualitative Field Research to nursing and sociology doctoral students at UCSF and conducts an annual seminar on grounded theory at the University of San Francisco for doctoral students in the Department of Education. Throughout her career, she has served as a grounded theory consultant to researchers and students, both national and international, from a variety of specialties.

Senior Editor's Preface

My early involvement with Grounded Theory came about as a result of my membership in our university research committee, specifically when assessing proposals from students embarking on their PhDs. A number of proposals were presented where the methods section described a research approach that appeared to circumvent the usual requirements. It seemed as if students were embarking upon their research without a clear research aim or plan of action, and that this could be justified by invoking the precepts of grounded theory. In many cases, my colleagues and I concluded that this was simply a device for students to bypass the usual process of scrutiny; the proposal was turned down, with a request for the methodological issues to be dealt with more clearly and adequately.

Although I had spent part of my time as an undergraduate studying social sciences, and had completed a PhD in sociology, by this time (mid-1990s) I was teaching and researching in the areas of Computing and Information Systems (IS), focusing largely on IS development methods and ways in which such systems might be modelled mathematically. In the ensuing years, my own research and teaching reverted to my earlier interests in the social sciences, and I found that within the area of academic IS these issues were taking on far more importance, supplementing and challenging the more technically oriented perspectives.[1]

Thus I found that some of the research students in my own area were now proposing to develop PhDs using the methods of the social sciences—including the grounded theory method (GTM). My scepticism with regard to GTM might well have continued had not one student persisted with his proposal, despite my concerns. He showed me how the method had been used within IS itself, argued for its value, and also demonstrated how many of those claiming to use the method either failed to grasp its full implications or relied on a highly selective misreading of the key texts.[2]

Prompted to learn more about GTM, I read the 'primary' sources of Glaser & Strauss, Glaser's later works, and those of Strauss and Corbin; also some 'secondary' sources which either claimed to adopt the method or where the method was discussed in more general terms. Seeing that GTM was becoming part of the methodological armoury of IS research, in 2001 I prepared a paper on GTM in general and on its use in IS in particular (Bryant, 2002a). In that paper I argued that GTM was clearly a valuable and important methodological advance, but that many of its precepts and early statements were in need of extrication from what we would now understand to be an outdated epistemological stance, redolent of positivism and naïve empiricism. Soon after submitting the paper, I happened upon the work of Kathy Charmaz, in particular her contribution to the second edition of *Handbook of Qualitative Research* (Charmaz, 2000) in which she proposed a distinction between *objectivist* and *constructivist* GTM. Here was a similar argument to my own, albeit hers was far more informed and nuanced.

I contacted Kathy, and sent her a copy of my paper; she was kind enough to send me an encouraging reply and point to other sources in a similar or related vein. A short time later I came across Glaser's response to Charmaz's chapter and, after discussing it with Kathy, submitted my own reply to Glaser (Bryant, 2003). In the meantime I had also republished my original paper (Bryant, 2002b), which had led to an exchange with Cathy Urquhart, a researcher with a track record of using GTM in the field of IS.

By 2004 I had established a group of young researchers, all doing PhDs, some of whom were using GTM in a variety of areas and countries. Kathy Charmaz was completing work on what was eventually published as *Constructing Grounded Theory* (2006); surely destined to become a standard introduction to the method. We discussed the idea of a collection of papers extending and elaborating upon the constructivist trend within GTM, and approached SAGE with a proposal. The editor, Patrick Brindle, not only welcomed the idea but also suggested we think about something on a far larger and wider scale. SAGE already published handbooks on many methods, but there was no handbook for GTM; surely an oversight that required some remedy.

Our proposal was received with enthusiasm by the reviewers to whom it was sent for comment; indeed several requested that they drop their anonymity and be invited to contribute. The aim was always to publish the Handbook in 2007; 40 years since the publication of *The Discovery of Grounded Theory*. The list of potential contributors was largely prepared on the basis of names suggested by Kathy and, largely because the requests came from her, we achieved a positive response from almost all of those approached.

In the meantime, I made direct contact with Barney Glaser, finally meeting him at a conference in Stockholm in 2005, and again at his London GT Seminar in early 2006. Although I am sure that there are several chapters in this Handbook with which Barney will not agree, he has offered encouragement throughout. In preparing the Editors' 'Introduction,' I followed one of Glaser's basic precepts and treated the chapters 'all as data.' As a consequence, I treated my reading as a coding exercise, on the basis of which I was able to produce an outline for our Introduction.

One of the questions often posed by students is: 'Does applying GTM necessarily result in a Grounded Theory?' They rarely ask the more profound question: 'Can one produce a Grounded Theory without using GTM?' During the period in which I was preparing the Handbook (late 2006) I attended a tribute to Enid Mumford, a pioneer researcher who applied the socio-technical framework developed at The Tavistock Institute to contexts in which people were coping with the introduction of new technology, particularly computer-based technology.

Mumford's work (e.g. 1981, 1996) was based on meticulous fieldwork in locations as varied as coalmines, docks, offices, and hospitals. It was undertaken as a form of Action Research but, in terms of the outcome, the theoretical results can be seen to be clearly grounded. Thus just as there are many researchers claiming to do GTM, so there are others who are doing GTM without realizing it. This Handbook is aimed at both groups, as well as those who wish to learn more about the method 40 years on.

While preparing this Handbook, Barney Glaser emailed me to ask what 'main concerns are you trying to resolve with the forthcoming handbook?' to which I replied 'I see the handbook as a resource for researchers—both relatively new and experienced—who are keen to find out more about GTM. From my experience many researchers have only a vague idea about GTM: and usually a largely inaccurate idea at that. The chapters in the handbook will offer some indication of the principles behind the method, and that is why I think your statement about FGT will be critical; and it will lead people to investigate the issue further by reading your book on FGT.' This in turn evoked Barney's rejoinder: 'Your vision of the handbook is *right on.*'

NOTES

1 These ideas and these developments are discussed in my recent book *Thinking Informatically* (2006).
2 These ideas were further developed in a joint paper with the student in question, Kobus Smit; see Smit & Bryant, 2000.

REFERENCES

Bryant, A. 2002a. Reply to Urquhart's Response to Bryant, 2002. *The Journal of Information Technology Theory and Application*, vol. 4, no. 3, pp. 55–57.
Bryant, A. 2002b. Re-grounding Grounded Theory. *The Journal of Information Technology Theory and Application*, vol. 4, no. 1, pp. 25–42.
Bryant, A. 2003. Doing Grounded Theory Constructively. A Reply to Barney Glaser. In *Forum Qualitative Sozialforschung/Forum: Qualitative Social Research*. Retrieved March 17, 2007, from http://www.qualitative-research.net/ fqs/fqs-eng.htm (*now included in CSA Abstracts* http://www.csa.com/factsheets/ socioabs-set-c.php).
Bryant, A. 2006. *Thinking Informatically: A New Understanding of Information, Communication, and Technology*. Lampeter, UK: Edwin Mellen.
Charmaz, K. 2000. Grounded Theory: Objectivist and Constructivist Methods. In Denzin, N.K. and Lincoln, Y.S. (eds), *Handbook of Qualitative Research*, 2nd edition, pp. 509–535. Thousand Oaks, CA: SAGE.
Charmaz, K. 2006. *Constructing Grounded Theory: A Practical Guide Through Qualitative Analysis*. London: SAGE.
Mumford, E. 1981. *Values, Technology and Work*. The Hague: Martinus Nijhoff.
Mumford, E. 1996. *Systems Design: Ethical Tools for Ethical Change*. Basingstoke: Macmillan.
Smit, J. & Bryant, A. 2000. Grounded Theory method in IS Research: Glaser vs. Strauss. Retrieved March 17, 2007, from http://www.lmu.ac.uk/inn/documents/2000-7.pdf

Acknowledgements

This handbook is a collective, emergent endeavor. We are most appreciative of our authors' efforts, their reviewers' comments, and the insights of our advisory board members. We thank Patrick Brindle, our editor at Sage, for his interest in and support for the project, and the production staff at Sage for transforming manuscript copy to published pages. A summer research award from the School of Social Sciences at Sonoma State University gave Kathy Charmaz some valuable clerical assistance.

Introduction
Grounded Theory Research: Methods and Practices

Antony Bryant and Kathy Charmaz

PRE-EMINENT QUALITATIVE RESEARCH METHOD

The Grounded Theory Method (GTM) comprises a systematic, inductive, and comparative approach for conducting inquiry for the purpose of constructing theory (Charmaz, 2006; Charmaz & Henwood, 2007). The method is designed to encourage researchers' persistent interaction with their data, while remaining constantly involved with their emerging analyses. Data collection and analysis proceed simultaneously and each informs and streamlines the other. The GTM builds empirical checks into the analytic process and leads researchers to examine all possible theoretical explanations for their empirical findings. The iterative process of moving back and forth between empirical data and emerging analysis makes the collected data progressively more focused and the analysis successively more theoretical.

GTM is currently the most widely used and popular qualitative research method across a wide range of disciplines and subject areas. Innumerable doctoral students have successfully completed their degrees using GTM. An extensive and expanding literature on the method has developed in research reports where it has been used, and in discussions concerning its general precepts and how it might best be understood, developed, and taught to others. Its extensive use in specific practice professions has led to significant advances in those practice fields. Using its originators Barney G. Glaser and Anselm L. Strauss's (Glaser & Strauss, 1967) own terms, GTM has 'grab' and 'fit'; it is clearly 'a good thing'.

GTM is now so much a part of the methodological inventory of so many disciplines and subject domains that scholars may forget that it only came into existence 40 years ago with the publication of Glaser and Strauss's initial publication, *Awareness of Dying* (1965a). Soon after, the key canonical text, *The Discovery of Grounded Theory* (1967) followed. Indeed as Stefan Timmermans and Iddo Tavory discuss in Chapter 23, based on a keyword search in databases of sociological publications, GTM did not become the dominant qualitative methodology until the late 1980s. Furthermore, they associate this rise to pre-eminence with the publication of Anselm Strauss's *Qualitative Analysis for Social Scientists* (1987) followed soon after by Strauss and Corbin's 'user-friendly' *Basics of Qualitative Research* (1990).

Whether or not Timmermans and Tavory are correct in their interpretation of their data, by 2000 Titscher, Meyer, Wodak, and Vetter could report in their bibliometric survey of qualitative methods that for the period 1991–1998, GTM received 2622 citations in the Social Science Citation Index out of a total of 4134 citations to all types of methods, quantitative as well as qualitative—almost 64% of the total; with the remaining percentage shared between 11 other methods. Noting their congruent findings with those of others such as Coffey, Holbrook, and Atkinson (1996), and Lee and Fielding (1996), Titscher et al. argue that these findings 'suggest that grounded theory is the most prominent among the so-called *qualitative* approaches to data analysis. *This does not mean that the methodologies developed by Anselm Strauss and Barney Glaser are used to any great extent*' (2000: 74, italics added). Lee and Fielding's correct assessment of the discrepancy between claiming use of the method and actual evidence of this continues today. This *Handbook* aims to substantiate the attributes and contributions afforded by GTM, at the same time clarifying the ways in which researchers have developed and adapted it in use. The *Handbook* also demonstrates how GTM has been influential and influenced by other methods in various fields and disciplines.

Titscher et al. explain the predominance of GTM in part by the enormous number of citations of Glaser and Strauss's *The Discovery of Grounded Theory*, *Awareness of Dying*, and *Time for Dying* books, whereas other approaches do not have such specific and widely acclaimed core texts. (Kearney, in Chapter 6, describes these three texts as 'the definitive GT tutorial'.) Yet, as Lee and Fielding note: '[W]hen qualitative researchers are challenged to describe their approach, reference to *grounded theory* has the highest recognition value. But the very looseness and variety of researchers' schooling in the approach means that the tag may well mean something different to each researcher' (1996: 3.1).

Certain perceptive readers might, at this stage, take exception to our focus on qualitative research in this introduction. They might point out that Glaser strongly maintains that GTM is a method that can use all forms of data: qualitative and quantitative. Glaser has consistently made this argument over the years, but it is worth noting that the full title of Glaser and Strauss's book was *The Discovery of Grounded Theory: Strategies for Qualitative Research*.[1]

In a similar way, ambiguous and contested meanings of the term 'Grounded Theory' itself become readily apparent. As used most commonly in the literature, the term Grounded Theory can lead to confusion. In some cases it refers, correctly, to the result of the research process, i.e. a grounded *theory*; but in many other cases it refers to the *method* used in the research process (Charmaz, 2003).

Strictly speaking a Grounded Theory is exactly that: A theory that has resulted from the use of the GTM. In common parlance, however, the term refers to the method itself, and the title of the *Handbook* adopts and follows this usage. In some individual chapters, as well as in this Introduction, the authors have adopted the term Grounded Theory Method (GTM) to refer to the method. The term Grounded Theory (GT) then refers to the result of using that method. Quotes from specific sources use the original authors' own terms. In most cases, the context in which the authors use the term resolves any actual ambiguity. The methods world will have to accept that the phrase Grounded Theory has now become part of common parlance, resonating with both meanings: the method and the resulting theory.

GROUNDED THEORY METHOD: A CONTESTED CONCEPT

The contested status of grounded theory methods, however, is not so easily resolved. Gallie (1956) first propounded the idea of an 'essentially contested concept' in 1956; specifically with regard to political terms such as 'power' and 'democracy'. Since then, scholars have often applied the label of 'contested concept' to any term that elicits substantial disagreement. Gallie himself offered a set of clear 'minimal criteria' for scholars to view a concept as *essentially contested*. Bryant's (2006) explanation of Gallie's criteria follows:

(1) the concept must be 'appraisive in the sense that it signifies or accredits some kind of valued achievement', i.e. deemed to be significant and valuable;
(2) the achievement 'must be of an internally complex character, for all its worth is attributed to it as a whole';
(3) this complexity of praiseworthy achievement leads to a variety of descriptions of the nature and process of the achievement;
(4) the achievement must be 'open', in the sense that there has been 'considerable modification in the light of changing circumstances' which could not have been predicted;
(5) those who use the term must recognize that their specific use 'is contested by those of other parties ... to use an essentially contested concept means to use it against other uses and to recognize that one's own use of it has to be maintained against other uses'. It has to be used 'aggressively and defensively';
(6) there must be some 'original exemplar whose authority is acknowledged by all the contestant users of the concept', failing which there is the risk of 'radical confusion';
(7) the continuous competition for acknowledgement should enable the 'original exemplar's achievement to be sustained and/or developed in optimum fashion'.[2]

When applying Gallie's criteria to GT/GTM, it certainly qualifies as a contested concept, and labeling it as such usefully allows us to identify the following aspects:

(1) 'Appraisive'. GTM clearly fulfils this criterion, as has already been pointed out, the method has 'high recognition value' and claims for its use provide partial validation of a researcher's study.

(2) 'Internally complex character'. This criterion certainly applies in the sense that the achievement of GTM has been to redefine the character of qualitative research, and of social research methods in general. Only the most myopic and outdated overview of even quantitative research methods could fail to acknowledge the impact of GTM.
(3) 'Variety of descriptions'. This criterion is a central feature of GTM; with an embarrassment of riches in terms of 'variety', albeit with many authors contending that some descriptions of the method have moved well beyond its claimed confines.
(4) 'Considerable modification in the light of changing circumstances'. Again another criterion that is all too evident in the paths taken by its proponents since 1967.
(5) 'Used aggressively and defensively'. The GTM literature is replete with examples of precisely such efforts. Diverse researchers often take Glaser's position, and those who work with him, to be that his writings embody 'classic GTM', with all other forms being secondary, partial, or not GTM at all but rather mere 'description' or Qualitative Data Analysis (QDA). In fact, Glaser now seems far more amenable to the possibility of alternative conceptions of GTM than in the past. Other grounded theorists, while recognizing Glaser's unique and continuing contribution and influence, would maintain that their chosen perspective on GTM holds at least equivalent validity. In addition, methodologists who do not claim grounded theory allegiance have raised criticisms of the method and of how various researchers have used it. These criticisms range from its emphases on induction, agency, and presumed emphasis on micro studies to disapproval of some grounded theorists' small samples and trite analyses as well as inattention to epistemological questions and integration with extant literatures.
(6) 'Original exemplar'. No problem here; the original exemplar is *The Discovery of Grounded Theory* or the combined GTM tutorial provided by *The Discovery of Grounded Theory*, *Awareness of Dying*, and *Time for Dying*. Having a clear original exemplar does not, however, preclude 'radical confusion' since several candidates for additional exemplars draw either from Glaser's writings or those of Strauss, and some users of GTM, particularly in fields outside traditional social science still seem unaware of the divergences among them (see Smit & Bryant, 2000).
(7) 'Continuous competition for acknowledgement'. Again this criterion is readily apparent in regard to GTM. We would like to think that this *Handbook* exemplifies the diverse ways in which the original exemplar's achievement has been sustained in optimum fashion.

In sum, GTM is a contested concept, yet we argue that its contested nature does not detract from its value and contribution. On the contrary, it accentuates the ways in which the method has redrawn the methods map, brought to the fore some of the central practical and philosophical methods issues, and initiated a flourishing interest in methods enhancement and development. The *Handbook* serves as an indication of this rich profusion and promise.

GLASER AND STRAUSS AND BEYOND: MASTERS AND APPRENTICES

The two founders of GTM have left their indelible marks upon this method, far more so than is the case with founders of other methods. Moreover, the ways in which Glaser and Strauss each went in distinct directions after their initial collaboration have also had significant impact on the method. The considerable growth in interest in GTM dates from the late 1980s, the period following their divergence. Thus many researchers who claimed use of the method in the early

1990s often did so with near exclusive reference to Strauss and Corbin's work, assuming it to be a seamless development from *The Discovery of Grounded Theory*. By the late 1990s, however, only those researchers who had not come across Glaser's (Glaser, 1992) arguments would have been unaware of the distinct differences between Glaser's and Strauss's writings about GTM.

Strauss died in 1996, but his ideas continue to have currency, and as many of the chapters in the *Handbook* evidence, to some extent our authors reaffirm his contribution to grounded theory. Indeed Timmermans and Tavory argue that Strauss's work in the late 1980s, particularly *Qualitative Analysis for Social Scientists* (1987) and *Basics of Qualitative Research* (Strauss & Corbin, 1990) re-established Strauss's role in GTM. Although long recognized by many symbolic interactionists, many other scholars now see and stress the links between Strauss's early work and that of the American pragmatists such as Mead and Dewey, and the writings of Peirce, as crucial influences on his initial contribution to GTM, and to his later methodological writings. Janice Morse and Jörg Strübing in particular discuss these issues in Chapters 11 and 27, respectively, and Adele Clarke and Carrie Friese build on Strauss's pragmatism. Strauss's later writings also come closer to the centre of attention, particularly his *Continual Permutations of Action* (1993), to which no fewer than seven contributors refer. Thus scholars see Strauss's contribution to the GTM canon as having a far wider reach than narrow methodological questions and prescriptions because it goes well beyond the early collaborative work with Glaser, the later book on *Qualitative Research*, and the first edition of *Basics of Qualitative Research*.

Glaser continues to write about and teach GTM. His chapter here summarizes his recent ideas on formal grounded theories, and over the past few years he has produced an extensive range of books and edited collections of examples of GTM research. He continues to offer his Grounded Theory Seminar, attracting students from around the world, and states that he has despatched copies of his books to recipients in more than 40 different countries. Glaser claims continuity between the initial GTM statements, such as *The Discovery of Grounded Theory*, and his later writings. He defines his position as being that of 'traditional' or 'classic' GTM, thereby distancing his view of the method from Strauss and Corbin in particular, but also from many other writers claiming the GTM mantle. In some regards, his position has changed from dismissing any other version of the method as invalid, towards a more accommodating view that at least acknowledges the existence of disparities between newer variations of the method and his authentic GTM.

Glaser played an enormous role in shaping GTM. From the outset, however, the method became more than the combined work of Glaser and Strauss. Using the current methodological terminology we might now talk of Glaser and Strauss each, individually, acting as a *lens* that refracted diverse and profound traditions (both theoretical and methodological) towards the focal point of GTM. Yet at a more empirical and immediately personal level, Glaser and Strauss had from the outset worked with Jeanne Quint on research about death and dying at the

University of California, San Francisco. Their various publications are listed in the footnotes in the introduction to *Awareness of Dying*. Quint (later Quint Benoliel) went on to develop her work based on this initial collaboration to the extent that the Washington State Nurses Hall of Fame has honoured her, and included the comment that, 'Her commitment to caring for the dying began with an early study with Barney Glaser and Anselm Strauss in which she assessed the way in which dying patients were cared for'. This commentary continues:

> To say that Jeanne Quint Benoliel is a 'living legend' is an understatement. She has trans-formed the field of care for dying people. She was the first to bring the family into care for the dying. Her research, joined with Ruth McCorkel's, continued to focus on system distress, enforced social dependency, and health outcomes for patients and the families. Taken together, Jean's contributions have helped shape the field of palliative care and hospice care. She has made legendary contributions to nursing that bring honor to the discipline. Retrieved March 23, 2007 from (http://www.wsna.org/hof/inductee.asp?id=2).

As many of the contributors to this *Handbook* indicate, Glaser and Strauss came from very different backgrounds, and their specific trajectories certainly exerted profound influences both on their early statements and examples of GTM, and on their later divergence. More critically, and again something some of our contributors comment on and demonstrate, the method spread in its early years through a form of apprenticeship and mentoring of doctoral students in sociology and nursing at the University of California, San Francisco (UCSF). A number of the contributors to this *Handbook* studied with Glaser or Strauss or both and, as their chapters testify, these experiences were formative and enduring.[3]

Glaser continues active promotion of GTM, and has a large group of adherents who rely upon his guidance and support in their work: both face-to-face and via E-mail. Yet even with the vast reach now possible using electronic forms of communication, this growth via apprenticeship can only account for a minute proportion of those using GTM. Certainly, key GTM figures of the second generation of Glaser and/or Strauss's former doctoral or postdoctoral students such as Kathy Charmaz, Adele Clarke, Juliet Corbin, Susan Leigh Star, Phyllis Stern, Janice Swanson, Carolyn Wiener, and Holly S. Wilson, among others, have sought to continue this tradition with their teaching and mentoring. Nonetheless, the method itself has now taken on a life of its own as evidenced by the wide range of contributions to this *Handbook*.

Given some of the key ideas about GTM, that it should produce mid-range theories grounded in the data, 'fit' the context, and generate applicable and useful analytic explanations, it is important to note that even from the outset a significant strand of practice-oriented research was manifest. Two of the three founding texts (*Awareness of Dying* and *Time for Dying*) had clear practical ramifications that Quint specifically developed. Indeed Quint's development from early collaborative work with Glaser and Strauss led to her 'legendary contributions' to the professional practices and strategies for palliative and hospital care, and represents an early and notable exemplar of this central characteristic. It also explains to some extent why GTM has sustained the interest of people working in care and associated medical and support areas, often combining professional employment with their research activities. Quint demonstrated the usefulness of conceptualizing issues in professional practice and explicating their consequences.

In sociology in the USA, qualitative research attracted women and the UCSF doctoral program in sociology itself enrolled more women than men. During the early years of the program, most of the men who completed their degrees entered applied areas that seldom included qualitative research. After the decline of American sociology in the late 1970s, the doctoral program at UCSF narrowed its focus to medical sociology and offered specializations in women's health and ageing; all of these areas interested women students in the program.

CAUSES, CONTEXTS, AND CONDITIONS OF
THE DEVELOPMENT OF GROUNDED THEORY

GTM developed in very specific circumstances. The initial research projects from which the method emerged had been undertaken in the wake of Anselm Strauss and Barney Glaser each suffering a close family bereavement. The Appendix to *Awareness of Dying* makes it clear that an important factor in their work on death and dying came initially from Strauss's experience in dealing with the illness and death of his mother in the early 1960s. Glaser joined forces with Strauss some 6 months after the research project had begun (around 1960), having himself just suffered the loss of his father. They worked together, and also with Jeanne Quint, publishing a number of papers mentioned in the footnotes to the opening pages of *Awareness of Dying*, first published in 1965. They also published some methodological papers at this time, including a joint paper 'Discovery of Substantive Theory: A Basic Strategy for Qualitative Analysis' (1965b) and Glaser's paper 'The Constant Comparative Method of Qualitative Analysis' (1965). These articles provided much of the groundwork for the more extended and polemical statement of the method to be found in *The Discovery of Grounded Theory* when it appeared in 1967.

Chapter 1 provides further details on the respective backgrounds of Glaser and Strauss, as do other contributors, but scholars often ignore the deeply personal motivation that animated Glaser's and Strauss's commitment to GTM from the start. A similar personal commitment remains an important factor to this day amongst many GTM practitioners as many chapters in this handbook very much evidence both in content and style of presentation.[4] Yet had early grounded theory works simply gained their inspiration from the originators' personal commitment, then it is unlikely that the method would have flourished in the ways it has. Glaser and Strauss, together and individually, brought with them: (1) a shared dissatisfaction with current trends in US social science research; (2) a wide range of ideas drawn from their distinctive backgrounds and experiences; and (3) an innovative and perceptive orientation to the practices and skills required for research in contemporary social settings. The chapters by Eleanor Covan, Susan Leigh Star, and Phyllis Stern each attend, in some manner, to how Glaser's and Strauss's particular individual experiences, training, temperament, and interests influenced the background and development of the method. We do not wish to imply that the emergence of GTM can simply be understood in terms of a biographical concoction of the two; but neither do we disavow that these issues have impact.

None of our contributors has sought to apply either Glaser's 'Six Cs': '*Causes, Context, Contingencies, Consequences, Covariances,* and *Conditions*' (see Glaser, 1978) or Strauss and Corbin's 'conditional matrix' (1990, 1998) to the development of GTM itself, but it would be an interesting exercise to apply these two approaches as heuristic devices to shed light upon the originators' trajectories, convergence, and divergence.[5] Seeking to account for the emergence and subsequent development of GTM in terms of the *Causes, Context, Contingencies, Consequences, Covariances,* and *Conditions* might well be an illuminating exercise, albeit one open to the criticism of constructing post hoc reifications rather than shedding light on important conjunctures. Similarly Strauss and Corbin's (1990) conditional matrix might be able to provide an alternative conception of the shared framing of GTM and its originators' subsequent differences.

Indeed using these two approaches might provide a way in which the explanatory power and shortcomings of each could be assessed. In addition it would contribute to a key deficiency in much of the GTM-related literature, i.e. a lack of in-depth use of key strategies of the method itself. Far too many references to GTM fail to get much beyond a few slogans or mantras supposedly corroborated by reference to key texts, as if the rich detail and complexities magically flow from the latter. For instance, any attempt to apply the conditional matrix would result in the realization that the 1990 version differs significantly from the 1998 one (Charmaz, 2005, 2006; Clarke, 2005). Strauss was a theorist of action, not of individuals. For him, action formed the core of experience and of sociological analysis. The 1990 version of *Basics of Qualitative Research* better represents Strauss's emphasis on action and interaction and their relation to meso and macro social contexts, although the linked spirals of the 1998 version imply trajectory and connections. Thus tracing a path around the 1990 version of the conditional matrix (see Strauss & Corbin, 1990) would encompass the range and type of structural conditions influencing and being affected by incorporating the co-founders' methodological actions taken together as well as viewed separately. A similar exercise might be attempted for GTM itself as it has developed since the 1960s.

This point exemplifies one of the key strengths of the method: Its ability to give rise to and illustrate the practical use of key research practices and conceptual tools, albeit with the likelihood that such facilities and potentialities will themselves give rise to limited and mechanical applications and to the emergence of new and syncretic forms of the method itself. Several contributors make this point; e.g. Margaret Kearney, notes that students subjected Strauss to constant pressure in the 1980s and 1990s to outline simple step-by-step recipes for generating grounded theories. Strauss responded by offering heuristics, rules-of-thumb, that all-too-often students saw as virtual rules to be followed regardless of the research context.

A CELEBRATION OF DIFFERENCE?

We have deliberately entitled this introduction 'Grounded Theory Research: Methods and Practices', since we both firmly see many of the developments from *The Discovery of Grounded Theory*-vintage GTM as strengths and enhancements of GTM, rather than as dissipations and diversions. Our view does not imply that we welcome all such developments. For instance, we have not found axial coding to be a productive research strategy, because it relies far too much on preconceived prescriptions. In addition, we have serious reservations about the conditional matrix in either of its forms. Such techniques cannot be mechanically applied. In an analogous way that extant concepts should earn their way into a grounded theory analysis, so too should using preconceived methodological tools. Such use should only occur after researchers carefully assess whether a given technique has earned its way into their respective methodological repertoires for their specific research problems (Charmaz, 2007). Thus in his chapter, Bruno Hildenbrand provides an example of a good fit between the conditional matrix and his developing analysis.

Ultimately, the maturity of a method will most likely result in the development of a range of related strands, some of which may well appear to be vastly different from the original. The progenitors of GTM have changed, modified, or eliminated major methodological strategies themselves. Carolyn Wiener points out that Strauss dispensed with writing memos directly and instead relied on transcriptions of team meetings. Glaser (2003) recently changed his stance on the grounded theory quest to discover a single basic social process. Certainly, such developments will test the tolerance of the method practitioners and of the key statements of the method itself. In so doing, disputes will arise concerned with issues such as the core features of the method, the possible and viable interpretations of its key characteristics, whether or not some new or hybrid form of the method is actually a valid or legitimate variation rather than an anathema, and the extent to which particular applications or exemplars of the method-in-use demonstrate its flexibility or undermine its integrity. This is not unique to GTM, Bob Dick's chapter charts a similar set of developments in the context of Action Research.

Two important, and related, issues arise in this regard: First, to what extent are statements about methods prescriptive, advisory, or heuristic? Second, at what point do the differences between variations outweigh the similarities? The first issue concerns the ways in which researchers and writers regard the invocations of GTM texts. Some scholars see methods statements as detailed prescriptions for research practices and procedures, while others look upon them as guidelines or heuristics. These ambiguities pertain to GTM but, moreover, apply to all statements about methods. Responsibility for the adopted orientation lies at least as much with the reader (practising researcher) as the writer (methods author). Some methods are offered by their progenitors from the very start as a basis for variation and interpretation, while others are couched far more towards the prescriptive end of the spectrum.

In practice, the initial intentions of the methods progenitors do not really seem to matter. Some researchers will advocate strict adherence, but others will seek to follow or develop variations; with ensuing arguments concerning whose approach has greater validity or authenticity. The resulting tensions have particularly affected the history and development of GTM, especially once Glaser and Strauss themselves took their different paths.

The originators taking different paths leads to the second issue: At what point do such differences lead to a move from 'variations on a theme' to 'a different method in its own right'? This question holds fundamental relevance for GTM, since anyone looking at the range of statements and exemplars on offer will need to take some stand in this regard. Clearly, a fairly specific and widely acknowledged group of initial, canonical texts include statements or exemplars of the method: *The Discovery of Grounded Theory*, *Awareness of Dying*, and *Time for Dying* are the obvious ones. Yet the subsequent trajectories of Glaser and Strauss severely undermine taking these texts as a basis for a sustained and seamless understanding of GTM.

Glaser contends that his writings since these early statements do indeed continue to offer a genuine continuation of and adherence to the early GTM sources. The alternative path taken by Strauss, particularly in his collaboration with Corbin, attests to at least one other point of view. Furthermore, at least since Charmaz's chapter in the second edition of the *Handbook of Qualitative Research* (2000), further diversification of the method has occurred, although the underpinnings of her view were apparent in her 1990 article, 'Discovering Chronic Illness: Using Grounded Theory'. At the simplest level, we have the Glaserian school of GTM, the Strauss and Corbin school, and the Constructivist. The integration of methodological developments of the past 40 years distinguishes Constructivist Grounded Theory. This version emphasizes how data, analysis, *and methodological strategies* become constructed, and takes into account the research contexts and researchers' positions, perspectives, priorities, and interactions.

Many scholars would agree that GTM has three versions; nevertheless, for some scholars, GTM is actually far more diverse. In Chapter 21, Norman Denzin lists seven different versions of GTM; 'positivist, postpositivist, constructivist, objectivist, postmodern, situational, and computer assisted'. The distinctions between some of these remain unspecified, and some overlap. In any case, the most articulated forms of the method fall fairly readily into the three given above.

GROUNDED THEORY METHOD AS A FAMILY OF METHODS

Anyone contemplating the GTM landscape must grasp the inherent complexity of what might be termed the 'family of methods claiming the GTM mantle'. This point may not seem significant to experienced researchers, but to those new to research, particularly if faced with methods examinations and submissions to research committees, the issues are immediate and vital. Understanding them allows novices to make informed choices and to articulate rationales supporting their choices.

Consideration of GTM as a 'family of methods' deliberately evokes Ludwig Wittgenstein's concept of 'family resemblances' which he introduced in his *Philosophical Investigations* to demonstrate how similarities are often based on judgements around ideas that are not amenable to clear and precise definitions. Thus according to Wittgenstein, we all know what a 'game' involves. We can successfully apply this term to many diverse activities that do not all share common attributes, but do share some common characteristics with some other games. Wittgenstein writes:

> Consider for example the proceedings that we call 'games'. I mean board-games, card-games, ball-games, Olympic games, and so on. What is common to them all? Don't say: There must be something common, or they would not be called 'games' but look and see whether there is anything common to all. For if you look at them you will not see something that is common to all, but similarities, relationships, and a whole series of them at that. To repeat: don't think, but look! (Wittgenstein, 1953, aphorism 66).

Note that Wittgenstein's admonition 'don't think, but look!' is similar to many GTM statements concerning the primacy of grounded observation over preconceptions. More critically for our present discussion, his argument centres on similarities and relationships that can apply to GTM itself. Every contributor to this *Handbook* has studied, applied, taught, and/or written about GTM. Yet each one will have his or her own ideas of what precisely constitutes GTM, and these specific (idiosyncratic) ideas form a family of resemblances in much the same way as Wittgenstein describes them.

Wittgenstein states:

> I can think of no better expression to characterize these similarities than 'family resemblances'; for the various resemblances between members of a family: build, features, colour of eyes, gait, temperament, etc. etc. overlap and criss-cross in the same way. And I shall say: 'games' form a family (Wittgenstein, 1953, aphorism 67).

Now we can readily extend this metaphor of family resemblances so that, just as in real families, membership becomes contested or individuals become excluded. Given the pre-eminence of GTM, many researchers have good reason to claim the mantle of GTM in some manner, and for others to challenge what they regard as illegitimate claims and claimants. Correspondingly, those who see the method as fostering incomplete data collection or mundane explanations will distance themselves from it, as do those who are antagonistic towards inductive qualitative research.

Unlike Wittgenstein's example of games, however, novices cannot obviously and intuitively grasp GTM. Rather, it takes a good deal of effort and insight to develop sufficient confidence with the method to make these sorts of judgements. Indeed, in putting this *Handbook* together, we intend our readers to view it as a basis for discussion and debate from which students can learn, and upon which experts can apply their insights; certainly not as the only statement about the method, albeit one with some definitive status.

Teaching GTM often requires that instructors treat a set of procedures as if they were rules. Yet learning how to *use* GTM necessitates moving beyond rules to a more profound, more nuanced, and more resilient understanding of the key principles of the method. Thus Strauss worried about students' persistent requests for a clear set of procedures for doing GTM. Ironically, however, Strauss and Corbin's *Basics of Qualitative Research* achieved its popularity to some extent precisely because it seemed to offer just this sort of GTM manual. Some have termed it a cookbook approach, in which the authors discuss the ingredients, procedures, and outcomes in explicit detail, with clear instructions derived from decomposing complex activities into small-scale, simpler tasks. Yet a cookbook can also provide a foundation from which imaginative cooks can develop their own versions of the recipes. (Kearney notes in Chapter 6 that, as GTM grew in popularity, Strauss was constantly asked for a restatement of the method in recipe form.)

We argue for viewing GTM as a family of methods along the lines suggested by Wittgenstein. The *Handbook* then indicates the extent to which scholars invoke differences of approach and of substance, and specify the relationships between their respective approaches and substantive analyses. Many of the contributors themselves offer ideas about the essential properties or features of GTM; Stern's paper specifically focuses on this issue. In some cases the authors define a set of criteria. For instance Wiener states that she considers the following to be 'integral to following GTM':

- data gathering, analysis and theory construction proceed concurrently;
- coding starts with first interview and/or fieldnotes;
- memo writing also begins with first interview and/or fieldnotes;
- theoretical sampling is the disciplined search for patterns and variations;
- theoretical sorting of memos sets up the outline for writing the paper;
- theoretical saturation is the judgement that there is no need to collect further data;
- identify a basic social process that accounts for most of the observed behaviour.

Urquhart outlines a set of guidelines, five in all, which centre on:

- doing a literature review for orientation;
- coding for theory not superficial themes;

- use of theoretical memos;
- building the emerging theory and engaging with other theories;
- clarity of procedures and chain of evidence.

Jane Hood argues that three features of GTM distinguish it from any other research methods: '(1) theoretical sampling, (2) constant comparison of data to theoretical categories, and (3) focus on the development of theory via theoretical saturation of categories rather than substantive verifiable findings'. She terms these the 'troublesome trinity', since as well as being 'essential properties of Grounded Theory' they are 'also the most difficult for researchers to understand and apply'. Hood directs her entire chapter to demonstrating distinctive properties of GTM, differentiating it from what she terms the 'Generic Inductive Qualitative Model'. As many readers already know, Glaser has consistently sought to distinguish between GTM and what he terms 'Qualitative Data Analysis' (QDA).

Other authors make somewhat less expansive statements about the 'core' of GTM. Thus Karen Locke argues that at its heart GTM consists of a set of 'research procedures and practices that help us to initiate, organize and carry forward our thinking relative to our engagements with the field, for example, coding, continuous comparing, iterative sampling in light of developments in thinking, diagramming, memo writing, and so on'. Meanwhile Denise O'Neil Green, John W. Creswell, Ronald J. Shope, and Vicki L. Plano Clark see the method as 'a qualitative research design in which the inquirer generates a general explanation (a theory) of a process, action, or interaction shaped by the views of a large number of participants'.

Other contributors and GTM researchers will perhaps have their own particular ways of summarizing the key features of the method. One of us has recently presented a specific account, which includes the following summary:

> Grounded theory involves taking comparisons from data and reaching up to construct abstractions and then down to tie these abstractions to data. It means learning about the specific and the general—and seeing what is new in them—then exploring their links to larger issues or creating larger unrecognized issues in entirety. An imaginative interpretation sparks new views and leads other scholars to new vistas. Grounded theory methods can provide a route to see beyond the obvious and a path to reach imaginative interpretations (Charmaz, 2006: 181).

GROUNDED THEORY PARADOXES AND PERPLEXITIES, COMPLEXITIES AND CONUNDRUMS

A close reading of the chapters in this *Handbook* brings to the fore a number of major issues concerning GTM, some of which are certainly paradoxical and confusing to novice researchers, and perhaps even to those with more experience. Following Glaser's maxim 'all is data', we subjected the chapters for this *Handbook* to a light-touch coding exercise that resulted in a series of themes or concepts highlighting many key issues regarding GTM and its use in current research practice.

What is grounded in GTM: the categories, the concepts, or the theory?

This query is one of those deceptive questions; at first sight hardly worth asking, but upon reflection it raises a whole series of critical issues. The obvious and immediate answer is 'the theory'; after all it is the Grounded Theory Method. But this response then leads one to ask about the relationship between the theory, the concepts and/or categories, and the data. The categories must surely be 'grounded' in the data, since they give rise to the theory; or in Glaser's terms theories are systematically generated according to the procedures of GTM.

This answer, however, results in a further consideration: What does 'grounding' mean? Glaser correctly admonishes those researchers who fail to rise above what he terms 'description'. Yet he also criticizes those who leap to generate theoretical statements without regard for systematic data collection and analysis, and calls such statements 'immaculate conjectures' or 'immaculate conceptualizations'. Again the traps for the novice and the unwary are legion without further insight and guidance. A researcher embarking upon use of GTM will have to avoid the Scylla of 'mere description' on the one side, and the Charybdis of 'immaculate conceptualization' on the other.

One problem actually lies in the way in which the term data is understood in GTM, and the ambiguities in the early GTM works. Several contributors (e.g. Holton, Kearney, and Locke) point out that data play a double-edged role in GTM. The method certainly encourages, even commands, researchers to gather data in one form or another; and many GTM researchers seem guided by the motto 'everything is data'. But this motto is not meant to imply that 'data is everything', on the contrary, as Kearney remarks in Chapter 6, 'Glaser and Strauss were much more comfortable writing *at a distance from data* than are authors of current qualitative reports in the practice disciplines' (stress added).

GTM products that really have 'grab' and 'fit' probably do so because the researchers have managed to sustain this balancing act between 'grounding' and 'distancing', thereby producing substantive conceptualization. Again Kearney sums this up by noting that Glaser and Strauss favoured 'theoretical density over descriptive amplification'. This observation leads us to consider two other related issues: the nature of data and the sense in which GTM research encompasses and perhaps even requires researchers to make imaginative leaps from the data.

Data

The term 'data' is central to the early writings of GTM, and indeed continues to act as a pivotal identifier for the method. Yet, as we point out in Chapter 1, and as other contributors such as Adele Clarke and Carrie Friese, Katja Mruck and Günter Mey, Virginia Olesen, and Susan Leigh Star would concur, the term itself is fraught with problems that the GTM literature itself ignored. In our earlier works (for example, Bryant, 2002, 2003, 2006; Charmaz, 2006; Charmaz & Mitchell, 2001), each of us has individually sought to incorporate key admonitions with regard to the use of the word, yet still retain the main strengths of GTM.

In the realm of IT or ICT (Information and Communications Technology) the term data has similar centrality and accompanying ambiguities, which can illustrate similar problems arising in GT. People distinguish between data and 'information', explaining the relationship between them in terms along the lines of '[D]ata is therefore raw material that is transformed into information by data processing'.

This sort of imagery appears in most popular textbooks for students of computing and information systems. It implies that human beings and computers 'process' information from data, in much the same manner as petrol is refined from crude oil. Thus, this mechanistic imagery obscures the issue of 'meaning', and mistakes the ways in which humans act in the world. We are not automatons, taking in data and then somehow processing it. As one of us has argued elsewhere (Bryant, 2006), in the context of IS and Informatics, people cannot engage directly with anything to do with data. Scanning a book into a computer is a data process; someone trying to read it (and make sense of it) immediately is in the realm of information, because it inevitably involves meaning.[6] In GTM, the very acts of defining and generating data place the researcher in the realm of meaning.

The contributions by Ian Dey, Bob Dick, Sharlene Hesse-Biber, Jo Reichertz, and many others make similar points. In GTM, the relationship between data, however defined and grasped, and the researcher is one founded on action, interaction, and interpretation. As Mruck and Mey, and Olesen imply, reflexive scrutiny of these processes helps the researcher to locate and position their data (and themselves) without reifying these data or their resulting analyses. The early GMT texts understandably emphasized the importance of 'the data', in contrast to the theoretical flights of fancy that Glaser and Strauss saw as predominant in sociological research at the time. But we are now in the position where GTM has taken its place in the methodological armoury, and the danger is that researchers will over-emphasize the role of data at the expense of other facets of the method. Hence, a number of contributors to the *Handbook* meticulously locate the role for imagination, serendipity, 'abduction', and reflexivity in GTM.

Induction, deduction, abduction

GTM is categorized as an inductive method. Induction can be defined as 'a type of reasoning that begins with study of a range of individual cases and extrapolates from them to form a conceptual category' (Charmaz, 2006: 188). In effect, it means moving from the particular to the more general; in the context of GTM it implies moving up from the detailed descriptive to the more abstract, conceptual level. One of the problems with induction is that this type of reasoning involves a leap from the particular to the general, and may rely on too limited a number of individual cases or an idiosyncratic selection. To an extent GTM overcomes these problems with the ideas of theoretical sampling (see Chapter 7 by Jane Hood and Chapter 11 by Janice Morse, respectively) and the distinctions between substantive and formal grounded theories (see Chapter 4 by Glaser and Chapter 6 by Kearney, respectively). Indeed a close reading of *The Discovery of Grounded Theory* and many other GTM books indicates a far more sophisticated philosophical position than students often glean, much less those who only glance at the texts in order to substantiate their GTM claims. Conversely, as Timmermans and Tavory explain, some of the statements on offer, particularly from 'objectivist' GTM sources, provide ammunition for critics of GTM to label it as an 'epistemological fairy tale'.

In the light of the work of those who have traced Strauss's ideas back to the American Pragmatists and the work of Charles S. Peirce, the inductive nature of GTM is now seen as only part of the story: 'abduction' plays a key role. As a way of reasoning:

> Abductive inference entails considering all possible theoretical explanations for the data, forming hypotheses for each possible explanation, checking them empirically by examining data, and pursuing the most plausible explanation (Charmaz, 2006: 188).

The chapters by Strübing and Locke mention abduction, but Jo Reichertz deals specifically with the topic, remarking on the 'secret charm of abduction' since it combines both the rational and the imaginative aspects of research; the former by defining a logical form of inferencing, and the latter by acknowledging the role played by insight and institution. Although no specific mention of the term abduction appears in any of the writings of Glaser and Strauss, or Strauss himself, a strong case can be made that *The Discovery of Grounded Theory* and some of the other GTM works of Glaser and Strauss, collectively and individually, have abductive strands and implications, particularly when they raise issues such as theoretical sensitivity. Indeed, Reichertz makes the important point that attending to the process of abduction reunites the topics of the logic of discovery and the logic of validation or justification; bringing both into the realm of methodological consideration. Whatever one's view on abduction, and its role in GTM in practice, this new attention to the topic helps underscore how GTM far transcends the 'naïve Baconian inductivism' of which it has been accused (Haig, 1995).

Grounded Theory Method: simple yet skilful

One of the recurrent themes in many chapters is that GTM, far from being some mystical complex approach, is in fact 'simple' and straightforward. Thus Lora Lempert notes that memo making is not mystical but simple; Judith Holton sees the solution to the chaos of coding inundation as 'relatively simple', as also is recognition of the point at which to stop collecting data. Carolyn Wiener points out that, with regard to the method of constant comparison, 'the basic rule is simple'. Conversely many contributors make the point that several key facets of

GTM rely on extensive experience and skill on the part of the researcher. Wiener notes that one of the key characteristics of the team in which she worked with Strauss was that 'All of us were skilled at coding but he was especially gifted at it'. Hesse-Biber argues that one of the most difficult skills in learning qualitative analysis 'is the ability to see what is in the data'.

This paradox or ambiguity is particularly evident in discussions concerning *theoretical sensitivity*. Almost all of those who address theoretical sensitivity, comment to the effect that it is an acquired skill that does not come easily or naturally. Holton rightly asserts that '[T]heoretical sensitivity requires two things of the researcher—analytic temperament and competence'. Udo Kelle deals with this issue at some length, and he concludes that 'the previously presented two basic rules, (1) to abstain from forcing preconceived concepts, and (2) to utilize theoretical sensibility in this process, are obviously difficult to reconcile'. Moreover he notes that in the years following publication of *The Discovery of Grounded Theory* the 'apparent antagonism between "emergence" and "theoretical sensitivity" remained a major problem for teaching the methodology of grounded theory'.

Theoretical sensitivity is thus a problematic concept. It is crucial in the application of GTM. But who has theoretical sensitivity? How do you get it? Who judges it? Glaser and Strauss locate it within the researcher. Certainly, some researchers have more developed theoretical proclivities than others. Abduction helps here. Being able to entertain a range of theoretical possibilities to account for a surprising finding gives the researcher material for making systematic *theoretical comparisons* in relation to the particular finding. Making theoretical comparisons not only means knowing something about theory, and at least intuitively understanding how to go about theorizing, but also means being able to play with theoretical ideas before becoming committed to a single theoretical interpretation.

GTM rightly appeals to novice researchers because it encourages them to develop their own theories rather than merely fine-tuning existing ones. They may become conceptual entrepreneurs themselves rather than just work for theoretical capitalists. Nonetheless, this point obscures the fact that use of GTM, at least as much as any other research method, only develops with experience. Hence the failure of all those attempts to provide clear, mechanistic rules for GTM: there is no 'GTM for Dummies'. GTM is based around heuristics and guidelines rather than rules and prescriptions. Moreover researchers need to be familiar with GTM, in all its major forms, in order to be able to understand how they might adapt it in use or revise it into new forms and variations.

Codes, categories, concepts

The terms 'code', 'category', and 'concept' occur as central ones within GTM writings. Some writers use two or more of these terms synonymously. Star poses the specific question 'What is a code?' and gives as a response that it 'sets up a relationship with your data, and with your respondents'. She does not use the term category, but does use the term concept implying that it operates at a higher level of abstraction than a code. Lempert states that 'codes capture patterns and themes and cluster them under a "title" that evokes a constellation of impressions and analyses for the researcher'; and she uses the term category as a higher level code which has grown in complexity and abstraction, so subsuming other codes. Kelle distinguishes between 'data, codes and the emerging categories', and also notes that Glaser's discussion of *Theoretical Sensitivity* (1978) introduced a distinction between substantive codes and theoretical codes. Kelle sees the latter as 'terms which describe possible relations between substantive codes and thereby help to form theoretical models'. He adds that '[T]he word "codes" or "conceptual codes" is thereby used as synonymous for "categories and their properties"'. Holton equates a code with a category, and quotes from another author who equates a category with a concept; but her main focus is on the ways in which the GTM researcher develops concepts and decides upon a core category. Glaser stresses the importance of a core category in developing SGTs (substantive grounded theories) and then using this core in the conceptual move towards FGTs (formal grounded theories). Kelle invokes set theory and Venn diagrams to achieve some clarification of the terms *category* and *property*, but perhaps researchers need to clarify further distinctions between *code* and *category* and *concept*.[7] It would seem that the best working model places these terms in a hierarchy from bottom to top: respectively code, category, concept. The resulting hierarchy will not, however, appeal to those GTM researchers who see the relationship between category and concept as far more intricate. Whichever approach researchers adopt, Glaser's fundamental question 'what category is this data the study of?' must still be posed.

Theoretical codes, coding paradigms

Glaser and Strauss, individually, noted that the early founding texts of GTM were far from perfect. Glaser's chapter seeks to provide clarity and guidance on the topic of Formal Grounded Theory (FGT), noting that some of the earliest statements about FGT contained ambiguous or incomplete ideas. Both Glaser and Strauss sought in their later, distinct writings to deal with other issues of ambiguity or potential misunderstanding (see Strauss & Corbin, 1994). In some cases these efforts generally produced positive results; but in other cases, they netted fewer obvious benefits. We have already pointed out that the concept of a *coding paradigm* is problematic and to an extent undermines the power of GTM itself. A similar case can be made about Glaser's introduction of his *Theoretical Sensitivity* in 1978. To a novice researcher, Strauss's coding paradigm and Glaser's theoretical codes appear to undermine one of the basic principles of GTM: an open-minded, framework-free orientation to the research domain at the outset. Kelle points out that Glaser: (1) does not clearly explain use of these codes; (2) the codes themselves mix 'logical' with 'substantive' issues; and finally (3) 'the employment of such an unordered list for the construction of "grounded theories" poses grave difficulties if the researcher does not have a very broad theoretical background knowledge to hand concerning the different theoretical perspectives entailed in the list'. Glaser himself has distanced himself from these codes in recent years, and as Kearney argues, Strauss remained ambivalent in dealing with the demands to offer formulae or rules-of-thumb for the application and use of GTM.

Verification and validation

Glaser and Strauss initially developed GTM as a move away from grand theory verification. They aimed to offer an alternative to young sociological researchers who, in colourful imagery, were almost exclusively tied to acting as 'proletariat testers' to their masters, the 'theoretical capitalists' (Glaser & Strauss, 1967: 10). Hence their concern in *The Discovery of Grounded Theory* with 'generation' as opposed to 'verification'. But this concern then begs the question of how grounded theories themselves can be verified or validated.[8] Dey raises this issue in his discussion of how the distinction between the 'context of discovery' and the 'logic of validation' can become sullied if grounded theorists use the same data both for discovery and for validation. He quotes Kelle who argues that 'the prerequisite of independent testing requires that a hypothesis is not tested with the empirical material from which it is developed'.

Accepting the notion of such independent testing is problematic for GTM (unless we aim for *theorizing* rather than verification) because the method itself depends on coterminous data gathering, analysis, and conceptual development. Dey advises GTM researchers to be alert to these distinctions, so that '[I]f we think of validity as the extent to which a theory is well-grounded empirically *and* conceptually, then we can better appreciate the importance of theoretical consistency as well as the accuracy or acuteness of our empirical interpretations. When we develop categories, we need to take account of their theoretical underpinnings and implications as much as their efficacy with regard to the data'. Reichertz, following Peirce, states that the outcome of abductive inference can never be verified, however extensive the testing: 'All that one can achieve, using this procedure, is an intersubjectively constructed and shared *truth*'. Peirce found the idea of absolute certainty 'irresistibly comic', and so saw truth claims as at best provisional. Discussions about verification are not unique to GTM, but still remain part of current discourse on epistemology, science, and general claims to understand the real world.

Using the literature

Ever since the publication of *The Discovery of Grounded Theory*, concerns have arisen regarding how students and researchers should approach and use the existing literature relevant to their research topic. Holton states her view starkly, the researcher should enter the domain with 'no preconceived problem statement, interview protocols or extensive review of literature'. Stern notes this precept approvingly, but also remarks that pressures from one's professors, funding committees, and other approval mechanism may work against being able to post-pone a literature review to later (post-conceptual) stages of the research. Lempert however clearly states that she deviates from this aspect of classic GTM, not for the reasons given by Stern, but for pragmatic reasons:

> In order to participate in the current theoretical conversation, I need to understand it. I must recognize that what may seem like a totally new idea to me—an innovative breakthrough in my research—may simply be a reflection of my ignorance of the present conversation. A literature review provides me with the current parameters of the conversation that I hope to enter ... It does not, however, define my research (see Chapter 12 in this *Handbook*).

Lempert's point suggests a larger problem occurring in some studies that claim grounded theory methods. Researchers may report ideas as new that have been developed in relevant literatures, sometimes by other grounded theorists. Careful *analysis* of relevant extant literatures after developing one's grounded theory can provide cues for raising its theoretical level and indicate which conversations to enter.

Barry Gibson wonders how researchers develop theoretical sensitivity without some familiarity with relevant literature. Similarly, Timmermans and Tavory point to the various statements along the lines of Holton's as the reason that many novice researchers are left in 'confused awe'. The recommendation that the researchers should enter the research domain with an open mind is sound, but many contributors point out two key flaws in taking this at face value. First, in keeping with Dey (1999; Chapter 8), an open mind does not imply an empty head. Anyone starting research will most certainly have some preconceived ideas relevant to the research area. A researcher can account for these ideas in some way, but certainly should not simply ignore them. Second, the advice about post-poning exploration of the literature usually emanates from experienced researchers, who themselves have developed an extensive knowledge of a vast mass of literature together with a general familiarity with key topics and an array of concepts at their fingertips. Wiener notes Strauss's skills in analysis and cod-ing that clearly derived from his wide experience and reading. Similarly Glaser can reel off numerous examples of substantive and formal GTs, as well as many others that do not quite make the grade. Here again, the balance arises between reliance on the literature to provide the framework to start with, something that Glaser and Strauss particularly took issue with, and having a level of understanding to provide an orientation as Lempert advises.

Grounded Theory Method and Symbolic Interactionism

The relationship between GTM and Symbolic Interactionism elicits clear disagreements. Clarke and Friese state unambiguously that '[W]ith deep roots in symbolic interactionist sociology and pragmatist philosophy, the grounded theory method can be viewed as a theory/methods package with an interpretive, constructionist epistemology'. Glaser has been at pains to counter this assertion, devoting a specific article to countering precisely this easy identification (Glaser, 2005).

Symbolic interactionism and grounded theory have strong compatibilities. Both the theoretical perspective and the method assume an agentic actor, the significance of studying processes, the emphasis on building useful theory from empirical observations, and the development of conditional theories that address specific realities. Like symbolic interactionists, grounded theorists assume that people act, as individuals and as collectivities. The symbolic interactionist emphasis on meaning and action complements the question grounded theorists pose in the empirical world: What is happening? (Glaser, 1978).

To find out and interpret what is happening takes the researcher into meanings of action, which may be unstated or assumed. This point speaks to the major divide among grounded theorists implied above: those who treat what they see or hear and record as objective and those who see both what research participants' actions and researchers' recordings and reports as constructed. The latter position treats the research process itself as an object of scrutiny and thus embraces contemporary currents in symbolic interactionism.

The dual emphases on an agentic actor and action in both grounded theory and symbolic interaction lead researchers into attending to process rather than assuming structure. Subsequently, grounded theorists attempt to define fundamental processes and symbolic interactionists view social life as somewhat indeterminate and open-ended because it consists of interactional processes. These points reveal the pragmatist underpinnings of both symbolic interactionism and grounded theory, and have animated Strauss's work. It follows that the resulting theories would be contingent on specific conditions and modifiable as those conditions change. Glaser in particular (Glaser, 1978, 1992; Glaser & Strauss, 1967) has stressed the modifiability of grounded theories. Simultaneously, however, he advocates moving towards a general, abstract level, and thus addresses explanatory 'why' questions. Symbolic interactionists have produced many studies of local phenomena that answer 'how' questions. Symbolic interactionists can and do use grounded theory strategies to advance inquiry that answers why questions without severing finished studies from the conditions of their production (see, for example, Casper, 1998; Star, 1989).

The fit between symbolic interactionism and grounded theory is extremely strong. Perhaps we should phrase the question, in pragmatist language, as follows: Do symbolic interactionism and grounded theory work as a theory-method package? Yes, absolutely. Whether they constitute a unitary theory-methods package is another question. Charmaz (1990) has long maintained that researchers from varied theoretical persuasions can adopt grounded theory strategies with sound results. Beginning from another theoretical perspective means that a researcher invokes a different or additional set of sensitizing concepts to begin the research process (Charmaz, 2005). Yet, in any case, where one starts a grounded theory study is seldom where one ends.

Grounded Theory Method and sociological theory and practice

When Glaser and Strauss published *The Discovery of Grounded Theory*, they clearly set their sights on challenging specific people and practices predominating in US social sciences at the time. In the ensuing 40 years, the people and practices have changed. GTM now perhaps joins the orthodoxy of the social sciences, although several authors depict how qualitative researchers in general and GTM practitioners in particular continue to be marginalized in US social science faculties. They also make the point that adhering to some of the central precepts of GTM is difficult in a culture where research aims and objectives have to be submitted for vetting to research boards, funding committees, and ethical approval procedures in advance of the research being undertaken; and where, once approval is granted, any deviation from the proposal requires further formal approval.

In *The Discovery of Grounded Theory*, Glaser and Strauss singled out various figures, including C. Wright Mills and in particular his book *The Sociological Imagination* (1959), as a target of their criticism of existing sociological methods:

> Much of C. Wright Mills' work, we believe, is exampled with only little theoretical control, though he claimed that data disciplined his theory. In contrast, grounded theory is derived from data and then illustrated by characteristic examples of data (Glaser & Strauss, 1967: 5).

We share the position with many contributors to this *Handbook*, that GTM has now matured and in many regards this maturity has resulted in a revised account of the balance of skills and perspectives required for GTM. That three authors make specific mention of Mills, but in affirmative terms rather than disapproving ones, indicates the maturity of GTM. Locke and Hildenbrand each make the connection between the abductive or playful aspects of GTM, with Hildenbrand noting that Strauss in his later work referred to *The Sociological Imagination* as an example of the ways in which the grounded theorist must be *creative*. Covan sees parallels between GTM and *The Sociological Imagination* in which Mills argued for the necessity of understanding social situations by encompassing three dimensions: individual biographies, history, and social structure, and which 'is, of course, grounded in the creative process of generating theory in consideration of the same dimensions'. Lempert argues that Mills's book exemplifies a formal theory with 'analytic power' and extensive application.

Covan makes the interesting point that Glaser and Strauss share some key ideas with Durkheim. Both *The Discovery of Grounded Theory* and Durkheim's *The Rules of the Sociological Method* are based on the claim that social facts exist and that the study of these facts is a true science. Moreover, Durkheim was advocating empirical study, in opposition to the prevailing views of Comte; echoing the criticisms voiced in *The Discovery of Grounded Theory*. Durkheim stated that 'up to the present, sociology has dealt more or less exclusively with concepts and not with things' (1938: 18–19). Covan concludes that '[L]ike Glaser and Strauss, Durkheim seemed to be motivated to explain not only how to "do sociology," but why his way was legitimate'. Moreover they shared a belief that while lay inter-pretations of reality were a resource for theorizing, the sociologist must tran-scend these. One main distinction between Durkheim's *The Rules of the Sociological Method* and GTM, however, is that Durkheim advocated classifica-tion in advance of the research activities, which GTM specifically rejects.

Serendipity and theoretical development

Several of the contributors allude to 'serendipity'. Covan rightly points to the footnote on page 2 of *The Discovery of Grounded Theory* where the authors argue that although Merton referred to the 'theoretic functions of research', he failed to develop this to encompass anything like GTM. The closest he came, according to Glaser and Strauss, was in using the term 'serendipity', which they define as 'an unanticipated, anomalous, and strategic finding that gives rise to a new hypothesis' (Glaser & Strauss, 1967, p. 2). Glaser and Strauss distance GTM from serendipity, since they stressed the purposive nature of GTM in developing theoretical insights, as opposed to what might seem to be an accidental and contingent manner. Yet GTM has taken on the mantle of serendipity in dif-ferent ways. In 1998, Glaser stressed the 'subsequent, sequential, simultaneous, serendipitous and scheduled' (Glaser, 1998: 15) nature of grounded theory. Wiener cautions the GT researcher to be 'ready for the serendipitous opportunity'.

Nevertheless, in the work on GTM and abduction, the concept of serendipity has taken on renewed importance. Reichertz does not specifically use the term 'serendipity' but takes great care in explaining that abductive reasoning involves 'assembling or discovering, on the basis of an interpretation of collected data, such combinations of features for which no appropriate explanation or rule in the store of knowledge already exists. This discovery causes surprise'. Moreover it results in the search for a new theory or hypothesis, precisely the grounded development of concepts and/or theories that lies at the heart of GTM. If it wasn't always apparent that GTM is all about serendipity, then it certainly is now.

Diagrams

A clear split divides those who see diagrams as critical and those who deprecate them. If a researcher proffers a diagram to Glaser, he wants to know what it means, and that implies writing or talking about it; Stern echoes this view in Chapter 5. Lempert sees diagrams as 'central in Grounded Theory work. They create a visual display of what researchers do and do not know. As such, they bring order to the data and further the total analyses'. Clarke (2005; Clarke and Friese, Chapter 17) goes even further in her approach to *Situational Analysis* which centres on the production of diagrams in various forms and at various stages.

Indeed, the division of opinion appears less marked if one notes that Lempert specifically addresses the researcher and what the researcher knows. Thus a researcher can offer a diagram as a possibly helpful way of generating concepts from what might otherwise be a chaos of data. As Lempert says, the diagram furthers the analysis, but may not provide a way of expressing it to others. Glaser bases his criticism squarely on this latter aspect of research, and GTM specifically addresses the issue of writing about one's research.

Writing Grounded Theory

An emerging trend within GTM quite correctly stresses the importance of writing about one's research. Stern specifically addresses the importance of 'skilful writing', and many GTM teachers stress that if one has carefully and consistently written memos in the course of one's research, then, once sorted, these can provide the basis and structure for the eventual research report. A related concern about skilful writing concerns those grounded theorists who present their reports to some extent in literary terms. Dey refers to this literary turn when he discusses the role of narrative in GT research. He particularly notes how a narrative framework can provide 'a vehicle for contextualizing and integrating the various elements'; in effect a form of 'grounding'. Whether or not most grounded theorists can effectively emulate this form, the attention paid in GTM literature to 'skilful writing' and forms of expression can provide a starting point for discussion with relevance to all types of research and their dissemination.

Use of support software

Increasingly, grounded theorists adopt software to expedite their analyses. We contend, however, that ultimately the research process must remain under the control of the researcher(s). Glaser and others are correct to be wary of use of software, particularly when researchers come to rely upon it. Yet, cases abound where use of some form of electronic repository, plus sorting and retrieval facilities has proved useful. Researchers must understand both the benefits and the dangers of use (and reliance upon) software support. Dey and Hesse-Biber each offer arguments in favour of its use. Dey in particular sees software as encouraging 'a more diligent and disciplined approach to the auditing of the creative process'. Glaser remains adamantly opposed to any use of GTM software support largely because he sees it as undermining researcher's creativity, and wasting large amounts of precious time and effort; he devotes a specific chapter to his concerns in *The Grounded Theory Perspective II* (Glaser, 2003: Chapter 3). Hesse-Biber offers an alternative view; 'software supports structure, enriches the learning process; Conversely use of technology may destroy the intimacy between researcher and data'. In any case, whatever one's views might be, the computer is now ubiquitous and so will be incorporated in diverse ways in all and any research settings and projects.

CONCLUSION: GTM IS ABOUT DEVELOPING GROUNDED *THEORIES*

No overview of grounded theory would be complete without a word about theorizing, the professed purpose, and promise of GTM. If the purpose of the method is to create the product (a coherent grounded theory), then how does the researcher go about it? In brief, theorizing in GTM means developing abstract concepts and specifying the relations between them. Thus, how researchers arrive at these concepts becomes a crucial part of theorizing and of grounded theory practice, more generally.

Theoretical concepts in GTM result from iterative processes of going back and forth between progressively more focused data and successively more abstract categorizations of them. Researchers focus on treating their most significant categories to further analysis and raising them to concepts in their emerging theories. Yet their means of making these theoretical moves are by no means transparent. Current discussions of GTM often address tensions between possibilities of emergent categories and the practice of theorizing. The notion of emergence has held a central place in grounded theory logic, and rhetoric. Some grounded theorists argue that categories emerge automatically when researchers study, compare, and successively focus their data. Others avow that emergence does not occur independently from interpretation and, subsequently, they cast doubt on any claims to emergence. For them, however implicit, ideas always inform categories and words alone always impart meaning.

We propose that the two positions are not necessarily mutually exclusive; nor should they be. Grounded theory strategies allow for imaginative engagement with data that simple application of a string of procedures precludes. This engagement with data creates a space where the unexpected can occur; thus, unexpected events and experiences may emerge. In keeping with Mead (1932) and Durkheim (1938), an emergent phenomenon has new and different properties from its antecedents. If so, then a grounded theorist's categories would have new and different properties from the pieces of data that prompted the researcher's idea for the category. Emergent categories arise from the researcher's skill in defining these new properties through the successively more analytic comparative processes of comparing data with data, data with code, code with code, code with category, and category with category. In short, grounded theorists can build on an epistemologically sophisticated view of emergence that allows for possibilities of emergent (but never wholly inductive) categories in the practice of theorizing.

This *Handbook* has been developed to provide a resource for researchers eager to develop their theory-building skills through engagement with a wide range of perspectives on GTM; its features and ramifications; its intricacies in use; its demands on the skills and capabilities of the researcher; and its position in the domain of research methods. As such, the 27 chapters have been divided into six sections: I Origins and History; II Grounded Theory Method and Formal Grounded Theory; III Grounded Theory in Practice; IV Practicalities; V Grounded Theory in the Research Methods Context; and VI Grounded Theory in the Context of the Social Sciences.

NOTES

1 Chapter VII of *The Discovery of Grounded Theory* concerns 'Theoretical Elaboration of Quantitative Data', and so does lay the basis for Glaser's valid contention that GTM can use all kinds of data. But we would still hold to the generally accepted view that GTM is a qualitative research method, even if it can incorporate quantitative data: this characteristic is also true for many other qualitative methods.

2 This summary is taken from Bryant, 2006, where it is used with reference to the term 'information' (pp. 39–42).

3 See the chapters in this *Handbook* by Stern, Covan, Clarke, and Star, all of whom studied with both Glaser and Strauss.

4 Barney Glaser is fond of stating that 'Grounded Theory is more than a methodology, it's a way of life', and this is far less far-fetched than might appear at first glance.

5 Kearney, Gibson, Greene et al., and Hildenbrand discuss the conditional matrix; and they and several others discuss the role and nature of Glaser's *theoretical codes*.

6 Bryant, 2006.

7 Readers should refer to the *Discursive Glossary* for some of the different characterizations of these and other GTM terms.

8 Although in some contexts, particularly software development, the two terms have distinct meanings, here 'verification' and 'validation' are treated as synonyms.

REFERENCES

Bryant, A. (2002) Re-grounding grounded theory. *The Journal of Information Technology Theory and Application*, 4, 25–42.

Bryant, A. (2003) A constructive/ist response to Glaser. In *Forum Qualitative Sozialforschung/Forum: Qualitative Social Research*. Retrieved 15 March 2007 from http://www.qualitative-research.net/fqs/fqs-eng.htm (*now included in CSA Abstracts* http://www.csa.com/factsheets/socioabs-set-c.php).

Bryant, A. (2006) *Thinking Informatically: A New Understanding of Information, Communication, and Technology*. Lampeter, UK: Edwin Mellen.

Casper, M. (1998) *The Making of the Unborn Patient: A Social Anatomy of Fetal Surgery*. New Brunswick, NJ: Rutgers University Press.

Charmaz, K. (1990) Discovering chronic illness: Using grounded theory. *Social Science & Medicine*, 30, 1161–1172.

Charmaz, K. (2000) Grounded theory: Objectivist and constructivist methods. In N. K. Denzin & Y. S. Lincoln (Eds.), *Handbook of Qualitative Research* (2nd ed., pp. 509–535). Thousand Oaks, CA: SAGE.

Charmaz, K. (2003) Grounded theory. In M. Lewis-Beck. A. E. Bryman, & T. Futing Liao (Eds.), *The SAGE Encyclopedia of Social Science Research Methods* (pp. 440–444). London: SAGE.

Charmaz, K. (2005) Grounded theory in the 21st century: A qualitative method for advancing social justice research. In N. K. Denzin & Y. S. Lincoln (Eds.), *Handbook of Qualitative Research* (3rd ed., pp. 507–535). Thousand Oaks, CA: SAGE.

Charmaz, K. (2006) *Constructing Grounded Theory: A Practical Guide Through Qualitative Analysis*. London: SAGE.

Charmaz, K. (2007) Constructionism and grounded theory. In J. A. Holstein & J. F. Gubrium (Eds.), *Handbook of Constructionist Research*. New York: Guilford.

Charmaz, K. & Henwood, K. (2007). Grounded theory in psychology. In C. Willig and W. Stainton-Rogers (Eds.), *Handbook of Qualitative Research in Psychology*. London: SAGE.

Charmaz, K. & Mitchell, R. G. (2001) Grounded theory in ethnography. In P. Atkinson, A. Coffey, S. Delamont, J. Lofland, & L. H. Lofland (Eds.), *Handbook of Ethnography* (pp. 160–174). London: SAGE.

Clarke, A. (2005) *Situational Analysis: Grounded Theory after the Postmodern Turn*. Thousand Oaks, CA: SAGE.

Coffey, A., Holbrook, B. & Atkinson, P. (1996) Qualitative Data Analysis: Techniques and Representations. *Sociological Research Online*. Retrieved 15 March 2007 from www.soc.surrey.ac.uk/socresonline Vol. 1, No. 1.

Dey, I. (1999) *Grounding Grounded Theory: Guidelines for Qualitative Inquiry*. London UK: Academic Press.

Durkheim, E. (1938) *The Rules of the Sociological Method*. New York: The Free Press.

Gallie, W. B. (1956) Essentially contested concepts. *Proceedings of the Aristotelian Society*, 167–198.

Glaser, B. G. (1965) The constant comparative method of qualitative analysis. *Social Problems*, 12, 436–445.

Glaser, B. G. (1978) *Theoretical Sensitivity*. Mill Valley, CA: Sociology Press.

Glaser, B. G. (1992) *Basics of Grounded Theory: Emergence vs. Forcing*. Mill Valley, CA: Sociology Press.

Glaser, B. G. (1998) *Doing Grounded Theory: Issues and Discussions*. Mill Valley, CA: Sociology Press.

Glaser, B. G. (2003) *The Grounded Theory Perspective II: Description's Remodeling of Grounded Theory Methodology*. Mill Valley, CA: Sociology Press.

Glaser, B. G. (2005) The impact of symbolic interaction on GT. In *The Grounded Theory Perspective III*. Mill Valley, CA: Sociology Press.

Glaser, B. G. & Strauss, A. L. (1965a) *Awareness of Dying*. Chicago: Aldine.

Glaser, B. G. & Strauss, A. L. (1965b) Discovery of substantive theory: A basic strategy for qualitative analysis. *American Behavioral Scientist*, 8, 5–12.

Glaser, B. G. & Strauss, A. L. (1967) *The Discovery of Grounded Theory: Strategies for Qualitative Research*. Chicago: Aldine.

Glaser, B. G. & Strauss, A. L. (1968) *Time for Dying*. Chicago: Aldine.

Haig, B. D. (1995) Grounded theory as scientific method. *Philosophy of Education*. Retrieved 15 March 2007 from www.ed.uiuc.edu/EPS/PES-Yearbook/95_docs/haig.html

Lee, R. M. & Fielding, N. (1996) Qualitative data analysis: Representations of a technology: A comment on Coffey, Holbrook and Atkinson. *Sociological Research Online*, Vol. 1, no. 4. Retrieved 15 March 2007 from http://www.socresonline.org.uk/socresonline/1/4/lf.html

Mead, G. H. (1932) *The Philosophy of the Present*. LaSalle, IL: Open Court Publishing.

Mills, C. W. (1959) *The Sociological Imagination*. New York: Oxford University Press.

Smit, K. & Bryant, A. (2000) Grounded theory method in IS research: Glaser vs. Strauss. *Research in Progress Papers*, 2000–7. Retrieved 15 March from http://www.leedsmet.ac.uk/inn/documents/2000–7.pdf

Star, L. S. (1989) *Regions of the Mind: Brain Research and the Quest for Scientific Certainty*. Stanford, CA: Stanford University Press.

Strauss, A. L. (1987) *Qualitative Analysis for Social Scientists*. Cambridge: Cambridge University Press.

Strauss, A. L. (1993) *Continual Permutations of Action*. New York: Aldine de Gruyter.

Strauss, A. L. & Corbin, J. (1990) *Basics of Qualitative Research*. Thousand Oaks, CA: SAGE.

Strauss, A. L. & Corbin, J. (1994) Grounded theory methodology: An overview. In N. K. Denzin & Y. S. Lincoln (Eds.), *Handbook of Qualitative Research* (pp. 273–285). Thousand Oaks, CA: SAGE.

Strauss, A. L. & Corbin, J. (1998) *Basics of Qualitative Research* (2nd ed.). Thousand Oaks, CA: SAGE.

Titscher, S., Meyer, M., Wodak, R. & Vetter, E. (2000) *Methods of Text and Discourse Analysis*. Thousand Oaks, CA: SAGE.

Wittgenstein, L. (1953) *Philosophical Investigations*. Retrieved 15 March 2007 from http://www.galilean-library.org/pi1.html

PART I

Origins and History

Grounded Theory in Historical Perspective: An Epistemological Account

Antony Bryant and Kathy Charmaz

The Grounded Theory Method (GTM) was 'discovered' in the 1960s, as Barney G. Glaser and Anselm L. Strauss titled their pioneering book, and simultaneously conveyed a crucial epistemological premise about creating scientific knowledge. In this chapter we seek to offer an account of this development by locating its foundations against the epistemological background of the time, and note how epistemological shifts have impinged on grounded theory in the intervening decades. Throughout the chapter, we will use GTM to indicate that we discuss the method, rather than the theoretical product, a *grounded theory*, of using the method. We emphasize the specific historical context of social research and the content and direction of sociological inquiry just before and during the time Glaser and Strauss were writing as a team. We not only show that Glaser and Strauss articulated and developed important trends in social research, but also that they brought innovative methodological strategies to these trends that inspired generations of new scholars to pursue qualitative research.

The foundations of GTM are rich and varied. Glaser and Strauss articulated them in a complex methodological mix from what in effect are four founding texts: *Awareness of Dying* (1965), *The Discovery of Grounded Theory* (1967), *Time for Dying* (1968), and *Status Passage* (1971). Yet for many researchers, both advocates and critics of GTM, the method revolves largely around a very limited reading of *The Discovery of Grounded Theory*. In earlier papers we have termed this reading 'the grounded theory mantra', which in its minimal form comprises the claim that 'theory emerges from the data'. We, too, return to the early works but informed by considered readings of varied grounded theory statements and of epistemological shifts and developments during the past five decades.

Whatever the reasons for this complex mix of sociological and personal factors constituting the GT mantra, this self-referential, and often self-reverential, orthodoxy is clearly breaking down, as the variety and scope of the chapters in this *Handbook* indicate. In part, this change has come about as a result of the numerous and varied applications of the method. Thus, if we are to have more than a shattering of orthodoxies into a plethora of do-as-you-please versions of GTM, such developments must also be accompanied by an understanding of the epistemological bases of Glaser and Strauss's original method and the historical context in which it arose, our central concerns in this present chapter.

Any research method makes epistemological claims; a method must indicate why its application will lead to a development of knowledge, otherwise researchers would have no basis for choosing it in the first place. GTM makes explicit claims to an extent, however, in its founding texts, these claims are often couched in ambiguous terms and with reference to, and in sharp contrast with, existing ideas of what constituted 'proper' research procedures. Moreover, when reading these statements some 40 years later, it is crucial that readers understand something of the context within which they appeared and the rationales and motivations behind their appearance. Hence, we address epistemological issues pertinent to GTM and those related to 1960s sociology in the USA.

EMERGENCE OF GROUNDED THEORY

Glaser and Strauss derived the GTM through analysing their own research decisions, most notably in their analyses of procedures and practices in hospitals dealing with the terminally ill (*Awareness of Dying*). Glaser's background comprised a rigorous training in quantitative methods and middle range theories, working at Columbia University under the guidance of both methodologist Paul F. Lazarsfeld and noted theorist and sociologist of science Robert K. Merton.[1] Strauss, in contrast, had a background in symbolic interaction, derived from his studies with the Chicago School and its emphases on pragmatist philosophy, George Herbert Mead's social psychology, and ethnographic field research. We realize that what scholars call the Chicago School glosses over the diverse methodological and theoretical approaches that the Chicago faculty evinced (see Abbott, 1999; Bulmer, 1984; Fine, 1995; Platt, 1996); however, we adopt the term here to indicate the pragmatist, symbolic interactionist, and ethnographic traditions at Chicago.

Glaser and Strauss, each in his own fashion and from specific perspectives, argued against growing disciplinary trends and sought to transcend the shortcomings (as they saw them) of these early influences. Like many works,

The Discovery of Grounded Theory continued and advanced earlier conversations with each author's mentors and, in Strauss's case, with numerous Chicago School and symbolic interactionist colleagues. Glaser and Strauss's individual backgrounds and trajectories brought them together at University of California, San Francisco, in the 1960s and early 1970s, from which the GTM emerged; perhaps their subsequent separate paths contributed to their methodological divergence in later decades.

Through developing this method, Glaser and Strauss aimed to provide a clear basis for systematic *qualitative* research, although Glaser has always argued that the method applies equally to quantitative inquiry. They intended to show how such research projects could produce outcomes of equal significance to those produced by the predominant statistical-quantitative, primarily mass survey methods of the day. What they also achieved was a redirection of positivist-oriented concern among qualitative researchers seeking reliability and validity in response to criticisms from quantitative methodologists. Glaser and Strauss offered a method with a solid core of data analysis and theory construction. Their method contrasted with the strategy of those who sought procedural respectability through collection of vast amounts of unanalysed, and often un-analysable, data.

In so doing, Glaser and Strauss simultaneously positioned themselves against the quantitative orthodoxy and, whether or not they were aware of it, offered a way of mimicking this orthodoxy: the same but different. Their logic proved to be a source not only of major strengths but also of weaknesses in their method. A key strength, and one still central to GTM, is that it offers a foundation for rendering the processes and procedures of qualitative investigation visible, comprehensible, and replicable. GTM builds on methodological concepts of empirical grounding derived from the quantitative orientation, together with an explication of how to apply the kinds of analytic steps long practiced, but seldom articulated, by theoretically oriented Chicago School field researchers. The key weaknesses of Glaser and Strauss's statement of the GTM resided in the positivist, objectivist direction they gave grounded theory, which we discuss below.[2]

In their early work, Glaser and Strauss offered a method that could claim equivalent status to the quantitative work of the time. Theorizing need not have central recourse to quantitative foundations and studies, instead data could generate more than numerical data. Such research findings must amount to more than impressions and resorting to ethereal theorizing or suppositions. In seeking to provide a firm and valid basis for qualitative research, their early position can be interpreted as justification for a naïve, realist form of positivism, which holds that the veracity of a theory can be determined simply by recourse to 'the data'. Whether or not Glaser and Strauss each individually realized it, their approach (both together in their early GTM writings and later in their separate works) implies far more than this view; but for a variety of reasons the data-oriented positivist idea of the method predominated, and has only recently been critically exposed and challenged. We seek to show at this juncture that this positivist view constitutes only a partial reading of GTM, and that other, more profound perspectives were present even in the earliest writings.

It was hardly surprising that GTM in the 1960s took on the mantle of the prevailing positivist view of knowledge and applied it to qualitative research, hence the focus on data, fit, etc. After all, these foci reflected Glaser's perspective and positivist heritage and they reflected concerns expressed by fellow qualitative researchers who sought to defend qualitative inquiry (see, for example, Becker, 1958; Becker & Geer, 1960; Bruyn, 1966; Dean & Whyte, 1958; Deutscher, 1966, 1970; Filstead, 1970). The title of Glaser and Strauss's methods manual, *The Discovery of Grounded Theory*, attests to a clear epistemological orientation that assumes that reality can be discovered, explored, and understood. From this perspective, reality is unitary, knowable, and waiting to be discovered.

Yet Strauss's earlier essay, *Mirrors and Masks* (1959/1969) indicates that he was well aware that people's perspectives shaped how they view objects. He wrote, 'Classifications are not *in* the object; an object gets classified from some perspective' (p. 48). This point speaks to the explicit continuity of Strauss's thinking with pragmatism and, in particular, Mead's (1934/1962) notion of the multiplicity of perspectives. Taken to its logical extension, Strauss's position suggested that the objectivism of an external reality and the constructionism in theory development was a problematic issue when he stated, 'It would appear that classification, knowledge and value are inseparable' (p. 23). Several years after publication of *The Discovery of Grounded Theory*, Schatzman and Strauss (1973) alluded to this tension in their field research manual, 'As he [sic] scans his ON's [Observational Notes] he recognizes the fullness, clarity and incontrovertibility of distinct experiences in the field. These are not *soft data*; these are as hard and true as he could make them from his experiences' (p. 106). Their nod to the researcher's experiences hints that what the researcher can observe in the field shapes the analysis, and weakly intimates that previous experiences may also have some impact (see Glaser & Strauss, 1967: Chapter 11); but their strong truth claims challenged assertions that qualitative data was *soft* and therefore unreliable.

Such truth claims tended to privilege the researcher's knowledge over those actors involved in the research context. Thus, in *Time for Dying* (Chapters 2 and 3), evidence abounds that Glaser and Strauss understood that the concept of *trajectory* explained how staff defined, planned, and re-interpreted patients' experiences in the unit. They even point to the ways in which nurses engaged in 'reconstructing' a woman's story (p. 21). Yet this perspective is never applied directly to the researcher. To us, this silence implies that the researcher is immune from this process of constructing and re-constructing. Chapter 11 of *Time for Dying* concerns how people are actively involved in defining aspects of their lives and their situations; but Glaser and Strauss do not apply this reflexive insight to themselves as researchers and authors.[3] Interestingly, however, Glaser (1991) recalls that, as a new sociologist, Strauss urged him to study how other sociologists researched and conceptualized their work and to 'try to grasp their conceptualization not as something to believe, but as the author's perspective on the data from an historical or "school" point of view and see this perspective as data itself!' (p. 12). By 2001 (p. 48), Glaser states, 'All knowledge is not perspectival. Description is perspectival; concepts that fit and work are variable'. Here, Glaser alludes to his position that grounded theory is a type of variable analysis analogous to quantitative manipulation of variables.

We can identify pressing reasons why a straightforward scientistic[4] view of grounded theory might have predominated over more nuanced positions in the 1960s, and perhaps even been advisable in order to secure funding, promotion, and career development. Qualitative research was clearly seen as second-rate, a poor relation (if related at all) to rigorous statistically based research. The reputability and quest for legitimate academic status of qualitative research demanded that it should claim some basis of validity equal to that of quantitative practices, so why not try to establish a 'scientific' basis for applying and validating qualitative research? In part this stance coincided with the prevailing ideas of researchers throughout the social science disciplines who, for the most part, tended to assume they were engaged in studies of an external reality and that all observers would see much the same things in the field.[5] Many scholars saw the social sciences as cast very much in the same mould as the natural sciences, and believed that if the social sciences did not yet actually fit that mould, then they certainly *ought* to fit it. (This view particularly pertained to the USA where sociologists built on the work of Talcott Parsons, Robert Merton, and others working in the structural-functional tradition. Simultaneously, their methodological counterparts created major survey research centres that obtained substantial Federal funding and conducted studies for government agencies.[6])

From our view today, *The Discovery of Grounded Theory* was far too readily open to a reading anchored in a clearly positivist epistemology; something that became readily apparent in the ensuing decades, if it was not as obvious at the time of first publication. Nonetheless, Glaser and Strauss's detailed studies from this period offer many intimations and arguments that show that they understood the research process in a more complex way. Chapter 11 of *The Discovery of Grounded Theory* was specifically concerned with 'Insight and Theory Development', arguing that researchers could and should provide insight and imagination as key characteristics of inquiry itself. In both *Awareness of Dying* and *Time for Dying*, the authors offer clear indications that the research process is at least as much about dialogue as about data and analysis. However, no one, including Glaser and Strauss, took up these points as central issues for GTM in the immediate aftermath of the publication of *The Discovery of Grounded Theory*.

Schatzman and Strauss (1973) did devote space to watching and listening as well as to interviewing as part of the research process and, more recently, Glaser (2001, 2002) has advocated passive observation in the field. Indeed Glaser (1978, 1992, 1998) has long advocated active and repeated scrutiny of the data and of subsequent emerging codes and categories through constant comparative analysis.

He argues that these constant comparisons serve to abstract major properties of categories from the data and, thus, render the analysis objective. This process is markedly different from blindly gathering vast amounts of data. For Glaser (2001), abstraction eliminates the need for situating the data in its context. He argues that creating abstract categories moves the analysis to a general conceptual and more theoretical level, and increases its parsimony by covering a wide range of empirical indicators.

Some evidence exists that Glaser and Strauss and other early GTM adopters discussed these issues, and Glaser sometimes seems to engage with them in his writings. By 1994, Strauss and Corbin stated that their version of grounded theory meant doing interpretive work. As Corbin (1998) points out, Strauss, however, attended to his work, not to debates about it. Thus, for a host of reasons, some of the richness of the early GTM expositions disappeared as the method gathered momentum to become by far the most popular and widely-claimed qualitative research method despite criticisms of its epistemological naïveté (Emerson, 1983; Katz, 1983), slipshod attention to data collection (Lofland & Lofland, 1984), questionable justification of small samples (Charmaz, 2006), production of trite categories (Silverman, 2001), presumed incompatibility with macro questions (Burawoy, 1991; Layder, 1998), and hints of being unscientific (Spalter-Roth, 2005). Despite these criticisms, the method has led to jobs, journal articles, and funded research in addition to inspiring researchers to engage in qualitative inquiry.

SOCIAL CONSTRUCTIONIST CHALLENGES IN SOCIOLOGY

In order to re-establish the full intensity of GTM, one needs to understand the major epistemological shifts that developed concurrently with GTM itself in the 1960s. These developments had, and continue to have, a profound impact on sociology and beyond. *The Discovery of Grounded Theory* (1967), *Awareness of Dying* (1965), and *Time for Dying* (1968) were published during a time of reappraisal and renewal in sociological discourse. Critiques of quantification together with social constructionist statements in several sectors of the discipline had spurred this reappraisal, beginning in the 1950s. Such diverse luminaries as Herbert Blumer (1954, 1956), Pitirim Sorokin (1956), and C. Wright Mills (1959) had long called for redirecting the sociological enterprise away from 'variable analysis' (Blumer, 1956), 'abstract empiricism' (Mills, 1959), and 'fads and foibles' (Sorokin, 1956). Throughout his career, Blumer called for direct study of the empirical world by gaining firsthand knowledge of it. In his culminating essay, he enjoined sociologists to 'respect the nature of the empirical world and organize a methodological stance to reflect that respect' (1969: 60). For Blumer, symbolic interactionism meant exactly what he subtitled his book: perspective and method. Sorokin valued intuitive, less concrete ways of knowing in an age when social scientists dismissed research problems unsuited for quantification. Mills sought to tackle social structure from a critical perspective and to address pressing social issues that lay beyond the consciousness and tools of positivist social scientists who had donned the cloak of neutrality.

Meanwhile, Goffman (1959, 1961, 1963) arrived on the sociological scene. He combined Chicago School interactionism and a micro version of Durkheimian structuralism in his compelling studies of the self, identity, and social organization that inspired generations of graduate students. Goffman did not engage in epistemological battles about method; indeed his acute observations appeared to be the dispassionate recordings of a distanced observer (see Goffman, 1989). His growing opus, however, testified that a single observer could construct incisive analyses when *embedded* in the research setting. Ultimately Goffman achieved the balance between exhaustive knowledge gained through immersion in the setting and dispassionate analysis that cut to the core of social experience.

Strauss played a significant role in advancing Chicago School social constructionist analyses well before his collaboration with Glaser. Granted, he wrote *Mirrors and Masks* (1959/1969) as a theoretical essay, but based *Images of the American City* (1961) on collected data. He also supervised a large field research project that culminated in *Psychiatric Ideologies and Institutions* (Strauss, Schatzman, Bucher, Erlich, & Sabshin, 1964), which depicted how staff constructed, maintained, and defended treatment ideologies. In one of the most important constructionist statements of the day, Strauss and his colleagues (1963) theorized the organization of the hospital as a 'negotiated order', constructed through collective and individual action, not as a stable structure separate from human involvement. In some ways this negotiated order can now be seen as an incipient form of his later work on social worlds and arenas.

In 1967, *The Discovery of Grounded Theory* immediately took its place as a classic statement articulating Chicago School strategies for qualitative inquiry that *Awareness of Dying* had already exemplified. Moreover, by 1966 another sociological classic had appeared: *The Social Construction of Reality* by Peter Berger and Thomas Luckmann, followed by Harold Garfinkel's *Studies in Ethnomethodology* in 1967.[7] These two books seriously challenged conventional positivistic epistemologies because they explicitly argued that people constructed their realities through their ordinary actions, a position that is also implicit in Glaser and Strauss's empirical works.

In some cases, subsequent social constructionist statements came perilously close to the extreme of arguing that in fact no external reality existed; a clearly non-tenable position. Other less extreme forms of social constructionism appeared to end in complete relativism, according equal status to all and any representations of reality. We certainly do not subscribe to either of these positions, but we do stress the importance of recognizing that social actors' understanding of the world is socially constructed, but not in any arbitrary or ad hoc fashion. Indeed this sustained and never completed process of construction has to be understood as the core of what is now fairly readily grasped as 'structuration', whereby the structure 'is both the medium and the outcome of the practices which constitute social systems' (Giddens, 1981). Although students of the time may have been influenced by all three of the books mentioned above, the authors did not explicitly engage each other in subsequent works.

We certainly do not wish to suggest that social scientists immediately took up the implications of all or any of these works. However, by the early 1970s, Berger and Luckmann's, and Garfinkel's books were standard fare on under-graduate sociology reading lists, and *The Discovery of Grounded Theory* had inspired graduate students in sociology and particularly in nursing to pursue qualitative research with far more confidence. In addition, Thomas Kuhn's *The Structure of Scientific Revolutions* had appeared in 1962, and was sufficiently well-known among theorists and philosophers in the social sciences for a second edition to appear in 1969 with a postscript in which Kuhn responded to his critics. By the early 1970s, within the general domain of the social sciences, the issues of epistemology, science versus non-science, and the relationship between knowl-edge and knower(s) had emerged as central concerns. Scholars increasingly rec-ognized the import of the sociology of knowledge and its production. Thus, there is good reason to argue that by the late 1960s and early 1970s, social scientists should have been aware that the epistemological grounds of inquiry had shifted.

In the USA, these shifts informed theorists and sociologists of knowledge but the gap between theory and methods remained a chasm in the broader discipline of sociology. Relatively few methodologists of either quantitative or qualitative persuasions traversed the new epistemological ground in their empirical research. Moreover some who had followed these epistemological shifts may not have known how to act upon them in research practice.[8]

Further challenges to traditional positivist approaches in sociology emanated from Garfinkel's concept of ethnomethodology, essentially endowing or recog-nizing the methodological skills of all social beings' collective construction of their everyday lives through interactive practices. Ethnomethodological studies demonstrate that social actors ascribe meaning to situations through socially shared interpretive practices. Social actors know how to enter into social con-texts, and they know how to ensure that social interaction is initiated and sustained. Early ethnomethodology projects often consisted of interventions into social set-tings with the aim of exposing these taken-for-granted actions by deliberately undermining them. Garfinkel built on Schutz's phenomenology and Weber's *verstehen*, which meant beginning study with an empathetic understanding of how social actors defined their situations.[9]

Social constructionist and ethnomethodological studies taught researchers that data don't speak for themselves. The cognizant other (the researcher) engages data in a conversation. As we have already pointed out, early GTM sources, such as *Time for Dying*, appear to invoke a similar concept but restrict it to non-researchers. Garfinkel's work broached the question of how social stability was maintained and enforced by making such stability a problem rather than a given. This question stood in stark opposition to the prevailing Parsonian

structural-functionalist theoretical assumptions of the day, where order and stability was assumed, and equilibrium was the status quo. Garfinkel coined the
terms 'cultural dope' and 'psychological dope' to symbolize specific weaknesses
of the Parsonian position:

> By 'cultural dope' I refer to the man-in-the-sociologist's-society who produces the stable
> features of the society by acting in compliance with preestablished and legitimate alterna-
> tives of action that the common culture provides. The 'psychological dope' is the man-in-
> the-psychologist's-society who produces the stable features of the society by choices among
> alternative courses of action that are compelled on the grounds of psychiatric biography,
> conditioning history, and the variables of mental functioning. The common feature in the
> use of these 'models of man' is the fact that courses of common sense rationalities of judg-
> ment which involve the person's use of common sense knowledge of social structures over
> the temporal 'succession' of here and now situations are treated as epiphenomenal
> (Garfinkel, 1967: 68).

Garfinkel aimed to show how ordinary people, acting on their common sense
knowledge, construct their routine, taken-for-granted behaviour. For Garfinkel,
routine behaviour and everyday routine practices were accomplishments, not
givens. Taken together, people usually followed taken-for-granted rules and thus
enacted the routine practices that constituted social life: Garfinkel termed his
approach to common sense knowledge the 'documentary method':

> The method consists of taking an actual appearance as 'the document of', as 'pointing to',
> as 'standing on behalf of' a presupposed underlying pattern. Not only is the underlying
> pattern derived from its documentary evidences, but the individual documentary evidences,
> in their turn, are interpreted on the basis of 'what is known' about the underlying pattern
> (Garfinkel, 1967: 78).

In other words, Garfinkel sought to position the commonsense methods of the
actors themselves at the very centre of sociological research. As we shall see, his
approach bears some resemblance to the founding texts of GTM, but also differs
in some key respects. Glaser and Strauss also maintain a clear distinction
between lay accounts ('walking surveys' in Glaser's current term) and expert
GT-based ones.

The main point to take from Garfinkel, however, is that social stability is an
accomplishment that may be already established in some sense, but has to be
continually maintained and sustained by those social actors present in any given
context. Hence Garfinkel had his students engage in mischievous interventions
that upended people's taken-for-granted expectations about how interaction
should proceed. By disrupting the routine grounds of behaviour, Garfinkel's
'experiments' laid bare the rules that govern situations and the relationships
within them. These experiments included such startling actions as treating
your mother as if she is your landlady, standing facing the back in an elevator,
moving ever closer to people at parties or looking just over their shoulders when
talking to them, and taking literally things that are said as pleasantries.

Berger and Luckmann argued, in a similar fashion, that people construct social
stability through their everyday actions, but did so from a position within the

1960s domain of 'the sociology of knowledge'. We would now understand their standpoint as a form of social constructivism or situated cognition. Essentially, their book extended the argument developing from Marx's statement from *The 18th Brumaire:* 'Men make their own history, but they do not make it as they please; they do not make it under self-selected circumstances, but under circumstances existing already, given and transmitted from the past'. Although Berger and Luckmann developed their ideas primarily from the work of Alfred Schutz, their work also complements that of Mead and other Chicago School symbolic interactionists.

> It is important to keep in mind that the objectivity of the institutional world, however massive it may appear to the individual, is a humanly produced, constructed objectivity ... In other words despite the objectivity that marks the social world in human experience, it does not thereby acquire an ontological status apart from the human activity that produced it ... Society is a human product. Society is an objective reality. Man is a social product. It may also already be evident that an analysis of the social world that leaves out any one of these three moments will be distortive (Berger & Luckman, 1966: 61).

Together the core concerns of Garfinkel, and those of Berger and Luckmann, encourage scrutiny of the nature of social research and the role of the social researcher, but still rendered them as essentially ambiguous or inherently problematic. Taken to its logical conclusion, although few researchers did, the researcher can no longer assume a position of disinterested observer; any effort to do so must at the very least engage the above issues, and raise perennial issues for sociologists. The accounts of social actors must be understood to be a central resource for social investigation and research; but the status of these lay sources raises a conundrum. Garfinkel's subversive demonstrations lead to infinite regress or a complete dismantling of any sociological project; as such later ethnomethodologists such as Sacks (see Silverman, 1998) moved beyond earlier methodological experiments and sought to show how systematic investigation of the social world was possible, while still allowing for a constructivist orientation.

To an extent, Glaser and Strauss offer intimations of this key development. They intended to show how interactions construct and reaffirm structure, albeit with a focus directly on awareness contexts or time expectations rather than social stability. With their concern for aspects such as 'fit' and 'substantive theory', however, their attention was directed away from wider epistemological and methodological issues. Consequently they neglected to develop the ramifications of their own position on objectivity directly or to challenge notions of a disinterested observer. Their empirical work, however, revealed social constructionist assumptions in detailing research participants' practices that produce the studied world.

In direct opposition to some of the trends identified above, however, Glaser and Strauss adamantly maintained the view that researchers' expert knowledge superseded that of their research subjects. Hence, they adhere to a distinctly different starting assumption and trajectory from Garfinkel. Yet such a view could no longer be taken-for-granted. For Garfinkel, experts' accounts are simply yet another form of document, running parallel to common-sense material. Social researchers are 'doing social research' just as their 'subjects' (for example, nurses) are 'doing nursing'; the former have no better claim to knowledge and insight than any other account. Glaser and Strauss, throughout *The Discovery of Grounded Theory*, maintain that systematic theorizing can claim an elevated status; a position that Glaser (2001, 2002) sustains throughout his writings. (Strauss, in contrast, would likely agree that researchers are 'doing social research', but would argue that by conceptualizing the processes in the field, we offer a useful account of actual phenomena.)

When we consider all of these developments exemplified by Garfinkel, and Berger and Luckmann, that pertain to ideas put forward in *The Discovery of Grounded Theory*, Glaser and Strauss's critique of quantitative sociology splits in two. They direct one part of their critique perfectly and tellingly at the procedural orthodoxy of the day. The other part, however, fell short of a target that rapidly changed form and moved beyond its earlier confines. The accepted wisdom underlying the entire project of being scientific and objective was in the process of transformation in light of a vast array of challenges with which we still contend, whether we wish to or not. Although its origins can be traced back to a period well before the mid-twentieth century, the 1960s marked the point from which all researchers would have to engage problems of 'science', 'knowledge', 'data', and 'objectivity' following the publication of and attending debate around Thomas Kuhn's *The Structure of Scientific Revolutions*. Given our intent to draw attention to precisely these concerns within the context of GTM, and the fact that several other chapters in this collection mention precisely these aspects, it is necessary to outline Kuhn's ideas at some length before explaining their importance for GTM and research methods as a whole.

THOMAS KUHN'S CHALLENGE TO CONVENTIONAL SCIENCE

Kuhn's book first appeared in 1962, as part of a series of monographs under the general title of *The International Encyclopaedia of Unified Science*.[10] Ironically science would never be unified in quite the same way again in the wake of its publication. Kuhn's book aroused sufficient controversy in the scientific arena, and among historians and philosophers of science, that in 1969 a second edition was published, including an extended 'Postscript' taking issue with the plethora of comments and critiques the first edition had provoked.

In essence, Kuhn's argument centred on the ways in which scientists 'do science' in the normal run of things, normal being the operative word. Kuhn coined the term 'normal science' defining it as the activities undertaken by scientists in a field where research could be 'firmly based upon one or more past scientific achievements, achievements that some particular scientific community acknowledges for a time as supplying the foundation for further practice' (Kuhn, 1969: 10). These achievements had to have some basic attraction that ensured that a group of scientists felt sufficiently drawn towards them, and they also had to leave open a sufficient range of issues for further research.[11] Kuhn's term for such a context of existing and acknowledged achievements plus open-ended issues was *paradigm*, a source of much misunderstanding since that date, partly an effect of the many ways in which he used and developed the term in his book.[12]

Kuhn built his conception of paradigm change on the foundations constructed by Ludwik Fleck (1935/1979) who remained unnoticed in the USA until long after Kuhn had become an icon in the philosophy and history of science. Fleck presaged the social constructionist view of science, and Kuhn's notion of paradigm. Fleck recognized that 'facts' arose from what he called 'thought collectives', or groups of scientists who shared a language, set of principles, and way of thinking about the scientific problems that they encountered. Thus, for Fleck, facts did not exist independently in an external reality separate from scientific observers; instead, they were constructed by scientists. Researchers have not yet fully mined the implications of Fleck's brilliant contribution, as Löwy has averred (1988, 1990). Kuhn's analysis, however, captured the imagination of those 1960s sociology graduate students interested in epistemology and qualitative inquiry.

The outcome of Kuhn's argument was that historians and philosophers of science (and many others) came to understand science as a collective activity centred on traditions, authorities, institutions, networks, and community solidarity at least as much as on some unquenchable thirst for truth and knowledge. More critically, Kuhn laid out an argument that stressed the ways in which science as a communal activity actually could be seen to work against innovative thinking, since 'normal science often suppresses fundamental novelties because they are necessarily subversive of its basic commitments'. This suppression or inhibition was not merely a sociological phenomenon, with authoritative figures freezing out those who sought to challenge the paradigmatic orthodoxy; although this was and continues to be an important aspect of the institutionalization of science.[13] In its starkest form, Kuhn's position amounted to arguing that scientists viewed the world through the prevailing paradigm of their discipline; it acted as a cognitive lens or filter. Those who were outside the discipline, or who challenged the paradigm in some way, often did so because they *saw things differently* or *saw different things*.

Many social scientists enthusiastically adopted Kuhn's ideas, sometimes in ways with which Kuhn himself disagreed. Some saw Kuhn's work as undermining the orthodox view of what constituted science and scientific practice, simultaneously demolishing the science/non-science distinction. Claims to 'being scientific' no longer amounted to anything special: science was a form of belief, resting on assumptions and traditions not unlike other belief-systems.

More critically, and more pertinently for our purposes, Kuhn's work fed into the growing critique of positivism, and so further undermined the scientific orthodoxy with its view of what constituted 'proper science', 'scientific method', and where the distinction between science and non-science could be clearly drawn.

Ultimately this path can lead to a relativist free-for-all, but at the very least it confounded any attempt to develop the social sciences in the same mould as the traditional view of the physical sciences.

Whatever one's views of the trends exemplified and embodied in the work of Garfinkel, Berger and Luckmann, and particularly Kuhn, by the mid-1970s a body of well-founded opinion had emerged that at the very least offered an alternative view of the social sciences and how the social world could and should be studied; and also questioned the coherence of the exemplars held up to these disciplinary upstarts as paragons of academic and intellectual virtue, the hard sciences, and positivist scientific practices.[14]

GROUNDED THEORY METHOD: GATHER YOUR DATA WHILE YOU MAY

The four founding texts and the trajectory of GTM clearly emanate from a profound dissatisfaction with the prevailing approach of university-based social research in the USA in the 1960s. Glaser and Strauss took issue from the very start with two key features of the established institutional orthodoxy: (1) the primacy accorded to *verification* of existing theories; and (2) what they term 'theory generated by logical deduction from *a priori* assumptions' (1967: 3). Hence, they stressed developing or generating novel theories as opposed to verification of existing ones, and urged social researchers to go into the field to gather data without a ready-prepared theoretical framework to guide them.

Not surprisingly, Glaser and Strauss over-emphasized the faults of those they challenged and under-emphasized the problems of the alternative they proposed. In particular, their early work placed huge emphasis on 'data', albeit not in the sense of what they saw as the near-mindless 'data gathering' that was the procedural order of the prevailing deductive verificationism; but data itself was posited as non-problematic, something to be observed in 'phenomenalist' fashion by a disinterested researcher. Certainly Glaser and Strauss were equally concerned that analysis accompanied data collection, rather than being postponed until its completion. They introduced the term 'constant comparison' to aid and abet ongoing analysis; but the imagery of research being 'grounded in the data' was unfortunately bound to elevate 'data' to prime position precisely at a time when the term data itself was increasingly problematic.

In part this preoccupation with data arose because Glaser and Strauss, in addition to focusing on the very real deficiencies of social research, were also inordinately keen to uphold qualitative social research as a scientifically respectable practice which had to be learned and in which specific expertise had to be developed. They were quite explicit about this position. Indeed, they stressed that any method must adhere to scientific rigour, and that the generating of sociological theory is the sole job of sociologists. Professionals and lay people 'cannot generate sociological theory from their work. Only sociologists are trained to want it, to look for it, and to generate it' (Glaser & Strauss, 1967: 6–7).

Glaser and Strauss amplified this position by detailing how they conceived of the 'interrelated jobs of theory in sociology' (Glaser & Strauss, 1967: 3), namely:

> (1) to enable prediction and explanation of behaviour; (2) to be useful in theoretical advance in sociology; (3) to be usable in practical applications—prediction and explanation should be able to give the practitioner understanding and some control of situations; (4) to provide a perspective on behaviour—a stance to be taken toward data; and (5) to guide and provide a style for research on particular areas of behaviour (Glaser & Strauss, 1967: 3).

These five theoretical jobs would be acceptable to even the most 'verificationist', empirical sociologist. But taken together with their stress on inductive data gathering, Glaser and Strauss offer a fairly succinct summary of a scientistic[15] or positivist position. In short, they presented a view of scientific practice and theory of knowledge that the ideas of Kuhn et al. already had challenged, if not undermined, as we described earlier. Their scientistic position may well have been at odds with what they each actually sought to advocate, but in the ensuing decades the inherent positivism in statements such as these came to efface much of the rich profundity of their early writings.

The key positivist feature of GTM in many of its classic texts is the various exhortations about 'data'. Data is an unproblematic concept for positivists; it is simply what one observes and notes down in the course of doing one's research. So too for Glaser and Strauss in the 1960s, and for many GTM proponents since then. How researchers define, produce, and record data largely remains unexamined. This uncritical stance towards data emanates from the assumption that data reside in an external reality that researchers can access and examine in a straightforward manner. Glaser (1978, 1992, 2002) insists that researchers let data emerge, and must not preconceive them either through applying extant concepts or asking extensive questions of research participants. Glaser does not acknowledge that researchers' own standpoints, historical locations, and relative privileges shape what they *can* see.[16]

In particular, Glaser's constant refrain has always been 'all is data'; right up to the present day. As it stands, this stance might not be too problematic; except that it is often taken to mean 'data is all'; in other words the inductive gathering of data will somehow lead to the emergence of concepts and a grounded theory. Glaser's stance implies that the researcher does not need to be concerned with quality of the data, range of data, amount of data, access to data, or accuracy of data.

INDUCTION, DEDUCTION, ABDUCTION

Glaser and Strauss were always keen to demonstrate that their method was *inductive*, as opposed to the conventional *deductive* approaches they were challenging. They did not couch their criticism of 'theory generated by logical deduction from *a priori* assumptions' in philosophical or methodological terms as such. Rather they pointed to the failure of this prevailing approach to generate new theories. This is a key point. A good deal of debate had always occurred about the nature of appropriate methods for the social sciences dating back to the nineteenth century, in particular the *Methodenstreit* (methods conflict) originating in the German-speaking world in the 1880s, and to which Weber and Sombart contributed. In the 1960s, this debate was re-ignited as the works of Karl Popper, Jurgen Habermas, and others were published.

Put in simple terms, the problem of induction is that merely because one has collected a limitless number of seemingly identical observations, one has no certainty that generalizing from these observations produces a valid conclusion. One aspect of the problem of induction is that of failing to see the exception. Thus if one is sitting on a riverbank, one might observe several swans swimming past. They are all white in colour and, after counting 10, 20, ... 100, or more, one might be tempted to conclude that 'all swans are white', unaware that the black swan went by sometime earlier, or will pass by soon after one ceases making observations. The other problematic aspect of induction was clearly stated by David Hume in the eighteenth century as follows: 'It is impossible, therefore, that any arguments from experience can prove this resemblance of the past to the future; since all these arguments are founded on the supposition of that resemblance'. In other words, similarity is in the eye of the researcher; deciding that two or more observations are similar is itself a part of the research process, and cannot be seen merely as some mechanistic form of counting occurrences and accruing a mass of data.[17]

In the wake of such work, use of terms such as induction and deduction in any methodological context needed to be handled with some attention to the developing discussions. All that Glaser and Strauss could offer was an exhortation to apply an inductive method, with no reference to the body of arguments about the problems of induction. Although good reasons for their silence may have existed in the 1960s, followers of GTM continued along this path which even proponents of the method have described as 'naïve Baconian inductivism' (Haig, 1995).

We do not suggest that deductive reasoning is better than inductive reasoning, nor do we treat Glaser and Strauss's criticism of the prevailing methods in social sciences in the USA at the time as without foundation. We do wish to alert people to the silences and lacunae in their early writings, which Strauss and Corbin (1994) acknowledge when they state, 'Because of the partly rhetorical purpose of that book [*The Discovery of Grounded Theory*] and the authors' emphasis on the need for *grounded* theories, Glaser and Strauss overplayed the inductive aspects' (p. 277). These deficiencies have become more problematic in the intervening period, but are now being remedied, in many cases by the sort of work that has been accomplished by many of the contributors to this volume.

Further evidence of Strauss's awareness of some of these issues appear in *Mirrors and Masks*:

> ... any particular object can be named and thus located in countless ways. The **naming** sets in within a context of quite **differently related classes**. The nature or essence of an object does not reside mysteriously within the object itself but is dependent upon **how it is defined** (p. 20). [our emphasis]

The direction of activity depends upon the particular ways that objects are classified (p. 21).
… it is the definition of what the object 'is' that allows **action** to occur with reference to
what it is taken to be (p. 22). [our emphasis]

Strauss was influenced by the writings of Dewey, Peirce, Mead, and Blumer. He saw research as an analytic interplay between analysing inductive data, conceptualizing them, and then checking these conceptions through further data gathering which brings in deductive elements. His approach uses *abductive* reasoning. The logic of abduction entails studying individual cases inductively and discerning a surprising finding and then asking how theory could account for it. The researcher subsequently puts all these possible theories to test by gathering more data to ascertain the most plausible explanation. Abductive reasoning resides at the core of grounded theory logic: it links empirical observation with imaginative interpretation, but does so by seeking theoretical accountability through returning to the empirical world (see also Chapter 10 by Reichertz and Chapters 26 and 27 by Locke and Strübing, respectively).

GROUNDED THEORY METHOD: MOVING BEYOND THE MANTRA

Glaser and Strauss stated from the outset that their method is based on induction; and they clearly used the term in the sense of building from the specific to the generic. Their rationale for this in the 1960s was clearly to distinguish their approach from the hypothesis-driven *deductive* method that, as far as they were concerned, characterized the social and behavioural sciences at the time, at least in the USA. The standard model of social science research in the 1960s was one in which graduate researchers drew out hypotheses from the works of the grand old men of social theory, and then sought to test those hypotheses in social settings. Glaser and Strauss gave researchers a way out of this model by offering a clear rationale for doing fieldwork without having recourse to the grand theories and grand theorists. Parsons, Merton, and Lazarsfeld had broken with the earlier trend, generating their own grand theories or, in Lazarsfeld's case, a methodology to gather 'facts'. As Glaser and Strauss state, 'But even these few have lacked methods for generating theory from data, or at any rate have not written about their methods. They have played "theoretical capitalist" to the mass of "proletariat" testers' (Glaser & Strauss, 1967: 10).

Thus, Glaser and Strauss had sound reasons for their clarion call for an inductive approach. Given the period in which their first books appeared, it was not surprising that their concept of induction was fairly uncomplicated and easily led to a staunch position of *phenomenalism* as defined above. Examples are easy to find in their early work, but also in their later writings. Glaser and Strauss continually refer to theory being 'grounded in the data', with theory almost mystically 'emerging' from the data. Such statements are often quoted as the mantra of the grounded theorist. Like a mantra, it is continually chanted but rarely questioned or examined. Indeed today numerous publications claim to use GTM that do no more than refer to *The Discovery of Grounded Theory* and quote the mantra—and perhaps subsequently elicit major criticisms (see Atkinson, Coffey, & Delamont, 2003; Spalter-Roth, 2005). A few examples from early and late GTM publications will serve as illustrations of Glaser and Strauss's views, both when they wrote in concert and later when they published separately and when Strauss co-authored with Corbin:

- [t]he basic theme in our book is the discovery of theory from data systematically obtained from social research (Glaser & Strauss, 1967: 2).
- Theory based on data can usually not be completely refuted by more data or replaced by another theory. Since it is too intimately linked to data, it is destined to last despite its inevitable modification and reformulation (Glaser & Strauss, 1967: 4).
- … the generation of theory from such insights [sources other than data] must then be brought into relation to the data, or there is great danger that theory and empirical world will mismatch (Glaser & Strauss, 1967: 6).
- The first step in gaining theoretical sensitivity is to enter the research setting with as few pre-determined ideas as possible—especially logically deducted [sic], a prior [sic] hypotheses. In this posture, the analyst is able to remain sensitive to the data by being able to record events and detect happenings without first having them filtered through and squared with pre-existing hypotheses and biases (Glaser, 1978: 2–3).
- A theory must be readily modifiable, based on ever-emerging notions from more data (Glaser, 1978: 4).
- A researcher does not begin a project with a preconceived theory in mind (unless his or her purpose is to elaborate and extend existing theory). Rather, the researcher begins with an area of study and allows the theory to emerge from the data (Strauss & Corbin, 1998: 12).
- Creativity manifests itself in the ability of researchers to aptly name categories, ask stimulating questions, make comparisons, and extract an innovative, integrated, realistic scheme from masses of unorganized, raw data (Strauss & Corbin, 1998: 13).
- Although we do not create data, we create theory out of data (Strauss & Corbin, 1998: 56).
- One would hope that by 'sticking to the data' the analyst is left out of the interpretive process, but this is highly unlikely (Corbin, 1998: 123).

Ironically, Strauss and Corbin (1994) take a different stance towards data when they state, 'Theories are always traceable to the data that gave rise to them—within the interactive context of data collecting and data analyzing, in which the analyst is also a crucially significant interactant' (pp. 278–279).

GTM: MOST WIDELY USED QUALITATIVE METHOD

For a variety of reasons GTM steadily gained in popularity, initially in the social sciences and eventually well beyond, moving out into any discipline where research involved contact with human subjects in specific situations. By the late 1990s, surveys indicated that among published papers reporting on qualitative research, two out of every three claimed to be using GTM (Titscher et al., 2000). One reason for GTM's popularity was that claiming to use the method allowed a degree of licence to the researcher, particularly in the early stages of producing a proposal, and hence use of GTM would later be claimed in published accounts. Haig (1995) called GTM a 'useful umbrella term', conceal-ing more than it revealed; and this strand of criticism certainly has some basis. Given its popularity it is not surprising that the method has received wide atten-tion, including many extended critiques, they are much testimony to its widespread use as they are to any inherent weaknesses.

Many of the criticisms can be allayed with reference to the extended body of research that has accrued since the 1960s. This body of work is not monolithic. There is, as most readers of this *Handbook* will already realize, the fundamental dichotomy between the two founders, but this is by no means the only contour to be traced through GTM research over the past 40 years. The variation in use and implementation of the method across a wide range of topics, disciplines, and researchers is far more important. As a result, a large and growing body of work claims use of GTM that can itself now be cited, and used as guidance—and some-times as warning. Until comparatively recently, most researchers claiming to be using GTM cited only a very small and constrained portion of this literature. In recent years, however, this trend has started to change and citations to GTM have moved beyond the confines of Glaser and Strauss, plus either Strauss and Corbin or Glaser on his own. This trend reflects the health and vigour of the method. In many regards, GTM is developing in a manner similar to Action Research (AR; see Chapter 18 by Dick). AR can be traced back to the pioneering work of Kurt Lewin and others, but is now identifiable in many different approaches all of which retain key characteristics of the early formulations, but each of which has taken those insights and developed them according to different contexts, dis-ciplinary conventions, conceptual and theoretical engagements, and forms of implementation. This diversity needs to be seen as a basis for discussion and exchange of ideas, not an excuse to erect barriers between one 'true' version of GTM and all others, inevitably deemed to be impostors or diluted forms of 'the one authentic method'.

We have demonstrated here that GTM developed against a background of increasing discussion and questioning of fundamental philosophical precepts; a process that extended well beyond the narrow confines of philosophy seminars, going deep into the social sciences and beyond. As a result, the emergence of GTM is a history of not only chasing a moving target (i.e. scientific rigour) but also one that is doubling back on itself and meeting 'qualitative' and 'interpretive' strategies coming at it from elsewhere. As a consequence the pop-ularity of GTM is double-edged. In its early formulations, it provided a justification for doing qualitative research, but it did so initially by imposing a positivist mantle on that process. Later, others have shown how this mantle can be stripped away (e.g. Bryant, 2002; Charmaz, 2000, 2006; Clarke, 2005; Dey, 1999; Locke, 2001). We need to understand this trajectory, and to some extent dismantle the method from its initial formulations. Although this project may prove disagreeable to some of its proponents, it will have a significant impact on the ways in which the method is both practiced and justified.

One key problem is that GTM literature on the method itself from the late 1960s to at least the early 1980s remained almost untouched by any of these epistemological developments that we have discussed.[18] This point may also be true for many other research methods, but it is far more critical for GTM because the founding manifesto of the method specifically addressed key issues such as the role of the researcher, the concepts of data and induction, and the generation of theory. And all of these have extensive ramifications, particularly in the light of the developments in philosophy of science, epistemology, and the sociology of science from the early 1960s onwards.

For whatever reasons, neither Glaser nor Strauss demonstrated sustained engagement with these conceptual developments throughout their various publications. Glaser was initially a student of Merton, and so it might be expected that he would have attended to debates in the sociology of science, but he has always made it clear that he rapidly moved away from Merton's stance on many key issues.[19] Strauss may have stood at the periphery of the various critiques of positivism and scientific method at the time. From his own intellectual formation, he certainly adopted the pragmatist study of action and understood the methodological implications of symbolic interactionism, which raised similar issues about contingency, multiplicity of meaning, observers' values, and provisional truth.[20] Strauss and Corbin mention several of these issues in their 1994 chapter and Strauss demonstrates his awareness of the methodological implications of pragmatism in *Continual Permutations of Action* (1993).

So we are left with a conundrum; one which may eventually be resolved, but at this stage we can only take note of it and move on. In doing so it is important to note that the very popularity of GTM attests to its profound attraction and usefulness; but we must distinguish between what is key to the method, and what needs to be discarded or reformulated if the method is to shake off its reputation for being positivist, philosophically naïve, and a refuge for the methodologically indecisive.

Many of the chapters in this *Handbook* demonstrate the rich and varied uses of GTM, and all in some way attest to its value and attraction as a method. In summary we can offer the following benefits and attractions of GTM. This method:

- fulfils a need to justify qualitative approaches (justification of process);
- justifies qualitative research in terms familiar to quantitative researchers—data, validity, systematic, empirical, etc. (justification of ontology);
- and thus keeps the gate-keepers placated and satisfied (justification by publication and acceptance);
- offers a rationale for researchers as they begin their research—the method eliminates and precludes need for hypotheses and conjectures at the start (justification of methodological flexibility and indeterminacy);
- warns against an unexamined or too briefly considered application of extant ideas and theories and instead urges fresh theorizing (justification of open-mindedness);
- requires a comparative approach;
- keeps the analyst engaged through adopting emergent guidelines.

GROUNDED THEORY METHOD: AN EPISTEMOLOGICAL RE-ARRANGEMENT AND RE-ENGAGEMENT

For over a decade, the basic principles of GTM have come under fire both from within and without the GTM community. In philosophical terms, some scholars (e.g. Layder, 1998) have accused GTM of naïve inductivism; and the method has been labelled as positivist. Several scholars take these criticisms as sufficient reason to argue that the method is fundamentally flawed; yet others have sought to distinguish between particular versions or aspects of GTM, pointing out how the method can overcome these criticisms. Hence we have made the distinction between 'objectivist' and 'constructivist' GTM (see Bryant, 2002, 2003; Charmaz, 2000, 2002, 2006).

To an extent, we can see the objectivist—constructivist distinction as an attempt to distinguish between the *essences* and the historical *accidents* of GTM, i.e. between the core aspects of the method, without which it wouldn't be GTM, and the aspects which can be traced back to the historical context within which GTM developed, and which can therefore be dispensed with. Any attempt to tease out and separate these two categories would, however, quickly come to grief. What some would regard as essential to GTM, others would see as accidental. At this stage we prefer to delineate the variety of ideas and developments within and around GTM.

What is critical, however, is to re-position GTM in the light of the current philosophical and epistemological landscape. This repositioning will allow us to understand such issues as those shaping the research process, the roles, social locations, perspectives of the researcher, the production of data, and the dialectical relations between sensitizing concepts and induction. Closer attention to these issues enables us to situate our grounded theories, see complexity, and to avoid the hegemonic reach of over-generalization with its erasure of positionality, difference, time, and location (see also Clarke, 2005). Such repositioning will also allow us to move beyond simple criticisms that label GTM as positivist or limited to micro-analyses.

The various debates since the 1960s have resulted in far more acceptance of uncertainty and indeterminacy in knowledge claims. We may all yearn for certainty, but most knowledge claims are couched in provisional terms. When even the findings of the 'hard' sciences (usually held up as the paragons of truth and knowledge) are couched in terms of context, probability, ambiguity, and uncertainty, then no one can demand anything more from the softer sciences. Ironically, Glaser and Strauss had clear intimations of exactly this position in their discussions of substantive and formal theories, and Glaser's recent work makes some important observations on this topic.

So although clear positivist strands are evident in the original GTM texts, these books also hold insights that can provide the basis for a very different interpretation of the method. More importantly, we can usefully and successfully build on its key features of 'theoretical agnosticism' (Henwood & Pidgeon, 2003: 138), coding for actions and theory construction, successive comparative analyses, inductive-abductive logic, memo-writing, theoretical sampling, and theoretical integration.

Furthermore Glaser and Strauss's objectives for developing GTM can also be brought into line with recent developments in science and technology studies. The arguments raised against the grand theorizers, the 'theoretical capitalists' (Parsons, Merton, etc.) can be seen as a call to members of the varied parts of the academic sociological community to work against prevailing paradigms, to challenge the way 'things are done around here'. *The Discovery of Grounded Theory* can be read very much as the call of the outsider pointing out the deficiencies of existing orthodoxies. Glaser's participation in the discipline certainly fits the bill of a productive (and provocative) outsider. While Strauss was much more enmeshed in sociological and academic circles but as a central figure in Chicago School sociology, he stood outside of the functionalist trend towards increasing quantification and challenged it.

Thus, we can see GTM as originally a way of trying to encourage, support, and guide researchers who wanted to work outside 'normal social science' (1960s USA style). And scholars can still see GTM as a call for 'thinking outside the paradigm' in its key ideas of aiming at new conceptual insights based on direct hands-on research, even if the advice regarding exposure to existing literature and current research findings is anomalous and ambivalent. Re-reading *The Discovery of Grounded Theory* in the light of Kuhn's writings and current social constructionist work[21] leads to a reinterpretation of Glaser and Strauss's exhortations. Their characterization of 'verification' and 'theoretical capitalists' parallels Kuhn's concept of 'normal science', although Glaser and Strauss restrict themselves to institutional issues, and do not touch on the epistemological ones. In order to break out of normal science, researchers must constantly strive for innovative insights and fresh conceptualizations. GTM can provide a way of building the confidence to do so, even when one is just starting out as a researcher

A repositioned GTM solves numerous epistemological problems. It takes a middle ground between realist and postmodernist visions (Charmaz, 1995; Charmaz & Mitchell, 1996). This approach adopts Blumer's assumption of an 'obdurate reality' but views reality as multiple, subject to redefinition, and somewhat indeterminate (see Strauss & Fischer, 1979a, b). Furthermore, a repositioned GTM moves further into interpretive conceptual frames and further away from deterministic variables. This GTM builds on the fluid, interactive, and emergent research process of its originators but seeks to recognize partial knowledge, multiple perspectives, diverse positions, uncertainties, and variation in both empirical experience and its theoretical rendering. It is realist to the extent that the researcher strives to represent the studied phenomena as faithfully as possible, representing the 'realities' of those in the studied situation in all their diversity and complexity. A repositioned GTM assumes that any rendering is just that: a *representation* of experience, not a replication of it. It is interpretivist in acknowledging that to have a view at all means conceptualizing it. Data are always conceptualized in some way. Thus the generalizing impulse in classical grounded theory, its strain towards parsimony and subsequent reductionism, the beliefs in discovery and distanced observation, all become problematic. A repositioned GTM bridges defined realities and interpretations of them. It produces limited, tentative generalizations, not universal statements. It brings the social scientist into analysis as *an* interpreter of the scene, not as the ultimate authority defining it. And this method acknowledges the human, and sometimes non-human, relationships that shape the nature of inquiry.

ACKNOWLEDGEMENTS

We thank Adele E. Clarke, David Maines, Andrew Roth, David Silverman, and Sharlene Hesse-Biber for their thoughtful comments on earlier drafts of this chapter. They each had intriguing insights and raised important questions that challenged us to clarify our position.

NOTES

1 Lazarsfeld was the Head of the Bureau of Applied Social Research, a noted centre for survey research.

2 One of the reviewers objected to this aspect of our chapter, arguing that Glaser and Strauss 'were well beyond' issues such as positivism—perhaps a statement with which Glaser would still concur. We contend that claims about data must at least engage with the issues of positivism and constructivism, even if those making the claims end up with an epistemological position far different from ours.

3 Kathy Charmaz adds, in the 1960s, theoretically oriented qualitative researchers discussed notions of reality as constructed but treated their own data as given in an external world. At that time, Anselm often noted that various research team members observed much the same processes. He portrayed this phenomenon—often with delight—as testifying to the strength of their interpretations of the reality in question, that they had captured 'it'. I was acutely aware then that Anselm did not see that the 'objectivity' of the team reflected their largely shared class, race, and generational backgrounds and acceptance of professional, i.e. medical, assumptions. One can also read the dying books as reflecting the staff position, not the patient's or their families.

4 Scientism being defined as the belief that (natural) science is the highest (perhaps the only true) form of knowledge as well as process of acquiring knowledge—specifically in its positivist or empiricist form. In short, scientism involves the worship of science.

5 We leave it to readers to decide if the status and funding issues had any impact on the cognitive ones—or vice-versa.

6 We are indebted to Adele Clarke for this point and also for noting that it was no accident that Columbia University housed the Bureau of Applied Social Research and the University of Chicago established the National Opinion Research Center as survey researchers displaced Chicago School field research.

7 Garfinkel had published most of the chapters earlier but having them in book form brought greater attention to them. His approach gave rise to two related methodologies: ethnomethodology, and conversational analysis. Both challenged positivistic methodological practices of the day and conceptions of scientific theorizing. Ironically, 40 years later, many social scientists view conversational analysis as the most positivist of the qualitative methodologies.

8 Patrick L. Biernacki, for example, was well-schooled in the epistemological debates of the 1960s, but his 1986 book reflected his training in positivistic grounded theory from Glaser. In contrast, Virginia Olesen was explicitly influenced by Schutz, as is evident in her co-authored book (Olesen & Whittaker, 1968), and also recalls being influenced by the interactionists of the time (personal communication to K. Charmaz, July 9, 2006).

9 Severyn T. Bruyn (1966) also primarily built on Schutz and Weber, with some consideration of George Herbert Mead, to develop a humanist methodology on a phenomenological foundation. Bruyn articulated methodological procedures although not in great detail. He devoted much of the book to theoretical discussions of ways of knowing and to expanding traditional concepts of validity, reliability, and verification to take subjective meaning into account.

10 The series was founded by Rudolf Carnap, in 1938, together with the sociologist Otto Neurath (both having earlier been members of the Vienna Circle of logical positivists) and the pragmatist philosopher, Charles W. Morris. The idea was to publish a series of monographs dealing with issues in the philosophy of science, particularly those concerning mathematics and empirical science. (See entry in Encyclopaedia Britannica.)

11 Kuhn termed these issues 'puzzles', a deliberately demeaning term.

12 The term has become so misused since Kuhn's time that its use is now almost entirely restricted to those impelled to express themselves in the most unreflective forms of management-speak. The ultimate expression of this is, of course, to be found in the popular American animated sitcom, *The Simpsons*:

Network Executive: We at the network want a dog with attitude. He's edgy. You've heard the expression 'Let's get busy'? Well, this is a dog who gets *biz-ay*; consistently and thoroughly.

Krusty: So he's proactive?

Executive: Oh, God yes! We're talking about a totally outrageous paradigm.

Writer: Excuse me, but 'proactive' and 'paradigm'? Aren't those just buzzwords that dumb people use to sound important? Not that I'm accusing you of anything like that … I'm fired aren't I?

13 Recent examples of this institutionalized exclusion can be found in the Artificial Intelligence community in the 1970s and 1980s where the rule-based paradigm effectively suppressed the connectionist or network-based one. Also the current penchant for string theory amongst leading physicists is claimed by its detractors to operate in a similar fashion. For a grounded theory treatment of struggles to establish theoretical dominance in science, see Susan Leigh Star, *Regions of the Mind: Brain Research and the Quest for Scientific Certainty* (1989). She documents how brain localizationists suppressed the challenges from brain diffusionists to establish the ruling theory of brain functioning.

14 This is putting it very mildly, and a slight caricature might add some additional insight. Charmaz's chapter in the 2nd edition of the *Handbook of Qualitative Research* argues that there are two alternative positions: objectivist and constructivist. The argument for a constructivist position effectively undermines the objectivist one.

15 Scientism can be defined as 'science's belief in itself as the highest, or even only valid form of knowledge'.

16 Awareness of earlier developments in the sociology of knowledge by Karl Mannheim (1952, 1954) could also have led to similar realizations about the significance of standpoint, perspective, and historical location for seeing the empirical world.

17 So a black 'swan' might simply be re-classified as something else, so preserving the integrity of swans as white.

18 During this period, numerous grounded theory studies in the experience of chronic illness and sociology of science adopted social constructionism.

19 At his GTM seminar in London (April 2006), Barney Glaser admitted that he 'was a sociologist of science … for about one whole day … I think it was a Wednesday!' Nonetheless Merton's emphasis on middle-range theories, positivist views of science, and structural-functional perspective did influence him.

20 Clarke (2005) takes this position further with her agreement with Star (1989) and Fujimura (1992) that symbolic interaction and grounded theory constitute a theory/methods package and her argument that this package always contained postmodern elements.

21 Vibrant established and emergent constructionist research is evident in such diverse areas as health and illness, information systems, communications, criminology, ageing, social psychology,

and science and technology studies. Significant influences in research settings are not limited to human actions. The growing literature on relationships with animals, for example, suggests how they may influence the form and content of inquiry (see, Irvine, 2004; Sanders, 1999). Clarke (1998) emphasized how scientists' access and use of research animals affected the development of the field of reproductive biology and sociologists and geographers have documented how the built environment affects social life and social research (see, for example, Lofland, 1998; Milligan, 2003a, b).

REFERENCES

Abbott, A. (1999) *Department & Discipline: Chicago Sociology at One Hundred*. Chicago: University of Chicago Press.

Atkinson, P., Coffey, A. & Delamont, S. (2003) *Key Themes in Qualitative Research: Continuities and Changes*. New York: Rowan and Littlefield.

Becker, H. S. (1958) Problems of inference and proof in participant observation. *American Sociological Review*, 23, 652–660.

Becker, H. S. & Geer, B. (1960) Participant observation: The analysis of qualitative field data. In R. N. Adams & J. J. Preiss (Eds.), *Human Organization Research: Field Relations and Techniques* (pp. 267–289). Homewood, IL: Dorsey Press.

Berger, P. & Luckmann, T. (1966) *The Social Construction of Reality: A Treatise in the Sociology of Knowledge*. Garden City, NY: Anchor Books.

Biernacki, P. (1986) *Pathways from Heroin Addiction: Recovery without Treatment*. Philadelphia: Temple University Press.

Blumer, H. (1954/1969) *What is wrong with social theory?/Symbolic Interactionism: Perspective and Method* (pp. 140–152). Englewood, Cliffs, NJ: Prentice-Hall.

Blumer, H. (1956) Sociological analysis and the 'variable'. *American Sociological Review*, 21, 683–690.

Blumer, H. (1969) *Symbolic Interactionism: Perspective and Method*. Englewood Cliffs, NJ: Prentice-Hall.

Bruyn, S. T. (1966) *The Human Perspective in Sociology: The Methodology of Participant Observation*. Englewood Cliffs, NJ: Prentice-Hall.

Bryant, A. (2002) Re-grounding grounded theory. *Journal of Information Technology Theory and Application*, 4, 25–42.

Bryant, A. (2003) A constructive/ist response to Glaser. In *Forum Qualitative Sozialforschung/Forum: Qualitative Social Research*. Retrieved 15 March 2007 from http://www.qualitative-research.net/fqs/fqs-eng.htm (now included in *CSA Abstracts* http://www.csa.com/factsheets/socioabs-set-c.php).

Bulmer, M. (1984) *The Chicago School of Sociology: Institutionalization, Diversity, and the Rise of Sociology*. Chicago: University of Chicago Press.

Burawoy, M. (1991) The extended case method. In M. Burawoy, A. Burton, A. A. Ferguson, K. Fox, J. Gamson & N. Gartrell (Eds.), *Ethnography Unbound: Power and Resistance in the Modern Metropolis* (pp. 271–290). Berkeley: University of California Press.

Charmaz, K. (1995) Between positivism and postmodernism: Implications for methods. In N. K. Denzin (Ed.), *Studies in Symbolic Interaction* (17: 43–72). Greenwich, CT: JAI Press.

Charmaz, K. (2000) Grounded theory: Objectivist and constructivist methods. In N. K. Denzin & Y. S. Lincoln (Eds.), *Handbook of Qualitative Research* (2nd ed., pp. 509–535). Thousand Oaks, CA: SAGE.

Charmaz, K. (2002) Grounded theory analysis. In J. F. Gubrium & J. A. Holstein (Eds.), *Handbook of Interview Research* (pp. 675–694). Thousand Oaks, CA: SAGE.

Charmaz, K. (2006) *Constructing Grounded Theory: A Practical Guide Through Qualitative Analysis*. London: SAGE.

Charmaz, K. & Mitchell, R. G. (1996) The myth of silent authorship: Self, substance, and style in ethnographic writing. *Symbolic Interaction*, 19, 285–302.

Clarke, A. (1998) *Disciplining Reproduction: Modernity, American Life Sciences, and the Problems of Sex*. Berkeley: University of California Press.

Clarke, A. (2005) *Situational Analysis: Grounded Theory after the Postmodern Turn*. Thousand Oaks, CA: SAGE.

Corbin, J. M. (1998) Alternative interpretations: Valid or not? *Theory & Psychology*, 8, 121–128.

Dean, J. P. & Whyte, W. F. (1958) How do you know if the informant is telling the truth? *Human Organization*, 17, 34–38.

Deutscher, I. (1966) Words and deeds: Social science and social policy. *Social Problems*, 13, 233–254.

Deutscher, I. (1970) Looking backward: Case studies on the progress of methodology in sociological research. In W. J. Filstead (Ed.), *Qualitative Methodology: Firsthand Involvement with the Social World* (pp. 202–216). Chicago: Markham Pub. Co.

Dey, I. (1999) *Grounding Grounded Theory: Guidelines for Qualitative Inquiry*. San Diego: Academic Press.

Emerson, R. M. (1983) Introduction to theory and evidence in field research. In R. M. Emerson (Ed.), *Contemporary Field Research* (pp. 93–107). Boston: Little Brown.

Filstead, W. J. (1970) Introduction. In W. J. Filstead (Ed.), *Qualitative Methodology: Firsthand Involvement with the Social World* (pp. 1–11). Chicago: Markham Pub. Co.

Fine, G. A. (Ed.) (1995) *A Second Chicago School? The Development of a Postwar American Sociology*. Chicago: University of Chicago Press.

Fleck, L. (1935/1979) *The Genesis and Development of a Scientific Fact*. In T. J. Trenn & R. K. Merton (Eds.). University of Chicago Press: Chicago.

Fujimura, J. (1992) Crafting science: Standardized packages, boundary objects and 'translation'. In A. Pickering (Ed.), *Science as Practice and Culture* (pp. 168–214). Chicago: University of Chicago Press.

Garfinkel, H. (1967) *Studies in Ethnomethodolgy*. Englewood Cliffs, NJ: Prentice-Hall.

Giddens, A. (1981) *A Contemporary Critique of Historical Materialism*. London: Macmillan.

Glaser, B. G. (1978) *Theoretical Sensitivity*. Mill Valley CA: Sociology Press.

Glaser, B. G. (1991) In honor of Anselm Strauss: A collaboration. *Social Organization and Social Process: Essays in Honor of Anselm Strauss* (pp. 11–16). New York: Aldine de Gruyter.

Glaser, B. G. (1992) *Basics of Grounded Theory: Emergence vs. Forcing*. Mill Valley, CA: Sociology Press.

Glaser, B. G. (1998) *Doing Grounded Theory: Issues and Discussions*. Mill Valley, CA: Sociology Press.

Glaser, B. G. (2001) *The Grounded Theory Perspective: Conceptualization Contrasted with Description*. Mill Valley, CA: Sociology Press.

Glaser, B. G. (2002) Constructivist grounded theory? In *Forum Qualitative Sozialforschung/ Forum: Qualitative Social Research*. Retrieved 15 March 2007 from http://www.qualitative-research.net/fqs-texte/3-02/3-02glaser-e-htm

Glaser, B. G. & Strauss, A. L. (1965) *Awareness of Dying*. Chicago: Aldine.

Glaser, B. G. & Strauss, A. L. (1967) *The Discovery of Grounded Theory: Strategies for Qualitative Research*. Chicago: Aldine.

Glaser, B. G. & Strauss, A. L. (1968) *Time for Dying*. Chicago: Aldine.

Glaser, B. G. & Strauss, A. L. (1971) *Status Passage*. Chicago: Aldine Atherton.

Goffman, E. (1959) *The Presentation of Self in Everyday Life*. Garden City, NY: Doubleday Anchor Books.

Goffman, E. (1961) *Asylums.* Garden City, NY: Doubleday Anchor Books.

Goffman, E. (1963) *Stigma.* Englewood Cliffs, NJ: Prentice-Hall.

Goffman, E. (1989) On fieldwork. *Journal of Contemporary Ethnography*, 18, 123–132.

Haig, B. D. (1995) Grounded theory as scientific method. *Philosophy of Education.* Retrieved 15 March 2007 from www.ed.uiuc.edu/EPS/PES-Yearbook/95_docs/haig.html

Henwood, K. & Pidgeon, N. (2003) Grounded theory in psychological research. In P. M. Camic, J. E. Rhodes & L. Yardley (Eds.), *Qualitative Research in Psychology: Expanding Perspectives in Methodology and Design* (pp. 131–155). Washington, DC: American Psychological Association.

Hume, D. (1772) *An Enquiry Concerning Human Understanding.* Retrieved 15 March 2007 from www.marxists.org/reference/subject/philosophy/works/en/hume.htm

Irvine, L. (2004) *If You Tame Me: Understanding our Connection with Animals.* Philadelphia: Temple University Press.

Katz, J. (1983) A theory of qualitative methodology: The system of analytic fieldwork. In R. M. Emerson (Ed.), *Contemporary Field Research* (pp. 93–107). Boston: Little Brown.

Kuhn, T. S. (1962) *The Structure of Scientific Revolutions.* Chicago: University of Chicago Press.

Kuhn, T. S. (1969) *The Structure of Scientific Revolutions* (2nd ed.). Chicago: University of Chicago Press.

Layder, D. (1998) *Sociological Practice: Linking Theory and Social Research.* London: SAGE.

Locke, K. (2001) *Grounded Theory in Management Research.* Thousand Oaks, CA: SAGE.

Lofland, L. H. (1998) *The Public Realm: Exploring the City's Quintessential Social Territory.* Hawthorne, NY: Aldine de Gruyter.

Lofland, J. & Lofland, L. H. (1984) *Analyzing Social Settings* (2nd ed.). Belmont, CA: Wadsworth.

Löwy, I. (1988) Ludwik Fleck on the social construction of medical knowledge. *Sociology of Health & Illness*, 10, 133–155.

Löwy, I. (1990) Ludwik Fleck: From philosophy of medicine to a constructionist and relativist epistemology. In I. Löwy (Ed. & Trans.), *The Polish School of Philosophy of Medicine: From Tytus Chalubinski to Ludwig Fleck (1896–1961)* (pp. 215–227). Boston: Kluwer Academic.

Mannheim, K. (1952) *Essays on the Sociology of Knowledge.* New York: Oxford University Press.

Mannheim, K. (1954) *Ideology and Utopia: An Introduction to the Sociology of Knowledge.* New York: Harcourt, Brace, and World.

Marx, K. (1852) *The 18th Brumaire of Louis Napoleon.* Retrieved 15 March 2007 from http://www.marxists.org/archive/marx/works/1852/18th-brumaire/ch01.htm

Mead, G. H. (1934/1962) *Mind, Self and Society.* Chicago: University of Chicago Press.

Milligan, M. (2003a) Displacement and identity discontinuity: The role of nostalgia in establishing new identity categories. *Symbolic Interaction*, 26, 381–403.

Milligan, M. (2003b) Loss of site: Organizational moves as organizational deaths. *International Journal of Sociology and Social Policy*, 23, 115–152.

Mills, C. W. (1959) *The Sociological Imagination.* New York: Oxford University Press.

Olesen, V. L. & Whittaker, E. W. (1968) *The Silent Dialogue: The Social Psychology of Professional Socialization.* San Francisco: Jossey Bass, Inc.

Platt, J. (1996) *A History of Sociological Research Methods in America, 1920–1960.* New York: Cambridge University Press.

Sanders, C. (1999) *Understanding Dogs: Living and Working with Canine Companions.* Philadelphia: Temple University Press.

Schatzman, L. & Strauss, A. L. (1973) *Field Research: Strategies for a Natural Sociology.* Englewood, Cliffs, NJ: Prentice-Hall.

Silverman, D. (1998) *Harvey Sacks: Social Science and Conversation Analysis*. Cambridge UK: Polity.

Silverman, D. (2001) *Interpreting Qualitative Data* (2nd ed.). London: SAGE.

Sorokin, P. A. (1956) *Fads and Foibles in Modern Sociology and Related Sciences*. Chicago: H. Regnery.

Spalter-Roth, R. (2005) Putting the Science in Qualitative Methodology. *Footnotes (p. 6)*. Washington, DC.

Star, L. S. (1989) *Regions of the Mind: Brain Research and the Quest for Scientific Certainty*. Stanford, CA: Stanford University Press.

Strauss, A. L. (1959/1969) *Mirrors and Masks*. Mill Valley, CA: The Sociology Press.

Strauss, A. L. (1961) *Images of the American City*. New York: Free Press.

Strauss, A. L. (1993) *Continual Permutations of Action: Communication and Social Order*. Chicago: Aldine.

Strauss, A. & Corbin, J. (1994) Grounded Theory Methodology—An Overview. In N. K. Denzin & Y. S. Lincoln (Eds.) *Handbook of Qualitative Research* (pp. 273–285). Thousand Oaks, CA: SAGE.

Strauss, A. L. & Corbin, J. M. (1998) *Basics of Qualitative Research*. Thousand Oaks, CA: SAGE.

Strauss, A. & Fisher, B. (1979a) George Herbert Mead and the Chicago tradition of sociology, Part 1. *Symbolic Interaction*, 2 (Spring), 9–26.

Strauss, A., & Fisher, B. (1979b) George Herbert Mead and the Chicago tradition of sociology, Part 2. *Symbolic Interaction*, 2 (Fall), 9–19.

Strauss, A. L., Schatzman, L., Bucher, R., Erlich, D. & Sabshin, M. (1963) The hospital and its negotiated order. In E. Freidson (Ed.) *The Hospital in Modern Society* (pp. 147–163). New York: Free Press.

Strauss, A. L., Schatzman, L., Bucher, R., Erlich, D. & Sabshin, M. (1964) *Psychiatric Ideologies and Institutions*. New York: Free Press.

Titscher, S., Meyer, M., Wodak, R. & Vetter, E. (2000) *Methods of Text and Discourse Analysis*. London: SAGE.

2

The Discovery of Grounded Theory in Practice: The Legacy of Multiple Mentors

Eleanor Krassen Covan

The notion that sociologists need to tell others about the necessity of generating social theory that is both structurally relevant and pertinent to one's data, one that has 'fit and grab' was an idea Glaser and Strauss shared when they published *The Discovery of Grounded Theory* (1967) 40 years ago. That explanation was necessary and that observation of data was required for theory generation were not new ideas, however, having been adumbrated in the work of others. As all students of epistemology know, knowledge is cumulative. Theoretical ideas and the methods for generating them emerge as generations reconsider the conclusions of earlier scholars.

C. Wright Mills's *The Sociological Imagination* (1959) is an intriguing concept, suggesting that we can understand social situations if we examine them from the point of view of the interplay among three dimensions: individual biographies, history, and social structure. Grounded theory is, of course, grounded in the creative process of generating theory in consideration of the same dimensions.[1] The interplay of these dimensions is particularly important to my endeavor in this chapter, explaining the legacy of multiple mentors as it relates to the process of learning grounded theory. The grounded theory method of understanding, like all other methods of understanding social reality, is not static; it changes even in the process of teaching it to student cohorts.

Relatively few students have been fortunate to have studied at the University of California, San Francisco (UCSF) with both Barney Glaser and Anselm Strauss, simultaneously, in the decade following their having published *The Discovery of Grounded Theory* (1967). My cohort was at UCSF from 1974–1980.[2] We learned about grounded theory through reading the grounded theory text, participating in seminars about the method led by the authors of the book as well as their colleagues, through personal communications about grounded theory with Glaser and Strauss, and most importantly by using the method under their direction. Most others have learned about grounded theory from books alone or by studying with one or the other great mentor or a student of one or both of them. Now, in 2006, many are learning from the students' students.

To thoroughly understand the impact of multiple mentors on students of grounded theory and its students would require working beyond the scope of this chapter because the task would be longitudinal in design. Understanding differs between students of sequential cohorts, and even among students of the same cohort. Such a study would require a considerable time span as each student brings his or her own intellectual lineage to the study of grounded theory and builds a new lineage in the process of developing a career. One would have to consider the dynamic intellectual lineages to which generations of students have been (and continue to be) exposed, and to subsequently examine the productivity of cohorts of students who claim to be 'doing grounded theory.' I intend to present just a glimpse of the legacy of grounded theory mentors by considering those aspects of their legacy that they shared with me personally, and to discuss how this legacy has perhaps influenced the careers of a few members of my own cohort and the emergent careers of the students we are teaching.

As I examine my education, I recall having been taught the importance of the sociological imagination with regard to the interplay between individual biography and social structure at Temple University, long before I was a student at UCSF. I needed Anselm Strauss, however, to help me to appreciate what Mills may have meant by the importance of history and cohorts. Strauss was quite willing to engage me in conversations about the importance of history and cohorts, especially with regard to explaining how meaning is negotiated in the context of social interaction. To this end we discussed the fact that somehow I had received an undergraduate liberal arts education thinking that studying history meant contemplating political systems, warriors, explorers, battles, and dates exclusively, with no analyses of the consequences of those experiences for ordinary citizens let alone the consequences of those citizens' actions for political systems. Strauss's personal dismay as we discussed gaps in my education revealed that my dismissal of history beforehand was a consequence of the fact that I had never been fortunate to take a course taught by a social historian. I began to understand the impact of the interplay between history and personal biography when Strauss had me contemplate my personal epistemological philosophy. In the context of the history of sociological thought, he challenged me to compare my prior knowledge of sociology with that of other students in my cohort. He was so determined to make sure that I understood the importance of cohorts that even my French foreign language exam involved discussing with him an article about 'cadrés' of students in French universities. In consequence, Strauss helped me to recognize that I bring my history with me, even as I use my sociological eye anew.[3] I imagine him smiling as I write a history of becoming a grounded theorist.

SOCIAL AND BEHAVIORAL SCIENCES AT UCSF (1974–1980)

At the time that we became students of Glaser and Strauss in 1974, I don't think that anyone in my cohort considered themselves to be a student of grounded theory. Indeed we were all enrolled in a four quarter sequence of courses that audaciously had been labeled, 'The Discovery of Social Reality.'

Each course exposed us to methods of qualitative data analysis, and we hoped that we would learn enough to eventually complete a PhD dissertation. In reminiscence, during our era in the UCSF Department of Social and Behavioral Sciences, we were taught only qualitative research methods which were infused throughout the curriculum. If we did not know it beforehand, we quickly learned that no matter who chaired the department at any particular time, it was Anselm Strauss who provided the leadership.[4] He told us that he had created the medical sociology program by recruiting others who were comfortable with qualitative methods, and it had been he who negotiated placement of the program in the School of Nursing, because the administrative structure of the School of Nursing provided him with the autonomy he needed to develop his curricular ideals. Since UCSF is a medical center, it was no coincidence that in the doctoral program we were reading numerous articles and research monographs about medical sociology, debating not only the research conclusions, but also the philosophical and epistemological assumptions behind the qualitative methods used in those studies. We read qualitative research articles and monographs exclusively, which included structural ethnography, ethnomethodology, naturalistic observation, and phenomenology, in addition to grounded theory. As we learned about the variety of qualitative research methods in other courses, we were never told that we were expected to write dissertations using the grounded theory method. Nor did faculty tell us that we had to be *symbolic interactionists*. Nevertheless, as Anselm Strauss led, many followed.[5]

For my cohort, *The Discovery of Social Reality* sequence was introduced in a single lecture by Anselm Strauss, but really began with a course co-taught by Virginia Olesen and Leonard Schatzman focusing on fieldwork, field notes, and the use of memos in the analysis of field data. Among other foci, Virginia Olesen taught us the importance of research ethics, especially with regard to negotiating entrée to a field site. While she taught that it was perhaps acceptable to observe behavior in public settings, she warned us not to assume that such observations were 'unobtrusive measures.' Schatzman seemed most interested in teaching us how to write three kinds of field notes and later expanding them into memos that would become our analyses of field data. This typology of notes included observational notes or ON (simple descriptions of what we were noticing in the field); methodological notes or MN (comments about what we were doing or needed to do in the future, later expanded to compare our methods to those of other fieldworkers); and theoretical notes or TN (notes to ourselves about theoretical ideas related to the social setting, eventually expanded by comparisons to what existed about the situation in the social science literature). During this Olesen/Schatzman seminar, we also learned much about the social history of Schatzman's relationship with Anselm Strauss. He had been Strauss's protégé at Indiana University before being recruited by Strauss to be on the faculty at UCSF. He was fully committed to the theoretical perspective of symbolic interaction, teaching us, as he entertained us with numerous examples of his own field experiences, about the utility of this perspective.

The prior experiences of students in qualitative methods in general and in writing about field experiences in particular varied tremendously. We were asked to submit both our raw field notes and a final analytic paper for grading purposes. I suppose in retrospect that the first course was designed to even out our playing field although at least one student thought that Olesen's purpose was to 'guard against grade inflation.' We certainly all learned how to write field notes and added this skill to our methodological repertoires. Some of us had previously been steeped in survey research; others were more knowledgeable when it came to case studies or ethnography. At the time we finished this course most of us still had no inkling of grounded theory, since neither Schatzman nor Olesen exhibited any interest in it.

THE RULES OF SOCIOLOGICAL METHOD: ADUMBRATIONS OF GROUNDED THEORY

In my second quarter at the University of California, San Francisco, I had the experience of rereading Durkheim's *The Rules of the Sociological Method* (1938) and reading Glaser and Strauss's *The Discovery of Grounded Theory* (1967) simultaneously in a seminar on epistemology taught by Fred Davis. Having studied Durkheim's text previously in a theory class at Temple University taught by Dean MacCannell,[6] I was startled by what I saw as obvious similarities between the two works. I now understand that I compared the two texts in an attempt to reconcile the disparate intellectual lineages to which I had been exposed. As the reader may find it helpful to understand the importance of reconciling intellectual lineages in the emergence of new theories, let me digress by explaining what fascinated me at the time in relation to what I now understand about the contributions of my mentors.

In 1975, I recognized that each book was a methods text starting with a critique of other methods of sociological analysis. Durkheim was encouraging sociologists to begin with the observation of social facts that he referred to as 'things' and in doing so he criticized Auguste Comte noting, 'up to the present, sociology has dealt more or less exclusively with concepts and not with things' (1938: 18–19). Glaser and Strauss opened *The Discovery of Grounded Theory* (1967: 1) by critiquing the fixation of sociologists with the notion of how accurate facts could be obtained and rigorously tested. I noticed that both of the methodological works also include a brief discussion of how sociology is needed by the lay audience. Durkheim (1938: 37) stresses that the scientist had to reject lay interpretations of reality, while at the same time realizing that these interpretations 'serve as suggestions and guides' for his analysis. His work can be seen as an adumbration of the Glaser and Strauss idea that lay beliefs can be used as the starting point in the generation of theoretical categories. The authors all stress that the sociologist must transcend lay concepts. Durkheim states that such concepts are 'crudely formed … they do not coincide exactly with scientific concepts' (1938: 37). Glaser and Strauss similarly state that the sociologist must 'do what the laymen cannot do—generate general categories and their properties … and so a different perspective' (1967: 30).

That data 'exist' and were to be revealed through observation was an assumption in both works. Durkheim, however, wrote more about social facts and Glaser and Strauss wrote more about observing social processes and grounded theory. Data, for Glaser and Strauss, just as for Durkheim, are different from the ideas that are in the minds of the average citizen (including the mind of the average sociologist). Accordingly, they taught that the job of the sociologist is to generate social theory from the data themselves, not from their own minds exclusively. Although the minds of sociologists are like those of other people, we were taught that sociologists must learn a style of analysis that relies on everyday experience, yet transcends that experience. The existence of data was reified to such an extent that I remember thinking that their omnipresence might allow independent action on the part of the data themselves. I initially was somewhat puzzled by such conceptual positivism because it seemed quite inconsistent with other things that I was hearing from Anselm Strauss. In class, as he taught us about 'symbolic interaction,' he told us unequivocally that 'society,' 'group consciousness,' and even 'shared definitions of the situation' are mental constructs to be avoided. My confusion lingered as I wrestled with the notion that concepts could emerge from observation of data. Which concepts were acceptable and which were not remained unclear as I began to consider how I would 'do grounded theory.' When I questioned Fred Davis about this, he suggested, 'Sometime you will have to discuss the implications of the decided tendency to reify concepts in grounded theory with Glaser and Strauss' (F. Davis, personal communication, February 10, 1975).

When further reading revealed to me that while Durkheim as well as Glaser and Strauss were suggesting a similar method for beginning sociological analysis (observation of data), the methods were actually quite different, perhaps as they were developed with different purposes. While the comparative method is paramount in both *The Rules of the Sociological Method* and *The Discovery of Grounded Theory*, Glaser and Strauss's goal was to provide strategic advances over the method used by earlier comparativists (1967: 22). Durkheim's major concern for comparisons was connected with his insistence that sociology must become a science. In order for sociology to accomplish this feat, it was going to be necessary to establish sociological proofs. Durkheim placed primary emphasis on verification. He states, 'Sociological explanation consists exclusively in establishing relations of causality' (1938: 125). Because it is necessary to have at least two events in order to determine that one event produces another, a comparative framework became essential to Durkheim's work. 'A social fact can be explained only by another social fact' wrote Durkheim (1938: 145). Durkheim also believed that in order for relationships among facts to be useful they had to be general and happen repeatedly. Further comparisons were then necessary (1938: 133).

Glaser and Strauss agree that comparisons can be used to establish facts and to verify theories (1967: 23–27). Indeed they explained that all general methods of data analysis including grounded theory, experimental designs and statistical analysis rely on the logic of comparison (Glaser and Strauss, 1967: 21). Since Glaser and Strauss were not interested in verifying existing theories, they noted that comparisons were particularly useful when employed to generate and discover new categories for analysis. Thus if comparisons expose a seemingly deviant case, it is no cause for alarm. An exception becomes another variable to be accounted for and classified in a grounded theory (Glaser and Strauss, 1967: 22). In *The Discovery of Grounded Theory*, Glaser and Strauss note the importance of continuing the comparative process and of analyzing extreme cases throughout the research process as a guide to theoretical sampling. Durkheim also used comparisons to classify, but the idea of a continual process of generating categories and classifying them was absent from his method. Durkheim believed that phenomena should be defined and classified in advance of all analysis as soon as observations had been made. Unlike Glaser and Strauss, he saw classification as separate from the analytical process rather than as an inherent part of that process. In a footnote in *The Discovery of Grounded Theory* (Glaser and Strauss, 1967: 2), discussing Robert Merton's writing about 'serendipity' (Merton, 1949), Glaser notes that Merton came close, but hadn't understood the intrinsic value of the comparative process to generate theoretical hypotheses.

The chapter on theoretical sampling provides the best explanation of what set Glaser and Strauss apart from those who had been following Durkheim's rules as it outlines what they meant concerning the selection of groups for comparison. Although others have tried to clarify theoretical sampling, the best explanation remains in *The Discovery of Grounded Theory*:

> Theoretical sampling is the process of data collection for generating theory whereby the analyst jointly collects, codes, and analyses his data and decides what data to collect next and where to find them, in order to develop his theory as it emerges (Glaser and Strauss, 1967: 45).

The authors explain that a researcher cannot predetermine groups that will logically separate all categories in an emerging theory. They note that a method of sampling pre-determined population groups differs from theoretical sampling in that population sampling is theoretically useful for verifying facts for only a single theoretical category (Glaser and Strauss, 1967: 50), by holding variation constant for that particular category. Theoretical sampling instead uses many different comparison groups, such that differences within groups are eventually minimized and differences between groups are eventually maximized to develop theories of the widest scope. Choices of comparison groups must therefore be altered, with the analysis of each relevant theoretical category (Glaser and Strauss, 1967: 55–60).

For Durkheim, data had to be seen as real, directly observable entities, if sociology were ever to become a complete and legitimate science, commanding the same respect accorded any of the natural sciences. Facts similarly had to be regularly ordered since Durkheim believed that experimentation was of critical importance in the verification of social facts. Glaser and Strauss were less concerned with verifying existing social facts than they were with using these facts to form the core of their theoretical analysis and the generation of new sociological theories. Accordingly, the very existence of social facts seemed even less problematic for Glaser and Strauss than it had been for Durkheim. Glaser and Strauss assumed that real data exist and must be observed directly if theories that are being developed are to 'fit and work' in the situation under analysis. Theories that are [only] logically deduced, they said, can lead sociologists far astray, while theory that is grounded in data endures for centuries (Glaser and Strauss, 1967: 4). The Glaser and Strauss notion of *grounded theory* is very close conceptually to Durkheim's notion of *social facts*. Perhaps there is a subtle difference in the sense that for Durkheim both suicide rates and explanations of suicide using concepts of anomie and altruism are social facts. Glaser and Strauss may on occasion distinguish their observational data from theory derived from such observations. I believe the concepts can be equated, however, especially when one considers the early collaborative efforts of Glaser and Strauss (Glaser and Strauss, 1965) and their insistence that collection of data and the analysis of data were not different processes (Glaser and Strauss, 1967). What differed, of course, between Durkheim's work and that of Glaser and Strauss in their early work together are the kinds of data that were studied. Theory based on data about awareness of dying contexts was derivative of interviews and participant observation data while Durkheim's typology of suicide was derived from suicide rates.

INDIVIDUAL CONTRIBUTIONS

Although Glaser and Strauss wrote *The Discovery of Grounded Theory* as a team, data exist in the form of their later individual writings and from personal communications from which we can learn their individual contributions. From personal communications, for instance, I know that the homage to Durkheim's *Suicide* (1951 [1897]) as exemplary of the notion that grounded theories will endure was all Glaser's, whereas it was Strauss who defended his particular kind of observation of data (field observations). Glaser and Strauss also each confirmed that my content analysis demonstrated that *The Discovery of Grounded Theory* did indeed share many of the assumptions posited by Durkheim in his early work. It was Glaser who told me that this was a conscious decision on his part while Strauss noted that content analysis can be useful to make such discoveries[7] (Glaser, 1975; Strauss, 1975; personal communication).

From *The Rules of the Sociological Method* and *The Discovery of Grounded Theory* texts, alone, one may learn something about the legacy of mentors. If we add the history that is typically revealed in curriculum vitae, we can make presumptions about who contributed what in *The Discovery of Grounded Theory* text based on who studied with whom. Considering just the footnotes, the intellectual lineages of the authors are revealed. Thus we see that in *The Rules of the Sociological Method*, Durkheim who argues for the study of social facts and who had cited Comte previously is eventually cited by Robert Merton (1949, 1973). Merton, in turn, argues that sociologists should engage in the study of middle range theories starting with aspects of social phenomena. Presumably it is Glaser who cited his mentor in *The Discovery of Grounded Theory*. Glaser attributes many of the ideas in *The Discovery of Grounded Theory* to Merton with whom he had studied at Columbia beginning in 1955, particularly those ideas about relevance (Glaser, 2005a). For reasons which should now be obvious, I would presume that all citations in *The Discovery of Grounded Theory* text to Merton and Lazarsfeld were written by Glaser and that those to Blumer, Park, and Becker were written by Strauss reflecting his mentors and peers at the University of Chicago. As both Glaser and Strauss were sociologists, other intellectual lines are more difficult to distinguish as each was exposed to Max Weber's notion of *verstehen* for example (Weber, 1930).

As time has passed since the publication of Durkheim's book, his rules for sociologists which emphasized the comparison of 'not isolated variations but a series of systematically arranged variations of a wide range' (Durkheim, 1938: 135), became diluted at best in the sense that the words are now used as a slogan rather than a guiding principle. Instead of beginning with the observation of social facts, some sociologists began to think of social theories of limited scope, while seated at their desks, or based on very limited empirical data. Perhaps every generation needs to be reminded of the danger of grand theorizing with insufficient data. In any case Merton's comments on theories of 'middle range,' that were generated after study with Lazarsfeld, were echoed by Glaser who reminded his own students that evidence was needed to support our thoughtful predictions. The legacy that Glaser passed on to students was that grand theorizing without data was the wrong way to 'do' sociology. It is helpful in explaining Strauss's independent legacy to note that Mead, Blumer, and Park would surely have agreed that grand theorizing without direct observation of data was a bad idea.

We learn much more if we analyze all of the publications in a career. Glaser's solo authored work includes 13 subsequent books on applications of grounded theory.

There, for example, he clarifies numerous times that, in his vision, grounded theory is much more than a method for symbolic interaction. He believes that grounded theory provides the tools for many theoretical perspectives including nursing, social work, management, higher mathematics, and international information networks (Glaser, 2005b). Glaser proudly notes that most applications of grounded theory including his began with a dissertation. Subsequently many textbooks and journal articles have been written by Glaser's students to explain grounded theory to researchers in disparate disciplines (Charmaz, 2006; Goulding, 2002; Hansen and Kautz, 2005; Locke, 2001).

After 40 years, epistemological debates continue among scholars about how to conduct social research and especially about how to do grounded theory. The debate now includes many who practice their craft in ways never discussed in *The Discovery of Grounded Theory*, especially as the technology to record field notes has also evolved. Some record interviews verbatim, fearful of missing a single word of datum; others describe population sampling in addition to theoretical sampling. Perhaps all we have in common beneath our tangled roots is that our goal is to induce a theory from our starting point—which is our data however disparately we define them.

LEARNING GROUNDED THEORY

Since 'continuous comparative analysis' is a universal social process employed by everyone who attempts to accumulate knowledge, I suppose that other students in my cohort also may have compared *The Discovery of Grounded Theory* to other books that they had read previously. Doing so came naturally to me, because I had practiced such a style of exegesis while a student at Temple University. Regardless, as a group we finally began the last two quarters in *The Discovery of Social Reality* sequence that were both taught by Barney Glaser. I remember being very frustrated at that time, not because of what I was being taught, but instead by what was missing in the instruction process.

I wanted a script, a sequential list of what to do first, second, third, etc. We had been asked to read *The Discovery of Grounded Theory*, but for us that text provided a philosophy rather than a detailed description of how to *do* grounded theory. To the extent that details of the method are present in that work, I perceived them more in terms of what not to do than what to do, since I was trying to reconcile the differences between two intellectual lineages. The only methodological certainty I gleaned from the *The Discovery of Grounded Theory* was that I was to begin inductively by collecting and simultaneously analysing my own data, rather than deductively with a hypothesis generated from existing sociological literature. I knew that I was supposed to make several comparisons, but I wasn't sure what to compare. By 2006, most students are presented with articles, textbooks, and edited volumes that have been written by students of Glaser and Strauss (see, for example, Charmaz, 2006; Goulding, 2002; Schreiber and Stern, 2001).

Other texts are available, written by sociologists who were motivated to write them perhaps in consequence of their own frustration as students, or in response to questions that emerged when they began teaching grounded theory methods to their own students. In addition, when applying for research grants, funding agencies require that one's methods be explicated. A comparison of these texts reveals that they are all very different from one another. Each perhaps is a personal interpretation of the method that the authors have used in their own research, guided, in addition, by their personal biography. I, for example, have used grounded theory in a secondary analysis of anthropological ethnography and I subsequently published a description of the methods I used so others would understand what I had done (Maxwell and Maxwell, 1980). None of the articles, textbooks, or edited volumes provides a description of the method that was demonstrated in seminars attended by my particular student cohort from 1974–1980. Never, for example, were the concepts of *axial coding* or *situational matrix* discussed. These concepts came about several years later when Strauss and Corbin (1990) collaborated. What the works have in common is that each comes closer to a scripted set of directions, than contained in *The Discovery of Grounded Theory*.

Although it is somewhat ironic that we learned to process grounded theory philosophically by 'doing grounded theory' inductively, it is not a surprise as I was recently reminded by Phyllis Stern that in the decade of the 1970s *process learning* was a hot topic. Everyone seemed to be defining *learning* by *doing* (P. N. Stern, personal communication, June 8, 2006). We were learning how to do grounded theory by copying the methods that were demonstrated to us in our classes. Strauss would lead a seminar to demonstrate anecdotal comparisons, for example, by asking us to supply him with data on the basic social process of negotiating. Strauss was at that time working on his book *Negotiations: Varieties, Contexts, Processes, and Social Order* (1978). He used our comparisons to illustrate that who knows what about a situation can be used advantageously in the context of sales, explaining how salesmen maximize their advantage when selling automobiles. In many other instances, learning to do grounded theory took the form of discovering what to do next by continually comparing whatever we happened to be doing to what our classmates and mentors were doing. In essence, we were both teaching and learning grounded theory methods from one another without written instructions.

To be more accurate, I will add that my cohort was taught 'grounded theory' in particular as Glaser demonstrated the method, in the last two quarters of the *Discovery of Social Reality* sequence. Glaser's seminars were supplemented, however, by personal communications with Strauss who sometimes came to class, and who often met with us individually. It was thus usually Glaser who defined concepts such as properties, dimensions, basic social processes, or cutting points, illustrating them using data supplied by students in his seminar. To demonstrate grounded theory methods, Glaser and students 'read data aloud.' We were told that we could compare segments in the data, by analyzing them 'line-by-line.'

As we read, Glaser would encourage us to discover patterns in the data, patterns that might be dimensions, properties, or cutting points. Robert Broadhead (personal communication, May 31, 2006) told me that he emulated Glaser's line-by-line method of coding when he taught the graduate qualitative methods course at the University of Connecticut in the 1980s and 1990s because, 'I found that useful for getting students thinking creatively.'

There was much more to Glaser's grounded theory analysis, however, because while most of the students were comparing only segments of the data before us, he was adding anecdotal comparisons. In *The Discovery of Grounded Theory* the authors had explained that anecdotal comparisons are those where, 'through his own experiences, general knowledge, or reading, and the stories of others, the sociologist can gain data on other groups that offer useful comparisons' (Glaser and Strauss, 1967: 67). In any event, Glaser was adding to the comparisons by inserting the data that were in his head, from personal history, knowledge of other studies, and the like. Some of us were confused about when to move from our own data to what we thought we knew ourselves from other contexts. We had been told not to 'review the literature' before beginning to analyze our data, and thus we typically had much less relevant information in our heads than did Glaser. Many were impressed with Glaser's apparent genius for discovering the basic social processes from which we could frame our dissertations. Some, however, were annoyed because Glaser never told us exactly when the literature should be read. Others were put off, not by Glaser's knowledge of the literature or his personal talent, but by his ego, as he literally beamed with pride over each of his discoveries which impacted negatively on our vulnerable egos.

Strauss's teaching style was very different. I cannot recall that he used Glaser's line-by-line reading of data as he demonstrated the grounded theory analytic process, and when he chose to illustrate concepts such as anecdotal comparisons, as noted previously, he had us supply the comparisons. He would employ the Socratic method to engage us in discussions about our data as well as his, and to thus guide us in the discovery process. He was always patient as he asked question after question about data, almost never telling us what he knew was there until we had made discoveries ourselves as we answered his questions. From both mentors (and more so because we were also taught by Leonard Schatzman, Virginia Olesen, and Fred Davis, who all eschewed labeling themselves as grounded theorists) we eventually learned to write theoretical and methodological memos and to employ the comparative process of theoretical sampling to enrich the process of generating emerging theory.

Glaser's line-by-line reading of data may have inspired some grounded theorists to recommend recording data from interviews 'verbatim.' Such recording was never recommended by Glaser or Strauss, however. Both taught that recording field notes or interviewer notes was more important than verbatim text because they provided the context for who said what at any particular time. Some comments could be recorded for purposes of quotation if they seemed to illustrate a point. Strauss, in particular, taught us not to worry about missing something by not recording it even noting that we need not waste our time in verbatim transcriptions. He stressed that if something were important, we would see it or hear it again.

I also recall his saying that even the absence of something important would be discovered as we reflected on what we had observed through discussion with others or through memos to ourselves about our interviews or field notes. In the fieldwork text he co-authored with Schatzman (Schatzman and Strauss, 1973), he advocated the use of observational, methodological, and theoretical notes, discussed earlier in this chapter in the process of discovering what is important. In *The Discovery of Grounded Theory* one finds similar advice:

> From the point of view of generating theory it is often useful to write memos on, as well as code, the copy of one's field notes. Memo writing on the field note provides an immediate illustration for an idea. Also, since an incident can be coded for several categories, this tactic forces the analyst to use an incident as an illustration only once, for the most important among the properties of diverse categories that it indicates. He must look elsewhere in his notes for illustrations for his other properties and categories. This corrects the tendency to use the same illustration over and over for different properties (Glaser and Strauss, 1967: 108).

Now that I have more than 30 years of research experience, including several as editor of an international journal, I am much better at 'doing grounded theory' than I could ever have been as a student. That is because I now have a great deal of experiential data in my own head, providing me with a wealth of anecdotal data on theory and research methods. This suggests that collaborating with others in grounded theory studies may be helpful as multiple researchers obviously cumulate more experience than one does alone. Grounded theory perhaps, like the study of the Jewish mystical system of *Kabala*, is best performed by mature theorists who possess the wisdom of experience, or at least in collaboration with those with lots of experience. (See Chapter 14 for Carolyn Wiener's description of how collaboration through team meetings can facilitate the emergence of grounded theory.)

When attempting to summarize what my cohort of grounded theory students have in common, I stumbled on Howard Becker's website in which he refers to the 'So-Called Chicago School of Sociology.' In describing his generation he notes:

> We were, instead, confused by the mélange of contradictory viewpoints, models, and recommendations the department presented to us. And each of us made what we could of it, emphasizing what we could use, ignoring what we couldn't ... The result of this—of each person inventing his own private Chicago—was that no two of these Chicagos were exactly alike. There were many things that people who had been trained there at a particular time shared, but there were also enormous differences (Becker, 2006).

My cohort was also similarly confused by contradictory viewpoints in the department and beyond, and we too have invented our own private means of doing grounded theory.

GROUNDED THEORY AND ME

I began the PhD program at UCSF while employed by anthropologists as a research associate on a federally funded cross-cultural study of the aged. My part of the project involved designing a codebook that would be used to summarize information about the social position of the aged. The data to be coded were to be abstracted from published ethnographies on more than one hundred societies. The codebook would be used in quantitative analyses to predict which variables best explained the social position of the aged. The two Principal Investigators were Philip Silverman and Robert J. Maxwell. The latter was my husband at the time. Maxwell and Silverman had been classmates at Cornell University during the 1960s where they had been introduced to the Human Relations Area Files. Using the technology of the 1950s, universities had copied the entire texts of ethnographies, storing them in Xerography and microfilm in libraries across the country thus making them available to others for secondary analysis as a large qualitative data set. Silverman and Maxwell were attempting to practice the cross-cultural survey methods that they had been taught by their mentor, Jack Roberts. Roberts had worked with G. P. Murdock on the first cross-cultural surveys that led to the creation of the Human Relations Area Files (HRAF). The codebooks of earlier cross-cultural surveys had been added to the HRAF ethnography files, such that the initial data bank of ethnographies, then also included a system of numeric codes in the margins that demonstrated how ethnographies could be compared on variables that had interested the anthropologists. Although there were codes in the HRAF about the aged (categories 886, 887, and 888), Silverman and Maxwell believed that their study would best be accomplished by reading entire ethnographies and creating their own codes rather than beginning with the codes in the HRAF.[8, 9]

One might think that being a research associate on a federal grant would be an advantage when developing a dissertation proposal because I entered the doctoral program with readily available data. It presented a hurdle in my case; the Maxwell/Silverman data were being quantified and I was in a department with an expressed preference for qualitative data analysis. When I first discussed the cross-cultural study with Anselm Strauss, he led me to consider whether I might be happier at UC Berkeley where Neil Smelser was known for his cross-cultural studies. Strauss worried that it would be impossible to study the position of the elderly from ethnographic texts because the structure of these texts often excluded detailed descriptions of what anthropologists had observed in the field. When I brought examples of my data to *The Discovery of Social Reality* seminar, fortunately Barney Glaser enthusiastically endorsed my data and provided me with the confidence necessary for success. When classmates questioned how I could analyze data from ethnographies, Glaser explained that my dissertation would begin with an analysis of the social organizational properties that were specific to the aged and that these were well represented in ethnographic texts. He encouraged me to work with him, Anselm Strauss, and Leonard Schatzman on my qualitative study (Maxwell, 1979). Of course, I remained at UCSF. Although Glaser guided me both theoretically and methodologically, he was overjoyed when Strauss agreed to chair my dissertation committee. He hoped that in doing so Strauss would become convinced that grounded theory would work with any kind of data, including the secondary analysis of data originally collected using perspectives other than symbolic interaction. I later decided to refer to my data as 'scenes.' In most instances they were descriptions of intergenerational activities that I abstracted from the ethnographies. Some scenes included the ethnographers' interpretations of those activities. Other scenes were descriptions of who was present or absent at a community event. Glaser helped me to explain that in grounded theory everything was data and that my scenes could be compared to each other just as my classmates were comparing their field notes. I wrote an article in 1980 entitled, 'Search and Research in Ethnology: Continuous Comparative Analysis,' to explain the methods used in my dissertation to those of the symbolic interaction lineage including Strauss and Schatzman, and to anthropologists of the cross-cultural survey lineage including my husband and Phil Silverman.

Although I do not teach a formal course in qualitative data analysis at UNC Wilmington, I have presented data analysis workshops at international conferences attended by persons who hail from many traditions. The methods I teach and how I deliver the workshop are similar to the methods I learned from Barney Glaser and Anselm Strauss. I prefer to have students bring data to the workshops, but when they do not, I use anecdotal data that they supply to illustrate how to do grounded theory. Others in my cohort also juggled academic lineages when learning grounded theory. Phyllis Stern describes writing her dissertation:

> As a nurse student in a group of sociology students I managed to weather the Glaser storm … I learned enough sociological jargon to ask, 'Where's the ladies room?' I never became fluent … I remain pleased with the theoretical framework I developed on discipline in step-father families … The most helpful nurse on my committee was Shirley Chater; I gave her the label of the patron saint of doctoral students. Shirley explained to us that getting a doctoral degree in large part is the political process, part of the task is knowing your own power, knowing what to say, whom to say it to, and when to say it. Shirley could talk research in any form, and she *got* what I came up with, unlike my Chair Betty Highley, also a nurse, who didn't (P. N. Stern, personal communication, June 8, 2006).

Stern, whose work appears in this volume, has started her own lineage by teaching grounded theory to an entire generation of nursing students. Understanding that the nursing lineage requires precise description of just about everything, she has attempted, not always successfully, to teach students that they can be creative with anecdotal data and precise in their interviews simultaneously. Stern has co-authored an edited volume with Rita Schreiber, one of her former students, on using grounded theory in nursing (Schreiber and Stern, 2001). Another of Stern's students, Judy Wuest, has taken grounded theory in the direction of influencing public policy in Canada where she has been studying the impact of policy on women who have been abused by men (Wuest and Merritt-Gray, 1999). Wuest has also been writing about how to combine the intellectual lineages of nursing and grounded theory (Wuest, 2007). While Stern does not recommend recording verbatim interviews and rarely has done this herself,[10] some of her students, including Duff (2002), have done so to satisfy the expectations of others on their dissertation committees.

Like Phyllis Stern, Carolyn Wiener also recalls that she began the doctoral program with no background in sociology. Although she told me that she 'had no problem with the ambiguities of qualitative research' having a preexisting aversion to putting ideas in boxes, she explains that she 'did have some problems at first with "getting" grounded theory.' She recalls many discussions about the difference between properties and dimensions. Explaining what she learned from Glaser and Strauss she notes:

> My work has been influenced by Barney's disciplined approach to following the tenets of grounded theory, by his insistence on a basic social process and his description of this overall process and its sub-processes as a 'little logic', and by his use of gerunds in expressing this logic in order to denote change over time. Anselm had a greater influence on me, since I worked with him not only as a student but as a colleague, for a total of 25 years. Although he was at times laid back in his strict adherence to the orthodoxy of grounded theory, the tenets were so ingrained in him that he used them even when he wasn't explicit about their use. What I learned from him was his masterful creativity regarding theoretical sampling and the constant comparative. His utilization of the latter always covered an extensive scope since he had such a wide range of interests and I benefited from his conviction that imaginative comparisons could be fruitful … (C. Wiener, personal communication, May 28, 2006).

While all of Carolyn Wiener's work has been grounded in grounded theory, others such as Robert Broadhead have moved into survey research. His vitae now indicates that his work involves community demonstration projects to prevent and combat HIV infection in Connecticut, Russia, Vietnam, China, and Thailand (R. S. Broadhead, personal communication, May 31, 2006). Marsha Rosenbaum's career has been eclectic. Like Judy Wuest, she has used grounded theory to impact social policy. From 1977 to 1995, Rosenbaum was the principal investigator on National Institute on Drug Abuse-funded studies of heroin addiction, methadone maintenance treatment, MDMA (Ecstasy), cocaine, and drug use during pregnancy. Although unable to contact Rosenbaum personally, her publications indicate a willingness to be pragmatic and inclusive in terms of data collection and analysis.

I was unable to receive comments from everyone in my UCSF cohort which is why so much of what I have written about the legacy of multiple mentors describes my own experience. Obviously, others will review our cohort's history differently. It is cathartic to reexamine the legacy of our mentors, at least once in a career. For me personally, a brief reminiscence experience is a prelude to moving on. For another description of the legacy of grounded theory from one whose knowledge of grounded theory's history has more breadth, perhaps, than my own, I refer you to Barney Glaser's work, 'The Roots of Grounded Theory,' a keynote presentation he delivered at the 3rd International Qualitative Research Convention in August 2005, as well as his work in this volume.

NOTES

1 Barney Glaser was a PhD student at Columbia University at the time C. Wright Mills was writing *The Sociological Imagination*.

2 In addition to students who completed the PhD program in sociology graduating in the years from 1979–1980 (Robert Broadhead; Elizabeth Cauhape, Eleanor Krassen Maxwell [the author]; Marsha Rosenbaum, Robinetta Wheeler, and Carolyn Wiener) the *Discovery of Social Reality* cohort discussed in this chapter included Phyllis Noerager Stern who earned her DNS in Family Health Nursing in the summer of 1976.

3 Strauss was referring to the concept of 'sociological eye' published by his colleague, Everett Hughes (1984).

4 Strauss discouraged conflict among his faculty in the Department of Social and Behavioral Sciences by encouraging everyone to 'do good work.' There was nevertheless some disharmony during the time my cohort was at UCSF. This disharmony eventually cost Glaser a tenure track position within the department and also resulted in Fred Davis accepting a position on the campus of UC San Diego. Carroll Estes was recruited during this period. As a scholar of the political economy of aging, her arrival began a new era in which study included a combination of qualitative and quantitative methods among students interested in her work.

5 Strauss may have used his position of leadership to encourage others to develop intellectual lineages of their own provided that they wrote about methods that would elevate the overall position of qualitative research. Other texts that are still in circulation include the book he co-authored with Leonard Schatzman, *Field Research: Strategies for a Natural Sociology* (Schatzman and Strauss, 1973), and the text co-authored with Juliet Corbin, *Basics of Qualitative Research: Grounded Theory Procedures and Techniques* (Strauss and Corbin, 1990). Perhaps because of Strauss's reputation for leadership in symbolic interaction, many students believe that grounded theory must be derivative of symbolic interaction, despite the fact that these co-authored works are about qualitative methodology rather than about symbolic interaction. Barney Glaser certainly insists that symbolic interaction is only one of many philosophic traditions to benefit from employing grounded theory techniques.

6 MacCannell who had studied sociology at Cornell University during the early 1960s, taught graduate theory courses at Temple University from 1970–1978. He later joined the faculty at UC Davis.

7 Glaser and Strauss did agree that although their text shared certain assumptions with Durkheim, they had no intention to reinterpret Durkheim's rules for a new generation of sociologists.

8 Much of the work of Jack Roberts involved the cross-cultural analysis of games. While not a grounded theorist in terms of academic lineage, his theories were generated by methods of continuous comparison of ethnographic data supplemented with anecdotal data from his own milieu such that the resulting theories about play and games have 'fit and grab.' I consider them to be grounded theories. Anyone interested in games or in how cross-cultural surveys might be used in combination with quantitative data analysis to generate grounded theory is advised to review his work. In particular, see Roberts and Sutton-Smith, 1966.

9 For a more detailed description of how cross-cultural studies are done today, see, Silverman and Messinger, 2006: http://www.csub.edu/ssric-trd/modules/sccs/sccsin.htm

10 Stern and I have been collaborating on a study of life histories of her surviving classmates who were trained in the cadet corps nursing program during the 1940s. These interviews have been video recorded to facilitate analysis by both of us, as we work together separated by distance. As well, the recordings have value to historians who work with oral histories.

REFERENCES

Becker, H. S. (2006) 'The Chicago School, So-called.' Retrieved 6 June 2006 from http://home.earthlink.net/~hsbecker/chicago.html

Charmaz, K. (2006) *Constructing Grounded Theory: A Practical Guide Through Qualitative Analysis*. Thousand Oaks, CA: SAGE.

Duff, D. (2002) Families with a Member Experiencing Severe Traumatic Brain Injury. Unpublished PhD dissertation, University of Calgary.

Durkheim, E. (1938) *The Rules of the Sociological Method*. New York: The Free Press.

Durkheim, E. (1951 [1897]) *Suicide: A Study in Sociology*, Translated by John A. Spaulding & George Simpson, New York: The Free Press.

Glaser, B. (1975) Personal Faculty/Student Communication between Barney Glaser and Eleanor Krassen Maxwell.

Glaser, B. (2005a) 'The Roots of Grounded Theory,' a keynote presentation given at the 3rd International Qualitative Research Convention, Johor Bahru Malaysia, August 23.

Glaser, B. (2005b) 'The Impact of Symbolic Interaction on Grounded Theory.' Chapter 10 in Glaser, B. *The Grounded Theory Perspective III*, Mill Valley, CA: Sociology Press.

Glaser, B. & Strauss, A. (1965) *Awareness of Dying*. Chicago: Aldine.

Glaser, B. & Strauss, A. (1967) *The Discovery of Grounded Theory: Strategies for Qualitative Research*. Chicago: Aldine.

Goulding, C. (2002) *Grounded Theory: A Practical Guide for Management, Business and Market Researchers*. Thousand Oaks, CA: SAGE.

Hansen, B. H. & Kautz, K. (2005) 'Grounded Theory Applied—Studying Information Systems Development Methodologies in Practice,' Proceedings of the 38th Annual Hawaii International Conference on System Sciences (HICSS'05), p. 264b. Track 8.

Hughes, E. C. (1984) *The Sociological Eye*. New Brunswick, NJ: Transaction Books.

Locke, K. D. (2001) *Grounded Theory in Management Research*. Thousand Oaks, CA: SAGE.

Maxwell, E. K. (1979) Modeling Life: The Dynamic Relationship Between Elder Models and their Protégés. PhD Dissertation, University of California, San Francisco. Ann Arbor, University Microfilms International.

Maxwell, E. K. & Maxwell, R. J. (1980) Search and research in ethnology: Continuous comparative analysis. *Behavior Science Research*, 15, 219–243.

Merton, R. K. (1949) *Social Theory and Social Structure*. Glenco, IL: Free Press.

Merton, R. K. (1973) *The Sociology of Science*. Chicago: Chicago University Press.

Mills, C. W. (1959) *The Sociological Imagination*. Oxford: Oxford University Press.

Roberts, J. R. & Sutton-Smith, B. (1966) Cross-cultural correlates of games of chance. *Behavioral Science Notes*, 1, 131–144.

Schatzman, L. & Strauss, A. L. (1973) *Field Research: Strategies for a Natural Sociology*. Englewood Cliffs, NJ: Prentice Hall.

Schreiber, R. S. & Stern, P. N. (2001) *Using Grounded Theory in Nursing*. New York: Springer.

Silverman, P. & Messinger, J. (2006) 'Introduction to the Standard Cross Cultural Survey Module,' SSRIC Teaching Resources Depository. Retrieved 11 June 2006 from http://www.csub.edu/ssric-trd/modules/sccs/sccsin.htm

Strauss, A. (1975) Personal Faculty/Student Communication between Anselm Strauss and Eleanor Krassen Maxwell.

Strauss, A. (1978) *Negotiations: Varieties, Contexts, Processes, and Social Order*. San Francisco: Jossey-Bass.

Strauss, A. & Corbin, J. (1990) *Basics of Qualitative Research: Grounded Theory Procedures and Techniques*. London: SAGE.

Weber, M. (1930) *The Protestant Ethic and the Spirit of Capitalism*. New York: Scribner.

Wuest, J. (2007) Grounded theory: The method. In P. Munhall (Ed.), *Nursing Research: A Qualitative Perspective* (pp. 239–272). Sudbury, MA: Jones and Bartlett.

Wuest, J. & Merritt-Gray, M. (1999) Not going back: Sustaining the separation in the process of leaving abusive relationships. *Violence Against Women*, 5, 110–133.

3

Living Grounded Theory: Cognitive and Emotional Forms of Pragmatism

Susan Leigh Star

INTRODUCTION

Scientific writing often encodes powerful emotive narratives. Enshrouded, archived, hidden away in government white papers and documents, read and unread, lives every passion and drama common to all human activity. However, what scientists do (often including ourselves) is fundamentally inaccessible to most of the world. People may see a map of a genome or a syringe full of experimental medication. These are just the end products, however, of a web of relationships, what Lave and Wenger have called communities of practice. Lave and Wenger make the strong claim that membership in these communities *constitutes* learning and science (Adler and Obstfeld, in press; Bowker and Star, 1999: Chapter 10; Lave and Wenger, 1991; Obstfeld, 2005). These relationships are usually invisible to readers of science and technology (Star and Strauss, 1999; Suchman, 1987). Part of the reason for this is precisely that scientists rely on the relational, not the concrete reified world.[1] Relations between people, between different perceptions of objects, between nature and politics, between laboratories and administrations, to name but a few, *are part of the relational world*. Another aspect is that scientists are normatively discouraged to write directly about this invisible part, and untrained in its analysis. This includes the love, the suffering, the dedication, covering up, and forming selves in the scientific world (see, Clarke, 1998, for how this has appeared in the work of reproductive scientists and those studying sex). Most scientists write in a kind of encrypted voice, a language that relies on this invisible work, and its extremes of isolation and specialization (Latour, 1987).

Popular notions of science support this quiet suppression of passion. This includes simplistic notions of 'science as truth'; science or scientific medicine as concerning the heroic search for new discoveries and cures; and scientists as dispassionate judges of pure results. Although these norms are slowly changing in some fields, there are yet many barriers to overcome. The conventional way of writing even forbids the use of the first person (which, undeniably, is at best awkward with multiple authors, and 'we' implies another valuation altogether). The standards and formal classifications that pervade science always represent treaties between conflicting passions and desires, yet what could look more innocuous or boring? (Bowker and Star, 1999; Star, 1999).

Thus forming a scientific self entails a peculiar kind of pain and of joy that remains almost unspeakable. It leaks out in so-called popular science articles: the rage of an ecologist at seeing habitats destroyed, for example. It leaks out in memoirs and biographies: for example, in Evelyn Fox Keller's biography of Barbara McClintock (1983). In our own social science, it leaks out in the form of reflexivity, personal narrative, poetry, visualization, and performance art (Star, 1998). These genres are an accepted part of social sciences in a few places (although often at great cost, see Laurel Richardson's 1996 account of writing a poem instead of an article about her research on single mothers, and its reception at the American Sociological Association).

This chapter has a long genesis in my own learning, teaching, and living of grounded theory and Pragmatist philosophy. In all of the books and articles about grounded theory, I keep searching for a particular answer: how does it feel to do grounded theory? Am I alone in feeling intense emotion while doing analysis? Or in the feeling that I am, in some sense, always doing grounded theory? As a sociologist, I don't believe of course, that anyone has pure or unique experiences, except as they combine to form a unique biography. C. Wright Mills's idea of 'personal troubles and public problems' (2000) or the feminist notion that *the personal is political* is always the beginning heuristic for me, rather than the idea that I am alone or unique. This takes a few years to develop, I think. In other words, even to ask the question, 'Am I the only one?' presupposes the answer: of course not. So when I called my student, Olga Kuchinskaya, to talk about what I was writing, her voice filled with relief at my words, and she described her own feelings of doing analysis as quite similar to this. So encouraged, I took a deep breath and began.

As a graduate student, I searched for years for teachers who would not try to divorce me from my life experience, feelings, and feminist commitments. At the same time, I didn't want just a 'touchy-feely' sort of graduate education; I also needed to satisfy the love for stringent analysis I had developed as an undergraduate. I wouldn't have known how to say it, exactly, then, but I was looking for a way simultaneously to incorporate formal and informal understandings of the world.

I sought a methodological place that was faithful to human experience, and that would help me sift through the chaos of meanings and produce the eureka of new, powerful explanations. I also wanted a way of understanding the world that I could carry with dignity in my world as a feminist activist and as a working poet.

A tall order, to be sure.

A PATHWAY TO GROUNDED THEORY

After my undergraduate degree, I began my choice of graduate programs (as one often does at the age of 21), by following a lover to Santa Cruz, California. I enrolled in a PhD program in philosophy of education at Stanford. This program was unusual in that it promised many of the things I looked for, including faculty interested in qualitative methods and in comparative, historical studies of learning. However, no doubt due to my own lack of knowledge of philosophy or of the world of education, I found myself mute in most of the community-building efforts there. As serendipity would have it, one of the key professors in the small program was on leave; and I was unable to make the translations between philosophy and social science. We read John Dewey and I was intrigued, but his writings were not yet animated for me. (Years later, with the addition of empirical data and a community of grounded theory scholars, I would fall in love with Dewey. I actually wept when I found out he was no longer alive. But back to my brief chronology.)

In the midst of my confusion and intellectual loneliness, I saw a poster in the Education library, announcing the University of California at San Francisco's (UCSF) Program in Human Development. It said that UCSF offered an interdisciplinary program in adult development, which would include questions about how people choose career paths; ethnicity and how it intertwined with aging in different communities; and what developmental events in adulthood couldn't be predicted (even the concept of adult development seemed radical to me). I applied to the program and was accepted, and I began my studies at UCSF that autumn.

I had also noticed in passing, on my way to UCSF, that Anselm Strauss was an 'adjunct' faculty in the program. I was happy about that, as Glaser and Strauss's *The Discovery of Grounded Theory* had been used successfully by a friend in her feminist, qualitative dissertation. I had even read *The Discovery of Grounded Theory* (Glaser and Strauss, 1967), a manifesto for freedom from the sterile methods that permeated social sciences at the time. But I didn't know exactly how to use it. For my senior undergraduate thesis in psychology, I had instead used George Kelly's personal construct theory (1955, 1963), which I liked for its open, recombinant possibilities in eliciting people's priorities and categories. The personal construct method is an analytic tool for eliciting an individual's core repertoire of concepts, and how they are ordered for importance in use. The map that results is called a 'repertory grid.' In its spatial representations of concepts, it resembles aspects of Clarke's powerful situational analysis, which offers a methodological guide for mapping social worlds and larger-scale arena formed by the intersection of many social worlds, as for example in the formation of a scholarly discipline. Her book is a seminal 'second generation' example of Straussian grounded theory (Clarke, 2005).

I had used personal construct theory with the goal of finding out how women experienced (or did not experience) the paradigm shift to feminism that seemed to be going on all around me (in the mid-1970s, in Boston). I added, in order to scale up the psychological approach, a pair of theoretical works that spoke to the formation of widespread shifts in consciousness (the term current at the time); Thomas Kuhn's *The Structure of Scientific Revolutions* (1970) and Mary Daly's *Gyn/Ecology* (1978/1990) to examine the nature of large-scale changes in thought. Unlike grounded theory, however, my methodological approach lacked much inveiglement in people's lives. That is, without fieldwork, it was not possible to observe the personal constructs in the contexts of action, in the full spectrum of messy and formal acts in which humans participate. I had hopes of deepening this earlier work toward anthropological/qualitative sociological methods when I arrived at UCSF.

There was much to recommend in the Human Development Program. In classes, I was introduced to phenomenological and dialectical psychology, in particular the work of Klaus Riegel (1978) and of L. S. Vygotsky (1986). We read the emergent critiques of moral developmental psychologist Lawrence Kohlberg (1981). These included Carol Gilligan's feminist alternatives to Kohlberg's developmental steps that she saw as lacking context, uncertainty, and nuance in women's lives (1993). As well, I had the opportunity to delve into the cross-cultural critiques of Kohlberg's USA-centric moral developmental model. These many critics accused Kohlberg of taking American individualism, cognitivism, and logic, and claiming that these are universal values. All of these readings helped push me from the individual as a unit of analysis toward communities, organizations, and complex relations as foremost.

At the same time, however, I continued to lack a satisfying method, or a deeper methodology that would allow me to move forward in my general intellectual project. In retrospect, I would now say that I lacked a community of people who would help me develop my earlier intuitions about eliciting dimensions important to respondents, and how it might link with larger structural analyses. Most of the people in Human Development found George Kelly 'a bit old-fashioned,' or just not comprehensible. While accepting gender as a variable, as a group they were fairly uninterested in qualitative, empirical explorations of engendering in various social formations, different experiences of becoming a woman or a man in various racial and ethnic groups, different cohorts, different sexual orientations, etc. I found the statistical approaches offered as methods completely hollow for answering my burning questions. Furthermore, the justifications for using statistics seemed rather scientistic to me, e.g. 'no one will believe you unless you use numbers' or 'qualitative research is not generalizable' (without being able to say why not).

As an activist, these blind and authoritarian directives angered me; I had been well trained as an undergraduate by feminist science critic Ruth Hubbard and feminist philosopher Mary Daly to question authority in such academic statements. I began to remember Glaser and Strauss, and upon inquiry, realized that I was eligible to take classes in other departments at UCSF. However, when I went to my advisors in Human Development, I was discouraged from taking classes from Strauss, as he was, according to one advisor, 'not a real sociologist.' (And thus I was introduced to the politics of qualitative research.)

By the following year, I determined that I would take qualitative classes in spite of my advisors' resistance. I began the long sequence of courses in fieldwork and grounded theory analysis in the Social and Behavioral Science Department, working first with Leonard Schatzman and Virginia Olesen, and then, finally with Barney Glaser and Anselm Strauss. I will not continue with this detailed personal chronology, beyond noting some of the lessons learned in my search for teachers and methods:

- Simply finding grounded theory was not self-evident. It meant walking a twisted path, full of contingency and accidental proximities.
- The formation of this path was/is not accidental, however full of contingencies it may be. Rather, it forms the basis for creating a critical map of my emerging intellectual commitments. In my first fieldwork class, a prerequisite for the grounded theory sequence, Leonard Schatzman's first lesson was to get us to write down 'how we ended up here' (at UCSF). This itself became the data for beginning to analyze complex social processes, and how to name them and begin to seek dimensions in the search itself. I was astonished that such exploration could itself be analyzed as a sociological phenomenon. A posting on a bulletin board, a love relationship, a chance meeting or phrase, can be considered as data. In this, a reflexive move analyzing life decisions becomes a tool for deepening one's repertoire of concepts and commitments. Today, I would call it the building of an intellectual infrastructure.
- In bringing both contingencies and commitments to explicit, overt analysis, one creates the chance to reflect on a somewhat unconscious set of choices, and to include the heart of method as a part of lived experience.

Grounded theory is an excellent tool for understanding invisible things. It can be used to reveal the invisible work involved in many kinds of tasks, as I have written about elsewhere (Bowker and Star, 1999; Star, 1991a, b, 1998; Star and Ruhleder, 1996; Star and Strauss, 1999). This includes invisible work in the acquisition and practice of method. *The longer one practices grounded theory, the more deeply imbricated it becomes in daily life*. This, of course, results in examining the various forms of invisible work one does as an analyst. For example, among those I have found in my own life are:

- Carrying nineteenth century heavy, dusty volumes of patient records from a consulting room to a small attic chamber; waiting to retrieve them until the consulting physicians were done with the room in which they were stored (Star, 1989);
- Explaining bisexuality and various sexual practices to a young, eager, and naive respondent, in order to create a cordial space for conducting an interview;
- Having to ask elderly lesbians to sign a legal release form explaining that, since at the time sodomy and certain other sexual practices were illegal, they might be arrested if they spoke of

having had fellatio or anal sex (the Human Subjects Committee at San Francisco State, required us to do this, not distinguishing genders or life experiences: you can imagine how silly I felt explaining this to a 75-year-old lifelong lesbian);
- Learning local parking regulations and practices in some 50 different genetic laboratory locations, from Vancouver to Missouri and beyond, during multi-sited fieldwork to help develop a tool for communication across a scientific community.

Abstracting from this short list, one can see various forms of work that are not discussed in the final published reports. This invisible work includes managing my embarrassment at asking personal questions in an interview about sexual practices and identity/emotion work (Charmaz, 1991; Corbin and Strauss, 1988). It includes the manual labor of carrying the heavy records book from place to place. All fieldworkers have similar stories (never get an anthropologist talking about plumbing in far away places, especially over dinner). In my work as a sociologist of science, I came up with the code, 'deleting the work.' Scientific journals are full of articles that delete the development, setting, communication practices, and 'grunt work' involved in doing science. Of course, as a scientist, this insight applies to me as well.

CODE: GETTING TO 'OUT OF BOUNDS'

What is a code? When I have taught grounded theory, I have explained going through the data repeatedly, looking for several sorts of things. These include anomalies, distaste, liking one person more than another, a shock of recognition as a respondent uses a phrase in local jargon that captures something about the site or acts (an in vivo code). I've taken students through the classical teachings of fieldwork, including the especially helpful *Doing Fieldwork: Warnings and Advice* (1971) by Rosalie Wax and Sanjek's *Fieldnotes* (1990), an edited volume that begins with Jean Jackson's provocative essay, 'I Am a Fieldnote.' Why these two books in particular? I hadn't really thought about it in depth before, however, in writing this essay I see that both are written in clear, deeply personal terms, and they do not take the object of analysis, or the methodological procedures for granted. They include emotions, especially joy, mourning, confusion, and anxiety. (Code: *When emotions break through.*)

What is a code? A code sets up a relationship with your data, and with your respondents. One of the core mandates of sociology is the ability to ask the question, 'Of what is this an example?' For instance, when I studied nineteenth century physiologists doing brain experiments on great apes, I was asking questions about, inter alia, the nature of experiments, how materials are obtained, the role of social movements in restricting science (antivivisection, for example), and how one simian was turned into part of 'the brain,' an abstract map of the human brain.

Abstracting includes this sort of dialogue with imaginary others: sociologists, or advisors, other writers, or clients. Abstracting means to drop away properties from the original object. (Code: *abstracting away intimacy.*) This does not require a full specification of properties in the tradition of analytic philosophy; rather, this occurs by comparison, in the Pragmatic and grounded theory senses, as outlined above. In fact, one is simultaneously discovering new specific properties and then merging them or dropping them in the face of comparisons. This is an open-ended, sprawling type of research, indeterminate, and structured by one's own ability to manage 'grounded abstractions' and 'local emotions' while continuing to develop theoretical sensitivity.[2]

For example, a couple of months ago I saw a bobcat in my driveway; a beautiful wild animal, poised there. I wanted to pet it, to get to know it, to help it— all sorts of emotions welled up in me. (Code: *when emotions break through// wildness.*) Fear for my own smaller cats, wondering why it was in my driveway, after many years here, I had never seen this before. I begin to analyze the bobcat. (Codes: *Wild, pity, beauty, fear, out of bounds.*) Then, my thoughts were of myself and our small settlement here in the mountains. We are out of bounds, too. We have no gas or sewage, and coyotes, deer, and quail are much more common than people. But the bobcat and I are not the same. However, I keep thinking about out of bounds and what it means to each of us.

In a research project, I would have hundreds of codes and many sorts of comparisons to make. But in my daily life, I also think this way. As Everett Hughes put it, 'What do a priest and a prostitute have in common?' It seems a shocking comparison, but then you begin to see the circumstances, the context, of their work. They both listen to people's confessions; they work with people one-on-one (usually) in a setting that invites these sorts of intimacies, they listen rather than reveal their own lives, and so forth (Hughes, 1970). By comparing, yet going back again and again to the data, we preserve something of what we see in both of these lines of work; something also of the shock of the new, and the new way of seeing that is more abstract than before. However, as I dip back into the data, I refresh my image of the people over and over. (Coding, question of constant comparison: *abstracting away* and *the breaking through of emotions simultaneously* invoke *out of bounds. Can I take this comparison through more experiences and expand it?*)

RESOURCES

I pause at this point for an incomplete list of resources for doing grounded theory in research, before discussing some of the affective and Pragmatic approaches I take in my own work. Kathy Charmaz's recent textbook, *Constructing Grounded Theory: A Practical Guide through Qualitative Analysis* (2006) provides an extremely clear, suggestion- and example-filled guide to beginning to use grounded theory. In particular, the chapter on coding makes much of my work in this essay easier. It examines the *how* of coding, something that has been much discussed, but often with a lack of clarity, and confusing internal contradictions. An earlier attempt, in Barney Glaser's *Theoretical Sensitivity* is also full of good suggestions, but is somewhat cramped for some users by an idiosyncratic language of logic that was never broadly picked up in the sociological or professional communities (1978). The book is also a little difficult to obtain and read. (I speak here from teaching experience.) Thus, this welcome update from Charmaz represents and clarifies quite a bit of Glaser's work in *Theoretical Sensitivity*. Similarly, Strauss's *Qualitative Analysis for Social Scientists* (1987) has several compelling examples that help one intuit the nature of coding, and a Q&A section at the end that is helpful. For the simple mechanics of handling field notes as a beginning, Schatzman and Strauss's *Field Research* (1973), remains useful in dividing codes into types: methodological, observational, and substantive. However, its language does not connect well to later usage (that is, more advanced usage and later scholarship). Adele Clarke's excellent new book, *Situational Analysis* (2005), helps to fill in this gap. Her approach focuses on arenas and social worlds, and in particular the problems associated with analyzing disciplinary growth and change. This will be useful for those wishing to analyze changes in science, industry, politics, or social movements (or combinations of these), and in facing the initial 'messiness' of the data and the nature of developments. It does not focus overly much on the epistemological processes of coding per se. However, combined with Charmaz's book and the insights provided in this volume, Clarke helps build an indispensable scaffold for moving between the cognitive, affective 'close-in' aspects of grounded theory to the larger-scale changes in the current world. As with all grounded theory, all these works advocate moving from data to analysis, and back again, recursively.

Long ago, Herbert Blumer (Strauss's teacher and student of George Herbert Mead) called for the following of 'hunches' through data, intrinsically a personal biographical approach at the beginning. Glaser spoke of 'life-cycle' sources for topics although not for coding; for example, both he and Strauss lost a parent close to the time of the writing of several books on death and dying [*Awareness of Dying*, 1965; *Time for Dying*, 1968; and *Anguish*, 1970 (see the excellent discussion of these in Chapter 1)]. This personal experience was always fascinating to me, but neither Glaser nor Strauss were very interested in exploring or discussing the nature of how their own emotions were used as sources for analysis (either in their methodological writing nor in their classes). Which, of course, being obsessed with invisible work, makes me even more curious.

The above is a very incomplete sketch of work on grounded theory, meant primarily to point to new resources and to understand the dearth of material for answering the question, 'where do codes come from?'

A RECIPE FOR THE COGNITIVE-EMOTIONAL GENERATION OF 'A CODE' IN GROUNDED THEORY

Object relations

What is a code? What do a bobcat and a sociologist have in common? We are both a bit out of bounds, myself in what I am writing and thinking, and she in crossing the driveway and peering up at my house. Using the above codes of emotions breaking through and abstracting simultaneously, I enrich the notion of out of bounds. My first reaction comes from a sense of attachment (remembering that attachment can be positive and/or negative). At some emotional level, I want to know this bobcat. I feel kinship with her. She is beautiful. I feel somewhat attached to her, as if I would like to capture her wildness and beauty and make it part of me. But I know that to do so in real life would be to kill that beauty. So I begin to think with 'grounded theory feelings' about this little relationship. As I think about this, and abstract the relationship, a code forms that both adds and subtracts from the experience. Out of bounds is not the total of my experience or relationship with the bobcat. However, the combination of empathy, or attachment, and abstraction, is even more powerful than either alone. In working with biologists, I have felt this dual vision: if they see a subject within their expertise, they are compelled to name it, often in Latin. Almost simultaneously, they will say something empathic, like 'hey there, little fella,' or 'what a beauty,' or, as frequently, sorrow about the condition of its habitat. In fact, each part of science has some version of this double vision (see Keller, 1983; or Star and Ruhleder, 1996, on 'the worminess of the worm' in a genetics nematode laboratory).

A code, then, is a matter of both attachment and separation. When I am able to hold both *simultaneously*, I experience the joy and grief of adulthood. To speak of 'life cycle' reasons for topics: I grew up in a very close-knit, rural family, one that had very specific ideas about how things are done. Yet my reading (I seemed to have been practically born reading) implied other worlds, where these assumptions were not taken for granted. Gradually I began to nurture the notion that *somewhere else* was a place to reconcile these things. This required that I step out of bounds with respect to my extended birth family. This was emotionally hazardous, and it took me many years to trust my own experience of the world, and to balance many forms of attachment and separation, or abstraction and intimacy. From this experience I have drawn many projects related to marginality, outsiders, membership, or lack thereof, and invisible work.

Within psychological theory, the simultaneous attachment-separation idea is found extensively in the object relations model of familial and social dynamics. Perhaps most notably, the work of D. W. Winnicott (1965) on separation and transitional objects captures the dynamics of this developmental process. Winnicott has been primarily remembered for his studies of infant and child development. He was also a vital, imaginative theorist, moving from his clinical work to theory (and then back again). Although he was a psychoanalyst, his links with the Freudian school do not appear (to me) to be overly dogmatic or even central. Concepts such as 'separation anxiety,' 'pathological attachment,' and 'good-enough mothering' belong to him; he also was relentlessly both theoretical and material. His work on transitional objects has (not unlike the work of Gregory Bateson, 1972) impacted scholars from many disciplines, and has been used to revitalize much of the analysis of love and loss.

Winnicott believes the infant learns gradually (in the best case) to attach to the parent in many small ways, and to experience those separations that are bearable for it. Maturity means holding larger and multiple separations along with attachment, not total separation (abstraction) nor total attachment (total intimacy), but a balance. In the words of Winnicott (1965):

> It is generally acknowledged that a statement of human nature is inadequate when given in terms of interpersonal relationships, even when the imaginative elaboration of function, the whole of fantasy both conscious and unconscious, including the repressed unconscious, is allowed for. There is another way of describing persons … of every individual who has reached to the stage of being a unit … it can be said that there is an *inner reality* to that individual, an inner world which can be rich or poor and can be at peace or in a state of war … if there is a need for this double statement, there is need for a triple one; there is the third part of the life of a human being, a part that we cannot ignore, an intermediate area of *experiencing*, to which inner reality and external life both contribute. It is an area which is not challenged, because no claim is made on its behalf except that it shall exist as a resting-place for the individual engaged in the perpetual human task of keeping inner and outer reality separate yet inter-related (p. 230).

One way for achieving this maturity is learning to manage the anxiety produced by separation, or the smothering of too much attachment, through the use of what Winnicott called a transitional object: with young children, this is often a blanket, a doll, or some other small prized possession. The transitional object belongs a little to each world: the old world of being attached, and the new world of growing up, leaving, going away, abstracting.

Codes in grounded theory are transitional objects

Codes allow us to know more about the field we study, yet carry the abstraction of the new. When this process is repeated many times, and constantly compared across spaces and across data, it is also possible reflexively to grow. In grounded theory, this is known as theoretical sampling. Codes are part, also, of the third space of development, the 'holding space' of experience. Theoretical sampling stretches the codes, forcing other sorts of knowledge of the object. The theory that develops repeats the attachment-separation cycle, but in this sense taking a code and moving it through the data. In so doing, it fractures both code and data. Again, it calls up some anxiety, and at the same time, perhaps causally, it calls for authority. There isn't any roadmap, and to make it worse, as one practices constant comparison across data sets and even outside 'normal' ethnographic data (Strauss, 1970), one constantly loses and gains, attaches and separates.

Let me give an example of this from my own work, and foreshadow how this appears in Pragmatist problem-solving. Some years ago, I became interested in the gap between how people act, and how they are represented online and on paper. Part of this insight came from doing fieldwork in an artificial intelligence [AI] laboratory and a neurophysiology laboratory, another part of it a reflection on my training to self-censor my feelings in the narrative of my research. One of the first family of codes I developed concerned simplification in scientific work (Star, 1983). I examined the different ways that scientists, in writing up their results, discarded 'unruly' data such as that gathered from women, black people, and bald men. The ideal research object was a white, middle-class 10-year-old boy. Unruly data included several codes about the work itself: discarding anomalies, substituting reliability for validity (a code I would return to throughout my work), and all the sorts of formatting constraints that writing for scientific journals contain, and that implicitly inhibit the 'unruly data' of the investigator as well as the subject.

As this study grew into various studies of computer use, creation of classification systems, and other ways scientifically of representing human behavior, it became increasingly important for me to immerse myself in Pragmatism. Much of the modern current of computer critique, particularly in artificial intelligence and in classification, has been purely logical and cognitive, including the philosophy of mind and of language (but see the very important exception of Suchman, 1987, and her colleagues). The inspirational philosophers included Heidegger, Wittgenstein, John Searle, and Quine. I wrote one paper, accepted for publication, that attacked much of this work by questioning how AI used humans as research material. Then I sat with the paper, and with myself, and realized that I had to choose between becoming a scientific gadfly, or getting on with the project of seeing *how* these philosophers and computer scientists worked together; on understanding the impact of different forms of computing, and what work was being done to create visions of the human mind.

I withdrew the paper, which had been accepted for *AI and Society,* as I made the choice to return to studying work. I felt ashamed of myself, as if I had come close to becoming a sort of muckraker. In any event, this decision stood me in good stead, as I began working more closely with computer scientists as colleagues, not themselves solely as ethnographic subjects. Following the precept of 'analyze consequences, not antecedents,' I took this aspect of Dewey's work and outlook to heart. I ended up writing my first book on the coordination of work from different lines of work in early (nineteenth century) neurophysiology and brain research (Star, 1989).

So the doing of grounded theory, at its most basic, is, among other things, an emotional challenge and a call to methodological maturity. With other sorts of analysis, such as focus groups or surveys, one primarily is seeking to extract data from respondents. A focus group is face-to-face, but not long-term; in some survey research, it is often delegated such that one never meets a respondent (Roth, 1966). (Of course, this varies considerably, and I am *not* saying that the joining of experience/affect with abstraction is the unique purview of grounded theory.)[3]

The long haul

Over a lifetime of research, some people have a sense of a *life's work*. For Strauss's festschrift, I wrote:

> Every passionate scientist has a mystery at the center of his or her research. In exactly the
> ancient senses of mystery and passion, there are questions or sets of questions that can

never be solved, only wrestled with, embraced, and, one hopes, transformed. The primacy of work is just such a mystery in the work of Anselm Strauss, and his profoundly fertile transformations have given rise to a new way of framing an old sociological/philosophical question: the relationship between the empirical/material on the one hand, and the theoretical abstract on the other. Here I call this the relationship between the visible and the invisible (Star, 1991b: 265).

It may be a very useful exercise for one to question oneself, at any career stage, about the nature of one's own passions and mysteries. (For those interested, my own passions are most closely spelled out in Bowker and Star, 1999; Star, 1991b, 1998; Star and Griesemer, 1989.) Of course, in setting out this comparison with object relations, I realize that there is an infinite regress in possibility. Where does attachment come from? If I say, as many would, that they arise from the body, the unconscious, and one's biography, this takes my point from a chapter to someone else's life-work. At the same time, I hope this recognition of affect, attachment, and deep feelings will legitimate aspects of doing grounded theory that are rarely written about, although frequently talked about in some circles, perhaps most often in a teacher's counsel during the dissertation process. I was lucky beyond measure in having Strauss as an advisor I trusted completely.

PRAGMATISM

Pragmatist philosophy challenges one to accept the invitation to adulthood offered by object relations as interpreted above. It is an occupation of the third space, and through grounded theory, the implication of codes as transitional objects both emotionally and analytically. Learning grounded theory was not divided from learning about Pragmatist philosophy and also about early Pragmatist-informed sociology and social psychology. As graduate students, we trained simultaneously in method and theory, and were encouraged to use both philosophers and other sociologists as sources for comparison, coding, ontology, and epistemology. We nearly always read the originals, not textbooks.

We emphasized the early Chicago School and its relationship with Dewey, James, Mead, and later, Bentley.[4] We joined a community of practice with profound historical roots. Below, I take several Pragmatist tenets, and relate them to the attachment-separation balance I have presented.

Consequences, not antecedents

One of the simplest and most difficult tenets of pragmatism is that understanding is based on consequences, not antecedents. One does not build an *a priori* logic, philosophical analysis with pre-set categories, or as 'verificationist' social scientists, as Barney Glaser so mordantly termed them. Rather, the process is backwards to most modes of analysis. In a sense, to follow the language of this essay, one bares one's soul to the elements, and sees what happens. 'What happens' is a matter of several things. An interruption to experience (or as I teach it, an anomaly that gets one's attention in the data) was actually consistent with Peirce's notion of abductive thinking. Both Dewey and Mead posited that a fact is the result of an interruption to experience. Earlier, William James's notion of how we form habits, and react to their disruption, presages this formulation.

A reflection, based in a community and dialogue, about the nature of the experience, results in a new object (a more formal code, or the result of theoretical sampling, in Strauss's terms). This idea of the chain *experience-interruption-reflection-object* dates back in complex ways to Dewey's first paper, 'The Reflex Arc Concept in Psychology' (1896). There, Dewey argued that perception is not continuous, but constantly interrupted and in a way that demands interpretation. A reflex is not a matter of a continuous stream of 'information' hitting the black box of the brain, but rather a constant feat of interpretation, as routine acts and ways of seeing are interrupted, interpreted, and revised. Thus, from James's 'blooming, buzzing confusion,' we arrive at humanness through the constantly offered interpretations of our family, community, nature, media, art, animals, and all others.

Choosing among conflicting interpretations means constant struggle for selfhood, that is, how one shapes a body of interruptions and interpretations, and comes to incorporate integrity and authority in action. In this, Pragmatism is neither modern nor postmodern, but orthogonal to the terms of those debates, including positivism vs. interpretation (or realism vs. relativism). Choices are complexly mediated by close-in cultures, and also by cultures-at-a-distance, including media.

A glimpse here, then, of what underlies attachment and separation: the fluid whisperings (and sometimes demands) of others in childhood, mediated then and in adulthood by history and the growing self. It constantly challenges the input–output model with the attachment-separation-transitional object formation. Dewey's *The Quest for Certainty* (1929a) scales up from the 'Reflex Arc' paper, and examines how philosophers and other scholars use pre-set models, concepts, and methods. He deems this a quest for certainty, a shelter from the emotional storm in a sense, although he uses few affective words to describe this. I would say that this quest for certainty (for example, for a single model that pre-explains most events in the world) is a way of shielding ourselves from the powerful pain of the attachment-separation grief (in part, at least). In doing grounded research, this is a moment to return to the data, bringing the subject-object-mediation back to coding and categorizing.[5]

The objective reality of perspectives

The maturity implied by constantly practicing the object relations side of grounded theory/Pragmatism may actually be the scariest aspect of doing grounded theory. In so doing, one becomes a methodological maverick and, in the earlier stages of one's career, this can be costly. In addition, practicing this philosophy directly challenges the binary and well-guarded division between interpretation and Reality. Interpretation is poetry. Reality is science. They are meant to be kept apart. Putting them together is asking for trouble.

I came to sociology of science as a Pragmatist, at the beginning of what later would be called 'the science wars,' a bitter, divisive brawl where 'constructivist theorists' (or interpretive theorists) were pitted against 'realist scientists.' Positivist scientists saw the work of much of the new program of sociology of science (beginning in roughly 1976) as anti-science. This included their attempts to see science as just another kind of work, as something that changes historically and culturally, and as a process subject to developmental contingencies and politics. Constructivism is a complex argument, not merely a know-nothing attitude. Participants often had high stakes in their approach to science, much of it quite personal, as well as a social world (community of practice), shared ideology, and collective practice. Their examination of realist science was met with indignation by traditional scientists. For example, those exploring the cultural and historical aspects of physics were seen as mystical dreamers, or even fools: 'Are you saying that if I jump off a building I won't fall to the earth?' Well, no. But constructivists were, for the most part, interested in exploring the meaning of say, falling, as culturally constituted; of injury and the body as having different meanings in different times and places. The world, as it had been explained by scientists to date, appeared as both brutal and universalist (except perhaps for art, religion, and the like) and reactive in just the way that Dewey saw in the reflex arc model.[6]

Delicately dissecting, situating, and making the world ontologically and epistemologically open to revision was not of interest to the traditional science warriors. They were quite threatened by the prospect of cultural relativism as applied to science. Often citing 'Nazi science' or 'Lysenkoism' as examples of what may happen as a result of relativism or constructivism, this group of scientists ridiculed sociology of science as if we were know-nothing yahoos who sought to ridicule science.

From the Pragmatist view, the response to this quarrel is to examine questions of responsibility, location, consequences, and authorship. Pragmatists see 'universalism' as agreements across a large number of communities of practices and cultures, nothing more or less. It does not exist in some *a priori* analytic reality. People always interpret events from a situated and complexly principled point of view. For example, death means the end for some religions, a transition for others, a transformation for still others. These are radically varying views of an experience we all undergo. If one respects interpretation, they are not, however, universal. Nevertheless, those things with powerful scope and scale consensus are to be respected, most of the time as being just that; this does not, however, mean that one must sign on to the belief in ontological or epistemological universality.

The classic article of Pragmatist philosopher George Herbert Mead, 'The Objective Reality of Perspectives,' gives a kind of mandate for the *ontological primacy of interpretation* (1927/1964). Mead argues that a perspective is a way to stratify and order nature. That stratification, he asserts, comes from the development of a perspective, ancient and slowly accrued, or more novel, no matter. These stratifications are 'the only form of nature that is there.' This means that as an analyst, the confidence and authority accumulated by attachment-separation-transition (uncountable times, sometimes recursing, sometimes accruing, sometimes taking other shapes and textures) must come to the fore as an author, when one writes. This can be psychologically difficult.

I believe that this difficulty is akin to something Barney Glaser once called 'flooding,' a common experience in grounded theory. One has a plethora of codes, comparisons, and provisional ways of arranging the data. But so much seems worthy. How to weed? How to choose? In his book, *Memory Practices in the Sciences*, Bowker (2006) analyzes the continually changing nature of the past. In *The Mnemonic Deep*, he notes that even a name has multiple, tangled origins and aesthetics, for example in naming new species. The illusion of the completed and perfected is only that, a story we make up in order to give legitimacy to our own authority. But as we plumb the mnemonic deep, we find exactly the same challenge as with 'contemporary' data. The gap between the romantic story of the past and the messy, attached, feeling-full past can be painful and misleading, just as can pluralistic ignorance ('I must be the only one') in social groupings. As Dewey (1929b) said in *Experience and Nature*:

> Romanticism is an evangel in the garb of metaphysics. It sidesteps the painful, toilsome labor of understanding and of control which changes sets us, by glorifying it for its own sake. Flux is made something to revere, something profoundly akin to what is best within ourselves, will and creative energy. It is not, as it is in experience, a call to effort, a challenge to investigation, a potential doom of disaster and death (1929b: 51).

Here both Bowker and Dewey capture the visceral terror of authority in research (see also Becker, 1986). Part of it is an attempt, as Mead would say, to nail down 'the specious present' (1932). We live between the past and the present, poised and vulnerable, despite the romantic call to prior solutions. In this sense, Pragmatism reverses our commonsense temporality, and challenges us to a profound heterochronicity.

The human skin: philosophy's last line of defense

I will conclude with some points from the Pragmatist political scientist Arthur Bentley (1935, 1954), who, like Dewey, had a long and productive career and produced several important books before joining forces with John Dewey. Much of his work on science and organizations, including that on relativity theory and on beliefs and fact (written in the 1920s and 1930s), resonates profoundly with more recent sociology of science. He is less well known than Dewey, except perhaps for their co-authored *Knowing and the Known* (1970 [1954]), one of Dewey's last publications.

One essay of his, now available in a volume of his reprinted papers, has had a profound impact on my own work in science. The article, 'The Human Skin: Philosophy's Last Line of Defense,' argues that philosophers use the skin (the edges of the body) as an epistemological border and barrier, in fact out of a kind of superstition (1954/1975). To the extent that the object of analysis in Pragmatism and in grounded theory is nearly always a form of action, this idea crystallizes a central challenge for, in fact, all of sociology and philosophy of science. The idea of action as the central unit of analysis has been discussed in all of the grounded theory books cited here, and in Strauss's most complete theoretical statement, *Continual Permutations of Action* (1993).

If action is the unit, some unknown interiority (perhaps the brain, perhaps the gene, perhaps memory or history) cannot form the antecedent basis for action. An action always ramifies and continues, at least those sorts of action of importance for sociological analysis. Actions traverse the skin. They do not originate in individuals, but rather as a result of relations, the 'between-ness' of the world. Thus, Bentley's work, at least as much as Dewey's is a radical refutation of individualism. It calls to Durkheim's notion of the *sui generis* aspect of social facts, that is, that relations between many people constitute a level and unit of analysis that are whole and infungible (1938). The continuous nature of the act, and how and/or when you take that as your basic unit of analysis, changes perception of the world. Perhaps we might call this continual permutations of analysis.

CONCLUSION: LIVING GROUNDED THEORY

In conclusion, I would like to return to how grounded theory permeates my way of seeing the world, in connection with Pragmatism. Embedded in my everyday action, it is a powerful tool, almost a spiritual tool to decenter my own assumptions and constantly remind me to try to take the role of the other, in Mead's words. This has developed over a long period of time (I have been doing this for about 29 years, a baby really in terms of learning). However, I do have a sense of a life-work, as mentioned above. So in this sense, both temporally and spatially, grounded theory helps to form my biography as well as my way of seeing perceiving day to day. The risk of adding different studies together, of following various paths connected to science, technology, medicine, and information, is that I will fall into a confused compilation of theory, and measure it according to the conventional world of academia. The joy or goal, conversely, is to understand what I write as a wild, imaginative window on the world. I hope that I have the courage to allow one study to interrupt the experience of another.

How does one create a life-work and remain open; open to the data, open to being wrong, to redoing one's own work, actively to seek out new views and mistakes? For me, that has come through the privilege of teaching grounded theory, and of collaborating with people who like to work this way. That is, to embrace a continuous, embedded, imbricated, multiple, constantly compared way of making sense of myself. I hope this essay is helpful in understanding the emotional depths and life-work of living grounded theory and Pragmatism. The growing community of analysts, critics, and students is my ground of reflection, and we give each other the courage to go on.

ACKNOWLEDGMENTS

Thanks to Olga Kuchinskaya for a good discussion of the emotional aspects of coding and choice; to Pat Lindquist for teaching me to write and to grow; to Geoff Bowker, for anchoring my experience and helping me braid my projects together in my own idiosyncratic way; and to John Staudenmaier, for being my friend. Kathy Charmaz, Tony Bryant, David Obstfeld, and anonymous referees provided invaluable insights.

NOTES

1 Another way of 'seeing' the web of relationships in science is examining cases where people attempt to export the science in the absence of those relationships. For a brilliant example, see Wenda Bauchspies's ethnography of the acceptance of science as a 'stranger' (1998), in the sense classically developed by Simmel (1950).

2 My thanks to Kathy Charmaz for her very perceptive comment about this.

3 One *may* do grounded theory on any data, but qualitative analysis is really not very good at predicting elections or understanding large-scale demographic change. It may be very useful in companionship with other methods, but that is a statement more honored in the breach than the practice.

4 We did read Peirce as well, and some of the more minor philosophers, but at that time Peirce was not emphasized to us; he was presented by Strauss as being of a much older generation, and few of us gravitated toward his work alone. Nor were we encouraged to do so. Kathy Charmaz notes that he was more emphasized in her cohort at UCSF than he was in mine.

5 My thanks again to Kathy Charmaz.

6 And reactive in just the way that Dewey saw in the reflex arc.

REFERENCES

Adler, Paul S. and David Obstfeld (in press) 'The Role of Affect in Creative Projects and Exploratory Search.' *Industrial and Corporate Change.*

Bateson, Gregory (1972) *Steps to an Ecology of Mind*. San Francisco: Chandler.

Bauchspies, Wenda (1998) 'Science as Stranger and the Worship of the Word.' In Shirley Gorenstein (Ed.), *Knowledge and Society 11* (pp. 189–211).

Becker, Howard S. (1986) *Writing for Social Scientists: How to Start and Finish Your Thesis, Book, or Article*. Chicago: University of Chicago Press.

Bentley, Arthur (1935) *Behavior, Knowledge, and Fact*. Bloomington, IN: Principia Press.

Bentley, Arthur (1954) *Inquiry into Inquiries: Essays in Social Theory*. Ed. and with an introduction by Sidney Ratner. Boston: Beacon Press.

Bowker, Geoffrey (2006) *Memory Practices in the Sciences*. Cambridge, MA: MIT Press.

Bowker, Geoffrey and Susan Leigh Star (1999) *Sorting Things Out: Classification and its Consequences*. Cambridge, MA: MIT Press.

Charmaz, Kathy (1991) *Good Days, Bad Days: The Self in Chronic Illness and Time.* New Brunswick, NJ: Rutgers University Press.

Charmaz, Kathy (2006) *Constructing Grounded Theory: A Practical Guide through Qualitative Analysis.* Thousand Oaks, CA: SAGE.

Clarke, Adele E. (1998) *Disciplining Reproduction: Modernity, American Life Sciences, and 'The Problems Of Sex.'* Berkeley: University of California Press.

Clarke, Adele (2005) *Situational Analysis: Grounded Theory after the Postmodern Turn.* Thousand Oaks, CA: SAGE.

Corbin, Juliet and Anselm Strauss (1988) *Unending Work and Care: Managing Chronic Illness at Home.* San Francisco: Jossey-Bass Publishers.

Daly, Mary (1978/1990) *Gyn/ecology: The Metaethics of Radical Feminism.* Boston: Beacon Press.

Dewey, John (1929a) *The Quest for Certainty: A Study of the Relation of Knowledge and Action.* New York: Minton, Balch.

Dewey, John (1929b) *Experience and Nature.* NY: Norton.

Dewey, John (1981) [1896] 'The Reflex Arc Concept in Psychology.' In J. J. McDermott (Ed.), *The Philosophy of John Dewey* (pp. 136–148). Chicago: University of Chicago Press.

Dewey, John and Arthur Bentley. 1970 [1954]. *Knowing and the Known.* Boston, Beacon Press.

Durkheim, Émile (1938) *The Rules of Sociological Method.* Chicago: University of Chicago Press.

Gilligan, Carol (1993) *In a Different Voice: Psychological Theory and Women's Development.* Cambridge, MA: Harvard University Press.

Glaser, Barney G. (1978) *Theoretical Sensitivity: Advances in the Methodology of Grounded Theory.* Mill Valley, CA: Sociology Press.

Glaser, Barney G. and Anselm L. Strauss (1965) *Awareness of Dying.* Chicago: Aldine.

Glaser, Barney G. and Anselm L. Strauss (1967) *The Discovery of Grounded Theory: Strategies for Qualitative Research.* Chicago: Aldine.

Glaser, Barney G. and Anselm L. Strauss (1968) *Time for Dying.* Chicago, Aldine.

Hughes, Everett (1970) *The Sociological Eye.* New York: Aldine.

Keller, Evelyn Fox (1983) *A Feeling for the Organism: The Life and Work of Barbara McClintock.* New York: W. H. Freeman.

Kelly, George A. (1955) *The Psychology of Personal Constructs.* New York, Norton.

Kelly, George A. (1963) *A Theory of Personality: The Psychology of Personal Constructs.* New York: W. W. Norton.

Kohlberg, Lawrence (1981) *The Philosophy of Moral Development: Moral Stages and the Idea of Justice.* San Francisco: Harper & Row.

Kuhn, Thomas (1970) *The Structure of Scientific Revolutions.* Chicago: University of Chicago Press.

Latour, Bruno (1987) *Science in Action.* Cambridge, MA: Harvard University Press.

Lave, Jean and Etienne Wenger (1991) *Situated Learning: Legitimate Peripheral Participation.* Cambridge: Cambridge University Press.

Mead, George Herbert (1927/1964) 'The Objective Reality of Perspectives.' In A. J. Reck (Ed.), *Selected Writings* (pp. 306–319). Chicago: University of Chicago Press.

Mead, George Herbert (1932) *The Philosophy of the Present.* La Salle, IL: Open Court Publishing Co.

Mills, C. Wright (2000) *The Sociological Imagination.* Oxford: Oxford University Press.

Obstfeld, D. (2005) Social Networks, the *Tertius Iungens* Orientation, and Involvement in Innovation. *Administrative Science Quarterly,* 50, 100–130.

Richardson, Laurel (1996) 'Ethnographic Trouble.' *Qualitative Inquiry,* 2, 27–30.

Riegel, Klaus F. (1978) *Psychology, Mon Amour: A Countertext.* Boston: Houghton Mifflin.

Roth, Julius A. (1966) 'Hired Hand Research.' *American Sociologist*, 1, 190–196.

Sanjek, Roger (1990) *Fieldnotes: The Makings of Anthropology*. Ithaca: Cornell University Press.

Schatzman, Leonard and Anselm L. Strauss (1973) *Field Research: Strategies for a Natural Sociology*. Englewood Cliffs, NJ: Prentice Hall.

Simmel, Georg (1950) [1908] 'The Stranger.' In Kurt Wolff (Ed.), *The Sociology of George Simmel* (pp. 402–408). Glencoe, IL: Free Press.

Star, Susan Leigh (1983) 'Simplification in Scientific Work: An Example from Neuroscience Research.' *Social Studies of Science*, 13, 205–228.

Star, Susan Leigh (1989) *Regions of the Mind: Brain Research and the Quest for Scientific Certainty*. Stanford: Stanford University Press.

Star, Susan Leigh (1991a) 'Power, Technologies and the Phenomenology of Standards: On Being Allergic to Onions.' In John Law (Ed.), *A Sociology of Monsters? Power, Technology and the Modern World. Sociological Review Monograph,* 38 (pp. 27–57). Oxford: Basil Blackwell.

Star, Susan Leigh (1991b) 'The Sociology of the Invisible: The Primacy of Work in the Writings of Anselm Strauss.' In David Maines (Ed.), *Social Organization and Social Process: Essays in Honor of Anselm Strauss* (pp. 265–283). Hawthorne, NY: Aldine de Gruyter.

Star, Susan Leigh (1998) 'Experience: The Link between Science, Sociology of Science and Science Education.' In Shelley Goldman and James Greeno (Eds.), *Thinking Practices* (pp. 127–146). Hillsdale, NJ: Lawrence Erlbaum.

Star, Susan Leigh (1999) 'The Ethnography of Infrastructure.' *American Behavioral Scientist*, 43, 377–391.

Star, Susan Leigh and James Griesemer (1989) 'Institutional Ecology, "Translations," and Boundary Objects: Amateurs and Professionals in Berkeley's Museum of Vertebrate Zoology, 1907–1939.' *Social Studies of Science*, 19, 387–420.

Star, Susan Leigh and Karen Ruhleder (1996) 'Steps toward an Ecology of Infrastructure: Design and Access for Large Information Spaces.' *Information Systems Research*, 7, 111–134.

Star, Susan Leigh and Anselm Strauss (1999) 'Layers of Silence, Arenas of Voice: The Ecology of Visible and Invisible Work.' *Computer-Supported Cooperative Work: The Journal of Collaborative Computing*, 8, 9–30.

Strauss, Anselm (1970) 'Discovering New Theory from Previous Theory.' In Tomotsu Shibutani (Ed.), *Human Nature and Collective Behavior: Papers in Honor of Herbert Blumer* (pp. 46–53). Englewood Cliffs, NJ: Prentice Hall.

Strauss, Anselm (1987) *Qualitative Analysis for Social Scientists*. Cambridge: Cambridge University Press.

Strauss, Anselm (1993) *Continual Permutations of Action*. New York: Aldine de Gruyter.

Strauss, Anselm L. and Barney G. Glaser (1970) *Anguish: A Case History of a Dying Trajectory*. Mill Valley, CA: Sociology Press.

Suchman, Lucy A. (1987) *Plans and Situated Actions: The Problem of Human-Machine Communication*. New York: Cambridge University Press.

Vygotsky, L. S. (1986) *Thought and Language*. Cambridge, MA: MIT Press.

Wax, Rosalie H. (1971) *Doing Fieldwork: Warnings and Advice*. Chicago: University of Chicago Press.

Winnicott, D. W. 1965. *The Maturational Processes and the Facilitating Environment; Studies in the Theory of Emotional Development*. London: Hogarth.

PART II

Grounded Theory Method and Formal Grounded Theory

4

Doing Formal Theory

Barney G. Glaser

Is there such thing as formal grounded theory (FGT)? Yes there is; despite the fact that it has received scant attention since it was first mentioned and anticipated in our book *Awareness of Dying* (Glaser & Strauss, 1965) where we said:

> And in its turn, substantive theory may help in formulating formal theory. It may also contribute to the formulation of new formal theory grounded on careful comparative research ... Consequently, if one wishes to develop a systematic formal (or general) theory of awareness contexts, he must analyse data from many substantive areas (p. 276).

We then defined formal theory in Chapter IV of *The Discovery of Grounded Theory* (Glaser & Strauss, 1967) and again, I defined it in Chapter 9 of *Theoretical Sensitivity* (Glaser, 1978). Furthermore, Anselm and I wrote one FGT, *Status Passage* (Glaser & Strauss, 1971) and I produced a formal theory on organizational careers in my reader, *Organizational Careers* (Glaser, 1968).

Our words in *Awareness of Dying* 40 years ago and our subsequent efforts still hold true today. These efforts are awaiting the many good and excellent substantive grounded theories (SGT) ready to be broadened and generalized into FGT. Several researchers of worthy SGTs are asking for this instruction and inspiration. In reading over 25 qualitative methods books and a few quantitative methods books, I found not one indexing to formal theory (see References and Further Reading). There are just a few indexings to generalizations and generalizing, with no relation to their use in FGT. I found only a few mentions of FGT in these texts, usually in conjunction with SGT, as the next step, but the mention goes no further. The mentions are not a clear appeal to future research. They are mentioned only in passing; they are unclear, and even slightly wrong. The promise offered by doing FTG is not noted or emphasized. In short, the scant attention to

FGT means that it is virtually ignored. The scant attention paid to FGT is because it both does not fit the typical qualitative data analysis (QDA) methodological model and so much GT is remodeled by QDA (Glaser, 2003) that the next step is not in view or just not there to take. Here follows a typical example from the collection edited by Gilgun et al. (1992). After a linear list of substantive researches, Snyder says:

> Further because these theories have been systematically induced from the actual experiences of individuals they also constitute what Glaser and Strauss referred to as grounded theory (p. 31). Examining similar constructs across substantive areas yields formal theory (p. 129). My second recommendation is the construction of formal theory that is developed for a formal or conceptual area of sociological inquiry … comparative study of the conceptual frameworks induced from the social construction of anger, fear, grief, etc. provide additional rungs on the ladder toward development of formal grounded theory (p. 63).

Fine, but after this brief mention and promise of FGT, there is absolutely no push to do it, no procedural direction to go in. This illustration is just one of many examples that make the same observation, from which I derive the need for this paper and my forthcoming book (Glaser, 2006). It has been no better since this 1992 example to the present. I wish to focus on FGT as a reality, not just a promise.

Do some FGTs exist under a different name? Barely any; none that are systematically generated according to the rigorous procedures of generating grounded theory. There exist 'immaculate conceptions' that draw on some data even though mainly conjectured. There exist particularistic formal theories based on lots of experience, but not systematically researched. Exemplars of these theories are cited by Lincoln and Guba (1985): 'Like many other theorists, Simmel based his ideas about society on his own direct, non-systematic observations. And Goffman characterized his methodological approach: "The method that is often resorted to here—unsystematic, naturalistic observation—has very serious limitations"' (pp. 91–92). We can all think of further examples from our disciplines.

Walking surveys generate particularistic formal theories all the time as 'they know', but it is not research. Like many other professionals, lawyers and doctors are walking surveys who do this to the maximum, passing off their formal theories as coming from 'professionals who know' after years of practice. Walking surveys are grounded in the vicarious and actual experience and knowledge of the person. Stake (1983) calls them 'naturalistic generalizations, which develop within a person as a product of experience. They derive from the tacit knowledge of how things are … they seldom take the form of predictions, but lead regularly to expectation. They guide action' (p. 282).

Literature reviews abound, which often could have been, but are not FGTs. The literature citations are usually mildly added or accumulated for simple descriptive comparison of similarities and differences and not used for systematic generation of conceptual theory on a category. I examine at length the role of literature in generating formal theory in Chapter 5 of my forthcoming book *Doing Formal Grounded Theory*.

FORMAL GROUNDED THEORY DEFINED

So what is a FGT? Let us be clear. There are many very good SGTs out there. Many people feel their 'grab' conceptually and see the general implications of the core category everywhere they look. As Strauss and I wrote in 1967:

> A [SGT] theory at such a conceptual level, however, may have important general implications and relevance, and become almost automatically a springboard or stepping stone to the development of a grounded formal theory … [SGT] not only provides a stimulus to a 'good idea', but it also gives an initial direction in developing relevant categories and properties and possible modes of integration [theoretical codes] (Glaser & Strauss, 1967: 79).

For example, Odis Simmons's (1993) renowned paper on 'cultivating' easily leads to almost forgetting his substantive area (the milkman and his customer) to seeing cultivating everywhere in the human scene. His paper on cultivating for profit leads to cultivating for fun, recreation, social gain, love, etc. Other authors get what I call core fever. They see their core operating everywhere. For example, Hans Thulesius's (2003) renowned paper on balancing in palliative care leads him to see balancing everywhere. Or a substantive theory on the comparative failure of scientists (Glaser, 1964) leads directly to the need for a theory of comparative failure in work or even more generally, in all facets of social life. Or a substantive theory of deviance disavowal of people with visible handicaps leads to one concerned with deviance disavowal by a much wider range of impaired persons or other forms of visible, usually legitimate deviance.

Thus seeing the core category working beyond the immediate substantive area studied engenders a need to study it generally. For example, Barry Gibson's discovery of cautionary control among dentists to avoid contracting HIV, easily leads to wanting a formal theory of cautionary control which goes on in all facets of life, for all size units: traffic control, terrorist control, sanitary disease control (especially operating rooms), and so forth. The general implications of a core category lead to the need for generating a formal theory of the core by looking at data and other studies within the substantive area and in other substantive areas using the conceptualizing constant comparison method. Extending the theory of a core variable's general implications is the next obvious research step after doing a SGT.

Thus FGT can be defined as a theory of a SGT core category's general implications, using, as widely as possible, other data and studies in the same substantive area and in other substantive areas. For example, a well known theory of becoming a nurse (Davis & Olesen, 1970), is easily formalized by comparing it constantly to other data and theory about becoming a doctor, becoming a lawyer, becoming a pilot, becoming an accountant, etc. to arrive at a theory of becoming a professional. This FGT of becoming can be made even more general by looking at nonprofessional becoming, and even more general by looking at becoming a person in a culture; which we call socialization. From these examples, we see that FGT generalizations are conceptual *not descriptive*, and thus abstract of time, place, and people. As I have said in my book on conceptualization compared to description (Glaser, 1998), description is very soon stale-dated.

Further, a FGT's generalizations about a core category are abstract of time, place, and people until their application. When they are applied to a situation, a context and/or conditions, the FGT concepts are adjusted to suit. For example, for a FGT of cautionary control, tossing caution to the wind as some dentists do to avoid the expense, does not apply to operating rooms, where expense is not a concern; or does not apply to a traffic intersection where costs of an accident can run very high.

Thus FGT is simply a conceptual extension, however possible by research, of a SGT's core category using GT generating procedures, particularly theoretical sampling and conceptualizing constant comparison. FGT is *not* so-called 'grand theory', general theory, elaborated theory, middle range theory, etc. It has no predetermined level of abstraction. It will end up at the level of abstraction that the data and studies bearing on the core category (and the energy and resources of the theorist) will allow it. It is not as Dey (1999) says, a necessarily higher level of abstraction, although it may end up so. It depends. But keep in mind that FGT is not 'august' or 'high fallutin' theory.

FGT is not speculatively remote from data, especially the data it purports to explain. It is based on data and studies based on data. FGT methodology insists that; no matter how general (how broad in scope or abstract) the theory, it should be generated by that back and forth interplay with data that is so central to GT methodology. Models or theoretical codes used in previous SGTs to bring out a core category should not necessarily be used for genuine grounding in the current FGT. The models may change for the core category. For example, Richard Ekins (1995) tried to use awareness context theory with cross-dressing and came up with a variation of going from a closed to an open awareness context. He added progressive displays from closed to open awareness. The reader will discover that FGT becomes a very powerful tool of explanation. For example, a theory of credentializing nurses easily leads to a FGT on how to credentialize for quality control in all occupations.

The reader may question: Can one generalize from a single case SGT? Isn't one case too particularistic? Of course, but people do it anyway, researchers and laymen alike. General implications abound at all levels. What FGT does is to broaden the base of generalizing 'to and from'. FGT allows generalizing on a core category from several substantive areas with more multivariate conceptual complexity. In sum, FGT is nothing more than extending the general implications of a core variable by sampling more widely in the original substantive area and in other substantive areas and then constantly comparing with the purpose to conceptualize the general implications. It increases the SGT in breadth and depth of explanation.

CLARIFYING THE FORMAL GROUNDED THEORY DEFINITION

In *Awareness of Dying* (Glaser & Strauss, 1965) and *The Discovery of Grounded Theory* (Glaser & Strauss, 1967), our definition of FGT was somewhat too confusing for its lack of specificity, although the idea and quest were clearly there. We were responding to the general implications of the core variable however unspecified at that time. Awareness context had tremendous grab. Anselm and I said, in *Awareness of Dying*, that we anticipated the formulation of FGT, but did not quite define it nor understand it. We said:

> In the preceding chapter we remarked that substantive theory faithful to the empirical situation cannot be formulated by merely applying formal theory to the substantive area. A substantive theory must be first formulated in order to see which parts of diverse formal theories … can then further the substantive formulation. And in its turn, substantive theory may help in formulating formal theory. It may also contribute to the formulation of new formal theory grounded on careful comparative research … Consequently, if one wishes to develop a systematic formal (or general) theory of awareness contexts, he must analyse data from many substantive areas. When advancing a substantive theory to a formal one, the comparative analysis of groups is still the most powerful method for formulating credible theory (p. 276).

In *The Discovery of Grounded Theory*, we began to define FGT. We said:

> By substantive theory we mean theory developed for a substantive or empirical area of socio-logical inquiry, such as patient care, geriatric life styles, etc. … By formal theory we mean theory developed for a formal or conceptual area of sociological area such as status passage, stigma, deviant behavior, etc. Both types of theory may be considered 'middle range'; they fall between minor working hypotheses of everyday life and the 'all-inclusive' grand theories. Substantive and formal theories exist on conceptually ordered distinguishable levels of generality which differ only in terms of degree. In any one study each type of theory can shade at points into the other. The analyst, however, should focus clearly on one level or the other (p. 177).

This latter definition, which has been subsequently repeated several times in the methods literature, leads to some confusion. Its focus on levels of generality adds to the confusion. Most writers picking up on generality level have defined FGT wrongly, by focusing on a conceptual area, which is vague. This vagueness leads easily to focusing on a theoretical code (see Glaser, 2003) such as a process or range instead of a core category. This vagueness also leads to QDA comparative description focusing on descriptive differences and similarities about the conceptual area, not on constant comparisons for conceptualization. A lot of descriptions about status transitions is not FGT. Dey (1999), after trying to handle the level of abstraction confusion, comes up with this definition:

> Thus the difference between substantive and formal theories lies in their degree of conceptual abstraction. We can move from one to the other by focusing on a high level of generality and incorporating material from other substantive areas with the same formal theoretical import. In short, the distinction between formal and substantive theory might be better recast in terms of degrees of abstraction in which theory at any level has some combination of both substantive and formal elements. This still allows for a distinction in terms of theoretical emphasis, for theory may focus on either capturing the complexities of specific cases

or on the generating (or condensing) of generalities across a range of cases. However, it also implies a less clear-cut division between theoretical tools to capture individual complexity and those we might use to make generalizations (p. 41).

This statement leads to no product-oriented direction. It is uncertain and leads the researcher into confusion, not a clear direction to which a clear methodology can be attached. Our lack of clarity at the start in the late 1960s confused thinking about FGT. Dey faults us on making such a 'rigid distinction' between substantive and formal, which was somewhat inaccurate due to our lack of early clarity. Now, the reader can see the clear distinction between SGT and FGT given in the definition above. As a researcher, it is clear which way to go in generating by constant comparisons. Unfortunately, Dey's confusion also comes from seeing substantive theory as really descriptive, not conceptual, when he refers to capturing individual complexity of the substantive case and seeing SGT shading into FGT with no clear separation.

Karen Locke, in *Grounded Theory in Management Research* (2001), does better with our former lack of specificity. She says:

> In *The Discovery of Grounded Theory*, Glaser and Strauss make much of the difference between substantive and formal theory. They view formal theory as the sociologist's goal. However, to be valid, they insist that it be developed from a substantive grounding in concrete social situations. Thus substantive theory is prior to formal theory, and it is closely linked to the practice domain. It represents the close connection to the empirical reality... When we speak of formal theory, however, we usually refer to those areas of inquiry that operate at a high level of generality, such as systems theory. In Glaser and Strauss's view, substantive and formal theory are clearly related. Substantive theory can provide a link to more formal theory, but this is achieved by working empirically to develop conceptual categories at a higher level of abstraction and generality (p. 35).

Locke, in following our early lack of specificity in defining formal theory, is clearly led into thinking that any general category is generated at a higher level of abstraction when doing formal theory. Our clear definition here will set this vagueness to rest. Let the level of abstraction fall where it may, as the generation of formal theory pursues the general implications of a core variable. Now the FGT researcher has a clear path. Generality of 'what' is brought into clear focus also. Jane Gilgun and colleagues (1992) follow our same lack of conceptual focus and specificity. She says:

> Grounded theory can be of two general types: substantive and formal (Glaser & Strauss, 1967). In substantive grounded theory, the concepts and hypotheses that researchers develop are based on data focusing on one area of study. Discovering similar concepts and hypotheses across areas of study, time and setting and informants leads to formal theory (p. 37).

Clearly in these definitions, which lack conceptual specificity, the general implications of a core variable and its resultant applications is missing. Alvesson and Skoldberg (2000) respond to the lack of specificity in our early definition of FGT. They say, 'The difference between substantive and formal theory is not, however, altogether clear' (p. 31). They refer to differences in 'entities' and 'properties' in each type of theory and 'distinguishable levels of generality which differ in terms of degree', but they are not totally clear in trying to clear up our early definition. They say, 'The whole thing boils down to a matter of a lower or higher level of generality, and in reality there are not just two levels, but an arbitrary number of them'. Of course, level of generality is involved, but it is not the crucial dimension in my specific definition above. It emerges. Finally, in their conclusion section, they offer what they hope will clear up our lack of specificity by adding what they call a 'golden rule' to our early definition:

> Try to effect an epistemological break with the actor level in the formal grounded theory. The formal theory would then account for the deep structure and the substantive theory for the surface structure, upon which this is based. Such a golden rule would counteract much of what we see as the fundamental weakness in Glaser and Strauss's position while trying to preserve its strengths (p. 65).

I am not sure what they mean, but they are still using the generality level difference in an effort to handle the confusion brought on by our early statement lacking specificity on what FGT is. One reason for their miss of seeing the generalizing of a core category is that they consider it a constant resolving of a main 'worry'. This is not correct and too strong. The core category constantly resolves a main concern in a substantive area of action; this concern being the general goal that motivates participation, or structures to keep working. Whether or not worry is involved in a FGT, and it usually is not, is another issue that may or may not emerge. Their effort is commendable but the lack of clarity remains. Lastly, and briefly, Kearney (2001) alludes to what formal theory is, with typical over-generality and a kind of assuming that everyone knows what FGT is. She says:

> Grounded formal theory is middle-range theory grounded in substantive qualitative research. Glaser and Strauss (1967) conceived of grounded formal theory as describing a discrete kind of human experience that could be demonstrated across situation and contexts (p. 228).

This is a QDA remodelling, dropping the level of generality to description. It is no wonder, given our early over general definition of FGT and these examples of methodologists trying to clear it up, that there has been scant attention given to generating FGT. There was no clear generation path to it as there is for SGT. Indeed, FGT, now defined and specified, is just about the general implications of a core category generated from a substantive theory, which is a core variable with 'grab' and just pressuring to be generalized. FGT is not about a theoretical code (TC) such as structural process, an authoritarian structure, a range, a set of dimensions, a reward system or status congruency, etc. (see Glaser 2003) which are models for generating either SGT or FGT. The theoretical code used will emerge for a FGT as it does for a SGT. Do not confuse FGT with elaborating a theoretical code, however complex, such as an escalating basic social process model.

The core category may be somewhat, or very, abstract, like cultivating or creditializing compared to professional becoming or cautionary control respectively but it is still substantive in relevant meaning and fit. It just extends the core category in breadth and depth to more substantive areas within and without, or beyond, the original area. The FGT abstractness varies and is emergent and is not to be preconceived. Its degree of 'middle range' will vary. Furthermore, a FGT is not a 'grand theory' about a TC such as systems maintenance or deviant theory, situational analysis (Clarke, 2005), role theory, or status transitions (Glaser, 1994: 380). The GT researcher is modest and grounded. He is not a generator of immaculate conjecture. To repeat, FGT is just about a core category, such as moral reckoning or supernormalizing, no matter what TC emerges or what level of generality emerges. It is not to be confused with elaborating TCs or necessarily generating a higher level of generality. It just generates the general implications of a core variable such as pluralistic dialoguing. It has a clear product-oriented focus. It does not wander throughout a conjectural, conceptual realm.

GENERAL IMPLICATIONS

In *The Discovery of Grounded Theory* (Glaser & Strauss, 1967) we wrote:

> Since substantive theory is grounded in research on one particular substantive area, it might be taken to apply only to that specific area. A theory at such a conceptual level, however, may have important general implications and relevance and become almost automatically a springboard or stepping stone to the development of a grounded formal theory (p. 79).

There are three main dimensions of general implications:

- FGT in generating the general implications focuses only on conceptually general categories and hypotheses, not on descriptive differences and similarities. The conceptual generalities are arrived at through the constant comparative method of analysis.
- Conceptual generalities are highly applicable when conditioned and/or contextualized for a suitable and particular application; for example, how to apply cautionary control to the operating room or to traffic at street intersections or to flight travel security. The FGT conceptual hypotheses are applicable because they have fit, relevance, and workability; in short, because they were grounded.
- The doing of FGT generalizations are motivated by the pressure to generalize a core category that has grab; e.g. cautionary control, etc. The researcher of the SGT sees it everywhere, such as balancing.

Let me consider each in turn.

CONCEPTUAL GENERATING

In April 2005, my daughter Bonnie Glaser wrote:

> I have an idea for one of your next books. It should be about how a grounded theorist takes a SGT they have already done and builds on it ... through more research using theoretical sampling, emergent fit, building formal theory. In general, how to do more research and write about the general implications of theories that are already done... this is soooo important and people aren't really sure (without asking you) how to go about it. Alvita Nathanial wants to do a FGT on moral reckoning and Antoinette McCallin on pluralistic dialoging. Both asked me to ask you how.

This chapter begins to outline some answers to their questions but here I would point out it is the conceptual generality of their core categories of SGTs that taps general implications. In short, the general implications of a core category are expanded by generating grounded conceptual categories about it, from many different areas using the constant comparative method. FGT does NOT expand general implications by doing descriptive generalization, with its QDA need for accuracy, context, unit condition, harping on indicators, or describing a general law. The core category is expanded by abstract conceptual generalizations based on grounded research. The researcher uses constant comparison to generate concepts NOT to discover descriptive differences and similarities.

Furthermore the researcher cannot generate FGT from speculation and/or particularistic experiences. Nor can the researcher properly generate FGT theory bits (one sentence theories) from just one piece of data that is just one indicator. Theory bits come easy, as I said in *The Grounded Theory Perspective* (Glaser, 2001), as a researcher or reader of the research sees general implications of a core category everywhere and by human nature fits the concept to what situation he sees. One can see supernormalizing in sports everywhere and spout indicators of it; hence theorizing them even though the category came from dealing with heart attack victims. Theory bits undermine doing FGT. Some, none the wiser, may even take a theory bit about a substantive category as FGT. A SGT discussion seems formal to them. Not so: the generating research by conceptual comparisons must be done to yield a FGT. Conceptual generality is abstract of time, place, and people, yet can be applied. Thus FGT revolves around this abstract power of conceptual generality.

APPLICATION

General implications of a core category and its subcore categories generated in a FGT are applicable because people see them in other places (virtually everywhere) and automatically contextualize and condition them. For example, getting others to visualize deteriorization easily leads to seeing worsening progressions that are hard to get others to recognize. Lars Dahlgren (a student of Sven Stybern, a major supporter of GT) and colleagues (2004) emphasize the application function of abstract GT categories in worldwide public health problems. They say:

> Finally some words about generalization. GT strives at creating abstract knowledge from concrete observations. This means that the ultimate ambition is to discover theories on a level which will make is possible to apply them to a wide range of situations or contexts. Once discovered concepts leave the level of people, they become the focus of the research … The aim is to construct formal theory from substantive cases (p. 137).

This conceptualization leads to generalization that can then be brought back to many empirical areas with fit and relevance. Certainly, SGT concepts can be applied, but FGT conceptualizations have a wider, more grounded range. In 1978, I wrote, 'I am always amazed, given the pressure to generalize, the ease of doing

it with GT and the fact that all substantive grounded theories have general implications' (Glaser, 1978: 94).

FGTs, since they are grounded, have content references that fit and are relevant, thus can be applied as the researcher contextualizes almost automatically.
As the FGT builds, the applicability of its categories grows, and its categories
gain credibility and their ready modification becomes easy according to the context and conditions where it is applied. Thus the abstract power of FGT is very
empirically rooted. It is not based on speculative, conjectured, reified concepts.
A well-grounded FGT will, indeed, yield complex multivariate applications of
a core category. Thus abstract theory when grounded by generating using GT
procedures is very practical. FGT is much more that just a higher-level abstract
theory floating nowhere to be used. FGT's abstraction allows its application over
a wide range of empirical areas virtually forever, as opposed to descriptive
generalizations which are rooted in one empirical area and soon stale dated.

Janice Morse recognized this up to a point. She said in her article, 'Theory
Derived from Qualitative Research' (1997: Chapter 9), 'Generalizability is
obtained when the theory is recontextualized to another setting. The use of
abstract concepts in practice is difficult, and theory must provide an adequate
linkage to make such concepts relevant for use in the clinical setting' (p. 163).
She is right, except that generating SGT and FGT is not that difficult in providing
the 'link between concepts and recommendations for practice', since they are
linked to data.

Williams (2003) has not heard of, or perhaps not understood, GT and especially
FGT when he states, 'The problem with grand theory is that its sweep is often just
too grand.... We conclude that it is hard, though not impossible to link grand
theory to research' (p. 33). We grounded theorists know that it all boils down to
using grounded theory procedures to generate FGT to solve the link issue. FGT is
practical theory that fits and is relevant. It does away with applying conjecture and
the generalizations of particularistic views. Grounded abstraction generates application. SGT and FGT categories may appear context stripped or context free
because of their abstraction, and they are until recontextualized for application.
Application is an interaction of effects. Concepts recontextualized get applied and,
in turn, application incorporates comparisons with the context which generates
categories and properties; hence, more meaning for the FGT of the core category.

Context is a general word for environment, setting, ambience, larger picture
immediate situation, local normative frame of reference, etc. FGT gives both
access and control categories to a context as its application helps us to understand and explain what is going on in the context. FGT, when applied, creates
conditions for shared perspectives, interpretations, consequence predictions, and
normative views about relevant matters of whatever area it is applied to. The fit
of FGT sensitizes the applier (whether academic, consultant, or layman) to the
context's problems as both are flexibly modified to support needed change.
By constant comparisons, application modifies the FGT as it is applied.
Contextualization provides controllable footholds in the applied to area.

Thus the conceptual application is probable and modifiable to fit the area as opposed to the application of descriptive generalization which never really fits and is soon stale-dated. Thus, for example, in a FGT of cautionary control, there is the hypothesis that the greater the concern, the greater the cautionary control. Airplane travel and operating rooms have great concern, thus great techniques of cautionary control. Wet side walks and steps and dental practice have some concerns of danger and just use signs or warnings. Karen Locke saw this applicability when she wrote, 'A conceptual category has analytic generalizability when it can plausibly account for a large number and range of empirical observations. Glaser and Strauss (1967) speak of this when they describe a theory as being generally applicable' (p. 39). David Silverman (2000) also recognizes the applicability of FGT when he writes, 'this paper does not simply offer lists of common sense categories, but combines them into an analytic scheme which holds out the possibility of generating formal theories of the kind that Glaser and Strauss (1967) recommend and which may well have practical relevance' (p. 287). The reader may now be thinking of more properties of applying FGT, including its overlap with SGT as it merely extends SGT in breadth and depth. See also Hind et al. (1992).

THE PRESSURE TO GENERALIZE

As I have said, the pressure to generalize a core category is strong. It has grab; it is often a high impact dependent variable of great importance; it is hard to resist; it happens automatically with ease. Researchers tend to see their core category everywhere, such as Hans Thulesius seeing 'balancing' everywhere, or Helen Scott trying to use balancing in her study of integrating temporal, flexible distance study into a structured life. She says, 'then trying balancing and it didn't work, but it nearly did' (personal communication, 27 May, 2005). The probability of a core category being applicable in another area makes it easy to try and hard to resist.

It is normal for people to generalize the particular in everyday parlance. In science, the pressure to generalize a research fact or concept is legion. As Ian Dey said, 'We could not survive in the world without understanding particular events in all their complexity: but nor we could survive without comprehending some generalizations about how and why things work as they do' (p. 222). Generalizing is safe with a grounded category when modifiably applied. FGT generates many of these categories as a FGT about a core category is generated. In contrast, and in spite of the pressure to generalize hence to see general implications, many researchers miss this pressure because of the caution against generalizing descriptions in the QDA literature. It is a 'no no' and dangerous. For one of many examples, see Lincoln and Guba (1985: Chapter 5), 'The only Generalization is there is no Generalization' (p. 110). As a result, there is precious little in qualitative and survey methods books on how to generalize and a lot on how dangerous it is to do so. Thus researchers do not learn how to organize research to generalize, even if they wish to do it. Grounded general implications are forestalled, frustrated, or simply killed easily in spite of the pressure. The researcher then sticks with fact finding, descriptions, and, if needed and tempted, speculative generalizations.

The reverse applies also in somewhat less measure. Some researchers wish to keep their fact finding special. They do not want their precious, notable finding to be swallowed up in a generalization and therefore lose its singular impact. This finding fetish is prolific in 'tiny topic' research in which precious descriptive specifics are the goal. There is little or no need to see beyond the borders of the specific descriptive study (e.g. Devereux et al., 2005).

METHOD NEEDED

The above assertions imply that a procedural method is needed to generate FGT. Clearly it is what is needed to respond to the pressure to generalize widely for those researchers on the verge of doing FGT. Many FGTs are waiting to happen because of the needed method. To mention a few core categories awaiting an FGT, they are moral reckoning, pluralistic dialoguing, visualizing deterioration, supernormalizing, cautionary control, credentializing, cultivating, solutioning, rehumanizing, constructing relevance, relationship power abuse, fluctuating support networks, infra-controlling, untenable accountability, covering, psychic accompanying, particularizing the universal, privatizing public tracts, etc. A clear method is needed to prevent falling back into descriptive QDA as the research areas widen and also to prevent responding to this need by falling into logical-deductive speculation when widening the relevance and fit of SGT. For examples of immaculate conception, unfettered by systematic data, see Zetterberg (2005) or Anderson (2005). I am sure the reader has many more examples in mind.

I hope to hinder the natural tendency of researchers to fall back into generalized 'theory bits' founded on only one incident, as useful as that seems at the time, when more research becomes too much. I also want to help many SGT researchers to do FGT who feel they cannot yet or are not ready to try. In deference to grand theories and the idols who speculate them (the theoretical capitalists of our profession), a method of doing FGT will take its place both in our social psychological and sociological disciplines. Speculation will never disappear. I simply add another source of formal theory; the method for which is needed to round out, perspectivize and raise issues in discussions on abstract levels. FGT, as defined above, needs method, direction, and clarification to get it into being a resource for formal theory. I hope to go beyond the illustration level on method that Anselm used in his paper, 'Awareness Contexts and Grounded Formal Theory' (Glaser, 1994). He said:

> Barney Glaser and I have written many pages together, but we have never offered a set of images for how one might develop a particular formal theory. I will try to do that … giving

a few of the steps I am now following in developing a theory of awareness contexts. My talk is meant to show a theorist at work, rather than to offer a prescriptive set of generalized steps in the formulation process (p. 360).

The reader will judge my success in generating a clear method after reading my work. In *Theoretical Sensitivity* (Glaser, 1978), I wrote:

> We are far more humble when it comes to generating formal theory. We remain convinced that it should be grounded, but are not sure yet, as with grounded substantive theory, of the resolutions to many specific problems of generation. For example, in choosing a core variable for a formal theory, what are the grounds for its relevancy, how does one integrate the theory, where next to theoretically sample, how dense should formal theory be? Indeed, why generate formal theory at all? Once the analyst is cut loose from the grounding of a specific substantive area, answers to these questions are not readily apparent. At times it seems that formal theory can 'go' just about any way that an analyst desires (p. 142).

Twenty-six years of experience later, I hope to resolve in this chapter some solutions to these problems that were in question in 1978. My experience is not as vast as it is in generating SGTs but I have been involved in generating four FGTs: awareness contexts, status passage, organizational careers, and cautionary control, and I have touched on many aspects of generating FGT in my many books. I hope to bring all these writings and experience together into a method. Without many, many, FGTs as yet, the method needed cannot be totally explicated and derived from what does not exist. Yet enough FGTs do exist for the first method clarification and formulation of procedures which are warranted. In 1967, we said:

> The processes by which a substantive theory is advanced to a formal one, we should emphasize, since our experience and knowledge is least extensive in this area, most of our discussion will be concerned with general rules, positions and examples of initial effort at generating formal theory. More specific procedures await the time when enough sociologists will have generated FGTs that their procedures can be codified (Glaser & Strauss, 1967: 80).

Forty years after *The Discovery of Grounded Theory*, the time for codifying such procedures has arrived. The details of this method will also stop the free for all on how to do FGT that exists in the QDA literature. FGT will be open to and dependent on a method, henceforth. Albeit no doubt modifications will subsequently occur as we learn more by their doing. Please remember that I am merely trying to systematize with grounding by research procedures which up to this point comprises the natural tendency, unsystematically, to do FGT by generalizing general implications seen all around us. The method, I explicate, will be a conceptual generalizing model, not a descriptive approach, as used by Kearney (2001). She said:

> I went on to pull together studies of women's adjustment to illness and trauma, addiction recovery and experience in violent relationships using GT analysis techniques to synthesize what should be useful in health care practice. I developed a target for formal theory development that was a variation on the original Glaser and Strauss model. I consciously decided to work toward relevant and recognizable models of specific health phenomena, using multiple studies of single phenomena rather than ... aim for broader theory that extended beyond health related contexts. My goal ... lowered mid-range theory (p. 228).

Needless to say, it is probably OK to extend a SGT, however limited, to just several cases within a substantive area, but in her case, it forestalled conceptualization by constant comparison in favour of synthesizing descriptions of similarities and differences. She missed that conceptual FGT is also very practical for health related applications when applied by contextualization. Until we have a method to do FGT and thereby build on an extant SGT, it will be easy to continue confusing excellent SGTs such as Davis's on deviance disavowal, with others that are merely descriptive (Glaser, 1994: 376).

The inspirational, strengthening aspects of the needed method are clear. Advanced grounded theorists want to generate FGT but do not know quite how. A method will inspire them and give them the strength to try. Alvita Nathanial, an experienced author as well as grounded theorist, wrote (personal communication, 12 April 2005), 'I need your advice. I am seriously thinking about writing a proposal to submit to develop a formal theory of moral reckoning. Tell me what type of sample/sampling you think would be effective for this project'. Antoinette McCallin, generator of a theory on pluralistic dialoguing, wrote (personal communication, 22 May 2005), 'Formal theory development—I am interested in this although wonder if I have enough experience as a GT researcher to develop just yet. Disadvantage, it sounds sophisticated and wonder if I have the GT skill yet'. Her skill learned from doing a SGT is enough, which I trust will overcome her doubts. Both Alvita and Antoinette, independently, talked with my daughter, Bonnie, to encourage me to try the writing-up of the FGT method. It is needed.

END THOUGHTS

Since FGT and SGT are so tied together, much of what I will write about FGT reflects back on SGT and will help understand it. And the reverse is true as much SGT goes into FGT. I will try to keep the distinction clearly separate where appropriate. Much of this will be a gathering together and rearranging of material already written in my previous books on GT, while adding the thoughts of other methodologists and adding my extensive experience and knowledge of written SGTs. Nevertheless, I am rethinking these writings on FGT in order to put them into a coordinated, condensed, and compiled perspective for the method needed by researchers looking forward. Future researchers doing FGT will provide formal theory for users such as academic lecturers, frame oriented researchers, intelligent laymen in command posts, consultants, and news commentators. They will find its relevance, fit, and workability better than immaculate, speculative general theory. FGT is not easy to assimilate. It often takes time, two or three readings, to assimilate. Many may not like it as they like SGT. They can find it too abstract, too opaque. Of course, it's the users choice, but the relevance and fit of FGT solves a bit of one's 'too abstract' problem since it easily relates to (has general implications for) the real world. Core categories tend to be seen going on 'everywhere' beyond the SGT area.

FGT emerges as natural as researchers and academics talk substance. They often base their theory bits on particularistic, educated, but immaculate speculation and on current studies. FGT beefs up the current studies part with external validity and credibility. FGT emerges as natural if a researcher of a SGT continues his research into other studies in the same or other substantive areas. The method set forth will help this beginning generation of FGT. The method will also jump-start the stall on formal theorizing among those who are shy, but should be generating FGT. Undeniably, FGT, as SGT, is not for everyone, but it is for many more who could generate it and use it than do. It is obviously for those users and researchers adept at conceptualizing. They must cope with its high density, tight, unrelieved conceptual integration. Its reading can go slow for the attentive reader.

I am here trying to put and encourage FGT into its rightful place in the world of social–psychological research. It neatly fits into the 'golden age of rigorous qualitative analysis'. As I try, the reader must remember that FGT is *not* the development of a theoretical code, nor grand, speculative theory. It is purely and simply the conceptual extension of the general implications of a core category.

FURTHER READING

Burawoy, M., Burton, A., Ferguson, A. A. & Fox, K. (1991) *Ethnography Unbound*. Berkeley, CA: University of California Press.

Creswell, J. (1998) *Qualitative Inquiry and Research Design*. Thousand Oaks, CA: SAGE.

Creswell, J. (2003) *Research Design, Qualitative, Quantitative and Mixed Methods Approaches*. Thousand Oaks, CA: SAGE.

David, M. & Sutton, C. (2004) *Social Research: The Basics*. London: SAGE.

Denzin, N. & Lincoln, Y. (Eds.) (2000) *Handbook of Qualitative Research*. Thousand Oaks, CA: SAGE.

Fowler, F. (2002) *Survey Research Methods*. Thousand Oaks, CA: SAGE.

Glaser, B. G. (1992) *Basics of Grounded Theory Analysis*. Mill Valley, CA: Sociology Press.

Glaser, B. G. (Ed.) (1993) *Examples of Grounded Theory*. Mill Valley, CA: Sociology Press.

Glaser, B. G. (Ed.) (1995) *Grounded Theory 1984 to 1994*. Mill Valley, CA: Sociology Press.

Glaser, B. G. (Ed.) (1996) *Gerund Grounded Theory, The Basic Social Process Dissertation*. Mill Valley, CA: Sociology Press.

Glaser, B. G. (2005) *The Grounded Theory Perspective: Theoretical Coding*. Mill Valley, CA: Sociology Press.

Granovetter, M. (1974) *Getting a Job: A Study of Contact and Careers*. Chicago: University of Chicago Press.

Gummesson, E. (1999) *Total Relationship Marketing*. Oxford, UK: Butterworth-Heinemann.

Heaton, J. (2004) *Reworking Qualitative Data*. Thousand Oaks, CA: SAGE.

Hesook, K. & Kollak, I. (Eds.) (1999) *Nursing Theories, Conceptual and Philosophical Foundations*. London: Springer-Verlag.

Marshall, C. & Rossman, G. (1999) *Designing Qualitative Research* (3rd ed.). Thousand Oaks, CA: SAGE.

Miles, M. & Huberman, A. (1994) *Qualitative Data Analysis*. Thousand Oaks, CA: SAGE.

Miles, M. & Huberman, A. (Eds.) (2002) *The Qualitative Researchers Companion*. Thousand Oaks, CA: SAGE.

Morse, J. (Ed.) (1992) *Qualitative Health Research*. Thousand Oaks, CA: SAGE.

Morse, J. (Ed.) (1994) *Critical Issues in Qualitative Research Methods*. Thousand Oaks, CA: SAGE.

Punch, K. (2003) *Survey Research, The Basics*. Thousand Oaks, CA: SAGE.

Schreiber, R. & Stern, P. (Eds.) (2001) *Using Grounded Theory in Nursing*. New York: Springer Publishing.

Schutt, R. (2004) *Investigating the Social World*. Thousand Oaks, CA: SAGE.

Silverman, D. (Ed.) (2004) *Qualitative Research, Theory, Method Practice*. London: SAGE.

Stebbins, R. (2001) *Exploratory Research in the Social Sciences*. Thousand Oaks, CA: SAGE.

Wolcott, H. (1994) *Transforming Qualitative Data, Description, Analysis and Interpretation*. Thousand Oaks, CA: SAGE.

REFERENCES

Alvesson, M. & Skoldberg, K. (2000) *Reflexive Methodology: New Vistas for Qualitative Research*. London: SAGE.

Anderson, B. (2005) Some Proposals for a Social Psychology of the Virtues. Paper presented at the 37th World Congress of the International Institute of Sociology, Stockholm.

Clarke, A. E. (2005) *Situational Analysis: Grounded Theory after the Postmodern Turn*. Thousand Oaks, CA: SAGE.

Dahlgren, L., Emmelin, M., Winkvist, A. & Epidemiology and Public Health Sciences. (2004) *Qualitative Methodology for International Public Health*. Umeå: Umeå University.

Davis, F. & Olesen, V. (1970) *Becoming a Nurse*. Glencoe, IL: Free Press.

Devereux, P. G., Bullock, C. C., Bargmann-Losche, J. & Kyriakou, M. (2005) Maintaining support in people with paralysis: What works? *Qualitative Health Research, 15*, 1360–1376.

Dey, I. (1999) *Grounding Grounded Theory: Guidelines for Qualitative Inquiry*. San Diego, CA: Academic Press.

Ekins, R. (1995) On Male Femaling. In B. G. Glaser (Ed.), *Grounded Theory 1984–1994* (pp. 721–744). Mill Valley, CA: Sociology Press.

Gilgun, J. F., Daly, K. & Handel, G. (Eds.) (1992) *Qualitative Methods in Family Research*. Newbury Park, CA: SAGE.

Glaser, B. G. (1964) *Organizational Scientists: Their Professional Careers*. Mill Valley, CA: Sociology Press.

Glaser, B. G. (1968) *Organizational Careers: A Sourcebook for Theory*. Chicago: Aldine Publishing Company.

Glaser, B. G. (1978) *Theoretical Sensitivity: Advances in the Methodology of Grounded Theory*. Mill Valley, CA: Sociology Press.

Glaser, B. G. (Ed.) (1994) *More Grounded Theory Methodology: A Reader*. Mill Valley, CA: Sociology Press.

Glaser, B. G. (1998) *Doing Grounded Theory*. Mill Valley, CA: Sociology Press.

Glaser, B. G. (2001) *The Grounded Theory Perspective: Conceptualization Contrasted with Description*. Mill Valley, CA: Sociology Press.

Glaser, B. G. (2003) *The Grounded Theory Perspective II: Description's Remodeling of Grounded Theory Methodology*. Mill Valley, CA: Sociology Press.

Glaser, B. G. (2006) *Doing Formal Grounded Theory: A Proposal*. Mill Valley, CA: Sociology Press.

Glaser, B. G. & Strauss, A. L. (1965) *Awareness of Dying*. Chicago: Aldine Publishing Company.

Glaser, B. G. & Strauss, A. L. (1967) *The Discovery of Grounded Theory: Strategies for Qualitative Research*. Hawthorne, NY: Aldine de Gruyter.

Glaser, B. G. & Strauss, A. L. (1971) *Status Passage*. Chicago: Aldine Atherton Inc.

Hind, P. S., Chavez, D. E. & Cypress, S. M. (1992) Context as a source of meaning and understanding. *Qualitative Health Research, 2*, 61–74.

Kearney, M. H. (2001) New directions in grounded formal theory. In R. S. Schreiber & P. N. Stern (Eds.), *Using Grounded Theory in Nursing* (pp. 227–246). New York: Springer Publishing Company.

Lincoln, Y. S. & Guba, E. G. (1985) *Naturalistic Inquiry*. Beverly Hills, CA: SAGE.

Locke, K. (2001) *Grounded Theory in Management Research*. London: SAGE.

Morse, J. (Ed.) (1997) *Completing a Qualitative Project, Details and Dialogue*. Thousand Oaks, CA: SAGE.

Silverman, D. (2000) *Doing Qualitative Research*. Thousand Oaks, CA: SAGE.

Simmons, O. (1993) The milkman and his customer: A cultivated relationship. In B. G. Glaser (Ed.), *Examples of Grounded Theory: A Reader* (pp. 4–31). Mill Valley, CA: Sociology Press.

Stake R. E. (1983) The case study method in social inquiry. In G. Madaus, M. Scriven & D. Stufflebeam (Eds.), *Evaluation Models. Viewpoints in Educational and Human Services Evaluation*. Boston: Kluwer-Nijhoff.

Thulesius, H., Håkansson, A. & Petersson, K. (2003) Balancing: A basic social process in end-of-life cancer care. *Qualitative Health Research, 13*. Thousand Oaks, CA: SAGE.

Williams, M. (2003) *Making Sense of Social Research*. London: SAGE.

Zetterberg, H. I. (2005) How Sociology May Cope with Some Findings from Linguistics and Philosophy of Language. Paper presented at the 37th World Congress of the International Institute of Sociology, Stockholm.

5

On Solid Ground: Essential Properties for Growing Grounded Theory

Phyllis Noerager Stern

INTRODUCTION

One essential quality of true grounded theory is that it makes sense; put simply, the reader will have an immediate recognition that this theory, derived from a given social situation, is about real people or objects to which they can relate. Furthermore, it must be clear that the developed theory comes from data rather than being forced to fit an existing theoretical framework. Integration of the finished product needs to be executed in such a way that every component is in harmony with every other component with the precision of joined chemical particles. Additionally, while it must fit the social scene studied, it needs to be of sufficient abstraction that it can apply to the larger world of social psychological and social structural situations. Finally, the author needs to place the developed theory within the work of other social scientists and demonstrate how it goes beyond what has been known.

The mathematicians DeMillo, Lipton and Perlis (1979), writing for the journal, *Communications of the Association for Computer Machinery*, argued that the success of a piece of research is a social process wherein peers either accept or reject findings based on whether they make sense or not. They added that no one reads the proofs (method section) because they're so boring. Published grounded theory (GT) needs to be written in such a way that it makes *sense* to the audience. This, of course, is true of any research, whether quantitative or qualitative; what the reader wants to know is how will these findings make an impact on my life, my work, and my psyche. Only hardcore methodologists (among whom I count myself) will examine the method section for errors in sample size, means of analysis, or accuracy of data transcription. However, the researcher who follows the essential qualities of the method will put forth a piece of work that does make sense. In this chapter, I detail the vital elements of making sense, connection to the target group, groundedness in data, integration, abstraction, modifiability, relatedness to existing theory, and delivering the message to the reader by skillful writing. Following the advice of Glaser (1978) and Wuest (2006), I've organized this chapter around concepts found in published research that I'm most familiar with or, put another way, my own research.

As grounded theory is a method, I find that in order to describe its essential elements, I need to write in terms of the methodology. For me, the beauty of the method lies in its everything-is-data characteristic; that is to say, everything I see, hear, smell, and feel about the target, as well as what I already know from my studies and my life experience, are data. I act as interpreter of the scene I observe, and as such I make it come to life for the reader. I grow it.

MAKING SENSE

In a class on evidence-based practice, my colleague Dr. Deborah Cullen mentioned a piece of research on breast feeding that claimed that adults who had been breastfed longer than 4 months as newborns tended to be obese, while those who were nursed only 4 months were not (personal communication, September 2004). Deborah is a respiratory therapist by profession, while I am a maternity nurse by training. I am dedicated to the merits of breastfeeding for both child and mother (why else would female mammals have breasts), so I was enraged: I countered that the World Health Organization, the US Center for Disease Control, the American Academy of Nursing, the American Pediatric Association, and anyone in their right mind, knows that breastfeeding for a year (if the mother's employment makes this possible) is the way to go. Only then did I begin to take apart the methodology of the research: a retrospective study where there were any number of intervening variables but above all else it just didn't make sense.

Has *my* work always made sense? My audience decides that. In my early research on discipline in stepfather families (Stern, 1978), I argued that the newcomer to the group, the stepfather, should refrain from enforcing rules, that is, engage in discipline, until the mother and child agreed that it was OK. This makes sense to most people, but family therapists argued that it was necessary for the parents to agree on the rules for child behavior prior to forming a union (a seemingly impossible task for two biological parents to do, since things keep coming up and people evolve). I pointed out that the child whose mother defers to the stepfather would feel abandoned, but therapists remained unconvinced.

Even though I managed to publish a fair amount about what I found (Stern, 1978, 1982a, b), family therapy wise I came to believe I was beating a dead horse, therefore, rather than carving out a career path that followed the trials and successes of stepfamilies, I moved on to other areas of study (Stern, 1981; Stern, Tilden & Maxwell, 1980). Twenty-eight years later, I felt cleansed when I heard popular television psychologist Phil McGraw (Dr. Phil, n.d.) point out that stepparents can never act as the primary disciplinarian of stepchildren because they have no history with the child, and that the biological parent is a child's first love.

GETTING THE DATA

As a rule, social scientists (to include clinical psychologists, social workers, sociologists, nurses, and the like) tend to rely on interview and observational data because they are interested in human interactions in a variety of circumstances. Glaser has always described GT as a method that can be used with any kind of data, and in his 2005 publication, *The Grounded Theory Perspective III*, he reemphasized that grounded theory is a method that can be used with any data, including statistical data, rather than as a tool solely to analyze qualitative, inductive materials. In this chapter, I'm writing about the techniques that are most useful to those in the helping professions; inductive qualitative interaction

The sample for a ground theory study needs to be both wide and prompted by the emerging theory. For example, at a certain point in my stepfather study, I realized that my sample was made up of mostly middle class white people and their school age children; thus I sought out families with teenage or older children. This is an example of theoretical sampling, i.e. directing the data search to advance the developing theory. The families with teenagers tended to be in crisis mode, but I'm not sure whether that was a feature of being stepfather families or a norm of adolescent rebellion, which seems to be common in intact families. One finding that was consistent across families was their focus on their *stepness*; they failed to realize that many of their interactions were common in intact families as well. The time of the study, the 1970s, was before the plethora of stepfamily support groups materialized so that, in the main, these families had no way of knowing they were basically OK, and much like intact families. I used the snowball method to contact potential participants, therefore it's no surprise that, during the years 1975–1976 when I was collecting data, the middle class white families referred me to stepfamilies of their own ethnic group. Today, I could just go to the neighbors in my integrated housing development for referrals to a variety of cultural groups. Although, to be fair to myself, in that period in time the emphasis in the scientific community was on homogeneous samples. At some time during the 1980s, we evolved to the point where we stopped thinking of non-whites as 'the other' and began including multiethnic people, and even women.

Theoretical sampling consists of collecting data that will advance the theory. When Covan did her 1998 study of residences of a retirement community, it was a well-known fact that women spent their senior years taking care of their frail partners. Had she failed to interview men as well as women, she might have reinforced this belief. However, what she found was that both members of the couple protect one another's frailty: perhaps she has become incontinent of urine in her old age, and he shields her from public scrutiny in the supermarket; it may be that he has trouble getting out of bed, and she helps him with that; or it is possible that his success in business provided the capital for their comfortable life style.

When is enough enough?

The sample for GT study needs to be representative, but it's unnecessary and perhaps defeating to collect huge amounts of data. As Glaser (1998) pointed out, these large files tend to go unanalyzed, or researchers becomes overwhelmed with the sheer volume they have to deal with, and loses the fundamental processes going on in the area of study. There is no way of knowing beforehand the size of the sample for a GT study, but professors, ethical review boards, and funding agencies want an estimate before approving the research. This is a point I am unwilling to go to fight to a grizzly end, so I make up a number based on what was adequate in previous work I have done. The number can be corrected later if necessary. I usually guess at 20 to 30 interviews and/or hours of observation adequate to reach saturation of the categories. Most methodology authors advise learners that saturation is reached when the learner hears nothing new. In the stepfather study, following the GT rules about constant comparison of data, I had developed a conceptual framework by the time I did the final interview. I realized I had reached the point of saturation when the stepfather of a couple I was interviewing was telling me how when he was a small child he stood witness as his mother shot his father dead, *and I was bored*. I made all the right noises to the couple, but I knew that my data collection for that study had come to an end. I thought more interviewing was unnecessary in expanding the category I had developed: integration in stepfamilies around child discipline. In the fire study (Stern & Kerry, 1996), my sample exceeded 100 individuals, but I only conducted about 30 of these interviews; two master's students collected the rest to partially fulfill their thesis requirements (Kerry, 1991; Northrup, 1989). It was relatively simple for me to pull together a multicultural group: by that point in my history I had a number of non-white friends and acquaintances who could refer me to a variety of ethnic groups. In addition, I often traveled internationally, and I always quizzed the locals on the appropriate ritual followed when someone they knew had a home fire. Robert Stebbins (2006) suggested that, instead of studies with large numbers of participants, the researcher may find a series of smaller related studies to be more fruitful in discovering social reality as viewed by the actors. This makes perfect sense, as one can not *unknow* what one knows; therefore every study is subject to the impact of the researcher's previous work.

Worrisome accuracy

Worrisome accuracy is Glaser's (1998) term.[1] He wrote this about tape recording interviews:

> One of the strongest evidentiary invasions into grounded theory is the taping of interviews. The confusion is between the traditional use of the interview as complete evidence for substantiating or verifying a finding compared to grounded theory's use of interviews for conceptualization or for generation of concepts and hypotheses (p. 107).

Both Glaser and Strauss advised their students against paying attention to the accuracy of the interview data, that the 'cream' (essential information) would rise to the top, and stick in the investigators mind. They did encourage field notes as a way of keeping track of what went on in interviews and observations. Strauss dictated his field notes to a tape recorder; other than that he shunned them. Students are uncomfortable trusting to their memory and allowing the cream to rise to the top, but when they bring their transcribed interviews to me for help with coding, I never do a line-by-line analysis because there is so much filler to skip over. Rather, I do a search and seizure operation looking for cream in the data. I'm not suggesting that tape recording will ruin a researcher's chances of developing a solid grounded theory, but I have found that, in the years since Glaser and Strauss's 1967 publication *The Discovery of Grounded Theory*, researchers have placed more and more emphasis on the accuracy of collected data rather than concentrating on the developing theory. These researchers are in grave danger of developing a rich description of the social scene rather than a theoretical one. Description is important to our knowledge, but it's not theory, and researchers need to be as accurate about what they're calling their method and findings. I suspect that this transition of method has arisen from the researcher's need for agency funding. For much of the twentieth century, only those researchers who proposed using tests and measurement as a way of finding truth were entitled to grant dollars. Thus qualitative researchers were driven to looking as much like hard scientists as possible in order to get financial support for their work.

Another element to be considered was the academic placement of Glaser and Strauss as professors in the School of Nursing at the University of California, San Francisco. As a natural outcome, the nurse scholars there were many of the first to see GT as a way of telling the story of the work they do. Use of the method spread quickly to the larger community of nurses. But a problem evolved in that nurses in their practice arena absolutely and positively have to be accurate; so it has been only with great difficulty that they have been able to 'wing it' in the classic grounded theory sense. Some are unable to free themselves of the culture of their profession.

Of late I have been working with doctoral students from Thailand. These students have limited English, and I have no Thai, but we manage. They do their interviews in Thailand, and then translate them into what can only be called Pidgin English. One student, upon conferring with her advisor in Thailand via electronic mail, was told that her translations needed to be so accurate that when converted back into Thai, a panel of Thai speakers could understand them. I explained to the Thai professor that 'I watch him with corner eye' (student's translation) transmitted the same essential meaning as 'I watch him out of the corner of my eye' (standard English). To my way of thinking, researchers need to focus on the accuracy of their discovered truth, rather than the less important what-did-they-say-exactly.

Analyzing the data

We have an embarrassment of method authors to which the student of GT can refer, each one approaching the process of analyzing data differently. I suspect that this is because although analyzing data is 'the way a guy thinks' (Schatzman, personal communication, 9 October 1970), as individuals, we all process information differently. Grounded theory as an analytical activity is a largely cerebral process, which makes it hard to explain using words. As Dey, in writing about grounded theory, mused (cited in LaRossa, 2005: 837), 'There is an irony—perhaps a paradox—that a methodology that is based on "interpretation" should itself prove so hard to interpret.' I don't think you can *do* grounded theory unless you consult the original architects of the method (Glaser & Strauss, 1967). I confess that I had great difficulty understanding *The Discovery of Grounded Theory* (because it was couched in the language of sociology of which I had limited knowledge) until I had *done* a grounded theory, however Glaser's 1978 book, *Theoretical Sensitivity*, is a must for anyone who is serious about covering the essential elements of the method. In 1980, I became famous in my professional world by writing an article in which I offered up an English language translation of grounded theory from the original sociologese of the *Discovery* book (Stern, 1980). GT had become a buzzword in academic nursing, but researchers had no clear direction about how to do it (they didn't speak sociologese either).

MAKING MEMOS, SORTING MEMOS

Making memos (memorandums) is a process the analyst uses to keep track of what they think about the data: what coded data seems to cluster together, just what is the problem for these people, is it the material loss of a home by fire, or is it the fact that other people lack an understanding of their grief, what life experiences have I had that are similar, and what did I do about them? (Everything is data.) If data are the building blocks of the developing theory, memos are the mortar. The analyst must write out their memos because unwritten inspired theorizing at night wafts away, the next morning it's gone, and the grounded theory never materializes.

Making memos goes on throughout the study. Once categories have been developed, clustered, and expanded, the analyst needs to sort them according to categories and properties. Sorting 'by hand,' as Glaser (2003) advises, requires a great deal of space (the dining room table or the living room floor serve as ideal venues for this work). The idea is to make labels to act as rubrics for all known categories and their properties. Life isn't that tidy, and neither is memo sorting: it turns out that new labels are needed as categories collapse upon one another, and memos turn out to be misfiled and belong to another category. Sorting helps the analyst integrate the theory; in the physical display of their thought processes, the appearance of the theory begins to take shape.

USING TECHNOLOGY PROPS

Several computer programs have been developed that help the analyst to keep track of data. However, artificial intelligence has not advanced to a state that allows a machine to solve human problem-solving techniques. I read the first few of these computer-assisted studies when I served as Editor of the journal *Health Care for Women International*, and I determined that the findings suffered from premature closure: they were thin and pat. But then I read the excellent work of MacDonald and Green (2001) and Milliken and Northcott (2003), which destroyed my prejudgment. The analysis is in the hands of the researcher; if electronics can help them to manage data, then OK. However, Glaser advises that computer assistance gets in the way of the process of sorting memorandums. Sorting is a vital part of analysis. According to Glaser (2005), sorting is a creative activity:

> Tempting one's creativity is actuated by this process. Fear that one does not have creativity stops this type of sorting and causes the fleeing to computer retrieval of data on each category, resulting in full conceptual description [Glaser's term for research that fails to reach the theoretical level]. Hand sorting releases the creativity necessary to see a TC [theoretical code] in the memos, as the analyst constantly compares and asks where each memo goes for the best fit (p. 36).

Charmaz (2006) omits any mention of computer-assisted analyses. As a risk taker and a thrill seeker, I find hand coding and hand sorting exciting, and maybe a little dangerous; every time you present your research you risk your reputation, since someone in the audience may think you're a fool, and may say so. You have no statistics, no proofs, no software evidence that your take on a scene is meaningful. Fear of public shame may be the best impetus for making sense.

THEORETICAL CODES

Theoretical codes are tools for looking at a variable in an abstract rather than a substantive way. According to Charmaz (2006), 'theoretical codes specify possible relationships between categories you have developed in your focused [substantive] coding' (p. 63). In 2005, Glaser wrote that symbolic interactionism (SI) is nothing more than a theoretical code and, at that, overused by social scientists. He even went so far as to blame the use of SI for the glut of descriptive studies being produced as opposed to grounded theories. He chided Milliken and Schreiber (2001) for suggesting that symbolic interactionism is essential to grounded theory. I've always thought of SI as a kind of backdrop for grounded theory, an assumption that people act and react based on their relationships, but I don't see it as *the* theoretical code that can bring a study together. Theoretical codes help me see the limits of a variable. For example, in the study about survivors of home fires (Stern & Kerry, 1996), once we had determined that in the circumstance of a single dwelling destroyed by fire, as opposed to an apartment building or a city, there was no appropriate grief ritual in place (a ritual connected to need), we had to find the extent of this 'unconnected' ritual.[2] Using the 'cutting point' theoretical code, we were able to reexamine our data for instances of ritual that *was* connected to need. We found connected ritual to be the rule for rural dwellers as opposed to city dwellers, because, as one participant explained to us, 'We need to look out for one another to stay alive.' (Glaser introduced examples of theoretical codes in 1978, 2001, and 2005.)

SELLING THE PRODUCT THROUGH SKILLFUL WRITING

Unless your published research hooks the potential audience, it may go unread. Selling the product begins with the title. While you want to be sure the title is web friendly (i.e. it will get a hit by a scholar doing a literature search), it needs to be catchy. Most of my students have developed read-me titles for their work, a few choice examples include 'Discovery of nursing gestalt in critical care nursing: The importance of the gray gorilla syndrome' (Pyles & Stern, 1983); 'Living on the cutting edge: A study of work satisfaction among operating room nurses' (Wood, 1989); 'Becoming strangers: the changing caregiving relationship in Alzheimer's disease' (Wuest, Ericson & Stern, 1994); 'Falling apart: A process essential to recovery in male incest offenders' (Scheela & Stern, 1994); and 'Tactful monitoring: How Thai caregivers manage their schizophrenic relatives at home' (Dangdom, Stern, Yunibhand & Areewan, 2006). In my long career, the publication that has been cited most often outside of the nursing profession is a chapter I wrote for one of Jan Morse's method books, *Eroding Grounded Theory* (Stern, 1994). It was an OK piece of work, but I'm convinced that it was the title that caught the attention of social scientists.

Once you have the reader's attention, you need to keep it. Writing may not be the most important component of growing theory but it's one with which most neophyte researchers have difficulty. Their discovered theory seems so clear to them that they forget that the reader was elsewhere when they took that arduous journey from data to theory, so they fail to explain their work thoroughly. As Wuest (2006) advised, new researchers fail to realize how much analysis goes on in the writing; it's only when you see it on the paper that the final integrated theory is clear. Wuest also pointed out that she had learned from Glaser (1978) to write about the theory rather than the people. In order to accomplish this she described how she writes the concepts first, then adds confirming data later, and still later relevant literature. This is sound advice, because the whole point of doing GT is to develop a theory rather than spinning a yarn. However, the writer does need to be something of a storyteller, because if they fall short of holding the reader's attention, their peers will fail to accept the research. While writing about this social situation in a theoretical way, the author nevertheless needs to convey the emotional impact of the problem and the processing of it on the participants: GT comes from the field of social psychology and psychological impact on the target group needs to be illuminated. In a review of a submitted manuscript on a sensitive subject, my suggestion to the author was, 'If there's heartbreak you need to break the reader's heart.' LaRossa (2005) gives full credit to the art inherent in the research process. To this end, I often advise students to read fiction for its rhythm and flow or articles in a quality magazine like *The New Yorker*. When Glaser (2005) stressed that GT is a method that can be used in ways other than analyzing a social scene, he suggested that one can use it with documents or numbers thus developing a formula. But if your formulaic analysis reaches this level of abstraction, you need to be a skillful writer indeed to explain it in terms that the reader will understand.

The figure

Which brings me to another point: the figure. Depicting the emerging hypothesis in a diagram can help the researcher in putting their theory together, but then the diagram needs to be described using words. The figure is a diagram, and that's all it is; it's something that helps you with your work. Rarely have I found a figure helpful in understanding findings, an exception is LaRossa's (2005) figure showing how axial coding works. I've never understood the term 'axial coding,' where it came from or why it had been introduced into the GT lexicon. I've always had a hunch that Strauss was taken with the Saul Bellow novel *The Adventures of Augie March* (1953); in the novel, Augie believes that there must be an axis somewhere that would explain what life is all about (p. 258).

Murky writing vs standard English

My notation for this section is 'funny words.' There seems to be a penchant among grounded theory writers to either make up new words, or borrow words from another discipline when writing about the method or the findings from a study; axial coding is an example (Strauss & Corbin, 1990). The purpose of writing up the findings from GT research is to add to our knowledge of a given area of study; if the writer wants to use funny words, they need to provide the reader with a straightforward explanation of the term. At the very least, the reader ought to be able to find the word in an English language dictionary. In December 2005,

I chaired an oral examination of a dissertation by Richard Charles Mitchell, a Canadian PhD candidate attending the University of Stirling, 'The UN Convention on the rights of the child in (post) modernity: An autopoietic analysis of human rights education policies in Scotland and Canada.' When the letter of request arrived, I figured the mystery of the title would be explained in the body of the work. Never the less, I queried my colleagues for a hint. One knew of the UN Convention, but no one had a clue about what an autopoietic analysis might be. The term sounded vaguely biology related, and I asked a bench-biologist friend of mine if he could solve the puzzle; he went to the World Wide Web, and found the term related to a self-renewing-closed system. When the thesis arrived, I found no explanation on any of the 1000 pages. (That's right, 1000 pages.) At the oral exam, Richard explained that the term comes from systems theory, and his point was that although there is a good deal of political resistance in Canada to teaching children what their rights are, the power of the UN Convention is such that the process is spreading in spite of right-wing opposition. I wanted to know why he didn't just write it that way; further, I emphasized my belief that findings should be scripted in such a way that a reasonably bright, secondary school senior could understand them. The story ends well: with editorial changes and the addition of a glossary of terms, Richard became Dr. Mitchell.

ON THE SHOULDERS OF GIANTS

> ... a dwarf standing on the shoulders of a giant may see farther than the giant himself (Robert Burton, in *Bartlett's familiar quotations*, 1980: 258).

When you write up your grounded theory, you may feel like a giant when in reality you are the dwarf: it is because of everything you have read, seen, heard, and felt that you have been able to pull your thesis together. Therefore, it is important to situate your work within the body of related literature, both because it's academically honest to give credit to other researchers, and because you need to demonstrate how you built upon it so that you *can* see further. Ideally, the search of literature comes after the construction of the theoretical framework, but because of the rigidity of professors, ethical reviewers, and funding agencies, all of whom demand a thorough literature review prior to starting data gathering, you may be stuck with a lot of information that lies outside of your analysis of the gathered data. This rigidity makes two points clear: (1) although GT may be '... the way a guy thinks' (Schatzman, personal communication, October 1970), in most of the scientific world, the way a guy thinks has little relevance, but the way a computer handles data is seen as a way to bring forth truth, and (2) in order to get your doctorate, pass ethical review, and receive grant funding, you'll do whatever it takes. Undertaken after data analysis, reviewing the work of other researchers completes and enriches the research. Rather than verification, your job is to demonstrate how your work *adds* a new dimension, an element that heretofore was unknown.

When I did the stepfather study, I searched the literature published in the 35 years before I started my research, and found only 12 articles, most of which were on stepmothers. Outside of some statistical information (Bohannan, 1975), most of the published work on stepfamilies was irrelevant, because the authors assumed the biological parent had been widowed. There was one exception: the social workers Fast and Cain (1966) suggested that any attempt the stepparent made to replace the missing parent would cause role confusion. They suggested further that the stepparent adopt the role of wiser older friend. As I examined my data, I discovered a number of techniques stepfathers used to become a friend to stepchildren; thus I was able to go beyond Fast and Cain but, had I not read their work, I might have missed the point about this process of resolving discipline issues. I was then able to abstract these properties of befriending to fit any authority figure new to a job (a new head nurse for example). I read far and wide in the psychosocial literature, the family dynamics literature, and lay publications on fathering, most of which helped me understand what I was seeing and hearing, and trying to put together, but Fast and Cain gave me my eureka moment.

CODA

Another essential quality of doing grounded theory is that it thrills the investigator: if the researcher fails to be emotionally involved with the data and its analysis, they may be doing it wrong. The method is a jealous lover that takes over the researcher's waking and sleeping hours; although I guess any research project does that (the phrase, 'absent-minded professor' comes to mind).

A final word about making sense: I draw the readers attention to the advice of DeMillo, Lipton and Perlis (1979) to rely on peer review; and to rely on my advice, let your peers help you, but never let them defeat you. Especially in the publication field: there's always another draft, or another journal. You're invincible!

NOTES

1 It would be easy take pot shots at Glaser's lack of accuracy in his published method books as, despite repeated suggestions that he hire a professional proofreader, he seems unwilling to depart from the cottage industry flavor of Sociology Press (he even spelled my name wrong in his 2005 book). Although his publications lack academic panache, and although he seems to have a need to reaffirm that he does GT better than anyone (he names names), as one of the *founders* of the *grounded theory movement*, one needs to acknowledge that his descriptions of the method must be valid.

2 Our first thought was that there is no grief ritual for victims of home fire, until Jan Morse pointed out that there's no such thing as *no* ritual (she has double PhD in anthropology and transcultural nursing). So we went back to the data and found what we called 'connected' ritual (connected to need) and 'unconnected' ritual. In unconnected ritual, the acquaintance says the following, 'How terrible!' 'Was anyone hurt?' 'Did you have insurance?' 'Let me know if I can do anything,' often followed by, 'Lucky you, you'll have all new things.'

REFERENCES

Bartlett's familiar quotations. (1980). Boston: Little Brown. (Original work, Robert Burton, 1621. *The anatomy of melancholy*.)

Bellow, S. (1953). *The Adventures of Augie March*. London, UK: Penguin.

Bohannan, P. (1975). Stepfathers and the mental health of their children. Western Behavioral Science Institute. La Jolla, CA: Research Report.

Charmaz, K. (2006). *Constructing Grounded Theory*. Thousand Oaks, CA: SAGE.

Covan, E. K. (1998). Caresharing: Hiding frailty in a Florida retirement community. *Health Care for Women International*, 19, 423–439.

Dangdom, P., Stern, P. N., Yunibhand, J. & Areewan, O. (2006). Tactful monitoring: How Thai caregivers manage their schizophrenic relatives at home. Qualitative Health Research Conference, Alberta, Canada.

DeMillo, R. A., Lipton, R. J. & Perlis, A. J. (1979). Social process and proofs of theorems and programs. *Communications of the Association for Computer Machinery,* 22, 271–280.

Dr. Phil. (n.d.). Retrieved June 30, 2006 from http://www.drphil.com/articles/article/243

Fast, I. & Cain, A. C. (1966). The stepparent role: potential disturbances in family functioning. *American Journal of Ortho-psychiatry*, 36, 485–491.

Glaser, B. (1978). *Theoretical Sensitivity*. Mill Valley, CA: Sociology Press.

Glaser, B. (1998). *Doing Grounded Theory*. Mill Valley, CA: Sociology Press.

Glaser, B. (2003). *The Grounded Theory Perspective II*. Mill Valley, CA: Sociology Press.

Glaser, B. (2005). *The Grounded Theory Perspective III*. Mill Valley, CA: Sociology Press.

Glaser, B. & Strauss, A. L. (1967). *The Discovery of Grounded Theory*. Chicago: Aldine.

Kerry, J. (1991). Managing burning: Victims of body and home fire. Unpublished masters thesis, Dalhousie University, Halifax, Nova Scotia, Canada.

LaRossa, R. (2005). Grounded theory methods and qualitative family research. *Journal of Marriage and Family*, 67, 837–857.

MacDonald, M. & Green, L. W. (2001). Reconciling concept and context: Dilemmas of implementation in school-based health promotion. *Health Education and Behavior*, 28, 749–768.

Milliken, P. J. & Northcott, H. C. (2003). Redefining parental identity: Caregiving and schizophrenia. *Qualitative Health Research*, 12, 100–113.

Milliken, P. J. & Schreiber, R. S. (2001). Can you 'do' grounded theory without symbolic interactionism? In Schreiber, R. S. & Stern, R. S. (Eds.), *Using Grounded Theory in Nursing*, 177–190. New York: Springer.

Mitchell, C. M. (2006). The UN Convention on the rights of the child in (post) modernity: An autopoietic analysis of human rights education policies in Scotland and Canada. PhD Thesis, University of Stirling, UK.

Northrup, D.S. (1989). Fire loss: Transformative progression from victim to survivor. Masters Thesis, Dalhousie University School of Nursing.

Pyles, S. H. & Stern, P. N. (1983). Discovery of nursing gestalt in critical care nursing: The importance of the gray gorilla syndrome. *Image*, 15, 51–57.

Scheela, R. & Stern, P. N. (1994). Falling apart: A process essential to recovery in male incest offenders. *Archives of Psychiatric Nursing,* 8, 91–100.

Stebbins, R. A. (2006). Concatenated exploration: Aiding theoretic memory by planning well for the future. *Journal of Contemporary Ethnography,* 35, 483–494.

Stern, P. N. (1978). Stepfather families: Integration around child discipline. *Issues in Mental Health Nursing*, 1, 50–56.

Stern, P. N. (1980). Grounded theory methodology: Its uses and processes. *Image*, 12, 20–23.

Stern, P. N. (1981). Solving problems of cross-cultural health teaching: The Filipino childbearing family. *Image*, 13, 47–50.

Stern, P. N. (1982a). Affiliating in stepfather families: Teachable strategies leading to integration. *Western Journal of Nursing Research*, 4, 75–89.

Stern, P. N. (1982b). Conflicting family culture: An impediment to integration in stepfather families. *Journal of Psychosocial Nursing*, 20, 27–33.

Stern, P. N. (1994). Eroding grounded theory. In Morse, J. (Ed.) *Critical Issues in Qualitative Enquiry* (pp. 212–223). Newbury Park, CA: SAGE.

Stern, P. N. & Kerry, J. (1996) Restructuring life after home loss by fire. *Image: The Journal of Nursing Scholarship*, 28, 9–14.

Stern, P. N., Tilden, V. P. & Maxwell, E. K. (1980). Culturally-induced stress during childbearing: The Filipino-American experience. *Issues in Health Care of Women*, 2, 129–143.

Strauss, A. & Corbin, J. M. (1990). *Basics of Qualitative Research*. Newberry Park, CA: SAGE.

Wood, H. D. (1989). Living on the cutting edge: A study of work satisfaction among operating room nurses. Masters Thesis, Dalhousie University School of Nursing.

Wuest, J. (2006). An approach to doing and thinking about grounded theory. In P. Munhall (Ed.), *Nursing Research: A Qualitative Perspective*, 239–272. New York: Jones & Bartlett.

Wuest, J., Ericson, P. K. & Stern P. N. (1994). Becoming strangers: The changing caregiving relationship in Alzheimer's disease. *Journal of Advanced Nursing,* 20, 437–443.

6

From the Sublime to the Meticulous: The Continuing Evolution of Grounded Formal Theory

Margaret H. Kearney

Complexity has fascinated and puzzled me much of my life. How to unravel some of that complexity, to order it, not to be dismayed or defeated by it? How not to avoid the complexity nor distort interpretations of it by oversimplifying it out of existence? This is, of course, an old problem: Abstraction (theory) inevitably simplifies, yet to comprehend deeply, to order, some degree of abstraction is necessary (Strauss, 1993: 12).

The role of theory in a complex world is a continuing puzzle. In introducing his last major work, above, my teacher Anselm Strauss was revisiting a core concern of Dewey and many others before him. Nevertheless, Strauss went on to present a carefully grounded and highly abstract formal theory of action as the engine of social structure and process. His theorizing about human complexity was grounded in systematic comparisons of findings from distant and disparate sources and was confident in its conclusions while remaining interested in other variations. Many of us have struggled with both these issues: what constitutes adequate grounding, and what degree of abstraction is appropriate in a postmodern age?

THE USES OF THEORIES AND SATISFACTIONS OF THEORIZING

Theories are efficient handles by which to grasp large volumes of information.[1] Practice disciplines such as my own, nursing, need theories as efficient ways to communicate our current understandings of the dynamic conditions of human lives and behaviors. We have a pressing need to manage large amounts of complex multi-sourced information, whether numerical data or qualitative text. Like symbolic interactionists, health professionals have long observed that humans use internal working models (Kleinman, 1987; Pridham, Knight & Stephenson, 1989), however temporary, to understand their worlds and direct their behavior. Educators, psychologists, lawyers, social workers, and others also draw on theories to predict and control outcomes. Admittedly, theories turn over with ever-increasing rapidity as knowledge proliferates, but we are uneasy during periods of theoretical transition.

Grounded theory research provides tools to achieve abstraction without completely sacrificing complexity. Since my days at Strauss's seminar table, these methods have been a rewarding means of creating theory that makes accessible real-life complications and contingencies in a dynamic and sometimes elegant way. Grounded theory analysis can portray conclusions as dynamic and interactive, rather than as a single common outcome. That is, a fully developed grounded theory does not simply posit that A always leads to B, but rather that the degree to which A leads to B and what that relationship looks like depends on a range of factors that influence A, B, and the relationship between them.

But the act of putting theories 'out there' and claiming their value in public can be an uncomfortable venture in a postmodern era, as has been well articulated by Clarke (2005). If we are uncertain about the legitimacy of theory in a postmodern age, we should be in even more distress when faced with formal theory. Formal theories exacerbate the tension between our need to create rules of thumb to get things done and our postmodern awareness that the complexity of life can never be fairly captured in any theory. I (and maybe others) manage this discomfort by rushing to point out my theories' groundedness ('see, this quote from a real person demonstrates the dynamic in that diagram'), by crafting caveat clauses of ever-increasing complexity ('but remember, this work is almost a work of fiction, arising out of my own situated sensibility, and may only be useful for others in my discipline at this point in time working with people just like these, and is only as useful as you find it ...'), and by congratulating myself on their aesthetic elegance as solutions to messy problems ('isn't it ingenious, how that metaphor captures that angst-ridden double bind, and how that diagram aligns all those interacting forces?').

Simultaneous with the postmodern concern over the hazards and potential injustices of generalization is the current movement in the practice disciplines to privilege evidence over theory. Research findings now carry high social value, and the greater the volume of raw data from which they have been derived, the greater the value, in my view. Urgent effort now goes into management of the proliferating volume of research reports. Health care practice (for example) now relies heavily on mathematically assisted meta-analyses to summarize clusters of numerical research results.

In a similar effort to derive a more cross-cutting level of evidence from clusters of related single qualitative studies, meta-synthesis has arisen as a set of techniques for pooling and reaching conclusions about common characteristics of an aspect of human experience across situations and groups. These meta-synthesis methods are still in formative stages, and many challenges have yet to be overcome. These will be discussed in more depth later, but they include taking into account all of the ways in which the constituent studies were shaped by differences in sample characteristics, the investigator's discipline, training, frame, and agenda; time and place of original data collection; approach to data analysis; constraints of the publication venue; and other influences that are unknown and inaccessible to the later analyst. Yet these techniques may offer an approach to bridge summary and complexity: to capture some overarching principles of the way social interaction works, while retaining representation of differences and uniqueness in the separate research ventures.

I have argued (Kearney, 1998a) that grounded formal theorizing is a form of meta-synthesis and can capture the different effects of inter-study variations on outcomes of interest. I have used the term grounded formal theorizing to describe my meta-synthesis work in nursing. Was this label misapplied? Is the grounded formal theory described by Glaser and Strauss an early version of meta-synthesis, or a qualitatively different product? What level of abstraction denotes a formal theory? Is formal theory even of interest to postmodern qualitative scientists?

A twenty-first century examination of grounded formal theories and theorizing is warranted. This reconsideration is the focus of this chapter. The work labeled grounded formal theory by Glaser and Strauss will be reviewed and contrasted with newer efforts by others, and the methods of grounded formal theory construction described in those original and newer works will be outlined. The contributions of several experts will be considered as strategies to enable grounded formal theorizing in a postmodern age.

WHAT DOES GROUNDED FORMAL THEORY LOOK LIKE?

Theorizing and grounding by Glaser and Strauss

The development of grounded formal theory followed closely on the publication of the first substantive grounded theories and their methods. Even a superficial tour of a few major works reveals important differences from our current conventions of research reporting and more importantly of research thinking. Strauss described his first large-scale research venture, *Psychiatric Ideologies and Institutions* (1964), as 'virtually a grounded theory study, but only implicitly so' (1993: 12). A team of researchers spent several years studying two psychiatric institutions and produced an intricate portrait of social organization and interaction in these public and private hospitals, demonstrating a number of interactionist concepts (awareness contexts, negotiation, status passage, processual social order) that would be revisited in his work with Glaser and beyond. Meticulous field methods with concurrent theorizing were portrayed in a vivid and highly practical methods chapter that stands today as a resource for grounded theory researchers, although the words grounded theory never appeared.

Even in this early work, Strauss's interactionism led him toward a constructivist view, reflecting appreciation of standpoint and situation. He demonstrated sensitivity to concerns of stance and reflexivity and noted his appreciation of the theoretical influence of diverse backgrounds and standpoints among his research team. When asking hospital team members about an incident, for example, 'we regarded the information as relevant to their positions on the team and evaluated it in that context' (1964: 34). The work's last sentences were, 'We do not claim that our own perspective is the only useful one for study of these various types of human association or even that it should dominate studies of hospitals. But we do argue for its investigative power' (1964: 377). Strauss carried this particular interactionist banner throughout his scientific career, noting that social organization was negotiated and processual, affected by a continual stream of contingencies, and always in the eye of the beholder. Theory was not unitary or universal, even at this early stage.

Although we would recognize the 1964 psychiatric hospitals study as grounded theory, Strauss clearly indicated in his 1993 retrospective that the grounded theory method as depicted in *The Discovery of Grounded Theory* (1967) was formulated 'in close and equal collaboration' with Barney Glaser (Strauss, 1993: 12). Indeed, Glaser was the first author on all three books from the pivotal project that brought these men together and produced the grounded theory method. When Glaser and Strauss embarked in 1962 on a Division of Nursing-funded study of care of dying patients, grounded theory as a method had yet to be labeled and articulated. By the end, three of the four books from that project (*Awareness of Dying*, 1965; *The Discovery of Grounded Theory,* 1967; and *Time for Dying*, 1968), stood as a definitive grounded theory tutorial.

While *The Discovery of Grounded Theory* is the most widely cited source for the original grounded theory method, *Time for Dying* included an Appendix that gives life to the rigor of grounded theory fieldwork and adds a great deal to the more decontextualized depiction in *The Discovery of Grounded Theory. Awareness of Dying* included a valuable expansion on the validity checks for useful grounded theory, going beyond understandability, fit, generality, and control to include the requirements that concepts bridge abstraction and reality, and that access variables be identified through which individuals can influence processes and outcomes:

> Our concepts are both analytic and sensitizing. By *analytic* we mean that they are sufficiently generalized to designate the properties of concrete entities—not the entities themselves— and by *sensitizing* we mean that they yield a meaningful picture with apt illustrations that

enable medical and nursing personnel to grasp the reference in terms of their own experiences … these concepts provide a necessary bridge between the theoretical thinking of sociologists and the practical thinking of people concerned with the substantive area (Glaser & Strauss, 1965: 263).

As they developed this substantive project, Glaser and Strauss were gathering material to demonstrate their claim that grounded formal theory would make these findings meaningful on a larger scale. For example, in *Time for Dying*, they noted the contribution of their newly discovered concepts to larger theoretical projects in the field of sociology. They linked dying to the previously articulated concept of status passage and began to explore the concept of structural process, the interaction among individual and group activities, and the institutional structures they co-create. They viewed their substantive study as contributing directly to formal theory, and they called for further exploration of applicability across contexts.

The cooperative venture of the *Time for Dying* study gave birth to the ideas and processes of both substantive and formal grounded theory. In the chapter on grounded formal theory in *The Discovery of Grounded Theory,* Glaser and Strauss drew on their experiences together in the *Time for Dying* study to lay out the idea and approach of grounded formal theory development, a methods description that varied little over the next several decades. Soon thereafter, *Status Passage* (1971) was introduced as a grounded formal theory. Citing Glaser's *Organizational Careers* (1968) as the only other example to date, Glaser and Strauss thus fulfilled their earlier recommendation, neatly closing the era of co-authorship. In 1978, Strauss published the third of the four book-length grounded formal theories, *Negotiations*.

Strauss went on, in 1985, to publish, with Fagerhaugh, Suczek, and Weiner, *The Social Organization of Medical Work*. The same meticulous fieldwork was used, funded by a 5-year grant and involving the three authors other than Strauss in seven hospitals over a prolonged period. Having reached a pinnacle in analytic expertise, they abandoned solo coding and memo-writing early on, in favor of using audiotaped weekly team meetings to do their theorizing work out loud. When ideas crystallized into major findings, memos were written and built upon, but transcribed team meetings became the main memo form. The inescapable subjectivity of qualitative fieldwork also was noted:

[T]he personal experiences of each project member enriched both the data collection and the analysis. We emphasize this particularly because of firmly held canons, widespread among social scientists, about the biased subjectivity of personal experience, which ought therefore to be carefully screened out of research like potential impurities from drinking water (Strauss et al., 1985: 294).

The presentation of the work was also resistant to the values of the time. By 1985, social science investigators had begun to pull back from univocal assertions and documentary control and instead allow readers direct access to participant voices. The era was dawning in which minimally altered data would be privileged over even expert analysis. Strauss had recognized a movement toward letting data speak for themselves, yet acknowledged without apology that despite the trend toward voluminous exemplification of points with quotes and field notes, he had persisted in his established approach of supporting his theorizing claims with a systematic set of comparisons completed by a group of experts off-stage, rather than flooding the book with a profusion of 'raw' data:

> Many quite esteemed and excellent monographs use a great deal of data—quotes or field note selections ... Most of these monographs are descriptively dense, but alas theoretically thin. If you look at their indexes, there are almost no new concepts listed ... furthermore, the linkages made by the author among the phenomena represented by his or her concepts are often not especially numerous, nor are variations specified by noting the relevant conditions, consequences, associated strategies, etc. ... In our monographs ... we attempt to analyse data closely ... so as to construct an integrated and dense theory. So the interview and field note quotations tend to be brief ... We think twice about loading a theoretically oriented monograph with too many chunks of descriptive material and are fairly deliberate about those that are included (Strauss et al., 1985: 296).

The same representation decisions were applied in formal theorizing, as will be seen.

Much of Strauss's work in the 1980s and early 1990s was directed at helping others to gain access to grounded theory methods. In his final full-scale creative work, *Continual Permutations of Action* (1993), he began the work with a personal retrospective on his evolution from pragmatist interactionist beginnings and ended it with a contextualization of how his theory of action animates social order, presented as only one option among many, but one that was generalizable without being deterministic or reified, based on an expandable network of social conditions and contingencies.

After reviewing Strauss's findings and methods descriptions in the original works, I suggest that he left a set of interactionist tools for looking at human societies that is enriched but not clearly discounted by twenty-first century perspectives. But the grounding in both the substantive and formal works of both Glaser and Strauss looked different from what we are now accustomed to seeing in many practice discipline research reports. Verbatim quotations or field note excerpts were rare. Findings were stated without data, citation, or direct referential support. Instead, various formulations of what came to be known as a conditional matrix were used to ground theoretical conclusions in systematically saturated variations, from micro to macro levels of influence. A profusion of systematically identified and conceptually framed examples supported each hypothesis, reflecting great scope in fieldwork and library work accompanied by deep and thorough grounded theorizing.

Indeed, Glaser and Strauss were much more comfortable writing at a distance from data than are authors of current qualitative reports in the practice disciplines. Much of their narrative was written in a 'formalizing' or highly abstract style, reflecting the rhetoric of their discipline and era. They wrote in the present tense. Claims were not delimited to a unique geocultural or historical setting. For example, they theorized about hospitals in general and death in general, after presenting the conditions under which their project took place. The processual nature of social order was reflected not in caveats and disclaimers about limited transferability, but in a conditional matrix (Strauss, 1993) serving as an accessible repository for the variations in situation that would produce variations in action. This rhetorical and analytic strategy was carried through Strauss's career with only minor variations. Only in his later instructive writing (e.g., *Qualitative Analysis for Social Scientists*, 1987) was documentary evidence such as drafts, diagrams, and analysis session transcripts routinely drawn upon for illustrative purposes.

By the end of his career, Strauss had passed a postmodern social science crossroad. He and Glaser had laid a path for theorizers, full of parsimonious explanations of complex human dynamics but unsettling to some in its cross-cultural and cross-historical generalization. A second path branched off for scientific describers, making limited claims rooted in carefully documented, minimally interpreted evidence. Strauss nodded to the ever-widening latter path, accessible to many, but continued on the more difficult one, accessible methodologically to only a few. The skills honed by Glaser and Strauss made grounded formal theory possible, but they had limited company on that road.

What Glaser's and Strauss's Grounded Formal Theory Looks Like

Organizational careers

The first work labeled grounded formal theory appeared in 1968. Glaser framed the work as a start at formal theory, rather than a finished product. (None of their formal theories was presented as anything but a starting point or one option among many.) Glaser made the distinction between substantive theories of specific kinds of situations (scientific careers, juvenile delinquency) and formal theories of more cross-cutting human phenomena (organizational careers, deviance), but noted in a passage borrowed from *The Discovery of Grounded Theory* that both substantive and formal theories are middle-range theories: 'They fall between the "minor working hypotheses" of everyday life and the "all-inclusive" grand theories' (Glaser & Strauss, 1967: 3).

In the reader entitled, *Organizational Careers: A Sourcebook for Theory* (1968), Glaser clustered over 60 contextually diverse excerpts from the substantive works of himself and others on the roles and dynamics of individuals within organizations, with brief initial and section introductions laying out the larger theoretical claims for which the substantive works served as source and illustration. To illustrate the breadth of topics covered in this theory, the book includes sections on recruitment to organizational careers, career motivations within organizations, loyalty to organizations, promotion and demotion, succession in organizational roles, moving between organizations, and career patterns of executives and workers. The sections include excerpts from studies of public and private organizations, including various industries, the military, academia, research, medicine, law firms, and the post office, with certain researchers' work recurring in each section and others used only occasionally.

Glaser used his previous work on scientists' organizational careers as a substantive case, and explained that he excerpted the other contributors' original works 'to bring out general ideas, accompanied by sufficient data to understand their grounding' (1968: 6), believing that an abundance of data was unnecessary, and that his editing had produced 'a continuous flow of theoretical ideas on careers, uninterrupted by the normal tedium of many research presentations' (1968: 6).

The theorizing in this volume, presented in the introduction to each section of excerpted works, is a catalog of conditions affecting various aspects of the phenomenon. For example, in the introduction to the section on recruitment, Glaser noted the influence of attributes of the individual, their coworkers, the careers in that discipline, the organization's characteristics, and the sociopolitical environment. Recruitment is shaped by the candidate's and organization's appraisals of each other. Recruitment may be direct or mediated, internal or external, and decisions may be hard or easy to reverse, and inclusive or arbitrary. Each party considers anticipated consequences of the offer and its acceptance. Introducing the section on career motivations, Glaser suggested that career motivations are constantly changing, most affected by the problems and contingencies of the individual's career stage, but also shaped by messages received from others within the organization about its goals and a changing degree of investment in those goals, and the various kinds of motivators offered by the organization itself. This first step toward theorizing beyond specific arenas was rudimentary in its presentation and more focused on influences on the core human experience than on how that experience is co-created by individual and organization, but it represented an important shift in grounded theorizing toward study of dynamics that cross social worlds.

Status passage

Published in 1971, *Status Passage* was again introduced by Glaser and Strauss as a first attempt at formal theory. The authors introduced status passage as an old idea and a longstanding shared interest, but one ripe for revival and revision with the aid of their interactionist view of status as not fixed but continually changing. They defined status passage as conscious movement between social roles or sets of internally and externally defined expectations, and suggested that these passages occur continually over time and are not necessarily regularized or prescribed.

Glaser and Strauss achieved considerable success in this first and only shared formal theory venture. The work is indeed complex and dense, two characteristics they valued in grounded theories, yet parsimonious, in that core constituent ideas of status passage and the important contingencies that affect it were clearly threaded through the 'far-out comparisons' of the examples. This success may have been supported by their method of theorizing, which Strauss later applied to *The Social Organization of Medical Work*:

> Because so much relevant data and theory was 'in us' from our previous work, the principal mode used to generate theory was to talk out our comparisons in lengthy conversations,

and either record the conversation or take notes. We ... studied relevant literature for more data and theory. These conversations went on almost five days a week for three months. At this time we gave up in exhaustion, and with the realization that we could begin to write it all up ... At some points Xeroxing our notes and studying them helped to maintain continuity and coverage (Strauss et al., 1985: 192–193).

Their presentation differed from Glaser's formal theory book. Examples from others' work were cited and footnoted rather than reproduced, producing greater cohesion and integration in the text, and a more nimble format for dramatic comparisons in close succession. This think-out-loud analytic style and highly synergistic collaboration, coupled with a minimal documentation system, no doubt enabled in the final text the easy movement among examples as varied as art collectors, hippies, religious converts, Latin-American physicians, and Chinese biochemistry students.

Negotiations

In the introduction to the 1978 *Negotiations: Varieties, Contexts, Processes, and Social Order*, Strauss situated his interest in negotiation as one of the dynamics of negotiated social order. He proposed to extend his previous work by exploring actors' theories of negotiation, the subprocesses of negotiation (such as making trade-offs, taking kickbacks, compromising, paying off debts, and reaching negotiated agreements) and their conditions and consequences, and to lay out the dimensions or major variations of negotiations across various contexts, both to enhance the literature on negotiation and that on social order. Cases from his own and others' studies were explored, ranging from psychiatric hospitals to insurance companies, corrupt politicians, and the Nuremberg trials, from face-to-face interpersonal negotiations to bargaining between nations. Strauss outlined the macro-to-micro interaction of conditions shaping negotiation and social order and proposed that no social institution or phenomenon can be fully studied without an appreciation of the dynamic role of silent and overt negotiation in creating and sustaining it.

The paradigm he put forth, with its catalog of conditions, contexts, subtypes, and kinds of action, was offered as a starting point for later theorizing but was already considerably denser than the previous two formal theories had been. Strauss noted that he was uncertain about the value of a completely abstract general theory of negotiation, or of any general theory for that matter, because he viewed all human activity as inseparable from social context and structural conditions, the full range of which no theory could ever predict. Again he presaged constructivist concerns.

Awareness contexts

Never considered finished or granted a volume of its own, the emergent formal theory of awareness contexts was alluded to across the decades by both Glaser and Strauss and later played an influential role in Strauss's theory of action and processual order. Awareness context never was fully explored in its own right, perhaps because it was a condition for action rather than an action in itself.

It was perhaps best captured in a lecture by Strauss at UCSF in 1979 that was reprinted by him in 1987.

In this talk, he recalled being inspired during the analysis of *Awareness of Dying* to ponder various conditions of awareness of social status: visible and invisible, stigmatized and praiseworthy, debatable and certain, erroneous and correct, etc. He described drawing on research on such diverse examples as gay identity, various disabilities, racial minority status, student nurses' public and private identities, and criminal guilt. He considered various means of altering or protecting awareness, including betrayal, rectification, and secret-keeping. He closed the speech with an invitation to suggest other examples of awareness contexts that could enrich his ongoing theorizing, and called for more attention to formal theory, to counterbalance the preponderance of attention to substantive ones.

Continual permutations of action

Strauss's 1993 work was a culmination of a lifetime of theorizing and teaching, and brought together theoretical gleanings from many of his major substantive works. In this last large work, Strauss formally set out assumptions of action from his own increasingly constructivist interactionist perspective, supported them in eight highly varied substantive case examples, and concluded with a highly formal and closely argued summary of the implications of this understanding of action for his increasingly mature theory of negotiated order, now termed processual ordering. *Continual Permutations of Action* was the most formal of Strauss's theories in terms of abstraction and scope but was not termed a formal theory in title or text. (Perhaps, by this time, formal theory dominated his horizon and needed no self-indicating label.) Here the presentation of formal theory had moved beyond Glaser's brief introductions of others' excerpted work and the theory-driven chapter structure of *Status Passage* to the stand-alone theoretical presentation followed by the extended author-interpreted case examples refined in *Negotiations*. Strauss's prose leads a reader deftly between the micro and macro and between the substantive and formal, while keeping the overarching model in view. This was indeed a fitting final opus, and an inspiration to theorists who follow.

HOW IS GROUNDED FORMAL THEORY CONSTRUCTED?

Formal theory methods as depicted in The Discovery of Grounded Theory

A chronological review reveals that across the writing of Glaser and Strauss, the descriptions of formal theory methods vary little, if at all. Parts of the chapter in *The Discovery of Grounded Theory* devoted to this purpose were replicated verbatim in several later descriptions. In each case, Glaser and Strauss defined formal theory as distinguished from substantive theory only in degree of abstraction and generality across contexts. In their structure and function and in their discovery and development, they were viewed as the same. The main agenda was to describe and recommend means of arriving at formal theory, but no step-by-step approach was offered, perhaps because the methods were represented elsewhere in the chapters on substantive theory development.

In *The Discovery of Grounded Theory*, Glaser and Strauss suggested several approaches to formal theorizing. They defined a one-area formal theorizing approach as simply deleting the specifics of a substantive theory while making the assumption that it applied more generally. This was termed a rewriting technique, unimpeded by attention to the original data. They offered examples of converting a theory of dying as an unscheduled status passage to a theory about unscheduled status passage in general, or a theory about cohesiveness in small groups of college women to one of cohesiveness in small groups in general. They criticized the rewriting approach as dissociated from data, untested for fit and work, and suitable mainly as a starting point. We can view this strategy as simply erasing the particulars from a localized theory but not checking to see whether it fit or worked beyond its situation of origin.

Glaser and Strauss much preferred what they termed a multi-area formal theory, and this is the approach that was seen in all their own formal theorizing. Awareness contexts and status passages were used as examples. In this approach, studies of diverse and often quite disparate social groups would be selected based on theoretical sampling, and then systematically compared using the same techniques as in substantive theory development. For example, awareness contexts were said to exist in car sales, pool halls, racial 'passing,' international spying, and circus clowning. These would vary in visibility of status to others, number of players involved, ratio of insiders to outsiders, position, stakes, and so forth. These systematic comparisons could lead to hypotheses about the role and impact of various combinations of conditions on resulting actions.

Theoretical sampling consisted of seeking out specific variations of specific conditions in other situations and groups, often involving library work to find substantive studies. The process of theoretical sampling for formal theorizing described in *The Discovery of Grounded Theory* is essentially the same as was recommended for substantive theory, but instead of seeking out live examples within a single milieu under study, one would seek out examples collected by others in more disparate settings and conditions. The library or bookshelf, rather than the human activity surrounding a researcher in the field, becomes the pool from which to elicit theoretical comparisons.

Glaser and Strauss also acknowledged that there was a third strategy for formal theorizing, in which formal theory could be formulated directly from diverse datasets. They noted that this would require a lot of work and discipline and would lack the advantage of a starting point of a substantive theory. They cautioned that this approach would require first organizing and reviewing massive amounts of data, and they offered this approach only as one hypothetically available but not recommended. In concluding the chapter, Glaser and Strauss acknowledged that formal theory was not universally popular in sociology at the time.

The discipline favored a high degree of specialization in small substantive fields, and formal theory already was viewed by some as depersonalized and too distant from everyday life. Yet Glaser and Strauss defended grounded formal theory as more trustworthy than logico-deductively-derived theory and more useful for understanding new situations and stimulating new research.

Formal theorizing methods in Organizational Careers

In Glaser's introduction to this 1968 reader, he excerpted a number of passages of methods description from *The Discovery of Grounded Theory* and expanded the rationale for formal theory somewhat, citing the need for formal theories to manage increasing volumes of information. At the same time, however, he empha-sized the need for multiple formal theories, because no single theory would ever capture all the relevant facets of all phenomena.

Glaser offered his work as an example of the multiple-area approach to formal theory previously promoted in *The Discovery of Grounded Theory*. He described his choice of substantive articles on organizational careers as based on ideational variation and theoretical relevance and indicated that the sequencing of chapters was designed to display variations in an understandable order. Glaser went on to discuss the importance of selecting materials based on the desired population scope and conceptual level of the theory. He concluded by explaining the char-acteristics to be considered in generating a dense theory: the types, degree, or continua of a category, its conditions and contingencies, major consequences, structural context, social and structural processes that create or maintain it, and so forth, language that foreshadowed the six Cs he would later offer as a theo-retical coding strategy (Glaser, 1978). Although the product of this first venture, in its use of extended excerpts with brief introductory commentary, was not as smoothly presented as later formal theorizing, his explication provided a more enriched model of theorizing than had been offered in the brief chapter of *The Discovery of Grounded Theory*.

Methods in Status Passage

The methods of development of *Status Passage* (Glaser & Strauss, 1971) as formal theory were described in a concluding chapter, starting with the verbatim borrow-ing of previous text on the now-familiar distinction between substantive and formal theory, reasons for selecting materials for comparison, and how formal theory can be made more profound. They also described the brainstorming method of cooperative analysis detailed above. Making an important new point, they indi-cated that saturation was not possible in grounded formal theory, so they expected that additional categories of status passage might well be deemed important by others. Yet they observed that the theory of status passage as offered was extremely dense and tightly integrated, and apologized for the resulting slow reading, despite inclusion of only a third of what they had written for the project.

Glaser and Strauss concluded with a forceful claim for the value of formal theory as a road map for conditions to explore when facing an unfamiliar but related area, whether as researcher or practitioner. They described drawing on their formal theory of status passage when they were confronted with problems in research on training programs and illness careers, and on negotiation theory in their consulting work, when interactions were bogged down or participants were immovable. Their increasing demand as consultants by this time may stand in itself as testimony to the practical relevance of their theorizing.

Methods in Theoretical Sensitivity

In the chapter on formal theory in Glaser's 1978 work, he again began with excerpted previously published explanatory text and then discussed for the first time the role of substantive basic social processes as starting points for formal theorizing. Glaser noted that this required an experienced grounded theorist who could identify situations and literature that were relevant and avoid logical elaboration beyond the substantiating data. He warned against assuming that a formal theory applied to a substantive area even if it sounded relevant. The chapter concluded with text from previous works, including the instruction for reading formal theory given to readers of *Organizational Careers*, although there was no formal theory to read in this methods volume.

The 'Recipe' in qualitative analysis for social scientists

The only major variation in the presentation of formal theory methods was found in Strauss's 1987 introduction to his 1979 talk at UCSF on awareness contexts. To aid the later reader, Strauss offered as preamble the following 'rules of thumb' (pp. 241–242, cited here verbatim with small deletions indicated by ellipses):

1. Choose a phenomenon, and give it a name, for this will be your core category to which all your codes will relate.
2. Select and examine some data in which your phenomenon, named as the core category, appears. The data may be drawn from an interview, fieldnote, newspaper account … or from your own or someone else's experience.
3. Begin to code these data in the usual fashion: dimensions, subcategories, etc., and in accordance with the coding paradigm.
4. Begin to write theoretical memos incorporating your initial ideas and the results of your coding.
5. Employ theoretical sampling, seeking your next data in a different substantive area. This will yield new subcategories and begin to give variance to the previous analyses.
6. Continue to do that, theoretically sampling within the same substantive areas but also in widely differing ones …
7. At every step of the analysis, think comparatively—not merely to suggest new theoretical samples (sources, events, actors, organizations, processes) but to enrich your specific codes and theoretical memos.
8. … Be very aware of how all codes that you develop bear on the core phenomenon, and make the connections as *specific as possible* [italics in original].

This simple recipe reflected the demands on Strauss in his later career to revisit the basics of grounded theory technique at every turn, as diverse and expanding audiences attempted to grasp and apply the principles of the method. Yet one could not generate a grounded formal theory using this recipe, any more than one could generate a substantive theory from a set of named procedures without definitions or examples. The only conceivable purpose of this list was to demonstrate that building formal theory is like building substantive theory (equally easy and convenient) and to encourage them to do it. From the review of later grounded formal theory that will follow, it would appear that few, if any, took him up on the challenge.

Newer grounded formal theory contenders: Are they, or aren't they?

Formal theory: Deductive and mathematical models
As early as 1980, Freese depicted the state of formal theorizing in sociology as a 'babelized' mix. What is meant by the term formal theory clearly varies across fields. I found comparatively few publications labeled formal theory in current serials. The kind of work most commonly labeled formal theory in the sociological and practice discipline literature at this writing is the mathematically generated formula derived from a collection of quantitative datasets. Examples were an empirical test of predictors of status hierarchies using quantitative data from work groups, fraternity friendships, and play among infant quintuplets (Gould, 2002); a predictive model from demographic data of the likelihood of stopping childbearing after having a boy (Yamaguchi, 1989); and a model predicting the effect of high school students' friends' norms and attitudes and school peer culture on individual students' study habits and academic engagement (Bishop et al., 2004). In a slightly different deductive approach, Bengtson and Roberts (1991) reported a theory of intergenerational solidarity in aging families. After creating a taxonomy of concepts from the literature, a proposed predictive model was tested twice, revised, and then tested as a structural equation model on data from a new sample of elderly parents and their adult children.

Viewed from the definition of Glaser and Strauss, these works could be labeled 'grounded,' in that they were induced from literature or data, but not all would be termed 'theory,' in that the mathematical models make no claim to apply beyond their data of origin, and only Bengtson and Roberts' (1991) work might be viewed as 'formal,' in that the mathematical models did not cross boundaries into diverse substantive areas of human activity. The current weighting of 'hard' data over insightful observation may explain the popularity of computer modeling, in which researchers allow correlations among data to determine the level of importance of theoretical relationships.

Glaser's and Strauss's conclusion decades ago that formal social-psychological theories were on the way out of style appears to have held up today, a decline no doubt accelerated by the current fear of decontextualization and abstraction I have observed earlier. In a similar observation, sociologists of knowledge

Lynott and Lynott (1996) observed that over the past several decades, the predominant earlier styles of formal theorizing on aging (individual-oriented and researcher-absent approaches that ignored sociopolitical and perspectival influence) had been effectively challenged by feminist and political concerns, leading to their expectation that critical and multiple theories were the likely direction in the near future. Thus the scarcity of formal theories may be due to both sociological and epistemological shifts in recent years.

Contemporary grounded formal theories
No grounded formal theories labeled as such were found in social science serials when searched using computerized academic citation databases and tables of contents of major journals. One unpublished report of a doctoral thesis in executive management at Case Western Reserve University was found in a Google search. Apprey (2006) analyzed the ethics of the transfer of project ownership in ethnonational conflict resolution. Apprey had a significant track record of international fieldwork and writing on the psychohistorical aspects of international relief and reconstruction work, and had written a series of papers on the psychosocial processes of ethnocultural conflict resolution as captured by grounded theory means. He explained that his grounded formal theory was a formal theory because it theorized beyond the substantive areas of his original data collection, but he quite skillfully used techniques derived from meta-ethnography (Noblit & Hare, 1988). Apprey conducted a reciprocal translation of the results of qualitative studies of two peacemaking agencies' approaches to conflict resolution and identified the results (a list of seven propositions about the emotional work of conflict resolution) as a new model applicable beyond the local examples in a variety of ethnonational conflict situations. This work was carefully done and met our definition of grounded theory, but it did not reach the level of scope that Glaser and Strauss would term formal theory, as the conclusions were limited to a single arena of human interaction.

The work of three authors in current health science literature, all nurses, may represent variations of grounded formal theory. My own work started with a methods description (Kearney, 1998a) directly derived from the Glaser and Strauss works depicted earlier in this chapter. I made a careful distinction, however, between the cross-phenomenon goals of Glaser's and Strauss's grounded formal theory and my own aim of synthesizing substantive studies of the same phenomenon in different populations without rising much above the level of abstraction of the original works. The topics to which I applied this method included women's recovery from addiction (Kearney, 1998b) and serious illness and trauma (Kearney, 1999), and women's experience of violent relationships (Kearney, 2001a) and changing health behaviors (Kearney & O'Sullivan, 2003). Only the illness recovery and health behavior change analyses extended beyond a single substantive phenomenon. In each of these ventures I applied analytic techniques of traditional grounded theory (theoretical sampling, constant comparative analysis, increasingly theoretical coding, and testing of hypothesized relationships) to the text of qualitative research reports, while treating as analytic contingencies the original analysts' times, disciplines, apparent clinical standpoints, and methodological variations. My goal was to produce clinically useful models for health care providers dealing with these problems in populations and locations similar to those of the constituent studies. Yet I generally stopped short of what Glaser and Strauss would have accepted as formal theory.

Writing with similar clinical goals, Finfgeld (1999) synthesized six studies of courage among ill persons, three of which were her own, using a method termed meta-interpretation. This was depicted as guided procedurally by meta-ethnography, but inspired epistemologically and methodologically by Strauss and Corbin's 1990 grounded theory method. Data elements from the constituent reports were coded and ordered according to the 'grounded theory paradigm prescribed by Strauss and Corbin' (p. 805) using techniques of dimensionalization and search for variation. The product was a model portraying a shared general response crossing several life situations, and could be described as 'formal' in that it crossed several situations, but perhaps not as fully developed 'theory,' in that commonalities rather than variations were the main goal.

In 2001, Wuest proposed a theory of women's caring across personal and professional contexts and situations as a step toward grounded formal theory. The theory of precarious ordering was developed by theoretical sampling of new data, theorizing from her own extensive previous substantive studies, and analysis of work of others. Like her two nurse colleagues, in her formal theorizing, Wuest claimed a departure from Glaser in limiting her focus to studies that shared substantive characteristics, but her topical lens was focused more widely across substantive areas than in two of my studies. It is unclear whether Wuest returned to her original interview data and generated completely new categories or built from the theories she had previously produced from those data. It is likely that both approaches were used, as the resulting theory, elegantly integrated, includes subprocesses she had previously identified.

Grounded formal theorizing by other names
At least three qualitative researchers and research teams have been going about developing theory across substantive populations and studies without applying the label of grounded formal theory. The extensive work of Morse, a persistent and articulate proponent of qualitatively derived theory, cannot be adequately represented here, but she has progressively built a theory of suffering and comfort care (e.g., 1999, Morse et al., 2002) that is at a fairly high level of abstraction. Most of Morse's work has been single studies extending previous work into new theoretical areas, but over time examples of overt synthesis of multiple studies on related phenomena have also appeared. For example, in 1991, Morse and Johnson concluded an edited volume of students' grounded theory studies with a chapter depicting the illness-constellation model, synthesized from the student-developed grounded theories and consisting of four stages: uncertainty, disruption, striving to regain self, and regaining wellness, each with a number of stage-specific human responses.

Minimizing suffering was identified as the core process in the model. This was a more comprehensive and higher-abstraction model than its constituent theories, and meets the criteria of a grounded formal theory, although that label was not applied. The label of grounded theory fell away as Morse subsequently developed her own language for qualitatively derived theory development. It is difficult to detect any difference in the overall mechanism and final product from grounded formal theory, although epistemological differences may be inherent. The volume and attention to detail is impressive by any name.

Paterson and colleagues analyzed over 250 qualitative reports about chronic illness, using a new articulation of meta-study (Paterson, Thorne, Canam & Jillings, 2001). In this approach, the group sought to improve the product of qualitative meta-synthesis of study findings by separately analyzing the theoretical context and methods of research in a substantive area and integrating the results of all three analyses. The process of meta-study was described as constructivist and interpretive, but its goal was midrange theory that would provide a deeper understanding of the problem in question. The analysis and synthesis process, based on Miles and Huberman's hypothetical path analysis strategy (1994), was indistinguishable from grounded theory techniques, in that models were hypothesized and their support in existing data was systematically explored with iterative modification of the model.

Separately and together, Paterson and colleagues published a number of reports of this project, including the Shifting Perspectives model of chronic illness (Paterson, 2001, 2003), embedded assumptions in fatigue studies (Paterson et al. 2003), and the shifting conception of chronic illness over time from one of loss and burden to one of wellness in illness, transformation, and normality (Thorne & Paterson, 1998). As the researchers may have hoped, the most illuminating products were those that focused on the disciplinary and sociocultural influences on chronic illness experience, and how those previously unlabeled frameworks shaped care and interaction and ultimately the ill person's experience.

Sandelowski has made major contributions to the methods and methodology of meta-synthesis, as will be noted below. She also produced a theoretical model from three of her studies of the transition to parenthood in fertile and previously infertile couples (1995), which had clear characteristics of clinically focused grounded formal theory. Yet, like Morse and Paterson and colleagues, she did not choose to link the techniques or goals to grounded formal theory.

EVOLUTION OF GROUNDED FORMAL THEORIZING

The formal theory ventures since Glaser and Strauss have not ventured very far beyond the substantive scope of their constituent studies. Types of illnesses or health behavior problems are generalized to chronic illness or health behavior in general, and specific conditions of parenting are generalized to slightly larger groups of parents. Finfgeld's study of courage and Morse's ongoing work in illness and comforting appear to be the most abstract and cross-cutting but still remain bounded within study of health and illness experience.

The practice disciplines of these post-Glaser and Strauss grounded formal theorists have important influence on the scope of these theories. Most are concerned with the practicalities of providing health and illness care, and one (Apprey) with cross-ethnic conflict resolution. Speaking from my own discipline, nurses' enthusiasm for grounded theory techniques stems from its great potential for clinical application. Nurses specialize within illness phenomena. They appreciate the intricate particularities of cancer experience, for example, as compared to heart attack or parenting an ill child. Nurses may not be particularly interested in formal theory at higher levels of abstraction if it is harder to apply to a specific substantive context or conveys obvious simple knowledge that they have long held.

Perhaps the most interesting contrast between the formal theories of the originators and those of the next generation is in the grounding: how supporting evidence is conceived of and included. Later theorists all demonstrated and exemplified each theoretical claim using verbatim data of various kinds, whereas Glaser and Strauss felt no such obligation. Glaser edited out the supporting data in *Organizational Careers* and, in their work together and in Strauss's work afterward, they favored theoretical density over descriptive amplification.

Our value shift over time regarding evidence has at least four possible origins: the discipline and skill level of the researcher, the era within which the work took place, and the overarching goal of the formal theory project. Practice disciplines have been increasingly pressured by scientism and exhorted to provide the evidentiary basis for each practice decision. As a result, practitioners are most comfortable stating theoretical claims when they can be accompanied by cases in point. Furthermore, few have been trained in the world of theory and theorizing. Practitioners are schooled in rapid access to and appraisal of experimental research, but rarely in the ability to recognize and link concepts within textual or observational data.

The 1960s–1980s shaped the work of Glaser and Strauss, and the 1990s–2000s shaped the work of later theorists in radically different ways. Scientists of the earlier era were generally more comfortable with pronouncements about human interaction presumed to be globally applicable and less preoccupied with the interpretive nature of even empirical research. Those in the contemporary period are acutely sensitized to issues of locality and partiality, power and control, and voicing and narrative. Shifts in both discipline and era have combined to produce qualitatively different goals for formal theorizing from those held by Glaser and Strauss in the earlier time. Contemporary formal theorists appear to seek models that stay close to the ground (substantive areas) and close to their grounding (in original data). The results, increasingly visible today, are a plethora of substantive semi-formal theories closely wrapped in supporting data trails. In building new products from existing qualitative material, the goal is more often metasynthesis or meta-summary, in which findings are pooled to create not a higher level of abstraction, but a better substantiated substantive theory.

In my own goals for stronger formal theorizing in my practice discipline, I stop short of demanding a broader scope than the naturally occurring boundaries of illness and recovery phenomena. Accepting that this is a divergence from the original vision and practice of Glaser and Strauss, I find that article-length rather than book-length theorizing is more easily brought into the practice arena, and article-length theories must perforce narrow their focus to capture all the relevant conditions and particularities. My goal is to retain complexity while providing a road map through the important details.

WHAT NEXT, FOR PRACTICE DISCIPLINES?

Making the best of meta-synthesis

Strengthening technique
Given the need to manage large amounts of substantive evidence amid the movement away from formal theorizing in practice disciplines, several directions can be considered. First, to support multiple close-to-the-ground substantive or semi-formal theories with closely adherent exemplar data, stronger techniques for meta-synthesis are warranted. In less skilled hands, the common meta-synthesis is a generalized but mostly uninformative set of category labels, presented as the shared aspects of a target experience. The product is both less substantive and less well substantiated than the contributing studies from which it is drawn. Despite the ideal of creating something distinct from quantitative meta-analysis, in effect most qualitative meta-synthesis achieves the same goal, albeit with less methodological rigor: the goal of demonstrating a kind of pooled effect size, a decontextualized claim to evidence.

As I have explored elsewhere (Kearney, 2001b), the approaches to (and names for) meta-synthesis have proliferated in the last decade. While rarely involving formal theorizing, meta-synthesis does have potential utility. It can salvage some knowledge from the critical mass of small and often weak qualitative studies on many topics of interest to practice disciplines. Although 20 studies, each with 6 shallow interviews, offer little individually, when viewed together by a skilled analyst, some patterns may emerge that can be useful. Another benefit is increasing cross-paradigm credibility by increasing sample size. Although this tactic ignores the idiographic case orientation of qualitative research (Sandelowski, 1996), it may help move certain findings into arenas where they would otherwise be discounted.

Meta-synthesis methods can be strengthened. Sandelowski and Barroso provided clear and replicable techniques for representation of the frequency and intensity of shared findings in their development of the meta-summary approach (2003). They described methods of extracting and abstracting findings and calculating their frequency of occurrence across studies and intensity of occurrence within studies. This low-inference approach, as they have termed it, enables the integration of less than stellar qualitative reports, while providing a useful platform for further theorizing when the constituent material allows.

Capturing context in theorizing across substantive studies

I made an attempt to salvage situatedness in my conception of grounded formal theorizing (Kearney, 1998a) by treating the historical and sociocultural context of constituent studies as conditions that shaped the findings of each study and contributed to their shared aspects and variations. This effort can be extended. The advantage of the grounded theory approach is that constant comparative techniques and theoretical sampling provide mechanisms for incorporating variations into the final product of formal theory. The disadvantages are that this maneuver is extremely difficult to enact without grounded theory training and, unlike in substantive theory development, one has fewer options for dealing with questions that arise about published work completed by others long in the past. When one has no way of gauging the impact of unmeasured and unreported contextual influences on a phenomenon, conventional grounded theory methods provide no easy way of telling that story.

Paterson and colleagues have called for a separate discursive and critical analysis of the context of constituent literatures and offer the meta-study method (2001) as a valuable contribution. This approach enables exploration of positional and perspectival variations as data in themselves. They effectively instructed newer practitioners to step out of the empiricist view of text as 'true' data and remember that each constituent substantive study was shaped by an era, a discipline and methodology, and at least one individual; and that meta-synthesis cannot be conducted without taking those aspects into consideration in distinct and separate analyses.

Along these lines, but using data close to hand and on related topics, McCormick and co-authors (2003) brought together their own analyses from distinct projects to develop what they called an interpretation of interpretations. In a collaborative fashion, they articulated the background theories and epistemologies of their individual studies and considered them in the analytic process, with the outcome including insights into broader sociopolitical and cultural phenomena affecting the constituent studies.

Sandelowski (2006) moved farther in this direction by suggesting that the inevitable layers of interpretation obscuring original participants' experiences must be tackled head-on. She proposed a 'quadri-hermeneutic' stance toward qualitative material, incorporating the usual treatment of the material as empirical representation but adding three critical/discursive treatments: analyzing for the series of interpretive acts that have intervened between the experiencing subject and the final report, critically appraising the political and ideological context of individual studies and their social worlds of origin, and considering issues of authority and representation. These four kinds of interpretation of a body of qualitative work have value independently but also can be presented in combination, better equipping readers to judge the potential contribution to practice.

Applying theorizing to context

Clarke's (2005) situational analysis moved sociopolitical and discursive context from background to center, offering an important and effective counterweight to the increasingly intrapsychic focus of much current grounded theorizing in the practice disciplines. She aimed to explore differences rather than commonalities and to replace the static conditional matrix with more fluid and multi-relational representations of networks of influence, intentionally stopping short of formal theorizing. Drawing on Foucault, Clarke called attention to the power relationships creating and created by discourse, and offered a means to represent invisible and silent sociocultural forces that impinge on action. Described as complementary and supplementary to traditional grounded theorizing (p. 291), situational analysis provides techniques for capturing positionality and movement among social actors and discursive forces. Clarke described using the familiar techniques of theoretical sampling, coding, and memoing to create and refine three types of maps, while deliberately seeking out the visual and historical narratives and objects that shape action in a given social world. In *Situational Analysis*, sociologist Clarke took a definitive step away from positivist formal theory and toward a sensitized relativism, but she simultaneously refocused grounded theorists on larger social forces that are rarely represented in typical small-scope grounded theorizing in the practice disciplines.

Meta-study, quadri-hermeneutics, and situational analysis offer languages and techniques with which I and other postmodern grounded formal theorists can more deliberately and thoroughly sensitize our work to issues of standpoint and context. In the focus on close-up comparisons within bounded collections of empirical evidence that predominates in the practice disciplines today, these approaches incorporate reminders about important influences on individual and social action that often escape our gaze.

A CALL FOR STRONGER FORMAL THEORIZING
WITH POSTMODERN GROUNDING

Glaser's and Strauss's analytic approach retains much utility and potential today. Their formal theory work and particularly Strauss's *Negotiations* and *Continual Permutations of Action* achieved an ease of movement between abstraction and complexity, moving back and forth from the sublime to the meticulous. Dynamic principles of continually evolving, action-based, processual social order were systematically refracted in kaleidoscopic variations of types and context derived from and demonstrated in close-to-the-ground examples.

If bolstered by attention to social discourses and objects using techniques offered by Paterson, Sandelowski, and Clarke, Glaser and Strauss's approaches to analysis have much to offer practice disciplines today. I am not recommending that we shed our postmodern sensibility and revert to writing in the present tense using only masculine pronouns, and I doubt that we will be released completely from our burden of footnoting and citation, but systematic and artful theorizing from diverse and well researched contexts is still of value.

Yet few today have the thinking skills to systematically catalog and test many of the dimensions and properties of contemporary phenomena of interest. Most of us lack working practices like the analysis-by-discussion method modeled in the creation of *Status Passage* and *Social Organization of Medical Work*, perhaps being too preoccupied with grounding our work in empirical data to risk speculative discussion of conceptual variations. In the practice disciplines, training and practice in systematic conceptualizing appears of little interest. Mathematical meta-analysis techniques for neutralizing and summarizing numerical facts for evidence-based practice are the new gold standard, to which little is added by the masses of relatively uninterpreted and decontextualized verbatim speech too often presented as qualitative research.

Meanwhile, in the absence of rigorous theorizing, old unsubstantiated models continue. Techniques such as situational analysis help push us away from our data to conceptualize about forces 'out there' that continue to shape or constrain action within arenas of concern. Socio-politically and historically informed grounded formal theorizing has the potential to pry open oppressive structures of thought and practice, and may even enable us to conceptualize alternative paths.

NOTES

1 For the purpose of this chapter, I will define theories as temporarily acceptable generalizations about the influences on and consequent variations in human action. Substantive theories are limited in origin and application to a specific kind of human experience or interaction, whereas formal theories are depictions of the predictors and dynamics of forms of social action and interaction that are general enough to be applied across a wide range of instances and contexts.

REFERENCES

Apprey, M. (2006). A formal grounded theory on the ethics of transfer in conflict resolution. Retrieved May 10, 2006, from weatherhead.case.edu/edm/archive/files/year2/Apprey—revised%20SYRP1%209-9-05.pdf

Bengtson, V. L. & Roberts, R. E. L. (1991). Intergenerational solidarity in aging families: An example of formal theory construction. *Journal of Marriage and the Family, 53*, 856–870.

Bishop, J. H., Bishop, M., Bishop, M., Gelbwasser, L., Green, S., Peterson, E., et al. (2004). Why we harass nerds and freaks: A formal theory of student culture and norms. *The Journal of School Health, 74*, 235–251.

Clarke, A. E. (2005). *Situational Analysis: Grounded Theory after the Postmodern Turn.* Thousand Oaks, CA: SAGE.

Finfgeld, D. L. (1999). Courage as a process of pushing beyond the struggle. *Qualitative Health Research, 9*, 803–814.

Freese, L. (1980). Formal theorizing. *Annual Review of Sociology, 6*, 187–212.

Glaser, B. G. (Ed.) (1968). *Organizational Careers: A Sourcebook for Theory.* Chicago: Aldine.

Glaser, B. G. (1978). *Theoretical Sensitivity: Advances in the Methodology of Grounded Theory.* Mill Valley, CA: Sociology Press.

Glaser, B. G. & Strauss, A. L. (1965). *Awareness of Dying*. Chicago: Aldine.

Glaser, B. G. & Strauss, A. L. (1967). *The Discovery of Grounded Theory: Strategies for Qualitative Research*. New York: Aldine de Gruyter.

Glaser, B. G. & Strauss, A. L. (1968). *Time for Dying*. Chicago: Aldine.

Glaser, B. G. & Strauss, A. L. (1971). *Status Passage*. Chicago: Aldine Atherton.

Gould, R. V. (2002). The origins of status hierarchies: A formal theory and empirical test. *The American Journal of Sociology, 107*, 1143–1178.

Kearney, M. H. (1998a). Ready to wear: Discovering grounded formal theory. *Research in Nursing & Health, 21*, 179–186.

Kearney, M. H. (1998b). Truthful self-nurturing: A grounded formal theory of women's addiction recovery. *Qualitative Health Research, 8*, 495–512.

Kearney, M. H. (1999). *Understanding Women's Recovery from Illness and Trauma*. Thousand Oaks, CA: SAGE.

Kearney, M. H. (2001a). Enduring love: A grounded formal theory of women's experience of domestic violence. *Research in Nursing & Health, 24*, 270–282.

Kearney, M. H. (2001b). New directions in grounded formal theory. In R. Schreiber & P. N. Stern, Eds. *Using Grounded Theory in Nursing* (pp. 227–246). New York: Springer.

Kearney, M. H. & O'Sullivan, J. (2003). Identity shifts as turning points in health behavior change. *Western Journal of Nursing Research, 25*, 134–152.

Kleinman, A. (1987). Explanatory models in health-care relationships: A conceptual frame for research on family-based health-care activities in relation to folk and professional forms of clinical care. In J. D. Stoeckle, Ed. *Encounters between Patients and Doctors: An Anthology* (pp. 273–283). Cambridge, MA: MIT Press.

Lynott, R. J. & Lynott, P. P. (1996). Tracing the course of theoretical development in the sociology of aging. *The Gerontologist, 36*, 749–760.

McCormick, J., Rodney, P. & Varcoe, C. (2003). Reinterpretations across studies: An approach to meta-analysis. *Qualitative Health Research, 13*, 933–944.

Miles, M. B. & Huberman, A. M. (1994). *Qualitative Data Analysis: An Expanded Sourcebook* (2nd ed.). Thousand Oaks, CA: SAGE.

Morse, J. M. (1997). Responding to threats to integrity of self. *Advances in Nursing Science, 19*, 21–36.

Morse, J. M. (1999). Linking the concepts of enduring, uncertainty, suffering, and hope. *Image: Journal of Nursing Scholarship, 31*, 145–150.

Morse, J. M. (2001). Toward a praxis theory of suffering. *Advances in Nursing Science, 24*, 47–59.

Morse, J. M. & Johnson, J. L. (Eds.) (1991). *The Illness Experience: Dimensions of Suffering*. Newbury Park, CA: SAGE.

Morse, J. M., Hupcey, J. E., Penrod, J. & Mitcham, C. (2002). Integrating concepts for the development of qualitatively-derived theory. *Research and Theory for Nursing Practice, 16*, 5–18.

Noblit, G. & Hare, R. (1988). *Meta-ethnography: Synthesizing Qualitative Studies*. Newbury Park, CA: SAGE.

Paterson, B. L. (2001). The Shifting Perspectives model of chronic illness. *Journal of Nursing Scholarship, 33*, 21–26.

Paterson, B. L. (2003). The koala has claws: Applications of the shifting perspectives model in research of chronic illness. *Qualitative Health Research, 13*, 987–994.

Paterson, B. L., Thorne, S. E., Canam, C. & Jillings, C. (2001). *Meta-study of Qualitative Health Research: A Practical Guide to Meta-analysis and Meta-synthesis*. Thousand Oaks, CA: SAGE.

Paterson, B., Canam, C., Joachim, G. & Thorne, S. (2003). Embedded assumptions in qualitative studies of fatigue. *Western Journal of Nursing Research, 25*, 119–133.

Pridham, K. F., Knight, C. B. & Stephenson, G. R. (1989). Mothers' working models of infant feeding: Description and influencing factors. *Journal of Advanced Nursing, 14,* 1051–1061.

Sandelowski, M. (1995). A theory of the transition to parenthood of infertile couples. *Research in Nursing & Health, 18,* 123–132.

Sandelowski, M. (1996). One is the liveliest number: The case orientation of qualitative research. *Research in Nursing & Health, 19,* 525–529.

Sandelowski, M. (2006). 'Meta-jeopardy': The crisis of representation in qualitative metasynthesis. *Nursing Outlook, 54,* 10–16.

Sandelowski, M. & Barroso, J. (2003). Creating metasummaries of qualitative findings. *Nursing Research, 52,* 226–233.

Strauss, A. (1978). *Negotiations: Varieties, Contexts, Processes, and Social Order.* San Francisco: Jossey-Bass.

Strauss, A. L. (1987). *Qualitative Analysis for Social Scientists.* Cambridge: Cambridge University Press.

Strauss, A. L. (1993). *Continual Permutations of Action.* New York: Aldine de Gruyter.

Strauss, A. & Corbin, J. (1990). *Basics of Qualitative Research: Grounded Theory Procedures and Techniques.* Newbury Park, CA: SAGE.

Strauss, A., Fagerhaugh, S., Suczek, B. & Weiner, C. (1985). *The Social Organization of Medical Work.* Chicago: University of Chicago Press.

Strauss, A., Schatzman, L., Bucher, R., Ehrlich, D. & Sabshin, M. (1964). *Psychiatric Ideologies and Institutions.* London: The Free Press of Glencoe, Collier-Macmillan Ltd.

Thorne, S. & Paterson, B. (1998). Shifting images of chronic illness. *Image: Journal of Nursing Scholarship, 30,* 173–178.

Wuest, J. (2001). Precarious ordering: Toward a formal theory of women's caring. *Health Care for Women International, 22,* 167–193.

Yamaguchi, K. (1989). A formal theory for male-preferring stopping rules of childbearing: Sex differences in birth order and in the number of siblings. *Demography, 26,* 451–465.

7

Orthodoxy vs. Power: The Defining Traits of Grounded Theory

Jane C. Hood

Conventional field research is also exciting work, but, as we have detailed, it lacks the more extensive commitment to discovery of theory displayed by research utilizing theoretical sampling (Glaser & Strauss 1967: 76–77).

INTRODUCTION

Since the publication of *The Discovery of Grounded Theory*, the number of researchers claiming to base their work on grounded theory (GT) principles has steadily increased. According to the Social Science Citation Index, there were 101 journal article citations to *The Discovery of Grounded Theory* in the 1970s, 296 in the 1980s, 472 in the 1990s, and 605 between 2000 and 2006. However, the use of the term 'grounded theory' has proliferated even faster than have citations to Glaser and Strauss. An Academic Premier search for 'grounded theory' in the text of journal articles from a variety of disciplines finds just 17 articles mentioning GT in the 1970s, 81 in the 1980s, 1485 in the 1990s (when more journals were indexed) but 4357 in the just the first 6 years of this century (see Figure 7.1).

Clearly, it has become popular for sociologists to describe their qualitative methods as 'grounded theory.' However, as Charmaz (2006) points out, a great many people claiming to be using GT methods are not doing anything that would

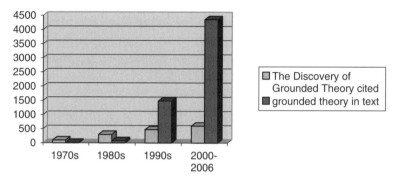

Figure 7.1 Comparison of relative growth of citations to *The Discovery of Grounded Theory* and mentions of 'grounded theory' in the text of articles 1970–2006. Reproduced with kind permission of Springer Netherlands.

be recognizable as such even when using the most inclusive definition of the term. For example, a student recently queried a qualitative research listserv claiming to have 'finished' a GT study and said that she 'was ready to begin concept analysis and instrument development' (message posted to QUALRS-L, September 19, 2006). For some authors, use of the term 'grounded theory' is simply a justification for engaging in a qualitative data analysis or doing some form of coding. For others, 'grounded theory' simply means building theory inductively from data. However, since qualitative research designs are usually inductive and necessarily involve analyzing data by coding for themes and patterns (Maxwell, 2005), what distinguishes Grounded Theory from the generic inductive qualitative design? And does this distinction matter? What, if anything, is to be gained by distinguishing between 'grounded theories' or 'grounded theory methodologies' and 'Grounded Theory' (with capital letters)? I contend that blurring the distinction between Grounded Theory and the generic inductive model risks losing the unique power of Grounded Theory. Without constant comparative analysis, theoretical sampling, and theoretical saturation of categories, we have lost the power of the method. In this chapter I argue that these processes are critical to the development of grounded theory and are often misunderstood and improperly used: authors say that they have done theoretical sampling or used the constant comparative method when they have not actually done so. This chapter draws upon examples of the misappropriation of Grounded Theory terminology for methods that belong instead to the generic inductive qualitative model (GIQM).

THE GENERIC INDUCTIVE QUALITATIVE MODEL

Because sociologists so often identify all things qualitative with 'grounded theory,' many of us would not be able to explain how the generic inductive model differs from grounded theory. What do I mean by the GIQM? Joseph Maxwell's

Qualitative Research Design (2005) provides an excellent example of this kind of model:

(1) Questions get at processes rather than 'variance.' Process questions ask 'how' rather than 'whether or not,' or 'how much' (Maxwell, 2005: 74–75).
(2) Researchers normally move back and forth among data collection, data, analysis, study design and focus, and emerging theory. However the GIQM allows for the use of existing theory in developing one's question as well as in interpreting results (Maxwell, 2005: 43–47).
(3) Samples are purposeful ones that allow theoretical (cross population) generalizations (Maxwell, 2005: 115–116).
(4) Analysis of data begins with the first observation and continues as additional data are collected.
(5) Researchers write copious memos of many sorts (concept maps, interpretive memos, research process memos) from the start of the project.
(6) Coding focuses on themes and sometimes theoretical categories.
(7) Data collection stops when additional cases no longer add new information.

Most of these points require little additional explanation. However, since some readers may be unfamiliar with the distinction between variance and process questions and others may not have learned about cross-population generalization, I will elaborate upon each of these topics.

Variance vs. process questions

At least two or three times a year, students will come to me with a question having to do with the effect of one variable on another while at the same time telling me that they want to do a qualitative study with a purposeful sample of one category of cases. For example, the student may want to know what practices lead to the best learning outcomes in an on-line course. In other words, the student wants to know the relative effects of variables X_1, X_2, and X_4 on variation in Y. For this kind of question, researchers need to design a true experiment that randomly assigns treatments to two or more comparison groups or use data from a survey with a relatively large random sample. These designs allow one to calculate effect sizes statistically, something that one simply cannot do without either a random sample or random assignment within a subject pool. If the student wanted to gain an understanding of the various ways in which students structure their on-line learning experiences and discover a variety of real life contingencies that affect the learning process, then using focused open-ended interviews with a purposeful sample would make sense.

Cross-population generalizations

As Maxwell (2005) and others (Patton, 1990; Schutt, 2004) have explained, the logic of generalizing from non-probability samples is very different from that governing statistical generalization. Rather than generalizing results from a sample to the population from which that sample was chosen as one does in survey research, qualitative researchers describe their samples in so much detail that readers can then decide whether or not to generalize conclusions to similar cases observed by other researchers. The criteria for making such decisions are theoretical rather than statistical. In their Appendix to *Awareness of Dying*, Glaser and Strauss (1965:191–192) describe this generalization procedure as 'the discounting process.' For example, in deciding whether or not to apply findings from my study of 'Urban University' janitors (Hood, 1988) to other janitors, it would be important to know whether or not the other janitors were also members of the American Federation of State, County, and Municipal Employee (AFSCME) union working at a public university that was forcing them to change from night to day shift. However, the general finding that the timing of work can change the nature of work can be and has been generalized to other categories of shift workers in many settings (Melbin, 1987).

In order to generalize findings from a single case or category of cases to similar ones in other populations, any kind of qualitative researcher needs to be able to answer the question: 'What is my case a case of?' What is theoretically important about my case? In the janitor study, I was looking at 'dirty work' that was both more visible and more stigmatizing by day than it was at night. My findings could therefore apply to other dirty work done in shifts.

Whether the researcher is doing an ethnography, narrative analysis, or small sample interview study, many or all of the GIQM traits are likely to characterize a study that is both inductive and qualitative. Because Grounded Theory methods are both inductive and qualitative and because Glaser and Strauss's work has helped to shape qualitative methods in the social sciences over the past 40 years, several elements of Grounded Theory overlap those of the GIQM. This overlap most likely contributes to the confusion researchers experience when attempting to use GT methods. What, then, are the key elements of Grounded Theory, and which of these set Grounded Theory apart from the GIQM?

GROUNDED THEORY (1967)

The key components of Grounded Theory as described in *Discovery* (Glaser & Strauss, 1967) are:

(1) A spiral of cycles of data collection, coding, analysis, writing, design, theoretical categorization, and data collection.
(2) The constant comparative analysis of cases with each other and to *theoretical categories* throughout each cycle.
(3) *A theoretical sampling process based upon categories developed from ongoing data analysis.*
(4) The size of sample is determined by the '*theoretical saturation*' of categories rather than by the need for demographic 'representativeness,' or simply lack of 'additional information' from new cases.
(5) The resulting *theory* is developed inductively from data rather than tested by data, although the developing theory is continuously refined and checked by data.
(6) Codes '*emerge*' from data and are not imposed *a priori* upon it.
(7) The substantive and/or formal theory outlined in the final report takes into account all the variations in the data and conditions associated with these variations. The report is an *analytical product rather than a purely descriptive account. Theory development is the goal.*

At first glance, the GT and GIQM models appear to be very similar. However a closer look will discern the major difference between the GIQM and GT which is the emphasis upon discovery of new theory developed from data. Although the GIQM allows for this kind of discovery, it does not *require* it. As Maxwell admits, his own dissertation study of the Inuit in Canada (2005: 45) suffered from his framing the results in terms of two competing pre-existing theories. Although Glaser and Strauss do not rule out the possibility that pre-existing theory may prove to be relevant to grounded theories, they advise that we compare our new theoretical findings to those in the literature after we have developed our grounded theories from the data (1967: 34).

COMPARING THE GENERIC MODEL TO GROUNDED THEORY

I have summarized the differences between the two models in Table 7.1. The main difference between the two is that Grounded Theory is guided by the theoretical relevance of each additional slice of data, and new data are selected because of their probable theoretical importance. Glaser and Strauss (1967: 46–47) even go so far as to say that after having developed one's core categories, one can save time on transcription by not transcribing material that is irrelevant to those categories (1967: 69). This focus on emerging theory and theory driven data collection is very different from data collection in conventional ethnographies which strives to provide thick description of all that can be observed in a given setting regardless of theoretical relevance.

Using Table 7.1 as a guide, I will compare the two models systematically. For this comparison, I have chosen David Karp's (1985) study of the academic careers of aging professors. This very interesting and well-written small-sample qualitative study is one of a great many examples of research attempting to follow GT guidelines but which is actually using the Generic Inductive Qualitative Model. I chose this study because the author tried to use both theoretical sampling and constant comparative analysis and because he directly cited Glaser and Strauss (1967). There are, no doubt, many other examples that could be used to illustrate the difference between the GIQM and GT, but since Karp's study is a very good illustration, I have chosen to use it, with all due apologies to the author of this very interesting article.

Question
Whereas research governed by the generic model may ask descriptive and interpretive questions such as 'How do female professors' careers differ from those of their male colleagues?' Grounded Theory research typically elucidates a process. As Kathy Charmaz (2006) points out, the titles of GT studies typically start with a gerund, and these studies focus on action and process. A GIQM small-sample interview study such as David Karp's (1985) research on gender, family, and academic careers often starts with equal numbers of interviewees

Table 7.1   Comparison of the Generic Inductive Qualitative Model with Grounded Theory

	Generic Model	Grounded Theory
Question	Descriptive, process, interpretive	Process primarily
Sample	Purposeful; may be either contingent or *a priori*; criteria may be demographic.	Purposeful; criteria are theoretical and contingent upon categories developed from initial data. Sample is never chosen based upon *a priori* criteria.
Research process	Inductive and *usually* cyclical moving back and forth among questions, data gathering, and data analysis.	Inductive and *must* be cyclical.
Data analysis	Focus on themes and interpretation comparing cases to each other.	Focus on development of theoretical categories via the constant comparative method comparing data both to each other and to theoretical categories.
Memos	Memoing is critical and memos may be of many types.	Memoing is essential. Memos are more often interpretive and theoretical.
Criteria for ending data collection	Added data yield little new information or insight.	Added data do not serve to further develop key theoretical categories
Generalizability	Theoretical or cross population generalizability to like cases.	Theoretical generalizability via the 'discounting process.'
Range of theory	Substantive to middle range formal theories.	Substantive to middle range formal theories.
Design	Develops and becomes increasingly focused during the research process. Goal is interpretation of rich data.	Develops and becomes increasingly focused during the research process. Goal is a theory that emerges from the data analysis.

in two demographic categories and results in a detailed interpretive analysis of the difference between respondents in those two categories. A Grounded Theory study, in contrast, might have developed a question such as 'How do women become relegated to the lower ranks of the academic ladder?' or 'What process produces "the higher, the fewer pattern"?' Rather than focusing on a comparison between men's and women's careers, Karp would have used the results of this comparison as a starting place and then might have gone on to discover key elements in the academic ladder that distinguish between upwardly mobile and stagnated careers. He might then have sampled on one or more of those categories instead of (or in addition to) gender. If the way in which careers are gendered emerged as a key contextual category, Karp would sample for the gendering of careers. Are all careers equally gendered? What conditions contribute to the gendering process? How does the gendering process work? These are the kinds of questions grounded theorists ask. Instead, Karp presents his results descriptively as modal categories. He observes, for example, that:

> Because of the time clock they are on, the women are not, like the men their age, thinking about *leaving a mark*. They are too busy *making a mark* (Karp, 1985: 17).

In other words, Karp's detailed descriptive analysis becomes a comparison and contrast between the patterns of men's and women's careers in the context of marriage and family. A Grounded Theory study would instead have focused on processes and would have resulted in new core categories around which those processes were organized. Theory emerging from this process would do much more than illustrate the ways in which married men's and women's academic careers differ; it would also show us a mechanism underlying that difference and might even offer a formal theory about the gendering process that could be applied in settings other than academia.

Sampling

Qualitative studies typically use some form of purposeful sampling. The researcher may decide ahead of time to study 'academic males in their fifties' as Karp did and then use a snowball or other sampling frame to locate people fitting that description. When researchers decide what categories of people or situations to sample and how many of each they want to include, they are using what I call an '*a priori*' purposeful sample. However, if on the basis of their analysis of the first several cases they decide to sample other categories, they are using a 'contingent' purposeful sample. When Karp decided to add an equal number of middle-aged women to his study of middle-aged academic men after interviewing a few women by way of comparison, he changed his sampling process from an *a priori* to a contingent one.

In selecting his sample, Karp took care to 'reflect variation by gender, academic discipline, and type of discipline,' but he kept age constant ending up with 23 males and 24 females with an average age of 54 years (1985: 11) (see Figure 7.2). Karp describes his sampling strategy as follows:

SELECTED CHARACTERISTICS OF THE STUDY SAMPLE

	MALES	FEMALES
Number of Respondents	23	24
Average Age	54.7	54.3
Academic Rank		
Assistant	1	9
Associate	9	8
Full	13	7
Average Number of Years Since Last Professional Degree	23.8	15.5
Discipline Area		
Natural Sciences	6	3
Social Sciences	12	13
Humanities	5	8

Figure 7.2   Table I from Karp 1985.

The sample is not a statistically representative one, but is a 'theoretical' sample, the result of a 'snowball' process. After each interview, the respondent was asked for additional names of persons 'of whom it would be useful for me to interview' (Karp, 1985: 10).

In describing his sampling procedure as he does, Karp follows a common pattern of equating purposeful with theoretical sampling (Coyne, 1997) as well as assuming that the snowball process is an attribute of theoretical sampling. In fact, as Coyne and others have pointed out, all theoretical sampling is purposeful sampling, but not all purposeful sampling is 'theoretical' in the way that Glaser and Strauss are using the term. What would Karp have done differently if he had used theoretical sampling, and what difference might this change have made in his study?

Karp started with an interest in the ways in which professional men might be restructuring their work identities and adjusting priorities among work, family, and other life spheres. He purposefully chose middle-aged academic men and used snowball sampling to acquire a sample of males who varied by rank and disciplinary area. Because these men were all middle-aged, only one was still an assistant professor. After interviewing 10 of these men, Karp decided to try interviewing some women of the same age just to see what he would find. The results were so interesting that Karp then chose to add an equal complement of women resulting in a final sample of 23 men and 24 women with an average age of 54 years. Among Karp's findings was his observation that women's careers began later in life so that, even though the women and men were of the same chronological age, the women regarded their male colleagues as their 'seniors.' In the process of building his sample, Karp used snowball sampling to locate respondents to fit his purposeful sampling frame that was defined by gender, age, discipline, and rank.

In contrast to Karp's contingent and purposeful sampling strategy, a GT theoretical sampling process would look very different. Rather than filling cells defined by demographic criteria chosen because they made a difference in outcome, Karp would have used theoretical codes emerging from his analysis such as 'devotion to male's career' or 'costs of getting back in to career' to guide his sampling. And instead of using concepts from the work and family literature, such as 'two-person/one career' to describe his findings, Karp might have more fully developed some of his emic codes such as 'the standard version,' a term that his women respondents used to describe careers characterized by detours into marriage and family. As one of Karp's respondents said:

We were programmed for the standard version of what an educated woman was supposed to do. You were supposed to marry an educated man and bring up children that you were supposed to educate (Karp, 1985: 13).

A focus on the 'standard version' code might have led Karp to look for women who did not follow the standard path and to compare them with women who did. A Grounded Theory version of the code might be 'adopting the standard version.' A GT researcher would then want to know which conditions allow women to deviate from the standard version. What conditions push women into the standard path? Does sexuality affect the choice of the standard path? Karp might then have sampled on one or more of these conditions. Although Karp does not say so, it appears that all of his respondents were in heterosexual marriages. Would partnered lesbians also have been propelled into 'adopting the standard version'?

Karp mentions that some women were told by department chairs (as I was in the 1980s) that professional work and raising a family were not consistent with each other for women (Karp, 1985: 15). Were all the women told this? Were there any examples of women in family-friendly settings? Instead of building his analysis on 'typical' cases, Karp could have looked for more atypical ones and sampled on 'family friendliness' of institutions or 'conditions for retention.' Had he done so, Karp might have developed a theory about what attributes of a work place affect the ease with which academics can combine work and family.

In addition to work and family issues, Karp's study also deals with the concept of 'professional' as opposed to chronological age. Women who had entered academic life after raising families were the age-peers of full-professor male colleagues but the professional-peers of much younger male assistant professors. Karp reports that men and women had different interpretations of the same chronological age and that women, unlike men, were painfully aware of the difference between the two kinds of 'aging.' As one of his respondents said:

> The only reason I know my age is that my doctors asked me the other day. A big thing for me has to do with the difference between professional and chronological age. Professional age makes so much more sense in terms of what is meaningful out there. So you use your degree as the basis for determining your professional age. It has nothing to do with feeling terribly old. It has to do with getting recognition out there for your profession (Karp, 1985: 22).

The notion of varieties of 'aging' yardsticks and their contexts and consequences could be the basis for theoretical sampling that would have led the study in still a different direction with 'marking age' as a core category. As the reader can see, theoretical sampling can go on forever. Memoing and focusing on one pivotal core category help the GT researcher avoid non-productive tangents. Building one's study on theoretical rather than demographic categories is more likely to result in new theory instead of either pure description or a simple analysis of the differences between two demographic categories.

Research process

Karp describes his research process as follows:

> Like most qualitative research studies, the analytical foci of this project have evolved as the data were collected (Karp, 1985: 11).

Karp also describes how he wrote copious memos and revised his interview guide as the focus of the study evolved. This cyclical process is typical both of

Grounded Theory and some GIQM studies. However, let us compare Karp's process to Glaser and Strauss's description of theoretical sampling:

> Theoretical sampling is the process of data collection for generating theory whereby the analyst jointly collects, codes, and analyses his data and decides what data to collect next and where to find them, in order to develop theory as it emerges (Glaser & Strauss, 1967: 45)

Since Karp's process was guided by purposeful sampling that was not also theoretical, he did not use the research cycle 'in order to develop his theory as it emerges,' and therein lies the difference between a GIQM spiral and a GT one.

Data analysis

Karp's analysis focused on comparison of cases to each other and made frequent use of concepts in the work family literature such as Spradley and Mann's (1975) idea that women in male worlds are subject to a 'handicap rule.' By concentrating on the comparison of the men's and women's data and not comparing data against emerging theoretical codes, Karp left out a key element of constant comparative analysis. Comparing bits of data to each other is a place to start rather than end the process of constant comparison. Here is Glaser and Strauss's description of the constant comparative process:

> While coding an incident for a category, compare it with the previous incidents in the same and different groups coded in the same category … This constant comparison of incidents very soon starts to generate theoretical properties of the category (Glaser & Strauss, 1967: 106).

In his analysis, Karp describes some theoretical codes that might well have been worth developing. For example, Karp talks about the process of 'getting back in' and the price some women paid for it. 'Getting back in' could have been developed as a core code. Women asking what they were worth, divorces resulting from women's choices, and the actions of male gatekeepers might all have been related codes some of which could be properties of the category 'getting back in.' In this instance, Karp's study might have become one about 'getting back in.' Karp instead thought that 'the logic of constant comparative analysis require(d) that we draw on the experiences of men in order to place the women's lives in proper perspective' (1985: 10). Once more, by using demographic rather than inductively developed theoretical categories to guide his analysis, Karp lost the power of the Grounded Theory methods that he was trying to employ. Thus, instead of a Grounded Theory, Professor Karp produced a fascinating, nuanced, and insightful description of the ways in which re-entry women's careers differ from those of their established male colleagues.

Memos

Writing interpretive memos throughout the research process is a critical component of both the GIQM and GT methods. Karp tells us that 'consistent with the process of inductive grounded theory' he wrote many memos on emerging themes in the data and refocused his interviews as necessary (Karp, 1985: 11–12). Using memos to focus one's inquiry and staying close to the data in order to 'clarify areas of substantive richness' is an excellent idea. Doing so is the best way of avoiding a formless mass of unanalyzable data at the end of one's study. And Karp is right that memoing is a critical part of grounded theory. However, GT memos are more heavily focused on 'theoretical' rather than 'substantive' richness. Both the GIQM and GT rely heavily on memoing, but GT memos are more often used to develop theoretical categories and their properties. Nonetheless, I suspect that a study of memos written for each kind of study would find some overlap in memo types. It is the type of memoing and not the existence of it that sets GT apart from the GIQM (see Chapter 12).

Criteria for ending data collection

Whereas statistical sampling ends when the researcher has collected data from all available elements in the predetermined sample, *inductive and contingent* non-probability sampling ends when the 'saturation point' is reached. That point is normally determined by the discovery that additional interviews are yielding so little new information that more interviews would be a waste of time (Schutt, 2004: 299). Grounded Theory also uses the concept of saturation to describe the point at which one may stop collecting new data. However, 'theoretical saturation' of categories is very different from the concept of substantive saturation commonly used in the GIQM. The concept of 'theoretical saturation' is as difficult to explain as it is for most researchers to understand. Using my own research on two-job families, I will do my best (Hood, 1983).

The core category in *Becoming a Two-Job Family* (Hood, 1983) is 'provider role definition.' My study revolves around the process whereby and the conditions under which the male provider role is redefined by two-job couples after a wife returns to work. As I added more data to my study by adding couples, interviewing husbands alone, and re-interviewing both husbands and wives, I developed codes for secondary, and co-providing spouses as well as co-provider, traditional provider, and super-provider husbands. Although the provider role terms I used were not original, my categories were completely grounded in the data. For example, traditional or primary provider husbands typically described their wives' earnings as 'icing on the cake' and insisted that their wives' money was used for 'extras' while their own money 'put the food on the table' (see Hood, 1986). In addition, I developed codes for the relative importance of work/family roles for each respondent. Role priorities, I discovered, were directly related to the ease with which a person *relinquished* all or part of a former role. Men who could not think of themselves as anything but a paycheck had a much harder time sharing the provider role (as well as housework and parenting) than did men who saw themselves as fathers and husbands as well. Since I had to finish my dissertation, I cannot claim to have fully saturated the 'provider role definition' category, but I did use all the relevant data in the many interviews I did with the 16 couples and managed a few rounds of theoretical sampling. More theoretical sampling would no doubt have yielded richer theory and full theoretical saturation.

Generalizability

The GIQM and GT are most similar with regard to the way in which generalizations are made. In fact, the rule for generalizing from non-probability samples extends across all kinds of studies using any kind of non-probability sample. Known variously as 'cross population' generalization or the discounting process, the rule simply states that one can generalize to cases similar to the ones the researcher has studied. However, GT researchers are interested less in the generalization of specific substantive findings and more in the generalizability of formal theory that can be applied across a variety of settings. For example, in her work on people dealing with chronic illness, Charmaz found that people who could not predict the outcomes of their illnesses managed uncertainty by 'living one day at a time' (Charmaz, 1991: 178–181). Building on this very well elaborated substantive theory about chronic illness, other Grounded Theorists might theoretically sample a variety of 'uncertainty contexts' in which people are confronted with personal or health crises with unpredictable outcomes. Such contexts might include families of prisoners charged with first-degree murder, children anticipating a parental divorce and the dissolution of their families, or couples hoping to become parents through the process of open adoption. In each case, the outcome and its consequences are unpredictable and uncontrollable. People faced with such situations often do so 'one day at a time' because to do otherwise risks overwhelming disappointment or paralyzing fear. By extending theoretical sampling to other contexts and using the constant comparative process to elaborate and refine the 'one day at a time' strategy, a Grounded Theorist might move Charmaz's substantive theory about managing chronic illness towards a middle range formal theory about strategies for dealing with uncertain outcomes in a variety of frightening situations.

Range of theory

Both GIQM and GT often result in substantive theory that can be generalized to other similar cases. However, the process of theoretical sampling and theoretical saturation of categories allows the GT researcher to develop both substantive and formal theory of the middle range that is applicable far beyond the setting in which it was developed. Nonetheless, just as Karp did not pursue the many possible theoretical threads discovered in his GIQM research, GT researchers, under pressure to finish dissertations or publish articles, often stop after uncovering a process or describing a single core code. To move towards formal theory, one must go further. In her study of women recovering from depression, Schreiber developed a core category that could be generalized beyond the people she studied but probably only to others like them (Schreiber, 1998). Schreiber discovered that the process of 'cluing in,' a shift in Gestalt of self-understanding, distinguished between women who recovered and those who did not. As Schreiber writes:

> After cluing in a woman is seeing with clarity, a time when the woman is able to look back and accept where she has been and what she has experienced (Schreiber, 1998: 274).

By using theoretical sampling to look for women who had and had not 'clued in,' Schreiber was able to saturate this category. Schreiber could then conclude that 'cluing in' was a necessary condition for recovery from depression for depressed women, and we may very well be able to extend her findings to recovery from depression in general.

Design
Both the GIQM and GT models develop and focus the research design as the study progresses, but the GT study is driven by the developing theory, whereas the GIQM study is driven by substantive import.

ORTHODOXY VS. POWER

By now, I hope that the reader understands the difference between the Generic Inductive Qualitative Model and Grounded Theory. As we have seen, the difference is (1) theoretical sampling, (2) constant comparison of data to theoretical categories, and (3) focus on the development of theory via theoretical saturation of categories rather than substantive verifiable findings. (Given that these three essential properties of Grounded Theory are also the most difficult for researchers to understand and apply, perhaps we should refer to them as the 'Troublesome Trinity.') As you may have noticed, I have referred primarily to Glaser and Strauss (1967) and not as much to the subsequent work of Corbin and Strauss (1990) or even Charmaz (2006). However, I think that all three brands of GT (Glaserian, Straussian, and Charmazian) rest upon these three principles even though they vary somewhat in how each is implemented. Whereas Glaser sometimes thinks of categories as variables and Charmaz chooses not to, both advocate consistently comparing pieces of data to emerging categories, and that process is critical to Grounded Theory.

Lest the reader be tempted to accuse me of advocating a fundamentalist, Trinitarian orthodoxy using *The Discovery of Grounded Theory* as my bible, I should point out that this orthodoxy is limited to the three principles. Beyond those principles, I see a great deal of room for grounded theorists to vary from the methods and epistemology outlined in *The Discovery of Grounded Theory*. As far as I am concerned, one can, as Charmaz has, use a constructivist rather than an objectivist approach and still retain the power of GT, and one may, as Lempert does in Chapter 12, incorporate standpoint theory and the use of literature reviews into GT without giving up theoretical power. I would not go so far as to encourage forcing data into pre-existing categories, of course, but I see no need to be purist about the use of the literature to develop one's theoretical sensitivity as long as one's codes are entirely supported by the data. However, without theoretical sampling, constant comparison of data to theoretical categories, and theoretical saturation of categories, one should not claim to be using Grounded Theory.

CONCLUSION

Unfortunately only a handful of studies have used the Troublesome Trinity correctly. Both Charmaz's study of chronic illness (Charmaz, 1991) and Schreiber's study of depression (Schreiber, 1998) are examples. Most other researchers claiming to be doing GT confuse purposeful with theoretical sampling and misunderstand the constant comparative process. For many, the term 'grounded theory' refers simply to attaching codes to data or not using statistics. Claiming to use Grounded Theory without using any of the most important attributes of the approach is misleading and has made the term 'grounded theory' meaningless in the social science literature. GT is a powerful tool for discovering theory in inductive qualitative studies. However, qualitative researchers will not have this tool at their disposal until and unless they understand the difference between Grounded Theory with capital letters and the Generic Inductive Qualitative Model.

REFERENCES

Charmaz, K. (1991). *Good Days, Bad Days: The Self in Chronic Illness and Time.* New Brunswick: Rutgers University Press.

Charmaz, K. (2006). *Constructing Grounded Theory: A Practical Guide Through Qualitative Analysis.* London: SAGE.

Corbin, J. and A. Strauss (1990). *The Basics of Qualitative Research.* Thousand Oaks, CA: SAGE.

Coyne, I. T. (1997). Sampling in qualitative research. Purposeful and theoretical sampling; merging or clear boundaries? *Journal of Advanced Nursing,* **26**, 623–630.

Glaser, B. G. and A. L. Strauss (1967). *The Discovery of Grounded Theory.* Chicago: Aldine.

Hood, J. C. (1983). *Becoming a Two-Job Family.* New York: Praeger.

Hood, J. C. (1986). The provider role: Its meaning and measurement. *Journal of Marriage & Family,* **48**, 349.

Hood, J. C. (1988). From night to day: Timing and the management of custodial work. *Journal of Contemporary Ethnography,* **17**, 96–116.

Karp, D. A. (1985). Gender, academic careers, and the social psychology of aging. *Qualitative Sociology,* **8**, 9–28.

Maxwell, J. A. (2005). *Qualitative Research Design: An Interactive Approach.* Thousand Oaks, CA: SAGE.

Melbin, M. (1987). *Night as Frontier: Colonizing the World after Dark.* New York, London: Free Press, Collier Macmillan.

Patton, M. Q. (1990). *Qualitative Evaluation and Research Methods.* Newbury Park, CA: SAGE.

Schreiber, R. (1998). Clueing in: A guide to solving the puzzle of self for women recovering from depression. *Health Care For Women International,* **19**, 269–288.

Schutt, R. K. (2004). *Investigating the Social World.* Thousand Oaks, CA: Pine Forge.

Spradley, J. P. and B. J. Mann (1975). *The Cocktail Waitress: Woman's Work in a Man's World.* New York: Wiley.

PART III

Grounded Theory in Practice

8

Grounding Categories

Ian Dey

Grounded Theory advances the claim that categories are 'grounded' through the process by which they are generated. This claim raises several questions, not less interesting or important for apparently being obvious. First, we must ask what categories are and what role they play in the analytic process. Second, we must ask what it means to 'ground' categories. What claims to knowledge does this imply? Our task is to clarify what kind of aspirations the grounding of categories might imply for analysis. Third, we must ask how this 'grounding' can be accomplished. This question concerns not just the status of knowledge but the practicalities of its production. One reason grounded theory has become so popular as a form of qualitative research is the attention its exponents have given to addressing such practicalities. The expansion of postgraduate education and research has generated demand for more explicit procedural guidelines for qualitative analysis. This has prompted the 'codification' of grounded theory, expressed in the formalization of its analytic procedures and an emphasis on 'coding' as a major analytic procedure or even its analytic core. This codification has been encouraged by the development of software to support qualitative analysis, often tacitly inspired by or explicitly supportive of a grounded theory approach. We must ask, therefore, how coding can contribute to the grounding of categories and what are the practical challenges of this analytic approach.

Though sometimes equated, coding does not exhaust the analytic process; one can even question whether it is integral to it. There are elements in grounded theory which point in different directions: a focus on process, an emphasis on theoretical sensitivity, and the centrality of a storyline around which analysis can coalesce. Though eclipsed somewhat by the centrality assigned to coding, these raise further questions about the role of categories and the ways they can be grounded in the analysis. Indeed, it is perhaps through addressing these questions that we can anticipate the most innovative methodological developments in qualitative analysis. In grounded theory, coding is usually conceived within a particular analytic perspective, centred on 'theoretical sampling' and aspiring to 'theoretical saturation'. But the practical import of these methodological injunctions is problematic. A further question concerns whether and how categories can be grounded when theoretical sampling is limited and theoretical saturation unattainable. To translate: how do we know when our categories are sufficiently grounded that we can stop producing and analysing data? A final question (at least for this chapter) requires reflection on reflexivity and replication. Reflexivity is in fashion, and we must therefore ask what and how it can contribute to the grounding of categories. But it remains equally pertinent to ask whether and what replication can contribute to this task. In addressing these questions about the grounding of categories, my aim is to stimulate reflection about underlying methodological assumptions rather than to identify and illustrate a set of particular procedures. Despite my occasional foray into prescription, I am less intent on telling readers what to do than in encouraging them to think critically about what they are doing.

To begin at the beginning: what are categories and what role do they play in the analytic process? Glaser and Strauss described categories as 'conceptual elements of a theory' (1967: 36). Categories emerge initially from a close engagement with data, but can achieve a higher level of abstraction through a process of 'constant comparison' which allows their theoretical elaboration and integration. To stay with a well-known example, the category 'perceptions of social loss' among nurses is elaborated by exploring the various 'loss rationales' that nurses develop, or investigating the implications of differing perceptions of loss for the quality of patient care (Glaser & Strauss, 1967: 42). We can think of categories as forming the theoretical bones of the analysis, later fleshed out by identifying and analysing in detail their various properties and relations.

Glaser (1978) presents the meaning of categories in terms of the indicators through which they are observed. Thus the category social loss is not to be defined abstractly but in terms of particular ways in which nurses respond to patients. However, indicators are used not to substantiate a category empirically through description but rather to elaborate the category through exploring its different dimensions (Glaser, 1978: 43). Though not endorsing the concept-indicator model, Charmaz (2006) characterizes it as 'a method of theory construction in which the researcher constructs concepts that count for relationships defined in the empirical data and each concept rests on empirical indications' such that 'the concept is "grounded" in the data' (2006: 187).

Nevertheless, categories play a dual role in grounded theory which transcends the classical definition of concepts in terms of indicators. They can be both 'analytic' and 'sensitizing'. They allow us to conceptualize the key analytic features of phenomena, but also to communicate a meaningful picture of those phenomena in everyday terms. They allow us to classify phenomena, but also to construct relationships among the different elements of a theory. They provide a parsimonious conceptual structure which allows for rich theoretical elaboration. This raises some questions about the role of categories in grounded theory. Can categories be analytic and sensitizing, rich and parsimonious, explain as well as classify? In envisaging a dual role for categories Glaser and Strauss went beyond classical conceptions of classification and anticipated future developments in the study of categorization in cognitive psychology and linguistics (Dey, 1999).

These disciplines treat categorization as central to thinking, 'virtually all cognitive activity involves and is dependent on the process of categorizing' (Bruner et al., 1986: 246), but also as problematic. How do we use categories to sort out and order our experience of the world? The grounding of categories depends on understanding this process, especially insofar as grounded theory relies on naturalistic enquiry that emulates rather than repudiates everyday thinking.

In the classical model, categories are based on comparison: 'A category is, simply, a range of discriminably different events that are treated "as if" equivalent' (Bruner et al., 1986: 231). We identify similarities between various features of objects and events, which we use as a basis for formulating categories and assigning phenomena to them. This account assumes that categories are identified through correspondence to key features in the phenomena that we can observe. Categorization proceeds according to set criteria or rules which allow the unambiguous assignation of phenomena to designated categories. In the classical model, categories are indeed categorical and express a clear and complete conceptualization of phenomena in terms of common features. A well-defined category will have attributes that are jointly sufficient and singly necessary to identify the category. Only members of the category will possess all these attributes, and all the members of the category will possess each one of them. Thus 'the key characteristics of defined categories are that membership is all or none and that membership can be unambiguously determined by reference to a rule' (Medin & Barsalou, 1987: 461).

Research has identified several problems with the classical account. One is that categorization is always approximate and provisional; though it may converge on an adequate and stable representation of invariant features of phenomena it is always subject to revision through further observations of 'confusable alternatives' (Harnad, 1987). Another problem is that for many categories 'it is not possible to specify a rule that identifies all of its members and only its members' (Medin & Barsalou, 1987: 461). For example, not all birds fly, and not all creatures that fly are birds. Research has also found that often categorization does not proceed through the invocation of rules at all but through comparison with recalled or prototypical exemplars (Rosch, 1978). When we categorize a chicken as a bird, we tend not to review its features systematically in terms of some complicated taxonomy (beak, wings, feathers, flight); we prefer to think of its resemblance to some prototypical example, like a robin.

This implies that categories lack clear boundaries defined by an unambiguous set of criteria; categories are fuzzy and category membership is a matter of degree (McNeil & Freiberger, 1994). There may be no characteristics common to all members of a category, just as Wittgenstein (1953) suggested that the category 'game' applies to activities bearing only a family resemblance with no features common to all. Though we can recognize card games, ball games, board games, and mind games as 'games', we cannot readily identify a set of characteristics shared by all of them. We can recognize similarities (some are competitive, some involve skill) but there is no single defining feature common to every game (cf. Hahn & Ramscar, 2001: 257–258).

The 'Roschian revolution' focused attention on the role of prototypes or exemplars in categorization and inspired a variety of theory-based accounts of categorization (Hahn & Ramscar, 2001; McGarty, 1999). Murphy and Medin (1985) for example argue that category coherence is not achieved by comparing features but is theoretically informed: we have a 'theory' that birds are warm-blooded creatures with wings and feathers which often fly (cf. McGarty, 1999). From this perspective, categories and categorization depend on our conceptual understandings of the world, rather than on similarity between characteristics. Lakoff (1987) too rejects the classical account of categories as (more or less accurate) representations of the world because categorical judgements are informed by an underlying cognitive context that is shaped through interaction. Thus the category 'bachelor' cannot be reduced to a rule identifying men who are not married: we would hesitate to describe the Pope as a bachelor. It is applied with respect to what Lakoff calls an 'idealized cognitive model' of society involving assumptions about marriage, eligibility, and marriageable age. Thus categories are not simply generated by data, but through judgement in terms of some cognitive frame of reference by which we make sense of experience. According to Lakoff, these idealized cognitive models are generated through basic experience and categories are often derived (or extended) through the use of metonymy or metaphor (cf. Lakoff & Johnson, 1980). Their invocation is motivated by the varying cognitive contexts in which category judgements are made. In the same vein, research has shown that 'similarity is an insufficient principle to constrain category formation' since 'perceived similarity changes in context-dependent ways and with knowledge and experience' (McGarty, 1999: 59). The emphasis on theory in the sense of underpinning conceptual understandings has become so pervasive that a recent review sets out to defend similarity as a central element in categorization (Hahn & Ramscar, 2001). However, one can recognize the importance of theory without discounting the role of similarity in forming and utilizing categories.

The dual role of categories envisaged in grounded theory is quite consistent with an approach that emphasizes theory as well as comparison. The recognition that categories are theoretically informed (or motivated) creates a conceptual space for the sensitizing role of categories that is recognized in grounded theory but that is otherwise hard to find in the classic concept-indicator model.

Lakoff's account of the idealized and often metaphorical nature of knowledge provides a perspective within which sensitizing concepts can do their work. The theoretical approach also explicitly acknowledges a causal as well as a comparative dimension in categorization. Research by Ahn and Dennis (1999) suggests that causal status is important in categorical judgements. In categorizing, people take account of causal relations, attaching more weight to causal powers or attributes (e.g. with wings a bird can fly) than consequential ones (e.g. so it can nest in trees). Thus categorization may play a central role in causal inference, but not only or even mainly through the constant comparison of events to identify concurrence in the classic mode. In everyday thinking, people are more inclined to look for and use information about causal mechanisms than to rely on covariation. This may be partly due to the high information costs of identifying or communicating about covariation, but as McGarty notes it is also consistent with the use of theoretical principles (or entities) to characterize and explain behaviour. Thus categorization in everyday thinking may already invoke or imply an explanation, supporting the central explanatory (and parsimonious) role which categories are assigned in grounded theory.

That categories are already implicated in explanations (and vice versa) underlines another important point to emerge from recent psychological research. In the classical model, the main role of categories is to describe phenomena through classification. But categories can play other roles important in analysis. We can use categories to discriminate among new data or to make inferences. Indeed, for some psychologists, the ability to make inferences is the critical role of categorization. For example, I may want to know if something is an apple, not to distinguish it from some other object but so that I can eat it. It is worth distinguishing these different roles, for they have different requirements and implications. To discriminate effectively requires what psychologists call high 'cue validity', this means that having an attribute implies a high probability of belonging to a category. To infer attributes from category membership, however, requires high 'category validity', a high probability that belonging to the category means having the attribute. These requirements do differ. We can infer that every bachelor is an adult male (this has high category validity) but being an adult male has low cue validity for being a bachelor. Another potentially important distinction is between the role of categories in explanation and communication, since the way we generate categories for explanation may differ from how they are 'justified, compared and communicated with other people' (McGarty, 1999: 242).

Take grounded theory itself as an example. What attributes of grounded theory have high category validity? In other words, what do we know for sure about a theory which claims to be a grounded theory? We might expect that it aims to theorize a social process; that it focuses on understanding the intentions and strategies of actors involved in that process; that it proceeds through exploring the process in a variety of settings; and that it involves systematic analysis of data through categorization and comparison. However, given that the various guidelines and interpretations of grounded theory can be 'opaque and confusing' (LaRossa, 2005: 838) even this set of core characteristics is likely to be contentious; LaRossa himself identifies a quite different set of principles, in which for example 'the micro-analysis of written texts' figures prominently. What about high cue validity? We might expect a study that generates theory by analysing data through a set of systematic coding procedures to be a grounded theory, though there is no agreement as to the appropriate set of coding procedures to adopt. Though coding may confer high cue validity (an understandable concern for aspiring graduate students) note that it did not figure at all in the attributes I proposed with respect to high category validity. This lack of agreement about the basic characteristics of grounded theory may itself be attributed to differences between the explanatory and communicative roles of categorization, since the purpose of legitimation figures more fully in the latter.

There are several points worth emphasizing in this account of categories and their role in analysis. One fundamental point is that it is important to take account of on-going research on the use of categories and categorization in everyday thinking if we are to understand their role in grounded theory. Though this is a rapidly developing and changing field, research already suggests that the classical model is deficient in several respects. The reduction of concepts to indicators, the focus on features (which are given) rather than attributes (which are identified), the assumption of clear rules for assignation, unambiguous membership and crisp category boundaries, the centrality of comparison, and the critical role of similarity are all contested. In contrast, psychologists now emphasize resemblance to remembered or prototypical cases, motivation and context, knowledge and theory, causal relations as well as properties, inference as well as classification. The emerging picture of categories and categorization is certainly more complex, we now have several different accounts to contend with; these richer accounts are more consistent with the methodological evolution and theoretical ambitions of grounded theory.

WHAT DOES IT MEAN TO GROUND CATEGORIES?

When Glaser and Strauss wrote *The Discovery of Grounded Theory* they wanted to challenge grandiose armchair theorizing by developing a more effective means of generating theory. In place of the traditional method of deriving and testing hypotheses from existing theory they emphasized the virtue of generating theory through interaction with data. Their main message was that theory 'discovered' through data could be more relevant and productive since it would at least fit the immediate problems being investigated, as well as potentially opening up more fruitful lines of enquiry. A grounded theory was not speculative, since it derived directly from empirical observation, and was always substantive, even if it provided a basis for generating more formal and abstract theories. In this context, the grounding of theory refers to the use of data obtained through social research to generate ideas. Of course, Glaser and Strauss had some recommendations about effective ways to do this, by avoiding preconceptions, using systematic comparison, theoretical sampling, and so on. While grounding theory implies no more than the use of data to generate theory in practice, it has come to refer to some methodological guidelines to make this possible in principle.

What are these guidelines? In the light of the above discussion, it should be no surprise that we lack clear and consistent rules governing the classification of theories as grounded or otherwise. There is no agreement on what constitutes a grounded theory, only varying interpretations which bear a family resemblance. So there are various and conflicting answers to what makes a theory grounded. In the case of my own research on union opposition to redundancies (Wood & Dey, 1983), I tried to ground my theorizing about the process of resisting redundancy in a variety of ways. First, I tried to approach the subject without accepting the preconceptions of the 'industrial relations' literature, in which opposition to redundancy was typically perceived as an irrational obstacle to gains in productivity. I read more widely in fields with an interest in shopfloor organization, such as Marxism and the sociology of bureaucratic organization. This in turn helped me to realize a second aim, which was to explore in great detail and depth the accounts of key actors involved in the process. The preconceptions in the literature might have limited my capacity to listen and to hear what these activists had to say. Third, I looked at how activists tried to oppose redundancies in a variety of events and settings, so that different aspects of the process could be explored and clarified. Fourth, I analysed the resulting data systematically, categorizing contexts, events, and strategies in ways which allowed comparison and contrast, links and connections. Fifth, I tried to integrate emergent categories around a narrative which conveyed the interactive, shifting, and dynamic evolution of ideas and events. This was also a situated narrative, in that my intention was to provide a substantive account of union opposition to redundancies in a particular time and place. Had my intention been to develop more formal theory, I might have examined other forms of opposition at work in other settings. Thus my theorizing was grounded in practice through procedures which embedded emergent categories in the data being analysed.

The value of using data gathered through social research to generate ideas would hardly be controversial were it not for the persistent influence of a model of scientific endeavour which focuses almost exclusively on theoretical deduction and hypothesis testing. This model appeals to those who make comparisons (usually unfavourable) between the methodologies available to social and natural sciences. However, in relation to theory generation, it is not even a good model of natural science. It does fit well with some moments of scientific discovery; as when Einstein devised his general theory of relativity, and its prediction that light would be bent by the sun's gravity was tested during an eclipse in 1919. But even Einstein did not always develop theory by conducting thought experiments; his discovery of photoelectric activity (for which he received the Nobel Prize) was generated through his analysis of Brownian motion in a test tube. Consider also two of the most fundamental theoretical developments in modern science. Darwin's contribution to evolutionary theory was inspired by his thorough, exhaustive, and comprehensive observations of the natural world, most famously the variation in finch populations across the Galapagos Islands. More notoriously, the helical model of DNA devised by Crick and Watson was inspired by an uninvited perusal of the X-ray data taken by their colleague and rival Rosalind Franklin. Thus two of the major theoretical discoveries of modern science were generated through interaction with research data.

While the role of research data in generating theory can be readily accepted, any claim that theory can also be validated (and not just grounded) through this process of generation is more contentious. Glaser and Strauss do, at times, seem to flirt with this bolder claim. They cite the pace of social change, the short shelf life of social theories, and the difficulties of empirical testing as factors likely to limit further validation. They suggest that theory generated through interaction with data may in any case be sufficiently 'plausible' (Glaser & Strauss, 1967: 235) to seem relevant and useful to practitioners without resort to any further validation. This implies a fuller grounding of categories than would be required merely to generate theory.

Moreover, problems arise when we confuse or conflate the context of discovery with the logic of validation. As Kelle (2003: 485) argues 'the prerequisite of independent testing requires that a hypothesis is not tested with the empirical material from which it is developed'. A further prerequisite is that hypotheses are formulated with sufficient rigour to allow for a systematic confrontation with evidence. Data that provides a useful ground for generating theory usually provides a poor basis for testing it. If a theory emerges from data then that data can hardly provide the independent evidence required for a test of the theory. This is after all what keeps us in business: the research community provides the medium through which a theory can be tested, whether through replication, application, or evaluation. The requirements of discovery and validation differ. To discover theory, we can use a flexible, iterative, and adaptive approach to generating and utilizing data. In testing theory, we need to specify in advance what theoretical claims we are advancing and what data would count for their refutation or validation. Otherwise we are all too liable (given the weaknesses in our everyday thinking) to find what we are looking for in the data.

Some of the pitfalls of everyday thinking have been explored by Gilovich. We are inclined, for example, to identify patterns in data as meaningful that are a product of mere chance. Gilovich offers as an example a tendency to attribute running streaks in sport to character and behaviour (such as the acquisition or loss of confidence) rather than luck. We tend to misunderstand probability, assuming that the law of large numbers governs shorter sequences, underestimating, for example, the extent to which we might obtain a run of four heads in 20 tosses of a fair coin (the probability is 0.5). We tend to confuse necessary and sufficient causation. We tend to pay more attention to positive than negative instances. We tend to recognize or seek out evidence that confirms rather than refutes our expectations, even where we have no particular interest in the results. For example, if asked to assess whether things are similar, we look for evidence of similarity; conversely, if asked to assess whether things differ, we look for evidence of dissimilarity (Gilovich, 1993: 37). If we are interested in the results, our own preferences are liable to influence both the amount and the kind of information we examine: we are particularly poor judges of our own abilities and actions (Gilovich, 1993: 77–82). Where we do seek out countervailing evidence (nowadays a standard injunction in qualitative analysis) our inclination may be to explain it away rather than revise our assumptions. Moreover, 'once we suspect that a phenomenon exists, we generally have little trouble explaining why it exists or what it means. People are extraordinarily good at ad hoc explanation' (Gilovich, 1993: 21). Our preconceptions tend to bias our interpretations, so that confirmatory evidence is accepted without reflection, while 'we subject inconsistent information to more critical scrutiny than consistent information' (Gilovich, 1993: 53). Thus, gamblers spend more time explaining away their losses, while taking their wins for granted. The tendency to impute meaning may be valuable in many contexts, but it can also mislead us, especially given our inclination to exaggerate our own virtues and treat our beliefs as possessions to be protected from criticism and shown off to appreciative audiences. In testing theories, we can build in safeguards which discount the effects of chance, ensure that negative as well as positive instances are fully considered, evaluate the quality of evidence, protect against self-serving bias, and so on. But 'when we do not precisely specify the kind of evidence that will count as support for our position, we can end up "detecting" too much evidence for our preconceptions' (Gilovich, 1993: 58).

No doubt it was to counter such fallibilities that Glaser and Strauss warned about the dangers of preconceptions, emphasized the importance of emergence, and promoted a 'constant comparative' method as a means of producing fresh evidence with which to challenge and refine theory. Such safeguards are required given our predisposition to see patterns and order where there is none. However, 'the predisposition to detect patterns and make connections is what leads to discovery and advance' (Gilovich, 1993: 10). While the contexts of discovery and validation must be distinguished, it remains the case that the particular merits of grounded theory as a method of theory generation flow from grounding categories in data, even if this falls some way short of their full validation. Let us consider some of the ways in which this can be accomplished.

HOW CAN CATEGORIES BE GROUNDED?

One of the most striking but controversial recommendations of Glaser and Strauss was to avoid preconceptions and let categories 'emerge' from the data.

They thought preconceptions could be limited by not engaging in advance of the research with existing literature in the field of interest. They did not advise complete abstinence in this respect, but rather a wider engagement with ideas and evidence from other fields, not necessarily academic. Their aim was to sharpen rather than blunt theoretical sensitivity, by working with a wide range of cross-cutting and inter-disciplinary ideas (in my study of redundancy, I drew on other fields to counter-balance the predominant assumptions of the industrial relations literature). Their target was undoubtedly the researcher inclined to plough ahead along an established theoretical furrow regardless of the diversity and richness of the data, thereby diminishing its potential for stimulating theoretical innovation. Researchers drawing from a wider repertoire of theoretical ideas, such as those identified in Glaser's coding families (1978: 81), could avoid the blinkered vision of an established theoretical framework, at least by bringing to bear a range of theoretical perspectives.

This seems sound advice, not least because the intersection of different fields and frameworks seems more suited to stimulate new questions and fresh ideas. While recognizing the virtues of an eclectic approach, the proposal to discount the most immediately obvious and relevant literature seems more questionable. As I have suggested previously (Dey, 1993: 229), we should not confuse an open mind with an empty head. Even ideas drawn from the immediate field can provide a useful guide to analysis, providing that we keep an open mind about their cogency and relevance to the data. But what does it mean to keep an open mind? Bertrand Russell argued that an open mind is also likely to be a vacant one, for we cannot altogether avoid preconceptions if we want to make progress in a field. As Gilovich argues, 'the power and flexibility with which we reason depends upon our ability to use context, generic knowledge and pre-existing information' (1993: 52). The point is not to avoid preconceptions, but to ensure that they are well-grounded in arguments and evidence, and always subject to further investigation, revision, and refutation.

This message is underlined by the recognition that categories are not the self-contained concepts of the classical model but arrive already invested with meaning by underlying cognitive models. If categories are 'irreducibly cognitive' then it is vital to be alive to their relation to our underlying theoretical ideas and questions. This involves making the underlying theoretical context of categorization more, not less explicit. For example, consider the category 'voluntary redundancy', which is not simply a means of classifying and contrasting 'voluntary' with 'compulsory' redundancies but also acquires its meaning in terms of an historically specific strategy for managing industrial relations and labour force reductions. The argument that categories simply emerge from the data was doubtful even when it was first formulated. Perhaps it did not even convince its authors, given their emphasis on theoretical sensitivity and the value of bringing a wide repertoire of theoretical ideas to the data. Certainly Strauss and Corbin (1994) allowed a role for existing theory and previous research, provided their fit with data was assessed with rigour. Given the challenges discussed earlier to the classical (correspondence) model of category formation and utilization, it is even more doubtful now. If we want to ground our categories, we need to give as much attention to their theoretical provenance as to their empirical base.

In grounded theory, concern tends to focus on face validity, that is the degree to which the concepts we use are meaningful ways of interpreting the data that we investigate. However, other facets of validity are also important, including the degree to which our theoretical claims are consistent with well-established knowledge in the field. New interpretations need not be consistent with established knowledge, but any inconsistency is an occasion for further reflection and investigation. This can be considered construct validity, if interpreted as consistency in theory rather than with measurement through established indicators. If we think of validity as the extent to which a theory is well-grounded empirically *and* conceptually, then we can better appreciate the importance of theoretical consistency as well as the accuracy or acuteness of our empirical interpretations. When we develop categories, we need to take account of their theoretical underpinnings and implications as much as their efficacy with regard to the data.

The question of efficacy can no longer be reduced to adequate representation in terms of similarity and difference. Although constant comparison plays a critical role in grounded theory, it may do so in a way rather different from the standard conception of identifying patterns (or regularities) across the data. Pattern recognition is by no means irrelevant, but it is only part of the process of category generation. Given our predisposition to identify patterns even among chance products, we need to be more circumspect and ask which patterns are worthy of recognition, or further conceptual analysis, and why. Empirical regularities in the data are of little value unless we can answer these questions. Again, this suggests the significance of theoretical context and the need to consider pattern matching as indicative rather than decisive with regard to theoretical import. We can think of identifying patterns as primarily a theoretical enterprise if we consider patterns not as empirical regularities but as the underlying conceptualizations which can identify and describe in the most economical terms the empirical relationships (and not just superficial regularities) identified within the data. This is akin to the way a knitting pattern can produce a complex and colourful product. For example, an underlying pattern 6r4y9b (six red, four yellow, nine blue stitches or rows) may economically describe a product with regular variations in colour bands. Even where we can observe no obvious regularities, there may be an underlying pattern, as with the Penrose tile which combines in such a way as never to repeat (cf. Mirksy, 1997). Simple patterns can produce complex results, and social research can explore these by investigating the logic underpinning complex behaviours. This suggests that categories are grounded when they provide logical and economical accounts of empirical observations; they do not so much represent these observations as explain them.

Causal explanations are central to grounded theory as a method of analysing social processes, most notably in the analytic paradigm presented by Strauss and Corbin (1990). This directs our attention to causal links between conditions, interactions, and consequences in the evolution of a social process, not forgetting the strategic role of the various actors involved. Through a 'conditional matrix' (Strauss & Corbin, 1990: 163), we can consider a range of conditions (local to global) implicated in an event, adding depth to the analysis. The social process may be conceptualized in various ways, depending on whether it is stable or unstable, controlled or chaotic, continuous or discontinuous, and so on. From this perspective, categories can be grounded through a systematic appraisal of the contexts, dynamics, and results of interactive processes. This is typically presented as a process of connecting categories which have emerged through the initial analysis by a comparative investigation of their various properties and relations. If a causal condition seems important in one context, does it also figure in a different setting? The emphasis on theoretical sampling in grounded theory is driven primarily by the requirement of systematic comparison in a variety of settings of the factors encompassed by the social process under investigation.

The reconceptualization of categories noted earlier suggests a rather different approach. Psychological research suggests causality is not consequent upon categorization but integral to it. We do not categorize and then connect; we connect by categorizing. When we categorize, we typically invoke theories of how the world works and, in this way, our categories provide implicit guidelines for inference and prediction. Think of the category 'strike', for example, with all its metaphorical associations and its attendant connotations about and implicit explanations of the nature of industrial conflict. Categories can be grounded more adequately if we recognize and attend the causal assumptions which underpin them. Otherwise we may simply discover connections later which are already implicated in the categories we have generated at the outset. For example, the category perceptions of social loss identified by Glaser and Strauss is not a neutral description of an empirical state; the category already implies an event or process in which something has been lost. The category would have been far less effective in generating theoretical connections were this broader process not already embedded in the initial categorization. A categorization which focuses on loss and the value placed upon it by nurses and other professionals also gains theoretical purchase from our understanding of the causal mechanisms at work. It is the intelligibility of this causal process which gives the category its theoretical potency. As the psychologists have observed, in everyday reasoning we give more weight to evidence concerning causal mechanisms (or powers) than to evidence of covariation.

This is not to dismiss covariation, on which we may also rely for clues about causality. Regularities in the data can be suggestive if not in themselves conclusive. One virtue of constant comparison as a method in grounded theory is that it protects against the tendency to overinterpret data and find connections where there are none. The inclination to focus on positive evidence as confirmatory can be challenged through the systematic use of constant comparison. This is easily appreciated if we construct a simple two by two table through which to assess covariation. Take the proposition that the value placed on social loss affects patient care. This could give us a schema for checking evidence (see Table 8.1).

Psychological research suggests that we are especially inclined to infer causality when we find values in cell **a**. If we find cases where the sense of social loss is strong and the quality of patient care is good we are liable to infer a connection between these on the basis of covariation. However, the commitment to constant comparison also encourages us to consider the other cells. Are there cases (as in cell **b**) where patient care is poor despite a strong sense of social loss? Are there cases (as in cell **c**) where patient care is good despite a weak sense of social loss? Are there cases (as in cell **d**) where the sense of social loss is weak and patient care is poor? It is only through the systematic comparison of cases across all these cells that we can infer a relationship in any confidence.

We can ask these questions even without the aid of a 2×2 table, but this tabular representation can be an invaluable aid to logical analysis and evaluation. There has been some debate (see Heath & Cowley, 2004 for a review) about the place of deductive logic in grounded theory, given its general inclination to emphasize observation and inference, and a rather neglected affinity with abductive interpretation (Dey, 2004: 91–92; see also Haig, 1995) rather than hypotheses formulation and testing. However, the deductive logic which encourages us to search for evidence to confirm or refute our hunches by looking for the evidence in other cells seems an indispensable tool for analysis. Much the same point applies to numerical aspects of the data, of which qualitative researchers sometimes harbour suspicion because of the risk of reducing complex meanings to what can be measured. This is a reasonable point, but its implication is that numbers and measurement should be treated with due caution rather than dispensed with altogether.

Graphic representation provides another powerful means of grounding categorical analysis. In a sense, a table is itself a form of graphic representation, but only one among many. Matrices, for example, offer powerful means of data reduction and comparison which can help the analyst acquire a useful overview of the data. A matrix can allow documentation of all categories and their assignations across cases, allowing the overall distribution and weight of evidence to be assessed more easily (see Figure 8.1).

Table 8.1 Social loss by quality of patient care (illustrative)

	Quality of patient care	
Perception of social loss	Good	Poor
Strong	a	b
Weak	c	d

Figure 8.1 (which in computer-assisted analysis may be linked directly to its evidential base) sets out categories as a series of variables with values for each of the cases being analysed. The nature of a case is problematic in grounded theory, especially as Glaser and Strauss deliberately rejected a case-based approach to sampling in favour of analysing social processes comparatively across different settings. However, even settings can be treated as cases and used for systematic comparison without implying the kind of representation of larger populations that Glaser and Strauss were anxious to avoid.

Mapping provides an alternative means of graphic representation. Where matrices only imply relationships between categories, causal maps can represent them directly. Indeed recent work in economics suggests that graphic representation is not just a means of portraying relationships but can offer a conceptual tool for investigating causality in its own right. For example, Pearl (1999) has shown that graphic representation provides a systematic method of identifying (or eliminating) confounding variables in causal analysis, something that has been impossible to achieve through maths or statistics. A simple procedure for adding and removing connections between nodes provides a means of deciding whether the effect of one variable upon another is determined by adjusting for a third variable (Pearl, 1999: 11–12). He suggests that graphs have emerged 'as the fundamental notational system for concepts and relationships that are not easily expressed in any mathematical language', also that they 'both serve as models for determining the truth of causal utterances and as a symbolic machinery for deriving such truths from other causal premises' (Pearl, 1999: 9). Though this work depends on statistical evidence, Pearl points out that it opens the door

	Social loss	Patient care	Loss rationales	
A1	s	g	ab	
N1	w	g	bdf	
D1	w	p	ac	

Figure 8.1   Matrix representation of category assignments. *Note:* **Where s, g, a, b, etc. are values assigned for each category (values need not be mutually exclusive).**

to a useful blend of qualitative and quantitative analysis in investigations of causality. In this context, it is worth recalling that grounded theory originated as a method with a foot in both these camps.

Although grounded theory has a strong causal bent, in grounded theory we may also be interested in relations between categories other than causal connections. Categories provide a basis for formal classification as well as substantive connection and a powerful if less prestigious task may be the development of a useful schema for classification. This task is especially difficult in qualitative research because the categories we develop are rarely exclusive or exhaustive of the data (Becker & Geer, 1982). Despite the tendency to adopt hierarchical forms of classification, through which categories can be integrated or refined, in qualitative analysis as in everyday life the conditions for this (that categories are comprehensive and exclusive) are rarely achievable. Discussing the classic biological taxonomy, McGarty suggests that 'very few categories have a hierarchical organization that provides such a sound basis for interference' (1999: 211). He observes that the classical conditions for hierarchical organization of categories ('each lower-level category is entirely included within one category of the higher level but is not exhaustive of it') are rarely met. The theory-based model of categorization suggests that complex categories and sub-categories are derived not through identifying a set of common features but 'by virtue of their relation to the ideal case, where the models converge' (Lakoff, 1987: 76).

Fortunately the standard tree diagram used to represent hierarchical classification is only a special case of a broader mode of representation, for example through Venn diagrams, which illustrate the logical relationship between groups of things (sets), such as cases of overlap between categories. These have the advantage of requiring far less stringent assumptions, more consonant with the realities of everyday categorization (see Figure 8.2).

Figure 8.2 (devised to illustrate the point) shows how four different subcategories of social value might overlap and how various exemplars (occupational roles) are located with respect to these. Thus the doctor scores on three counts (work, status, and skills) while the athlete is recognized as having skills and status but not work; social work is characterized in terms of work without either status or skills. The diagram implies a value hierarchy without requiring any demanding assumptions regarding the relations between categories. All that has to be identified is the overlap between categories and the characteristics of exemplars.

As well as representing overlapping relationships between categories, mapping can provide a flexible means of situating and structuring relationships between a range of various empirical and theoretical elements in a developing analysis, such as social contexts or key events (Clarke, 2005). Mapping in this way can provide a means of preserving empirical complexities as well as supporting a flexible approach to theorizing relationships (cf. Charmaz, 2006).

The observant reader will have noticed that the discussion has so far proceeded without reference to the promised discussion of coding, despite

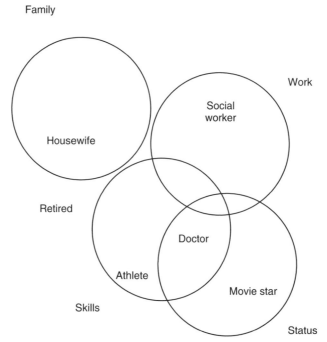

Family

Work

Social
worker

Housewife

Retired

Doctor

Athlete

Movie star

Skills

Status

Figure 8.2   Mapping overlapping categories: Dimensions of social value.

the strong association of coding with grounded theory. Given Glaser's talk of 'coding families' and the 'coding paradigm' of Strauss and Corbin, it is not surprising that coding has become a central analytic procedure in grounded theory, even setting aside the impetus imparted to this approach by the development of software packages for qualitative analysis. It has even been claimed that analysis is coding, though a more circumspect approach regards coding as only a preliminary means of managing and organizing data. Both of these perspectives have some merit, since coding can undoubtedly contribute a great deal to analysis as well as data management. Indeed, coding can contribute to analysis in a variety of ways (cf. Richards & Richards, 1994; Seale, 1999; Seidel & Kelle, 1995). One is by providing a system of indexing the data to mark up points of interest. Another is as a powerful tool for searching and retrieving categorized data. *Once data is coded*, we can identify all exemplars under particular category heads, a useful means of promoting comparison both within and across categories. A more sophisticated use of coding involves the interrogation of data in a manner akin to hypothesis testing. We can investigate covariation across categories and check out the evidence that supports or refutes various propositions we have come to entertain of the data. These are powerful methods of grounding categories and investigating their relationships but with regard to coding some important caveats must be observed.

The first point (always worth reiterating) is that coding is a metaphor (whether derived from coding language or statute) entirely inappropriate to the nature and requirements of analysis. The coding metaphor implies a one-to-one correspondence through the identification of clear rules and invariant features. As we have seen, this requirement is profoundly at odds with the theory-laden character of categorization. Categorization usually lacks the specificity, precision, and stability that coding implies; the metaphor becomes still more inappropriate once we acknowledge that our categories are provisional, prototypical, and permeable in nature. A second caveat concerns the focus on covariation which inevitably follows from the use of quasi-statistical techniques to interrogate the coded data, whether the search for correlations between categories or the investigation of 'if-then' relationships across categories. One risk here is that coding requires such an investment of time and effort that we treat the data thus reconceptualized as fixed rather than (as we would expect in grounded theory) provisional. In the paragraph above, the phrase 'once data is coded' misleadingly implies that coding are a single and secure operation, upon which subsequent analysis can be based. This is at odds with the contextual, provisional, and iterative character of categorical analysis. Our data is far from secure and, as argued earlier, are liable to provide a poor basis on which to test any emerging hypotheses. We also observed that covariation is not the only or even the main way in which we (non-statisticians) typically think about causal connections. Covariation plays a secondary role to the identification of causal powers and mechanisms. One risk of coding and interrogating data in this way is that the underlying theoretical, metaphorical, and causal dimensions of categorical analysis are neglected. Then we have to try to reconstruct the connections which we have fragmented through an inappropriate fragmentation of the data into different bits or segments. At the very least, it seems important to recognize that categories are embedded in cognitive models which already imply an integrative and relational element in categorization.

THE STORYLINE

One of the external examiners of my thesis on union opposition to redundancy remarked that it 'read like a novel'. Naturally I took this as a compliment at the time, but in retrospect the remark assumes a greater significance. Conveying to my readers the drama, uncertainties, and inconsistencies of events as they unfolded was a vital way of grounding my study of resistance to redundancies. It allowed the reader to appreciate the difficulties and dilemmas of union activists as they attempted to navigate and influence a turbulent and intractable set of events. A narrative framework provided a vehicle for contextualizing and integrating the various elements (power struggles, ideological commitments, pecuniary self-interest, intra-union conflicts) which characterized the social process.

One of the most interesting (if also challenging) features of grounded theory is its attempt to utilize different modes of analysis. Most obvious in this respect is the attempt to combine the variable analysis associated with quantitative methods with naturalistic enquiry rooted in the symbolic interactionist tradition of qualitative research (cf. Robrecht, 1995). One of the tensions in this marriage of methods lies in the use of approaches which variously emphasize or displace human agency. A third strand of enquiry less often recognized can be found in its focus on narrative. Strauss and Corbin suggest that the identification of a core category around which coding culminates follows from rather than precedes the explication of a storyline, that is, a descriptive narrative of 'the central phenomenon of the study' (1990: 116–117). Such a narrative might be a general descriptive overview of the research or little more than a brief abstract of the study; either way, it can stimulate the development of focus and integration. For Strauss and Corbin (1990) narrative is conceived largely in terms of the coding paradigm (conditions, interaction, consequences) if possible at a higher level of abstraction. Thus the explication of a storyline hints (but no more) at a more holistic, conjunctural, and multifactorial account of the data.

In this respect, grounded theory anticipates or echoes developments in historical analysis, where it has been argued that integration around a plot provides a means 'to integrate the variety of explanatory forms' into 'one intelligible whole to include circumstances, goals, interactions, and unintended results'; a plot provides a means of integrating a range of sub-stories into an overarching storyline (Polkinghorne, 1988: 49, 54). Polkinghorne discusses the ways in which historians have wrestled with the tensions between formal analysis and narrative enquiry over the past century. One important point to emerge from these debates has been the integral and distinctive contribution of narrative form to human enquiry more generally. In narrative explanation, the emphasis is on retrodiction rather than prediction; a conclusion has to be intelligible rather than predictable. The various elements of the story cohere in a way which encompasses chance events, unplanned encounters, unexpected incidents, and unanticipated consequences. This coherence is a matter of synoptic judgement in which various parts of the story are appreciated as a whole, rather than through logical deduction from premise to conclusion. Synoptic judgement involves 'configurational comprehension' so that 'things are understood as elements in a single and concrete complex of relationships' (Polkinghorne, 1988: 53). The elements themselves have to display a minimal logical coherence, notably chronological (such that causes precede effects) though interpretation of earlier events may depend on later outcomes. However, the grounding of a plot is more than just a matter of logical coherence among its various elements; it has to have some narrative or configurative coherence as well.

Even if narrative is more fragmented and diverse (cf. Andrews et al., 2003) than historians might allow, it is the basic way in which humans make sense of and structure experience and, as a method of enquiry, it is as relevant to the grounded theory analyst as the historian. The focus on process, both its temporality in terms of stages and sequences of events and its evolution through conditions, interaction, and consequences, suggests that narrative enquiry can play a critical role in grounded theory. It is not only the storyline identified by the analyst that is of interest. Actors (including agencies as well as individuals) engaged in the drama of events also constitute their experience in terms of unfolding stories and overarching plots. They categorize phenomena not just in terms of representing objects or events, but also their relationships within an overall configuration which makes sense (more or less) of experience. There are various culturally available means, or 'genres' (cf. Squire, 2004), through which such storytelling is enacted. Polkinghorne (1988: 55) for example discusses four 'tropes' proposed by White (metaphor, metonymy, synecdoche, and irony) which bear a close comparison with the various modes of categorization (including metaphor and metonymy) identified by Lakoff. Perhaps the idealized cognitive models which Lakoff sees as underpinning categories are themselves elements in the stories through which people make sense of their experience? If so, narrative enquiry may have a vital contribution to make to the grounding of categories.

This is not to suggest that an assimilation of fact and fiction as though narrative accounts were merely literary devices (cf. Czarniawska, 2004). Far from absolving one of the need to ground categories, narrative enquiry imposes further demands on the analyst, both in terms of representing process and explaining it (cf. Berlin, 1978: 131–133, on the challenges of historical enquiry). As Polkinghorne notes, narrative enquiry demands 'practical understanding on the part of the narrator' (1988: 144). Glaser and Strauss also hint at this in the emphasis they place on 'practical adequacy' as a test of a grounded theory, whether the researcher can 'make out' in the social world being studied (1967: 226–227) or the theory makes sufficient sense to practitioners that it is capable of practical application (1967: 244).

WHEN TO STOP

One of the attractions of grounded theory is that it offers practical advice about the nuts and bolts of doing qualitative research. As this is rarely articulated, it is all the more appreciated. The problem of 'when to stop' is an example of how grounded theory addresses the obvious (but awkward) questions that confront the researcher. To this question we have the answer: theoretical saturation, stop when the ideas run out. Categories are saturated when 'no additional data are being found whereby the [analyst] can develop the properties of the category' (Glaser & Strauss, 1967: 61). Adding further to the data makes no difference. Like a sponge which can hold no more water, the theory needs no more elaboration or refinement. The metaphor seems apt, so long as it is confined to the generation of ideas and not their validation. Despite their occasional flirtation with verification, Glaser and Strauss were quite explicit about the limited nature of theoretical saturation:

> ... the constant comparative method cannot be used for both provisional testing and discovering theory: in theoretical sampling, the data collected are not extensive enough

> and, because of theoretical saturation, are not coded extensively enough to yield provisional
> tests ... They are coded only enough to generate, hence to suggest, theory (Glaser & Strauss,
> 1967: 103).

Theoretical sampling too is considered as a tool of theoretical exploration not confirmation. The basic idea is to sample new settings which might illuminate through further comparison the properties and relationships of emerging categories. Thus the loss rationales of nurses in wards might be compared with loss rationales in other settings: residential homes or day care facilities for example. Or one might consider other kinds of social loss which are subject to professional intervention in different contexts (legal for example) and compare these with valuations in a medical setting. Theoretical sampling is conceived as an instrument for generating theory, not investigating cases. Once a theory is 'up and running', it is possible to be highly focused and selective in producing further data relevant to the elaboration or refinement of existing categories.

Despite its appeal, the idea of theoretical saturation itself needs further refinement. Consistent with their emphasis on emergent ideas, Glaser and Strauss at times seem to imply that saturation is a function of the data rather than the interpretation we make of it. Though theoretical sampling becomes increasingly focused and circumscribed, there remains a chance that additional data may 'explode' the theory (Glaser & Strauss, 1967: 73). Moreover, new interpretations can arise even as the study goes to press, 'so the published word is not the final one, but only a pause in the never-ending process of generating theory' (Glaser & Strauss, 1967: 40). How then can we be sure that we have achieved saturation? We may claim saturation without being able to prove it (Charmaz, 2006; Morse, 1995). Moreover, the saturation metaphor implicitly emphasizes the density of categorization rather than its parsimony. Elegance, precision, coherence, and clarity are traditional criteria for evaluating theory somewhat swamped by the metaphorical emphasis on saturation. Elaboration should not obscure the quest for refinement.

REFLEXIVITY AND REPLICATION

Robin Dunbar (1996) attributes human evolution to the motivating force of gossip. The recognition of language and in particular narrative as a central element in the organization of human experience has led to some scepticism about whether research claims can be grounded at all. The positive side of this scepticism has been a greater sensitivity to the 'authoritative' role of the researcher in the production of evidence (cf. Altheide & Johnson, 1994). The development of software for qualitative analysis has also encouraged a more diligent and disciplined approach to the auditing of the creative process. It is no longer enough to present a set of conclusions, supported and expanded by illustration from the evidential base. The reflexive researcher at the very least has to monitor and present the critical steps in the development of the analysis, so that these can be followed (and possibly disputed) by the reader. A dictionary of category definitions and their conceptual evolution through the analysis is one way to address this task. However, the dictionary metaphor is more in tune with the classical model, in which we spell out the criteria (indicators) through which our concepts relate to observations. With a greater appreciation of the cognitive aspects of categorization, our dictionary has to be complemented by an audit of the more metaphorical and narrative elements of the analysis. This suggests a shift in focus from coding and comparison to the rich role that other forms of theorizing can play in the analysis. The theoretical memo sometimes tends to be cast in the role of bit actor, perhaps with the best lines but nevertheless playing a subordinate part in the service of the main drama, seen as the development of a coding framework. Memos can be conceived mainly as adjuncts to codes and catalysts for their further development. Within the compass of a narrative framework, they may contribute more directly to theoretical development. The cryptic memo may be an appropriate medium (short and to the point) for sudden insights and creative intuitions, but the synoptic configuration required of narrative may benefit from a fuller engagement with memo writing as an integral part of the analytic process.

The impetus to develop a single narrative thread in grounded theory (around a core category) may survive the move to greater reflexivity, but this does suggest a more open and circumspect approach to the challenges of interpretation. A good plot does not preclude and indeed positively benefits from the potential for differing interpretations. The voice of the author becomes one among many and its claims to authority become more modest and, paradoxically perhaps, more persuasive. This perspective can be incorporated into the analytic process in various ways, such as exposing interpretations to the scrutiny of key informants or independent co-researchers.

Reflexivity can contribute to the grounding of categories by documenting their evolution through the analytic process. Insofar as this allows other analysts (at least in principle) to reproduce comparable results from the data, this could be described as internal replication. However, the data used to generate categories will always provide a poor basis for validating them. Can external replication play a role? As we have seen, Glaser and Strauss occasionally acknowledged but in general were rather indifferent to the demands of independent verification, having stressed the practical adequacy of theory in the reflexive interpretations of those practitioners who might apply it in different contexts. External replication is not dismissed, but largely takes a form attuned to the practical and contextual applications envisaged for grounded theory. Although Glaser and Strauss recognized and did not entirely relinquish the ambition to develop formal theory, they emphasized the role of theory generation in relation to what they called substantive theory. The distinction they drew between formal and substantive theory sometimes focused on levels of abstraction: 'patient care' was substantive while 'stigma' was formal (1967: 32). In practice, however, substantive theory is identified by its practical import and adaptability to specific contexts. In keeping with the original emphasis on substantive theory, Charmaz (2006) emphasizes the role and potential of grounded theory in generating contextually relevant plausible accounts. This implies a closer relationship between theory and practice, researchers and practitioners, than the more orthodox idea of replication through repetition. Even accepting that the test of a theory lies in its practical application, however, external replication requires some mechanisms for scrutiny and feedback from practitioners.

CONCLUSION

I began with a set of questions. Now I shall conclude with some key points. What are categories? Categories are inherently theoretical, implicitly explanatory, and often metaphorical and exemplary rather than rule-bound. What does it mean to ground categories? It means generating ideas through research in ways which root categories in evidence without providing a means of independent validation of any emergent theories. How can categories be grounded? This requires keeping an open mind, rooting categories in the data being analysed, seeking the underlying logic of apparently disparate events, recognizing causal inferences at work through our categorizations, checking, revising, and amplifying interpretations through comparison across settings, and using representational techniques to evaluate evidence and explore connections between categories. Does this mean coding? There are other approaches, such as narrative analysis which, because of their interpretive grab, may play a vital role in grounding our categories. When to stop? This judgement requires attention to the traditional criteria of good theorizing (elegance, coherence, clarity, precision) and not just exhausting the possibilities of refinement and elaboration. Is replication necessary? That may depend on the extent of our theoretical ambitions.

What constructive conclusions can we draw regarding the grounding of categories in grounded theory? Thanks to the recent and on-going work in psychology and linguistics, we are acquiring a more complex appreciation of the nature of categorization. The importance of exemplars, of metaphor, of causal assumptions, and cognitive models all open up new ways of thinking about the role categories can play in grounded theory. The grounding of categories becomes more obviously a conceptual as well as empirical challenge, requiring fuller reflection on the cognitive underpinnings of the categories we adopt. This in turn prompts a more open and critical engagement with current theory, a concern with construct as well as face validity, an attention to underlying logics as well as surface regularities, and an emphasis on causal powers/mechanisms as well as covariation. Various forms of graphic representation (matrices, mapping, graphs, tables, and Venn diagrams) offer powerful tools for grounding the substantive relations between categories. With important caveats, coding remains an important but less central means of grounding categories. Narrative offers an important (alternative) means of synoptic integration and interpretation. The elegance and cogency of interpretation loom larger in the criteria for judging theoretical adequacy. Reflexivity becomes important in writing about as well as classifying data. Replication through practical application invites a fuller collaboration with both informants and practitioners. Developing along these lines, grounded theory may in some respects differ from that envisaged by its originators, but not in its core ambition to generate theory of practical value grounded through systematic confrontation with evidence.

REFERENCES

Ahn, W.-K. and Dennis, M. J. (1999) Dissociation between categorization and similarity judgement: Differential effect of causal states on feature weights. In U. Hahn and M. Ramscar (eds) *Similarity and Categorization*. Oxford: Oxford University Press.

Altheide, D. L. and Johnson, J. M. (1994) Criteria for assessing interpretive validity in qualitative research. In N. K. Denzin and Y. S. Lincoln (eds) *Handbook of Qualitative Research*. London: SAGE.

Andrews, M., Sclater, S. D., Squire, C. and Tamboukou, M. (2003) Narrative Research. In C. Seale, G. Gobo, J. F. Gubrium and D. Silverman (eds) *Qualitative Research Practice*. London: SAGE.

Becker, H. and Geer, B. (1982) Participant observation: The analysis of qualitative field data. In R. Burgess (ed) *Field Research: A Sourcebook and Field Manual*. London: Allen & Unwin.

Berlin, I. (1978) *Concepts and Categories: Philosophical Essays*. In H. Hardy (ed). London: Pimlico.

Bruner, J. S., Goodnow, J. J. and Austin, G. A. (1986) *A Study of Thinking*. 2nd Edition. New Brunswick, NJ: Transaction.

Charmaz, K. (2006) *Constructing Grounded Theory: A Practical Guide through Qualitative Analysis*. London: SAGE.

Clarke, A. E. (2005) *Situational Analysis: Grounded Theory after the Postmodern Turn*. London: SAGE.

Czarniawska, B. (2004) *Narratives in Social Science Research*. London: SAGE.

Dey, I. (1993) *Qualitative Data Analysis: A User-friendly Guide*. London: Routledge.

Dey, I. (1999) *Grounding Grounded Theory: Guidelines for Qualitative Inquiry*. San Diego: Academic Press.

Dey, I. (2004) Grounded Theory. In C. Seale, G. Gobo, J. F. Gubrium and D. Silverman (eds) *Qualitative Research Practice*. London: SAGE.

Dunbar, R. (1996) *Grooming, Gossip and the Evolution of Language*. London: Faber and Faber.

Gilovich, T. (1993) *How We Know What Isn't So: The Fallibility of Human Reason in Everyday Life*. New York: The Free Press.

Glaser, B. (1978) *Theoretical Sensitivity*. Mill Valley, CA: Sociology Press.

Glaser, B. and Strauss, A. (1967) *The Discovery of Grounded Theory: Strategies for Qualitative Research*. Chicago: Aldine.

Hahn, U. and Ramscar, M. (eds) (2001) *Similarity and Categorization*. Oxford: Oxford University Press.

Haig, B. D. (1995) Grounded theory as scientific method. *Philosophy of Education 1995: Current issues*, 281–290. Urbana: University of Illinois Press. Retrieved 14 March 2007 from http://www.ed.uiuc.edu/EPS/PES-Yearbook/95_docs/haig.html

Harnad, S. (1987) Category induction and representation. In S. Harnad (ed) *Categorical Perception: The Groundwork of Cognition*. Cambridge: Cambridge University Press.

Heath, H. and Cowley, S. (2004) Developing a grounded theory approach: A comparison of Glaser and Strauss. *International Journal of Nursing Studies*, 41, 141–150.

Kelle, U. (2003) Computer-assisted qualitative data analysis. In C. Seale, G. Gobo, J. F. Gubrium and D. Silverman (eds) *Qualitative Research Practice*. London: SAGE.

Lakoff, G. (1987) *Women, Fire and Dangerous Things: What Categories Teach about the Human Mind*. Chicago: Chicago University Press.

Lakoff, G. and Johnson, M. (1980) *Metaphors We Live By*. Chicago: University of Chicago Press.

LaRossa, R. (2005) Grounded theory methods and qualitative family research. *Journal of Marriage and Family*, 67, 837–857.

McGarty, C. (1999) *Categorization in Social Psychology*. London: SAGE.

McNeil, D. and Freiberger, P. (1994) *Fuzzy Logic: The Revolutionary Computer Technology that is Changing our World*. New York: Touchstone.

Medin, D. L. and Barsalou, L. W. (1987) Categorization processes and categorical perception. In S. Harnad (ed) *Categorical Perception: The Groundwork of Cognition*. Cambridge: Cambridge University Press.

Mirsky, S. (1997) The Emperor's new toilet paper. *Scientific American*, 277, 1–15.

Morse, J. (1995) The significance of saturation. *Qualitative Health Research*, 5, 147–149.

Murphy, G. L. and Medin, D. L. (1985) The role of theories in conceptual coherence. *Psychological Review*, 92, 289–316.

Pearl, J. (1999) Statistics, causality and graphs. In A. Gammerman (ed) *Causal Models and Intelligent Data Management*. London: Springer.

Polkinghorne, D. E. (1988) *Narrative Knowing and the Human Sciences*. Albany, NY: State University of New York Press.

Richards, T. J. and Richards, L. (1994) Using computers in qualitative research. In N. K. Denzin and Y. S. Lincoln (eds) *Handbook of Qualitative Research*. London: SAGE.

Robrecht, L. C. (1995) Grounded theory: Evolving methods. *Qualitative Health Research*, 5, 169–177.

Rosch, E. (1978) Principles of categorization. In E. Rosch and B. B. Lloyd (eds) *Cognition and Categorization*. Hillsdale, NJ: Erlbaum.

Seale, C. (1999) *The Quality of Qualitative Research*. London: SAGE.

Seidel, J. and Kelle, U. (1995) Different functions of coding in the analysis of textual data. In U. Kelle (ed) *Computer-aided Qualitative Data Analysis*. London: SAGE.

Squire, C. (2004) Narrative genres. In C. Seale, G. Gobo, J. F. Gubrium and D. Silverman (eds) *Qualitative Research Practice*. London: SAGE.

Strauss, A. and Corbin, J. (1990) *Basics of Qualitative Research: Grounded Theory Procedures and Techniques*. London: SAGE.

Strauss, A. and Corbin, J. (1994) Grounded theory methodology: An overview. In N. K. Denzin and Y.S. Lincoln (eds) *Handbook of Qualitative Research*. London: SAGE.

Wittgenstein, L. (1953) *Philosophical Investigations*. Oxford: Blackwell.

Wood, S. and Dey, I. (1983) *Redundancy: Case Studies in Cooperation and Conflict*. Aldershot: Gower.

9

The Development of Categories: Different Approaches in Grounded Theory

Udo Kelle

INTRODUCTION

One of most crucial and fascinating ideas in *The Discovery of Grounded Theory* was that it would provide a methodological groundwork for directly deriving categories from data of social research. Thereby, grounded theory was meant to represent an alternative to the classical hypothetico-deductive approach which requires the construction of clear-cut categories and hypotheses before data are collected. However, the development of methodological guidelines for empirically grounded category building turned out to be much more challenging and difficult than initially thought. In *The Discovery of Grounded Theory*, the metaphor of 'emergence' was invented which had a far-reaching impact on the methodological debate but, at the same time, was difficult to be translated into tangible methodological rules. Glaser and Strauss's initial idea that categories would emerge from the data if researchers with sufficient theoretical sensitivity would apply a technique of constant comparison was difficult to realize in practice. Consequently, this idea was modified and refined several times in the ongoing development of grounded theory leading to a variety of different, new, and complex concepts like *theoretical coding, coding families, axial coding,*

coding paradigm, and many others, which supplemented and sometimes displaced the concepts of constant comparison and theoretical sampling from the early days.

The basic concept of category building through theoretically sensitive constant comparisons will be outlined in the first section of this chapter. It will be shown that the major problem of those concepts lies in the failure to explicitly conceptualize the role of previous theoretical knowledge in developing grounded categories. In the second section, I will discuss the progress which was made in this respect through the different approaches which Glaser and Strauss developed after they had finished their methodological cooperation in the late 1970s. I will focus on the most prominent differences between the Glaserian and the Straussian approach, comparing Glaser's notions of theoretical coding and coding families with the concept of coding paradigm put forward by Strauss and Corbin. The pros and cons of both modes of category building will be treated, and under which conditions and for which research questions these different approaches are best suited will be discussed.

The most basic challenge in grounded category building is to reconcile the need of letting categories emerge from the material of research (instead of forcing preconceived theoretical terms on the data) with the impossibility of abandoning previous theoretical knowledge. In the third section of the chapter, I will show how classical methodological concepts (especially the concept of empirical content) can be employed to distinguish between theoretical notions that force the data and concepts that support the emergence of new categories.

CATEGORY BUILDING THROUGH CONSTANT COMPARISON: THE BASIC RULES FROM *THE DISCOVERY OF GROUNDED THEORY*

How can theoretical categories be developed in the ongoing process of empirical research? The main purpose of Glaser and Strauss's first methodological book *The Discovery of Grounded Theory* was to show that empirical data can play a crucial role in that process: the book was written in order to give examples and rules for category building with the help of empirical data. Both authors wanted to provide an alternative to the hypothetico-deductive approach in sociology which demands that precise hypotheses are developed before data are collected. Consequently, Glaser and Strauss started *The Discovery of Grounded Theory* by criticizing the 'overemphasis in current sociology on the verification of theory, and a resultant de-emphasis on the prior step of discovering what concepts and hypotheses are relevant for the area that one wishes to research' (Glaser & Strauss, 1967: 1f). Contrary to the idea that the main purpose of empirical research is the testing of explicit theoretical assumptions, they proposed a method for the 'initial, systematic discovery of the theory from the data of social research' (p. 3) that would lead to the development of categories grounded in the data. But how can the grounding of categories be assured?

In *The Discovery of Grounded Theory,* the two most basic rules of category building are given which still form the backbone of category building in grounded theory:

- Categories must not be *forced* on the data, they should *emerge* instead in the ongoing process of data analysis.
- In developing categories, the sociologist should employ *theoretical sensitivity*, which means the ability to see relevant data and to reflect upon empirical data material with the help of theoretical terms.

The emergence of categories and their properties from the data

The most basic operations which provide the basis for category building are *coding* and the *constant comparison* of data, codes, and the emerging categories. Most interestingly, the term coding stems from the quantitative tradition of social research: there it means that predefined codes are used to qualify certain bits of data. For this purpose, units of analysis (e.g. paragraphs of a certain newspaper article in a research project about mass media, or an answer to an open ended question in a survey) have to be determined, and a precise coding scheme has to be constructed before the analysis. In this case, each code represents a value of a certain variable (for example, the value affirmation or disapproval of a variable called 'Evaluation of political events'). With the help of such a coding scheme, every unit of analysis can be investigated in order to find out whether a certain value of a variable applies to it; one may, for example, analyze paragraphs of newspaper articles in order to find out whether the authors express affirmation or disapproval for certain actions taken by the government. The purpose of this process is to count numbers of codes once the coding process is finished for all relevant data. Coding of that kind is always part of a hypothetico-deductive strategy and requires that the full coding scheme be developed before data are coded.

In a publication in 1960, Howard Becker and Blanche Geer adopted the term coding for the qualitative research tradition where it meant relating text segments in field protocols to certain predefined codes. The main purpose of qualitative coding *sensu* Becker and Geer was not to count codes but to be able to find all the different text passages which (in the researcher's opinion) refer to a certain topic:

> We have tentatively identified, through sequential analysis during the field work, the major perspectives we want to present and the areas … to which these perspectives apply. We now go through the summarized incidents, marking each incident with a number or numbers that stand for the various areas to which it appears to be relevant. This is essentially a coding operation … its object is to make sure that all relevant data can be brought to bear on a point (Becker & Geer, 1960: 280f).

Since an important aim of this process was to 'constitute proof for a given proposition,' this procedure still showed a certain proximity to a classical hypothetico-deductive approach. In their monograph *The Discovery of Grounded Theory,*

Glaser and Strauss distanced themselves from that approach by maintaining that their method was not meant as a technique for the (provisional) testing of hypotheses, but 'is concerned with generating and plausibly suggesting many categories, properties and hypotheses about general problems' (Glaser & Strauss, 1967: 104). For that reason, coding in grounded theory had to be conducted without a predefined coding scheme. Categories should 'emerge' from the data if the analyst 'starts by coding each incident in his data into as many categories as possible' (p. 105). This emergence of categories should be supported by the 'constant comparative method': while coding, the analyst constantly compares the already coded incidents (which usually means the text segments which relate to the incidents) with each other and with incidents not yet coded. 'This constant comparison of the incidents very soon starts to generate theoretical properties of the category' (p. 106).

From the early days of grounded theory, many users of the method found it difficult to understand the notions 'category' and 'property' and to utilize them in research practice, since these terms were only vaguely defined in *The Discovery of Grounded Theory*. Glaser and Strauss gave the following example: In their own research project about the interaction between nurses and moribund patients in hospitals they established the category 'social loss'; nurses tend to think about their dying patients in terms of the loss which their death would mean for their social environment (e.g. 'What will the children and the husband do without her,' p. 106). By constantly comparing incidents relevant for (and coded with) that category, they found various 'theoretical properties' of the category, for instance '... we realized that some patients are perceived as a high social loss and others as a low social loss, and that patient care tends to vary positively with degree of social loss' (p. 106). Whereas the notion 'category' can refer to any noun which the researcher found relevant for their research area, the notion 'property' is more difficult to grasp: are the concepts 'high social loss' and 'patient care' theoretical properties of the category 'social loss,' and what does that mean?

It is helpful here to draw on basic mathematical set or type theory to gain a better understanding of the relation between incidents, categories, and their properties: *objects* (i.e. *incidents* like text passages describing utterances of nurses about their patients) can be assigned to a certain class or type or category (e.g. 'utterances about social loss'). *Classes* or *types* or *categories* (these three notions can be treated as equivalent) can be divided into subclasses, subtypes, or subcategories. Subclasses or subcategories can themselves be divided into further subcategories. A basic idea of grounded theory is that the whole structure or system of categories should not be exclusively developed in a top-down manner by deriving subcategories from major categories. Instead, researchers are encouraged to find major categories by carefully comparing the initially found categories (which may later become subcategories) and by integrating them into a larger structure. A hierarchically ordered structure of subcategories can develop (see Figure 9.1). It becomes possible to differentiate incidents in the

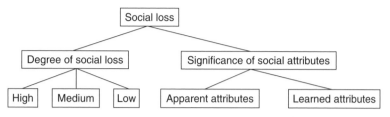

Figure 9.1   Hierarchical structure of (sub)categories.

data or text passages classified as dealing with social loss according to the subcategory 'degree of social loss' by forming further subcategories 'high social loss,' 'medium social loss,' and 'low social loss.' The whole range or set of these three subcategories then represents a theoretical property of the category social loss.

It is important to note that classes can always be divided into subclasses according to different criteria. Nurses use social attributes to calculate social loss, some of which are perceived immediately (like age, gender), while others are learned after some time (like social class, educational status). Thus, significance of social attributes could form a further subcategory of social loss with the two subcategories apparent attributes and learned attributes.

There are sets of (sub)categories which are mutually exclusive, while others are not. The subcategories high social loss, medium social loss, and low social loss form a range of mutually exclusive (non-overlapping) classes: there should be no incident which can be assigned to more than one of the three subcategories (which means that a certain utterance about a social loss cannot express simultaneously high social loss and low social loss). There are other categories or classes to which objects can be assigned simultaneously. Figure 9.2 demonstrates a very simple geometrical example for that. The 10 objects can be classified according to the category 'size' (with the subcategories small and big) and according to the category 'shape' (with the subcategories rectangular and circular).

In grounded theory, incidents and text segments can also be assigned to several categories in a similar (albeit more complicated) fashion: by carefully comparing text segments dealing with social loss, one may find that many of them can be also attributed to the category 'patient care' (since they contain nurses' utterances about how to care for dying patients) and to the subcategories

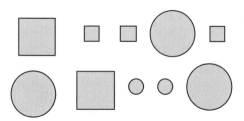

Figure 9.2

'intense patient care' or 'cursory patient care.' One may even find that text segments relating to high social loss can often be assigned to intense patient care which shows a possible relation between the two categories. This relation can likewise be regarded as a theoretical property of the category social loss.

By looking for commonalities and differences between incidents, the constant comparative method can thus reveal two different kinds of theoretical properties: possible sets of subcategories of a given category, and relations to other categories. The decisive question of constant comparison is thus: according to which criteria do the incidents vary? These criteria of variation form the categories or subcategories the analyst looks for, or they are at least suggestive of such categories. Thereby the analyst has to obtain the most basic rule of grounded theory: do not force preconceived categories on the data, but let the categories emerge from the data.

Theoretical sensitivity as a prerequisite for category building

Similar to the concepts 'category' and 'properties of categories,' many researchers who start their first grounded theory project will also find the idea of emergence difficult to apply in practice. In particular, the request 'literally to ignore the literature of theory and fact on the area under study, in order to assure that the emergence of categories will not be contaminated' (Glaser & Strauss, 1967: 37) can lead inexperienced users of grounded theory procedures to adopt an unrealistic idea about their work. Novices who wish to firmly observe the principle of 'emergence' often experience the search for categories as extremely tedious and a subject of sometimes numerous and endless team sessions, leading to a proliferation of categories which makes the whole process insurmountable. Often these researchers translate the instruction to let categories emerge from the data into a demand to transform every idea or concept which comes into their minds when reading the textual data into a category. In a methodological self-reflection, a group of junior researchers who had asked me for advice described this problem as follows:

> Especially the application of an open coding strategy recommended by Glaser and Strauss—the text is read line by line and coded *ad hoc*—proved to be unexpectedly awkward and time consuming. (...) Our attempts to analyse the data were governed by the idea that we should address the text *tabula rasa* and by the fear to structure data too much on the basis of our previous knowledge. Consequently every word in the data was credited with high significance. These uncertainties were not eased by advice from the corresponding literature that open coding means a 'preliminary breaking down of data' and that the emerging concepts will prove their usefulness in the ongoing analysis. Furthermore, in the beginning we had the understanding that 'everything counts' and 'everything is important'—even every marginal incident and phenomenon was coded, recorded in numerous memos, and extensively discussed. This led to an insurmountable mass of data ... (cf. Kelle et al., 2002, translated from German to English by Udo Kelle).

These researchers did not use line-by-line coding as a device for the initial breaking down of the data (as proposed by Glaser and Strauss), but as a tedious task of tracking down a 'complete and true meaning' in the data. Although such a procedure certainly goes against the intentions of the founders of grounded theory, it is interesting to note that the experience of these researchers underlines an important epistemological insight which is nowadays generally accepted: scientific observations are always 'theory laden' (cf. Hanson, 1965).

The idea that theoretical categories and propositions could be derived by simple ('inductive') generalization from observable data by researchers who have freed their minds from any theoretical preconceptions whatsoever before collecting empirical data manifests a rather outmoded view of scientific inquiry (nowadays often called 'naïve empiricism' or 'naïve inductivism,' cf. Chalmers, 1999). It is one of the most widely accepted insights of the philosophy of science and cognitive psychology that 'there are and can be no sensations unimpregnated by expectations' (Lakatos, 1978: 15) and that the construction of theoretical categories, whether empirically grounded or not, cannot start *ab ovo*, but have to draw on already existing stocks of knowledge. 'Both historical examples and recent philosophical analysis have made it clear that the world is always perceived through the "lenses" of some conceptual network or other and that such networks and the languages in which they are embedded may, for all we know, provide an ineliminable "tint" to what we perceive' (Laudan, 1977: 15). Empirical researchers (whether in the natural sciences or in the humanities) would need such 'lenses' or conceptual networks otherwise they would not be able to observe and describe meaningful events.

Certainly Glaser and Strauss did not overlook this problem, as one can easily see if one reads *The Discovery of Grounded Theory* with care. On page 3 they emphasize: 'Of course, the researcher does not approach reality as a tabula rasa. He must have a perspective that will help him see relevant data and abstract significant categories from his scrutiny of the data' (Glaser & Strauss, 1967: 3). Later they give a more detailed account of what they mean by the researcher's ability to 'see relevant data.' To discover grounded theories one needs 'theoretical sensitivity,' an 'ability to have theoretical insight into [one's] area of research, combined with an ability to make something of [one's] insights' (p. 46). But how can this ability be achieved? *The Discovery of Grounded Theory* contains only a few pages that address this question, comprising two advisory statements about how theoretical sensitivity can be enhanced:

1. The sociologist should harbor 'an armamentarium of categories and hypotheses on substantive and formal levels. This theory that exists within a sociologist can be used in generating his specific theory' (Glaser & Strauss, 1967: 46). Obviously existing theories can be clearly helpful in category building, and fruitful insights shall be drawn from them. Glaser and Strauss maintain that an empirically grounded theory usually combines categories and hypotheses which have emerged from the data with concepts arising from the researcher's previous theoretical knowledge.
2. A strong commitment to 'one specific preconceived theory' (Glaser & Strauss, 1967: 46), especially to 'grand theory,' must be avoided to get around the danger that categories of a 'pet theory' are forced on the data.

'Indeed the trick is to line up what one takes as theoretically possible or probable with what one is finding in the field' (Glaser & Strauss, 1967: 253).

This trick, however, is difficult to learn for many researchers. Given the concept of 'emergence,' so highly esteemed in *The Discovery of Grounded Theory*, and given the advice to abstain from reading literature about the field under investigation, some readers may be drawn towards the idea that theoretical concepts emerge from the data only if the empirical field is approached with no preconceived theories or hypotheses whatsoever. Others who wish to demonstrate 'theoretical sensitivity' may be worried that they will force inappropriate categories on the data when applying a specific sociological theory. It is obviously a challenging task to approach the empirical field without a predefined set of categories (which are applied on each empirical observation), and to hold various different theories in abeyance in order to use theoretical concepts only if they fit the data. Unfortunately, *The Discovery of Grounded Theory* neither gives clear-cut methodological rules nor practical examples about how previous theoretical knowledge can be fruitfully introduced in the process of category building. Thus the two basic rules presented previously, to abstain from forcing preconceived concepts, and to utilize theoretical sensibility in this process, are obviously difficult to reconcile.

THE GLASERIAN VS. THE STRAUSSIAN APPROACH: TWO WAYS OF THEORETICALLY INFORMED CATEGORY BUILDING

The Discovery of Grounded Theory invites empirical researchers to develop their own ideas instead of applying ungrounded theories in their empirical field and restricting the empirical work on the testing of hypotheses, which has a liberating and stimulating effect, especially on junior researchers or doctoral students. However, in the years following *The Discovery of Grounded Theory*, the apparent antagonism between emergence and theoretical sensitivity remained a major problem for teaching the methodology of grounded theory.

In their later writings, Glaser and Strauss undertook a variety of efforts to clarify the idea of theoretical sensitivity and to account for the necessary 'theory-ladenness' of empirical observation. Regrettably, these efforts led both authors in different directions and contributed to a major split between them. In 1978 (more than one decade after the publication of *The Discovery of Grounded Theory*), Barney Glaser tried to clarify the concept of theoretical sensitivity in his own monograph of that title. In doing so, he coined the terms 'theoretical codes,' 'theoretical coding,' and 'coding families' to describe a process whereby analysts have a great variety of theoretical concepts at their disposal to structure the developing categories and the emerging theory. Strauss developed a different conception: the most important categories shall be developed and related to each other by a so-called 'paradigm model,' a straightforward model of human action and interaction rooted in pragmatist social theory. (In his later writings Strauss gave up this strong inclination towards action.) These two models for grounding categories and their differences will be described and their advantages and disadvantages will be discussed in the following section.

Barney Glaser's model of theoretical coding

According to Glaser, one of the main reasons to write *Theoretical Sensitivity* was that the discussion of theoretical sensitivity turned out to be 'a major gap in *The Discovery of Grounded Theory*' (Glaser, 1978: 1). Glaser here attempts to unfold the technical aspects of theoretical sensitivity by inventing a new differentiation in the coding process. He distinguishes between 'theoretical coding' and 'substantive coding' while linking two different types of codes to these forms of coding: substantive codes and theoretical codes. (Codes or conceptual codes is thereby used as synonymous for 'categories and their properties.')

Substantive codes, which shall relate to the empirical substance of the research domain are developed during open coding, the first stage of the coding process. It could be either words informed by the language use of actors in the field (so called 'in vivo codes') or notions drawn from sociological terminology (which Glaser calls 'sociological constructs'). In order to establish relations between such substantive codes, the analyst needs theoretical codes which 'conceptualize how the substantive codes may relate to each other as hypotheses to be integrated into a theory' (Glaser, 1978: 72). Theoretical codes are terms which describe possible relations between substantive codes and thereby help to form theoretical models. The examples Glaser uses for such theoretical codes are formal and highly abstract concepts from epistemology and sociological 'grand theory' which make basic claims about the ordering of the (social) world. Terms like causes, contexts, consequences, and conditions, for instance may help to develop links between codes: by calling certain events (which were coded with the help of substantive codes) 'causes' and others 'effects,' the previously developed substantive codes can be integrated into a causal model.

Glaser then presents a list of so-called theoretical 'coding families,' merging concepts which come from various (sociological, philosophical, or everyday) contexts, for example:

- terms, which relate to the degree of an attribute or property ('degree family'), like 'limit,' 'range,' 'extent,' 'amount,' etc.
- terms, which refer to the relation between a whole and its elements ('dimension family'), like 'element,' 'part,' 'facet,' 'slice,' 'sector,' 'aspect,' 'segment,' etc.
- terms, which refer to cultural phenomena ('cultural family') like 'social norms,' 'social values,' 'social beliefs,' etc.

and fourteen further coding families containing notions from diverse theoretical backgrounds, debates, and schools of philosophy or the social sciences. Thereby, many of these terms can be subsumed under different coding families: the term *goal*, for instance, belongs to a coding family referring to action strategies

(*strategies family*) as well as to a coding family referring to the relation between means and ends (*means-goal family*).

The diverse coding families can obviously serve as a fund of concepts which may guide researchers in developing their ability to think about empirical observations in theoretical terms. However, their utility for the development of theoretical relations between the 'substantive codes' is limited. The reason for that is that one can make sense of coding families (which Glaser presents as an unsorted list of terms) only if one is clear about their inner relations and their embeddedness into greater conceptual networks. This can be easily demonstrated with regard to Glaser's first coding family (the six C's, which he obviously considers as the most important) referring (among other things) to causal relations. Terms denoting causal relations (like cause, condition, consequence, etc.), however, are in themselves not sufficient for the development of causal models. To construct a causal model about the relation between specific events it would be necessary to use substantial (i.e. sociological, psychological) categories which define those types of events which can be generally considered as causes and those which are usually to be seen as effects. By using merely a formal coding family denoting causal relations without reference to substantial categories, one could treat arbitrarily all kinds of events which can be found in the research field as causes and effects. To simply use the notion of causality while investigating youth delinquency could mean that one regards deviant behavior either as a cause or as an effect of negative sanctions. To choose between these two possibilities one would not primarily need formal terms (like cause and effect) but a theoretical code based on a sociological perspective. This could either (like classical learning theory or role theory) explain sanctions as a result of behavior or it could describe deviant behavior as a result of stigmatizing sanctions (like labeling theory). A crucial problem with Glaser's list of coding families is that it lacks a differentiation between formal or logical categories (like causality) and substantial sociological concepts (like social roles, identity, culture); both types of categories would have to be linked to each other in order to develop empirically grounded categories. Although Glaser's list of coding families certainly does not exclude such a sophisticated use of theoretical codes, the whole problem is not even mentioned in *Theoretical Sensitivity*. This causes problems particularly for novice researchers trying to make adequate use of the whole concept of theoretical coding: in a similar fashion to the notion of theoretical sensitivity, the concept does not entail a set of methodological rules applicable in research practice concerning how to structure the emerging categories with the help of theoretical knowledge. The problem is not so much that Glaser's list of coding families would not be sufficient to stimulate the discovery of possible theoretical relations between incidents in the data or between newly developed categories. It is rather that the employment of such an unordered list for the construction of grounded theories is very difficult if the researcher does not have a very broad theoretical background knowledge at hand concerning the different theoretical perspectives entailed in the list.

Anselm Strauss's concept of a 'coding paradigm'

In his book *Qualitative Analysis for Social Scientists*, published in 1987, Anselm Strauss goes one step further in explicating the concrete steps a researcher can take to develop categories from empirical data with a theoretical perspective in mind. The book had evolved from a research seminar set up to train students in grounded theory procedures (Legewie & Schervier-Legewie, 2004). Like Glaser before him (who used experiences from the seminar which he had run between 1968 and 1979 to author *Theoretical Sensitivity*), Strauss was aware of the difficulties novices 'have in generating genuine categories. The common tendency is simply to take a bit of the data (a phrase or sentence or paragraph) and translate that into a précis of it' (Strauss, 1987: 29). Many users of grounded theory procedures, novices in particular, often did not come to terms with developing true theoretical categories. Frequently, categories plucked from the data were only summaries or descriptions.

When Strauss wrote his own new methodological monograph, he and Barney Glaser had not worked together on joint research projects for some time. Although pages of the introduction are filled with extensive quotes from *Theoretical Sensitivity*, and some of the terms Glaser had invented were mentioned (for instance, *open coding*, *in vivo codes*, or *sociological constructs*), Strauss paid absolutely no heed to two concepts pivotal to Glaser's view on theoretical sensitivity: *theoretical coding* and *coding families*. Furthermore, Strauss invented the new term (coding paradigm) which he used to structure data and to clarify relations between categories:

> It is central to the coding procedures. Although especially helpful to beginning analysts, in a short time this paradigm quite literally becomes part and parcel of the analyst's thought processes. Whether explicit or implicit, it functions as a reminder to code data for relevance to whatever phenomena are referenced by a given category (Strauss, 1987: 27).

The coding paradigm comes into play during 'axial coding,' an advanced stage of open coding. Whereas open coding starts by 'scrutinizing the fieldnote, interview, or other document very closely; line by line, or even word by word. The aim is to produce concepts that seem to fit the data' (Strauss, 1987: 28), axial coding 'consists of intense analysis done around one category at a time in terms of the paradigm items' (Strauss, 1987: 32). This category forms the 'axis' around which further coding and category building is done and may eventually become the core category of the emerging theory.

Strauss elaborates further on the concepts 'coding paradigm' and 'axial coding' in *Basics of Qualitative Research* published together with a new co-author, Juliet Corbin (Strauss & Corbin, 1990). This book attempted to describe grounded theory procedures in a didactic step-by-step mode. The coding paradigm fulfils the same function as a Glaserian coding family; it represents a group of abstract theoretical terms which are used to develop categories from the data and to find relations between them. Similar to Glaser's coding families, the coding paradigm takes into account that the development of categories requires either a previously defined theoretical framework or at least the possibility to draw on a selection of such frameworks if one wants to avoid being flooded by the data

However, the coding paradigm turned out much more instructive for many grounded theory users than the coding family conception. While Glaser had proposed a long and only loosely ordered list of more or less related groups of sociological and formal terms, Strauss and Corbin advise the researcher to use one general model of action rooted in pragmatist and interactionist social theory (cf. Corbin, 1991: 36; Strauss, 1990: 7) to build a skeleton or 'axis' for the developing categories and their relations. Thereby, a general 'paradigm model' (Strauss & Corbin, 1990: 99) is established which determines the analysis of action and interaction strategies of the actors as the main purpose of grounded theory. Special emphasis is laid on the intentions and goals of the actors in this process. Categories developed during open coding shall be investigated whether they relate to: (1) *phenomena* at which the actions and interactions in the domain under study are directed; (2) *causal conditions* which lead to the occurrence of these phenomena; (3) attributes of the *context* of the investigated phenomena; (4) additional *intervening conditions* by which the investigated phenomena are influenced; (5) *action and interactional strategies* the actors use to handle the phenomena; and (6) the *consequences* of their actions and interactions. Thus the analyst is advised to identify types of phenomena, contexts, causal, intervening conditions, and consequences which are relevant for the most important category or categories in order to develop an 'axis' for the grounded theory. If, for instance, social aspects of chronic pain are investigated, the researcher shall try to determine action contexts in the data which are typical for patients with chronic pain as well as characteristic patterns of pain management strategies. Thereafter, it can be examined which pain management strategies are used by persons with chronic pain under certain conditions and in varying action contexts. This may then lead to the construction of models of action which provide the basis for a theory about action strategies generally pursued under conditions of chronic pain.

Pros and cons of the two approaches

Regarding the role of previous theoretical knowledge in the research process, one can now draw on two different versions of grounded theory which vary to a considerable extent. In 1992, Glaser attacked Strauss and Corbin in a monograph published in his private publication venture titled *Emergence vs. Forcing*. In this, Glaser accuses Strauss of having betrayed the common cause of grounded theory. By applying the concepts of axial coding and coding paradigms, researchers would force categories on the data instead of allowing the categories to emerge. Glaser's charges, which were written in an exceptionally polemical and even personally hostile manner, were never answered publicly by Strauss and Corbin. Nevertheless, several questions remain: which of the two approaches would better reflect the original intentions of grounded theory?

Which one would be better suited for developing categories from the data and which is more easily applicable in research practice?

All of the differing concepts 'theoretical sensitivity,' 'theoretical coding,' 'axial coding,' 'coding paradigm,' and 'coding families' represent attempts to solve a fundamental methodological problem which arises with the claim to let categories 'emerge' from the data: a strategy of investigation which approaches an empirical domain without any theoretical preconceptions is simply not feasible—such a method would yield a plethora of incoherent observations and descriptions rather than empirically grounded categories or hypotheses. The emergence of theoretical categories which can adequately describe phenomena in the empirical field is always dependent on the researcher's theoretical sensitivity, their ability to grasp empirical phenomena in theoretical terms. This competence demands an extended training and a broad background in sociological theory (cf. Glaser, 1992: 28). This is especially the case if the Glaserian approach is used: one would need an advanced understanding of different thoughts of school, their terminology, and their possible relations to make use of Glaser's list of coding families, to choose the coding families most adequate for the data and to combine different coding families in a meaningful way. Nevertheless, the methodological usefulness of this list is limited in more than one respect: novices in empirical research will have difficulties in handling the more or less unsystematic compilation of theoretical terms from various sociological and epistemological backgrounds. Researchers with broad theoretical background knowledge, and longstanding experience in the application of theoretical terms, will certainly not need such a list.

At first glance, Strauss and Corbin's 'coding paradigm' represents a more user-friendly concept, since it describes the construction of a theoretical framework for the development of empirically grounded categories in an explicit manner. By drawing on this concept, researchers with limited experience in the application of theoretical knowledge can use grounded theory methodology without taking the risk of being flooded by the data. Researchers may feel too constrained by the specific theoretical perspective embedded in the coding paradigm which stems from a certain theoretical tradition: philosophical and sociological pragmatism originating from the works of Peirce, Dewey, and Mead. Glaser's critique that the coding paradigm may lead to the forcing of categories on the data thus cannot be dismissed.

However, the conceptual design of the coding paradigm carries a broad and general understanding of action which is compatible with a wide variety of sociological theories (ranging from sociological phenomenology to Rational Choice Theory and even to functionalist role theory), and which is also entailed in several of Glaser's coding families: viewed from a Glaserian perspective, the coding paradigm can be regarded as a combination of aspects which Glaser disperses among different coding families, since it blends parts of the first coding family (the six C's, causes, contexts, contingencies, consequences, covariances, and conditions) with the 'strategy family' and the 'means-goal family.'

The coding paradigm presented by Strauss and Corbin in 1990 is specifically linked to a micro-sociological perspective on social phenomena emphasizing the role of human action and agency in social life. Interestingly, this perspective is also shared by Glaser who rarely includes terms from macro-sociological approaches into his coding families. Furthermore, in *Theoretical Sensitivity*, he himself asserts that coding and coded incidents have to be related to *actions* of the actors in the empirical domain. Finally, the concept of 'Basic Social Processes' which was crucial for Glaserian grounded theory particularly at that time shows strong associations to sociological pragmatism. Thus it is at least doubtful whether theoretical coding *sensu* Glaser was originally developed to foster a highly pluralistic use of theoretical codes, including the use of concepts from macro-sociological approaches (although theoretical coding can be definitely expanded in that direction). All of the substantive (as compared to the formal) coding families presented by Glaser in *Theoretical Sensitivity* show a strong relation to a micro-sociological perspective which places actors and their actions in the focus of analysis (with categories like strategies, tactics, maneuverings, identity, goals, anticipated consequences, and others). There is no coding family referring to system theory (with terms like integration, differentiation, or emergent properties). However, an analyst familiar with such a theoretical perspective may easily develop such a coding family and apply it, for instance, in a grounded theory about a certain organization. However, researchers with a strong background in macro-sociology and system theory may feel uncomfortable with Strauss and Corbin's coding paradigm, since such a micro-sociological and action-oriented approach goes contrary to their requirements.

Following the Straussian route by constructing one's own coding paradigm connected to the theoretical tradition one prefers would be one possibility to stick with grounded theory methodology without adopting the (meta)theoretical orientation of its founding parents. The methodology of grounded theory is undoubtedly open enough to allow for such a stance. The other possibility to avoid unwillingly introducing unwanted theoretical tenets is to draw on Glaserian theoretical coding while choosing and developing suitable theoretical codes and coding families using a theoretical approach one finds suitable for the area under study. In a grounded theory study about the process of care giving for elderly and frail relatives at home, for instance, one may use theoretical codes derived from decision theory (focusing on the intentions of the actors, as well as their perceived 'costs' and 'benefits' of care giving) or codes based on role theory (focusing on the expectations of the social environment). Such a strategy is clearly more flexible in regard to the variety of theoretical perspectives which can be used. However, one has always to keep in mind that such theoretical codes must not be 'forced' on the data (which means that they may only be used if the data material itself suggests their use: one may only apply an approach based on utility theory, for instance, if the research subjects did refer to what can be considered 'costs' or 'benefits' of the care giving situation). This makes such a strategy much more challenging for novices than the use of a readymade conceptual framework or coding paradigm.

As far as the role of previous theoretical knowledge is concerned, the crucial difference between Glaserian and Straussian category building lies in the fact that Strauss suggests the utilization of a specified theoretical framework based on a certain understanding of human action, whereas Glaser emphasizes that coding is a process of combining 'the analyst's scholarly knowledge and his research knowledge of the substantive field' (Glaser, 1978: 70) and has to be realized in the ongoing coding process, which often means that it has to be conducted on the basis of a broad theoretical background knowledge which cannot be made fully explicit in the beginning of analysis

Unfortunately, Glaser tends to exaggerate these differences and resorts to an inductivist rhetoric which produces a highly obscure image of empirical research. Therefore, he does not only expect a researcher working with grounded theory procedures to approach the research field without any precise research questions or research problems ('He moves in with the abstract wonderment of what is going on that is an issue and how it is handled,' Glaser, 1992: 22); he also burdens his method (and possible users) with unrealistic truth claims. Thus Glaser maintains: 'In grounded theory (...) when the analyst sorts by theoretical codes everything fits, as the world is socially integrated and grounded theory simply catches this integration through emergence' (Glaser, 1992: 84). 'Grounded theory looks for what is, not what might be, and therefore needs no test' (Glaser, 1992: 67). Such assertions display at least a gleam of epistemological fundamentalism (or 'certism'; Lakatos, 1978) and perpetuate the outmoded and positivistic idea that by using an inductive method empirical researchers may gain the ability to conceive 'facts as they are.' However, Glaser makes clear elsewhere that theoretical concepts do not simply arise from the data alone but require careful 'theoretical coding' (that means: the categorizing of empirical data on the basis of previous theoretical knowledge). Thus the suspicion arises that his 'emergence talk' does not describe a methodological strategy but simply offers a way to immunize theories from criticism with the help of a methodological rhetoric (claiming that researchers following the 'true path' of grounded theory can never go wrong since the categories have emerged from data).

Grounded theory was originally developed to provide an alternative to a strict hypothetico-deductive model of social research which restricts the function of empirical research to the testing of ready-made hypotheses. This experimental model of research represented a mainline approach towards methodology in social research at least in the 1950s and 1960s, although field studies conducted by famous ethnographers (like Malinowski or Margaret Mead) or outstanding sociological researchers (namely the members of the Chicago School) in the first decades of the twentieth century had demonstrated that field research in the social sciences cannot be pursued with the help of such a model. The concept of emergence which was meant to replace the deductive concept of hypothesis testing drawn from experimental research can provoke misunderstandings (namely the idea that categories emerge from the data if a researcher avoids the use of any theoretical preconception whatsoever). Qualitative researchers applying grounded theory methodology must therefore use the emergence concept in an epistemologically informed way: they must take into account that although qualitative research does not start with readymade and precise hypotheses, the development of categories from empirical data is dependent on the availability of adequate theoretical concepts. In the following it will be shown how the concept of empirical content can assist researchers in using their previous theoretical knowledge without forcing the data.

THE USE OF PREVIOUS THEORETICAL KNOWLEDGE IN CATEGORY BUILDING

If one sets aside Glaser's inductivist rhetoric, his concepts of theoretical codes and coding families represent a way systematically to introduce theoretical knowledge into the coding process without 'forcing' preconceived categories on the data. The conception of coding families make clear that certain types of theoretical knowledge are clearly helpful in deriving grounded categories from the data. Furthermore it allows for more theoretical pluralism than Strauss and Corbin's coding paradigm. However, as has been said before, the conception of coding families will be more difficult to employ for non-experienced researchers who may have problems in realizing the differences between theoretical knowledge, which forces the data, and theoretical concepts, which help with the emergence of suitable theoretical categories from the data. This situation may lead to the impression that theoretical sensitivity is merely an individual quality of researchers. However, if the use of previous theoretical knowledge is based on a sound methodological and epistemological basis novice researchers may easily learn to distinguish between theoretical notions that force the data and concepts that support the emergence of new categories. If that distinction can be made in a proper way the use of a predefined coding paradigm will also become possible: the researcher will then be able to select theoretical codes before the data are coded and to use predefined category schemes without abandoning basic principles of grounded theory (specifically the principle of discovering new patterns and relations in the data). But how can this task be achieved?

In the following text, it will be demonstrated that an understanding of classical methodological concepts like 'falsifiability' or 'empirical content' will be helpful for that purpose. A distinction between theoretical notions with *high empirical content* on the one hand and notions with *low empirical content* on the other hand can be an important tool for understanding the role of previous theoretical knowledge in developing grounded categories. Theoretical categories with high empirical content or high falsifiability are an essential part of a hypothetico-deductive research strategy, but can easily lead to forcing of the data if a grounded theory approach is used. Take the following hypothesis as an example: 'Young adults with a middle class background (defined in terms of income and educational status of their parents) have a better chance of attending university than young people with a working class background.' This hypothesis can be empirically tested (and thus be falsified if counter evidence is discovered during such a test), since each category in this statement can in principle be operationalized and measured (e.g. by defining young adults as 'men and women aged between 18 years and 25 years' or defining educational status as 'level of school leaving exam'). Categories and hypotheses of that type guide good quantitative social research, but the attempt to design a grounded theory project on such a basis would lead to methodological misuse: one would collect lots of material not suited to test the specific hypotheses and definitely disregard the richness of the data one can collect with the help of qualitative methods. The process of theory building in a grounded theory project can benefit from theoretical concepts with *low empirical content* which do not force the data but may serve as heuristic devices which will be discussed in the following two sections. In these sections I will present examples for two different types of heuristic concepts with limited empirical content which can be either utilized in open coding or as a means to define category schemes before data are collected: first, *theoretical notions*, definitions and categories drawn from 'grand theories' and second, *common sense categories* which relate to general topics of interest covered in the data.

Theoretical categories with limited empirical content as heuristic devices

A great number of theoretical notions, definitions, and categories drawn from grand theories (categories like identity, status, roles, systems, structure, values, and deviance), lack empirical content; they are so broad and abstract that it is difficult to directly deduce empirically contentful or falsifiable propositions from them which can be tested in a hypothetico-deductive framework. A proposition like 'A social role defines the expected behavior connected to a given social position' may serve as a good example of that. This statement has no (or very limited) empirical content which means that it is hard to imagine a direct empirical test which could disprove or falsify it: someone who tries to present a counter example (that would mean a social role not defining expected behavior connected to a social position) would even demonstrate thereby that he did not understand the meaning of such a statement: it is obviously not suited for being tested through empirical data. However, such theoretical categories can sensitize the researcher to identify theoretically relevant phenomena in their field. Herbert Blumer had proposed the term 'sensitizing concepts' to denote abstract notions which 'lack precise reference and have no bench marks which allow a clean cut identification of a specific instance' (Blumer, 1954: 7) and distinguished them from 'definitive concepts':

> Whereas definitive concepts provide prescriptions of what to see, sensitizing concepts merely suggest directions along which to look. The hundreds of our concepts—like culture, institutions, social structure, mores and personality—are not definitive concepts but are sensitizing in nature (Blumer, 1954).

Sensitizing concepts can fulfill an important role in empirical research, since their lack of empirical content permits researchers to apply them to a wide array of phenomena. Regardless how empirically contentless and vague they are, they may serve as *heuristic devices* for the construction of empirically grounded categories. A category like 'identity' may serve as an example for that. To operationalize such a category is much more difficult than to operationalize terms like 'university attendance' or 'educational status of parents.' And to directly derive falsifiable and testable propositions from that concept alone (that means without using any further concepts or empirical information) could be a troublesome task; the assertion, for instance, that individuals develop a certain identity in a given social domain does not imply a lot of information or empirical content by itself. Such a concept could be, however, extremely useful if one wants to formulate empirical research questions for a given substantive field: Does identity formation play an important role in the empirical domain under study? What processes of identity formation take place? By which means do empirical actors develop and defend their identity? Is the identity or self-definition of certain actors challenged by others? Which strategies do actors employ to defend and to maintain their identity if challenged? How do others counteract such strategies? Therefore, a sensible way to use a heuristic concept like identity in grounded theory research is not to derive a 'hypothesis,' which can be 'empirically tested' (like the hypothesis about the relation between social background and university attendance presented above), but to employ it as a conceptual frame which helps to understand empirical phenomena found in the research field. By employing a term like identity in a study about juveniles living in institutional care one may identify strategies how young people preserve and develop their identity under difficult circumstances. Identifying such strategies may lead to the development of empirically contentful statements (maintaining, for instance, that young people in care homes develop different strategies of identity formation compared to children in foster families) which can be further examined in subsequent research. Thus one can apply abstract theoretical categories with a general scope (which refer to various kinds of phenomena) but with limited empirical content (like identity or social role) as heuristic devices to develop empirically grounded categories with a limited scope and high empirical content (like 'identity formation of juveniles taken away from their parents and living in care homes in the UK').

A variety of concepts coming from differing theoretical approaches in sociology and social psychology can be used in such a way. It is also possible to use categories from schools of thought which are normally remote from qualitative research, like rational choice theory, as heuristic devices. A core assumption of rational choice theory is that human actors will choose the action which seems the most adequate for the achievement of a desired goal from a set of given action alternatives. However, without specifying *which* goals the actors pursue and *which* actions they consider to be adequate, the theory is like an 'empty sack' (cf. Simon, 1985). Thus, the core assumptions of utility theory contain almost no empirical content if they are not supplemented by auxiliary assumptions or 'bridge hypotheses.' Accordingly, rational choice theory may provide qualitative researchers with useful research questions, sensitizing concepts, and heuristic categories: one may, for instance, code incidents in the data which refer to the potential *costs* and *benefits* certain actions have for the actors, or one may code incidents which relate to the *intentions* and *goals* of the research subjects or to the *means* they use to reach their goals.

In this manner, a wide array of sensitizing categories from different theoretical traditions can be used to develop empirically grounded categories. Many researchers find it easier to let categories emerge if one stays with one particular theoretical tradition, however Glaser is certainly right with his frequent warnings that the utilization of a single pet theory will almost necessarily lead to the neglect of heuristic concepts better suited to the specific domain under scrutiny. There are heuristic concepts which capture a broad variety of different processes and events and nevertheless may exclude certain phenomena from being analyzed: thus the extended use of concepts from micro-sociological action theory (e.g. actors, goals, strategies) can preclude a system theory and macro-perspective on the research domain. A strategy of coding which uses different and even competing theoretical perspectives may often be superior to a strategy which remains restricted to a limited number of pet concepts. Furthermore, analysts should always ask themselves whether the chosen heuristic categories lead to the exclusion of certain processes and events from being analyzed and coded, since this would be an attribute of a category with high empirical content which refers to a circumscribed set of phenomena (akin to the definitive category 'young adults' excluding older persons).

Common sense categories

Another kind of heuristic categories which do not force data but allow for the discovery of empirically contentful categories are categories which refer to topics of interest contained in the data. Drawing on general commonsense knowledge can easily identify such 'topic oriented categories.' Categories like school, work, or family are simple examples of that, but topic oriented categories may be far more complex. They can also be related to specific local knowledge of the investigated field the researcher knows beforehand and thus mimic *in vivo* codes (although they are not discovered during open coding). However, as with heuristic theoretical concepts, one question remains of utmost importance: Does a certain code serve for heuristic purposes and can it thereby be related to important phenomena in the field or does it exclude relevant processes or events from analysis?

Suitable heuristic categories, whether developed from grand theory or taken from commonsense knowledge, do not force the data since they lack empirical content. This makes them useless for a hypothetico-deductive strategy; their strength is in the context of exploratory, interpretive research. Such categories fit various kinds of social reality and it will not be necessary to know concrete facts about the investigated domain before data collection takes place. Heuristic categories play the role of a theoretical axis or a skeleton to which the flesh of empirically contentful information from the research domain is added. The goal is to develop empirically grounded categories and propositions about relations between these categories. Category building of that kind starts by using heuristic concepts and proceeds to the construction of categories and propositions with growing empirical content.

The use of categories with high empirical content in grounded theory

It may be also possible to fruitfully employ categories and assertions with *high* empirical content in category building under certain circumstances. A researcher investigating the process of caregiving to frail and elderly people, for instance, may discover that Arlie Hochschild's category 'emotional labor' (Hochschild, 1983) helps the researcher to understand social interactions in the research field. This category, initially developed to describe typical patterns of action and interaction between flight attendants and air passengers, can thus adopt a heuristic function in the sociological investigation of another research domain, although it comprises more empirical content than terms like 'identity' or 'intentions': not all kinds of social interactions demand emotional labor and, compared to other sensitizing categories or propositions, the assumption that certain professionals are providing emotional labor can be falsified more readily.

The concept can be helpful for the analysis of social phenomena in certain areas. Consequently, it can be prudent in grounded theory research to use distinct and well-defined categories and propositions which contain enough empirical content to be empirically tested. The use of such concepts and the examination of hypotheses represent an older, well-established tradition in qualitative research. In the 1930s, researchers and methodologists coming from the Chicago School had proposed a research strategy named 'analytic induction,' which was used thereafter in numerous well-known qualitative studies: initial hypotheses are examined and modified with the help of empirical evidence provided by so-called 'crucial cases' (cf. Cressey, 1953: 104f; Lindesmith, 1946). By applying such a research strategy, one always carries the risk that theoretical categories are introduced which are not suited for the specific research domain and which are forced on the empirical data. The danger that heuristic concepts may contain too much empirical content is even prevalent with Strauss and Corbin's coding paradigm. Although it represents an understanding of purposeful and intentional human action useful for the description of a wide array of social phenomena, it may draw qualitative researchers towards a micro-sociological orientation which they do not necessarily share. The advice to use only categories with particular low empirical content may constrict inexperienced researchers, since not each heuristic concept can draw the researcher's attention to sociologically relevant phenomena. This danger relates to Glaser's coding families; novices in particular may be overstrained by the task to select the heuristic category most suited for their research field among a vast selection of theoretical schools of thought.

CONCLUDING REMARKS

The development of categories which are sufficiently grounded in the empirical data requires that researchers abstain from forcing theoretical concepts on the data. The process of category building is frequently described with the term 'emergence,' particularly in the earliest versions of grounded theory. This concept is obviously burdened with methodological problems while evoking empiricist ideas about researchers freeing themselves from any theoretical knowledge before approaching their empirical field. Glaser and Strauss did not overlook the fact, however, that researchers always have to draw on existing stocks of theoretical knowledge in order to understand, describe, and explain empirically observed phenomena. In *The Discovery of Grounded Theory*, they use the term 'theoretical sensitivity' to denote the ability to identify theoretical relevant phenomena in the data. In their further methodological writings, Glaser and Strauss elaborated this concept in quite differing directions. Previous theoretical knowledge may thus be used in different ways in the process of developing empirically grounded categories:

1. The strategy of 'theoretical coding' proposed by Glaser is especially interesting for experienced researchers with a broad background in sociological theory: if the researcher has a large stock of theoretical categories at hand and a deep reaching knowledge about their interrelations, they can easily start coding without any predefined category scheme in mind and may develop the relations between substantive codes by drawing on theoretical codes which in their opinion are suited best for the data. For that purpose, researchers can either resort to the coding families suggested by Glaser and combine them in meaningful ways or they may define their own coding families by using theoretical approaches not mentioned by Glaser.
2. Novice researchers may experience greater difficulties in selecting and combining the most appropriate coding families for their research domain. Therefore, they may benefit from using a predefined coding paradigm and thus avoid drowning in the data. This may include, but is not restricted to, the specific coding paradigm rooted in pragmatist theory of action recommended by Strauss and Corbin. As with Glaser's coding families, researchers may also construct their own coding paradigms. In doing so, one must be careful to draw on concepts which do not force the data but enhance theoretical sensitivity and can serve as heuristic devices.

A theoretically sensitive researcher employing an epistemologically informed concept of emergence would be able to differentiate between different types of theoretical categories (namely between definite and precise categories, and broad and general heuristic concepts) and to reflect on their differing functions in the process of empirically grounded category building. Whereas definite and precise categories are suitable to form empirically contentful and falsifiable hypotheses (which in grounded theory should only be formulated at fairly advanced stages of the theory building process), broad and abstract theoretical notions are especially helpful for the empirically grounded generation of categories, since their lack of empirical content gives them flexibility to describe a great variety of empirical phenomena. Heuristic categories of that kind represent lenses through which researchers perceive facts and phenomena in their research field. If the difference between empirically contentful categories and categories as heuristic devices is observed, one need not refrain from inventing theoretical categories during open coding but may also develop a theoretical axis or coding scheme before data are coded. The decisive question which helps to make the distinction between empirically contentful and heuristic theoretical categories is: does the category exclude interesting phenomena in the empirical field from being analyzed?

REFERENCES

Becker, H. & Geer, B. (1960). Participant Observation: The Analysis of Qualitative Field Data. In R. N. Adams, J. J. Preiss (Eds.), *Human Organization Research: Field Relations and Techniques* (pp. 267–289). Homewood, IL: The Dorsey Press.

Blumer, H. (1954). What is wrong with Social Theory? *American Sociological Review*, 19, 3–10.

Chalmers, A. F. (1999). *What is this Thing Called Science?* Maidenhead: Open University Press.

Corbin, J. (1991). Anselm Strauss: An Intellectual Biography. In David R. Maines (Eds.), *Social Organization and Social Process. Essays in Honor of Anselm Strauss* (pp. 17–44). New York: Aldine de Gruyter.

Cressey, D. R. (1953/1971). *Other People's Money. A Study in the Social Psychology of Embezzlement*. Belmont: Wadsworth.

Glaser, B. (1978). *Theoretical Sensitivity. Advances in the Methodology of Grounded Theory*. Mill Valley, CA: The Sociology Press.

Glaser, B. (1992). *Emergence vs. Forcing: Basics of Grounded Theory Analysis*. Mill Valley, CA: Sociology Press.

Glaser, B. & Strauss, A. (1967). *The Discovery of Grounded Theory: Strategies for Qualitative Research*. New York: Aldine de Gruyter.

Hanson, N. R. (1965). *Patterns of Discovery. An Inquiry into the Conceptual Foundations of Science*. Cambridge: Cambridge University Press.

Hochschild, A. (1983). *The Managed Heart. Commercialization of Human Feeling*. Berkeley: University of California Press.

Kelle, U., Marx, J., Pengel, S., Uhlhorn, K. & Witt, I. (2002). Die Rolle theoretischer Heuristiken im qualitativen Forschungsprozeß—ein Werkstattbericht. In Hans-Uwe Otto, Gertrud Oelerich, Heinz-Günter Micheel (Eds.), *Empirische Forschung und Soziale Arbeit. Ein Lehr-und Arbeitsbuch* (pp. 11–130). Neuwied und Kriftel: Luchterhand.

Lakatos, I. (1978). *The Methodology of Scientific Research Programmes*. Cambridge: Cambridge University Press.

Laudan, L. (1977). *Progress and its Problems. Towards a Theory of Scientific Growth.* London and Henley: Routledge & Kegan Paul.

Legewie, H. & Schervier-Legewie, B. (2004). 'Research is Hard Work, it's Always a bit Suffering. Therefore, on the Other Side Research Should be Fun.' Anselm Strauss in Conversation With Heiner Legewie and Barbara Schervier-Legewie. In *Forum Qualitative Sozialforschung/Forum: Qualitative Social Research.* Retrieved March 9, 2007 from http://www.qualitative-research.net/fqs-texte/3-04/04-3-22-e.htm

Lindesmith, A. R. (1946/1968). *Addiction and Opiates.* Chicago: Aldine.

Simon, H. A. (1985). Human nature in politics: The dialogue of psychology with political science. *The American Political Science Review*, 79, 293–304.

Strauss, A. L. (1987). *Qualitative Analysis for Social Scientists.* Cambridge: Cambridge University Press.

Strauss, A. L. (1990). *Creating Sociological Awareness.* New Brunswick: Transaction Publishers.

Strauss, A. L. & Corbin, J. (1990). *Basics of Qualitative Research. Grounded Theory Procedures and Techniques.* Newbury Park, CA: SAGE.

10

Abduction: The Logic of Discovery of Grounded Theory

Jo Reichertz

> We decided to write a book about methods in the mid-1960s. We felt that changes were in the air and wanted to write for the new generation—the people over 30 were already too bound by convention. Barney was more positive about the project. I was more sceptical because I was older. The title indicates what was important to us *The Discovery of Grounded Theory* (1967): unlike the usual method books which are concerned with verification, we were more interested in the discovery of theory 'out of the data'. Grounded Theory is not a theory but a methodology to discover theories dormant in the data' (Legewie & Schervier-Legewie, 2004).[1]

Grounded theory (GT), which Anselm Strauss refers to here in an interview decades later, is one of the most successful methods ever developed and has added a more qualitative note to social research. This is, however, not a result of the clarity and simplicity of this method established by Barney Glaser and Anselm Strauss but is rather due to the fact that it counteracts the common prejudice, which is to some extent entertained in science, that theories quasi emerge by themselves from the data (without any previous theoretical input). According to this belief, one only has to evoke the theory inherent in the data by means of suitable methods, the theory would then become apparent without the active actions of scientists. The theories are thus believed to emerge slowly in a process of gradual abstraction from the data. Therefore, one of the most famous quotations from *The Discovery of Grounded Theory* is the following: 'Clearly, a grounded theory that is faithful to the everyday realities of the substantive area is one that has been carefully induced from the data' (Glaser & Strauss, 1967: 239). The incorrectness of such an inductive procedure has already been proven by

Popper in general and, with respect to GT, by Kelle (1994, 2005) and by Strübing (2004: Chapter 27) in particular. Many users of GT therefore regard this approach as an inductive method and are of the opinion, 'that the approach signals a return to simple "Baconian" inductivism' (Haig, 1995: 2). Representative for many others, here is an example from *Qualitative Research in Sociology*: Grounded Theory 'is known as an inductive or ground-up approach to data analysis' (Marvasti, 2004: 84). At first the two founders of GT shared this view: 'From its beginnings the methodology of Grounded Theory has suffered from an "inductivist self misunderstanding" entailed by some parts of the Discovery book. Although this inductivism plays a limited role in research work of many Grounded Theory studies (including those of the founding fathers) it has often lead to confusion especially among novices who draw their basic methodological knowledge from text books' (Kelle 2005: Chapter 24).

The fact that original GT has split into two directions (differing in the emphasis on the meaning of prior theoretical knowledge for research) became evident in Strauss's *Qualitative Analysis for Social Scientists* (1987), and certainly was clear in *Basics of Qualitative Research* (Strauss & Corbin, 1990). In both texts it was argued that theoretical pre-knowledge flows into the data's interpretation while Glaser insists that the codes and categories emerge directly from the data. The differences were made public in Glaser (1992; see also Glaser, 2002). The differences have been the object of heated debates (Kelle, 1994; Kendall, 1999; Miller, 1999; Strübing, 2004) in the scientific literature since then.

This later position found in both Strauss and Strauss and Corbin takes into account that observation and the development of theory are necessarily always already theory guided. 'Every type of inquiry rests on the asking of effective questions' (Strauss & Corbin 1990: 73). Furthermore, it also allows for the fact that scientists must be in a position to modify or even reject concepts during and due to observation. With this logic of research, GT falls within the realm of abductive research logic. Neither Strauss nor Strauss and Corbin have systematized this logic of abductive discovery, nor have they linked it to the considerations of Charles S. Peirce, the founder of abduction. To an extent their work can be read in other ways.

This contribution aims to close this gap: The purpose of this chapter is to examine whether the logic of later GT (Strauss from the 1980s onwards) is actually abductive. This might contribute to a better understanding of the nature of empirically GT construction. First, an adequate description of the abductive logic following Peirce is needed and second, an assessment is required whether the GT of the later Strauss (together with Juliet Corbin) can be reformulated with the ideas and notions of Peirce. Thus my thesis is that GT was to a very small extent abductive from the start and became more and more abductive in its later stage; at least in the work of Strauss. Thus the Glaser–Strauss controversy can be characterized, at least in part, as one between induction and abduction.

ABDUCTION: A RULE-GOVERNED WAY TO NEW KNOWLEDGE

Social researchers who take an interest in the fluctuation of their own professional vocabulary have been able, for more than two decades, to witness the
flourishing of a concept which is around 400 years old: it concerns the term
abduction. The boom has been so significant that we sometimes hear talk of an
'abductive turn' (Bonfantini, 1988; Wirth, 1995). First introduced in 1597 by
Julius Pacius to translate the Aristotelian concept *apagoge*, abduction remained
quite unnoticed for almost three centuries. It was Peirce (1839–1914) who first
took it up and used it to denote the only truly *knowledge-extending* means of
inferencing (so he claimed) that would be categorically distinct from the normal
types of logical conclusion, namely *deduction* and *induction* (1973, 1976, 1986,
1992). Several decades were to pass before Peirce's ideas were systematically
received and adopted (Anderson, 1995; Apel, 1967; Fann, 1970; Hanson, 1965;
Moore & Robin, 1964; Reichertz, 1991, 2003; Tursman, 1987; Wartenberg, 1971).
   Today the term 'abduction' has become something of a byword within social
research (but not only there): educationists, linguists, psychologists, psychoana-
lysts, semioticians, theatre-scientists, theologians, criminologists, researchers in
artificial intelligence, and sociologists announce in their research reports that
their new discoveries are due to abduction. The great success of abduction, in my
opinion, may be traced back to two particular features: first to its indefiniteness
and second to the misjudgment of the achievements of abduction that derive
from this. Frequently, the use of the idea of abduction has led many of its users
to one particular hope, that of a *rule-governed* and *replicable* production of
new and *valid* knowledge. This hope is found, above all, in artificial intelligence
research and in a number of variants of qualitative social research (e.g. Charniak &
McDermott, 1985; Hemker, 1986; Knorr, 1985; Kreppner, 1975).
   These approaches have in common that they stress both the *logical* and also
the *innovative* character of abduction. For abduction is no longer treated as a
traditional, classical means of drawing conclusions, but as a new method that is
not yet incorporated into formal logic. However, it is, in every sense, a means
of inferencing. It is precisely in this quality of being a 'means-of-inferencing'
that we find the secret charm of abduction: it is a *logical* inference (and thereby
reasonable and scientific), however it extends into the realm of profound insight
(and therefore generates new knowledge). The secret charm of abduction lies
straight in this kind of inference-being: abduction is sensible and scientific
as a form of inference, however it reaches to the sphere of deep insight and
new knowledge. Abduction is intended to help social research, or rather social
researchers, to be able to make new discoveries in a logically and methodologically ordered way.
   This hope, to be able to make new discoveries in a logically and methodologically ordered way, is directed against Reichenbach (1938) and Popper (1934)
who, by separating the logic of discovery from the logic of justification, 'drove'
the first into the realm of psychology, and allowed only the second into the realm

of serious science. This separation should be reversed: the unfortunate disjunction of contexts of discovery and justification should be removed by means of abduction. A rethinking of this kind promises a great deal: liberation from the 'chance of a good idea' (Habermas, 1973: 147), and (it is hoped) 'synthetic inferences *a posteriori.*'

Because of this hope many social scientists have treated, and still do treat, abduction as a magic formula: always applicable when the cognitive basis of the process of scientific discovery is being investigated: 'The attempt to characterize the act of the generating of hypothesis and subjective recognizing no longer only than arbitrarily and not further analyzable but comprehend it in form of the abductive conclusion can perhaps show the way in a direction, which is in the humanities well-known as hermeneutic procedure of creating knowledge' (Kreppner 1975: 69). In my opinion, however, this hope is the result of a widespread misunderstanding of Peirce's position with regard to the differences between 'hypothesis' and 'abduction' as forms of inference. From the modern point of view it is beyond question that, up to about 1898, Peirce combined two very different forms of inference under the name of 'hypothesis.' When he became aware of this unclear use of the term 'hypothesis,' he elaborated a clear distinction in his later philosophy between the two procedures, and called the one operation 'qualitative induction' and the other 'abduction' (for more detail see Reichertz, 2003, also Eco, 1981). Many social scientists, with reference to the *achievements* of abduction, rely on Peirce's later work (in my view wrongly), but with reference to its *form* and *validity*, on his work on hypothesis. It is only on the basis of this 'hybrid meaning' that they succeed in designing a logical operation which produces new knowledge in a rule-governed way.

DEDUCTION, QUANTITATIVE AND QUALITATIVE INDUCTION, ABDUCTION

The social order around which humans (often but not always) orient themselves in their actions is constantly changing and is, moreover, 'sub-culturally fragmented.' The different order(s) therefore possess only a localized validity and are continually and, since the advent of the 'modern,' with increasing rapidity being changed by individuals who previously (up to a point) adhered to them (Eisenstadt, 2003; Foucault, 2004). Moreover, both the *form* and the *validity* of this order are bound to the meaning attributions and interpretations of the acting subjects. Social science explanations of actions aim at the (re)construction of the order that is relevant to the acting subjects. Admittedly this kind of order can no longer be derived from proven grand theories, first because these are, as a rule, not sufficiently 'local,' and second because they have frequently already been overtaken by constant social change. Thus, appropriate new views of the structure of social order must constantly be generated. For this reason it is highly sensible to examine as closely as possible the life practice that is to be understood, and (on the basis of these data) to (re-)construct the *new* orders. It is obvious that the examination must start from older views and so have some link to them.

If we are now to make a serious attempt, in (qualitative and quantitative) research, to evaluate collected data, in other words to typologize them according to particular features and orders of features, the question very soon arises of how we may bring a little order to the chaos of the data. This is only to a very small extent a matter of work organization (sorting of data) and much more a question of how the unmanageable variety of the data may be related to theories: either pre-existing or still to be discovered. In this undertaking (if one pursues the ideas of Peirce) we may, in ideal terms, distinguish *three* procedures and, in what follows, I shall subdivide the second procedure into two sub-groups; not because there are fundamental differences between the two, but rather because in this way the difference we have already spoken of between *abduction* and *hypothesis* or *qualitative induction* can be made clearer (for a fuller discussion of this, see Reichertz, 2003).

Subsumption

One type of data analysis consists of the procedure of *subsumption*. Subsumption proceeds from an already known context of features, that is from a familiar *rule* (e.g. all burglars who steal from a medicine chest are drug addicts), and seeks to find this general context in the data (e.g. the unknown burglar has robbed the medicine chest) in order to obtain knowledge about the individual case (e.g. the unknown burglar is a drug addict). The logical form of this intellectual operation is that of *deduction*: the single case in question is subordinated to an already known rule. Here a tried and trusted order is applied to the new case. New facts (concerning the ordering of the world) are not experienced in this way; we have deduced that the unknown burglar is a drug addict (knowledge that may be quite useful to the police, if the rule is true). Deductions are therefore *tautological*, they tell us nothing new. But deductions are not only tautological but also *truth-conveying*: if the rule offered for application is valid, then the result of the application of the rule is also valid.

Generalizing

A second form of analysis consists of extending, or *generalizing*, into an order or rule the combinations of features that are found in the data material. Proceeding from the observation that 'in the case of burglaries a, b, and c the medicine chest was robbed;' and the case-knowledge that 'Mr. Jones committed burglaries a, b, and c,' the inference is drawn that 'Mr. Jones always robs the medicine chest when he breaks in.' The logical form of this intellectual operation is that of *quantitative induction*. It transfers the quantitative properties of a *sample* to a totality, it 'extends' the single case into a rule. *Quantitative inductions* therefore are equally tautological but not truth-conveying. The results of this form of inferencing are merely *probable*.

One particular variant of the inductive processing of data consists of assembling certain qualitative features of the investigated sample in such a way that this combination of features resembles another (that is already available in the repertoire of knowledge of the interacting community) in essential points. In this case one can use the term that already exists for this combination to characterize one's 'own' form. The logical form of this operation is that of *qualitative induction*. From the existence of certain qualitative features in a *sample* it implies the presence of other features (e.g. At the scene of a crime I see a particular set of clues. In very many respects these agree with the pattern of clues associated with Mr. Jones. Conclusion: Jones is responsible for the clues). The observed case (*token*) is an instance of a known order (*type*). To summarize: if *quantitative induction* makes inferences about a totality from the quantitative properties of a *sample*, qualitative induction (in contrast) supplements the observed features of a sample with others that are not perceived. It is only in this sense that this form of induction transcends the borders of experience, that is, only the experience of the sample in question. This inference only extends knowledge to the extent that it proceeds from a limited selection to a larger totality. *Qualitative induction* is not a valid but only a probable form of inference, although it does have the advantage of being capable of operationalization (albeit with difficulty). Qualitative induction is the basis of all scientific procedures that find, in collected data, only new versions of what is already known.

Abduction

The third type of data processing (apparently similar, but in fact totally different) consists of assembling or discovering, on the basis of an interpretation of collected data, such combinations of features for which there is no appropriate explanation or rule in the store of knowledge that already exists. This causes surprise. Real surprise causes a genuine shock (and not only in Peirce's opinion) and the search for the (new) explanation. Since no suitable 'type' can be found, a new one must be invented or discovered by means of a mental process. One may achieve a discovery of this sort as a result of an intellectual process and, if this happens, it takes place 'like lightning,' and the thought process 'is very little hampered by logical rules' (Peirce, 1931–1935: Vol. V: 117). An order, or a rule, in this procedure must therefore first be discovered or invented, and this has to happen with the aid of intellectual effort. Something unintelligible is discovered in the data and, on the basis of the mental design of a *new* rule, the rule is discovered or invented and, simultaneously, it becomes clear what the case is. The logical form of this operation is that of *abduction*. Here one has decided (with whatever degree of awareness and for whatever reason) no longer to adhere to the conventional view of things. This way of creating a new 'type' (the relationship of a typical new combination of features) is a creative outcome which engenders a new idea. This kind of association is not obligatory, and is indeed rather risky. *Abduction* 'proceeds,' therefore, from a known quantity

(= result) to *two* unknowns (= rule and case). Abduction is therefore a cerebral process, an intellectual act, a mental leap, that brings together things which one had never associated with one another: A cognitive logic of discovery.

TWO STRATEGIES FOR PRODUCING ABDUCTIONS

If one is to take seriously what has been outlined above, one would have to come to the conclusion (pessimistic though it might be for everyday scientific practice) that abductive discovery of new things is dependent either on pure chance, a benevolent God, a favorable evolution, or a particularly well-endowed brain. Science as a *systematic* endeavor would, according to this definition, seem doomed to failure. However, even if one cannot *force* lightning to strike in an algorithmically rule-governed way, could there perhaps be ways of proceeding and precautions that would make it easier for the (intellectual) lightning to strike? Even lightning is not entirely unexpected. To extend the metaphor, it happens only as a consequence of a particular meteorological situation. In a storm one can look for the oak tree or seek out the beeches or even go to the top of the church tower. None of these steps will make it certain that lightning will come and strike; but the likelihood is nonetheless very much greater than with someone who only loves the sunlight, who always takes refuge in a cellar during a storm, and who (if he does happen to find himself in a storm) always tries to find out where the nearest lightning conductor is. In short, if discovery is truly related to accidents, then one can either give accidents a chance or deny or reduce the possibility.

Peirce himself cites two *macro-strategies* that are particularly well-suited to 'enticing' abductive processes or at least to creating a favorable climate for their appearance. One can be derived from the story where Peirce talks retrospectively about his talents as an amateur detective (Peirce, 1929). In this Peirce tells how, during a voyage at sea, his overcoat and a valuable watch were stolen. He was very alarmed, because the watch was not his own property. He therefore decided to recover the watch, by any means and as quickly as possible. He had all the crew called together and asked them to form up in a line. Then he walked along the line and addressed a few apparently inconsequential words to each of them.

> When I had gone through the row, I turned and walked from them, though not away, and said to myself: 'Not the least scintilla of light have I got to go upon'. But thereupon my other self (for our own communings are always in dialogues) said to me, 'but you simply *must* put your finger on the man. No matter if you have no reason, you must say whom you think to be the thief'. I made a little loop in my walk, which had not taken a minute, and I turned toward them, all shadow of doubt had vanished (Peirce, 1929: 271).

Peirce named one person as the culprit and subsequently, after a great deal of confusion (see Sebeok & Umiker-Sebeok, 1985 for a full description), it emerged that the man suspected by Peirce was indeed the thief. The stimulus for this individual initiative in matters of 'detection' was therefore provided by *fear*: not the fear of losing the value of the watch, but the fear of a 'life-long professional disgrace' (Peirce, 1929: 270). When, after his first conversations with the crew, he could not name a suspect, he increased, by an act of will, his pressure to do something. In this partially self-induced emergency situation, the abductive lightning struck.

Of course, abductions cannot be forced by a specific procedural program, but one can induce situations (and this is the moral of this episode) in which abductions fit. According to Peirce, the presence of *genuine doubt* or *uncertainty* or *fear* or *great pressure to act* is a favorable 'weather situation' for abductive lightning to strike. Peirce, however, develops another possible way of creating situations in which new knowledge may more frequently be obtained. For this to work the investigator, as Peirce advises, should let his mind wander with no specific goal. This mental game without rules he calls 'musement,' a game of meditation, or daydreaming. How one achieves the condition of daydreaming may be seen in the following formulation:

> Enter your skiff of musement, push off into the lake of thought, and leave the breath of heaven to swell your sail. With your eyes open, awake to what is about or within you, and open conversation with yourself: for such is all meditation! (...) It is, however, not a conversation in words alone, but is illustrated, like a lecture, with diagrams and with experiments (Peirce, 1931–1935: Vol. 6, 315).

To do this requires leisure, that is to say, freedom from an immediate pressure to act is a fundamental condition, without which the skiff will not be able to embark. This apparently contradicts quite vehemently the preconditions for successful abductions which Peirce sets out in his detection example. Admittedly, the contradiction is resolved if one looks for what is typical in the two 'abduction-friendly' settings. In both cases the procedures mean that the *consciously working mind*, relying on logical rules, is outmaneuvered. Peirce-the-detective allows no time for the calculating mind to busy itself with the solution of his problem, and Peirce-the-daydreamer switches off his power of logical judgment by entrusting himself to the 'breath of heaven.'

All measures designed to create favorable conditions for abductions, therefore, always aim at one thing: the achievement of an *attitude* of preparedness to abandon old convictions and to seek new ones. Abductive inferencing is not, therefore, a *mode of reasoning* that delivers new knowledge, and neither is it an *exact* method that assists in the generation of *logically ordered* (and therefore operationalizable) hypotheses or some new theory. Abductive inferencing is, rather, an attitude towards data and towards one's own knowledge: data are to be taken seriously, and the validity of previously developed knowledge is to be queried. It is a state of preparedness for being taken unprepared.

RESEARCH RESULTS: RECONSTRUCTION OR CONSTRUCTION?

Abductive efforts seek some (new) order, but they do not aim at the construction of *any* order, but at the discovery of an order which *fits* the surprising facts;

or, more precisely, which solves the practical problems that arise from these. The justification for this selective attention (which targets a new order) is not the greatest possible closeness to reality or the highest possible rationality. The justification is, above all, the *usefulness* which the 'type' that is developed brings to the question of interest. It can bring order and the means of linguistic representation, however these new 'types' are indispensable tools if one is to be able to make predictions about the future on the basis of a past that is hypothetically understood because it is ordered: they are indispensable when it is a matter of producing answers to the question of 'what to do next?' New orders, therefore, are also always oriented towards future action.

An abductive discovered order, therefore, is not a (pure) reflection of reality, nor does it reduce reality to its most important components. Instead, the orders obtained are *mental constructs* with which one can live comfortably or less comfortably. Abduction is something we all do, when there is a crisis or when we do not know what to do next. For many purposes, particular constructs are of use, and for other purposes, different constructs are helpful. For this reason, the search for order is never definitively complete and is always undertaken provisionally. So long as the new order is helpful in the completion of a task it is allowed to remain in force: if its value is limited, distinctions must be made; if it shows itself to be useless, it is abandoned. In this sense, abductively discovered orders are neither (preferred) constructions nor (valid) reconstructions, but *usable* (re-)constructions.

When faced with surprising facts, abduction leads us to look for meaning-creating rules, for a possibly valid or fitting explanation that eliminates what is surprising about the facts. The end-point of this search is a (verbal) hypothesis. Once this is found, a multi-stage process of checking begins. If the first step in the process of scientific discovery consists of the finding of a hypothesis by means of abduction, then the second step consists of the *derivation of predictions* from the hypothesis, which is deduction, and the third step consists of the *search for facts* that will 'verify' the assumptions, which is induction. If the facts cannot be found the process begins again, and this is repeated as often as necessary until 'fitting' facts are reached. With this definition Peirce designed a three-stage discovery procedure consisting of abduction, deduction, and induction. Finding and checking are, in Peirce's opinion, *two* distinct parts of a *single* process of discovery or research. If the finding stage is largely a result of a conscious and systematic approach, checking takes place according to operationalizable and rule-governed standards that are controlled by reason. *Certainty* about the validity of abductive inferences, however, cannot be achieved even if one subjects an abductively developed hypothesis to extensive testing; that is to say, deduces it from its consequences, then seeks to determine these inductively, and then repeats these three steps many times. Verification in the strict sense of the word cannot be done in this way. All that one can achieve, using this procedure, is an intersubjectively constructed and shared 'truth.' In Peirce's opinion even this is only reached if *all* members of a society have come to the same *conviction*.

Since, in Peirce's work, 'all' includes even those who were born after us, the process of checking can in principle never be completed. For Peirce, absolute certainty can never be achieved so: 'infallibility in scientific matters seems to me irresistibly comic' (Peirce, 1931–1935: Vol. I, X).

THE STRAUSS CONCEPT OF GT AND PEIRCE'S LOGIC OF RESEARCH

In early GT there were two strands, an inductive one, which worked on the assumption that categories and even theories emerge out of the data if only one looks closely enough, and a theoretical strand, which banked on the fact that prior knowledge about the world and scientific theories (apart from the data) are useful (cf. Kelle, 2005). In the later variant of GT by Strauss and Strauss and Corbin (in my further considerations I will only focus on this variant of GT), one can find both strands, the inductive and the 'theoretical' one, but with reversed emphasis. In the inductive variant by Glaser and Strauss, knowledge concepts or theories were officially and explicitly founded on induction (while the theoretical strand worked in the background), and in the later variant by Strauss and Corbin, theory was officially and explicitly founded on theoretical knowledge (while the inductive strand worked in the background; Strübing, 2004: 50ff). Strauss and Corbin have strongly emphasized this turn of their concept: 'Also, researchers are still claming to use "grounded theory methods" because their studies are "inductive"' (Strauss & Corbin, 1994: 276). Thoughtful reaction against restrictive prior theories and theoretical models can be salutary, but too rigid a conception of induction can lead to sterile or boring studies. Alas, grounded theory has been used as a justification for such studies. This has occurred as a result of the initial presentation of grounded theory in *The Discovery of Grounded Theory* that had led to a persistent and unfortunate misunderstanding about what was being advocated. Because of the partly rhetorical purpose of that book and the authors' emphasis on the need for grounded theory, Glaser and Strauss overplayed the inductive aspects (Strauss & Corbin, 1994: 277). Later GT claims to be more than a method for the coding of data. Even if coding is an essential part of research for Strauss, GT doesn't exhaust itself in coding (see Strübing 2006). Otherwise GT would run the risk of merely doubling the data on a more abstract level. It is therefore very unfortunate if the later GT is described as a coding paradigm. Strauss and Strauss and Corbin repeatedly pointed out that GT is 'a general methodology, a way of thinking about and conceptualizing data' (Strauss & Corbin, 1994: 275). Thus GT helps scientists to fulfill two tasks: the intellectual task of coding (open, axial, selective), and the intellectual task of developing and redeveloping concepts and theories while repeatedly moving to and fro between the collection of data, coding, and memoing (logic of research).

Of decisive importance for the question whether later GT makes use of abductive thinking[2] is therefore (a) whether it provides opportunities for the emergence of abductive conclusions at the level of single thinking acts, i.e. during concrete coding acts, or (b) whether the logic of research as a whole is abductive or not. Thus the central issue is neither whether GT works abductively in all cases and in all fields (this would be nonsense), nor whether one is allowed to revert to knowledge apart from the data (this primarily pertains to qualitative induction), but whether GT systematically counts on the appearance of new codes or hypotheses. 'Abductive' here does not simply mean that the research data is taken seriously and that the findings have to fit the data (this must be accomplished by all serious research) but essentially that the research is laid out in such a way that new hypotheses can and do appear at every level, that the interpretation of the data is not finalized at an early stage but that new codes, categories, and theories can be developed and redeveloped if necessary. If one takes a closer look at the work of Strauss and Strauss and Corbin to see whether there are methodical routines and practices within GT which favor the appearance of new hypotheses, much evidence can be found.

Example (a): One passage is very clear as regards 'induction' as a basis of coding. It here becomes apparent that Strauss doesn't mean the logical conclusion 'induction' at all but rather all the actions and attitudes which lead to a hypothesis, and exactly this is also addressed by Peirce with his considerations: 'Induction refers to the actions that lead to discovery of a hypothesis—that is, having a hunch or an idea, then converting it into an hypothesis and assessing whether it might provisionally work as at least a partial condition for a type of event, act, relationship, strategy, etc.' (Strauss, 1987: 11f).

Example (b): In Strauss's work, one can find repeated references at the level of the research logic to a permanent testing of verdicts once taken. Data elevation, coding, and the making of memos are related to each other in a three-step process: Hypotheses lists deduction of consequences and the testing of these consequences by means of the data and data analysis. This exactly corresponds to the logic of 'abductive' research: '(..) data collection leads quickly to coding, which in turn may lead equally quickly, or at least soon, to memoing. Either will then guide the searches for new data. Or they may lead directly to additional coding or memoing. Or—please note!—they may lead to inspecting and coding of already gathered (and perhaps already analyzed) data. That latter kind of "return to the old data" can occur at any phase of the research, right down to writing the last page of the final report of the theory' (Strauss, 1984: Unit 1, 18).

Furthermore, recurring references to the necessity of not only relying on existing knowledge but of creating new codes, categories, and theories can also be found in the work of Strauss and Strauss and Corbin: 'Creativity is also a vital component of the grounded theory method. Its procedures force the researcher to break through assumptions and to create new order out of the old. Creativity manifests itself in the ability of the researcher to aptly name categories; and also to let the mind wander and make the free associations that are necessary for generating stimulating questions and for coming up with a comparison that leads to discovery' (Strauss & Corbin, 1990: 27). The wording itself already reveals how close the ideas of Strauss and Corbin and Peirce are. In other text passages which refer to the flash-like discovery of the new, the common ground (including the abstract agreement) becomes still clearer: 'Yet, the most gratifying moments of research for analytically inclined researchers will be those that bear on their discoveries. They may be matters of quick flashes of "intuition," or major breakthroughs in understanding the meaning and patterns of events, or the deeper satisfaction of having solved the research's major puzzles' (Strauss & Corbin, 1990: 28).

In later GT one can find (in addition to the coding and the development of theories of a middle or long range) two intellectual operations: the finding of similarity (coding in known codes) and the development of the new (creating new codes). This kind of scientific work has its parallel in the distinction between qualitative induction and abduction as made by Peirce. The operation, the intellectual jump which 'states' things in common between acquaintance and data and codes in already known concepts is the first step: the qualitative induction (as executed above). This thinking act adds something to the data too. The second step is the intellectual jump which adds something very new to the data, something that they do not contain and that does not already exist as a concept or theory either. This is abduction.

The question whether GT (in the variant of Strauss and Corbin) contains an abductive research logic can therefore be answered with a resounding 'yes.' Fortunately, however, it does not only contain the logic of abductive reasoning but also that of qualitative induction. The logic of later GT thus permits abductive reasoning, counts on it, enables it, grants it place. More is not necessary.

One can, in conclusion, wonder why Strauss did not further develop the ideas of Peirce on abduction. Strauss undoubtedly knew the idea of abduction, because he mentioned it in his work at least once (cf. Strübing, 2004: 51). In connection with the question where our knowledge for induction, deduction, and verification comes from, Strauss stated (and this is indeed an important but not the crucial determinant for the new variant of GT) that this knowledge is nurtured by experience, but can also derive from theoretical pre-knowledge. 'They come from experience with this kind of phenomenon before—whether the experience is personal, or derives more "professionally" from actual exploratory research into the phenomenon of from the previous research program, or from theoretical sensitivity because of the researcher's knowledge of technical literature' (Strauss, 1987: 12).

Strauss adds in a footnote here: 'See the writings of Charles Peirce, the American Pragmatist, whose concept of abduction strongly emphasized the crucial role of experience in the first phase of research operations' (Strauss, 1987: 12). For Peirce, the fact that intellectual operations are nurtured by knowledge of every kind in the phase of discovery is not decisive for defining abduction, however, it is of crucial importance for him that new knowledge can be generated by means of this operation. In 'Study Letters of the FernUniversität' in *Qualitative Analysis in Social Research: Grounded Theory Methodology* (Strauss, 1984), the notion 'abduction' does not yet appear. In later documents, Strauss does without the explicit idea of abduction. Why did Strauss not use this term before? Did he not know it? As a pragmatist he would have had good reasons (and many opportunities) to see the parallels between his way of coding (particularly the open and selective coding) as well as his type of generating theory by 'coherent perception' and the abductive reasoning of Peirce.

The following deduction might illuminate the sudden but brief appearance of the word 'abduction' in the work of Strauss (which, if correct, is explained by this surprising fact): Anselm Strauss became acquainted with pragmatism and its research logic via Blumer via Dewey.[3] Strauss also mentions the influence of Peirce in some passages, but his notes are always very general. There is no evidence that Strauss has systematically studied the writings of Peirce, but Strauss's lack of citation to Peirce did not mean a lack of knowledge: he primarily knew Peirce as an action theorist, a semiotist, and a logician, so that for him as an empirist and 'working sociologist' in the tradition of the Chicago School there was no real need to look for notes in the work of Peirce as far as the logic of discovery is concerned. Strauss knew the concept of abduction from at least 1968 and when he got to know it he saw the parallels to his form of coding and generating theories,[3] but he did not further expound on these parallels. If he saw the chance to build a methodological basis (as a general theory) for his GT with the abductive research logic, he did not use it,[4] possibly because (due to restricted time resources) he focused on convincing other researchers of the fertility of its methodology and methods, rather than on coordinating its procedure with the conceptualities of the dominant methodology and on fastening it against criticism.

NOTES

1 Heiner Legewie and Barbara Schervier-Legewie led the 1994 Interview with Anselm Strauss. Ten years later it was published in *Forum Qualitative Sozialforschung*.

2 *The Discovery of Grounded Theory* contains many considerations that point to an abductive reasoning: 'The root sources of all significant theorizing is the sensitive insights of the observer himself. As everyone knows, these can come in the morning or at night, suddenly or with slow dawning, while at work or at play (even when asleep); furthermore, they can be derived directly from the theory (one's own or someone else's) or occur without a theory; and they can strike the observer while he is watching himself react as well as when he is observing others in action. Also, his insights may appear just as fruitfully near the end of a long inquiry as near the outset' (Glaser & Strauss, 1967: 251). Interestingly, the authors did not mention Peirce in this passage but explicitly referred to the secondary literature 'Nature of Insight' and 'Creative Work' in a footnote.

3 'Contributing to its development were two streams of work and thought: first, the general thrust of American Pragmatism (especially the writings of John Dewey, but also those of George Mead and Charles Peirce) and including its emphases on action and the problematic situation, and the necessity for conceiving a method in the context of problem solving' (Strauss, 1987: 5). For the history of grounded theory see: Kendall, 1999: 743f. In Strauss & Corbin, 1990, Peirce is no longer mentioned when the influence of pragmatism is discussed (see Strauss & Corbin, 1990: 24).

4 An insignificant, but nonetheless interesting, question is why Strauss used the term 'abduction' so many years later. My hypothesis is that the term 'abduction' (for a short time) found its way into

grounded theory methodology via Germany. The following reasons support this hypothesis: a study visit of Anselm Strauss to Germany fell in the time between Study Letters (written in 1982/1983 and published in 1984) and the publication of *Qualitative Analysis for Social Scientists* (1987). During this study visit he exchanged thoughts (by invitation of Hans-Georg Soeffner among others) with the research teams of Richard Grathoff (University of Bielefeld), Fritz Schütze (University of Kassel), and Hans-Georg Soeffner (FernUniversität Hagen). At that time, all of the above-mentioned researchers (Grathoff, Schütze, and Soeffner) dealt with the features of abductive reasoning. Hans-Georg Soeffner still remembers having repeatedly mentioned Peirce's notion of abduction to Strauss in connection with the possibilities of 'coherent perception' when coding. First, discussions about the parallels of abduction and Strauss's theory of research already took place in 1981/1982 when Hans-Georg Soeffner was in San Francisco (Hans-Georg Soeffner, personal communication in 12/2006; Strauss, 1987: XV).

REFERENCES

Anderson, D. (1995). *Strand of System. The Philosophy of Charles Peirce.* West Lafayette: Purdue University Press.

Apel, K.-O. (1967). *Transformation der Philosophie.* Frankfurt am Main: Suhrkamp.

Bonfantini, M. (1988). Semiotik und Geschichte: eine Synthese jenseits des Marxismus. *Zeitschrift für Semiotik* 10, 85–95.

Charniak, E. & McDermott, D. (1985). *Introduction to Artificial Intelligence.* Massachusetts: Addison-Wesley.

Eco, U. (1981). Guessing: From Aristotle to Sherlock Holmes. *Versus* 30, 3–19.

Eisenstadt, S. N. (2003). *Comparative Civilizations & Multiple Modernities.* Leiden: Brill.

Fann, K. T. (1970). *Peirce's Theory of Abduction.* The Hague: Nijhoff.

Foucault, M. (2004). *Geschichte der Gouvernementalität.* Frankfurt am Main: Suhrkamp.

Glaser, B. G. (1992). *Emergence vs Forcing: Basics of Grounded Theory.* Mill Valley, CA: Sociology Press.

Glaser, B. G. (2002). *Constructivist grounded theory?* In Forum Qualitative Sozialforschung / Forum: Qualitative Social Research. Retrieved March 10, 2007, from http://www.qualitative-research.net/fqs-texte/3-02/3-02glaser-e-htm.

Glaser, B. & Strauss, A. L. (1967). *The Discovery of Grounded Theory.* New York: de Gruyter.

Habermas, J. (1973). *Erkenntnis und Interesse.* Frankfurt am Main: Suhrkamp.

Haig, B. D. (1995). Grounded Theory as Scientific Method. Retrieved September 2006 from http://www.ed.uiuc.edu/EPS/PES-Yearbook/95_docs/haig.html

Hanson, N. R. (1965). Notes Toward a Logic of Discovery. In: Bernstein, R. J. (Ed.), *Perspectives on Peirce* (pp. 42–65). New Haven and London: Yale University Press.

Hemker, A. (1986). Ein Expertensystem für die Fehlerdiagnose in einem Hochenergiephysik Experiment. In: Fachbereich Physik an der Universität Wuppertal (Ed.), Wuppertal: Universitäts Press.

Kelle, U. (1994). *Empirisch begründete Theoriebildung.* Weinheim: Deutscher Studienverlag.

Kelle, U. (2005). 'Emergence' vs. 'Forcing' of Empirical Data? A Crucial Problem of 'Grounded Theory' Reconsidered. *Forum: Qualitative Social Research* Volume 6, No. 2. 2005, Retrieved September 2006 from http://www.qualitative-research.net/fqs-texte/2-05/05-2-27-e.htm

Kendall, J. (1999). Axial Coding and the Grounded Theory Controversy. *Western Journal of Nursing Research* 21, 743–757.

Knorr, K. (1985). Zur Produktion und Reproduktion von Wissen. In: Bonß, W. / Hartmann, H. (Eds.), *Entzauberte Wissenschaft* (171–178). Göttingen: Otto Schwarz.

Kreppner, K. (1975). *Zur Problematik des Messens in den Sozialwissenschaften.* Stuttgart: Klett.

Legewie, H. & Schervier-Legewie, B. (2004). 'Research is Hard Work, it's Always a bit Suffering. Therefore, on the Other Side Research Should be Fun.' Anselm Strauss in Conversation With Heiner Legewie and Barbara Schervier-Legewie. *Forum Qualitative Sozialforschung/Forum: Qualitative Social Research.* Retrieved March 9, 2007 from http://www.qualitative-research.net/fqs-texte/3-04/04-3-22-e.htm

Marvasti, A. B. (2004). *Qualitative Research in Sociology. An Introduction.* London: SAGE.

Miller, S. I. & Marcel, F. (1999). How Does Grounded Theory Explain? *Qualitative Health Research* 9, 538–551.

Moore, E. C. & Robin, R. S. (Eds.) (1964). *Studies in the Philosophy of Ch. S. Peirce.* Amherst: University of Massachusetts Press.

Peirce, C. S. (1929). Guessing. *Hound and Horn* 2, 267–282.

Peirce, C. S. (1931–1935). *The Collected Papers of Charles S. Peirce.* 8 Volumes. Cambridge: Harvard University Press.

Peirce, C. S. (1973). *Lectures on Pragmatism—Vorlesungen über Pragmatismus. Herausgegeben mit Einleitung und Anmerkungen von Elisabeth Walther.* Hamburg: Felix Meiner Verlag.

Peirce, C. S. (1976). *The New Elements of Mathematics.* 5 Volumes. Mouton: The Hague.

Peirce, C. S. (1986). Semiotische Schriften Bd. 1. Edited and translated by Christian Kloesel and Helmut Pape, Frankfurt am Main: Suhrkamp.

Peirce, C. S. (1992). *Reasoning and the Logic of Things.* (Ed.) K. L. Ketner. Cambridge: Harvard University Press.

Popper, K. (1934). *Logik der Forschung.* Tübingen: Mohr.

Reichenbach, H. (1938). *Erfahrung und Prognose.* Braunschweig, Wiesbaden: Vieweg.

Reichertz, J. (1991). Folgern Sherlock Holmes oder Mr. Dupin abduktiv? Kodikas/Code Vol. 4/1991, 345–367.

Reichertz, J. (2003). *Die Abduktion in der qualitativen Sozialforschung.* Opladen: Leske + Budrich.

Sebeok, T. & Jean Umiker-Sebeok (1985). 'Sie kennen ja meine Methode.' Ein Vergleich von Ch. S. Peirce und Sherlock Holmes. In: Eco, U./Sebeok, Th. (Hrsg.) *Der Zirkel oder: Im Zeichen der Drei* (28–87). München: Wilhelm Fink Verlag.

Strauss, A. L. (1984). *Qualitative Analysis in Social Research: Grounded Theory Methodology.* Study Letter. University Hagen.

Strauss, A. L. (1987). *Qualitative Analysis for Social Scientists.* New York: Cambridge University Press.

Strauss, A. L. & Corbin, J. (1990). *Basics of Qualitative Research: Grounded Theory Procedures and Techniques.* London: SAGE.

Strauss, A. L. & Corbin, J. (1994). Grounded Theory Methodology: An Overview. In: Norman K. Denzin (Ed.) *Handbook of Qualitative Research* (273–285). London: SAGE.

Strübing, J. (2004). *Grounded Theory.* Wiesbaden. VS Verlag.

Strübing, J. (2006). Wider die Zwangsverheiratung von Grounded Theory und Objektiver Hermeneutik. In: Sozialer Sinn. Vol. 2/2006.

Tursman, R. (1987). *Peirce's Theory of Scientific Discovery.* Bloomington, Indianapolis: Indiana University Press.

Wartenberg, G. (1971). *Logischer Sozialismus. Die Transformation der Kantschen Transzendentalphilosophie durch Ch. S. Peirce.* Frankfurt am Main: Suhrkamp.

Wirth, Uwe (1995). Abduktion und ihre Anwendungen. *Zeitschrift für Semiotik Bd.* 17, 405–424.

11

Sampling in Grounded Theory

Janice M. Morse

In comparison with other types of qualitatively derived theory, the theory emerging within grounded theory has a unique structure; one that links the researcher's developing concepts in stages and phases, as they change over time or appear in different forms. Because grounded theory is based on symbolic interactionism and processes of negotiating reality and documenting change, grounded theory sampling techniques must not only explicate the dimensional *scope* of the phenomena of interest, but also enable comprehensive description of the *trajectory* of the phenomena over time. Within this three-dimensional frame, researchers must not only develop the pertinent concepts and their relationships to each other, but also describe their actions, roles, and interactions as they respond to and adapt within particular situations.

The key to developing any comprehensive and dynamic theory is the use of astute and efficient methods of sampling. Research methods have been developed to provide principles and procedures to guide sampling in such complex grounded theory research, but those for guiding sampling *decisions* have been less clearly explicated. Therefore, in this chapter we will first review the principles of sampling that pertain to *qualitative research in general*, and then develop those that pertain *specifically to grounded theory*.

PRINCIPLES OF SAMPLING FOR QUALITATIVE INQUIRY

All qualitative sampling is dependent on three principles, and research strategies have been developed to meet the goals of effective and efficient gathering of adequate and appropriate data.

Principle 1. Excellent research skills are essential for obtaining good data

Obviously, the researcher's techniques at collecting or gathering data are critical to the amount of data needed in a study. When conducting an interview, experience enables the researcher to know at what points in the interview process to move the participant's narrative from the general to the specific, and when to interrupt the participant to ask for examples. Experience enables the researcher to know when to let the participant move forward in the narrative into new areas, or when to move back in the interview to obtain additional details. It takes skill on the part of the researcher to establish trust with the participant quickly and early in the interview process, so that adequate and accurate information may be obtained, and it is the researcher's skill that enables the researcher to sort the relevant from the less pertinent or irrelevant information, while the interview is ongoing. At the same time, the experienced researcher does not lead the participant nor interrupt, thereby cutting off a stream of potentially important data. These attributes of an excellent interviewer influence the quality of the data and ultimately the size of the sample: the better the data quality, the fewer the number of interviews and participants required in a study. In other words, the more targeted the content of the interviews, the better the data, the fewer interviews will be necessary, and the lower the number of participants recruited into the study. Of course, the same principles apply to observational data: the more smoothly the researcher approaches the setting and the participants, is incorporated into the setting with minimal disruption, or becomes a part of the scene, the better the researcher's observations. If the researcher's presence has less of an influence on the setting, participants will trust and assist the researcher more quickly, and are less likely to alter or conceal their behavior when the researcher is observing.

How do researchers become interview smart and savvy at observation? At the risk of becoming derailed in a chapter on *sampling*, because of the interrelationship of these dimensions they will be mentioned briefly here. Self-awareness of your research skills, the constant monitoring of the quality of your data, as well as the directions and analytic needs of the study, are essential to the nature of the sample. To become skilled at interviewing and observing requires practice and a careful self-critique of each interview transcript and field note. Ask of the interviews:

> Where is the story line? Was each question and interruption necessary and productive? Am I giving space to the participant to really tell their story? If using observational methods, ask: Is your involvement in the setting at an appropriate level or are signals present that your observing makes the participants uncomfortable?

Ensure that you are working inductively and appropriately bracketing other theory:

> Do you know the literature yet maintain sensitivity to your data? Are you asking questions of the data? Do you use the library and the published work on the topic to generate alternative explanations and hypotheses, or to confirm/endorse emerging findings?

Sampling ceases when saturation is achieved, however saturation is not an end point to the study but a stepwise decision that you are certain of some category or finding before moving forward at each phase of the analysis. It is researcher's certainty in the developing analysis that provides indicators for continuing or ceasing to sample on a particular domain. Only when the entire model is complete, does the study sampling cease.

Finally, one adage: *More bad data does not make good data*. If a sampling strategy is not working, is not yielding the kinds of participants that one needs in order to get good data, then change the strategy. To keep sampling and hoping that the data will improve with quantity is nonsense. Qualitative inquiry methods are flexible and do permit the researcher to discard unproductive strategies and adopt new ways of sampling. However, you should be cognizant that if you are changing strategies to recruit from a new setting or to try new techniques of recruitment, then ethical approvals from the necessary university and agency committees, as well as (for doctoral students) permission from one's own supervisory committee, are required.

Principle 2. It is necessary to locate 'excellent' participants to obtain excellent data

Spradley (1979: 25–26), in his description of ethnographic methods, listed the qualities of what he called an 'excellent informant.' These qualities hold true as much for grounded theory as ethnography. An excellent participant for grounded theory is one who has been through, or observed, the experience under investigation. Participants must therefore be experts in the experience or the phenomena under investigation; they must be willing to participate, and have the time to share the necessary information; and they must be reflective, willing, and able to speak articulately about the experience. Not all of those people who volunteer to participate in your study will have all of the characteristics of an excellent participant. In Spradley's study of urban nomads (or tramps), Spradley relied primarily on a homeless person he called 'Bill' to obtain the majority of descriptive data about the context. Bill exemplified most of the characteristics of those who lived on the street: he had held more than 50 jobs, had been arrested nine times for drunkedness, and he had spent more that 200 days in jail. He was therefore experienced, he was articulate, and the letters he wrote to Spradley are published in the first section of his book *You Owe Yourself a Drunk* (Spradley 1970) and provide the necessary context for the study. Bill had time to be interviewed, and was also willing to describe details of his daily life. Bill therefore had all the characteristics of an excellent participant.

While researchers also add the criterion that the participant must speak whatever language the researcher is working in, this is not essential, for some research must be conducted using translators. I prefer to add a criterion about the *ethnicity* of the participant. One of the problems in qualitative inquiry is that researchers often hold *quantitative* assumptions in relation to sampling and these rules are often inappropriately enforced by granting agencies (Morse 1995). Unfortunately, review boards and granting agencies sometimes expect the qualitative sample be representative of the population using demographic quantitative criteria, such as ethnicity, gender, age, economic status, and so forth, rather than obtaining a sample with characteristics necessary for qualitative inquiry (i.e. representative of the experience). In other words, the qualitative researcher must select participants to observe or interview who know the information (or have had or are having the experience) in which you are interested. This is a crucial difference. In quantitative research, the assumption is that all potential subjects in the population will know about, or have an opinion about, the research topic, and therefore a sample selected randomly will provide excellent data from a sample that is representative of the general population. When this quantitative perspective is used with a qualitative sample, researchers erroneously select their sample according to demographic criteria, rather than the conceptual/informational needs of the study. For instance, if a given population consists of 40% Caucasian, 20% Black, 20% Hispanic, and 20% other, then the qualitative researcher, incorrectly operating on quantitative assumptions, will construct a sampling frame according to these demographic characteristics, and solicit a sample of (assuming 20 people in total) 8 Caucasians, 4 Blacks, 4 Hispanics, and 4 'others.' This causes two serious problems:

(1) Data may be inappropriate. If this is the only criterion used, you are likely to have invited participants with no knowledge of your topic at all into your study. This means that from some of your participants you may get no data, or very poor information. Because qualitative researchers use a relatively small sample, and data are expensive to process, you cannot afford in terms of time and research budget to tolerate poor participants; and

(2) Paradoxically, it decreases cultural variation. If you, as the qualitative researcher, suspect that the experience you are investigating is influenced by culture, each of the above subgroups will provide data that will contribute variation due to *cultural* differences. If you decide to compare and contrast the perspectives of each cultural group (and this should have been dictated by your question), then data from each group must be analyzed separately, data (from each group) must be saturated and the results compared. In this example, the sample of 20 participants is too small to sort data pertaining to the topic of interest as well as by cultural subgroups that consist of only 4 participants each. If your research hypothesis demands such a complex cross-cultural study, then each sub-sample must be large enough to be saturated.

The most common outcome in a situation such as described above is that the researcher pools data from all of the cultural groups. This means that all cultural variation is lost in the analysis, which is probably the reverse of the researcher's intent in selecting a multicultural sample in the first place (see Morse 1995). Furthermore, it will take the researcher longer to reach saturation, as a larger sample will be required because of the increasing 'noise' (i.e. variation) in the data. Thus, in qualitative samples, the researcher must attend to the problem of non-homogeneous (i.e. diverse) samples, including culture, age, gender, or any of the sociological quantitative sampling criteria, and the most appropriate way to handle such variation, is to initially select a demographically homogeneous sample. Once you understand what the phenomenon is that you are studying, then it is appropriate to study the variations in meaning in different contexts and groups. Thus, a good qualitative sample must be purposely selected.

Qualitative sampling often begins by recruiting participants solely based on whether they have experienced the research topic in question. The most obvious way to locate such participants is to go find them where they are. So researchers should recruit intentionally (purposefully) from wherever these people may be: from support groups, classrooms, pubs, sports venues, or wherever they may gather. If the phenomenon is more difficult to identify, for instance you are interested in nonsmokers, or people with phobias, or mothers who are weaning their infants, then you may advertise in newspapers, on notice boards, or on the TV or radio, asking for people who may be interested in the study and *who meet the criteria*, to contact you.

Primary selection (Morse 1986) occurs when researchers advertise for a group with a specific experience, for instance, mothers who have weaned their infants, and who have nursed more than one baby, or men who have experienced a heart attack more than 6 months ago, or whatever the sampling specifications of primary interest. But we still have a problem: While those who contact us now meet our 'experience' criteria, we do not know if they also meet the additional Spradley criteria—that is, are they willing to participate, are they articulate, and are they reflective? People volunteer for research for many different reasons: they may be solely interested in any monetary reward offered for their time; they may simply want someone to talk to; they may want to become personally acquainted with the interviewers; and so forth. We usually cannot incorporate the strategies that ethnographers use to overcome this problem; that is, to get to know all possible participants and establish trust before inviting them into the study, so after primary selection is complete, we practice *secondary selection* (Morse 1989a). If it becomes clear that the interview is going poorly and that the participant does not have the information needed, we politely complete the interview, label and date the tape, but then do not have the tape transcribed, nor incorporate the data into the study. (Later, once we understand 'what is going on' in our study, we may need to incorporate this taped information into our data set after all.)

Principle 3. Sampling techniques must be targeted and efficient

In spite of the availability of computer programs to facilitate the management of qualitative data (i.e. sifting and sorting), the true essence of qualitative analysis is based in investigator-insight. Computer programs, while invaluable, merely assist in placing data in the best possible position to aid the researcher's cognitive work; such programs cannot *do* the analysis for the researcher. It is for this reason that collecting too much data results in a state of conceptual blindness on the part of the investigator. Excessive data is an impediment to analysis, and the investigator will be swamped, scanning, rather than cognitively processing, the vast number of transcripts, unable to see the forest for the trees, or even the trees for the forest, for that matter. Furthermore, because the researcher can conceptually manage only relatively small amounts of data, data that are included in analysis must be significant, pertinent, informative, exciting, and not mundane, obscure, irrelevant, or only tangentially related to the topic. Because human brains have limited capacity and can only hold and process so many ideas simultaneously, and tire easily, qualitative researchers cannot afford to sift through piles of substandard data.

Thus, excellent qualitative inquiry is inherently biased (Morse 2006). By biased, I mean it has been deliberately sought and selected. This bias is essential if we are going to do good work and this bias is not something that impairs the rigor of the research. In qualitative inquiry, as in many bench sciences, researchers seek the best examples of whatever it is that they are studying. We seek the optimal, rather than the average, experience. By using the worst—or best—cases, the characteristics of the phenomenon or experience we are studying become most obvious, clear, and emerge more quickly and cleanly, than by using cases in which the concepts and experiences are weak or obscured with other noise in the data. Once the phenomena or concepts of interest have been clarified, and the researcher knows what characteristics to look for, then the average or poorer, less optimal examples can then be examined, if necessary, later in the study.

This inherent bias in qualitative research is an incredibly important factor. It means that the use of randomly selected samples may impede and invalidate inquiry, for they cannot be guaranteed to be the 'best cases.' Qualitative samples should always include processes of purposeful selection according to specific parameters identified in the study, rather than processes of random selection, and should be evaluated according to certain demographic factors or other indices used in quantitative inquiry.

What is wrong with randomization? Processes of saturation are essential in qualitative inquiry: saturation ensures replication and validation of data; and it ensures that our data are valid and reliable. If we select a sample randomly, the factors that we are interested in for our study would be normally distributed in our data, and be represented by some sort of a curve, normal or skewed. Regardless of the type of curve, we would have lots of data about common events, and inadequate data about less common events. Given that a qualitative data set requires a more rectangular distribution to achieve saturation, with randomization we would have too much data around the mean (and be swamped with the excess), and not enough data to saturate our categories in the tails of the distribution. In other words, our sample would not be very efficient, and given that we could not verify (saturate) the categories, our categories may not be comprehensive (Morse 1989a). In fact, if we chose to use a random sample to prevent bias, exactly the opposite would occur: we would be introducing bias by not attending to the meaningful scope of the phenomenon. Thus, sampling in qualitative inquiry must be purposeful, with participants invited into the study according to their knowledge about the topic being researched, or type of information that is needed to complete or to complement our understanding. This 'type of knowledge required' differs according to the stage of inquiry, whether new categories are emerging in the data set, or whether the researcher is seeking to saturate or to verify the categories.

PRINCIPLES OF SAMPLING FOR GROUNDED THEORY

The primary key to excellence in grounded theory, as in all qualitative inquiry, is that both data collection and techniques of analytical conceptualization must be rigorous. While in this chapter I am primarily concerned with the former, as data are collected and analyzed concurrently, these two processes, data collection and analysis, cannot be separated. Excellent data are obtained through careful sampling. In grounded theory, sampling schemes change dynamically with the development of the research. The main types of sampling methods are:

1. *Convenience sampling.* Participants are selected on the basis of accessibility. This method of sampling is used at the beginning of a project to identify the scope, major components, and trajectory of the overall process.
2. *Purposeful sampling.* Participants are selected as indicated by the initial analysis of interviews. These interviews reveal how participants themselves partition the emerging phenomena. Participants may be speaking for themselves ('we'), or speaking for others ('they') (i.e. providing shadowed data; Morse 2001). The researcher will then proceed to sample according to the way this scheme sorts the phenomenon.
3. *Theoretical sampling.* Participants are selected according to the descriptive needs of the emerging concepts and theory. These needs dictate the sampling strategies and goals (Charmaz 2006; Glaser 1978).
4. *Theoretical group interviews* are used to expand on and to verify the emerging model. When conducting theoretical group interviews, participants are recalled in small groups, introduced to the preliminary findings, and subsequently asked to discuss and to provide further examples of the findings. Their insights are used to modify and saturate the emerging model.

Each of these types of sampling will now be discussed within the stage and context of a grounded theory project.

Convenience sampling

In grounded theory, the first task of the researcher is to obtain an overview of the overall process. There is a need to scope the phenomenon, to determine the dimensions and boundaries, as well as the trajectory of the project. First, the researcher uses *convenience sampling* (Richards & Morse 2007) to locate persons who are available who have already gone through, or have observed, the process (i.e. 'experts' who have experienced most of the phenomenon). Identifying the most appropriate participant group is crucial. Ask yourself: Will this experience provide excellent examples of the concepts of interest? The researcher then determines the obvious boundaries of the project (for instance, type of illness, or whatever boundaries may be possible) and advertises or seeks assistance in locating these people. The researcher may place an advertisement in the newspaper, or solicit participants from organizations providing services for those participants.

A common pitfall in qualitative inquiry is not to move beyond the convenience sampling. When this occurs, the researcher is likely to:

- ignore variation within the experience, or with the sample;
- define the phenomenon too narrowly, because of the lack of variation, and not scoping adequately to identify the boundaries;
- terminate sampling too soon (premature closure) because 'no new data are emerging,' believing that saturation has been reached.

Once a preliminary convenience sample is selected, a *snowball* or *nominated sample* may be used. In this case, the researcher requests introductions from the initial participants, to invite their friends and acquaintances to participate in the study. This type of sample is very useful in instances when the researchers are studying illicit or illegal behaviors, and participants would be otherwise difficult to identify.

Initially, *purposeful samples* are selected to maximize variation of meaning, thus determining the scope of the phenomena or concepts. If nothing is known about the phenomenon, sociological categories may be tentatively used to guide the purposeful selection of participants: groupings by age, gender, socio-economic class, employment, and so forth. A targeted research question may also guide selection. If your question compares genders, then obviously we would organize the sampling frame by attending to the characteristics of the sample by first separating male and female participants, carefully saturating other categories in both samples.

As discussed earlier, one problem is culture. Do we select participants from any cultural group? Or select them from a single cultural group? Remember that for each of these a priori decisions, a different product will result. If the combinations are large, then each subgroup will have to be saturated. Your decision has important ramifications for the overall size of your project. Thus sampling decisions cannot be made without considering the context, and the researcher should carefully consider what the results and the implications of each study might be, by doing an 'armchair walkthrough' (Richards & Morse 2007).

Grounded theory interviews, are usually unstructured, with the researcher initially asking the participants to 'I am interested in the gifts that nurses receive

---

Box 11.1 Planning your sample using an armchair walkthrough

I am interested in exploring patient gift-giving in hospitals.[1] Despite the fact that receiving a gift appears an innocuous, innocent—even polite—gesture, it is forbidden. Despite the fact that nurses are not supposed to accept gifts from patients, patients continue to give gifts, almost universally. Despite the fact that hospitals have created policy prohibiting the acceptance of gifts, nurses continue to accept gifts. [Note that, as the researcher, I begin by using my own knowledge of the phenomenon.] Astonishingly, there is little literature on this topic [the researcher does look in the library], but there are some theories of gift-giving in anthropology. These theories raise the question not previously considered, 'What is a gift?' Is a gift a planned, formal, wrapped present, complete with a card? Or can a gift be a single chocolate, offered spontaneously? Does it have to be a material thing, or can it be an action (such as a 'thank you')? By working inductively, I must remain open even to the definition of a gift, and let the participants define what a 'gift' is.

Now sampling: Who do I to talk to? At this stage, I consider all of the possibilities and the kind of data I would hear in an interview with each person. I could observe—go to each patient care unit and look at the gifts that have been given—the flowers, cards and chocolates are usually displayed at the nursing stations. If I interviewed patients and their relatives, I would get information probably on their discharge, about why they gave such gifts—and my study would be almost like an evaluation of care. I could interview hospital administrators, and find out why they developed such a policy, and if they have to censure nurses for accepting gifts; or I could interview experienced nurses about the gifts they had received and their perceptions, as recipient, of the gift. Should I interview any nurse? I have observed that gift-giving does not occur throughout the hospital. OR nurses, for instance, never receive gifts, and the nurses who receive the most are in obstetrics. In order to fully understand the purpose of the gift, I decide to interview nurses in different care areas. I decide I need to *comprehend the overall process*, by interviewing nurses from psychiatry, maternity, med-surg, gerontology, and pediatrics, keeping each data set separate, and comparing and contrasting these data. I prepare a notice. Because accepting a gift is a censured activity, I do not mention that in my advertisement.

PARTICIPATE IN RESEARCH!!

A researcher wishes to interview experienced nursing staff about nurse–patient relationships. Interviews will be conducted by phone, in your own time. Please call xxx-xxxx for an appointment.

Figure 11.1   Invitation to participate.

from patients. Tell me about any gifts you have received, and who gave them to you,' and the role of the researcher is primarily to listen without interruption. If the participant asks where they should 'start their story,' then the researcher may reply, 'Anywhere you wish.' On completion of the narrative, if any part of the story is unclear, the researcher may ask clarifying questions. If the interview is lengthy and the participant is tiring, then the researcher may interrupt the interview, and invite the participant to continue at another time. These recorded interviews are transcribed, and the coding is initially commenced according to the categories that appear most obvious. This may, however, be a temporary schema. Some analytic strategies will facilitate our understanding of the process, and ultimately the analysis: for instance, the researcher may, at the end of each interview, ask the participants to give their story a title (Kacen 2002). These titles (or 'supercodes') usually provide important clues into the major process or basic social/psychological process (or core variable) that the participants consider runs through the entire process. Another strategy is for the researcher to graph the trajectory of each interview by the main sequential events. Recognizing that such 'maps' are event-driven (and independent of calendar/clock time), then similar events may be identified, and these may form the initial stages and the transitions in the theory.

In summary, initial interviews with the convenience sample will provide the researcher with an overview of the entire process or trajectory, and sampling strategies should be selected according to availability, with attention to obtaining an overview of the entire trajectory.

Purposeful sampling

Once the general trajectory or process is identified, sampling strategies change. In this phase, *purposeful sampling* is used, with participants sought who are in or 'going through' the particular stage. This enables confirmation of the trajectory, a rich description of different stages as they are experienced. Points between changes or stages are called *critical junctures*. One further difficulty in grounded theory sampling is that coding begins immediately, as soon as data collection commences. Thus, the initial coding, done before the trajectory was identified and before the investigator was aware of the stages, may have codes from the first phase placed in the same category as similar codes from a later phase, but the process may have changed some characteristics in the data significantly. Thus changes, or small differences, become merged in the general category and lost.

Box 11.2 Planning your sample

The initial interviews in our gift-giving project revealed that gifts were given at different phases of the nurse–patient relationship, and for different reasons: they were given initially to *ensure safe care*; during the relationship to ensure continuity of care; and at the end of the relationship for reciprocity for care. The value of the gift reflected the worth or value of the nurses care and the type of relationship established. Gifts varied according to patient care area, from non-monetary gifts, such as a smile or a 'thank you' appreciated in the nursing home, but considered by psych nurses as an attempt by the patient to manipulate. Even the type of chocolates given by patients sent a message to nurses regarding how much patients appreciate their care, with low-priced chocolates signifying less appreciation than hand-made specialty chocolates. The monetary value of gifts was greatest for nurses who established a connected relationship with the patient. In trying to establish the boundaries of gift-giving, I was shocked to learn that even *complaints* were considered a reciprocal gift—something *given* in retaliation for poor care. I sample using the *snowball technique*: I ask nurses to refer their colleagues according to certain criteria: 'Can you refer me to a nurse who is caring for a difficult (or angry) patient?' Or I ask nurses to tell me about the time they cared for a difficult patient.

Now that I understand the connection between the nurse–patient relationship and the gift as a symbol of that relationship for a care need met (or not met) by the nurse, I sample *purposefully*, according to different types of relationships, and at different stages of the developing relationship.

Therefore, once the stages have been identified, the researcher is forced to recode data according to the trajectory. At this time, participants who are going through a particular stage, or who represent a particular typology, are invited to be interviewed. This enables a rich description of stages as they are experienced.

Critics consider the purposeful selection of participants according to the needs of the study to be the greatest weakness of qualitative inquiry. Yet, as discussed earlier, qualitative research must be a biased activity. We are solving problems detective-style, looking for clues, sifting and sorting, and creating a plausible case. Analysis is an active process of constantly asking questions. There may be blind alleys and mistakes, but once significance is recognized, data may be reorganized, resorted, and categories renamed, and such problems resolved.

Shadowed data

When participants are describing an event or phenomena, it is important to consider if they are speaking for themselves or for others. We speaking for others, we refer to this as *shadowed data* (Morse 2001). Participants may place themselves with a class *like them*, that is the *generalized self*, or unlike them, that is, the *generalized other*. These categorizations provide significant groupings in which further sampling should occur. Consider the following piece of text, describing dependency from a patient's perspective:

> S: Well as soon as I got home I started thinking like, the way I used to be. So, like, I was very limited in what I could do, and that was painful because my expectancies were high and I think that's pretty normal. When you've been very active and all of a sudden you can't do anything. I don't know if its humility or you've lost something. I think the biggest thing is you've lost a piece of yourself. The biggest thing I had to accept was other people helping me. Like right now I still need a certain amount of help. Like I'm not a person who could say well I can just, like these people who used to take off through the woods and they would go for miles by themselves and they'd never see another human being for months, see. So I'm different, I can't do that. I lost that part of being totally, totally, on my own.

I: Do you have any stories to tell me about that?
S: People don't know what to do when it comes to that. They don't know. People don't know if they should or they shouldn't. Some help you and think nothing of it and some people are—you can see them move and then they stop themselves.

Thus, in the above example, for purposeful sampling, the researcher would first verify that other participants considered similar experiences in similar groupings, and then move to sample to determine in which kinds of experiences or conditions participants would accept or refuse help. We read: 'I don't know if it's humility or you've lost something. I think the biggest thing is you've lost a piece of yourself.' Now we ask questions: What is *humility*? What are the characteristics of a person with humility? What are the boundaries and attributes of the concept? And then we *sample* further by seeking participants with those characteristics or experiences in situations in which humility is required. Similarly, we may also investigate what it is, or what is meant by 'losing a piece of yourself.' In this way, the project moves forward by sampling using the concepts in the interviews to guide the sampling frame.

Next, the researcher, using the text below, would seek out, from the patient's perspective, conditions or circumstances in which help is welcomed:

I: Yeah, that's awkward.
S: You can see that they are very concerned. The people I think are a little hesitant, I think they are concerned about what you are going to say or think. The ones that help you, there's some people that don't help. Like it's no big deal to them. They do it automatic and they more or less think well if you don't like it that's too bad, because I'm just trying to help. That's what their answer would be, I guess.
I: Which do you prefer?
S: I don't know. I think I would accept it both ways. Sometimes with—I want help, sometimes I don't want help.

By comparing and contrasting between stages, researchers can recognize differences, and then deliberately seek out additional participants who are in the midst of a particular stage along the trajectory that has been identified from the scoping with the convenience sample. This is a most important phase of the study: data should be rich and many examples obtained; coding should be copious and categories maturing.

Thus, having identified and classified the *types of relationships* from the nurses' stories, the grounded theory now proceeds by identifying the dynamic process of the changing relationships and strategies of negotiation that nurses and patients use to achieve the type of relations each needs: nurses to feel effective and satisfied in their work, and patients to feel safe. We saturate our data set by requesting stories from nurses about patients they recall, and sorting these stories now using processes of deduction, that is, by sorting these stories according to the characteristics of the relationship already identified. As our understanding of the nurse–patient relationship increases, we find negative cases—cases that do not fit our emerging model. Perhaps in the nurse–patient relationship example, we find relationships that are out of sync—ones where the patient tries to involve the

---

Box 11.3 Let us go back to our gift-giving study

We are now able to identify four types of nurse–patient relationships: clinical, therapeutic, connected, and over-involved. Each of these relationships have different purposes, meet different characteristics, are used in a different context, and are negotiated for different patient needs. *Clinical
relationships* occur when the contact between the caregiver and the patient is brief, the patient's
needs are minor. The nurse assesses the patient, provides the treatment, and the patient is satisfied
with the care provided. The communication is superficial and rote: for instance, 'Hello, how are you
today,' 'What can I do for you?' There is little person involvement by either the nurse or the patient,
and neither the nurse nor the patient may remember each other or recall the other's name.

   Therapeutic relationships are usually of short duration, the patient's needs are not serious or
life threatening, care is given quickly and efficiently. The nurse views the patient first as a patient,
and second as a person, and the patient expects to be treated as a patient. Usually, these patients
have other needs met by their support system. If they feel insecure, they may test the nurse (for
instance, to make certain that she will come if they use their call bell) and are able to feel secure
and confident with the nursing care provided. These patients will keep chocolates on their locker
to keep nurses returning to their bedside, and give gifts to the unit staff as a whole.

   Connected relationships are professional, but the nurse will consider the patient first as a
person, and second in their patient role. This means that care will be individualized, and the
nurse will bend or break rules, advocate for the patient, and buffer and protect the patient if
necessary. Trust will be established between the nurse and the patient, and the patient respects
the nurse's judgment and feels grateful. This gratitude is reflected in the gifts given the nurse.

   An *over-involved relationship* occurs when the patient is overwhelmed by extraordinary
needs and the nurse chooses to meet those needs. This may occur after only a short duration,
or occur once the nurse and the patient have had a prolonged time together. The nurse is committed to the patient as a person and this commitment over-rides her commitment to the
patient's treatment regime, the physician, the other patients, and the institution. The nurse
becomes a complete confidant of the patient and is sometimes accepted as a member of the
patients' family. From the institution's perspective, the nurse's judgment becomes 'clouded.'
Gifts given to these nurses are large, and considered professionally inappropriate.

---

nurse (and the nurses will not commit) or examples in which the patient will not
respond to the nurse's strategies of negotiation.

Theoretical sampling

The main principle of theoretical sampling is that the emerging categories, and
the researcher's increasing understanding of the developing theory, now direct the
sampling (Glaser 1978). Researchers deliberately seek participants who have had
particular responses to experiences, or in whom particular concepts appear significant. These participants are then asked to tell their story, adding to the existing
data set about a particular concept or category; the participants may also be asked
targeted questions, and the resulting data may be used to verify the theory in its
entirety. The participants may also be asked to supplement information about
linkages between two categories, hence contributing to the emerging theory.

   Negative cases, or participants who have not responded in the anticipated way,
or who have opposite reactions to the majority to a particular phenomenon, are
called negative cases. In grounded theory, negative cases are not discarded, but
rather integrated into the emerging theory. Negative cases are therefore a part of
the sampling process, and cannot simply be ignored or discarded. In the example discussed previously, we could seek persons who thought no one was willing
to help them. The trick in grounded theory is therefore to determine the differences between a negative case and what quantitative researchers refer to as

> **Box 11.4 Purposeful sampling**
>
> The last type of negative case we find are difficult patients, who do not respond and remain hostile towards caregivers and patients who are self-alienated and will not respond to staff. We collect data about how patients informally assess the nurse, and strategies about how nurses connect with patients. Factors that interfere with the development of trust such as the sharing of patient confidence in patient charts, multiple caregivers, interchangeability of nurses, and the lack of time for contact in the nurse. The theory is now developing nicely, but still has some 'thin' areas.

an outlier. Outliers are serendipitous errors, and if the participant is a true outlier, in both qualitative and quantitative inquiry, can be ignored, for example in our study of nurse–patient negotiation and gift giving.

Theoretical group interviews

I have labeled small discussion groups, deliberately convened to 'push' the analysis towards completion, as *theoretical group interviews*. These groups are intended to provide the final missing pieces of the puzzle, polish data collection, complete processes of saturation, or provide any other information that the researcher requires. During a theoretical group interview, participants are given a presentation of the ongoing analysis. Participants are then invited to facilitate analysis by adding information to areas that are 'thin,' resolving conundrums or ambiguities that the researcher may have about the emerging model, in order to provide insights into the application of the emerging model from their perspective, context, and daily life. Note that the participants are not being asked to 'confirm the analysis,' and that these group interviews are still a phase of data collection and analysis.

The structure of *theoretical group interviews* differs dramatically from that of group *validation interviews* assembled by the investigator to confirm an emerging model. In validation interviews, the participants are working deductively, and the researcher will be asking if the analysis 'makes sense to them' and seeking agreement/disagreement, asking participants to look for a match between their experiences and the emerging theoretical model.

TERMINATING DATA COLLECTION

The golden rule is that sampling ceases once saturation has occurred. But the problem is: how does the analyst know when saturation has occurred? At the

> **Box 11.5 Negative cases**
>
> If we took the nurse–patient project to this phase, we would invite two or three participant nurses (and perhaps separately, two or three expert patients), and present our findings regarding gift-giving and the process of negotiation, to elicit stories to confirm the theory and to enrich the data set. At the end of this stage, the concepts should be saturated, the theory should be diagrammed, and fully explicated.

descriptive level, no two participants ever report the same story with exactly the same description of whatever happened. However, researchers do not look for the sameness or replication of instances, but of the characteristics of instances. That is what analysis is all about. Let us consider the following example. In a study of childbirth in Fiji (Morse 1989b), I became aware that the value on modesty in the Fiji–Indian culture seemed to be strong enough to interfere with maternal and infant health. To confirm this hypothesis, let us search our data for instances that confirm or refute our hypothesis. We find:

> *Example 1.* While the literature states that infants should be fed when they are hungry, and at that time most Western hospitals usually practiced 'feeding on demand' (i.e. mothers feed their infants when they are hungry), infants in the Fijian hospital were all fed on a fixed schedule. A sign was placed in the corridor outside the ward reading 'Infant feeding: No admission.' You realize that this sign is to inform men not to go into the ward, where mothers are breastfeeding, obviously with their breasts exposed.
>
> *Example 2.* Arranged marriages are common. The lack of premarital contact removes the tension of premarital sex and its consequences. Further, when you inquire, you find out that the females are kept innocent about the 'facts of life': girls do not know about menstruation at menarche, and you are told that 'brides running away on their wedding nights are a "big problem".'
>
> *Example 3.* You follow this up and confirm that mothers do not know the sign of pregnancy when they become pregnant. They do not find out that they are expecting a baby until their mothers-in-law notice morning sickness or the enlarging abdomen is evident. This means they do not receive early prenatal care, and there is no change in their work role when they become pregnant: they continue to work in the sugar cane fields. Nurses inspect the hands of women in the prenatal clinic for calluses, especially in cases of pre-eclampsia, as an indicator of too little rest.
>
> *Example 4.* In addition to the above, you cannot obtain any information about traditional herbs or remedies that Fiji–Indian women use prenatally, and only some for postnatal use. You find that childbirth is, in Mead and Newton's (1967) terms, 'a time of defilement.' In contrast, there are many traditional remedies in the Fijian culture, for both prenatal and postnatal use.
>
> *Example 5.* The rules at the hospital for student nurses are as follows: Student nurses may not leave the hospital compound. If they wish to go into town in the afternoon, a staff nurse will accompany them. Nurses may not receive phone calls from 'boys.' If they do, their parents will be notified.
>
> *Example 6.* In the course of observation in the delivery room, you discover that primigravida (first time) mothers in labor do not know 'how the baby is going to get out.' You confirm this with patient after patient.
>
> *Example 7.* You read in the local newspaper that a community health nurse, going into a village to teach birth control, has stones thrown at her by the elderly women. They scream at her that 'their women are good and do not need that information.'
>
> *Example 8.* The nurses tell you: One night a young man came into the hospital and said his wife was in the car with a stomachache. The nurses took the stretcher and went out, to the car. The woman was in the back seat. When they went to lift her, they realized that she had given birth, and had not even removed her underwear. The nurses could not resuscitate the baby. They were upset and said to the father, 'Why didn't you tell us she had given birth— we would have hurried!' and he said, 'I was too embarrassed.'

At first glance, these eight examples are exceedingly diverse, but they are all culturally consistent, and all indicate the ramifications of a strong value of modesty on maternal and infant health. Were there any exceptions? Yes, some (there always are exceptions), but the cultural pattern was very clear. Note that these examples are exceedingly unlike at a concrete/descriptive level, but at a more abstract, thematic level, all reveal an underlying theme, that is, the high value of modesty that over-rides even the health of the mother or the infant. Once the researcher is convinced that they understand what they see, can identify it in many forms, and it appears culturally consistent, then the category may be considered saturated and sampling may cease.

SAMPLING DATA

The final aspect that is important in all qualitative inquiry is that sampling does not stop at the level of participants but, in contrast to quantitative inquiry, does not treat all data equally. Within an interview, the researchers may disregard some text (as not helpful or irrelevant), use some portions of the text for verification of other interviews, use some of the text or stories in the data as adding to the descriptions provided by other participants, or adding new data that is different and will start a new category. However, something else is important. All of the stories are not equal, some are *better illustrations*, or *better descriptions* than others, and researchers will tend to use those stories as examples more often than other stories (Morse 2003). This is not a bias—it is a fact that all data are not equal, and some will be favored over others; some will be useful; others useless, and, in some, the usefulness may not be immediately apparent. Hence, we also purposely sample from our data, selecting and sorting, prioritizing or back-staging, as we craft our analysis.

CONCLUSION

Directed sampling enables the development of a rich, well-scoped grounded theory that has been verified through the process of saturation, is sensitive to the trajectory, stages, and phases of the phenomenon being studied, and has well described transitions. All of the concepts are distinctly delineated, linked logically, well supported with data, and saturated. Effective and efficient sampling strategies, which change during the process of data collection and analysis, enable the researcher to complete the task with minimal waste, and without entering any conceptual blind alleys, to produce an excellent grounded theory.

NOTES

1 This project was published as Morse (1992a, b).

REFERENCES

Charmaz, K. (2006) *Constructing Grounded Theory: A Practical Guide Through Qualitative Analysis*. London: SAGE.

Glaser, G. (1978). *Theoretical Sensitivity*. Mill Valley, CA: The Sociology Press.

Kacen, L. (2002). Supercodes reflected in titles battered women accord to their life stories. *International Journal of Qualitative Methods, 1*(1), Article 3. Retrieved October 20, 2006, from http://www.ualberta.ca/~ijqm

Mead, M. & Newton, N. (1967). Cultural patterning of peri-natal behavior. In S. Richardson & A. F. Guttmaler (Eds.), *Childbearing: Its Social and Psychological Aspects* (pp. 142–226). Baltimore: Williams & Wilkins.

Morse, J. M. (1986). Qualitative and quantitative methods: Issues in sampling. In P. Chinn (Ed.), *Nursing Research Methodology: Issues and Implementation* (pp. 181–193). Rockville, MD: Aspen.

Morse, J. M. (1989a). Strategies for sampling. In J. Morse (Ed.), *Qualitative Nursing Research: A Contemporary Dialogue* (pp. 117–131). Rockville, MD: Aspen Press.

Morse, J. M. (1989b). Cultural responses to parturition: Childbirth in Fiji. *Medical Anthropology, 12*(1), 35–44.

Morse, J. M. (1992a). The structure and function of gift-giving in the patient–nurse relationship. In Morse J.M. (ed.) *Qualitative Health Research* (pp. 236–256). Newbury Park, CA: SAGE

Morse, J. M. (1992b). Negotiating commitment and involvement in the nurse–patient relationship. In Morse J.M. (ed.) *Qualitative Health Research* (pp. 333–360). Newbury Park, CA: SAGE.

Morse, J. M. (1995). NIH and the methodological melting pot (Editorial). *Qualitative Health Research, 5*(1), 4–6.

Morse, J. M. (2001). Using shadowed data (Editorial). *Qualitative Health Research, 11*(3), 291.

Morse, J. M. (2003). Undemocratic data (Editorial). *Qualitative Health Research, 13*(1), 3.

Morse, J. M. (2006). Biased reflections: Principles of sampling and analysis in qualitative enquiry. In J. Popay (Ed.), *Moving Beyond Effectiveness in Evidence Synthesis: Methodological Issues in the Synthesis of Diverse Sources of Evidence* (pp. 53–60). London: HAD.

Richards, L. & Morse, J. M. (2007). *Readme First for an Introduction to Qualitative Methods* (2nd ed.). Newbury Park, CA: SAGE.

Spradley, J. (1970). *You Owe Yourself a Drunk*. Boston: Little Brown.

Spradley, J. (1979). *The Ethnographic Interview*. New York: Holt, Rinehart & Winston.

12

Asking Questions of the Data: Memo Writing in the Grounded Theory Tradition

Lora Bex Lempert

Memo writing is essential to Grounded Theory methodological practices and principles. It is *the* fundamental process of researcher/data engagement that results in a 'grounded' theory. Memo writing is the methodological link, the distillation process, through which the researcher transforms data into theory. In the memo writing process, the researcher analytically interprets data. Through sorting, analyzing, and coding the 'raw' data in memos, the Grounded Theorist discovers emergent social patterns. By writing memos continuously throughout the research process, the researcher explores, explicates, and theorizes these emergent patterns. It is the methodological practice of memo writing that roots the researcher in the analyses of the data while simultaneously increasing the level of abstraction of his/her analytical ideas (Charmaz 2006). Ultimately it is the integration of these abstract analyses developed in memos that the researcher shares with a public audience.

Memos are uniquely complex research tools. They are both a methodological practice and a simultaneous exploration of processes in the social worlds of the research site. Memos are not intended to describe the social worlds of the researcher's data, instead, they *conceptualize* the data in narrative form. Remaining firmly grounded in the data, researchers use memos 'to create social reality' (Richardson 1998: 349) by discursively organizing and interpreting the social worlds of their respondents.

This chapter will explore some strategies for memo writing in the Grounded Theory tradition that I have learned and sometimes modified. The ideas presented necessarily reflect my own permutations, preferences, and excitement with the memoing process. The chapter is in many ways a sharing of the lessons of my research processes, garnered over 2 years at Anselm Strauss's UCSF seminar table and extended thereafter over various tables in his (and Fran Strauss's) home, and finally honed to my particular style over the years. Hopefully, it will generate opportunities for others to develop grounded theories that are richer, more complex, more nuanced, and more reflective of multiple social realities than those produced by other research strategies. I do not intend for this chapter to be the final word on memo writing; I intend only to share some of my own ideas. For me, memo writing is the dynamic, intellectually energizing process that captures ideas in synergistic engagement with one another and, through naming, explicating, and synthesizing them, ultimately renders them accessible to wider audiences.

FORMAL AND SUBSTANTIVE THEORY

Grounded Theory research products (reports, presentations, articles, books) are contributions to on-going substantive and theoretical conversations with researchers, practitioners, and interested audiences from different theoretical and methodological perspectives. For Grounded Theorists, participation in these conversations is predicated upon specific analytical assumptions. For example, while both formal and substantive theories must be grounded in data, they are not the same. A formal theoretical conversation offers an explanation of a set of phenomena that have broad social applicability. The theory emerges from the analytical examination of the phenomena in a variety of disparate situations (Strauss & Corbin 1990) and its robustness comes from its simultaneous use in many different contexts (Strauss 1987). Formal theory, consequently, is not specific to a group or a place, instead it applies to a wide range of concerns and problems across situational contexts (Strauss & Corbin 1998). For example, C. Wright Mills (1959) offered 'the sociological imagination' as a formal theory to explain how external societal influences are internalized and consequently become part of individual motivations, values, goals, and aspirations. Mills makes the connection between history and individual biography by drawing a distinction between personal troubles and public issues. The consequent analytic power of 'the Sociological Imagination' is evident in its extensive applications. Substantive theory, however, refers to an empirical area of sociological inquiry and *is* specific to groups and place. For example, if the researcher used Grounded Theory practice and principles, starting with the collection and analysis of rich, solid data, he/she would initially end up with substantive theory, that is, a theory about the substantive area on which he/she have conducted research (Glaser & Strauss 1967). The resultant research, for example, might focus on how 'reductions in force' in a local industry affect the marital relationships of 'downsized' workers; such a topic is specific to group and place. Substantive theory may be an end in itself, or it may presage formal theory. By taking analyses to higher levels of abstraction and conceptual integration in a variety of contexts and groups, Grounded Theory methodology provides the means to develop formal theories from substantive theories (Charmaz 1994). It is through development of both formal and substantive theories that our best research engages with the intellectual work of others. Memo writing is the preparatory step for this conversational participation.

MEMOS

Memos, conceived as adaptable narrative tools for developing ideas and elaborating the social worlds of research sites, form the infrastructure of a Grounded Theory research process. They are the narrated records of a theorist's analytical conversations with him/herself about the research data; as such, they provide particular ways of knowing. Memos are the analytical locations where researchers are most fully present (Charmaz 1983), where they find their own voices, and where they give themselves permission to formulate ideas, to play with them, to reconfigure them, to expand them, to explore them, and ultimately to distill them for publication and participation in conversation with others.

Memos, especially early ones, are speculative and may lack coherence and connection to one another. They record interpretations and incipient patterns emerging from the concrete realities of the social worlds of research sites. They cannot pretend to universal knowledge, but instead must acknowledge the situational limits of the researcher (Richardson 1998). This acknowledgement of the positionality of the researcher is one of my deviations from classical Grounded Theory rubrics.

RESEARCHER POSITIONALITY

In Grounded Theory's debut (Glaser & Strauss 1967) and in Glaser's (1978), Strauss's (1987), and Strauss and Corbin's (1990, 1998) expansion work, the researcher, as research instrument, was presumed to be the neutral knower. As long as the researcher followed the distinctly analytical Grounded Theory research practices throughout the research process, his/her work would result in the development of mid-level theory. The researcher's person (his/her social locations as a raced, gendered, classed, etc., research instrument) was not considered in the initial iterations of Grounded Theory principles and practice. None of these original theorists accounted for the positionality of the researcher in the research process. There were no discussions of the ways that researcher social locations affect the research process. But they do.

Scholars of color (Baca Zinn 1979; Campbell 1969; Collins 2000; Frazier 1949, 1957; Gayle 1971; Hakimu 1969; Swisher 1986; Wright 1979; Zavella 1996) and gender scholars (Finch 1984; Harding 1997; Hartsock 1987; Oakley 1981; Smith 1992) made political and methodological claims for synchronicity and epistemic privilege between researcher and the researched in the research process. In 1972, Merton, challenging the claims of the early race scholars (p. 10), drew on a discourse of 'a largely institutionalized reciprocity of trust among scholars and scientists' and argued that synchronicity was 'deceptively simple and sociologically fallacious' (p. 24). The burgeoning feminist discourse of the past 35 years has been divided, with some feminist theorists supporting epistemic privilege, e.g., in standpoint theory (see Collins 2000, or Harding 1991, for fuller discussion of this argument) while others echo many of Merton's critiques. Importantly, however, unlike that of Merton, the discourse of these feminist scholars has been centered in analyses of power, particularly in trying to understand how power operates in gendering the world (Cock & Bernstein 2002) and hence in gendering research practice and analysis (Naples 2003). Feminist dilemmas in fieldwork, for example, frequently focus on the power differentials between researcher and researched resulting from researcher positionalities (Wolf 1996). Despite methodologies intended to establish research situations as sites for building equality, the exchange between researched and researcher remains asymmetrical (Berik 1996; Feldman, Bell, & Berger 2003; Nama & Swartz 2002), with a fundamental power imbalance existing between researchers and study participants. In the process of conducting qualitative research, researchers necessarily 'take' the words, perspectives, experiences, and personal and cultural stories from their respondents. To consider the resulting negotiations of power between research and research respondents, I offer the language and practice of give-and-take in research practice (Lempert, 2007). Give-and-take is a conceptual framework where who will give, who will take, and what will be given and taken is ever-present as an interactional subtext between the researcher and the researched. It is continuously negotiated by all participants in the research process. Give-and-take is not planned, or formally adopted, as is 'reciprocity,' rather it emerges from opportunities present in research interactions (Lempert, 2007). These opportunities are reflected in memo writing, where, as Laurel Richardson (1998: 349) argues, researchers find out about themselves, and where knowledge of self and knowledge about subject are 'intertwined, partial, historical, local knowledges.'

MEMOING STYLE

While researcher 'knowledges' are often constituted in published work as linear 'Knowledge with a capital K,' memos are neither linear nor Knowledge. Reflecting the social lives that they interpret and the interactional social positions of the researcher and his/her respondents, memos, especially early ones, are often messy and incomplete, with undigested theories and nascent opinions. Ideas may be represented in fragmented phrases, in weird diagrams (narrated in memos, of course), half sentences, or long treatises. Whatever works is just fine in a memo: a memo need only be the account of a researcher talking to him/herself. Clarity and integration come with the expanding analysis.

While memoing *style* is error free, a misstep in memo writing can occur if researchers try to force closure on the data collection and the analytical process too soon. A problem sometimes experienced by novice grounded theory researchers is that they become frustrated with the uncertainty of sorting, coding, and memo writing. They produce a few memos that don't seem to be going anywhere, or at least anywhere with an immediately recognizable theory. When that happens, novice researchers sometimes latch on to an early descriptive pattern. Or conversely they may experience memoing fatigue, writing memo after memo after memo and feeling totally overwhelmed by all the memos that are interesting in and of themselves, but which don't appear to link to one another in any coherent fashion. As a result, inexperienced researchers might also force a too early analytical framework on the data. Both types of error lead to misjudgments regarding the completeness of the analyses. To avoid these missteps and to develop richly nuanced grounded theories, it is necessary both to embrace the uncertainty *and* to have extensive data to analyze. Researchers in the Grounded Theory tradition trust that uncertainty is ultimately generative of theory and that, as the analysis develops, the content of memos improves in depth and quality of conceptualization, and ultimately of integration.

Box 12.1 What Memos Do

- Provide a means for the researchers to engage in and record intellectual conversations with themselves about the data
- Clarify processes by explaining and defining properties and characteristics
- Allow researcher to gain the analytical distance that enables movement away from description and into conceptualization
- Record research and analytical progress, as well as thoughts and feelings, about data and directions for further collection and/or analysis
- Distinguish between major and minor codes and categories
- Maintain a 'storehouse of analytical ideas' (Strauss & Corbin 1998: 220) available for sorting, ordering, re-ordering, and retrieval
- Do what people in research situation probably cannot do, that is, identify patterns and their properties for both general and specific situations (Strauss & Corbin 1998)
- Facilitate the generation of theory

That memos serve as the fundamental link between data and emergent theory is worth repeating. They record an idiosyncratic and creative process of theory development. Theories do not, of course, arise full-blown as though from the head of Zeus; they start in bits and pieces and patterns of ideas that may lack coherence and connection. As incipient ideas are recorded and explored through the memoing process, they grow in complexity and association.

STARTING TO WRITE MEMOS

The process of memo writing in Grounded Theory is a learned skill, a practiced art; it is not mystical, or mysterious, or useful only to 'super' researchers. Memoing itself is simple and straightforward. It is the thinking behind memos that is necessarily complex and analytical. Perhaps because writing memos calls upon a researcher's *confidence* in his/her own expertise, training, and educational and experiential knowledge, i.e., 'tacit knowledge' (Belenky et al. 1986), some researchers new to Grounded Theory methodologies may be intimidated in their initial encounters with memo writing. It is important at those times to remember that memo writing is a skill and, like any other skill, it can be learned through practice. Consider the following topic:

To differentiate between description and analysis, reflect on the topic 'shelters for victims of domestic violence.' Descriptive treatment might focus on the numbers of victims, the ages of victims, the locations of shelters, the sponsors of shelters (grassroots, religious, feminist, etc.), funding revenues, staffing issues, conflicts within shelters, rules and regulations for shelter users, resources provided to users, and so on. Analytical development, in contrast, might focus on the rhetorical uses and meanings of 'shelter' or 'victim' or 'survivor' by different actors, or on comparisons of the definitions of the situation by differentially placed knowers, or on conditions for differing interpretations of need for shelter or worthiness as a consequence of abuse, or on the trajectories of couple relationships after a shelter stay, or on conditions for disclosure/ non-disclosure of a shelter site, or on victim negotiations of cultural tropes of abuse, or on a questioning of the utility of shelters in the struggle to end intimate, interpersonal violence against women. The following example is an excerpt from an analytical memo questioning the appropriateness of shelters as a strategy in the movement to end domestic violence against women in South Africa. The respondent is a direct service provider in the South African shelter system. The larger research study focused on service providers' definitions, perceptions, and/or understandings of intimate, interpersonal violence against women in South Africa leading to particular culturally appropriate remedial strategies (for the published paper, see Lempert 2003).

Memo
   Appropriateness: Question is not shelters or no shelters. False dichotomy. Are shelters appropriate? Are there contexts where they are or are not appropriate? Question is appropriate role for shelters in the fight against violence. Presently forefront, money poured into them—not cost effective—single trajectory.
   Respondent: 'Shelters, I know there's a need for shelters. I just hope and pray to God that we are not in damn shelters forever, OK. But I do understand that, for the interim, we need some shelters for those women that really need that assistance and help. I'm not too comfortable with a million and one shelters, I'm not ... I suppose yes, there is a need for that, but I would like to see that being limited, and not expanding, you know. Because what it's going to say to me is that if you have a million and one shelters, that we are not dealing with the issues.'

While she acknowledges the short-term need for sheltering women without other resources, she also identifies the '*shelter trap*,' that is, shelters can never be more than a short-term solution to a long-term problem. They deflect attention (and resources) away from the source of the problem—structural inequalities—'not dealing with the issues.' Shelters attend to the symptom, not the disease. They provide an easy 'answer' that makes politicos look like they're doing something, but they don't alter the context or change the power structure. Once funding resources are poured into shelters, it's difficult to get more resources for the bigger fight. Nonetheless, she acknowledges the need for immediate action to protect women.

This memo examines and names ('shelter trap') a process identified by the respondent that reflects a particular moment in time in a newly democratized society when social life is still in transition and when important decisions are being made about quality of life and about the means to ensure improved quality of life for women. It analytically summarizes her comments, categorizing them as 'shelter trap' and it raises additional analytical questions: Is sheltering an appropriate strategy in this context? Under what conditions is sheltering an appropriate response? Is sheltering a trap? Is sheltering too limited a strategy? These and additional questions then are developed in further memos.

When memoing a topic analytically, the researcher generates a set of categories, contrasts, comparisons, questions, and avenues for further consideration which are more abstract than the original topic, in this case 'shelters for victims of domestic violence.' The analytical memos explicate underlying processes and assumptions about the topic in the research site. Memo writing is a private conversation between the researcher and his/her data. Researchers, even veteran researchers, are not always going to be brilliant, or neat, or articulate, or theoretical. This memo excerpt, for example, uses short phrases and incomplete sentences to capture nascent ideas. Grounded Theory researchers should not let the burden of a theoretical outcome paralyse them at the beginning (or middle, or end for that matter) of memo writing. Not every memo is going to be relevant to the final narrative. Some may be totally irrelevant. And all memos are partial and provisional.

Box 12.2 Memo Don'ts

- Don't start out with the burden of thinking that you have to generate theory. (It will come, in the interim, think 'generate.')
- Don't force the data. (Aim for diversity and lots of levels of generalization.)
- Don't worry about the coherence of the memos. (If you know what you mean, that's sufficient. You can 'clean them up' in your final presentations.)
- Don't force the process by imposing linearity. (Forget cause and effect for a bit; look for convolution, complexity, and indirection.)
- Don't reinvent the wheel. (Use the literature.)

The starting point of memo writing is the first idea that occurs to the researcher about his/her data. In a memo, they link their idea to the 'stories' in the data. They ask questions of the data: What is this an example of? When does it happen? Where is it happening? With whom? How? Under what conditions does it seem to occur? With what consequences?

These sorts of questions work best for me when I begin with some form of diagram of a process that I've noted in my data. In Grounded Theory, diagrams are part of the process of analysis (Lofland & Lofland 1995). I think of diagrams as 'motion' in the data: events happening in relation to other events. It is that 'relation' that Grounded Theory researchers try to capture, however imperfectly, in memos. The following diagram and memo was one of the first in a case study of the mother of a paternally incested daughter. The mother in the study is a friend of mine. In 1997, at a pizza dinner with four girlfriends, she, an African American, disclosed to us, two white women and two African American women, that her husband's alleged sexual relations with her daughter had been the reason for her divorce several years earlier. She, of course, knew that I study intimate, interpersonal violence against women. A few days later, she asked me to write about her experiences. I did (Lempert 1999). This was one of the initial diagrams based on my interviews with her (Figure 12.1).

The in-depth interviews with Sarah (a pseudonym chosen by my friend, the respondent, that I use in memo writing and publications) relates the story of her daughter's disclosure of incest. The disclosure occurs in a residential mental health facility where the daughter, Michelle (another pseudonym), is being treated for an eating disorder. A portion of the memo about Sarah's description of Michelle's disclosure, what I call the 'telling anecdote,' follows:

> date
>   TELLING—re: telling anecdote—from the outset, Sarah resists the definition of the situation {her daughter's allegations of incest} and her resistance is supported by her related story, adding to its particular denial. Innocence is not the story, but it supports the authenticity of her resistance. Sarah's is the story of the clueless mother of an incested daughter.
>   How of Sarah's narration in relation to what (cultural discourses available to moms of ...) *How does she construct story in relation to her particular biography*? Seems to have trouble combining disparate themes of good mom/bad mom.
>   AMBIGUITY—lots of it—all of account is retrospective, so all of it is a reconstruction. 'no reason to believe' (1) re: what? Only has Michelle's word; his denial; no other evidence. (2) IF ... Then why? Motive? (3) How? How is she {Sarah} implicated? (4) EVIDENCE—circumstantial; Michelle has an eating disorder (check lit—think I remember this being a 'sign' of childhood abuse); adolescence—Michelle not dating—whole life was dancing, underlying gender assumption—expected to date (compare to closeted gay youth); guys don't meet Michelle's standards—family image story; relief—[of Michelle's] not dating = no pregnancy. (5) Where—context for disclosure? Disclosure without specifics. Michelle is in mental hospital for eating disorder (3rd or 4th hospitalization). They only have supervised visits.

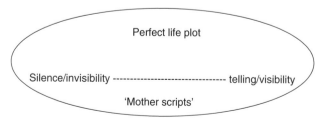

Figure 12.1   Initial diagram of early memo.

No opportunity to talk with her alone. Parents go monthly to sessions with Michelle. Michelle BLAMES Sarah.

This memo is one of my first 'passes' through the interview data. Since telling is a significant social act (Lempert 1996) that renders the invisible visible, that's where I started both conceptually and by location in the data. I theorized 'telling' in prior work on abused women, so I have a comparative framework that makes me attentive to this issue. I note Sarah's reported response within the context of larger sociological issues, i.e., definitions of the situation (and implicitly the Thomas & Thomas 1928 dictum: 'If situations are perceived as real, they are real in their consequences'). There are embedded sensitivities as well from C. Wright Mills in the question exploring the connection between Sarah's personal biography and the public issues surrounding the disclosure of incest. I use this 'tacit knowledge' (Belenky et al. 1986) to begin to 'ask questions of the data' (an Anselm Strauss 'mantra') and to provide elementary observational responses. My overall reading of the data at this stage is Sarah's presentation of self as 'the clueless mother of an incested daughter' and the ways that she constructs her story to support her cluelessness.

I am, for example, struck by the lack of 'evidence' available to Sarah and the consequential ambiguity that she struggles with. I need to *code* this phenomenon, that is, to name it and analyze its characteristics and relationships. In grounded theory, codes capture patterns and themes and cluster them under a 'title' that evokes a constellation of impressions and analyses for the researcher. I code this lack of evidence as 'AMBIGUITY' and I ask myself questions about it, reminding myself of the limits of the data (specifically its retrospective reconstruction) and I look for 'evidence' of Sarah's claims that she had 'no reason to believe' her daughter's allegations, that is, how does the code 'lack of evidence' contribute to the category 'ambiguity.' The conditions for ambiguity begin to emerge in the eating disorder, in the reported patterns of Michelle's adolescence, and in both the context and content of her disclosure. The consequence of ambiguity is Sarah's denial. EVIDENCE then emerges as another potential code for development, as does BLAME at the end of the memo. (Other memos then explore these codes. In early stage coding, I try to focus on one code per memo with references in text to other codes and, therefore, to other memos.) Also embedded in this memo are directions to myself for a focused literature review and a comparison (to closeted gay youth) that may generate additional dimensions. Overall then, the memo records my initial analysis, illuminates the gaps in that analysis, provides direction for work outside of the data, and furnishes an elemental foundation for further comparison, contrast, reconstruction, and refinement. I use caps, bold, italics, and underlinings as visual prompts to myself about relevance and importance, but also in anticipation of later searchings for phrasing, examples, and/or expositions. Caps, underlinings, bolds, and italics save me time in locating information.

When I get 'stuck,' when I'm developing categories, or when I think I 'have it,' I review memos, re-reading and re-reading and re-reading them.

The reviews often result in a shift in focus, or a reconfiguration of my analysis, or integrations of what were formerly disparate pieces of analysis, and/or a reconstitution of my argument. I integrate these changes in additional memos that become the basis for publishable work. These re-readings are what Lofland & Lofland (1995: 195) describe as '*analysis written on analysis*' (italics in original).

MEMOS AND LITERATURE

I use literature extensively when I conduct research, *as* I collect, code, memo, and write. This broad reading of the literature is another of my deviations from the proscriptions of classical Grounded Theory. Glaser & Strauss (1967), Glaser (1978, 1994), Strauss (1987), and Strauss & Corbin (1990, 1998) advocated delaying comprehensive use of the literature until after the analytical story emerged and stabilized. They cautioned against the pitfall of selecting data for a category that has been established by another theory, fretting that this singular selection would hinder generation of new categories and theories. Their caution was predicated in an assumption that novice (and some experienced) researchers would abandon the centrality of discovery in Grounded Theory and would instead attempt to force data into pre-existing categories. They sought a delicate balance between using pre-existing, theoretical, disciplinary knowledge as a sensitizing tool for comparative analysis and remaining unaffected, virtual research *tabulae rasae* or clean slates from the same existing theories.

While I concede the concern, my approach is personally pragmatic. In order to participate in the current theoretical conversation, I need to understand it. I must recognize that what may seem like a totally new idea to me (an innovative breakthrough in my research) may simply be a reflection of my ignorance of the present conversation. A literature review provides me with the current parameters of the conversation that I hope to enter. Utilizing comparisons from the literature alerts me to gaps in theorizing, as well as the ways that my data tells a different, or more nuanced, story (for example, see Lempert 1995). It does not, however, define my research.

Memos and diagrams evolve. They begin, as my first example demonstrated, simply and awkwardly but, as analysis progresses and as the literature informs, memos grow in complexity and abstraction. The following is an excerpt of portions of a more extensive memo further exploring the code AMBIGUITY. It incorporates both literature and analysis and additional codes of 'dichotomy' and 'coherence':

> date
>> Gergen 1992—When we tell one another our deepest secrets we use a public language (p. 128).
>> How does the mother of an incested daughter tell her story? How does she make sense of her daughter's allegations and her husband's denials? How does she explain her own ignorance of the aberrant sexual activity occurring in her home? What can her story tell others about the cultural scripts available to the mothers of incested daughters?

How does Sarah's narrative construct why she couldn't see {the incest} before? AMBIGU-ITY and image, cultural scripts offer no good choices—narrative swings between dichotomy—depressed mom vs good mom and creation of ideal family—neither one works. Ambiguity also in where to locate herself in the telling.

Gergen 1992—linear narratives, single narrative line is male model of story telling related to explicit goal state and is progressive—action moves toward goal. Women—story line is less demarcated and person is embedded in a variety of relationships. Women's lives and identities build around significant relationships in their lives—affects contents of stories and their formal structures, i.e., women are digressive and complex

{Sarah's} narrative is digressive and fails to achieve **coherence**—either/or dichotomy, maybe because of competing, contradictory recollections? Recollections can be competing; way of executing them, way of telling them can be different, either the emotion/lack of, doesn't have constraint of being coherent. More of a pastiche than a narrative with a devel-oping plot. **Coherence of story** linked to AMBIGUITY—if girl is sometimes an incest sur-vivor and sometimes a normal teenager, in order for mother to know this is happening, mother has to interact w/daughter when she is an incest survivor, not when she's other. How can you not know?—unreasonable that daughter would be incest victim 24 hrs a day. Not victim in identity, {she has} other identities. Sarah's interaction with Michelle's narrative becomes more analytically fluid.

While more abstract, this memo still does not meet conventional criteria for coherence. I am still in early conversation with myself about the data. I am using the ideas and theoretical insights of other researchers to inform and to sensitize myself to potential patterns in the data. I am asking more questions, more complexly analytical questions, than I am answering. My literature summaries are in the form of notes to myself. My analysis is contained in short phrases, half sentences, and, as yet, undeveloped avenues with the 'motion' between them captured by dashes and short phrases.

The author cited in this memo is not writing about incest. Gergen's work recounts the life histories of holocaust survivors. But she is theorizing respondent storytelling and her work serves as a comparative group. Sarah is attempting to mend the rift between the public disclosure of incest and her former, public construction of herself as a wife/mother in a 'happy' family. Sarah is an African American; her story is situated in an historically racialized context. As noted in the first memo, Sarah's presentation is a reconstruction. All life experience stories are selectively recounted and Sarah's is no exception. She is resisting the Mother Blame master narrative, but the cultural narratives available to the mother of an incested daughter are limited; they 'don't work.' My theoret-ical question is: Why not? The work of theorists like Gergen sensitizes me to potential answers as well as to forms and processes in Sarah's narrative.

I make notes to myself regarding the cultural question: How could a mother not know? And I try to answer that question by explicating some conditions under which a mother might remain unaware. Under the condition that the daughter is not a victim in her identity all the time, and the condition that the daughter has other equally significant identities (school girl, dancer, church member, etc.), a potential consequence is that her victimization remains unseen by her mother.

Another salient issue, highlighted in these portions and developed in other memos, is the problem of available cultural narratives. There are cultural narratives about mothers of incested daughters and cultural narratives about the sexual proclivities of African Americans. In this memo, I focus on the cultural narratives of mothers of incested daughters. The narratives 'don't work' in part because they are dichotomized. Sarah's presentation of herself as a 'good mom' is challenged by the incest. She declares her innocence, but she can't be a 'good mom' and be innocent, culturally they are mutually exclusive categories so no synthesis is possible.

The memo reflects more than Sarah's inconsistencies, it also reflects my perspective as a researcher able to 'see' the events from different angles. Grounded Theory analytical skills and practices require that I 'see' both the forest and the trees, that is, both the mezzo perspective reflected in socio-cultural stories of mother blame and the micro perspective of a mother's response to incest allegations that Sarah recounts. Memos are the locations for consideration of these synergistic accounts. As a category, ambiguity also problematizes Sarah's attempts to negotiate public discursive space with her story of obliviousness. She wants acceptance of her story, not blame for her ignorance. I'm trying to understand her experiences, to tease out the assumptions of the cultural narratives on mothers of incested daughters (as they intersect with master narratives of African American males), and to develop a coherent framework for making the analysis accessible to interested others.

Gergen's work alerts me to a rhetorical, cultural trap, specifically the social expectation of a linear story that might inform analysis of Sarah's episodic recounting of her experiences. Gergen posits the linear expectation as a male model of storytelling. Sarah's story may appear disjointed and episodic because she's resisting Mother Blame, because of the range of ambiguities, because no synthesis is possible, and/or because of a relational and digressive mode of relating her experiences. All of these possibilities are provisional; they remain active arenas for exploration in the data. Memo-writing has complicated the linear story; it is the place where rich complexity lies.

MEMOS AND RESPONDENT VOICES

Respondent voices are integral to Grounded Theory analyses. When studies include formal/informal interviews, the narrative voices of respondents constitute our data. Analyses are predicated on interpretations of their words and meanings. Memo writing distils this motion between respondent voices, 'data,' and the developing analyses. The early lessons from many high school English teachers: 'Good writing shows, it doesn't just tell,' can serve Grounded Theory researchers well. Data is the researcher's evidence; it is what we have to 'show' in support of our analyses. Providing data allows our audiences to participate in our unfolding analytical arguments. Including respondent voices in memos provides an immediate illustration of the analytical topic, keeps researchers grounded by keeping the data in the forefront of the analyses, and makes the data easily transferable to final written documents. We don't have to search for it. In the published document, respondent voices provide the details that enable the reader to draw the same conclusions and make the same inferences that authors do. Methodologically, it also prevents the overuse of singular examples (Charmaz 2006).

The following memo is a further development of AMBIGUITY, which started out as a code and which grew (through analysis and memoing) in complexity and abstraction into a category, subsuming other codes like 'evidence,' 'invisibility,' 'image,' 'holding together a shattered world' and linking them to the range of ambiguities present in Sarah's interview narrative. Portions of the memo follow.

> date
> EVIDENCE and 'emotion work' in AMBIGUITY:
> Sara needs tangible proof of the incest. Jackie is denying everything. She needs physical evidence, or evidence of hurt. Some examples she can interpret. They veiled their activities and that resulted in the invisibility of the abuse. Michelle actively shielded Sarah from knowledge. She withheld information that would have made knowledge possible (see EVIDENCE memo and Michelle's ambiguous anecdote).
>
> Ideology of family contributed to invisibility of the violence—tension between individual liberty and parental control. Privacy and respect accorded to individual family members, domestic autonomy, respect for individual.
>
> Sarah's strategic public construction of relationships and family as 'happy' trapped her. Jackie and Michelle controlled the information expressed publicly.
>
>> I think I went from I'm not gonna deal with this, I mean, I'm simply not gonna deal with this. I simply shut it right out, to pretty much believing it ... I guess for all practice purposes I had to make a choice. I mean if I had chosen him, if I'd chosen our marriage, I wouldn't have either of the kids ... I've always dearly, truly loved my kids, and I think, you know, it just wasn't the same for Jack. It wasn't, you know, we just weren't that happy. It just wasn't that good anymore. And I don't even know whether it was really ever that good. I think I was just hanging in there, you know, two kids, husband, [pet], two cars, you know, that image ... I don't know whether it's [that I] believed her more, it's like what she said and how she said it made me a believer. He didn't do anything that made me believe him.
>
> Sarah engages in 'emotion work' (Hochschild 1983) and uses it to distance herself from painful connections, get rid of her feelings and to escape from the situation, until that's no longer possible (see memo on Mother Blame).
>
> Her ideological center crumbled as she struggled to work through disappointment and betrayal. She necessarily accepts the failed narrative of her 'happy' family. She resolves her own uncertainty by making a cost/benefit choice.

While not fully developed, this memo is written in complete sentences. The analysis began to coalesce. The previously disparate pieces of analysis began through memo-writing to form themselves into a coherent story. The memo, including Sarah's voice, transposed to the following published argument (Lempert 1999: 47):

> The material evidence Michelle offered was an anecdotal story. Although Sarah recalled the incident, she used the narration to highlight the ambiguity that she experienced. Sarah actively constructed an image of herself as lacking knowledge of the clues that would, presumably, have led her to question her daughter. Lacking more definitive evidence, the allegations remained he-said/she-said conflicting versions of reality. Sarah was caught between the proverbial rock and a hard place. If she believed her daughter, then she lost her

husband; if she believed her husband, then she lost her daughter. Sarah's familiar and familial ideologies offered her no stable interpretations and no resolution of the ambiguities. For multiple reasons, Sarah reluctantly accepted Michelle's account:

> I think I went from I'm not gonna deal with this, I mean, I'm simply not gonna deal with this. I simply shut it right out, to pretty much believing it … I guess for all practice purposes I had to make a choice. I mean if I had chosen him, if I'd chosen our marriage, I wouldn't have either of the kids … I've always dearly, truly loved my kids, and I think, you know, it just wasn't the same for Jack. It wasn't, you know, we just weren't that happy. It just wasn't that good anymore. And I don't even know whether it was really ever that good. I think I was just hanging in there, you know, two kids, husband, [pet], two cars, you know, that image … I don't know whether it's [that I] believed her more, it's like what she said and how she said it made me a believer. He didn't do anything that made me believe him.

As Sarah confronted the 'truth' of the incest, she also confronted the 'truth' of her marriage. She reinterpreted the history of her marriage in a cost/benefit analysis and she chose to continue her relationship with her daughter.

INTEGRATING IN MEMOS

The most difficult feature of Grounded Theory methodology is integration (Strauss 1987; Strauss & Corbin 1990). It is hard intellectual work to keep categories analytical and to clarify analyses in memos. The process seems endless. Sometimes it feels like navel gazing, at other times like thinking in circles. Either response is a signal to 'take a break' from the data and analysis. Go work on the bibliography. Read more of the literature. Go for a walk. But then come back and re-read *all* of the memos. Treat them like data. Write memos on the memos. This step, looking for the cumulative patterns in the analyses and reforming the diagrams, is a heady process. It is energizing to begin to see your own ideas coalesce and your own theoretical insights emerge. Sometimes '*several possible modes of integration*' emerge, a seasoned researcher chooses one to develop (Lofland & Lofland 1995: 195, italics in original). She/he can go back later and develop the other(s). Remember 'there is no single way' to interpret social worlds (Lofland & Lofland 1995: 195).

DIAGRAMS IN INTEGRATION

Diagrams are central in Grounded Theory work. They create a visual display of what researchers do and do not know. As such, they bring order to the data and further the total analyses. The visualizations in diagrams enable Grounded Theorists to gain analytical distance which enables them to conceptualize the data in more abstract terms. Because they're less wordy than memos, diagrams can represent categories and their linkages more precisely and concisely. Grounded theory researchers use diagrams from the very beginning of their analyses.

Diagrams and memos are conjoined; both are necessary and simultaneous to a Grounded Theory research process. Like memos, diagrams are often messy, partial, and provisional. They also evolve, sometimes negate, and hopefully extend earlier configurations. More importantly, they reconceptualize data in visual form. They are more manipulable than memos, so they are often generative of new ideas, connections, and reconfigurations. At the integration stage, diagrams include most identified categories. Their inclusion forces researchers to see connections. It is important to diagram the emergent processes and then memo, in detail, the visual representation of the analysis.

In the memos provided here of the case study of the mother of a paternally incested daughter, I have focused analytical attention at the micro level. With a single respondent, what our quantitative colleagues label as $N = 1$, I did not have sufficient data for theoretical saturation or for claims of universality, and so I was not intent on developing a *core category,* or formal theory. Instead this work sought to develop substantive ideas and to understand Sarah's experience of disclosure and her processes of integration and re-integration. The context of her problem solving and subsequent constructions is the salient socio-cultural question directed toward mothers of incested daughters: How could you not know? Grounded in Sarah's reconstructions, I examined and problematized the conditions under which a mother, self-defined as a 'good' mother, could be unaware that paternal incest was occurring in her home. A mother's ignorance of incest is inherently a culturally discordant account.

My 'data' was Sarah's narrative collected from several informal discussions as well as two lengthy, open-ended taped interviews. Theoretical integration (and data evidence) required an examination of the mezzo and macro level influences on Sarah's biography, on the ways that her private troubles also reflected public issues (Mills 1959). Sarah's narrated story reflects the discrepancy between experience and the cultural narratives available to talk about them. My task was to theorize how Sarah's story might be deficient in terms of cultural standards, but still be consistent with the facts. My integration diagram is presented in Figure 12.2.

While I memo extensively on each portion of this diagram, including cutting and pasting from earlier memos to begin the publishable narrative, here I am only presenting portions of the memo about the *failed narrative* (which appears at the end of the diagram). Failed narrative is the end result of the dichotomized cultural narratives available to mothers of incested daughters; the category includes conflated codes like 'dichotomy' and 'coherence.' I tell Sarah's failed narrative (Lempert 1996: 43) as '... a challenge to the culturally circumscribed master narrative of mother-blaming that surrounds revelations of incest. By analyzing the ways that Sarah's fierce enactment of cultural and ideological images of "good wife" and "good mother" blinded her to the social processes that ensnared her, I demonstrate how the cultural resources available to reconstruct events, family, and self after disclosure of incest fail to capture the ambiguity and complexity of the experience.' Portions of the memo follow:

date
    She's resisting the mother blaming but there is no resistance model because as soon as you say you didn't know, then other {forms of} blaming {results} for not being a good mother.

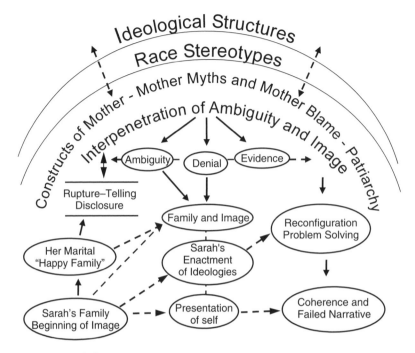

Figure 12.2   Final diagram.

Societal/cultural structures force us into dichotomous choices. Ideological structures don't relate to the ways that we live our lives; structure has nice, neat character but lived lives are messy. But we have to force messy lives into the [existing cultural story] structure, that's what {Sarah's} narrative is trying to do—a lot to put on a narrative. There are holes in the narrative where there's not good mapping. {I have to} deconstruct the cultural narrative in order to show where mapping doesn't work. Impossible task {for Sarah}—creating any narrative that bridges that gap is going to be a **failed narrative**. The gap between the reality of the good/bad mom and the ideological structure of either/or and {Sarah} is guilty for ignoring all the bad things, for not fixing them. Yet both are true. She is a good mother and a failed mother. True that she did all that she said she did. True that she was unable to protect her daughter from incest. Impulse to 'how can she not know' is largely based on wish and desire to force a kind of coherence on a story of social psychological disintegration.

The diagram for this memo, the integrated story that the data tells, includes a number of macro and micro categories that influence the invisibility of incest in the home of a 'good' mother. The story is told in this integration diagram and the previous and ensuing memos. Sarah's presentation of self/family was an on-going challenge to cultural narratives about African Americans. Her family background did not prepare her to consider even the possibility of incest in her life/family and, should the consideration have arisen, family 'image making' would have precluded interpretation of such information as 'incest.' There was no space for considerations of stereotypes. Her 'perfect life plot' was ruptured, first by Michelle's hospitalizations, but then more seriously by her allegations of paternal incest.

Disclosure of incest shatters the taken-for-granted world of the family unit. Yet ambiguity surrounded Sarah's daughter's initial and subsequent claims. Michelle provided no irrefutable *evidence*; Sarah was left with *ambiguity* and the interpenetration of ambiguity and image. Sarah wrestled alone with the ambiguities and uncertainties. Her problem-solving processes brought her to a solo meeting with Michelle and Michelle's therapist, both of whom enacted culturally supported *mother blame* narratives about Sarah's responses to Michelle's disclosure. Sarah was forced to choose between her daughter and her husband. A cost benefit analysis of her marriage enabled her to reluctantly choose her daughter.

Sarah's analysis reflects her resistance to cultural scripts (of mother blame and of African American sexuality) and her unsuccessful attempts to synthesize the dichotomies. Disclosure of incest required that Sarah reevaluate and reconstruct herself as a woman, as a wife, and as a mother. She drew upon the cultural models (of women, mothers, and African Americans) for both the form and content of a narrative through which she could construct meanings and interpret these life-shattering revelations. She actively resisted the stereotypical and stigmatized identities available to her as she tried to explain her meaning-making processes. The models left her with factual truths that were incongruent with the cultural means available to tell them. Ultimately, Sarah accepted that hers was going to be a *failed narrative*; it could not achieve cultural synthesis.

CONCLUSION

In this chapter I have provided strategies and examples of memo writing in the Grounded Theory tradition of research analysis. There are certainly other ways to turn raw data into published documents, but I'm not sure that they are as satisfying or as exciting as these. And although I remain foundationally true to the form and logic of classical Grounded Theory, I have also presented my own variations on the themes of Glaser and Strauss, Glaser, and Strauss and Corbin. I argue, for example, for the serious consideration of researcher positionalities and their effects, singly and in integration, on the research process. Human subject research is not neutral; human subject researchers are not separate and distinct from their research processes. Researchers have biographies and social privileges that affect their theoretical, philosophical, substantive, and methodological choices. Their research decisions are, implicitly or explicitly, ideological decisions. Grounded Theory practices must incorporate acknowledgments and analyses of these effects.

Additionally I argue for on-going researcher familiarity with the literature of the substantive area of study and its applicable theories. Engaging the literature provides the researcher with knowledge of the substantive area in sufficient depth to understand the parameters of the discourse and to enter into the current theoretical conversation. Moreover, Charmaz (2006: 163) suggests that literature reviews for research are themselves ideological sites 'in which you claim, locate, evaluate, and defend your position.'

Nonetheless, researchers who claim to use Grounded Theory methods in memo writing collectively adhere to fundamental principles. First, the purpose and intent of memo writing is discovery and theory development, not application. Second, extensive amounts of solid, rich data are the 'raw' materials for discovery. Analysis of this 'raw' data occurs through memo writing and diagramming. Third, Grounded Theorists write memos and create diagrams throughout the research process enabling them to shape the collection and subsequent analyses of data. Fourth, continuous memo writing, re-reading and re-writing, leads to progressively more abstract levels of theorizing.

As Hammersley and Atkinson (1983) note, memo writing forces the researcher to go through processes of explication and prevents aimless drifting through data. Rather than assume understanding on the basis of researcher insight, through memo writing 'one is forced to question *what* one knows, *how* such knowledge has been acquired, the *degree of certainty* of such knowledge, and what further lines of inquiry are implied' (Hammsersley & Atkinson 1983: 165). Early memos provide comparisons for later information. They begin the analytical processes. Refining memos builds structure, accounts for variations, and deepens both the complexity and quality of analysis. Spelling out the connections between codes and codes, between codes and categories, and between categories and categories is foundational to presentation of an integrated whole. It is through our integrated final analyses that we join the conversations of our peers.

ACKNOWLEDGMENTS

Special thanks to Lindsey Hill for her awesome talents manifested in transferring my messy final diagram into an accessible format, to Michael Gillespie for providing questions needing answers to new researchers learning Grounded Theory memo writing and, as always, to the Academic Women Writers.

REFERENCES

Baca Zinn, Maxine (1979) Field Research in Minority Communities: Ethical, Methodological, and Political Observations by an Insider. *Social Problems* 27, 2: 209–219.

Belenky, Mary Field, Clinchy, Blythe McVicher, Goldberger, Nancy Rule and Tarule, Jill Mattuck (1986) *Women's Ways of Knowing*. New York: Basic Books.

Berik, Gunnseli (1996) Skinfolk, Not Kinfolk: Comparative Reflections on the Identity of Participant-Observation in Two Field Situations. In Diane L. Wolf (Ed.), *Feminist Dilemmas in Fieldwork*. Boulder, CO: Westview, 72–95.

Campbell, Donald T. (1969) Ethnocentrism of Disciplines and the Fish-Scale Model of Omniscience. In Muzafer Sherif and Carolyn W. Sherif (Eds.), *Interdisciplinary Relationships in the Social Sciences*. Chicago: Aldine.

Charmaz, Kathy (1983) The Grounded Theory Method: An Explication and Interpretation. In Robert M. Emerson (Ed.), *Contemporary Field Research*. Boston: Little, Brown and Company, 109–126.

Charmaz, Kathy (1994) The Grounded Theory Method: An Explication and Interpretation. In Barney G. Glaser (Ed.), *More Grounded Theory Methodology: A Reader*. Mill Valley: Sociology Press, 95–115.

Charmaz, Kathy (2006) *Constructing Grounded Theory: A Practical Guide through Qualitative Analysis*. Thousand Oaks, CA: SAGE.

Cock, Jacklyn and Alison Bernstein (2002) *Melting Pots & Rainbow Nations: Conversations about Difference in the United States and South Africa*. Urbana and Chicago: University of Illinois Press.

Collins, Patricia Hill (2000) *Black Feminist Thought: Knowledge, Consciousness, and the Politics of Empowerment* (2nd ed). New York: Routledge.

Feldman, Martha S., Jeannine Bell and Michele Tracy Berger (2003) *Gaining Access: A Practical and Theoretical Guide for Qualitative Research*. Walnut Creek, CA: Altamira Press.

Finch, Janet (1984) 'It's Great to Have Someone to Talk to': The Ethics and Politics of Interviewing Women. In Colin Bell and Helen Roberts (Eds.), *Social Researching: Politics, Problems, Practice*. London: Routledge and Kegan Paul, 70–87.

Frazier, E. Franklin (1949) *The Negro in the United States*. New York: Macmillan.

Frazier, E. Franklin (1957) *Black Bourgeoisie*. New York: Free Press.

Gayle, Addison (1971) *The Black Aesthetic*. New York: Doubleday.

Gergen, Mary (1992) Lives as Texts: Symptoms as Modes of Recounting the Life Histories of Holocaust Survivors. In George C. Rosenwald and Richard L. Ochberg (Eds.), *Storied Lives: The Cultural Politics of Self-understanding*. New Haven: Yale University Press, 127–144.

Glaser, Barney G. (1978) *Theoretical Sensitivity*. Mill Valley, CA: Sociology Press.

Glaser, Barney G. (1994) *More Grounded Theory Methodology: A Reader*. Mill Valley: Sociology Press.

Glaser, Barney G. and Anselm L. Strauss (1967) *The Discovery of Grounded Theory*. New York: Aldine de Gruyter.

Hakimu Abd-l, Ibn Alkalimat (Gerald McWorter) (1969) The Ideology of Black Social Science. *Black Scholar* (December): 28–35.

Hammersley, Martyn and Paul Atkinson (1983) *Ethnography Principles in Practice*. London: Tavistock Publications.

Harding, Sandra (1991) *Whose Knowledge? Whose Science?* Ithaca, NY: Cornell University Press.

Harding, Sandra (1997) Comment on Hekman's 'Truth and Method: Feminist Standpoint Theory Revisited': Whose Standpoint Needs the Regimes of Truth and Reality? *Signs: Journal of Women and Culture* 22, 2: 382–391.

Hartsock, Nancy (1987) The Feminist Standpoint: Developing the Ground for a Specifically Feminist Historical Materialism. In Sandra Harding (Ed.), *Feminism and Methodology*. Bloomington: Indiana University Press, 157–180.

Lempert, Lora Bex (1995) The Line in the Sand: Definitional Dialogues in Abusive Relationships, *Studies in Symbolic Interaction* 18: 171–195. Reprinted in Strauss, Anselm and Juliet Corbin (Eds.) (1997) *Grounded Theory in Practice*. Newbury Park, CA: SAGE.

Lempert, Lora Bex (1996) Women's Strategies for Survival: Developing Agency in Abusive Relationships. *Journal of Family Violence* 11, 3: 269–289.

Lempert, Lora Bex (1999) 'An Unbelievable Kind of Thing': A Mother's Response to the Disclosure of Incest. In Mary Romero and Abigail J. Stewart (Eds.), *Women's Untold Stories: Breaking Silence, Talking Back, Voicing Complexity*. New York: Routledge, 37–52.

Lempert, Lora Bex (2003) Shelters: For Abused Women, or Abusive Men? As Aids to Survival, or as Rehabilitation Sites? *Agenda: Empowering Women for Gender Equity* 57: 89–100.

Lempert, Lora Bex (2007) Cross Race, Cross Culture, Cross National, Cross Class, But Same Gender: Musings on Research in South Africa. *NWSA Journal*

Lofland, John and Lyn H. Lofland (1995) *Analyzing Social Settings: A Guide to Qualitative Observation and Analysis* (3rd ed.). Belmont, CA: Wadsworth.

Merton, Robert K. (1972) Insiders and Outsiders: A Chapter in the Sociology of Knowledge. *American Journal of Sociology* 78, 1: 9–47.

Mills, C. Wright (1959) *The Sociological Imagination*. New York: Oxford University Press.

Nama, Nosisana and Leslie Swartz (2002) Ethical and Social Dilemmas in Community-Based Controlled Trials in Situations of Poverty: A View from a South African Project. *Journal of Community & Applied Social Psychology* 12, 4: 286–297.

Naples, Nancy A. (2003) *Feminism and Method: Ethnography, Discourse Analysis, and Activist Research*. New York: Routledge.

Oakley, Ann (1981) Interviewing Women: A Contradiction in Terms. In Helen Roberts (Ed.), *Doing Feminist Research*. London and New York: Routledge, 30–61.

Richardson, Laurel (1998) Writing: A Method of Inquiry. In Norman K. Denzin and Yvonna S. Lincoln (Eds.), *Collecting and Interpreting Qualitative Materials*. Thousand Oaks, CA: SAGE, 345–371.

Smith, Dorothy (1992) Sociology from Women's Experience: A Reaffirmation. *Sociological Theory* 10, 1: 88–98.

Strauss, Anselm L. (1987) *Qualitative Analysis for Social Scientists*. Cambridge: Cambridge University Press.

Strauss, Anselm L. and Juliet Corbin (1990) *Basics of Qualitative Research*. Newbury Park, CA: SAGE.

Strauss, Anselm L. and Juliet Corbin (1998) *Basics of Qualitative Research* (2nd ed.). Newbury Park, CA: SAGE.

Swisher, Karen Gayton (1986) Authentic Research: Interview on the Way to the Ponderosa. *Anthropology Education Quarterly* 17, 3: 185–188.

Thomas, William I. and Dorothy Swain Thomas (1928) The Child in America: Behavior Problems and Programs. New York: Knopf.

Wolf, Diane L. (1996) Situating Feminist Dilemmas in Fieldwork. In Diane L. Wolf (Ed.), *Feminist Dilemmas in Fieldwork*. Boulder, CO: Westview, 1–55.

Wright, Steven J. (1979) Why Don't More Blacks Study Blacks? *Change* 11, 7: 62–63.

Zavella, Patricia (1996) Feminist Insider Dilemmas: Constructing Ethnic Identity with Chicana Informants. In Diane L. Wolf (Ed.), *Feminist Dilemmas in Fieldwork*. Boulder, CO: Westview, 138–159.

13

The Coding Process and Its Challenges

Judith A. Holton

INTRODUCTION

Coding is the core process in classic grounded theory methodology. It is through coding that the conceptual abstraction of data and its reintegration as theory takes place. There are two types of coding in a classic grounded theory study: *substantive coding*, which includes both open and selective coding procedures, and *theoretical coding*. In substantive coding, the researcher works with the data directly, fracturing and analysing it, initially through *open coding* for the emergence of a *core category* and related concepts and then subsequently through *theoretical sampling* and *selective coding* of data to theoretically saturate the core and related concepts. *Theoretical saturation* is achieved through *constant comparison* of incidents (indicators) in the data to elicit the properties and dimensions of each category (code). This constant comparing of incidents continues until the process yields the *interchangeability of indicators*, meaning that no new properties or dimensions are emerging from continued coding and comparison. At this point, the concepts have achieved theoretical saturation and the theorist shifts attention to exploring the emergent fit of potential theoretical codes that enable the conceptual integration of the core and related concepts to produce hypotheses that account for relationships between the concepts thereby explaining the latent pattern of social behaviour that forms the basis of the emergent theory. The coding of data in grounded theory occurs in conjunction with analysis through a process of *conceptual memoing*, capturing the theorist's ideation of the emerging theory. Memoing occurs initially at the substantive coding level and proceeds to higher levels of conceptual abstraction as coding proceeds to theoretical saturation and the theorist begins to explore conceptual reintegration through theoretical coding.

There are a number of coding challenges that may confront those undertaking a grounded theory study. Among the most common challenges are those of preconceiving the study through the import of some standard qualitative research requirements, raising the focus of coding and analysis from the descriptive to the conceptual level and trusting one's intuitive sense of the conceptualization process to allow a core category to emerge, then being comfortable to delimit data collection and coding to just the core concept and those concepts that relate to the core. Those inexperienced in grounded theory methodology may worry about missing something when they leave the rest of the data behind but it is important to remember that grounded theory is about concepts that emerge from data, not the data per se. A fourth major challenge for many is the use of theoretical codes. Many who attempt grounded theory are captured by the energy of conceptual emergence at the substantive level and settle for a few good concepts but do not sustain the discipline and patience to systematically integrate those concepts through theoretical coding. This task is made more difficult if they have neglected the important process of memoing in conjunction with coding and analysis.

Developing one's skills as a grounded theorist takes practice; the method is best learned by cycling through the various procedures learning from each attempt and developing clarity and confidence in their application. This chapter will explore each of the aspects and challenges of coding as outlined above. Throughout the chapter, I have illustrated various aspects of coding by offering the reader details from my experience with the methodology as employed in my doctoral thesis (Holton, 2006).

THE CODING PROCESS

The conceptualization of data is the foundation of grounded theory development. The essential relationship between data and theory is a conceptual code. Coding gets the researcher off the empirical level by fracturing the data, then conceptualizing the underlying pattern of a set of empirical indicators within the data as a theory that explains what is happening in the data. Coding gives the researcher a condensed, abstract view with scope and dimension that encompasses otherwise seemingly disparate phenomena. Incidents articulated in the data are analysed and coded, using the constant comparative method, to generate initially substantive, and later theoretical, categories.

From the open coding of the first data collected to the final integration of emergent concepts through theoretical coding, issues and challenges often confront those new to grounded theory. There are numerous existing methodological guides that attempt to explicate the coding process as it pertains to a range of approaches that have been termed grounded theory. This chapter is not intended to sort through the plethora of advice offered or to serve as a 'how to' guide to any one approach. I will, however, try to situate the chapter within this broader research landscape.

I write as a classic grounded theorist. My perspective is rooted in the seminal work of Glaser and Strauss (1967) and the subsequent work of Glaser (1978, 1992, 1998, 2001, 2003, 2005). Despite the enthusiastic and widespread embrace of grounded theory by researchers within the qualitative paradigm, my perspective, by contrast, is shared instead with a growing number of theorists who view grounded theory not as a qualitative research method but as a general research methodology occupying its own distinct paradigm on the research landscape:

> A paradigm is an achievement that defines practice for a community of researchers. It defines practice because the achievement constitutes a model to be imitated and further extended—future research tries to fit itself to the same pattern as the original achievement. This definition of practice brings in its wake: the settling of the fundamental principles of the domain, the subsequent possibility of extremely precise research, a pedagogical tradition that trains succeeding generations in the use of the paradigm, a collection of institutions designed to promote the paradigm (professional journals, professional associations), and a worldview with metaphysical consequences (Klee, 1996: 135).

My stance is not in opposition to qualitative research, nor do I wish to suggest that classic grounded theory is a preferred or superior methodology. It is simply a different methodology, a distinct paradigm with its own principles and procedures for what constitutes valid research within this paradigm. For a classic grounded theorist, those studies done within the traditional paradigm of qualitative research and labelled as grounded theory frequently fall short of the criteria of a classic grounded theory. From the perspective of a classic grounded theorist, they have been remodelled to meet the criteria of the traditional, and dominant, qualitative paradigm (Glaser, 2003). Recognizing this distinction is important in advancing methodological scholarship within both paradigms.

Various scholars have positioned grounded theory as positivist (Charmaz, 2000), constructivist (Charmaz, 2000), interpretivist (Lowenberg, 1993), pragmatist (Locke, 2001), realist (Lomborg & Kirkevold, 2003; Partington, 2000, 2002; Patton, 2002), and neo-empiricist (Johnson et al., 2006). While Locke (2001: 1) quotes Denzin and Lincoln (1994: 508) in citing grounded theory as the 'most widely used qualitative interpretative framework in social sciences today', Smit and Bryant (2000) note the failure to clarify the basis on which grounded theory operates and the issue of methodology as causing some to view the method as a non-method. Much of this confusion can be attributed to particularized terminology used by various scholars to set out the boundaries and distinctions between and among the espoused research paradigms and associated issues of ontology, epistemology and methodology. Charmaz (2000: 524) attributes the confusion to a lack of explicitness in the seminal work of Glaser and Strauss (1967) and hence, the subsequent search to fit the method to accepted research paradigms.

Here, I believe, Charmaz has identified the crux of the matter and the futility of attempting its resolution through such a search. Grounded theory methodology, in the classic sense, does not fit within established research paradigms whether positivist, interpretivist, postmodern, or otherwise; rather, as a general methodology, classic grounded theory transcends the specific boundaries of established paradigms to accommodate any type of data sourced and expressed through any epistemological lens. Yet, the varying perspectives on what constitutes grounded theory and how it should be conducted presents the researcher with a baffling array of methodological options that have more the shape of a maze than a roadmap for guidance and clarification.

While articulating one's stance on the nature of knowledge and knowing is a prerequisite of any qualitative research design and, by association, any grounded theory study nested within the qualitative paradigm, classic grounded theory methodology transcends this concern. With Glaser's (1998) often quoted dictum, 'All is data' (p. 8) and its goal of conceptual abstraction, classic grounded theory methodology uses data of all types and media and accommodates a range of epistemological and ontological perspectives without having to espouse any one perspective; in essence, the methodology is epistemologically and ontologically neutral. While this stance may be at odds with qualitative research, where declaring a philosophical position is essential to the paradigm's interpretive perspective, it is entirely acceptable for the classic grounded theorist interested in the generation of conceptually abstract theory. Attributing meaning is not the goal of grounded theory; rather, its goal is to offer the reader a conceptual explanation of a latent pattern of behaviour that holds significance within the social setting under study. 'Without abstraction from time, place and people, there can be no multivariate, integrated theory based on conceptual, hypothetical relationships—descriptions cannot be related to each other as hypotheses as there is no conceptual handle' (Glaser, 2002a: 4). Thus, whether data are viewed as interpretative or objectivist is immaterial in classic grounded theory methodology as it is not the descriptive detail that concerns the grounded theorist but the abstract concepts that lie within the data.

Martin's (2006) review of Clarke (2005) and Charmaz (2006) gives us a hint of the divergent perspectives regarding grounded theory as posited by two established scholars from within the qualitative paradigm:

> Both authors treat a sacrosanct element of classic grounded theory, the core category or concept, as unnecessary or, worse, a barrier to understanding the phenomenon under study. Both accuse classic grounded theory of a lack of reflexivity about the research process, insensitivity to difference and variation, and oversimplification in its quest to create an integrative theory. The overall indictment is that grounded theory is out of step with the ways of thinking and talking about research brought about by postmodernism and other changes in scholarship through the 80s and 90s (pp. 119–120).

While such issues may concern those who view grounded theory as a qualitative method, they do not concern the classic grounded theorist whose goal is simply the discovery of conceptually abstract theory grounded in empirical data. As such, classic grounded theory methodology provides a systematic process for the abstract conceptualization of latent patterns within a social reality. While a systematic 'package' (Glaser, 1998: 12–20) of procedures, the methodology remains responsive to the researcher's intuitive sense of when to undertake each procedure and facilitates iterative cycling back and forth through successive engagements in data collection and analysis.

PRECONCEPTION

To remain truly open to the emergence of theory is among the most challenging issues confronting those new to grounded theory. As a generative and emergent methodology, grounded theory requires the researcher to enter the research field with no preconceived problem statement, interview protocols, or extensive review of literature. Instead, the researcher remains open to exploring a substantive area and allowing the concerns of those actively engaged therein to guide the emergence of a core issue. The conceptualization of this main concern and the multivariate responses to its continual resolution emerge as a latent pattern of social behaviour that forms the basis for the articulation of a grounded theory. Remaining open to discovering what is really going on in the field of inquiry is often blocked, however, by what Glaser (1998) refers to as the forcing of preconceived notions resident within the researcher's worldview, an initial professional problem or an extant theory and framework; all of which pre-empt the researcher's ability to suspend preconception and allow for what will emerge conceptually by constant comparative analysis.

One of the dominant preconceptions regarding grounded theory is the frequent attribution of its 'roots' to symbolic interactionism (Clarke, 2005; Goulding, 2002; Locke, 2001). Glaser (2005) has written at length on the impact of this 'takeover' (p. 141). While not discounting the influence of symbolic interactionism in the contribution of Anselm Strauss as co-originator of the methodology, to attribute grounded theory's origins thereto ignores the fundamental influence of Barney Glaser's training in quantitative methodology at Columbia University. As Martin (2006) suggests, 'It is really the analytic techniques out of Columbia, through Glaser, that gave qualitative researchers tools for systematic analysis' (p. 122). Pre-framing grounded theory through the theoretical lens of symbolic interactionism precludes other perspectives, pre-determines what data are used and how these should be collected, and limits the analyst's creativity in the analysis and conceptual abstraction of the data under study. This is not to suggest that classic grounded theory is free of any theoretical lens but rather that it should not be confined to any one lens; that as a general methodology, classic grounded theory can adopt any epistemological perspective appropriate to the data and the ontological stance of the researcher.

Concerns that arise through the researcher's professional training and experience often stimulate the initial research interest and can provide the motivation for pursuing a study. However, when the practitioner turns researcher, he/she carries into the field his/her own espoused values and accumulated experience and with this often comes the need to know in advance, to prescribe at the outset how the research should be framed, who should be engaged, and what outcomes should be anticipated. This instinctual practitioner perspective is, as well, frequently augmented by the structuring dictates of predominant research paradigms which call for the articulation of explicit theoretical frameworks in advance of fieldwork or analysis (Partington, 2002: 138–142).

Clarke's (1997, 2005) privileging of context as an essential consideration in the framing and analysis of a grounded theory study is another forceful example of preconception. Presuming the significance, indeed the centrality, of context as she does is merely forcing a preferred theoretical framework (what Glaser, 2005, calls a 'pet theoretical code') on a study from the outset. While accepting Madill, Jordan, and Shirley's (2000) contention that grounded theory may be applied within a contextualist epistemology (p. 10), for a classic grounded theorist context is merely another variable; thus, contextualizing meaning may or may not be relevant for a theory's explanation of how a main concern is continually resolved (Glaser, 2004). If it is relevant, it will emerge through the coding and constant comparison of conceptual indicators in the data. The relevance of context, like any other variable, must be earned in the emergent theory; it is not determined in advance by the analyst calling upon extant theoretical frameworks.

Marshall and Rossman (1999) offer 'analyst-constructed typologies', 'logical reasoning', and 'matrix-format cross-classifications' as strategies for data analysis (pp. 154–155). They do at least note Patton's (2002: 469–470) caution to be wary of the potential for such devices to manipulate the data through its forcing into artificial structures. A classic grounded theorist would echo this same caution. Marshall, however, appears not to have heeded this caution in her use of preconceived 'conceptual levers' (Marshall & Rossman, 1999: 148–149) in the data management for her own dissertation. Here she describes her use of role strain theory (Goode, 1960), sourced through her literature review, as a framework for analysing her data. While stating that she has employed 'constant comparative data analysis' (p. 149) to develop a grounded theory of women's socialization in male sex-typed careers, the classic grounded theorist is left wondering what the real concern of the women under study might have been and how they handled this concern. It is quite conceivable that the real concern of the women in Marshall's study may have had nothing to do with 'feminine identity and sexuality crises prompted by the demands of working in a male-normed profession' (p. 149). Their main concern may have been finding flexible child care services to accommodate unpredictable work schedules, finding time and opportunities to network, or structuring continuing professional development opportunities into an already over-subscribed life. Of course, it is impossible for us to know what their main concern may have been as Marshall's preconceived professional concern constrained the potential for the participants' main concern to emerge. Glaser (1978) offered the example of a sociologist's preconceiving a study of prostitution as a study of deviance when, from the perspective of the prostitutes under study, the main concern could be effective client servicing, a concern that would align them more appropriately with other service sectors: barbers, hair salons, auto repair, etc. Deviance as a dimension of prostitution would therefore have to earn its way into the emergent theory rather than being presumed from the outset (pp. 104–105).

The preconceiving practices of traditional training in qualitative research methodology that condition the researcher to know in advance can unwittingly condition the researcher to seeing new data through received concepts. In Konecki (1997), we see the impact of another preconceived theoretical framework: the conditional matrix (Strauss & Corbin, 1998). Konecki's interest in exploring the conditions for effective work by professional recruiters ('head hunters') has produced a solid piece of qualitative research; however, despite references to having produced a grounded theory, the study falls short of that goal. There is, of course, some possibility that the main concern of the recruiters may have focused on the effectiveness of their work and the time to find appropriate candidates, as Konecki's study suggests, but it is also quite possible that the core category of an emergent grounded theory may have been entirely unanticipated by his preconceived, discipline-bound perspective. It is this capacity for the emergence of tacit yet previously unarticulated explanations of social behaviour that delights the classic grounded theorist and motivates the effort to work at setting aside derailing preconceptions in undertaking a study.

Partington (2002) offers us another example of a preconceived theoretical framework imposed on an effort at grounded theory. His theoretical code of choice is Strauss and Corbin's (1990) 'paradigm model' which he simplifies to a mechanistic 'stimulus → organism → response →' framework and suggests its general utility for management research. In another guide to grounded theory for management, business, and marketing research, Goulding (2002) suggests Schatzman's (1991) dimensional analysis as an alternative approach to theorizing (pp. 79–83). What she really offers, however, is yet another preconceived theoretical framework to be forced upon the data. Later in her guide, Goulding cautions the reader that using grounded theory can be 'risky!' but advises that '[t]hese risks are of lesser concern for researchers who define their boundaries to begin with, explore the literature fully, identify key research questions, and collect data to answer them' (p. 156). These suggestions would most certainly reduce the risk of undertaking a grounded theory study. They would, in fact, remove all risk as no grounded theory would be involved. The process would be pure qualitative data analysis: a legitimate goal to be sure but not grounded theory.

These are but a very few of the examples of preconceived theoretical frameworks being forced upon what is intended as grounded theory. There are many others to be found in the numerous studies that masquerade under the guise of grounded theories while employing only selected aspects of the methodology. Glaser (2003) has written extensively on this propensity for remodelling.

Extensive review of extant literature before the emergence of a core category in a grounded theory study is another dimension of preconception that violates the basic premise of the classic methodology; that being, the theory emerges from the data not from extant theory. Extensive engagement prior to data collection and analysis also runs the risk of thwarting theoretical sensitivity by clouding the researcher's ability to remain open to the emergence of a completely new core category that may not have figured prominently in the literature to date. Practically speaking, preconception may well result in the researcher spending valuable time on an area of literature that proves to be of little significance to the resultant grounded theory. By contrast, in classic grounded theory methodology, the literature is just more data to be coded and integrated into the study through constant comparative analysis but its analysis and integration happens only after the core category, its properties and related categories have emerged, and the basic conceptual development is well underway, not in advance as is common to qualitative research methods. Unless pre-empted by preconception, emergence is natural with the resultant grounded theory often charting new theoretical territory.

FROM DESCRIPTION TO CONCEPTUALIZATION

To understand the nature of classic grounded theory, one must understand the distinction between conceptualization and description. Grounded theory is not about the accuracy of descriptive units, nor is it an act of interpreting meaning as ascribed by the participants in a study; rather, it is an act of conceptual abstraction. While tied to experience, conceptual abstraction directs attention to and isolates a part or aspect of an entity or phenomenon for the purposes of contemplation (Whitehead, 1925: 147). While the descriptive findings of a qualitative research study are most certainly valuable, they do not provide a conceptual abstraction. A grounded theory must offer a conceptually abstract explanation for a latent pattern of behaviour (an issue or concern) in the social setting under study. It must explain, not merely describe, what is happening in a social setting.

It is this ability to abstract from empirical indicators (incidents in the data under analysis) the conceptual idea without the burden of descriptive detail that distinguishes the coding process in classic grounded theory methodology. This abstraction to a conceptual level theoretically explains rather than describes behaviour that occurs conceptually and generally in many diverse groups with a common concern (Glaser, 2003). While a researcher's initial attempts at coding new data may very well be more descriptive than conceptual, a classic grounded theorist will endeavour to raise the conceptual level early on in the analysis process through the constant comparison of conceptual indicators in the data under study. Those trained in the requirements of qualitative research may, however, settle more readily into descriptive coding with its capacity to portray rich detail, multiple perspectives, and the voices of lived experience. For instance, where a qualitative researcher might record in vivo codes such as *boosting self confidence, growing as a person, learning to trust*, a classic grounded theorist, in asking 'what concept does this indicate', might code for *empowerment*, with the three descriptive codes serving as indicators.

For a classic grounded theorist, what matter are the concepts. The conceptual abstraction of classic grounded theory frees the researcher from the qualitative paradigm's emphasis on detailed description and elucidation of multiple perspectives. The skill of the grounded theorist is to abstract concepts by leaving the detail of the data behind, lifting the concepts above the data and integrating them into a theory that explains the latent social pattern underlying the behaviour in a substantive area (Locke, 2001). The result of a grounded theory study is not the reporting of facts but the generation of probability statements about the relationships between concepts; a set of conceptual hypotheses developed from empirical data (Glaser, 1998: 3, 22).

Morse (2004) recognizes the importance of raising qualitative research above the descriptive level of analysis. Unfortunately, her prescriptive procedures for developing qualitative concepts leave little scope for exercising the creativity and intuitive autonomy that are the hallmarks of classic grounded theory: the ability to fracture and interrogate the data for its conceptual essence, to constantly compare indicators for interchangeability, and the achievement of theoretical saturation. Her approach provides little allowance for the preconscious processing that enables the emergence of conceptual ideation and theoretical integration. Her structure may work well in qualitative analysis but would inhibit what Glaser (1998) describes as the 'subsequent, sequential, simultaneous, serendipitous, and scheduled' (p. 15) nature of grounded theory.

Various scholars within the qualitative paradigm have put forth strategies and guidelines for the coding process (Charmaz, 2006; Goulding, 2002; Partington, 2002; Patton, 2002; Strauss & Corbin, 1990, 1998). By comparison, the procedures espoused by classic grounded theorists may initially appear loose and perhaps even messy or confusing. These procedures as originally developed by Glaser and Strauss (1967) and extensively elaborated in Glaser's subsequent work (1978, 1992, 1998, 2001, 2003, 2005; Glaser & Holton, 2004) do require the researcher to grapple with both chaos and control. The chaos is in tolerating the uncertainty and subsequent regression of not knowing in advance and of remaining open to what emerges through the diligent, controlled, often tedious application of the method's synchronous and iterative processes of line-by-line coding, constant comparison for interchangeability of indicators, and theoretical sampling for core emergence and theoretical saturation. This discipline is simultaneously complemented by requiring the theorist to remain open to the innate creativity in preconscious processing of conceptual ideation and theoretical integration; a creativity characterized by the exhilaration of eureka sparks of discovery; what Glaser (1978, 1998) calls the drugless trip.

This excitement in generating concepts from data, however, derails some researchers. Captured by the imagery, or 'grab' (Glaser, 2001: 19–21), of the emerging concepts, they switch their attention from abstraction to description. By neglecting to stay with the full method of classic grounded theory, they are unable to tap its full potential in developing a conceptually integrated theory. 'To skip a step, particularly the middle ones associated with memoing and sorting, is to produce a theory with less conceptual density, less integration, less conceptual qualification, too much descriptive and conceptual flatness in places, and missed connections obvious to the astute reader' (Glaser, 1978: 16).

Baszanger's (1997) paper, 'Deciphering Chronic Pain', is an example of the kind of conceptual description that is frequently presented as grounded theory. While tempting us with the imageric grab of what Glaser would call a 'juicy concept' (Grounded Theory Seminar, New York, October 2003), and acknowledging that she has employed grounded theory techniques of 'constant comparative method of analysis and its coding procedures' (p. 5), Baszanger has not employed the full package of classic grounded theory methodology. Consequently, what we have is an ethnographic account of the way in which physicians at two different clinics manage the issue of deciphering chronic pain. She does not follow through in taking her conceptual description to a fully integrated theory that would offer us a conceptual explanation for the phenomenon under study. While we have a rich account of particularistic experiences, we are deprived of the full power of grounded theory to offer us an integrated set of conceptual hypotheses that would explain what is really going on in the process of deciphering chronic pain. Baszanger's account, however, offers excellent data for conceptual abstraction and the possible emergence of a grounded theory.

NAVIGATING THE CODING PROCESS

> In grounded theory the analyst humbly allows the data to control him as much as humanly possible, by writing a theory for only what emerges through his skilled induction. The integration of his substantive theory as it emerges through coding and sorting is his verification that the hypotheses and concepts fit and work and are relevant enough to suggest. They are not proven; they are theory (Glaser, 1992: 87).

The coding process is not a discrete stage as it is in some research methodologies but rather a continuous aspect of the analytic nature of classic grounded theory. As such, knowing how and when to engage in the various aspects of coding is essential to capturing the conceptual power of the methodology. This requires the analyst understand the distinctions between substantive coding and theoretical coding, between open coding and selective coding, as well as the cycling nature of constant comparison and theoretical sampling in progressing the analysis towards higher levels of conceptual abstraction, core emergence, and theoretical integration. Beyond understanding these distinctions comes the ability and the confidence to employ all aspects of coding as developed over time and with continued experience. The ability to intuitively trust in knowing when to move from one stage in the process to another builds with experience as the analyst gains confidence in exploring and confirming conceptual ideas as they emerge.

Theoretical sensitivity

The ability to conceptualize rests with the researcher's theoretical sensitivity; that is, their ability to generate concepts from data and relate them according to normal models of theory in general (Glaser, 1978: 1–17; 1992: 27–30, 49–60).

Theoretical sensitivity requires two things of the researcher: analytic temperament and competence. The required analytic temperament will allow the researcher to maintain analytic distance from the data, tolerate regression and confusion, and facilitate a trust in the power of preconscious processing for conceptual emergence. As to analytic competence, the researcher must be able to develop theoretical insights and abstract conceptual ideas from various sources and types of data. Reading widely in other disciplines is a recommended means of enhancing theoretical sensitivity (Glaser, 1998: 164–165; 2005: 7–10).

SUBSTANTIVE CODING

Substantive coding is the process of conceptualizing the empirical substance of the area under study: the data in which the theory is grounded. Incidents are the empirical data (the indicators of a category or concept) from which a grounded theory is generated. The process proceeds from the initial open coding of data to the emergence of a core category, followed by a delimiting of data collection and analysis for selective coding to theoretically saturate the core category and related categories.

Open coding

Beginning with line-by-line open coding of data and comparing incidents to each other in the data, the researcher codes the data in every way possible and asks a set of questions of the data: 'What is this data a study of?', 'What category does this incident indicate?', 'What is actually happening in the data?', 'What is the main concern being faced by the participants?', and 'What accounts for the continual resolving of this concern?' (Glaser, 1998: 140). These questions sustain the researcher's theoretical sensitivity, transcend descriptive details, and encourage a focus on patterns among incidents that yield codes. Line-by-line coding forces the researcher to verify and saturate categories, minimizes missing an important category, and ensures relevance by generating codes with emergent fit to the substantive area under study. It also ensures relevance of the emerging theory by enabling the researcher to see which direction to take in theoretically sampling before becoming too selective and focused on a particular problem. The result is a rich, dense theory with the feeling that nothing has been left out (Glaser & Holton, 2004: para. 50).

In grounded theory, it is essential that researchers do their own coding as coding constantly stimulates conceptual ideas. The researcher codes for as many categories as fit successive, different incidents. New categories emerge and new incidents fit into existing categories. Coding may feel very awkward at first, and the researcher may feel uncertain about labelling the codes, but this sense of uncertainty gradually subsides with continued efforts at analysis. Grounded theory's tandem processes of coding and memoing help to alleviate the pressure of uncertainty by challenging the researcher to stop coding and capture, in the moment, their conceptual ideas about the codes that they are finding. As coding and memoing progress, patterns begin to emerge. Pattern recognition gives the researchers confidence in the coding process and in their own innate creativity; it encourages the researchers to continue while offering guidance on where to go next in the data collection, coding, and analysis process.

It is, however, at this initial stage of open coding that the inexperienced grounded theorist may feel especially challenged and insecure. A linear, lock-step attempt at employing the method's procedures without having suffi-ciently grasped the iterative nature of the overall process can result in coding confusion. Jumping to selective coding before a potential core category has emerged; sorting memos prior to theoretical saturation; or becoming over-whelmed by the data and concerns with 'worrisome accuracy' (Glaser, 2004), particularly in the collection and transcription of qualitative interview data, can all result in coding chaos.

The solution, of course, is relatively simple if the researcher simply trusts and follows the procedures of classic grounded theory. As a starting point, selecting to use field notes enables the researcher to dispense with the meticulous and time-consuming efforts required to record and transcribe detailed interview data and mitigates being overwhelmed by its descriptive detail. While frequently discouraged by qualitative review panels and thesis committees as lacking sufficient rigour, field notes enable the grounded theory researcher to capture the essence of the participant's main concern and how that concern is resolved without the burden of laborious transcribing followed by the tedium of reading through and coding lengthy transcriptions.

By comparison, line-by-line coding of field notes enables the researcher to stay focused on what is really happening and facilitates coding on a higher conceptual level without the distraction of endless descriptive and superfluous detail. The process stays vibrant and generates active conceptual ideation about what is being coded; the researcher can direct energy to capturing this conceptual development through memoing of thoughts as the coding progresses and pat-terns begin to emerge. Giving up the assurance of taping and transcribing, how-ever, can be especially difficult for a seasoned researcher already trained and experienced in qualitative research requirements for detailed description. The impetus to shift from full coverage in data collection to field noting is also frequently discouraged by peer review and by thesis supervisors trained in traditional qualitative methods.

Like many new to classic grounded theory, initial efforts at open coding in my own doctoral research (Holton, 2006) were heavily influenced by earlier training in qualitative research methods. As a result, 155 codes were initially generated through open coding of data collected and analysed between October 2001 and February 2002; several of these codes were highly descriptive and, in some instances, somewhat repetitive. This is not unusual at the outset of a grounded theory study where the researcher wishes to remain as open as possible to what may emerge from line-by-line coding and not run the risk of precluding or predetermining what may eventually prove to be relevant to the emerging theory. The risk of this inundation, however, is that the analyst may be unable to transcend the descriptive detail and as a result miss the true conceptual power of classic grounded theory methodology. Here, the analyst must be patient in staying with the process while striving for a higher level of abstraction in the naming of codes. Classic grounded theory's practice of memoing analytic thoughts in tandem with the coding process can facilitate this conceptual transcendence.

As I advanced my competence in conceptual coding and the constant comparison of indicators, a significantly reduced list of 57 open codes emerged from continued data collection and analysis between February 2002 and January 2004. Several of the earlier descriptive codes were collapsed into the newer conceptual codes with only 13 codes from the original list appearing among the conceptual coding list.

Of course, as a grounded theorist develops her conceptual coding skills, she can more readily dispense with the initial descriptive codes and employ conceptual-level coding from the outset of the open coding process. This takes skill in conceptualization as well as a ready arsenal of conceptual labels; both are developed over time and with continued practice (see Box 13.1):

Box 13.1

At the outset of fieldwork, I collected the following excerpt from one interview:

'One … member described the challenge of working together on a large project such as Habitat for Humanity. I got very excited, and dreamed of how amazing that would be'.

My initial coding for this excerpt was *Excited by Challenge* and *Wishes & Dreams*. This excerpt was later re-coded as *Igniting Passions* (a code that emerged as a sub-core category in my theory). In this case, *Excited by Challenge* emerged as a property of *Igniting Passions*.

Another excerpt from early data collection and open coding was, 'I want to stay connected because it revitalizes me. It jazzes me!'

Initial coding for this excerpt was *Feeling Energized, Staying Connected* and the in vivo code, *It jazzes me!*; this excerpt was also later re-coded as *Igniting Passions*.

Another excerpt, 'It reminds me of the great things that are possible when people have a desire to work together and learn together'.

Initial coding was *Value of Participation* and *Motivation to Participate;* later re-coded as *Igniting Passions*.

Another excerpt, 'I loved the opportunity to be the court jester, either in a cow suit or by throwing out ideas that bordered on the absurd. And with so many of us vying for the hat with bells on it, the give and take just seemed to crank up the fun to a higher notch'.

Initial coding was *Playful Participation, Assumed Role, Feeling Energized*; later re-coded as *Igniting Passions*.

Constant comparison and theoretical sampling

As the twin foundations of grounded theory, the processes of constant comparison and theoretical sampling guide the development of the emergent theory. The purpose of constant comparison is to see if the data support and continue to support emerging categories. At the same time, the process further builds and substantiates the emerging categories by defining their properties and dimensions. Constant comparison resolves 'data overwhelm' (Glaser, 2003: 24). By alternating data collection with coding and conceptual memoing, the researcher is prevented from collecting redundant data as once a category has been saturated (i.e., no new conceptual properties or dimensions are emerging), the researcher ceases collecting additional data for that particular category. Early memoing of the emerging conceptual thoughts while actively engaged in coding and analysing enables the researcher to continuously build theoretical sensitivity. Early memoing also facilitates theoretical sampling as the researcher intuitively follows and develops conceptual ideas as they emerge through constant comparison.

The constant comparative process continues through open coding to selective coding and involves three types of comparison. First, incidents are compared to other incidents to establish the underlying uniformity and varying conditions of generated concepts and hypotheses. Then, emerging concepts are compared to more incidents to generate new theoretical properties of the concepts and more hypotheses. The purpose here is theoretical elaboration, saturation, and densification of concepts. Finally, emergent concepts are compared to each other with the purpose of establishing the best fit between potential concepts and a set of indicators, the conceptual levels between concepts that refer to the same set of indicators and their integration (theoretical coding) into hypotheses to become theory (Glaser & Holton, 2004: para. 53).

In conjunction with constant comparison, theoretical sampling is the process whereby the researcher decides what data to collect next and where to find them in order to continue to develop the theory as it emerges. As such, the process of data collection is controlled by the emerging theory. Beyond the decisions concerning initial collection of data, further collection cannot be planned in advance of the emerging theory. Instead, the researcher can only discover where next to collect data by first coding the initial data and then looking for comparison groups by which to saturate the emerging codes and their properties. By identifying emerging gaps in the theory, the researcher will be guided as to where and how to collect the next sources of data. The possibilities of multiple comparisons are infinite and so groups must be chosen according to theoretical criteria. The criteria (of theoretical purpose and relevance) are applied in the ongoing joint collection and analysis of data associated with the generation of theory. As such, they are continually tailored to fit the data and are applied judiciously at the right point and moment in the analysis. In this way, the researcher can continually adjust the control of data collection to ensure the data's relevance to the emerging theory (Glaser & Holton, 2004: para. 51).

Interchangeability of indicators

As noted above, grounded theory is based on a concept-indicator model of constant comparisons of incidents to incidents and, once a conceptual code is generated, of incidents to the emerging concept. The concept-indicator model requires concepts and their properties or dimensions to earn their relevance in the theory by systematic generation and analysis of data. This forces the researcher into confronting similarities, differences, and degrees in consistency of meaning between indicators, generating an underlying uniformity which in turn results in a coded category and the beginnings of the properties of that category. In the comparisons of further incidents to the emerging conceptual codes, codes are sharpened to achieve best fit while further properties are generated until the concepts are confirmed and saturated (Glaser, 1978: 62–65).

Constantly comparing incidents and thereby generating new properties of a concept can only go so far before the researcher discovers saturation of ideas through interchangeability of indicators (incidents). This interchangeability also facilitates transferability of the theory to other substantive areas and opens the potential for the generation of formal grounded theory (Glaser, 1978) (see Box 13.2).

Box 13.2

In Holton (2006), persistent and unpredictable change in the knowledge workplace emerged early in data collection and analysis as a significant concern of the research participants. The concept, *Changing Knowledge Workplace*, was later to prove significant to the emergent theory as one of the categories related to the emergent core category. As such, I continued to theoretically sample for indicators of this category. Through constant comparison, 51 indicators of the concept were coded to achieve theoretical saturation and to provide properties and dimensions.

The number of indicators per category is not as significant as the requirement to sample sufficiently to achieve theoretical saturation. The important thing is that each concept has earned relevance in relation to the theory, its relevance theoretically sampled for and sufficiently validated and its properties and dimensions identified through constant comparison and interchangeable indicators to theoretical saturation.

Core category emergence

As the researcher proceeds with constant comparison, a core category begins to emerge. This core variable can be any kind of theoretical code: a process, a typology, a continuum, a range, dimensions, conditions, consequences, and so forth. Its primary function is to integrate the theory and render it dense and saturated. In appearing to explain how the main concern is continually processed or resolved, the core becomes the focus of further selective data collection and coding efforts.

Charmaz (2004, 2006) discounts the relevance of the core category, suggesting that Glaser (2002b) advocates the explicit assertion of a main concern by the research participants and ignores that '[t]he most important processes are tacit' (Charmaz, 2004: 982). Here Charmaz misinterprets Glaser (2002b) who actually says that the core category is discovered as it emerges through iterative coding, conceptual memoing, and theoretically sampling for further data to pursue and develop conceptual leads, ensuring that all concepts earn their way into the emerging theory. Glaser also states that the core category merits its relevance and prominence by accounting for most of the variation in processing the concern or issue that has emerged as the focus of the study and by conceptually explaining the latent pattern of social behaviour that accounts for its continual resolution. Glaser discounts Charmaz's notion of a constructivist grounded theory by claiming that:

> She uses constructivism to discount the participant's main concern, which is always relevant to ongoing resolving behaviour, in favour of the researcher's professional concern, which is most often irrelevant to behaviour in the substantive area ... (Glaser, 2002b: para. 21).

This chapter does not afford the space for an extensive exchange of the multiple perspectives on what is and isn't fundamental to grounded theory. Suffice it to say that if one wishes to undertake a classic grounded theory study, then the emergence of a core category is an indisputable requirement.

It takes time and much coding and analysis to verify a core category through saturation, relevance, and workability. The criteria for establishing the core variable (category) within a grounded theory are that it is central, that it relates to as many other categories and their properties as possible, and that it accounts for a large portion of the variation in a pattern of behaviour. The core variable reoccurs frequently in the data and comes to be seen as a stable pattern that is increasingly related to other variables. It relates meaningfully and easily with other categories. It is completely variable and has a 'carry through' within the emerging theory by virtue of its relevance and explanatory power (Glaser & Holton, 2004: para. 54) (see Box 13.3).

Box 13.3

In Holton (2006), three categories emerged fairly early on as of some significant concern of the participants in the study: *Changing Workplace Context, Coping with Change, Humanizing Workplace.* Through further analysis, two new categories, *Dehumanization* and *Rehumanizing,* emerged as a better fit than *Humanizing Workplace.*

As the analysis progressed, *Rehumanizing* appeared to account for much of the variation around knowledge worker concerns with the changing knowledge workplace and the resultant dehumanization they experienced. *Rehumanizing* would subsequently emerge as the core category of the theory.

Delimiting for selective coding

Selective coding begins only after the researcher has identified a potential core variable. Subsequent data collection and coding is delimited to that which is relevant to the emerging conceptual framework (the core and those categories that relate to the core). By focusing on the core and other related categories, subsequent data collection can go very quickly; merely minutes, with a few field notes to be captured and analysed. In this way, the researcher can saturate the selected categories that form the basis of the emerging theory without collecting a lot of additional material that has no relevance to the developing grounded theory. This selective data collection and analysis continues until the researcher has sufficiently elaborated and integrated the core variable, its properties, and its theoretical connections to other relevant categories.

Delimiting occurs at two levels. First, as the theory integrates, it solidifies with fewer modifications needed as the researcher compares the next incidents of a category to its properties. Later modifications are mainly about clarifying the logic of the theory and integrating elaborating details of properties into the major outline of interrelated categories. As the researcher begins to discover an underlying uniformity in the categories and properties, the theory is reformulated with a smaller set of higher-level concepts. This second level of delimiting the theory reduces the original list of categories for coding. As the theory develops, becomes reduced, and increasingly works better in ordering a mass of data, the researcher becomes committed to it. This allows for a delimiting of the original list of categories for subsequent collecting and selective coding of additional data, according to the newly established boundaries of the theory. By delimiting the focus to one category as the core variable, only those categories related to that core are now included in the theory. This list of categories, now delimited for additional selective coding, is subsequently (and continuously) delimited through theoretical saturation of each category.

Theoretical saturation

One of the concerns often expressed by those new to grounded theory is when to stop collecting data. The answer is deceptively simple. One stops when one no longer needs to continue. The challenge is in how to recognize that the need no longer exists. Glaser (1978) describes this as the point of theoretical saturation (p. 71). As noted above, the constant comparison of interchangeable indicators in the data yields the properties and dimensions of each category, or concept. This process of constant comparison continues until no new properties or dimensions are emerging. At this point, a concept has been theoretically saturated. This 'intense property development' (Glaser, 2001: 191) produces the conceptual density necessary to lift the theory above description and enable its integration through theoretical propositions (hypotheses) as abstract conceptual theory. 'Once a category is saturated it is not necessary to theoretically sample anymore to collect data for incident comparisons. And of course, once many interrelated categories of a GT are saturated, theoretical completeness is achieved for the particular research' (Glaser, 2001: 192) (see Box 13.4).

Box 13.4

In Holton (2006), the core category, *Rehumanizing*, and 37 related concepts became the focus of selective data collection and coding. Continued delimiting, theoretical saturation, and conceptual integration confirmed the core category and 4 related categories as the basic social structural process of *Fluctuating Support Networks*. Additionally, 3 sub-core categories and 16 conceptual properties and dimensions of these sub-core categories were confirmed as the basic social psychological process of *Rehumanizing*. Constant comparison continued until the core and related categories were sufficiently saturated and further coding and constant comparison yielded no new conceptual ideation.

Memoing

The writing of theoretical memos is the core stage in the process of generating grounded theory. If the researcher skips this stage by going directly to sorting or writing up, after coding, she is not doing grounded theory (Glaser, 1978: 83).

Memos are theoretical notes about the data and the conceptual connections between categories. The process runs parallel with the coding and analysis process to capture the researcher's emergent ideation of substantive and theoretical codes and categories. Memo writing is a continual process that helps to raise the data to a conceptual level and develop the properties of each category. Memos also guide the next steps in further data collection, coding, and analysis.

They present hypotheses about connections between categories and their properties and begin the integration of these connections with clusters of other categories to generate a theory. The basic goal of memoing is to develop ideas with complete conceptual freedom. Memos are 'banked' and later sorted to facilitate the integration of the overall theory.

Memo construction differs from writing detailed description. Although typically based on description, memos raise that description to the theoretical level through the conceptual rendering of the material. Early in the process, memos arise from constant comparison of indicators to indicators, then indicators to concepts. These memos are often very brief, just a few lines. Later memos will be more extensive as they integrate the ideation of the earlier memos and will, in turn, generate new memos further raising the level of conceptualization. Sorting and writing memos generates additional memos. Memoing in conjunction with coding and analysis slows a researcher's pace, forcing a reasoning of the emerging theory as categories emerge and integrate. In this way, the researcher forestalls the premature adoption of a core category and final theoretical framework by ensuring their fit, relevance, and workability for the theory (see Box 13.5).

Box 13.5

In Holton (2006), during the constant comparison process, I had written over 400 memos capturing the conceptual and methodological development of my theory. These memos ranged in length from a few lines to several pages. The following offers a sample of the over 20 memos written in conjunction with more than 60 indicators of the category, *Igniting Passions*:

A2403 Memo 3 The Passion of Vocation August 3, 2003

Networks as keeping personal and professional passions from being eroded, depleted in the hectic, humdrum of daily organizational operations … 'Our job is our work … our practice is our passion'. Distinguishing between 'practice' and 'work'—between 'vocation' and 'job'.

A2403 Memo 6 Passionate Learning August 3, 2003

'really start to learn when they find a passion for a subject and then make a real connection to other learners and real time practitioners'. Individual passion for learning is stimulated and reinforced in community.

A703 Memo 11 Passion, Resistance & Bonding January 5, 2004

Re-reading field notes from interview with A, noted the many references to passion; in particular, the connection between passion and bonding of network members. Appears that the common passion that brings network members together—part of the likening that creates a network—is also the 'glue' that bonds network members. She goes on to describe the 'passionate few' as bonding due to the resistance they encounter from the formal system—'the resistance serves as a way to separate out those who really have a passion to keep working' … So … passion creates likening; resistance creates bonding and reinforces passions … a cyclic process that sustains member engagement in fluctuating networks.

Memo F 1504-7 Igniting Passions February 15, 2004

Passions are ignited by challenge—the 'against all odds' syndrome—finding mutual commitment to a goal that others consider impossible or crazy. Setting themselves apart from the 'masses', the ordinary—taking on a challenge and making it work—high achievement orientation—success is sweeter when shared. Believing in the impossible and then making it happen. (Field Interview D 502)

Memo F 1504-9 Igniting Passions February 15, 2004

There's a charge in being challenged and being creative in solving an issue, a problem that ignites passionate engagement within a network—draws members in. (Field Interview D 502)

Memo F 1904-6 Igniting Passions February 19, 2004

Passions are not always positive—they can also involve spirited outbursts of anger. This is particularly the case when the core group of a network have developed such a close group identity that it compromises their relationship with others in the external environment—insularity leading to intolerance—impacts upon ability of the network to function within the larger external environment of the formal organization—interactions become personalized and highly emotional—core becomes segregated—trust erodes and threatens sustainability … network members may limit/reduce their participation if they feel it jeopardizes their position within the formal organization—cannot risk the consequences. (Field Interview D 502)

Box 13.5 cont'd

Memo A 504-13 Igniting Passions April 5, 2004
There's a strong desire to continue to network once individual passions have been ignited. Passions are fueled by the desire to continue to experience the energy and synergy that result from mutual engagement—to work and learn and laugh together. There's a strong sense of fun, of pushing the envelope. The desire to continue to move the network forward creates its own sense of excitement and fuels a passionate belief in the ability to make a difference. (Field Interview O 290, O 3101-1, N 1201, O 3001)

THEORETICAL CODING

Conceptual elaboration concludes when the relationships among individually elaborated concepts emerge through the identification and use of appropriate theoretical codes to achieve an integrated theoretical framework for the overall grounded theory. Theoretical codes conceptualize how the substantive codes may relate to each other as hypotheses to be integrated into the theory. They help the analyst maintain the conceptual level in writing about concepts and their interrelations. Developing theoretical sensitivity to a wide range of integrating codes (processes, models, etc.) as used across a wide range of disciplines enhances a researcher's ability to see his/her emergent fit to a developing theory. Reading widely opens a researcher to serendipitous discovery of new theoretical codes from other disciplines. Latent patterns abound in social research as in nature; what patterns out in biology, for instance, may well conceptually pattern in sociology, in business, or in education. The more open one is to recognizing the larger integrative patterns around us, the more one can exploit their imagery in proposing theories of social behaviour (Glaser, 2005).

The researcher who does not reach outside extant theory for theoretical coding possibilities runs the risk of producing adequate but rather mundane conceptual theory. Such theory makes a limited contribution to knowledge and, although certainly preferable to purely conjectured theory, it will lack the impact that the creative emergence of a novel or non-traditional theoretical code may offer. The underlying imperative, however, is that the fit must be emergent and not imposed. To earn its relevance as a theoretical integrator of core and related variables in a classic grounded theory study, a theoretical code must go beyond spurious association. No matter how intellectually seductive, fashionable, or discipline-dictated a theoretical code may be, to cross the line from theoretical exploration to forced integration with a preconceived theoretical model undermines the generative nature of grounded theory.

Theoretical integration through hand sorting of memos

Theoretical sorting of the memos is the key to formulating the theory for presentation or writing. Sorted memos generate the emergent theoretical outline, or conceptual framework, for the full articulation of a grounded theory through an integrated set of hypotheses. The researcher's memos, once sorted and fully integrated, become the outline for presentation of the theory's publication.

This theoretical sorting is based on theoretical codes. As the researcher sees similarities, connections, and underlying uniformities, the theoretical decision about the precise location of a particular memo is based on the theoretical coding of the data grounding the idea. Facilitating the emergence of relevant theoretical codes requires close attention to the ideas memoed, submersion at the conceptual level, a balance of logic and creativity, openness to the unexpected, and confidence in following what emerges regardless of how counter-rational it may seem to extant theoretical perspectives.

Thus, rich, multi-relation, multivariate theory is generated through sorting. If the researcher omits sorting, the theory will be linear, thin, and less than fully integrated. Without sorting, a theory lacks the internal integration of connections among many categories. With sorting, data and ideas are theoretically ordered. This sorting is conceptual sorting, not data sorting. Sorting provides theoretical completeness and generates more memos (often on higher conceptual levels), furthering and condensing the theory. It integrates the relevant literature into the theory, sorting it with the memos. The researcher soon sees where each concept fits and works within the theory, its relevance, and how it will carry forward in the cumulative development of the theory. Sorting prevents over-conceptualization and pre-conceptualization, since these excesses fall away as the researcher zeros in on the most parsimonious set of integrated concepts (Glaser & Holton, 2004: paras 69–70).

In classic grounded theory, theoretical codes are not selected and imposed on data as a preconceived theoretical framework. To do so is to risk logical elaboration. Instead, theoretical sorting of memos forces the researcher to theoretically discriminate as to where each memoed idea fits in the emerging theory. Failing to recognize the essential requirement of hand sorting is, however, common in accounts of the methodology. Partington (2002) emphasizes the importance of avoiding a premature closure of the analysis and the need to press on in the search for negative cases in the data but makes no reference to careful hand sorting of memos for emergent integration of the theory. Locke (2001) and Goulding (2002) also overlook the importance of hand sorting conceptual memos.

While Charmaz (2006) provides a lengthy discourse on sorting, she seems to suggest that rather than allowing for the preconscious emergence of conceptual linkages through the often tedious hand sorting and re-sorting of memos, she advocates instead trying on various theoretical codes for possible fit; if not the basic social process, then perhaps Clarke's (2005) situational mapping or Strauss and Corbin's (1990, 1998) conditional matrix. Here again, we see the need to know in advance rather than thoughtful sorting of memos for emergent fit resulting in an overall conceptual integration with parsimony and scope (Glaser & Strauss, 1967: 110) (see Box 13.6).

Box 13.6

In Holton (2006), having achieved theoretical saturation of my core concept and related categories, I proceeded to review, hand sort, and integrate those memos related to the core, its properties, and related categories. As I began to sort memos and look for relationships between the various concepts, theoretical codes began to emerge as an abstract modelling of the latent structural patterns that integrated and explained the emerging theory. The first indication of emergent theoretical codes was memoed in an E-mail to Dr. Glaser, December 2003:

'Rehumanizing can be viewed as a structural condition affecting the nature of fluctuating networks of professional concern. These networks have always been there in the workplace as they are inherent to social organization generally—but today's increasingly compressed and dehumanized work environments (changing workplace context) have brought the need for rehumanizing to the fore as a means of addressing the main concern of those involved—coping with change thereby magnifying the BSPP [basic social psychological process] of rehumanizing as a structural condition of the BSPP of fluctuating networks. As such, the BSPP [basic social structural process] of fluctuating networks of professional concern has taken on the properties of the BSPP of rehumanizing including authenticity, depth/meaning, respect, safety, healing ... As a preliminary suggestion, the stages in the BSPP of rehumanizing may be finding, likening, igniting passions, kindred sharing, experimenting, bonding, sustaining. Some of these may be combined as research progresses; new ones may be identified ... the structural process (of fluctuating networks) is of significance because it explains the organization of behaviour (as emergent informal organization) to address the main concern of the participants—coping with change within the workplace—through a BSPP (rehumanizing) as antidote to the dehumanizing impact of traditional formal organizational structures. This is starting to feel 'right' for me—things are fitting into place and I can now see an overall conceptual framework around which to begin building the theory' (J. Holton, personal communication, December 29, 2003).

While continuing to consider basic social process as an appropriate theoretical code through which to integrate my emerging theory, I remained open to the emergence of other theoretical codes as I continued to hand sort and integrate memos. A final integration of the theory occurred in March 2004 with the emergence of an additional theoretical code—amplifying causal looping.

The concept *Igniting Passions* (as earlier illustrated in this chapter) was to emerge in a pivotal position as the catalytic middle stage, between the sub-core processes of *Finding & Likening* and *Mutual Engagement* (both amplifying causal loops), within the basic social psychological process of *Rehumanizing.*

Analytic rules for conceptual integration

There are several fundamental analytic rules that address issues regarding the sorting, carrying forward, and integration of concepts. These rules form the basis for the conceptual integration, organization, and writing up of the theory. Usually, the theory is presented as a conceptually abstract narrative that articulates each significant concept and then, through the articulation of theoretical propositions, the relationships between these concepts. Here I refer the reader to Glaser (1978: 120–127; Glaser & Holton, 2004) for further elaboration.

SKILL DEVELOPMENT IN GROUNDED THEORY

Morse (1997) suggests that qualitative researchers are theoretically timid and may be inhibited by what she sees as the hard work of conceptualization necessary to produce theory. While acknowledging the possibility of timidity, Glaser (2002a) refutes her assertion of the hard work of conceptualization, instead maintaining that many researchers simply lack knowledge and competence in conceptualization and, as such, they embrace with enthusiasm but without understanding. To truly understand classic grounded theory requires extensive study of the methodology in tandem with experiencing the method first-hand. While some like Dey (1999) would appear to dismiss the importance of first-hand experience in favour of adopting a sceptical stance from the sidelines, the resultant 'rhetorical wrestle' (Glaser, 1998) is ironically at odds with the fundamental premise of ensuring empirically grounding of one's theoretical (and methodological) contributions to knowledge. Yet, staying the course to develop that understanding is easily circumvented by straying into the mixed methods approaches prevalent in qualitative research and the diverse perspectives of the methodology that Glaser (2003) refers to as remodelled versions.

The decision to use classic grounded theory methodology is a 'full package' decision. It requires the adoption of a systematic set of precise procedures for collection, analysis and articulation of conceptually abstract theory. On the menu of research methodology, classic grounded theory is 'table d'hôte', not 'a la carte'. Generating grounded theory takes time. It is above all a delayed action phenomenon (Glaser, 1998: 220). Little increments of collecting and coding allow theoretical ideas to develop into conceptual memos. Significant theoretical realizations come with growth and maturity in the data, and much of this is outside the researcher's conscious awareness until preconscious processing facilitates its conscious emergence (Glaser, 1998: 50). Thus, the researcher must pace herself, exercising patience and accepting nothing until this inevitable emergence has transpired. Surviving the apparent confusion is important, requiring the researcher to take whatever time is necessary for the discovery process and to take this time in a manner consistent with her own temporal nature as a researcher: what Glaser (1998) refers to as personal pacing (p. 49). Rushing or forcing the process shuts down creativity and conceptual ability, exhausting energy and leaving the theory thin and incomplete.

As an experiential learning methodology, it is important that the grounded theorist stay actively engaged in continuing skill development by cycling through various projects and always having at least one project active (Glaser, 1978: 25–26). Reading and re-reading Glaser's work, while memoing about the methodology, also keeps cognitive processing alive. Critically reading substantive grounded theory papers and memoing conceptual thoughts is another way to gain insights into the methodology and to be able to distinguish a quality grounded theory or to see how or where another researcher may have come close but missed the full power of the methodology. Without active engagement through continuing field research and analysis as well as methodological reading, it is easy for many to leave behind their grounded theory skill development: especially those who have been trained in the dominant paradigm of qualitative research. The inevitable consequence is that they will begin, often unconsciously, to remodel the methodology to suit the dominant genre in their field or to compensate for inadequate or lost skill development.

Skill development seems to be particularly difficult for novice researchers who encounter resistance from thesis supervisors or peer reviewers who are trained in qualitative or quantitative methodologies and who express doubt or reservation about the full package approach of classic grounded theory. Without the confidence of experience gained through skill development or the power to challenge discipline or departmental authority, the novice researcher may feel pressured to abandon or compromise the proper procedures. The outcome diminishes the researcher's autonomy and confidence to engage with the methodology as intended. Glaser refers to this resistance propensity as the 'trained incapacity of novice researchers held to binding interpretations by the higher authorities of other research methodologies' (personal communication, July 10, 2004).

TECHNOLOGY ENTRAPMENT

Finally, perhaps just a brief comment on the use of technology for coding in grounded theory. Given the pervasive nature of technology, it is not surprising to see it surface as a tool for research. Traditional quantitative research methods have embraced technology's rapid and expansive processing capabilities to significantly reduce both the time and effort required to run multiple tests on vast data banks. Qualitative researchers have also explored the applications of various technologies to enhancing data collection and analysis. While various software programs purport to facilitate the coding and analysis of qualitative data and some methodologists advocate their use (Creswell, 2003; Morse & Richards, 2002; Richards, 2005), this facility does not lend itself to the coding and analysis of data in classic grounded theory methodology. As I trust the previous overview illustrates, the coding process in classic grounded theory is not a discrete phase but rather an intricate and integral activity woven into and throughout the research process. Despite the capacity of computer-assisted coding software programs for archiving and ready retrieval of coded data, the largely mechanistic mind-set that results from their application is not only time-consuming but also counter-creative to the conceptual ideation imperative for generating good grounded theory. Glaser (2003) devotes two chapters to the problems with computer-assisted data collection and analysis. Experienced classic grounded theorists continue to await a 'package' that can replicate the complex capabilities of the human brain for conceptualization of latent patterns of social behaviour.

REFERENCES

Baszanger, I. (1997). Deciphering Chronic Pain. In A. Strauss & J. M. Corbin (Eds.), *Grounded Theory in Practice.* Thousand Oaks, CA: SAGE, pp. 1–34.
Charmaz, K. (2000). Grounded theory: Objectivist and constructivist methods. In N. K. Denzin & Y. S. Lincoln (Eds.), *Handbook of Qualitative Research* (2nd ed.). Thousand Oaks, CA: SAGE.
Charmaz, K. (2004). Premises, principles, and practices in qualitative research: Revisiting the foundation. *Qualitative Health Research*, 14, 976–993.
Charmaz, K. (2006). *Constructing Grounded Theory: A Practical Guide Through Qualitative Analysis.* Thousand Oaks, CA: SAGE.

Clarke, A. E. (1997). A social worlds research adventure: The case of reproductive science. In A. Strauss & J. M. Corbin (Eds.), *Grounded Theory in Practice*. Thousand Oaks, CA: SAGE, pp. 63–94.

Clarke, A. E. (2005). *Situational Analysis: Grounded Theory After the Postmodern Turn*. Thousand Oaks, CA: SAGE.

Creswell, J. W. (2003). *Research Design: Qualitative, Quantitative and Mixed Methods Approaches* (2nd ed.). Thousand Oaks, CA: SAGE.

Denzin, N. K. & Lincoln, Y. S. (Eds.). (1994). *Handbook of Qualitative Research*. Thousand Oaks, CA: SAGE.

Dey, I. (1999). *Grounding Grounded Theory*. San Diego: Academic Press.

Glaser, B. G. (1978). *Theoretical Sensitivity: Advances in the Methodology of Grounded Theory*. Mill Valley, CA: Sociology Press.

Glaser, B. G. (1992). *Basics of Grounded Theory: Emergence vs. Forcing*. Mill Valley, CA: Sociology Press.

Glaser, B. G. (1998). *Doing Grounded Theory: Issues and Discussions*. Mill Valley, CA: Sociology Press.

Glaser, B. G. (2001). *The Grounded Theory Perspective: Conceptualization Contrasted with Description*. Mill Valley, CA: Sociology Press.

Glaser, B. G. (2002a). Conceptualization: On theory and theorizing using grounded theory. *International Journal of Qualitative Methods*, 1(2), Article 3. Retrieved June 1, 2006, from http://www.ualberta.ca/~ijqm/english/engframeset.html

Glaser, B. G. (2002b) Constructivist grounded theory? In *Forum Qualitative Sozialforschung/Forum: Qualitative Social Research*. Retrieved June 1, 2006, from http://www.qualitative-research.net/fqs-texte/3-02/3-02glaser-e-htm

Glaser, B. G. (2003). *The Grounded Theory Perspective II: Description's Remodeling of Grounded Theory Methodology*. Mill Valley, CA: Sociology Press.

Glaser, B. G. (2004). Naturalist Inquiry and Grounded Theory. In *Forum Qualitative Sozialforschung/Forum: Qualitative Social Research*. Retrieved June 1, 2006, from http://www.qualitative-research.net/fqs-texte/1-04/1-04glaser-e.htm

Glaser, B. G. (2005). *The Grounded Theory Perspective III: Theoretical Coding*. Mill Valley, CA: Sociology Press.

Glaser, B. G. & Holton, J. (2004). Remodeling Grounded Theory. In *Forum Qualitative Sozialforschung/Forum: Qualitative Social Research*. Retrieved June 1, 2006, from http://www.qualitative-research.net/fqs-texte/2-04/2-04glaser-e.htm

Glaser, B. G. & Strauss, A. L. (1967). *The Discovery of Grounded Theory: Strategies for Qualitative Research*. Hawthorne, NY: Aldine de Gruyter.

Goode, W. J. (1960). A Theory of Role Strain. *American Sociological Review*, 25, 483–496.

Goulding, C. (2002). *Grounded Theory: A Practical Guide for Management, Business and Market Researchers*. London: SAGE.

Holton, J. A. (2006). Rehumanising Knowledge Work through Fluctuating Support Networks: A Grounded Theory. Unpublished doctoral thesis, University of Northampton, UK.

Johnson, P., Buehring, A., Cassell, C. & Symon, G. (2006). Evaluating qualitative management research: Towards a contingent criteriology. *International Journal of Management Reviews*, 8, 3, 131–156.

Klee, R. (1996). *Introduction to the Philosophy of Science: Cutting Nature at its Seams*. New York: Oxford University Press.

Konecki, K. (1997). Time in the recruiting search process by headhunting companies. In A. Strauss & J. M. Corbin (Eds.), *Grounded Theory in Practice*. Thousand Oaks, CA: SAGE, pp. 131–145.

Locke, K. (2001). *Grounded Theory in Management Research*. London: SAGE.

Lomborg, K. & Kirkevold, M. (2003). Truth and validity in Grounded Theory—a reconsidered realist interpretation of the criteria: Fit, work, relevance and modifiability. *Nursing Philosophy*, 4, 189–200.

Lowenberg, J. S. (1993) Interpretative research methodology: broadening the dialogue. *Advances in Nursing Science*, 16, 57–69.

Madill, A., Jordan, A. & Shirley, C. (2000). Objectivity and reliability in qualitative analysis: Realist, contextualist and radical constructionist epistemologies. *British Journal of Psychology*, 91, 1–20.

Marshall, C. & Rossman, G. B. (1999). *Designing Qualitative Research* (3rd ed.). Thousand Oaks, CA: SAGE.

Martin, V. B. (2006). The postmodern turn: Shall classic grounded theory take that detour? A review essay. *The Grounded Theory Review*, 5 (2/3), 119–128.

Morse, J. M. (Ed.). (1997). *Completing a Qualitative Research Project: Details and Dialogue*. Thousand Oaks, CA: SAGE.

Morse, J. M. (2004). Constructing qualitatively derived theory: Concept construction and concept typologies. *Qualitative Health Research*, 14 (10), 1387–1395.

Morse, J. M. & Richards, L. (2002). *Readme First for a User's Guide to Qualitative Methods*. Thousand Oaks, CA: SAGE.

Partington, D. (2000). Building grounded theories of management action. *British Journal of Management*, 11, 91–102.

Partington, D. (Ed.). (2002). *Essential Skills for Management Research*. London: SAGE.

Patton, M. Q. (2002). *Qualitative Research & Evaluation Methods* (3rd ed.). Thousand Oaks, CA: SAGE.

Richards, L. (2005) *Handling Qualitative Data: A Practical Guide*. London: SAGE.

Schatzman, L. (1991). Dimensional Analysis: Notes on an alternative approach to the grounding of theory in qualitative research. In D. R. Maines (Ed.), *Social Organisation and Social Process*. Aldine De Gruyter: New York, pp. 303–314.

Smit, J. & Bryant, A. (2000). Grounded Theory method in IS Research: Glaser vs. Strauss. Retrieved July 3, 2004, from http://www.leedsmet.ac.uk/inn/document/2000-7.pdf

Strauss, A. L. & Corbin, J. M. (1990). *Basics of Qualitative Research: Grounded Theory Procedures and Techniques*. Newbury Park, CA: SAGE.

Strauss, A. L. & Corbin, J. M. (1998). *Basics of Qualitative Research: Grounded Theory Procedures and Techniques* (2nd ed.). Newbury Park, CA: SAGE.

Whitehead, A. N. (1925). *Science and the Modern World*. New York: Macmillan.

PART IV

Practicalities

14

Making Teams Work in Conducting Grounded Theory

Carolyn Wiener

INTRODUCTION

Few people outside of the health field had heard of cardiac catheterization, magnetic resonance imaging, echocardiographs, and the like in 1977, when Anselm Strauss began a team project investigating the impact of medical technology on patient care. The team he chose was comprised of two sociologists (Barbara Suczek and myself) and a nurse-sociologist (Shizuko Fagerhaugh, called by her friends and herein Shiz), all of whom were graduates of the Sociology Program at the University of California San Francisco (UCSF), which Strauss had founded and chaired. He and Shiz had done exploratory interviewing and field observation for several months in 1976, prior to receiving US Public Health (USPH) funding for this project, which originally covered the years 1977–1981. USPH support was subsequently extended for a further 2 years.

This chapter describes the project, sets forth the conditions that contributed to its success, and presents an analysis of the way using grounded theory as a team enhanced the results. Some of the conditions and the way the team acted upon them are personality-specific and/or unique to this project. Among the sociological factors described in this paper, however, are many that are more general and may serve as recommendations for qualitative social scientists who are contemplating team research.

DESCRIPTION OF THE PROJECT

The research design called for field observation on diverse hospital wards, chosen at first by selective sampling (Schatzman & Strauss, 1973) and later by theoretical sampling (Glaser, 1978; Glaser & Strauss, 1967; Strauss & Corbin, 1998). Observation occurred on various kinds of wards and departments in several different kinds of hospitals in order to maximize comparative analysis: a city-county hospital, a large urban community hospital, a military hospital, a university hospital, two small urban hospitals, and a suburban community hospital. In addition to the fieldwork, open-ended interviews were conducted with hospital personnel, patients and their family members, selected to pursue concepts and hypotheses that emerged over the course of the study. Other interviews were carried out with persons who represented special interests arising also from the emergent research: hospital architects, administrators, engineers, medical equipment innovators, designers, and researchers. The research, in keeping with grounded theory, led in directions unforeseen when writing the original research proposal. Anselm had a long-standing interest in professions and work (stemming from his origins in the Chicago School of sociology, known for its pragmatist philosophy) and, quite naturally, brought this perspective into the research. Most important was the influence of Everett Hughes on Anselm's thinking. For Hughes, the division of labor implied interaction. Allen and Pilnick (2006: 6) point out that Hughes regarded the division of labor 'as a poor term for the differentiation of function in social life as a whole, because it emphasized division rather than integration.' Anselm, as Hughes before him, was interested in the inter-relationship among professions and occupations within a system such as a hospital. Shiz, as the research progressed, became increasingly alarmed about the issue of patient, staff, and hospital safety and focused on that subject. I had not as yet written anything on health policy but developed an interest in bringing this subject to the project as the importance of this perspective became evident. Increasingly immersed in fieldwork, I could see that solutions presented in the literature for paramount issues (such as reducing the cost of health care, the need for professional consensus on treatment options, the neglect of 'patient power') were unrealistically simplistic. I was given full reign to pursue this course. Ultimately, the project spawned 10 co-authored papers and two co-authored books.

As we looked at the explosive growth of medical technology, we came to understand that its source lay not only in greatly increased knowledge but in the increasingly *chronic* and irresolvable character of illness. Heart transplant surgery, pacemakers, dialysis machines, chemotherapy, radiation therapy, and respiratory support had developed in the service of cardiovascular illnesses, renal diseases, cancer, and respiratory diseases. The patients we observed not only suffered from one or more of these chronic conditions but often were dealing with additional ones: arthritis, diabetes, Parkinson's disease, etc. Lewis Thomas (1974) popularized a term for the procedures, drugs, and machines we were observing, calling them 'halfway technologies,' meaning medical intervention applied in an attempt to compensate for the incapacitating effects of a disease whose course one is unable to do much about, or to postpone death. That chronic illnesses cannot be 'cured' but must be 'managed' makes them different in many respects from acute illnesses, the model around which the hospitals we were observing were traditionally built. We saw early on that enormous cost, the continuing expansion of health facilities, and a need for more and more highly trained personnel were characteristic of the type of technology we had set out to study. It became clear that until the basic questions about the mechanisms of disease in the various chronic illnesses were answered (and with some of them we are certainly closer now than we were in the late 1970s) patients and health care workers had to put up with halfway technologies. Although without question, as more than one commentator has aptly put it, for patients 'halfway is a long way to go,' issues arose as patients cycled through the hospital, then to the clinic or doctor's office, returned home, went back to the hospital during acute episodes, and again back to their homes. The problems of coordinating care had become immense. Also, as hospital costs rose, patients were being discharged earlier than in the past; sent home with equipment neither they nor their caregivers were trained to handle. 'Work,' therefore, performed by doctors, nurses, technicians, patients, and their caregivers, became a central focus of our research.

The team met weekly almost from the project's inception. Meetings were recorded and transcribed by the team secretary who, as she became bolder would add an editorial comment or two. The initial team meetings consisted of planning sessions, reports on recent fieldwork or interviewing, reports on literature search, and preliminary analysis of data. Early on, the weekly meetings took on a life of their own by turning into verbal-coding and memo-building sessions. Anselm's long experience and our shorter but intensive familiarity with grounded theory, gave us the confidence to side step line-by-line coding in favor of leaps into conceptualization in the form of memo writing. Although this unorthodoxy just 'happened,' Anselm wrote in a later memo that he liked the results of this experiment since work on these memos produced dense codes and examined their intricate relationships.[1] Each new fieldwork experience or memo sparked another memo, eventually reaching a total of over 200. Team discussions, often followed by a memo, also led to what Anselm called 'blue-skying conceptualization,' imaginative explorations of a topic. Barbara, for instance, after a discussion of the relationship between technology and depersonalization, wrote a memo sparked by a nurse's view that the epitome of depersonalization is for a patient to die in the hospital. Barbara looked at how depersonalization had become a shibboleth in an ideological war and conjectured, 'The hospital could well be, for some poor souls, the cleanest, pleasantest, most peaceful place they have ever been and the use of machines could represent concern, the ultimate in professional care. Depersonalization is a meaning, a subjective experience, conditional; who knows what patients think and why?'

As each of us completed observation and interviewing on a ward or in a department, a summarizing memo was prepared, discussed, and often amended. After a couple of years, there were meetings for which major memos were prepared. A typical major memo is one written by Shiz entitled 'Environmental Safety, Prevention and Minimization of Dangers/Catastrophe,' in which she reflected on the vastness of hospital safety concerns and analyzed each one (electric, fire, industrial, biohazard, radiation), discussed their tie-in with the total hospital, and examined the multiple roles and delicate balancing game of safety workers as policemen, enforcers, consultants, advisors, and educators. We later said, '… the analytic mode that emerged … from this particular research team's experience with its weekly meetings seemed generally to be exciting and satisfying, even seductive, while still seeming adequate to what we wished to accomplish' (Strauss et al., 1997: 294). When a potential topic grabbed one of us, she/he would volunteer to write a paper. We had agreed initially that all papers would be co-authored, with the writer as primary author and the rest listed in alphabetical order. (Somehow when this arrangement was made I forgot that my name started with a 'W.')

STRUCTURAL CONDITIONS

Anselm brought to grounded theory his deep immersion in, and appreciation of, symbolic interaction, defined succinctly by Charmaz (2006: 189) as 'a theoretical perspective derived from pragmatism which assumes that people construct selves, society, and reality through interaction.' This theoretical perspective became integral to the work of his students. The central question in his writings and teachings was: under what conditions does this process, event, or interaction happen and with what consequences? Thus, it is fitting to analyze first the structural conditions that contributed to the success of this project. Although the conditions are discussed here sequentially, they are not arranged in order of importance.

Loose research design

Unrestricted by the stringent requirements of current research proposals, Anselm had an established reputation and was able to obtain funding while maintaining a somewhat loose research design. Although I feel certain that we maintained an ethical standard in approaching and observing patients, there was no Committee on Human Research (CHR) at UCSF at the time, allowing us greater freedom and expanded opportunities as we went about the research. For example, at one point, while observing a repairman (on contract to the hospital) as he worked on a machine, I engaged him in conversation about his work. He invited me to go on rounds with him to various hospitals, an experience that added much richness to our understanding of machine breakdown (one of our major categories). This is in stark contrast with current research, where observation in hospitals not specified in the original proposal would require approval of the funding agency and the CHR.

Choice of team members

Asked by Barbara to what he attributed our compatibility, Anselm answered with no further amplification, 'I chose my team well.' We were all mature women, experienced researchers, and former students of his. Whether he could have foreseen that we would be amazingly non-competitive remains unknown since we were remiss in never asking him to explain more than the brief statement above. A visiting sociologist who spent a great deal of time with us, however, later summed up our interaction well, saying, 'There was a beautiful social relation among these four people' (Fritz Schuetze, personal communication, July 11, 2006).

Good balance of background, knowledge, and experiential history

One decidedly special attribute of the project was Anselm's experience in health care research, especially in hospitals and with chronically ill and dying patients. In addition to his own fieldwork, he had spent many hours reading, talking about and analyzing the field notes of his research associates on a study of pain management in hospitals. On that project he worked closely with Shiz. I, too, had worked for an intense year on that project, my first, and so had an understanding of the pathways to hospital research. Barbara had worked with Anselm investigating renal dialysis when it was new and patients were facing the problem of paying for it. She started this project knowing very little about the inner workings of the hospital and we both knew next to nothing about medical technology. Initially, as we observed heart-lung machines which have increased the number of candidates for surgery, intricate life-sustaining wires that keep low-weight infants alive, dialysis which was now funded and prolonging life for a previously compromised population, Barbara and I frequently remarked that we felt like Alice(s) in Wonderland. Shiz, on the other hand, was extremely alert to nurses' work, its challenges and impediments, and to tactics such as 'squirreling supplies,' an important category. We realized early on that the sociologists saw things the nurse took for granted, or that would remain invisible to an untrained eye, and vice versa.

Trusting and democratic relationship

As we worked together, our trust of each other became a stabilizing factor. Obviously, there was an asymmetrical relationship among Anselm and the rest of us in terms of status, experience, and authority. And yet, in no way was this a power situation. At team meetings, Anselm was the 'moderator.' He was not healthy at the time and could not do much fieldwork. All of us were skilled at

coding but he was especially gifted at it. At times, he would make an observation
or assign a code and Shiz, with her depth of hospital experience, would say, 'No,
I see it differently.' As the aforementioned visiting sociologist observed,
'Argumentation was harnessed as a means of generating knowledge.' Said
another, 'there was no artificial presentation of self to score points. All had an
egalitarian respect for each other' (Gerhard Riemann, personal communication,
August 9, 2006). A sociologist who went on to use the team approach in another
project with great success (Lessor, 2000) participated for a time in ours. Her
analysis is cogent:

> It seems to me that the reason grounded theory in the team works so well is that it
> continually opens up possibilities for contribution by all ... Sharing is essential to the process
> and 'research democracy' is built in. Now did we defer to Anselm when it came down to
> the definition of the situation? Perhaps we did. But we also argued for points of view
> (even I as a grad student and the lowest status member) (Lessor, personal communication,
> April 22, 2006).

The tone established by the principal investigator

Related to the above but worthy of a distinction from the above conditions is the
personality and style of Anselm himself. Charmaz (personal communication,
October 2, 2006) sees him as 'embodying the fluidity and belief in the democratic
process of Chicago school pragmatism—philosophy and practice become merged
in self and identity.' He ran team meetings just as he taught, in a relaxed manner,
fully in control but not domineering. His delight with 'juicy' data was palpable.
Moreover, there was no discomfort if one of us listened but remained silent.
We knew as the weeks went by that there would be different times when we could
hardly wait to spill forth our latest discoveries. Nor was there any scoffing at off-
the-wall comments. Someone would be motivated to tell a story, others would free-
associate, Anselm then turning the story around to look at it from different angles.
One session stands out in my mind. Surprisingly, no one volunteered to start.
Anselm then asked us how the machinery we were observing compared to the
home objects we knew so well: washing machine, dishwasher, even the toaster.
This led to an exceedingly fruitful instance of experiential comparison that is recommended in grounded theory. As categories emerged, Anselm would ask one of
us to write a memo. Similarly, one-on-one sessions were held with him as the need
arose: to work out a memo and later to work on the outline of a paper. These
meetings followed the same format of give and take that we had learned as his
students.

Unbound by Grounded Theory orthodoxy

Having co-authored the original grounded theory book (Glaser and Strauss, 1967),
Anselm had no compunctions about deviating from its precepts. For instance, none
of us was comfortable with the dictum that the literature in the substantive area
under study should not be reviewed until data had been collected and analyzed and

theory generation started. 'When the theory seems sufficiently grounded and developed, *then* we review the literature in the field and relate the theory to it through integration of ideas' (Glaser, 1978: 31). On the contrary, since the development of medical technology was a growing phenomenon, both the academic and the popular press were replete with articles that were useful to us from the very beginning of our research. If anything, remaining current was the pressing challenge. Unquestionably, these articles widened our horizons and enriched our interviews.

Flexible division of labor

As noted above, Shiz was our nursing expert. She came through with medically oriented and professionally oriented information when required, quite aside from the observations gathered by us in the field. Initially, she was interested in the impact of technology on nursing (Fagerhaugh, 1980). When she became alarmed about safety as a prominent issue, she was given full reign to follow this concern (Fagerhaugh et al., 1987). Similarly, my interest in health policy gradually evolved and I pursued this course (Wiener et al., 1980, 1982) while Barbara explored the unacknowledged and frequently invisible work that kin do (Suczek, 1981). As papers began to take shape in our minds, we were free to write first drafts, distribute them, and benefit from the cross-fertilization and raised level of analysis that followed.

Participation of visitors

Sociologists and sociology graduate students who had studied with Anselm (Irma Zuckerman, Roberta Lessor, and Diane Beeson) did some fieldwork for us and sat in on some meetings. Barbara Koenig, who, writing her dissertation, was doing research on plasmapheresis[2] as an illustration of the technological imperative in medical practice (Koenig, 1988), discussed this procedure with us. A nurse from Minnesota (Evelyn Peterson), who also had studied with Glaser, spent many months in San Francisco as part of her own research and joined us to contribute her experienced perspective. All of these discussions were mutually beneficial, enlarging our vision and theirs.

Over time, we were visited by a sociologist from Japan (Setsuo Mizuno) and a nurse from Switzerland (Ruth Quenzer). During the third year, a visiting professor from the University of Bielefeld, Germany, Fritz Schuetze, became a full working member of the team. Having foreign visitors who were not entirely at ease with the English language, forced us to explain ourselves more fully, refining our thinking in the process. In addition, we found that having an audience and welcoming outsiders' participation frequently fostered a deeper analysis of the data.

Reception of team members at research sites

Covering so many sites meant facing the challenge of entree more often than is true on many projects. Nevertheless, we encountered little in the way of problems.

On one occasion, I was told by the Chief of Obstetrics that, 'These women will not tell you anything that they haven't told me.' Despite this caustic assessment, he grudgingly agreed to my observation and interviews of soon-to-be and new mothers, their partners, and staff. Whether he acknowledged, or even knew of, his error regarding the fullness of the patient interviews on this ward, he never mentioned it again.

Undoubtedly, we benefited from the fact that hospitals had not as yet been heavily researched. To the contrary, the people we were studying were pleased that their work was being observed. Despite the usual problem of communicating the procedures and value of qualitative research, our explanation was accepted and we were given a great deal of freedom to pursue our data collection.

Increased number of sites covered

All of us were in different hospitals, looking at different types of wards and work, observing very different types of machinery. This variety, which could not be attempted by a sole researcher, greatly enhanced the comparative analysis that is essential in grounded theory research. Being able to compare and contrast the use of simple devices such as electrocardiograms (EKGs) to the complex machinery in the Intensive Care Unit, simultaneously rather than in retrospect, was invaluable.

Use of personal health experience as data

Most important to mention is how personal health experiences of each project member became data: 'We emphasize this particularly because of firmly held canons, widespread among social scientists, about the biased subjectivity of personal experience, which ought therefore to be carefully screened out of research like potential impurities from drinking water' (Strauss et al., 1997: 294). Anselm had a bout of severe illness during the fourth year of the project, my mother had a hospitalization, Barbara had a longstanding problem with her eyes resulting in numerous experiences with her physicians, Shiz helped guide her brother through a difficult surgery and through many complicated dealings with medical people. Some of those data were used in papers about patient and kin work, as well as in *Social Organization of Medical Work*. As we said there, 'What we have done is something in the spirit of people like Robert Park and Everett Hughes, both of whom poured their own living experiences into their constructions of sociological theory … In this regard, we have also followed the spirit of the philosophical movement called "pragmatism," which lies solidly behind the interactionist tradition in which we work' (Strauss et al., 1997: 295).

Regularity of team meetings

Knowing that team meetings occurred weekly underscored the need to stay current regarding reading transcriptions of meetings and one another's field notes and interviews. It also made the need to remain current in one's own transcriptions of interviews and field notes all the more necessary. Although the difficulty of these tasks increased as the data poured in, their importance cannot be emphasized enough.

APPLICATION OF THE BASIC TENETS OF GROUNDED THEORY

I turn now to the 'action' in symbolic interaction as applied in this team project. This action consists of use of the basic tenets that we considered integral to following the grounded theory method. A disclaimer is in order here lest I be accused of plagiarism. After years of using the language of grounded theory in writing and teaching, I no longer can distinguish between my own definitions of these tenets and those of Strauss, Glaser, or Corbin. If, in the following section, I have encroached upon their formulations, I have done so inadvertently.

Data gathering, analysis, and theory construction proceed concurrently

This is perhaps the hardest tenet an inexperienced researcher must face. It means that coding and memo writing begin with the very first interviews and/or field notes. How much easier it is to immerse oneself in the field and let the notes pile up without scrutinizing them. Yet, many an article has remained unwritten because a stack of unanalyzed notes and untranscribed tapes have become too daunting to tackle. Being a sole researcher increases this temptation while team participation makes the need to stay current more pressing.

Coding starts with the first interview and/or field notes

Field notes were written in great detail describing people, events, issues, conversations, and settings. We each transcribed our own interviews. Team coding, which entailed our variation on line-by-line coding as described above, consisted of converting these observations and interviews into categories, their properties, and dimensions: taking incidents and statements to an abstract level. There are numerous advantages to coding as a group. Although the first codes are frequently modified and given more precision as the research progresses, there is a human reluctance to ascribe early codes for fear of inaccuracy. As we coded in team meetings, however, just as we had as students, such inhibitions were decreased. Also, most novice grounded theory researchers find it difficult to move out of the specific to an abstract concept. Group coding makes it easier to see beyond the specific. Additionally, the mere fact that more brains are focusing on naming a code opened up more possibilities. Lastly, when a debate arose over naming a code, the ensuing discussion was more apt to lend it precision.

A word about in vivo codes, 'codes of participants' special terms' (Charmaz, 2006: 55). Grounded theory researchers are encouraged to use participants' language since this 'helps to preserve participants' meanings of their views and actions' (Charmaz, 2006: 55). An example in our research is 'bonding,' which refers to the necessity of close contact (touching and cuddling) for its long-term effects on parents and infants, a new concept in neonatal care at the time. Discovery of this code led to questions about 'bonding theory' and how its prevalence was affecting parents whose infants were hooked up to machinery and who therefore could not be held. Often, discussion of discovery of an in vivo code would be met with pleasure by another team member, who, having heard the same language had not as yet ascribed any importance to it.

Memo writing also begins with the first interview and/or field notes

Memos have a variety of functions. They may be written to delve into the deeper meaning of a code, to describe the significance of an observation, to capture an incident that appears salient but may not as yet have been coded, to question earlier observations. Memos may range from a couple of sentences to a number of pages. Headings on memos make it easier to sort them when one is farther along in the research and also to see where one memo cross-cuts with others, important in the building of a theory. In the process of transcribing or reviewing notes, it is important to stop to get the memo down on paper before it escapes one's notice. Team participation improved the quality and volume of memos as team discussion sparked new ideas or opened up new possibilities that were previously unappreciated. The following is a portion of a memo I wrote after a team discussion of 'sentimental work,' one of our categories. The memo refers to this work as it pertains to premature infants:

> We agreed I have to ask more about the frequent comments that 'they all have a distinctive personality,' i.e. when do they become more than a set of biological systems? This led to a discussion of *sentimental work*. Some of the infants can be taken out of their isolettes. Staff and parents touch it, hold it, feed it, talk to it. Isolettes are decorated with things like mobiles, picture of parents and siblings, balloons. There is an interaction among kin and staff, kin and baby, staff and baby. Can't interview baby, but if we assume there is something to *bonding theory*, then something is going on socially with the baby.

Memo writing allows the researcher to think through ideas about a category and its properties and to search for interrelationships with other emerging categories. Thus, the central requirement of memo writing is that it be done expansively and freely, unconstrained by the restrictions of formal writing, that is without attention to syntax, grammar, and spelling, and without internal debate over the issue of significance. Historian Jacques Barzun (1986: 8) captured this element well. What he says about first drafts, applies as well to memos: 'Convince yourself that you are working in clay, not marble, on paper, not eternal bronze; let that first sentence be as stupid as it wishes. No one will rush out to print it as it stands.' Although maintaining this aspect of memo writing would appear to clash somewhat with sharing memos with team members, it did not become an obstacle to spontaneity. Here is a memo of Barbara's that demonstrates the kind of conjecture that constitutes exploration of a category:

Machine storage/retrieval

... It doesn't end with finding a place to store equipment. Then you've got to be able to retrieve the stuff when you need it. How is it decided what gets stored nearby, what probably won't be used much? And what if it isn't used much but is absolutely necessary when it IS needed? Is there some sort of storage protocol? And who has charge of it? Some sort of general storage file clerk? With nurses floating in and out, it isn't possible for everyone to know how things are arranged, where what is, even IF there is a what. (My kids come home and put away dishes for me, and I can't find ANYTHING.)

The constant comparison technique is used to tease out similarities and differences and thereby refine concepts

If memos are the skeleton of the grounded theory method, use of the constant comparison is the full body. Comparison begins with the first codes. The basic rule is simple: while coding an incident for a category, we compared it with previous incidents coded in the same category in order to tease out a range of the code's properties, at every step, asking about opposites, variation, and/or continua. The following is part of a memo I wrote summarizing a team discussion comparing work in the Intensive Care Nursery (ICN) to work in the Dialysis Unit.

ICN	DIALYSIS
One to one watching, despite hook-up to alarm.	Patient is set-up and staff can listen for alarm.
Patient can't monitor self.	Patient is monitoring
Bad turn can be fast and serious.	Bad turn less likely (damage usually retrievable).
More diagnostic tasks (some have to be taken to other departments).	Diagnostic tasks at beginning and end of treatment.
Division of labor finer; staff is shaping; more systems; more procedures; more junctures; more crises.	Division of labor: patient and nurse (occasionally physician).
Shifting division of labor for different crises (pulmonary physician, pediatric surgeon).	Consistent division of labor.
Census very sporadic (adds to cost).	Census always full.
Sometimes over capacity, because don't want to lose future referrals.	Only occasional deviation from strict scheduling of patients.

In addition to making comparisons pertaining to data stemming from the project, thinking about outside comparative categories is encouraged in grounded theory. A case in point is the meeting described above where we compared home appliances to the high-tech machinery we were observing. Facility in thinking comparatively, whether with examples drawn from the popular or clinical literature, from the data, or from personal experience (e.g. home appliances) is the key element in finely shaping analytic questions. The researcher develops the skill of thinking in terms of variation, never settling for one answer but always pressing on with the query; under what specific (and different) conditions does this happen? This technique was honed in our team research due to the variety of sites being observed and the fact that wider personal experience was brought into the discussion. Since, in grounded theory, 'coding backward' (re-examining previous data for overlooked relevance) is not only acceptable but encouraged, team examination of an incident, observation, or comment would sometimes trigger comparison to data that heretofore had escaped notice.

Theoretical sampling is the disciplined search for patterns and variation

Since grounded theory research is inductive, one is constantly asking where do I look next to find out what I do not know? The answer lies not in haphazard search but rather in a way that will add to the analysis. The basic question one asks is: what groups or sub-groups of populations, events, and/or activities do I turn to next in order to find varying dimensions, strategies, and/or other action and for what theoretical purpose? At first, finding patterns and variation is the goal. Patterns, repeated versions of the same phenomenon, may emerge early or slowly in the research. The first time the phenomenon occurs, the researcher may have missed it. It may have gone by too fast, or she/he wasn't in a position to notice it, or she/he may have missed part of it. If it is repetitive, the next time it occurs the researcher is ready. Team discussion accelerated this search for patterns. Early on I remarked in a team meeting, 'I must be a jinx. Everywhere I go, the machine breaks down.' It was not long before we discovered that this was a highly important phenomenon, occurring more frequently than patients would wish to know, leading to massive consequences and the categories we developed of 'back-up' and 'tinkering.' (Regarding the latter, we thought of asking the publisher of *Social Organization of Medical Work* to design a cover picturing a nurse with screwdriver in hand but decided against it.)

The search for variation is more challenging but a crucial component of theoretical sampling. This is the reason we covered a range of wards and departments, from 'low tech,' such as radiology to observe X-ray technology, to 'high tech', such as cardiac scanners. In an effort to maximize variation, I would be in Labor and Delivery, observing the use of fetal monitors, a relatively simple machine but one with significant consequences, and Shiz would be in the Intensive Care Unit (ICU) observing patients who were hooked up to massive machinery. In team meetings, we would explore, for instance, what she had seen in the ICU.

Asking how do patients get there, we would discover extensive variation: referral from another ward, transfer from the Emergency Room, after surgery. This led to questions regarding priority, the physical structure of the hospital, space, and negotiated space (e.g. who gets 'bumped' and why), all in the service of our emerging theory. In this manner, the theory is being checked as the project proceeds.[3]

This procedure of theoretical sampling in no way interferes with a salient aspect of qualitative research: being ready for the serendipitous opportunity. Discovery, the cornerstone of grounded theory, consists of coming upon the unexpected and acting upon it, in keeping with Pasteur's oft-quoted comment, 'chance favors the prepared mind.' As noted above, machine breakdown, first observed as an anomaly, turned out to be a pattern. However, to observe the consequences of total breakdown was to carry this to an unexpected length. Thus, when Shiz heard on the radio that there was a power failure in the hospital she had been observing, she rushed to the Cardiac Care Unit to discover heart-lung machines being operated by hand (as well as other consequences of the break-down). Subsequently, she wrote a memo on how the breakdown highlighted dimensions of technology that might have otherwise been missed or taken longer to discover: gradations of machines from life-sustaining risk to no risk, and gradations of wards along the same dimensions. Similarly, when, by chance the garage door in one of the old Victorian houses owned by the University (buildings I passed daily) had been left open, I found a massive storage of old equipment, reminding me that in every department I had observed at least one 'old' machine covered in plastic. This led to a new awareness, new questions, and a new category, 'accelerated obsolescence.'

Theoretical sorting of memos sets up the outline for the writing of a paper or book

Glaser views theoretical sorting as 'an essential step in the grounded theory process that cannot be skipped' (Glaser, 1978: 116). In my own work, I honor this tenet by making file folders for major categories, as they emerge. In the folders I put relevant data: memos, pages with interview quotes, library notes, news clippings, scribbled items, cross-references to other files. At any phase in the research, sorting and re-sorting directs my theoretical sampling and may also generate additional memos.[4] This step was not followed in the team project. Since Anselm was the principal investigator, it was his prerogative to follow the line most comfortable for him, which was influenced by all of his previous research. From 1957, when he had observed residents and interns in a medical school (Becker et al., 1961), to 1958–1960, when he did fieldwork at two mental hospitals (Strauss et al., 1964) to 1960–1964, when he did field research in hospitals that culminated in two books about death and dying (Glaser & Strauss, 1966, 1968), to 1972–1974, when he conducted the study of pain in hospitals (Fagerhaugh & Strauss, 1977), a solid awareness had grown that the patients he had been observing in hospitals suffered from one form or another of chronic illness. He had sought funds for this project in order to study the technology which had led to changes in medical work and in the character and composition of the health occupations/professions, as part of the larger continuum of his work. In our team discussions, Anselm's earlier work, and the work of those of who had previously collaborated with him, were strongly present as we analyzed the data.[5] In addition, we had talked through sorting the data in the process of outlining our papers and books. In previous work, we all had used the term 'trajectory' in an attempt to transmit the fact that the patients we observed were going through more than a 'course of illness.' Gradually, what started as a 'sensitizing concept,' a concept that suggests a general sense of reference and guidance in approaching empirical instances (Blumer, 1954), became a major social process underpinning our analysis, described more fully below.

Theoretical saturation is the judgment that there is no need to collect further data

The standard definition of 'theoretical saturation,' as set forth by Glaser and Strauss, is that categories are considered saturated when gathering fresh data no longer sparks new theoretical insights, nor reveals new properties of these core theoretical categories. When Anselm collaborated with Juliet Corbin (1998: 136) a practical postscript appeared:

> ... In reality, if one looked long and hard enough, one always would find additional properties or dimensions. There always is that potential for the 'new' to emerge. Saturation is more a matter of reaching the point in the research where collecting additional data seems counterproductive; the 'new' that is uncovered does not add that much more to the explanation at this time. Or, as is sometimes the situation, the researcher runs out of time, money, or both.

After 4+ years, time and money were depleted and we were satisfied that we had adequately presented our findings. As with most projects, the writing of two books extended beyond this time. In fact, Anselm and I co-authored a third book, which dealt with current debates in health policy and their disjunction with our conclusions. Sadly, and in keeping with the reluctance to look at deficiencies in the American health care system that was prevalent at the time, publishers did not agree with our assessment of its 'timeliness' and it remains in manuscript form.

Identify a basic social process that accounts for most of the observed behavior that is relevant and problematic for those involved

Glaser, in his classes, called this a 'little logic.' He explains that most other categories and their properties are related to this core category and describes its important function for generating theory: '... through these relations between categories and their properties, it has the prime function of *integrating* the theory and rendering the theory *dense* and saturated as the relationships increase' (Glaser, 1978: 93). In previous work, and in his teaching, Anselm had used the term 'trajectory' to denote that since chronic illness brings most patients to the hospital, they likely have had previous experiences with health professionals, facilities, and medical care. Therefore, as Shiz and Anselm explained in their study of pain management (Fagerhaugh & Strauss, 1977: 23), 'the patient has had an illness career or trajectory, with its characteristic symptoms and associated experiences' (Fagerhaugh & Strauss, 1977: 23). In the books on dying in hospitals, the term 'dying trajectory' was used, meaning the course of death as defined by the participants to it. *Chronic Illness and the Quality of Life* found Anselm struggling with the knowledge that there are essential elements that are not captured in the common phrase 'course of illness.' In this book, he alluded to the shape of a trajectory (plunging straight down, moving slowly but steadily downward, vacillating slowly, etc.) pointing out that each type of chronic illness may have some range of variation in trajectory, but each tends to have a certain pattern (Strauss, 1975: 47). Our coding, memos, and animated team discussions now lent greater precision to the term, which became our basic social process: 'process' not in the sense of stages or phases but denoting change over time in patterns of action/interaction and in relationship with changes in conditions. Now we were determined to distinguish between a course of illness and an illness trajectory. Barbara, in a thoughtful memo, pointed out that we were borrowing from the physical sciences which provided an apt metaphor. She clarified that in ordinary usage the term describes the path of a projectile hurtling through space. Just as the speed and direction that launches a missile can be modified in flight by the push and pull of extraneous forces, so can the 'natural' course of a disease be altered by extraneous forces; here the interplay of medical, historical, psychological, economic, and social contingencies. As we observed 'halfway technology' in hospitals, we also became aware that patients had to learn how to operate technology such as dialysis machines, oxygen tanks, and hyperalimentation devices (which bypass the digestive system) at home. Seeing this stretch-out of the illness trajectory, we were now able to define it not only as the physical unfolding of disease, but the total organization of work done over the course of the disease, together with the impact that the consequences of the disease and its work exert on the lives of the people involved: patients, kin, and health professionals. In one of our first papers, we demonstrated the intertwining of trajectory and biography (Wiener et al., 1979). Looking at the 'birth trajectory,' we found that interwoven within it, giving it shape, are multiple biographies: ward, machine, medical specialty, hospital, staff, parents, and that of the infant itself. These biographies are also linked in complex ways with each other, with far-reaching consequences, which we spelled out in this paper. In two subsequent papers, we dissected the consequences of the burgeoning of technology in terms of the stretch-out of illness trajectories, the increase in treatment options, the challenge of balancing options, and the effect on patient power (Wiener et al., 1980, 1982). In *Social Organization of Medical Work* (Strauss et al., 1997), we pulled apart the types of work entailed in an illness trajectory (machine, safety, comfort, sentimental, and articulation work) and dealt with their interrelationship. In *Hazards in Hospital Care* (Fagerhaugh et al., 1987), we used the illness trajectory as a framework for organizing and managing clinical safety, demonstrating its efficacy in preventing, assessing, monitoring, and correcting error.

CONCLUSION

The goal in our papers and books was to identify the relationship among our various findings regarding conditions, interaction, and consequences. People often question the term 'grounded theory,' making it more complicated than need be. 'Grounded' simply means grounded in the data and was used initially by Glaser and Strauss to signal rejection of the conventional approach, whereby existent sociological theory was seen as the beginning of research and imposed upon new data. 'Grounded' was meant by them to mean that new theory was to be generated from new data. 'Theory' is even more misunderstood, perhaps due to its natural science imagery. By 'theory,' they simply meant an explanation of the inter-relationship between and among concepts, in order to present a systematic view of what is going on. Done properly, this method generates the intricate relationship among a wide number of concepts. While not setting out to develop a theory in this chapter, I find myself bound somewhat by the grounded theory philosophy and the need to underscore that the important element in assessing the success of our team project is the way conditions and action are reciprocal and ricochet off each other. Clearly, there are inter-relationships among the conditions that facilitated our team project, our use of this method (which I have called the 'action'), and the consequences (setting forth our findings in papers and books). Personality clashes or a dominating and hierarchical relationship among us would have led to a different outcome. There are also inter-relationships within the conditions and within the action. For example, the leadership tone, the choice of researchers, and the consequent trust that was established all affected one another.

Being asked to write this chapter has led me to fulfill a goal that all of us (including our visiting professor from Germany, Fritz Schuetze) had toyed with: analyzing why this project was such an outstanding experience. It has also been a bittersweet exercise, bringing back memories of Anselm and Shiz, now deceased and deeply missed, as well as reminders of Barbara's creative mind and probing questions. As we scrutinized the data, fretted, and laughed together, lifelong friendships developed. Looking back, I see that we can take pride in our productivity but also in the way we worked as a team, which, as has been made clear here, is in great measure attributable to Anselm Strauss's leadership. A few words I delivered at his memorial service are relevant:

> My fondest memories consist of sitting out on the beautiful deck at 18 Moore Place—every flower carefully tended by Fran and Anselm—and Anselm suddenly sparked by some observation I'd made, his eyes shining, his pencil drawing concentric circles on paper, representing

some image in *his* mind, and then my suddenly 'getting it.' One of Anselm's many gifts was that he always knew the greater part of teaching is listening and that a wide interest in all aspects of human behavior enhances not only the sociological endeavor but the sheer joy of being alive.

Anselm Strauss was an extraordinary man, who delighted in his work but did not feel proprietory toward it. He felt that his discoveries were not only 'out there' for other sociologists to draw upon but invited others to build new theory on his discovered theory, all in the interest of the enlargement of knowledge (Strauss, 1970). Most important, he respected the work of others provided they met his standards. I am privileged to have had him as a mentor, colleague, and friend, and we were privileged to have had him as the Principal Investigator of this project.

NOTES

1 This may represent the seeds of Anselm's view that grounded theory can be modified provided the basic tenets are upheld, a concept disputed by Barney Glaser. Anselm's criteria for such apostasy was pragmatic, i.e. to be judged by the results.

2 Plasmapheresis is a blood purification procedure used to treat several autoimmune diseases. It is also known as therapeutic plasma exchange.

3 Strauss and Corbin have likened this to the quantitative tenet of 'verification,' which has been disputed by Glaser (1992: 29). This is a debate I shall leave to others.

4 A reviewer of this chapter questioned this seemingly archaic system for storage and retrieval of data, given the huge technological advances that have occurred in the last three decades or so. This project covered the years 1977–1983, when such software was still being developed. Later, when I did research for *The Elusive Quest* (Wiener, 2000), I did not feel comfortable with the programs then available and found a 'hands-on' approach to the massive data I confronted more compatible with my needs. Spreading memos and other data on a large table and/or the floor, and playing with moving them around, allowed me to probe for relationships among categories, find a core category, and experiment with diagramming the overall scheme. This in no way detracts from the work of those who find storing and retrieving data electronically advantageous.

5 A reader of this chapter asked to what extent all of these experiences may have preconceived the data, raising the issue of the fine line between building on prior knowledge and seeing new experience through the filter of prior experience. This is first cousin to the question frequently asked by students: 'How do you know if others in the same research setting might not have come up with a different theory?' My answer to this query is always: 'Yes, they might. But that does not invalidate either one.' Both of these are questions of trustworthiness. Contrary to the expectation expressed in the first grounded theory book (Glaser and Strauss, 1967) that one can enter the research site with a *tabula rasa* mind, we all have biases, prior knowledge, and other influences that we carry with us. The best we can do is to be aware of them and be wary lest they affect our work. In the end, the value of the method and how it is utilized lies in the final product. If the theory presented is dense, consistent, and, as Glaser often said, 'explains most of what is going on,' others should be able to carefully scrutinize the research product (which in this case constituted many papers and books) and make a positive judgment about the method used and the integrity of the relationships set forth in the theory. Beyond that, it is for others, especially those who are motivated to build upon our work, to judge the usefulness of our categories and of our theory and to do the necessary research to discover new theory (Strauss, 1970).

REFERENCES

Allen, Davina and Alison Pilnick (Eds.). (2006). *The Social Organisation of Healthcare Work*. Oxford: Blackwell.

Barzun, Jacques (1986). *On Writing, Editing, and Publishing: Essays, Explicative and Hortatory* (2nd ed.). Chicago: University of Chicago Press.

Becker, Howard, Blanche Geer, Everett Hughes, and Anselm Strauss (1961). *Boys in White: Student Culture in Medical School*. Chicago: University of Chicago Press.

Blumer, Herbert (1954). What is wrong with social theory? *American Sociological Review*, 19: 3–7.

Charmaz, Kathy (2006). *Constructing Grounded Theory*. London: SAGE.

Fagerhaugh, Shizuko (1980). The impact of technology on patients, providers, and care patterns. *Nursing Outlook*, 28(11): 666–672.

Fagerhaugh, Shizuko and Anselm Strauss (1977). *Politics of Pain Management: Staff-Patient Interaction*. Menlo Park, CA: Addison-Wesley.

Fagerhaugh, Shizuko, Anselm Strauss, Barbara Suczek, and Carolyn Wiener (1987). *Hazards in Hospital Care: Ensuring Patient Safety*. San Francisco: Jossey-Bass.

Glaser, Barney (1978). *Theoretical Sensitivity*. Mill Valley, CA: Sociology Press.

Glaser, Barney (1992). *Basics of Grounded Theory Analysis*. Mill Valley, CA: Sociology Press.

Glaser, Barney and Anselm Strauss (1966). *Awareness of Dying*. Chicago: Aldine.

Glaser, Barney and Anselm Strauss (1967). *The Discovery of Grounded Theory*. Chicago: Aldine.

Glaser, Barney and Anselm Strauss (1968). *Time for Dying*. Chicago: Aldine.

Koenig, Barbara (1988). The technological imperative in medical practice: The social creation of a routine treatment. In M. Lock and D. Gordon (Eds.), *Biomedicine Examined*. Boston: Kluwer, pp. 465–496.

Lessor, Roberta (2000). Using the team approach of Anselm Strauss in action research: Consulting on a project in global education. *Sociological Perspectives*, 43(4): S133–S147.

Schatzman, Leonard and Anselm Strauss (1973). *Field Research*. Englewood Cliffs, NJ: Prentice Hall.

Strauss, Anselm (1970). Discovering new theory from previous theory. In T. Shibutani (Ed.), *Human Nature and Collective Behavior. Papers in Honor of Herbert Blumer*. Englewood Cliffs, NJ: Prentice Hall, pp. 46–53.

Strauss, Anselm (1975). *Chronic Illness and the Quality of Life*. St. Louis: Mosby.

Strauss, Anselm, Leonard Schatzman, Rue Bucher, Danuta Ehrlich, and Melvin Sabshin (1964). *Psychiatric Ideologies and Institutions*. New York: The Free Press of Glencoe.

Strauss, Anselm, Shizuko Fagerhaugh, Barbara Suczek, and Carolyn Wiener (1997). *Social Organization of Medical Work* (2nd ed.). New Brunswick, NJ: Transaction Publishers.

Strauss, Anselm and Juliet Corbin (1998). *Basics of Qualitative Research: Techniques and Procedures for Developing Grounded Theory* (2nd ed.). Thousand Oaks, CA: SAGE.

Suczek, Barbara (1981). Kin Work in a Technologized Hospital. Paper presented at the American Sociological Association Meeting, Toronto, Canada.

Thomas, Lewis (1974). *Lives of a Cell: Notes of a Biology Watcher*. New York: Viking Books.

Wiener, Carolyn (2000). *The Elusive Quest: Accountability in Hospitals*. New Brunswick, NJ: Transaction.

Wiener, Carolyn, Anselm Strauss, Shizuko Fagerhaugh, and Barbara Suczek (1979). Trajectories, biographies and the evolving medical technology scene: Labor and delivery and the intensive care nursery. *Sociology of Health and Illness*, 1(3): 261–283.

Wiener, Carolyn, Shizuko Fagerhaugh, Anselm Strauss, and Barbara Suczek (1980). Patient power: Complex issues need complex answers. *Social Policy*, 11: 30–38.

Wiener, Carolyn, Shizuko Fagerhaugh, Anselm Strauss, and Barbara Suczek (1982). What price chronic illness? *Society*, 19: 22–30.

15

Teaching Grounded Theory

Sharlene Nagy Hesse-Biber

STUDENTS' GROUNDED THEORY TALES

Eric is a graduating senior and has decided to take a qualitative methods course as an elective. He has taken his department's required methods course, which was primarily a quantitative methods course covering mostly survey and experimental research designs. He has little or no prior knowledge of qualitative methods and has no idea what grounded theory means.

I spoke to Eric about his experiences learning grounded theory in his current qualitative methods class. His story, to the best of my recollection, is similar to what many of my undergraduate students who are also novices to qualitative methods experienced in learning these skills:

> Eric: I have had no background in qualitative data analysis, so I had no idea what to expect. I am really confused these first few weeks, I mean, I thought my teacher was going to talk about going out and interviewing with a specific questionnaire. We are now told that we are not supposed to know what the questions are! I have no idea about this; I mean how can you interview someone without having very many questions? What is it that I am supposed to be looking for? What are the ideas I am supposed to be testing out? It's so strange to be in a situation where I feel like I am asked to row upstream without a paddle.

Kati is a graduate student who has taken a research methods course, so she has been exposed to qualitative and quantitative methods. The course covers a variety of quantitative and qualitative methods, but only one class session is devoted to grounded theory:

> Kati: I really don't know what to think if someone asked me about grounded theory. I mean I know it has to do with generating theory and not engaging in hypothesis testing,

but I really don't understand how you go from coding an interview to getting a theory. It all seems so abstract. Also, I really don't know if grounded theory is a theory or a method or both? Also, when I was taught about grounded theory it was mostly in a lecture format and what I read from my textbook in my methods course. I am at the point now that I need to start using some type of qualitative method for my dissertation proposal, but I have no idea how to do this. I mean I know the definition of what grounded theory means, but how do I use it? Apply it to my own research? I am really upset.

Deborah Piatelli is scheduled to graduate with her doctoral degree in a few months. She was asked to teach an undergraduate research methods course this semester. Deb reflects back on her early career as a graduate student.

Deb: During my first few semesters as a graduate student, I was very confused as to what grounded theory was: was it a method of analysis or a method of inquiry? Is any inductive analysis grounded theory? Is any study with an inductive question a grounded theory study? What constitutes a 'grounded theory' study? If I use grounded theory to analyse my data, is this a grounded theory study?

Contained within Eric, Kati, and Deb's experiences are many challenges that emerge in the learning of qualitative methods and grounded theory in particular. Students bump up against qualitative methods and generally expect them to be a variant of quantitative methods, wanting to test hypotheses and to follow a particular theoretical orientation. The teaching of grounded theory in particular often involves moving students from a deductive mode of thinking to an inductive one, but this transition poses some difficult challenges. Students may want to have a particular set of grounded theory steps to follow, thus grounded theory's inductive method with its upward spiral process can be confusing for students. Some students are not clear about what constitutes a grounded theory. Is being inductive the primary criterion when considering whether or not one is conducting a 'grounded theory'? Students are also unsure whether or not grounded theory is a method of inquiry or a method of analysis or both. We tackle issues of teaching grounded theory by beginning with a case study of the pedagogical issues involved in one college classroom.

TEACHING GROUNDED THEORY: A CASE STUDY

We begin with a case study that examines one college instructor's experience with teaching a grounded theory section of her undergraduate methods course. We will intersperse her experiences with the voices of those who have grappled with learning grounded theory and qualitative methods in general. We move to a general discussion of the pedagogy of grounded theory within the classroom setting and discuss teaching strategies that empower students' learning of grounded theory and address continued areas of student confusion. We then take up the challenges instructors and students face externally (outside their classrooms) by analyzing institutional barriers to the teaching and learning of grounded theory and qualitative methods in general at the departmental/disciplinary level.

TEACHING GROUNDED THEORY TO UNDERGRADUATES: WHAT WORKS, WHAT DOESN'T, AND WHAT CONFUSION REMAINS?

Setting the scene

Deborah Piatelli is an advanced graduate student in a department of sociology that has both qualitative and quantitative faculty and a qualitative and quantitative research program. She is teaching an undergraduate methods course and agreed to talk with me about her experience and to write some of her reflections on teaching grounded theory. I began by asking her to reflect on her own experience with learning and practicing grounded theory and asked how she planned to teach grounded theory to her undergraduate students. Deb located her discussion of grounded theory in the qualitative 'analysis' section of her course. Deb notes:

> Thus far in the course, we have applied a deductive approach to inquiry and analysis—the survey assignment. Some students have begun to experiment with an inductive analysis (open-ended survey questions) and have begun to develop inductive research questions for their research proposal.

Deb started out her course by talking about the differences between an inductive and deductive approach to research and stressed the different epistemologies inherent in these modes of knowledge building. Deb's pedagogical approach is very experiential: she does a lecture followed by an in-class exercise, usually having her students work in groups. There is often a take-home assignment for students to complete after an in-class exercise.

Let's look behind the scenes as Deb describes her reflections to me on how she will teach grounded theory to her students:

> Deb: It wasn't until I read Kathy Charmaz's work (2000) and began the process of constructing my dissertation proposal that I came to my own understanding that grounded theory is both a method of inquiry and a method of analysis. For me, grounded theory goes hand-in-hand with inductive inquiry. As a method of inquiry, a grounded theory approach resonates with the principles of my constructivist and feminist epistemology and shaped how I approached the research process from developing a research question, to collecting data, to theoretically sampling participants, to analysing data. As a method of analysis, grounded theory demanded the continuous interplay of data collection, analysis, and reflection that in turn allowed for emerging lines of inquiry and themes that may have gone unnoticed in a deductive or objectivist approach to data collection and analysis.

> Sharlene: You are about to teach the section on grounded theory to your students. What do you want to accomplish in teaching grounded theory?

> Deb: What I hope to accomplish in discussing grounded theory in the qualitative analysis section of the course is to give students a direct way to apply grounded theory to their interview assignment. By actually doing a grounded theory analysis on their interview data, I wish to give students an opportunity to experience the differences in analysing data deductively (survey) vs. inductively. How do students feel interpreting another person's words? Are there meanings behind the words on the page that the students factor into their codes? Will the student experience an 'ah ha' moment where an emergent theme

from the interview surprises them? How does the inductive analysis process influence how the students would choose their next participant and/or conduct their next interview? These are some of the reflections I will ask students to write about in their papers.

Getting a reading of students' experiences with the teaching of Grounded Theory

Deb and I co-created a short set of open-ended questions, and I asked her to distribute these questions to her students. I hoped to take stock of how students were thinking about the idea of grounded theory after Deb's initial lecture on it. Deb had spoken generally about inductive and deductive research, using grounded theory as an example of inductive research. From a perusal of the questionnaires, Deb's typical student was in his or her junior year with a smaller number who were sophomores or seniors (range: about 19–21 years). This was most students' first exposure to a methods course and their first introduction to grounded theory. In answer to the question, 'Can you tell me in your own words what you think "grounded theory" means?' most students had difficulty articulating what it was, although a few students brought in the idea of theory generation. There were, however, some very innovative responses:

- Theory that isn't all up high in the sky and keeps its head when stuff gets heavy.
- I think that 'grounded theory' is a theory that is based on some sort of subject matter already known.

Only two students articulated some of the basic tenets of grounded theory:

- I think grounded theory means to do research first and then develop a theory. In this way, the theory is 'grounded'—supported by the data.
- Generating theory from the interplay of data collection and analysis.

When I asked Deb to look over the students' responses to the questionnaire, she responded:

> Deb: I expected that students would describe grounded theory as (1) a part of the inductive method of inquiry where the researcher develops theory from the data and/or (2) a method of analysis—that data is collected and analysed simultaneously in order to generate a theory. I am surprised that only 9 students were able to offer some type of definition. Only 9 out of the 22 students actually answered the question. In the subsequent class, when I asked why many people did not answer the question, they said they didn't know how to define it, so they left it blank. Some said they thought it was a theory, but they were not really sure what type of theory it was. A few students admitted to not having done the reading.

Inside the classroom

Deb assigned several readings on grounded theory before presenting the first formal lecture on the topic to her students. She also assigned an in-class exercise and an out-of-class assignment on analyzing interview data they collected. Deb describes her teaching of grounded theory this way:

> Deb: Later in the semester, I held two classes on qualitative data analysis. The first was a 15-minute discussion on grounded theory as a method of analysis and a method of inquiry. Next, I demonstrated how I used grounded theory in my dissertation as both a method of analysis and inquiry, because their next assignment was asking them to use grounded theory as a method of analysis ... On the board, I detailed how I used grounded theory to build theory, stepping through the process of coding, category and theme development, and then to theory. In the next class, using HyperResearch, a computer software program for analysing qualitative data, I visually demonstrated how the coding process worked, moving from open coding to focused coding to category/theme development and eventually theory for one specific theoretical finding in my dissertation.

The in-class exercise

> Next, I broke the class into groups of four and distributed excerpts from an interview I conducted that had four segments. I asked them to individually begin open coding the first response in the interview. Once they finished I asked them to discuss the codes as a group. I asked them the following questions:
>
> • What did you decide to code? Did you highlight similar portions of the text?
> • Did you assign similar codes? If they were different, talk about your different interpretations.
> • What is your overall interpretation of what the respondent is saying in this response? Does the group agree or disagree?
>
> Interestingly, on average most students highlighted the same text, but labeled it differently. We had a good discussion on interpretation and most times we came to agreement on what the code definitions were and how they were similar. We noted all the codes on the board, after rectifying the definitions, and then we began the process of category/theme development. We repeated the process for all four segments of the interview. Next we reviewed the themes we generated and hypothesized about the theory—what was this person saying in the interview about the research question? All in all, the entire class agreed on the interpretation—which led us into a conversation about interpretive validity.

The assignment

> Their next assignment asked them to do an interview, transcribe it, and analyse the data using a grounded theory approach. They were required to generate at least one theme from their interview from the open coding process and then hypothesize about what theory might be generated about their research question. I'm still reading through the assignments, but the 10 I've read indicate that students certainly have grasped the process of grounded theory as a method of analysis. Most students generated 20 or so codes and several themes. Some took the discussion further in their papers and stated that they would modify their sampling approach (more theoretical vs. purposive) and many decided they would conduct a more open, exploratory type of interview and/or do the interviews in two phases. We also held a class devoted to discussing the interview assignment, and four themes emerged from these conversations: (1) Insider/outsider was experienced in almost all the interviews in the way it affected the data collected. In other words, students acknowledged that they needed to practice reflexivity before, during, and after the interview process. Many students realized that either their interview guides or their probing questions were biased, leading, or irrelevant to the participants' experiences; (2) Several students realized that their research questions required either more open or more structured interview guides; (3) A few students acknowledged that grounded theory was not an appropriate method of analysis for their data and research question; (4) A couple of students acknowledged that the interview method was

not a proper choice for their research question as they structured it—they should have made it more inductive.

After Deb's students completed their out-of-class assignment, we administered another questionnaire asking students to define the term 'grounded theory.' Here is a sampling of her students' comments:

- Grounded theory is a method of making a theory, where the theory is built from data collected instead of making a theory before collecting the data.
- To create a theory from the ground up.

If there remained any confusion, it was the voices of a few students who were still thinking more deductively and were citing the need to have a theory before gathering data. One stark illustration came from a student who defined grounded theory as 'a solid base theory used to begin research. Can be a foundation to be built upon.'

The questionnaire also asked, 'What is it (if anything) that is not clear to you about the term "grounded theory"?' While some students did not cite any ambiguities, many had some questions about the theory and methods. These questions centered on the distinction between induction and deduction, and there was also hesitation in giving up the idea of a prior theory or hypothesis.

> The only question I have is even though one builds the theory from the data, does the researcher still enter the process with a specific aim/hypothesis?

Additional points of confusion for students were the extent to which grounded theory is different from other inductive methods and when it can be used in a research project. Students wanted more practical applications of its use in research. Students were also asked to rate their overall ability to apply grounded theory to a research project using a five point fixed choice response with possible answers of 'excellent,' 'good,' 'moderate,' 'somewhat poor,' and 'poor.' Most students rated their ability as 'moderate,' although a few said 'good,' and one student selected 'somewhat poor.' No one chose the 'excellent' or 'poor' categories.

It appears that application of a grounded theory approach remains an issue for students; knowing what grounded theory is and applying it are two different learning challenges. I asked Deb what her thoughts were about teaching her research methods course next time.

> Deb: In thinking about next semester, I don't think I would introduce grounded theory in a different way or earlier in the course. For an undergraduate methods course, I think working with the concept of grounded theory as part of the inductive cycle, but also as a method of analysis, is almost enough for them to handle. I will however consider bringing in some research studies using grounded theory instead of using my dissertation in both classes. Perhaps discussing the studies in the first session and then using HyperResearch to demonstrate my own research might be more effective.

After reflecting on Deb's teaching experience and the comments of her students, it appears that utilizing a more *experiential approach* is of great value in helping students to understand the differences between 'inductive and deductive' approaches. Deb starts out her course by providing students with a basic understanding of methods as rooted in a specific type of *epistemological stance.* In doing this, she is already linking epistemology with methodology and method. Furthermore she focuses on differing epistemologies by contrasting a positivistic approach with an interpretative approach. She uses specific in-class and out-of-class assignments. Deb's comparison of survey research interviewing with in-depth interviewing reinforces this distinction for her students. It is also clear that students need specific examples of how other researchers carry out this mode of inquiry and analysis. Deb provides specific examples of both inductive and deductive approaches and uses her own dissertation research to give students a specific grounded theory analysis. Deb's use of computer-assisted software in the teaching of grounded theory further explicates the intricacies of a grounded theory analysis. Given the short period of time students spent on this topic, they obtained a moderate understanding of both the meaning and practice of grounded theory. It is clear that the standard undergraduate methods curriculum does not give students enough time to absorb and practice the skills they acquire. It also raises the questions of how students can solidify and follow up on the skills they acquire in a standard methods course, for these skills can easily atrophy over even a short period of time.

Our glimpse inside Deb's classroom has given us a perspective on the many 'internal challenges' teachers and students can experience when learning these new methods. We can categorize these challenges as a set of 'internal conundrums' in the teaching of grounded theory.

CONUNDRUMS IN THE METHODS CLASSROOM

- 'How can I get my students to understand the differences between an inductive research design and a deductive one?'

This question was of major importance to Deb as she prepared to teach her research methods course, and we can see that it appears to be a major conundrum when we review the literature on the teaching of qualitative methods and grounded theory (Fontes & Piercy, 2000; Huehls, 2005; Stoppard, 2002). Huehls (2005), who teaches graduate students, puts it this way:

Grounded theory may be particularly difficult for beginning student researchers to grasp because the process reverses the order of empirical research—hypothesis generation followed by data collection. The idea that theories can be generated from data—let alone qualitative data—contradicts the scientific tradition they were taught in elementary school science (p. 328).

Within her graduate-level qualitative classroom, Stoppard (2002) observes, 'The problem seemed to be that students were puzzled by the idea of doing research without using numbers or statistics' (p. 147). An overview of the literature on qualitative methods reveals that this is a common problem encountered by research methods teachers when their students embark on a research methods course. Many of these students expect the course to be presented with a quantitative model of research. As Hesse-Biber and Leavy note, 'The *quantitative research* design is typically presented as a "wheel" or a circle. The various parts of the research process make up the circumference and one can begin one's research at different parts of the wheel. The research process is also presented as a series of steps' (2006: 74; see also Crabtree & Miller, 1999: 9).

Figure 15.1 is best understood if we consider it as a metaphorical ladder (Crabtree & Miller, 1999: 8). This form of inquiry seeks the 'Truth,' and the arrows point only in one direction to reach this truth. It should be noted that while there is no interaction between the 'rungs' of this ladder, it is an important tool in that the researcher 'climbs a linear ladder to an ultimate objective truth' (Crabtree & Miller, 1999: 8).

Hein's (2004) report on his teaching of qualitative methods, and Deborah Piatelli's classroom experience in teaching grounded theory illustrate some of the same problems that were reported in Stoppard's evaluation of the classroom.

Step 9: Revise Hypotheses

⇧

Step 8: Conclusions

⇧

Step 7: Data Analysis

⇧

Step 6: Data Collection

⇧

Step 5: Instrumentation & Sampling

⇧

Step 4: Research Design (Methods)

⇧

Step 3: Hypothesis Formulation

⇧

Step 2: Literature Review

⇧

Step 1: Define Research

Figure 15.1   Diagram of the quantitative (positivistic) research process: Testing of theory (adapted from Crabtree & Miller, 1999).

All of these instructors observed how struggling students had difficulty under-standing a qualitative research paradigm. In particular, Hein traces his students' frustrations in making the transition from a quantitative to a qualitative way of thinking and what they perceive to be a lack of 'universal criteria for evaluating qualitative research' (p. 29). He also observes that there is a 'perceived lack of structure associated with the general process of developing themes to capture the meaning of excerpts' (p. 32) that can frustrate students. Similarly, Stoppard notes that learning qualitative methods can challenge students' perceptions of verity and knowledge. Stoppard (2002) uses a clever analogy and writes, 'Like the experience of learning a new language, students must juggle the ideas we discuss in class with a quite different set of assumptions in other courses' (p. 149). Both instructors found the complexities and tests of learning such a dynamic research method were unexpected challenges for their students. Deb also comments on this issue within her classroom environment. She notes:

> It's about getting students comfortable with trusting alternative forms of knowledge. In other words, the quantitative model relies on academic, scientific knowledge where the qualitative model relies on participant's knowledge. I felt students struggled in getting comfortable that we build theory from people's lives and also getting comfortable with their own interpretive voice. This really addresses the question students had in my course, namely 'It's a theory, but what kind of theory is it?'

Moving from a quantitative to a qualitative paradigm requires a set of skills on the part of the teacher and the student, for the environment within the qualitative classroom is dynamic, complex, and developing. An important strategy for enabling students who are enmeshed in a quantitative paradigm is to compare and contrast the elements of each research design. Some useful questions that might help students in the transition from one paradigm to the other are the following (Hesse-Biber & Leavy, 2006: 75):

- How would the quantitative model of research design be revised if one were to move to a grounded theory of social inquiry?
- What elements would remain, what elements would be added, discarded?
- How would you relate elements of the process to each other in a holistic manner?
- What is the role of theory or how does theory come into play in a grounded theory model?

With regard to this issue, Deb notes:

> Students felt a bit more comfortable when I explained that while they were constructing theory from their data, they still bring in literature/social theory. So they are not generating theory in isolation from other work. This is where their hypotheses or various theories can come into play—not used to construct the study, but rather coming into play during the study.

A quantitative paradigm assumes that knowledge is 'out there' waiting to be found, and the researcher's task is to be 'objective' and not allow their attitudes, values, and beliefs to enter into the research process. Grounded theory, in contrast, stresses the importance of the *symbolic meanings* individuals bring to the research process. The research becomes a *dynamic interaction* between the researcher and researched, and the goal is to generate a theory rather than to test a hypothesis. This does not mean, however, that qualitative researchers have no interest in 'testing' out their ideas in a process of analytical induction.

We can use Figure 15.2 as a guide to understanding the iterative relationship that exists between data collection, data analysis, and theory generation. Collectively, this relationship is known as *analytical induction*. There is an interdependent relationship between data collection and data analysis, for one is analyzing and building new ideas from new data throughout the entire process. This is an important exchange, for these new ideas are then used to explore and analyze other pieces of data. As Hesse-Biber and Leavy (2006) observe:

> There is a dynamic interaction between steps 6 (data collection), 7 (data analysis), and 3 (hypothesis formulation). Data collection (step 6) and data analysis (step 7) can lead to the creation of ideas/hypotheses concerning the data. This in turn might lead the researcher to collect specific types of data via a particular sampling procedure (step 5); an example of this step would be to sample specific cases to test out these ideas (theoretical sampling). The researcher moves back and forth in the steps of research almost as if he or she is doing a dynamic dance routine with unstructured steps (p. 76).

Indeed, this 'dance routine' is a useful tool to help us understand this fluid research process. Just as music may change unexpectedly at a dance, the data or conditions of a finding or analysis may change without notice. Like a dancer on the stage, the researcher is bound only by the spirit of his/her craft and the twists and turns of the research process. Many scholars and researchers, including Crabtree and Miller (1999), have also examined this unique 'dance-like' relationship in their studies.

What seems difficult to convey to the students is that grounded theory moves from order to disorder to order in a continuous cycle. One takes data in the form of interview transcripts, field notes, and documents and then decontextualizes it all.

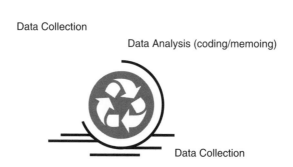

Data Collection

Data Analysis (coding/memoing)

Data Collection

Data Analysis

Figure 15.2   Diagram of the 'iterative' process in the analysis of data (adapted from Hesse-Biber & Leavy, 2006: 348).

This means that the researcher takes these data, segments the text, and finally sorts these segments by recombining and reconfiguring them into another level of order. The sequence begins again: order (level one) → disorder (level two) → order (level three).

- 'How can we bridge the differences in thinking about what it means to do deductive as opposed to inductive work so that our students understand different modes of inquiry?'

Let's look at a concrete example of how grounded theory moves from order to disorder to order. This example is adapted from Hesse-Biber and Leavy (2004: 411–412).

Grounded Theory: From order to disorder to order
The text in Box 15.1 was taken from one of my interviews with college-aged women (Hesse-Biber, 1996) and concerns their eating patterns and disordered eating habits. I began the process of re-ordering this text (recontextualizing) by coding the text and providing a label to a portion of the excerpted text. So, for example, the section of text that reads 'I always wanted to be the thinnest' was first coded 'thinnest' and 'prettiest.'

The first few codes listed are 'literal' codes, meaning that the words also appear within the text. These are descriptive code categories. The codes become more 'analytical' as we go down the code list, meaning that they are not linked as tightly to the text itself, but rely on the researcher's insights for drawing out interpretation. We are now moving toward a more 'focused coding' procedure that consists of building and clarifying concepts. 'Focused coding' employed in grounded theory starts to examine all the data in a category, by comparing each segment of data with every other segment working up to a clear definition of each concept. Such concepts are then named and become 'codes' (Charmaz, 1983: 117; Hesse-Biber & Leavy, 2004: 412). As Hesse-Biber and Leavy (2004: 412) note: 'Modifying code categories becomes important in *the development* of more abstract code categories which aid in the generation of theoretical constructs. This process, in turn, is essential to the generation of theory-building. One would only begin to do this type of coding after examining a number of interviews, retrieving the text associated with similar passages of text from other interviews, and seeing if common themes occur.'

Box 15.1 Excerpt from Interview (Hesse-Biber, 1996)

I always wanted to be the thinnest, the	>Thinnest, Prettiest
prettiest. I wanted to look like the girls	>look like girls in magazines
in the magazines. I'm going to have so	>boys will love me
many boyfriends, and boys are going	>positive body image
to be so in love with me, I won't have to	>provides economic resources
work and I'll be taken care of for the	>**Thin Rationale**
rest of my life	>Thin as a means of
	security
	>Media creates standards

As I continued to code additional interviews, I discerned some general themes emerging from the text. Two codes that are noted further down in this single text segment were 'thinness as a means of security' and 'media creates standards.' 'Thinness as a means of security' captures the words and goals of my respondent—that she wants to have a boyfriend, love, money, and to be taken care of. Indeed, when I read over other interviews with eating disordered women, I found there were additional reasons respondents wanted to be thin, namely, 'thinness as healthy,' 'thinness as empowering,' and so on. These insights (which I also developed as theoretical memos) eventually led to the development of a more encompassing analytical category I termed 'thinness rationales,' of which the code category 'thinness as a means of security' was a sub-set. A second analytical category, 'media creates standards' of behavior was discovered in a similar manner. As my interviewing with my respondents progressed, I found myself learning from the new analytical categories I created, constantly testing them out on newly collected data, asking: Did they apply? Are there any negative cases? I wove analytical memos (writing down my ideas of what it meant to be thin, for example) as I continued to interview and analyze my data.

Janet Stoppard (2002) offers one suggestion to offset students' concerns about moving toward the qualitative paradigm in her methods class. She added course materials that focused on the qualitative/quantitative debate since some of her students 'feared that quantitative methods would be dismissed, leaving them with little to hold on to' (p. 148). In her experience, this addition helped to assuage some of the students' worries and anxieties. Stoppard is not the first researcher to explore new ways of teaching these methods in the classroom. Several methods and exercises have been used to teach these methods to novice students. One method that has become particularly useful in helping students understand and appreciate the differences and linkages between these two different research design approaches is to introduce the underlying idea of two different epistemologies. Many qualitative research methods courses tend to avoid the philosophical issues regarding the basic assumptions of reality that underlie different research methods approaches. Epistemology asks: What is the nature of social reality? Who is a 'knower' and what can be known? In some cases, a research methods course may not have the time or inclination to answer these questions. Consequently, it is difficult for student researchers to get the idea that there are multiple points of view on social reality when they move from a quantitative to a qualitative paradigm of knowledge building. It is particularly challenging to grasp the notion that reality is socially constructed. It should be noted that teaching methods to students as a set of tools *short circuits* the underlying issues of epistemology and methodology. Instead there needs to be a more holistic perspective on the research process, one that links method to methodology and epistemology. Juliet Corbin (Cisneros-Puebla, 2004) is one of many scholars who are critical of this lack of emphasis on the philosophical traditions underlying the use of specific methods. Corbin's criticisms of her and Strauss's book, *Basics of Qualitative Research*, has led to the publication of a third edition containing a section that discusses epistemological traditions. Corbin notes:

> In the previous editions of *Basics* the section on philosophical underpinnings was removed by the editor because of what he stated was a lack of space. This time I will refuse to remove it. It is especially important to have this section now because we know that our perspectives and belief systems influence how we view and work with data. We want our readers to understand why it is important to look at experiences, feelings, action/interaction, to denote the structure or context in which these are located, and why it is important to study process (paragraph 21).

Juliet Corbin's message especially resonated with one of Deb's students in her methods course who wrote about the importance of epistemology. Having completed her research proposal for the course, the student notes:

> My desire to do an inductive study comes from my epistemological beliefs. I came to understand my epistemology or in other words my philosophical belief system about knowledge and how I believe knowledge is discovered, created, and known after learning how I most commonly shape a research question and what method of research I feel is most useful towards my research. After closely examining the various paradigms and perspectives of research methodology, my epistemology seemed to be most closely aligned with the critical perspective on social reality. By applying this framework, I truly think that my epistemological beliefs about research in the social science area can shine through ... I think it is almost impossible for a researcher to not have a point of view or have no biases related to a social issue. Most research should have a hint of the value-orientation of the researchers. I do not think a researcher can ever completely detach themselves from their research and close their opinion off from that subject.

THE INTERNAL CONUNDRUMS CONTAINED WITHIN GROUNDED THEORY METHODS THAT CONFUSE STUDENTS AND INSTRUCTORS

Some of the debate surrounding grounded theory centers on a controversy over the central tenets of the method. These tenets were originally espoused by Barney Glaser and Anselm Strauss in their work, *The Discovery of Grounded Theory* (1967), but a split occurred between the authors after the text's publication. Glaser (1978, 1992) and Strauss (1987) created separate theories and ideas that deviated from this earlier work and argued divergent ideas on grounded theory. These texts and others (Charmaz, 2000; Lincoln & Guba, 1985; Melia, 1996; Miles & Huberman, 1984; Robrecht, 1995; Seale, 1999; Strauss & Corbin, 1990) reflect the differences in how these theorists originally conceived the idea of grounded theory. Dey (1999) comments on this 'mixed marriage' within grounded theory and believes it has its origins in the combining of two rival analytical traditions:

> These traditions were represented on the one hand, by Glaser, who brought to grounded theory the rigor associated with the quantitative survey methods of sociological research at Columbia University; and on the other hand, by Strauss, whose background lay in 'symbolic interactionist' tradition of qualitative research as taught and practiced at the University of Chicago ... (p. 25).

In addition, Strauss and Corbin's (1990) emphasis on replication, generalization, and verification resembles more of a combination of inductive and deductive design, but Glaser asserts that this takes grounded theory away from its roots of theory generation. Glaser hoped theory generation would be a more open-ended, flexible process whereby the researcher 'should simply code and analyze categories and properties with theoretical codes which will emerge and generate their complex theory of a complex world' (Glaser, 1992: 71).

Babchuk (1997) points out that the practice of grounded theory in many disciplines has become an 'umbrella term' that consists of a range of practices. Research conducted in the field of education reflects the confusion in applying the method and/or 'ingenuity' on the part of researchers. He notes:

> These articles range from the use of only one of the grounded theory postulates (e.g., constant comparison) or use of grounded theory in conjunction with other methods, to using selected aspects of this methodology which analysts find convenient or appealing given the nature of their research, to utilizing most but not all of the recommended techniques outlined in one of the publications mentioned above (usually Strauss & Corbin, 1990), to attempting to carefully follow the full complement of rules and dictates. One begins to wonder if this diverse interpretation of grounded theory procedures is representative of the ingenuity of educators and their research designs or simply confusion over method, and whether this flexibility of application should be viewed as one of this methodology's strengths or one of its shortcomings (paragraph 11).

Kathy Charmaz (2000) stresses the differences between 'objectivist' and 'constructivist' approaches to grounded theory. There are tensions contained within different types of grounded theory that also echo students' confusion about induction versus deduction and between subjectivity and objectivity. As Charmaz notes:

> A constructivist grounded theory distinguishes between the real and the true. The constructivist approach does not seek truth—single, universal, and lasting. Still, it remains realist because it addresses human realities and assumes the existence of real worlds. However, neither human realities nor real worlds are unidimensional ... The constructivist approach assumes that what we take as real, as objective knowledge and truth, is based upon our perspective ... (p. 523).

She also observes that:

> ... objectivist grounded theorists adhere more closely to positivistic canons of traditional science ... They assume that following a systematic set of methods leads them to discover reality and to construct a provisionally true, testable, and ultimately verifiable 'theory' of it ... (p. 524).

It is therefore important for the researchers to reflect on their personal standpoint regarding grounded theory. What specific postulates of grounded theory do you want to emphasize in your teaching? What type of grounded theory and what specific tenets of grounded theory do you practice and teach? You might want to consider, for example, the level at which you are teaching qualitative methods—as an introductory undergraduate course or as a more advanced graduate course? Have your students had any previous experience in using a grounded theory approach as part of their prior research methods courses?

INDUCTIVE BIAS OF GROUNDED THEORY

Another issue related to the teaching and practice of grounded theory is rooted in students' confusion over what it means to practice 'induction.' This issue came up in the comments of Deb's students. One student wrote, 'It is hard to understand how no theory is supporting the data collection.' Deb also notes, 'Another student suggested the same question. We had discussions about this—does a researcher have to "go in blind" in order to do grounded theory? How is that possible?' Teachers of grounded theory echo the various student concerns expressed by some of Deb's students. They frame their concern around what they see as grounded theory's 'inductive bias' (Altricher & Posch, 1989: 23), which asserts the specific expectation that the researcher must enter the study with an unbiased mind. As Glaser and Strauss (1967) note, researchers should begin their work 'without any preconceived theory that dictates, prior to the research, "relevancies" in concepts and hypotheses' (p. 33). Glaser and Strauss ask the researcher to 'ignore the literature of theory' (p. 37) and enter a research study without any theoretical hunches. This tenet of grounded theory is a difficult task to accomplish and some researchers suggest that it is simply unrealistic and may force researchers to fit their ideas into preexisting categories. Strauss and Corbin (1994) suggest, however, that the inductive aspects of grounded theory may have been overstated and call for 'theoretical sensitivity' that acknowledges the importance of researchers taking into account their prior experiences and theoretical ideas. They note:

> Researchers carry into their research the sensitizing possibilities of their training, reading, and research experience, as well as explicit theories that might be useful if played against systematically gathered data, in conjunction with theories emerging from analysis of these data (p. 277).

Yet these diverging points of view on the extent to which prior knowledge finds its way into a research project remain confusing to students, and we can appreciate this issue, given the divergent points of view which emanate from the founders of grounded theory. Those students who follow Glaser's approach seek to know exactly how grounded theorists do away with their research and theoretical ideas on a given project. As Barbour notes:

> To portray data as speaking for itself ... sidesteps some difficult problems and risks ... We are unlikely to conceptualize a research question or to be able to formulate a research design that is fundable without explicit reference to existing bodies of knowledge and explicit or implicit reference to existing theoretical frameworks (2003: 1022).

Those who follow Strauss and Corbin's advice want to know: How do I follow the tenet of 'theoretical sensitivity' in the practice and teaching of grounded theory?

The inductive conundrum that lies within grounded theory can be a fruitful teaching moment for the instructor on the importance of 'reflexivity' in the research process:

> Reflexivity begins with an understanding of the importance of one's own values and attitudes within the research process and this begins prior to entering the field. Reflexivity means taking a critical look inward—a reflection on one's own lived reality and experiences, a self-reflection or journey. How does your own biography impact the research process? What shapes the questions you chose to study and your approach to studying them? How does the specific social, economic, and political context in which you reside impact the research process at all levels? (Hesse-Biber, 2007:129)

Reflexivity is the recognition that 'all knowledge is affected by the social conditions under which it is produced and that it is grounded in both the social location and the social biography of the observer and the observed' (Mann & Kelley, 1997: 392). A useful pedagogical tool to practice reflexivity in the class is the following 'reflexive exercise' (Hesse-Biber, 2007: 131).

> **Take 20 minutes and write down the various ways your position in society impacts the way you observe and perceive others in your daily life.** What particular biases, if any, do I bring to and/or impose on my research?
>
> - How do my specific values, attitudes, and theoretical perspectives influence the research style I take on? How do my values, attitudes, and beliefs enter into the research process? Do I only ask questions from my own perspective?
> - How does my own agenda shape what I ask and what I find?
> - How does my positionality impact how I gather, analyse, and interpret my data? From whose perspective do I perform these actions?

You might also ask your students to keep a research journal in which they reflect on their own research throughout the methods course. This can be quite helpful to students as they evaluate their own experiences in learning these methods. The next section of this text focuses on the problems and roadblocks students might encounter during this pivotal learning process.

STUDENTS' PROBLEMS WITH THE ANALYSIS OF DATA

Many instructors point out the difficulties students have at this stage of a methods course. Grant Blank (2004) observed that his graduate students struggled especially with a unit focused on creating code categories. He discovered that novice researchers are not wholly prepared for the demands of research. Blank found that:

> ... The most common mistake that students made was to underestimate the difficulty involved in creating a set of categories for the first assignment. Some students procrastinated. To these students, creating category schemes sounded relatively simple, but they found that it was not simple and they ran out of time (p. 193).

Blank is not alone in his observations, for many instructors have helped students face the surprises and unexpected challenges when inculcating skills in grounded theory and qualitative research. Many of these instructors have also discovered the importance of concrete examples and classroom exercises, and the 'hands-on' learning approach has become imperative to the teaching of these methods. Much of the literature focused on qualitative methods and the grounded theory approach praises the use of guided research projects and hands-on examples to help students grasp the concepts of these methods (Blank, 2004; Este et al., 1998; Janesick, 2004; Keen, 1996; Nyden, 1991). These exercises help students with skill building, but they also stress the importance of creativity in and engagement with qualitative data (McAllister & Rowe, 2003).

Qualitative data analysis programs are now widely used among qualitative researchers, but the assessment and evaluation of their use in the teaching of qualitative methods, especially grounded theory, is not widespread compared to our understanding of users' experiences with the usage of quantitative software data analysis packages. Many issues have been raised as to how to effectively incorporate these data analysis tools into the methods classroom. Questions are raised as to *when* to introduce software into the teaching of qualitative methods. How can instructors assess student learning of grounded theory with software? We address some of these pedagogical issues in the next section.

Computer-assisted software to assist with a grounded theory: A software tale

I asked Deborah Piatelli to describe her students' experiences in using computer-assisted software in her methods classroom:

> Some students said they used SPSS for their survey data analysis (I said they could if they knew it but didn't require it). I found that students that used SPSS didn't do as good a job with their data analysis as students who did it by hand. What do I make of this? I think there is value in having students do data analysis manually the first few times, but also showing them the benefits of using computer software. When I introduced HyperResearch, I said that they should do a few interviews (in their first research project) by hand and then move to the computer. We went over the 'dangers' of using a computer package, but I said that once you do the analysis by hand you are able to discipline yourself on the computer (not doing search and code immediately for instance) and it becomes a very valuable tool. It's like not teaching kids math on a calculator.

Instructors introduce software into the teaching of qualitative analysis for a variety of reasons. Blank (2004) used qualitative software in his class to teach methods and, more specifically, to further his goal of teaching 'qualitative analysis that was practical, systematic, valid and verifiable' (p. 288). He also hoped that computer-assisted software programs would speed up the learning process. Blank based this argument primarily on the speed and ease computers bring to the research process. Blank asserts, 'Good qualitative software makes good research easier. Software supports structure by helping researchers organize their research. Flexible software makes the organization easy to change, thereby promoting flexibility and creativity' (p. 189). From this perspective, we can see how software packages would enrich and simplify the elaborate learning process that typifies qualitative methods. The computer also becomes a handy tool in this case because it speeds up the research process to give the researcher more time for other data and research matters (Smith & Hesse-Biber, 1996). For an overall discussion of the problems and prospects of computer-assisted software, see: Fielding and Lee, 1991, 1998; Kelle, 1995.

Not all researchers have welcomed computer software to qualitative research with open arms. Many scholars and researchers are dubious when considering the use of computers to 'accelerate' the research process, for they wonder how qualitative and grounded theory analyses can be accelerated and still maintain the intimacy that exists between the qualitative researchers and their data. Juliet Corbin (Cisneros-Puebla, 2004) contends that there is already a lack of theory building that is inherent in the teaching of qualitative research, and students' reluctance to take the time needed to analyze data does not bode well for the field. She argues, 'Students don't want to put in the long hard work that goes into theory building. Yet I don't understand how we can continue to develop the various professions without a knowledge base to build on theory, theory grounded in data' (paragraph 17).

Corbin's arguments are augmented by those of Moya Morison and Jim Moir (1998). These scholars argue that the use of CAQDAS may in fact create a barrier in a student's understanding of what it means to analyze qualitative data. They allude to other researchers' fears that computer software will dehumanize the research process and eliminate the personal aspects of data collection. Computers, they assert, have the possibility of 'drawing the researcher into literally a programmatic type of data analysis based upon the systematization of the research process' (p. 114). They also assert that the idea of computers 'freeing up time' endangers the idea of the researcher 'handling, reading, and re-reading ... as part of the analytic process' (p. 115). Morison and Moir also warn researchers not to jump into software analysis without some thought, for 'in some cases the user may also be aware of only a fraction of the software's capabilities' (p. 115). They suggest researchers err on the side of caution when selecting and contemplating software packages in qualitative research (see also Hesse-Biber, 1995).

Grounded Theory and CAQDAS

Some of the earliest developers of qualitative data analysis software programs explicitly used some elements of grounded theory principles in software they created (Muhr, 1991; Richards & Richards, 1991; Seidel & Clark, 1984). These early software features allowed patterns and themes to 'emerge' from the data. Lonkila (1995) further clarifies the connection between grounded theory and early CAQDAS programs by discussing the analytical procedures that the two have in common, which includes coding, constant comparison, creating linkages, memoing, and theory generation. Although the first researchers/developers of CAQDAS often found elements of grounded theory useful, for the most part, they did not intend for their software to mimic a grounded theory methodology (or any particular analytical model). Rather, they wanted their programs to assist with some of their more cumbersome analysis techniques; techniques that many other qualitative researchers—both those dedicated to grounded theory and those with other methodological preferences—also happened to employ.

While a grounded theory model of analysis had some influence on the developers of early CAQDAS programs, Fielding and Lee's (1996) research on user's experience with CAQDAS programs postulates that qualitative data analysis software does not compel its users to conduct their analyses in particular ways (see also Fielding & Lee, 2002).

Software can be quite helpful in the time crunch that many research methods teachers face, but it may do harm by giving students the impression that analysis is not tedious and difficult work. There is also concern that students might not realize that research is a trying, intricate craft if software is simplifying the less-palatable aspects of their research. The disagreement over the use of software in the classroom, especially with novice researchers, also raises concerns about when it is most appropriate to introduce software in the teaching of grounded theory analysis. Getting on board the software 'bandwagon' may pressure instructors, many of whom are also novices in this type of technology, to introduce software too soon. This is especially apt to happen in a survey of research methods course where students already spend little time learning about grounded theory. The outcome may ultimately be detrimental to students if they get the impression that qualitative analysis means having a program to do the analysis for you. MacMillan and Koenig (2004) noted that introducing software too early might create 'unrealistic expectations of the software as a methodology; the treatment of qualitative analysis as a single, homogenized category; and the use of grounded theory as a legitimating link between tool and method' (p. 179). The authors encouraged CAQDAS users to consider 'the method of analysis before the software tool and before the research process begins' (p. 184). They hoped this consideration might reduce possible misunderstandings. This argument clearly distinguishes the roles of method versus software and emphasizes the importance of introducing software into the research process at the appropriate time. These programs may not necessarily speed up the analytical process if students spend most of their time concentrating on the intricacies of the software package rather than analyzing the data themselves and thinking about what they mean. Este, Sieppert, and Barsky (1998) examine the pros and cons of software use in their research methods class by assigning students two projects: one with and one without research software. The authors note:

> Students felt that they were not missing any conceptual pieces if they started to learn qualitative research with the aid of software. One student suggested that even when she missed a conceptual piece on the methods side, she learned what she missed very quickly and had to go back to learn it. The computer only follows what the researcher asks it to do. If the researcher gives inappropriate commands, the negative results will be readily apparent (paragraph 9).

There are others who introduce computer technology at an early stage as a vehicle for student learning. Lynn Davie (1996) teaches her students qualitative methods with computers, but she chooses to use the machine itself as a tool rather than focus on particular software packages. Davie divides her class into learning groups that use computer communications programs to work and learn as a team. She uses the computers to create an encouraging environment in the classroom, and she has found that 'the most difficult skill in learning to do qualitative analysis is the ability to see what is in the data' (p. 454). Davie works to bolster students' writing skills to solve this problem. She creates 'learning circles' of about six students that allow the students to help and educate one another through this process. Computer communication was a pivotal aspect of this support system.

We have provided you with a series of issues and practical tips from bridging the qualitative and quantitative divide in the teaching of grounded theory to overcoming some of the hurdles inherent to the basic tenets of grounded theory analysis. However, there are ranges of issues that lie outside the classroom context that upend the teaching of interpretative methods and, in particular, grounded theory. These departmental and interdisciplinary issues determine and impact the ways in which research methods are taught. It is to this set of issues that we now turn.

EXTERNAL CONUNDRUMS IN TEACHING GROUNDED THEORY: THE TALE OF A HOUSE DIVIDED

There are important institutional barriers some teachers and researchers working within an interpretive paradigm may face outside of the classroom environment. Let's go 'behind the scenes' with Judith Preissle, a cutting edge researcher and teacher of qualitative methods in education, as she relates her own personal experiences with some of the institutional challenges of teaching and conducting qualitative research. We join Judith Preissle (Faux, 2004) in the midst of an interview discussing the 'challenges' she confronted in teaching qualitative methods and conducting qualitative research early in her career at the University of Georgia:

> Well, we've really had to educate the larger community on the kinds of expectations you might have with somebody who does something other than experimental, quasi-experimental,

and survey research. You are not going to typically publish as many separate pieces. You're going to do work and publish work that is going to look different. Generally it's been a supportive environment, it's still a demanding environment … When I started out, when I wanted to study something, I just went and studied it. And if I did anything bad, well, maybe my peers would fuss at me but I'm not sure that peer control is any more effective among researchers than it is among doctors and lawyers. So we've had this tremendous influence of federal regulation. I won't say of the ethics of research because although it is intended to promote more ethical treatment and more ethical interaction, it's really, it puts it in a bureaucratic framework and that has problems of its own. But it certainly is control. And I've been on our university IRB [Institutional Review Board], I don't know, 12 years. That has been a challenge. But that would be a challenge anywhere … just like anywhere else, we've been coming to grips on how you get pre-approval for research but you don't know how it's going to turn out, so that's been a struggle for us here, but that's a struggle everywhere. Maybe something unique to Georgia is that we're doing what we're doing using people from many, many, many units across the university and definitely all around the college. And … anything we do is put together with safety pins. I mean it looks really great from the outside but we've had a lot of administrative change and new administrators come in and they want their agenda and so we're still challenged with the task of institutionalizing this work, this program (paragraphs 85–86).

Many academic departments have become immersed in 'paradigm wars' as qualitative methods become more popular and challenge the ways of quantitative methods. Judith Preissle's (Faux, 2004) experiences illustrate the frustrations and challenges this conflict can create. There is a 'methods lag' that stretches across specific disciplines and a 'quantitative bias' that continues to surround federal regulation of the research process. The latter is especially true when one considers the terms of University Institutional Review Boards, for their quantitative framework remains a template for approval of a research project. Preissle's experience also raises an important conundrum for those whose practice of methods remains solidly within an interpretative model of understanding the nature of social reality.

- 'How does the qualitative methods teacher bridge the quantitative/qualitative divide within their particular department or discipline?'

Professors who teach research methods recognize changes in academic climate and are responding to the increased interest in qualitative and mixed-methods research. Yet there remains much resistance on the part of some faculty who are ideologically opposed to qualitative research in their academic departments. A faculty member may in fact be confronted with both active and passive resistance to the integration of a qualitative paradigm into their departments. Issues are also raised as to how to work with resistant faculty. In addition, there may also be faculty who want to have the opportunity to learn more about qualitative research but lack the necessary time, support, or resources to do so.

There are some important constraints to consider when you are thinking about offering a qualitative methods course, and these constraints become particularly important if your course offers a grounded theory perspective. One issue is the general extent to which the climate of your department is hospitable towards qualitative research. While qualitative methods have become more prevalent and accepted within the social sciences, a survey of Canadian qualitative researchers

(Rennie et al., 2000) found that '... the majority of arts/science graduate programmes in psychology in this country do not have any qualitative researchers on faculty and that, for those that do, the numbers are small' (paragraph 8). The study asserts that the status of qualitative research in Canadian universities is 'uneven' with departments of psychology showing a strong resistance to qualitative research, while departments of nursing, sociology, and educational psychology are welcoming this approach. This survey gives us a glimpse of the teaching climate in departments that are not necessarily hospitable to qualitative research, and we get to take a look at some of the external issues that qualitative researchers may find themselves in as a minority method within their departments.

The survey suggests that instructors teaching a qualitative course often experience feelings of isolation from other faculty members when they assume a more qualitative post-tenure identity. Very often the teaching of a qualitative course is marginalized in the curriculum as an elective course at best. Coupled with the paucity of professors teaching qualitative research is the increasing student interest in learning about this method; as a result, qualitative faculty felt overwhelmed with the responsibility and work of teaching and advising students. This became especially difficult when there were few additional faculty members available to support and supervise qualitative theses or dissertations.

Using this survey as a background to some of the external departmental teaching conflicts, let's go behind the scenes with Janet Stoppard (2002) as she relates the specific difficulties she has had with introducing a graduate qualitative methods course into the psychology curriculum at one Canadian university. What have been Janet's problems and prospects with introducing a qualitative approach into her department? Janet Stoppard's (2002) early methods training and research projects were, as she puts it, 'thoroughly orthodox, with an emphasis on experimental methods and statistics' (p. 144). It was only after her tenure and promotion that she experienced a growing dissatisfaction with quantitative methods. Her research on women and depression raised a series of questions that she felt could not be addressed solely by a quantitative approach. These questions included: 'Why do some women, but not others seek professional help when depressed?' and 'What strategies do depressed women use to cope when depressed?' (p. 144). She relates her own journey toward finding a qualitative perspective that enabled her to understand women's experiences with depression. Achieving a more qualitative research identity is one thing, but introducing a course in qualitative methods is quite another. She was especially challenged by the fact that she worked within a predominantly quantitative department. Janet notes that her proposal to offer a graduate course in qualitative methods was accepted by her quantitative department, but her initial concerns focused on what went on outside of her classroom:

> The first time I offered the course, things appeared to go fairly smoothly ... Almost immediately, however, things began to happen outside the classroom. Students who were not taking my course approached me with questions about using qualitative methods in the

research they were doing. Typically, these students wanted help with analysis of responses to open-ended items on questionnaires and advice on doing content analysis (p. 148).

Janet Stoppard's course began to impact the department's environment, and some faculty began to teach these methods and others expressed some receptivity. Although some faculty members were receptive, most were not. The lack of a supportive environment raised particular issues on whether or not it was in a student's best interest to provide a qualitative research perspective if that meant a student might face the risk of getting a poor grade. She notes:

> This situation is particularly likely to arise when faculty evaluations of students' work are based on differing epistemological assumptions. In one case, for instance, this type of disagreement resulted in a student being required to add a lengthy section to a paper in order to address the epistemological assumptions informing the work. In essence, this student was required to defend the choice of a qualitative paradigm (p. 149).

Janet Stoppard's experience raises several important questions that potential instructors should consider before they contemplate the teaching of a grounded theory course: To what extent are faculty in your department open to new ideas and epistemological approaches? How will students work with faculty members who have no knowledge of alternative methods? Barbour (2003) also experienced the challenge of introducing qualitative methods into a predominately quantitative discipline and notes, 'Many qualitative researchers employed within medical faculties find themselves occupying the position of "cuckoos in the nest," attempting to introduce a new approach within preexisting courses and formats' (p. 1024; see also Harding & Gantley, 1999). This point of view is also supported by Eakin and Mykhalovskiy's (2005) experiences in teaching qualitative research in the health sciences. They are able to relate to the emotional and professional strains of doing cross-disciplinary teaching. They found several roadblocks that made their task difficult. They observed, 'Educational resources and institutional supports for the development of qualitative research expertise are limited, the quality of training is uneven, and teaching experience is seldom shared' (paragraph 4). Like other researchers have found when studying this topic, the authors note that the introduction of qualitative methods can be bitter and a bit messy. They found both students and faculty were resistant and observed, 'Colleagues may feel uncomfortable with the implicit challenge to established research orthodoxies ... qualitative approaches can seriously challenge students' assumptions and ways of thinking' (paragraph 30). These observations and those of other qualitative pioneers demonstrate the hard road that is traveled when bringing new methods into a settled academic research environment. A department whose basic foundation is polarized along a qualitative/quantitative divide creates an environment that permeates the very structure of the curriculum and how and what research methods are taught and practiced. This atmosphere also determines whether or not these methods are seen as compatible or divided and the extent to which mixed methods approaches are entertained.

CONCLUDING REMARKS

We leave behind a range of still unanswered questions that are ripe for empirical research. We need to seriously consider the importance of pedagogy in our teaching practices, especially with regard to research methods. There is a sense that methods are only tools to be acquired and applied. There is also a lack of connection between methodology and epistemology in the way methods are taught. Several of the articles reviewed for this chapter noted the importance of relaying to students the idea that grounded theory is a 'craft.' Acquiring the skills needed for grounded theory means that students need to hone their skills over a period of time. Yet, we noted that methods instructors are often strapped for time, and many are teaching grounded theory as only a small section of a larger methods course. What makes the situation even more challenging and time consuming for the instructor is that many students come to the classroom lacking training in methods. Those that have some training are often rooted in the more deductive, hypothesis-based styles of testing. These skills have a pervasive impact on a student's ability to learn and accept new methods (like qualitative research skills and grounded theory) because much of their perception of reality is based in these deductive thinking patterns. Many texts have also noted the emotional impact that teaching qualitative methods can have on teachers, for they must be prepared to immerse students in a new world of thought and restructure the thinking processes that have been inculcated since childhood education. Janet Stoppard (2002) offers an especially telling portrait of a student's reaction to the new methods. She notes that one of her pupils actually felt '"queasy" when confronting the implications of a social constructionist epistemology for assumptions about reality' (p. 149). Most of the research we have cited, however, has generally concluded that students can accept new, challenging methods with a mentoring model of instruction and with a 'hands on' experiential classroom approach. This was one of the essential cruxes that we focused on in the teaching of qualitative methods and grounded theory.

These responsibilities, along with the heated climates that some teachers work in, make the task of teaching qualitative methods quite complicated, for there are many external constraints outside the classroom. These include departments or disciplines that do not value their paradigmatic point of view. There are issues involving the lack of adequate training of faculty who are now teaching grounded theory as novices, and many of these qualitative instructors come from a purely quantitative background. It is difficult for instructors to teach and mentor students if they have not had experiential training in the practice of grounded theory. Faculties' inexperience and unfamiliarity with grounded theory and qualitative research is a sensitive issue, and Juliet Corbin has been especially vocal in her criticisms. In a recent interview, the author of *Basics of Qualitative Research* discusses the lack of adequate mentorship for students who are working on qualitative research. Corbin (Cisneros-Puebla, 2004) asserts that while much excellent research in qualitative methods exists, it has become for others only '... fast solutions to doing data analysis. They are satisfied to pull out a few good themes without having to put the effort into doing an in-depth analysis that will lead to theme or concept development ... perhaps some of the problem lies in the lack of good mentorship. Many teachers of research and committee members are not trained as qualitative researchers, and therefore cannot give proper guidance to their students' (paragraph 17). While it seems feasible that computer technologies can serve to bridge the divide between quantitative and qualitative methods, computers may become a fast track way of skipping over important lessons that are crucial to grounded theory. The debate continues as to whether or not technology can be exchanged for mentorship in the learning and practice of grounded theory.

This is only one of many schisms that have emerged in the teaching of grounded theory. Conflicts in the teaching and practice of grounded theory can also be traced to the ongoing debate between Glaser's and Strauss's differing notions of grounded theory practices. The debate over grounded theory's definition and meaning has continued, and researchers are often divided on which grounded theorist they choose to follow. The questions that are asked are pivotal to the study of methods. Is grounded theory to be envisioned as an 'art form' with a heavy reliance on the creativity and experience of the researcher? Is it more a set of rules to be followed and adhered to? Will the practice of this craft fade with heavier reliance on computer-assisted learning of grounded theory? Can the two perspectives on grounded theory work hand-in-hand to find a happy medium? These questions and a myriad of others have challenged researchers and theorists for years, and scholars continue to explore these questions.

The teaching of grounded theory is still a developing art, with more stories, more experiences, and more trials and errors to be tested and explored as we seek the most effective teaching techniques. The training and experiences of teachers and students are dynamic, growing and rife with surprises, but the teaching of grounded theory must also be embedded in a longer-range discussion of how the teaching of research methods fits into the context of the student's undergraduate and graduate career. What are the short-term and long-term goals of depart- ments regarding their commitment to teaching and nurturing interpretative methods at the graduate and undergraduate level? There also remain pedagogi- cal questions that are ripe for empirical investigation: When should software tools be introduced and how do we protect students' needs and learning? What is an effective amount of classroom time? What kinds of exposure will give stu- dents a good grasp of the theory and practice of grounded theory? The answers are in the classrooms, the adventurous teaching ideas, and the bright future of qualitative methods that is waiting to be discovered by instructors and students alike.

ACKNOWLEDGMENTS

Thanks to Deborah Piatelli for her insights on pedagogy and grounded theory. Thanks also to the undergraduate students who agreed to share their classroom experiences with me. Much appreciation to my research assistants, Cooley Horner and Melissa Ricker, for their sharp editorial advice and research support.

REFERENCES

Altricher, H. & Posch, P. (1989). Does the grounded theory approach offer a guiding paradigm for teaching research? *Cambridge Journal of Education* 19(1): 21–31.

Babchuk, W.A. (1997). Glaser or Strauss?: Grounded Theory and Adult Education. Michigan State University, Midwest Research-to-Practice Conference in Adult, Continuing, and Community Education. October 15–17, 1997. Retrieved June 22, 2006, from http://www.iupui.edu/~adulted/mwr2p/prior/gradpr96.htm

Barbour, R.S. (2003). The Newfound Credibility of Qualitative Research? Tales of Technical Essentialism and Co-Option. *Qualitative Health Research* 13(7): 1019–1027.

Blank, G. (2004). Teaching qualitative data analysis to graduate students. *Social Science Computer Review* 22(2): 187–196.

Charmaz K. (1983) The grounded theory method: An explication and interpretation. In R.M. Emerson (ed.) *Contemporary Field Research: A Collection of Readings* (pp. 109–126). Prospect Heights, IL: Waveland Press.

Charmaz, K. (2000). Grounded theory: Objectivist and constructivist methods. In N.K. Denzin and Y.S. Lincoln (Eds.), *Handbook of Qualitative Research* (2nd ed., pp. 509–536). Thousand Oaks, CA: SAGE.

Cisneros-Puebla, C.A. (2004, September). 'To Learn to Think Conceptually'. Juliet Corbin in Conversation With Cesar A. Cisneros-Puebla [53 paragraphs]. *Forum Qualitative Sozialforschung/Forum: Qualitative Social Research* [On-line Journal], 5(3). Retrieved June 22, 2006, from http://www.qualitative-research.net/fqs-texte/3-04/04-3-32-e.htm

Crabtree, B.E. & Miller, W.L. (1999). *Doing Qualitative Research*. Thousand Oaks, CA: SAGE.

Davie, L. (1996). Learning qualitative research: Electronic learning circles. *Qualitative Health Research* 6(3): 453–457.

Dey, I. (1999). *Grounding Grounded Theory: Guidelines for Qualitative Inquiry.* London: Academic Press.

Eakin, J.M. & Mykhalovskiy, E. (2005, April). Teaching Against the Grain: A Workshop on Teaching Qualitative Research in the Health Sciences. Conference Report: A National Workshop on Teaching Qualitative Research in the Health Sciences [43 paragraphs]. *Forum Qualitative Sozialforschung/Forum: Qualitative Social Research* [On-line Journal], 6(2). Retrieved May 10, 2006, from http://www.qualitative-research.net/fqs-texte/2-05/05-2-42-e.htm

Este, D., Sieppert, J. & Barsky, A. (1998). Teaching and Learning Qualitative Research With and Without Qualitative Data Analysis Software. *Journal of Research on Computing in Education* 31(2): 138–155. Retrieved May 17, 2006, from Business Source Premier Database.

Faux, R. (2004, September). The Coming of Age of a Qualitative Researcher: The Impact of Qualitative Research in Education Past, Present, and Future. Judith Preissle in Conversation With Robert Faux [106 paragraphs]. *Forum Qualitative Sozialforschung/Forum: Qualitative Social Research* [On-line Journal] 5(3). Retrieved June 22, 2006, from http://www.qualitative-research.net/fqs-texte/3-04/04-3-20-e.htm

Fielding, N.G. & Lee, R.M. (Eds.) (1991). *Using Computers in Qualitative Research*. London: SAGE.

Fielding, N.G. & Lee, R.M. (1996). Diffusion of a methodological innovation: CAQDAS in the UK. *Current Sociology* 44, 2(2): 242–258.

Fielding, N.G. & Lee, R.M. (1998). *Computer Analysis and Qualitative Research.* Thousand Oaks, CA: SAGE.

Fielding, N.G. & Lee, R.M. (2002). New patterns in the adoption and use of qualitative software. *Field Methods* 14(2): 197–216.

Fontes, L.A. & Piercy, F.P. (2000). Engaging students in qualitative research through experiential class activities. *Teaching of Psychology* 27(3): 174–179.

Glaser, B.G. (1978). *Theoretical Sensitivity.* Mill Valley, CA: Sociology Press.

Glaser, B.G. (1992). *Basics of Grounded Theory Analysis.* Mill Valley, CA: Sociology Press.

Glaser, B.G. & Strauss, A.L. (1967). *Discovery of Grounded Theory: The Strategies for Qualitative Research.* Chicago: Aldine Publishers.

Harding, C. & Gantley, M. (1999). 'You only want me for my methods'. Paper presented at the Academic Departments of General Practice (AUDGP) Annual Conference, London.

Hein, S.F. (2004). I don't like ambiguity: An exploration of students' experiences during a qualitative methods course. *The Alberta Journal of Educational Research* 50(1): 22–38.

Hesse-Biber, S. (1995). Unleashing Frankenstein's monster? The use of computers in qualitative research. *Studies in Qualitative Methodology* 5: 25–41.

Hesse-Biber, S. (1996). *Am I Thin Enough Yet? The Cult of Thinness and the Commercialization of Identity.* New York: Oxford University Press.

Hesse-Biber, S.N. (2007). The practice of feminist in-depth interviewing. In S.N. Hesse-Biber & P. Leavy (Eds.), *The Feminist Research Practice: A Primer.* Thousand Oaks, CA: SAGE.

Hesse-Biber, S.N. & Leavy, P. (Eds). (2004). *Approaches to Qualitative Research: A Reader on Theory and Practice.* New York: Oxford University Press.

Hesse-Biber, S.N. & Leavy, P. (2006). *The Practice of Qualitative Research.* Thousand Oaks, CA: SAGE.

Huehls, F. (2005). An Evening of Grounded Theory: Teaching Process through Demonstration and Simulation. *The Qualitative Report* 10(2): 328–338. Retrieved August 17, 2006, from http://www.nova.edu/ssss/QR/QR10-2/huehls.pdf

Janesick, V.J. (2004). *'Stretching' Exercises for Qualitative Researchers* (2nd ed.). Thousand Oaks, CA: SAGE.

Keen, M.F. (1996). Teaching qualitative methods: A face-to-face encounter. *Teaching Sociology* 24(2): 166–176.

Kelle, U. (1995). *Computer-aided Qualitative Data Analysis: Theory, Methods and Practice.* London: SAGE.

Lincoln, Y.S. & Guba, E.G. (1985). *Naturalistic Inquiry.* Newbury Park, CA: SAGE.

Lonkila, M. (1995). Grounded theory as an emerging paradigm for computer-assisted qualitative data analysis. In U. Kelle (Ed.) *Computer-Aided Qualitative Data Analysis: Theory, Method and Practice.* London: SAGE.

MacMillan, K. & Koenig, T. (2004). The Wow factor: Preconceptions and expectations for data analysis software in qualitative research. *Social Science Computer Review* 22(2): 179–186.

Mann, S. & Kelley, L. (1997). Standing at the crossroads of modernist thought: Collins, Smith and new feminist epistemologies. *Gender and Society* 11(4): 391–408.

McAllister, M. & Rowe, J. (2003). Blackbirds singing in the dead of night? Advancing the craft of teaching qualitative research. *Journal of Nursing Education* 42(7): 296–303.

Melia, K.M. (1996). Rediscovering Glaser. *Qualitative Health Research* 6: 368–378.

Miles, M. & Huberman, A. (1984). *Qualitative Data Analysis: Sourcebook for New Methods.* Beverly Hills, CA: SAGE.

Morison, M. & Moir, J. (1998). The role of computer software in the analysis of qualitative data: Efficient clerk, research assistant or Trojan horse? *Journal of Advanced Nursing* 28(1): 106–116.

Muhr, T. (1991). ATLAS/ti: A prototype for the support of text interpretation. *Qualitative Sociology* 14, 4(2): 349–371.

Nyden, P. (1991). Teaching qualitative methods: An interview with Phil Nyden. *Teaching Sociology* 19: 396–402.

Rennie, D.L., Watson, K.D. & Monteiro, A. (2000, June). Qualitative Research in Canadian Psychology [27 paragraphs]. *Forum Qualitative Sozialforschung/Forum: Qualitative Social Research* [On-line Journal] 1(2). Retrieved May 8, 2006, from http://qualitativeresearch.net/fqs/fqs-e/2-00inhalt-e.htm

Richards, T.J. & Richards, L. (1991). The NUD.IST qualitative data analysis system. *Qualitative Sociology* 14, 4(2): 289–306.

Robrecht, L. (1995). Grounded theory: Evolving methods. *Qualitative Health Research* 5: 169–177.

Seale, C. (1999). Quality in qualitative research. *Qualitative Inquiry* 5: 465–478.

Seidel, J.V. & Clark, J.A. (1984). The ETHNOGRAPH: A computer program for the analysis of qualitative data. *Qualitative Sociology* 7(1/2): 110–125.

Smith, B.A. & Hesse-Biber, S. (1996). Users' experiences with qualitative data analysis software: Neither Frankenstein's monster nor muse. *Social Science Computer Review* 14(4): 423–432.

Stoppard, J.M. (2002). Navigating the hazards of orthodoxy: Introducing a graduate course on qualitative methods into the psychology curriculum. *Canadian Psychology* 43(3): 143–153.

Strauss, A.L. (1987). *Qualitative Analysis for Social Scientists*. New York: Cambridge University Press.

Strauss, A.L. & Corbin, J.M. (1990). *Basics of Qualitative Research: Grounded Theory Procedures and Techniques*. London: SAGE.

Strauss, A. & Corbin, J. (1994). Grounded theory methodology; An overview. In N.K. Denzin and Y.S. Lincoln (Eds.), *Handbook of Qualitative Research*. London: SAGE.

16

The Evolving Nature of Grounded Theory Method: The Case of the Information Systems Discipline

Cathy Urquhart

INTRODUCTION

This chapter examines the diffusion and adaptation of grounded theory method (GTM) in the academic discipline of information systems (IS), a relatively recent, evolving field. It also suggests some general guidelines for writing up grounded theory studies by drawing on information systems examples that can be of use to researchers from all disciplines who wish to exploit the method's theory building capabilities to the full. GTM has been used in the information systems discipline since the mid 1980s, but studies generating grounded substantive theories from using the method are still rare. This chapter discusses the adaptations that information systems researchers have made to the method, in a discipline that is part technical and part social, and reflects on possible reasons for those adaptations. This chapter discusses a number of issues that face information systems researchers when using GTM, including the issue of theory building and relating substantive theories to larger ones.

Information systems as a discipline has increasingly used qualitative research methods in the past 10 years (Klein & Myers 1999, Klein, Nissen & Hirschheim 1991, Markus 1997, Myers 1997, Schultze 2000, Trauth & Jessup 2000, Walsham 1995).

A natural consequence of an increase in qualitative methods has been an increase in the use of grounded theory method (Adams & Sasse 1999, Baskerville & Pries-Heje 1999, Lings & Lundell 2005, Orlikowski 1993, Toraskar 1991, Trauth 2000, Urquhart 1998, 1999). As the use of GTM matures in information systems, there have been some debates and discussions in the discipline about its use (Bryant 2002, Bryant, Hughes, Myers, Trauth, & Urquhart 2004, Howcroft & Hughes 1999, Hughes & Howcroft 2000, Urquhart 2001, 2002). This chapter aims to extend those debates and consider the following issues:

- How has GTM been applied in the information systems field? How suitable is GTM as a research method for information systems research? What are the characteristics of the field that first make grounded theory a suitable method, and what implications do these characteristics have for GTM use in the field?
- How has the use of GTM evolved in the information systems field? How has it been represented, and what have been the key debates thus far?
- Which strategies of use of GTM have been most widely adopted and why these? Is the full theory building potential of GTM being utilized in information systems?
- What guidelines of use might be useful for information systems researchers when applying GTM to IS phenomena?
- Are there any lessons for the use of GTM in general that can be derived from the experience of IS researchers?

HOW GTM HAS BEEN REPRESENTED IN INFORMATION SYSTEMS

Like many professional fields, information systems is a research discipline which has many 'contributing disciplines' (Lee 2001). In information systems these disciplines range from computer science, to management, to sociology. As in any discipline, the introduction of new ideas and methods tend to be initiated by one or two people. The subsequent development of those ideas and the acceptance of those ideas can be traced back as they are debated and contested in academic papers and conferences. Generally, the first useful application of the idea or method that is published widely is often taken as the working definition.

One of the earliest studies using grounded theory in information systems, Toraskar (1991), was published at a conference that had a small audience. An early characterization of GTM in IS was provided by Orlikowski and Baroudi (1991), where they referenced GTM as an example of an *interpretive* viewpoint. They quote Glaser and Strauss's (1967) statement that the primary endeavor is to describe, interpret, and analyze the social world from the participant's perspective, and that all rigid a priori researcher imposed formulations of structure, function, purpose, and attribution are resisted (Glaser and Strauss 1967, Orlikowski and Baroudi 1991: 15). It is probably true to say that Orlikowski's (1993) paper, which was published in *MIS Quarterly* (the top journal in information systems), was responsible for giving grounded theory widespread legitimacy as a research method in information systems. Orlikowski (1993) introduced and justified her use of GTM on three counts: first, it was useful for areas where no previous theory existed; second, it incorporated the complexities of the organizational context into the understanding of the phenomena; and third, that GTM was uniquely fitted to studying process and change.

Walsham (1995), as a part of a very influential article on case studies and interpretive research, considered GTM in relation to the three roles of theory outlined by Eisenhardt (1989): as an initial guide to design and data collection, as part of an iterative process of data collection and analysis, and as a final product of the research. Walsham pointed out that GTM would emphasize the last two. Acknowledging that Glaser and Strauss (1967) warned in strong terms against using theory to design research and to collect data, Walsham (1995) stated that it is possible to access existing knowledge of theory without being trapped in the view that it represents the final truth in the area. However, the reason for the injunction against researching the literature at an initial stage was not stated in Walsham's article: the concern that a researcher might stifle theory development by imposing concepts from the literature on the data, rather than allowing theory to emerge naturally. Strauss (1987) modified the original position by stating that the injunction applied less so to experienced researchers, who are already good at subjecting a theoretical statement to comparative analysis. Walsham (1995) also cited Layder (1993) who felt that GTM needed to break away from focusing on micro phenomena as this prevented the grounded theorist from enriching the research by considering macro structures (Layder continues these arguments in his 1998 book). The problem with these statements from Layder is that Glaser and Strauss (1967), from the beginning, acknowledged that substantive theory development (pertaining to the phenomena being investigated) can and should shade into formal theories, and devoted a whole chapter in their book to this issue. Glaser and Strauss never saw GT as only a micro theory. Both of them worked at organizational levels as well, and Strauss's interest in social arenas and social worlds led him beyond the micro level to the 'meso' level. Strauss and Corbin (1990) suggested, in their 'Canons' for judging a grounded theory study, that the broader conditions that affect the study be built into its explanation. Glaser (1978) suggests that formal models of process, structure, and analysis may be useful guides to integration of a theory. More recently, Clarke (2005) makes many helpful suggestions as to how to take a grounded theory to meso and macro levels.

There were two key (but erroneous in my view) perceptions of GTM resulting from Walsham's (1995) discussion of the role of theory in case studies; first, that GTM runs the risk of ignoring theory, and second, that GTM's focus on micro phenomena meant that it was impossible to engage the theory generated with broader and more formal theories. This view of GTM from one of the most influential and scholarly players in IS interpretive research most certainly had an impact, even though the discussion of GTM came by way of discussing use of theory in case studies, and was in fact a side issue. Walsham's paper was widely read and cited; the paper was a most positive influence in interpretive IS research in general: it contained intellectually compelling and relevant advice on the process of generalization that was possible from interpretive case studies.

Subsequently there have been a number of debates and discussion pieces about the use of GTM in IS, starting with Hughes and Howcroft (2000) who emphasized the use of constant comparison and theoretical sampling. They draw a useful analogy between the use of information system development method- ologies (ISDMs), and the use of GTM. They suggest GTM can be likened to an ISDM in that it can be used by individuals of differing experience and can be tailored to the contingencies of a situation. They note a number of adaptations, mainly at the procedural level of coding, and noted that evaluative criteria as recommended by Strauss and Corbin (1990) were rarely used. They are definitely of the view that adaptation of GTM in IS is both useful and desirable. They posit that the epistemological position of the researcher may influence that adaptation; that positivist researchers are more likely to treat the method literally whereas interpretivists might treat it more metaphorically.

My own work (Urquhart 2001) outlined experiences as a PhD student with using the method, and attempted to give some guidance to graduate researchers about application and philosophical issues. In it, I described in detail the experience of using GTM for the first time, giving details of coding, and also discussed my experience of using the Strauss and Corbin (1990) book. Like many people coming to GTM for the first time, I had been unaware that the 1990 book represented a most serious disagreement between the co-founders. Reading around the debate meant accessing the entire GTM canon and I understood why, for me at least, the 1990 book was so difficult to apply. I came to agree with Glaser (1992) that the application of a single coding paradigm (conditions, interaction among the actors, strategies and tactics, and consequences) constituted the 'forcing' of data, given that there were many other coding paradigms to choose from (Glaser 1978) and indeed, no coding paradigms are mentioned in the 1967 book. The single coding paradigm did not work with the dialogue between analysts and clients I was studying; I found it impossible to identify conditions and consequences. That said, I could identify strategies and tactics and this became the focus of a research question. At the suggestion of my PhD advisor, I looked at Spradley's (1979) domain analysis and the semantic relationships he suggested between domains such as 'is a kind of,' 'a way to,' 'a stage of,' 'a characteristic of,' etc. This worked well; Spradley's semantic relationships seemed more than adequate for theorizing.

From the vantage point of many years later, I now see that the problem with the Strauss and Corbin paradigm goes much deeper and also comprises a problem of coding procedure. Glaser (1978) talks of open coding, where initial codes are allocated at a line-by-line level, and selective coding, where the categories are grouped, then theoretical coding, where relationships between categories are considered. Charmaz (2006) points to axial coding as a further type of coding introduced by Strauss in 1987 (that of relating categories to subcategories); this is a most helpful way of describing axial coding. Thus it goes one step further at the selective coding stage, by simultaneously considering relationships as a sort of 'mini' theoretical coding. It also introduces, in my opinion, a needless level of complexity. It is complicated enough to group categories without simultaneously considering relationships, especially for a novice. It also narrows down the options for theorizing. Now I am in the interesting position of watching my graduate students be attracted to the apparent siren simplicity of the coding paradigm, agreeing to their use of it (in the interests of not being dogmatic), only to see them founder on the same rocks of complexity as I did 10 years ago.

One of the problems with the application of GTM in the information systems area is that we are a new discipline, and it's hard to conceive of a research method that has a 40-year history in a much older discipline, with many books and articles behind it. As a beginning researcher in IS, it seemed logical that one book would tell me all I needed to know. Again, there is a parallel with information systems development methodologies, where there is usually one authoritative manual or reference.

I also discussed in my 2001 work whether GTM carried with it some philosophical baggage: was it inherently positivist or interpretivist? The general consensus of commentators seemed to be that, based on the background of the co-founders, the Glaserian strand of GTM was positivist (with Strauss being interpretivist; see Annells 1996). It was the positivist elements of the Strauss and Corbin book that led me to consider the philosophical baggage of GTM. It's also interesting to note that, from the standpoint of diffusion of ideas about GTM, that I was influenced by key commentators from the field of nursing. Madill, Jordan, and Shirley (2000) argue quite convincingly that the philosophical position adopted when using grounded theory depends on the extent to which the findings are considered to be discovered within the data, or as the result of con-struction of inter-subjective meanings. I concluded that GTM could, and should, be used in either paradigm, and was dependent on the position of the researcher.

Bryant (2002), drawing on Giddens (1984), made the claim that GTM was inherently positivist and needed to be claimed from its positivist origins. My reply (Urquhart 2002) drew attention to the fact that most of the use of GTM in IS had been by interpretive researchers who were quietly retrieving it from its positivist sounding origins. GTM had to be viewed in the context of its time, and primarily as a method. I also called for a much more detailed consideration of the role that GTM could play in theory building for IS. The debate about GTM in IS was further elaborated in a conference panel (Bryant, Hughes, Myers, Trauth, & Urquhart 2004) which discussed whether it mattered that many uses of GTM in IS were not 'pure' applications of GTM and did not result in theory generation, and also the epistemological position of GTM. This panel took place at a conference that celebrated 20 years of qualitative methods use in IS: thus it provided an important summation of perspectives on GTM use in IS, and set some new directions toward an adaptive and flexible view of GTM.

The debate on the use of GTM in IS continues, with Urquhart and Fernandez (2006) discussing and naming four prevalent myths of GTM: the researcher as blank Slate, GTM is inflexible, GTM produces low level theories that don't do much, and GTM is positivist/interpretivist. The wider debate also continues, with the publication in *Academy of Management Journal* an article entitled 'What Grounded Theory is Not' (Suddaby 2006).

APPLYING GROUNDED THEORY IN INFORMATION SYSTEMS

How GTM has been applied in the field of information systems can be looked at from two perspectives; the type of phenomena it has been applied to, and how GTM has been applied. This section looks at those two issues.

IS phenomena and Grounded Theory Method

It is interesting to consider whether the nature of the field of information systems, and the phenomena which we study, has an impact on the way grounded theory is applied to research in the field. This is of course an important consideration for any field adopting GTM: how do the characteristics of the field influence that adoption? The interaction of technology, people, and processes is one that has exercised both sociologists and information systems researchers for some time. Going beyond the idea of technological determinism is an issue in both disciplines. In sociology, it has been said that the common sense dichotomies between the 'technical' and 'social' need to be challenged (Hutchby 2001). In information systems, the dichotomy between technical and social has been challenged by studies in information systems utilizing such theories as structuration theory (e.g. Orlikowski 1992, Walsham 2002), and actor network theory (Mitev 2000, Walsham & Sahay 1999). Orlikowski's 1992 application of structuration conceptualizes technology as both a product of human action and a medium of human action, enabled and constrained by interpretive schemes and norms. The interaction with that technology influences the institutional properties of the organization through reinforcing or transforming structures of signification, domination and legitimation (Orlikowski 1992: 410) In Walsham and Sahay's application of actor network theory, software is conceptualized as a black box, a frozen element of discourse that is not open to question by the actors in the network. It is also seen as a delegated actor that inscribes certain interests in the network (Walsham & Sahay 1999), for instance software that mandates certain organizational procedures

The position of technology itself in IS research has exercised researchers in the discipline for some time, as it has been tied up with debates about the identity of the discipline: what is distinctive about information systems as a research discipline, as opposed to management or sociology? One obvious difference is that IS researchers are concerned with the interaction of individuals, groups, and organizations with IT. Orlikowski and Iacono (2001), in a seminal article, have identified five conceptualizations of IT in IS research: The Tool View, the Proxy View, the Ensemble View, the Computational View, and the Nominal View. The application of these categories to a purposive sample of IS articles using GTM is provided in Table 16.1.

First, Orlikowski and Iacono define the 'Tool' view of technology as the 'common received wisdom' about what technology is and means. As the field has progressed, it has moved beyond these somewhat straightforward definitions. The last definition proffered under this category, Technology as Social Relations Tool, where it is recognized that technologies can and do alter social relations, represents the increased focus on this aspect by information systems researchers in the past 10 years, and acts as a basis for another definition, the Ensemble view of technology. The Ensemble view of technology takes the view that the technical artifact is but one element in a package to be applied in what has become known as the 'web of computing' (Kling & Scacchi 1982). All of the variants of the Ensemble view focus on the dynamic interaction between people and technology (Orlikowski & Iacono 2001). Table 16.1 indicates that many IS researchers have used grounded theory method in the Ensemble view, and this makes sense when one considers that grounded theory method is good for studying processes.

The Proxy view of technology, by contrast, takes the view that the critical aspects of technology can be represented by surrogate and usually (but not always)

Table 16.1   Categorizing IS GTM Studies according to Orlikowski and Iacono (2001)

	Grounded Theory studies in this category	Comment

Tool view of Technology
  as labor substitution tool
  as productivity tool
  as information processing tool
  as social relations tool
	Adam and Wood 1999,
	  Baskerville and Pries-Heje 1999,
	  Calloway and Ariav 1995,
	  Lings and Lundell 2005, Orlikowski
	  1993, Seeley and Targett 1997,
	  Yoong and Gallupe 2001	

Proxy View of Technology
  as perception
  as diffusion
  as capital
	Adams and Sasse 1999,
	  Crook and Kumar 1998,
	  Toraskar 1991
		The Adams and Sasse study
		  could also possibly fit into
		  the 'tool' category

Ensemble View of Technology
  as development project
  as production network
  as embedded system
  as structure
	Hughes and Wood-Harper 1999,
	  King 1996, Lehmann 2001, 2003,
	  Lopata 1991, Scott 1998, 2000,
	  Sjoberg and Timpka 1998, Trauth
	  and Jessup 2000, Urquhart 1999,
	  Whiteley and Garcia 1996
		The vast majority of these
		  studies fall into the
		  'embedded system'
		  classification

Computational View of Technology
  as algorithm
  as model
		No studies found using
		  grounded theory method
		  in this area

Nominal View of Technology
  as absent
	Fitzgerald 1997	Fitzgerald's study of developers
		  use of system development
		  methodologies a good
		  example of the 'technology
		  as absent' type of study

quantitative measures. It is interesting to note then, that grounded theory has occasionally been used for these types of studies, albeit infrequently. Glaser argues that GTM is as much of a quantitative approach as a qualitative approach, yet quantitative applications are rare both in IS and other disciplines.

The Computational view in information systems focuses expressly on computational power of computing; the capabilities of the technology to represent, manipulate, store and retrieve, and transmit information. It comes as no surprise that there are no grounded theory studies in this category. The lack of application in this area is far more due to the reliance on quantitative methods for this category than any consideration whether GTM would be useful in this area.

There is no reason in my view for not using grounded theory method in this category of research; presumably it would be useful in generating concepts about the technology, if not building theory. The potential for its use is exciting, given the unique inductive nature of GTM. There is a sense in which we should celebrate and characterize the adaptations made to GTM in information systems, as opposed to feeling that we need to adhere to a 'pure' version of grounded theory. That said, it is important for the ongoing development of GTM in information systems that those adaptations are conscious and recorded: it requires a thorough knowledge and understanding of the use and potential of GTM to understand how it might be deviated from. This is especially important given that many IS researchers apply GTM without knowledge of the intellectual differences between Glaser and Strauss, and the consequences of these differences for application of the method. Lings and Lundell (2005), for instance, do an excellent job of listing their adaptations of GTM and points at which they departed from the method. They noted the absence of a core category, no axial coding per se, and the constant feedback of generated theory to stakeholders as significant departures that were fully justified by the characteristics of their research problem.

Lastly, Orlikowski and Iacono define the Nominal view of technology, where technology is 'invoked in name but not in fact.' The topic of interest is usually of broad interest to the field, but there are no references to specific technology. One study was noted of this type, but there may be more. It is possible that the level of analysis in these types of study (broad) is seen as incompatible with the detailed level of analysis required by GTM.

How Grounded Theory Method is applied to IS phenomena

One thing that is immediately noticeable in GTM use in IS is that IS researchers commonly use grounded theory method to generate concepts, as opposed to generating theory. This is not unusual, other disciplines such as health, too, have reported that many researchers adopt GTM for a purpose other than developing theory (see Becker 1993, Benoliel 1996, Elliot & Lazenbatt 2005, Green 1998). A larger survey of 32 information systems articles using GTM and covering the period 1996–2005 (Lehmann, Urquhart, & Myers 2006), found that GTM use fell into four categories:

- Full use of the method (11 papers)
- Using the method to generate concepts (11 papers)
- Mixing grounded theory with other research methods (4 papers)
- Mislabeled as GTM (i.e. not following any known procedures of either Glaser, Strauss, or Strauss and Corbin) (6 papers)

Those researchers that made full use of the method usually produced a theory covering a substantive area, i.e. pertaining to the area of interest. Concepts were linked, building the theory, and this generally led to strong papers (it is perhaps noteworthy that two of these papers, Orlikowski 1993 and Urquhart 1999, received best paper awards from the journals in which they were published). Attempts were generally made to engage the emergent substantive theory with competing theories. None of the articles attempted to articulate a formal theory.

Some articles mixed grounded theory method with other methods; the most notable and successful example of this being Baskerville and Pries-Heje (1999) where the grounded theory generation was combined with action research. The grounded theory concepts applied in that study produced informed diagnosing, action planning, action taking, and learning cycles in the study. Open coding was used in the first instance. Subsequently these open codes were grouped into categories as per the axial coding stage (following Strauss and Corbin), but few connections were made. The major categories were used as a basis for an entity relationship diagram which informed the prototype and the second cycle. The paper illustrates how the categories produced at each stage informed diagnosing, action planning, action taking, and learning over two cycles. Some limited linkages between categories exist, but the focus is on the refined conceptual constructs. The interesting thing about this application of GTM is how the coding became the essence of the evaluating, learning, and diagnosis phases of the action research, in effect merging the theoretical sampling with action research.

The category of 'mislabeled' GTM generally contained papers where some coding had taken place, but the coding was descriptive and, in some cases, derived from previous literature. This last category is common in the health discipline, where GTM can be equated with qualitative research in general (Benoliel 1996), and sometimes there seems to be the assumption that GTM is equated with coding in general. There is also the sense that GTM's coding procedures are deemed to be superior to other coding procedures; as a well known and respected coding method, GTM then provides a convenient imprimatur for any coding procedure. This seems odd when one considers that the whole point of the method is to generate grounded theory, and that the method has theory in its name. More and more adaptations, and excellent formulations of GTM as contained in Charmaz (2006), will encourage more theory generation. In the IS discipline, the theory building aspect of GTM still remains largely untapped.

In general, for all of the papers examined in this survey, there was a correlation between the amount of references to the whole body of GTM literature (e.g. Glaser 1978, 1992, 1998, 1999, 2001, Glaser & Strauss 1967, Strauss 1987, Strauss & Corbin 1990, 1997) and the in depth application of the method. Strauss and Corbin (1990) has acted as a double edged sword in its contribution to the canon; it has played a vital role in popularizing GTM, making it accessible to graduate students and those new to qualitative research, however, it caused a rift between the two founders and, while the book is attractive in its simplicity, it has been my own experience, and that of my graduate students (and many other researchers; e.g. Kendall 1999, Melia 1996) that the prescriptiveness of the procedures limits the theory generation potential of the method. The purposive survey of IS articles also looked at the unit of analysis to which GTM was applied: 21 of the articles applied GTM to individuals as a unit of analysis; 6 applied GTM at the organization level; the remainder applied GTM at both levels. GTM is said to be particularly good for studying processes (Glaser 1978, Orlikowski 1993).

Looking at Orlikowski and Iacono's five categories of IS research, described in the previous section, there is a correlation between GTM use and interactional research. For instance, the Ensemble view of technology where the focus is on dynamic interaction between people and technology has a large number of articles represented in Table 16.1, and GTM is generally applied at the individual level of analysis in these studies. The same applies to the Tool category. It is harder to conceive of an individual unit of analysis in the Computational or Nominal category, and the lack of GTM articles in these categories bears this out.

One thing to consider in GTM application in IS is whether we need to be far more flexible as to what a unit of analysis might be; e.g. Lamp (2006) proposes using Glaser's (1978) coding families for the ontological analysis of IS research. This is a good example of an imaginative adaptation that is far removed from the original intent of grounded theory, yet leverages one of the most important aspects of GTM; the ability of GTM to help develop theoretical linkages between categories.

Untapping the theory building potential of GTM for IS

One thing that is clear from the above discussion is that the theory-building abilities of GTM remain largely untapped in IS. This is no different from other disciplines where this also seems to be the case, and where GTM is used for reasons other than developing theory (Becker 1993, Benoliel 1996, Elliot & Lazenbatt 2005, Green 1998). However, it is possibly more of an issue for IS; a new discipline which thus far has generated few theories of its own. There has been concern expressed (Weber 2003) that IS researchers are over reliant on theories from outside IS, and that there is too much emphasis on theory testing, as opposed to theory building. Weber identified four steps in theory building: first, articulate the constructs of a theory; second, articulate the relationships among the constructs of a theory; third, articulate the lawful state space by considering the values ('properties' in Grounded Theory parlance) for the constructs; and finally, articulate the lawful event space of a theory by identifying the changes in state of the constructs for which the theory is expected to hold. The first two steps are well represented in grounded theory method. The third and fourth steps are the 'substantive scope' of a Grounded Theory.

Whetten (1989) suggests *What, How, Why* and *Who, When, Where* as build-ing blocks for making theoretical contributions. Table 16.2 considers how these building blocks might apply to theory generated by GTM. Table 16.2 demon-strates that grounded theories are well within the conventional tenets of theoriz-ing as exemplified by Whetten. Furthermore, applying the Whetten definition to grounded theories gives a clear direction for grounded theorists to actively con-sider how the theories they build can shade ultimately into formal theories

One of the potential advantages of GTM for IS researchers is the obligation (Strauss 1987: 282) to engage with theories outside the narrow discipline area. Arguably one issue with IS research is our unwillingness to fully engage with

Table 16.2 Applying Whetten's building blocks to GTM

Whetten's (1989) building blocks of theory	Application in Grounded Theory Generation
What factors should be considered as part of the explanation of the phenomena of interest? Comprehensiveness and parsimony are important.	Deciding on which categories are 'core' categories, and selectively coding until saturation is reached.
How are the factors related? This introduces the relationships (often embracing causality[1]) between the what objects; objects and relationships form the 'domain' or 'subject' of the theory.	Relating categories through theoretical coding. The relationships between categories can be of many different types, not just causal. Glaser's coding families (1978) give many options for theory building, including causal relationships, hypotheses, strategies and tactics, etc.
Why. What justifies the selection of factors and the proposed (causal) relationships. What are the underlying psychological, economic, or social dynamics? Why should colleagues give credence to this particular representation of the phenomena? Why are the factors behaving like they do? This aspect of a theory supplies the plausible, cogent explanation for 'why we should expect certain relationships in the what and how data' (Whetten 1989: 491). Weick (1989) refers to this as relevance and Glaser (1978: 93) adds an element of urgency when he points out that theory should 'account for ... which is relevant and problematic for those involved.'	The substantive research problem in a grounded theory study can be justified in similar ways to other studies. Because the theory is grounded in data, this provides automatic justification for factors and relationships—it is empirically justified. More interesting is the suggestion that the underlying dynamics in the wider field of investigation be identified. In grounded theory terms, this can be seen as relating and extending the substantive theory to formal theories. Thus logic starts to accompany data as the basis for evaluation.
Who, where, when are the temporal and contextual factors that set the limit on the theory's range, i.e. determine how generalizable it is. Bacharach (1989) adds 'values' (which he defines as the theorist's assumptions, especially those of a paradigmatic nature) as another set of who-variables that bound a theory.	In grounded theory the substantive scope (and generalizability) can be extended by additional theoretical sampling. Additionally, there is an opportunity for quantification of the salient constructs in the theory

[1]Whetten (1989) elegantly bypasses the (positivist) argument that causality may not be testable by comment-ing that 'restrictions in methods do not invalidate the inherent causal nature of theory' (p. 491).

theories outside our own area: Weber (2003) suggests more scrutiny of high quality exemplars from other disciplines. Even where this is attempted, theories are often imported only in a partial way. Working out how a generated theory relates to other theories (substantive or formal) requires an altogether different type of engagement. GTM is uniquely positioned to help IS researchers generate theory, as it provides clear procedures for analyzing data, generating a theory, and then engaging that theory with other theories. It is these last two points that information systems researchers need to leverage; the rest of this chapter is devoted to some suggestions and guidelines as to how grounded theory can be used to its full potential in information systems research. As information systems researchers, we tend to forget that, as information technology pervades every aspect of modern life, it is vital that theorizing helps us to deal with the modern world.

GUIDELINES AND IMPLICATIONS

This section suggests some guidelines for the application of grounded theory in information systems that may be also helpful for researchers in other disciplines. Guidelines in themselves can be problematic for researchers. It should be said at the outset that I feel that guidelines should not be a straitjacket that confines the creativity of the researcher. When the Klein and Myers (1999) guidelines on interpretive field research were published, there was a debate within information systems (Baskerville, Sawyer, Trauth, Truex, & Urquhart 1999) as to whether the publication of such guidelines represented a new orthodoxy and would confine and constrain qualitative field research. The need for flexibility in guidelines for grounded theory is doubly underlined when one considers that the main problem with the presentation of the 1990 Strauss and Corbin book (ignoring the theoretical issues for a moment) is that with clarity comes a simplification, which can easily turn into prescriptiveness. This would seem at odds with the essentially creative and emergent nature of the grounded theory process. Also, this chapter has pointed to the need for adaptations when researching information systems phenomena. The unique juxtaposition of technological artifacts and people in information systems research means that there are all sorts of theoretical possibilities around that interaction and, as previously discussed, there is a very real need for theory of all kinds to be generated in this area, not only for the discipline, but for the wider world whose every day life is infused with technology. Accordingly, these guidelines are not prescriptive—they aim for flexibility.

Guideline 1: The preliminary literature review as orientation not defining framework

In practice, most researchers will conduct a literature review before embarking on fieldwork. The injunction that no literature that relates to the phenomena should be studied before coding the data is one of the most widespread reasons for the lack of use of grounded theory, and to some extent is based on a misconception. The advice is 'brought about by the concern that literature might contaminate, stifle or otherwise impede the researchers effort to generate categories' (Glaser 1992: 31). Strauss's (1987) opinion on this issue was that the advice about delaying the scrutiny of related literature applies full force to inexperienced researchers, but less so to experienced researchers. Strauss and Corbin (1990) acknowledge that researchers bring with them both life experience and knowledge of professional and disciplinary literature. Graduate students in particular often have no choice about whether to conduct a literature review, as it is often a Departmental requirement in many universities.

The most useful way to deal with the idea of delaying the literature review is to think about the reasons for the injunction: the fear that a researcher might 'stifle' their coding. There is no reason why a researcher cannot be self aware, and be able to appreciate other theories without imposing them on the data. Walsham (1995) puts this position most succinctly when he says that it is possible to access existing knowledge without being trapped in the view that it represents the final truth in that area. At the same time, there is a real need for the researchers to engage with other theories once their substantive theory has been generated. This often implies a retrospective sharpening of the literature review once the generated theory has been finalized.

I have found the idea of the literature review as an orienting process to be useful. The researcher then knows about current thinking in the field, but, critically, does not take a position about the research to be done. One useful way to conduct the literature review is to conceive it as aspects of a broad research problem, and organize broad categories of literature around that problem. For instance, in my grounded theory study of analysts and clients (Urquhart 1999), the literature was organized around Individual Issues, Social Issues, Epistemological Issues, and Environmental Issues, all aspects of the research problem. Urquhart and Fernandez (2006) suggest that a preliminary literature review is conducted 'on the understanding that it is the generated theory that will determine the relevance of the literature.' The literature review is revisited, and extended, once the theory has been generated from the data.

Guideline 2: Coding for theory generation as opposed to superficial coding

Coding is the plank on which theory generation is based. Lehmann, Urquhart, and Myers (2006) found that there was a distinct difference between studies that applied GTM to generate descriptive constructs, and those that went beyond description to generate theories. Researchers have a number of alternatives in the coding stages of Strauss and Corbin (1990) (open coding, axial coding, selective coding) or the coding stages of Glaser (1992) (open coding, selective coding, theoretical coding), or Charmaz (2006) (open coding, focused coding, axial coding, theoretical coding). The key thing is that all stages are followed to allow adequate conceptualizations which are the basis of the formed theory. Miles and Huberman (1994) give a useful set of characterizations about codes which are of assistance when assessing the data analysis component of grounded theory studies in information systems. They describe three types of codes which can be equated to analytic level: *descriptive* codes, attributing a class of phenomena to a segment of text; *interpretive* codes, where meaning is attributed with reference to context and other data segments; *pattern* (or linked) codes, inferential and explanatory codes which describe a pattern. Clearly, it is desirable that the researcher reaches the third stage, that of inferential and explanatory codes. Axial coding (Strauss & Corbin 1990) or theoretical coding (Glaser 1978) are essentially about relationships between categories, the very stuff of theory building.

In my experience, it is in defining the relationships between categories that researchers really achieve depth of theory. These relationships can come from Glaser's (1978) coding families, the coding paradigm of Strauss and Corbin, or indeed anywhere, as long as relationships are considered. During this stage, it often becomes clear that some categories are properties of others and, as thinking sharpens, category names often reflect analytic thinking as opposed to simply describing the phenomenon. One issue for grounded theory application in information systems is the level at which the data is to be coded. Line-by-line coding is recommended and demonstrably fruitful (Charmaz 2006, Urquhart 2001), as it forces the researcher to consider the data in a detailed and systematic manner; it is less likely in this circumstance that the researcher will impose a story on the data. Given the varied phenomena in the realm of information systems to which GTM can be applied, line-by-line coding may not always be appropriate. Where there are large data sets of organizational documents, for instance, it might be more appropriate to code at a paragraph or page level.

Guideline 3: Use of theoretical memos and diagrams to aid the theory building process

Charmaz (2006) calls memo writing a crucial method in grounded theory. As data analysis proceeds, different dimensions of the research problem are discovered (Dey 1993), and memos are ideal for clarifying those dimensions. Memos can also be used for theorizing about relationships between categories and expanding the definition of a category. They are an important part of understanding the data as the researcher lives with the data over a period of time. Breaking off to write about that data, especially when using constant comparison methods, enables all sorts of insights about the data and its context. In my own work, I have found that the memoing process enabled me to elucidate key theoretical developments in the analysis, and these memos invariably find their way into the final write-up. Strauss (1987) also recommends the use of integrative diagrams in conjunction with theoretical memos, where the relationships between categories are successively reconsidered. One advantage of using such diagrams is that the relationships between categories are more systematically considered than might otherwise be the case.

Guideline 4: Building the emerging theory and engaging with other theories

One of the major criticisms of grounded theory method is that it produces low-level theories that give detailed insights about an area, but it is then difficult to scale up that theory. This in turn can make it difficult to assess the contribution of an emergent theory, as it may be at too low a level to engage with competing theories in the area. Thus there is the phenomenon of the grounded theory study which provides rich insights into a substantive area but does not engage with the literature in a meaningful way. So there are two issues at stake: first how to generate a theory at such a level that it can be engaged with other theories, and second the manner of that engagement. Glaser and Strauss (1967) recommend the development of only one or two core categories. In my experience, most researchers in IS tend to produce more than two core categories. This may be because the phenomenon being studied is not necessarily a process (see the different categories of IS research suggested by Orlikowski & Iacono 2001) and may have many different and distinct elements. A more compelling general reason is that the bottom up derivation of the generated theory makes it difficult to think in a very abstract manner. The very strength of grounded theory (its unique tie to the data) may also be in fact the weakness of the method. One useful device is to group the major categories into overarching themes, and relate these themes to areas of theory. A similar tactic is to generate propositions.

Glaser (1978) makes some useful suggestions for scaling up a theory and engaging with other theories. First, the rewrite method, where the theory is rewritten to omit specifics. So, for example, instead of talking about the strategies used by analysts when talking to their clients, one could talk about the strategies used by professionals when dealing with their clients, and this can act as a starting point to relate to other theories. While there are no more data points sampled, it nevertheless provides a starting point. Second, the level of conceptualization can be raised by comparing it to the data from other substantive theories. Third, the theory can be analyzed by comparing it with other substantive theories in the area. Glaser also suggests that formal models of process, structure, and analysis may be useful guides to integration. So, in the field of information systems, meta theories such as structuration theory (Orlikowski 1992, Walsham 2002) or actor-network theory (Walsham & Sahay 1999) may be a useful lens through which to view the emergent theory. Glaser (1978) also makes the point that context is necessarily stripped away as one moves toward a formal theory, and that comparative analysis is used to compare conceptual units of a theory, as well as data. For instance, in my own work, I produced a substantive theory of how systems analysts and their clients negotiated requirements for a new system. I could see similarities with substantive theories in health about interaction between patients and health professionals. I could also relate the emergent theory to theories of negotiation (Strauss 1978).

Guideline 5: Clarity of procedures and chain of evidence

One of the strengths of GTM is its ability to provide a chain of evidence. For every aspect of the generated theory discussed, there are many examples in the data. Illustrating the theory with data contributes greatly to the plausibility of the research account, and also allows readers to assess for themselves the researcher's claims (Charmaz 2006). It is still unusual, in information systems and other disciplines, to see a clear description of how coding procedures were applied. Yet it is not difficult to supply an account of the coding with some examples. Sometimes this is due to lack of space, sometimes I suspect that researchers do not want to reveal that, somehow, they deviated from the method. Yet it is precisely these deviations, or adaptations as I prefer to call them, which will move forward the application of grounded theory in information systems.

GTM is a living body of knowledge and it is up to us as information researchers to render GTM as it is appropriate for our discipline. Charmaz (2006) is an excellent example of a cogent re-rendering of GTM for the twenty-first century, while retaining the strengths of GTM: its credibility through grounding in data. Adaptations of grounded theory in information systems show us that grounded theory method can be applied in innovative ways to varied IS phenomena. Examples include fusing GTM with Action Research (Baskerville & Pries-Heje 1999), using GTM for a software pre-evaluation framework (Lings & Lundell 2005), and applying GTM to ontological analysis of scientific articles (Lamp 2006). Of course, an adaptation of grounded theory requires knowledge of what is being adapted, so the adaptations can be accounted for and analyzed with regard to the strengths and original purposes of GTM.

CONCLUSION

This chapter has reviewed the status and potential of GTM as a tool for IS research, and has come to two major conclusions. First, that clearly documented adaptations of GTM are both necessary and useful in IS research, given the interaction of individuals and technology which is unique to the field. Second, that the potential of GTM for theory building is yet untapped in IS, despite calls in the field for IS researchers to build theory (Weber 2003). Looking at how GTM has been represented in IS academic writings, it can be seen that it has largely been adopted as a method by interpretive researchers attracted to its close tie to the data. Some perceptions of GTM in IS that might have contributed to this particular pattern of use is the idea put forward by Walsham (1995) that GTM ignores existing theory and that GTM generates micro theories and ignores broader conditions. Both ideas are a subtle but not uncommon misrepresentation of GTM; GTM does require researchers to engage with other theories *after* the theory has been generated, and there is a great deal of discussion in the classic texts of GTM about building formal theories from substantive ones. Also, the GT potential for theorizing broader conditions remains largely untapped.

GTM has been applied in the information systems field largely as a qualitative data analysis tool as opposed to a theory-building tool (Lehmann, Urquhart, & Myers 2006), with some notable exceptions such as Orlikowski 1993. GTM has actually been applied to most categories of IS research except studies focused on the capabilities of technology, where people are absent. However, I've suggested that there is no reason why GTM could not be applied to this category as these studies are often exploratory in nature.

I have also offered some guidelines that could assist the application of GTM in IS, namely (1) Preliminary Literature Review as Orientating Framework, (2) Coding for Theory Generation, (3) Use of Theoretical Memos and Diagrams, (4) Building the Emerging Theory and Engaging with other Theories, and (5) Clarity of Procedures and Chain of Evidence. These guidelines are not meant to be prescriptive, but to provide a framework for IS researchers to tap the potential of GTM. It is also my hope that these guidelines are helpful for all researchers using GTM as the method does not discriminate between disciplines.

For the moment, the full power of GTM as a theory building tool for IS is largely unharnessed by IS researchers. It is my hope that this chapter, and the guidelines suggested here, will encourage researchers to consider the ability of GTM to generate ground breaking theories, and how we can relate that to larger theory building efforts in IS and other disciplines. Only then can we say that we are truly leveraging the unique potential of GTM to build theory, in all its variations and richness of method.

ACKNOWLEDGMENTS

I'd like to acknowledge Hans Lehmann, Walter Fernandez, Tony Bryant, and Michael Myers for many hours of enlivening discussions and debate on GTM as we all attempt to harness the potential of GTM in information systems, in different and stimulating ways. I'd also like to thank Kathy Charmaz for her thoughtful and insightful comments that have helped shape this chapter.

REFERENCES

Adam, L. and Wood, F. (1999) An investigation of the impact of information and communication technologies in sub-Saharan Africa. *Journal of Information Science* 25(4): 307–322.

Adams, A. and Sasse, M. A. (1999) Users are not the enemy. *Communications of the ACM* 42(12): 40–47.

Annells, M. P. (1996) Grounded theory method: philosophical perspectives, paradigm of inquiry, and postmodernism. *Qualitative Health Research* 6(3): 379–393.

Bacharach, S. B. (1989) Organisational theories: some criteria for evaluation. *Academy of Management Review* 14(4): 496–515.

Baskerville, R. and Pries-Heje, J. (1999) Grounded action research: a method for understanding IT in practice. *Accounting, Management and Information Technologies* 9(1): 1–23.

Baskerville, R., Sawyer, S., Trauth, E., Truex, D. and Urquhart, C. (1999) The uses and abuses of evaluative criteria for qualitative research methods. In O. Ngwenyama, L. D. Introna, M. D. Myers and J. I. DeGross (Eds.), *Information Technology in Organizational Processes: Field Studies and Theoretical Reflections on the Future of Work*. Boston, Kluwer: 293–295.

Becker, P. H. (1993) Common pitfalls in published grounded theory research. *Qualitative Health Research* 3(2): 254–260.

Benoliel, J. Q. (1996) Grounded theory and nursing knowledge. *Qualitative Health Research* 6(3): 406–428.

Bryant, A. (2002) Re-grounding grounded theory. *Journal of Information Technology Theory and Application* 4(1): 25–42.

Bryant, A., Hughes, J., Myers, M. D., Trauth, E. and Urquhart, C. (2004) 20 Years of applying grounded theory in information systems: a coding method, useful theory generation method or orthodox positivist method of data analysis? In D. T. B. Kaplan, D. Wastell and T. Wood-Harper (Eds.), *Information Systems: Relevant Theory and Informed Practice*. Norwell MA, Kluwer.

Calloway, L. J. and Ariav, G. (1995) Designing with dialogue charts: a qualitative content-analysis of end-user designers experiences with a software engineering design tool. *Information Systems Journal* 5(2): 75–103.

Charmaz, K. (2006) *Constructing Grounded Theory: A Practical Guide Through Qualitative Analysis*. Thousand Oaks CA, SAGE.

Clarke, A. (2005) *Situational Analysis: Grounded Theory after the Post Modern Turn*. Thousand Oaks CA, SAGE.

Crook, C. W. and Kumar R. L. (1998) Electronic data interchange: a multi-industry investigation using grounded theory. *Information & Management* 34(2): 75–89.

Dey, I. (1993) *Qualitative Data Analysis: A User Friendly Guide for Social Scientists*. London, Routledge.

Eisenhardt, K. M. (1989) Building theories from case study research. *Academy of Management Review*, 14, 532–550.

Elliot, N. and Lazenbatt, A. (2005) How to recognise a 'quality' grounded theory research study. Australian Journal of Advanced Nursing 22(3): 48–52.

Fitzgerald, B. (1997) The use of systems development methodologies in practice: a field study. *Information Systems Journal* 7(3): 201–212.

Giddens, A. (1984) *The Constitution of Society*. Cambridge, Polity.

Glaser, B. G (1978) *Theoretical Sensitivity: Advances in the Methodology of Grounded Theory*. Mill Valley CA, The Sociology Press.

Glaser, B. G (1992) *Emergence vs. Forcing: Basics of Grounded Theory Analysis*. Mill Valley CA, The Sociology Press.

Glaser, B. G. (1998) *Doing Grounded Theory: Issues and Discussions*. Mill Valley CA, The Sociology Press.

Glaser, B. G. (1999) The future of grounded theory. *Qualitative Health Research* 9(6): 836–845.

Glaser, B. G. (2001) *The Grounded Theory Perspective: Conceptualization Contrasted with Description*. Mill Valley CA, The Sociology Press.

Glaser, B. G. and Strauss, A. L. (1967) *The Discovery of Grounded Theory: Strategies for Qualitative Research*. Chicago, Aldine Publishing Company.

Green, J. (1998) Grounded theory and the constant comparative method. *British Medical Journal* 316(7137): 1064–1065.

Howcroft, D. and Hughes, J. (1999) Grounded theory: I mentioned it once and I think I got away with it. 4th UKAIS Conference, London.

Hughes, J. and Howcroft D. (2000) Grounded theory: never knowingly understood. *Information Systems Review* 1: 181–199.

Hughes, J. and Wood-Harper, T. (1999) Systems development as a research act. *Journal of Information Technology* 14(1): 83–94.

Hutchby, I. (2001). *Conversation and Technology: From the Telephone to the Internet*. Cambridge, Polity Press.

Kendall, J. (1999) Axial coding and the grounded theory controversy. *Western Journal of Nursing Research* 21(6): 743–757.

King, S. F. (1996) CASE tools and organizational action. *Information Systems Journal* 6(3): 173–194.

Klein, H. K., Nissen, H. E. and Hirschheim, R. (1991) A pluralist perspective of the information systems research arena. In H. K. Klein, H. E. Nissen and R. Hirschheim (Eds.), *Information Systems Research: Contemporary Approaches & Emergent Traditions*. Amsterdam, North-Holland, Kluwer.

Klein H. K. and Myers, M. D. (1999) A set of principles for conducting and evaluating interpretive field studies in information systems. *MIS Quarterly* 23(1), 67–93.

Kling, R. and Scacchi, W. (1982) The web of computing: computer technology as social organization. *Advances in Computing* 21: 1–90.

Lamp, J. (2006) An Ontological Analysis of Scientific Works, Working Paper, School of Information Systems, Deakin University, Australia.

Layder, D. (1993) *New Strategies for Social Research*. Cambridge, Polity Press.

Layder, D. (1998) *Sociological Practice: Linking Theory and Social Research*. London, SAGE.

Lee, A. (2001) Editors comments. *MIS Quarterly* 25(1): iii–vii.

Lehmann, H. P. (2001) Using grounded theory with technology cases: distilling critical theory from a multinational information systems development project. *Journal of Global Information Technology Management* 4(1): 45–60.

Lehmann, H. P. (2003) An object oriented architecture model for International information systems? An exploratory study. *Journal of Global Information Management* 11(3): 1–18.

Lehmann, H., Urquhart, C. and Myers, M. (2006) Putting the 'Theory' back into Grounded Theory: A Framework for Grounded Theory Studies in Information Systems, University of Auckland Working Paper.

Lings, B. and Lundell, B. (2005) On the adaptation of grounded theory procedures: insights from the evolution of the 2G method. *Information Technology and People* 18(3): 196–211.

Lopata, C. (1991) Adaptation processes during the implementation of an information-system: preliminary-results from a longitudinal investigation. *Proceedings of the ASIS Annual Meeting* 28: 246–250.

Madill, A., Jordan, A. and Shirley, C. (2000) Objectivity and reliability in qualitative analysis: realist, contextualist and radical constructionist epistemologies. *British Journal of Psychology* 91: 1–20.

Markus, M. L. (1997) *The Qualitative Difference in Information Systems Research and Practice. Information Systems and Qualitative Research*. London, Chapman & Hall.

Melia, K. M. (1996) Rediscovering Glaser. *Qualitative Health Research* 6(3): 368–373.

Miles, M. B. and Huberman, A. M. (1994) *Qualitative Data Analysis: An Expanded Sourcebook* (2nd ed.). Newbury Park CA, SAGE.

Mitev, N. N. (2000) Towards social constructivist understandings of IS success and failure: introducing a new computerised reservation system, *Proceedings of the 21st International Conference on Information Systems*, Brisbane, Australia, 10–13 December, edited by W. J. Orlikowski, P. Weill, S. Ang, H. C. Krcmar and J. I. DeGross, pp. 84–93

Myers, M. D. (1997) Qualitative research in information systems. *MIS Quarterly* 21(2): 241–242.

Orlikowski, W. (1992) The duality of technology: rethinking the concept of technology in organizations. *Organization Science* 3(3): 398–427.

Orlikowski, W. J. (1993) CASE tools as organizational change: investigating incremental and radical changes in systems development. *MIS Quarterly* 17(3): 309–340.

Orlikowski, W. J. and Baroudi, J. J. (1991) Studying information technology in organizations: research approaches and assumptions. *Information Systems Research* 2: 1–28.

Orlikowski, W. J. and Iacono, C. S. (2001) Research commentary: desperately seeking the 'it' in it research: a call to theorizing the it artifact. *Information Systems Research* 12(2): 121–134.

Schultze, U. A. (2000) Confessional account of an ethnography about knowledge work. *MIS Quarterly* 24(1): 3–41.

Scott, J. E. (1998) Organizational knowledge and the Intranet. *Decision Support Systems* 23(1): 3–17.

Scott, J. E. (2000) Facilitating interorganizational learning with information technology. *Journal of Management Information Systems* 17(2): 81–113.

Seeley, M. E. and Targett, D. (1997) A senior executive end-user framework. *Information Systems Journal* 7(4): 289–308.

Sjoberg, C. and Timpka, T. (1998) Participatory design of information systems in health care. *Journal of the American Medical Informatics Association* 5(2): 177–183.

Spradley, J. P. (1979) *The Ethnographic Interview*. Fort Worth, Harcourt Brace Jovanovich College Publishers.

Strauss, A. (1978) *Negotiations: Varieties, Contexts, Processes and Social Order*. San Francisco, Jossey-Bass.

Strauss, A. (1987) *Qualitative Analysis for Social Scientists*. Cambridge, Cambridge University Press.

Strauss, A. and Corbin, J. (1990) *Basics of Qualitative Research: Grounded Theory Procedures and Techniques*. Newbury Park CA, SAGE.

Suddaby, R. (2006) What grounded theory is not. *Academy of Management Journal* 49(4): 633–642.

Toraskar, K. (1991) How managerial users evaluate their decision support: a grounded theory approach. In H. K. Klein, H. E. Nissen and R. Hirschheim (Eds.), *Information Systems Research: Contemporary Approaches & Emergent Traditions*. Kluwer, North Holland.

Trauth, E. M. (2000) *The Culture of an Information Economy: Influences and Impacts in the Republic of Ireland*. Dordrecht, Kluwer Academic Publishers.

Trauth, E. M. and Jessup, L. M. (2000) Understanding computer-mediated discussions: positivist and interpretive analyses of group support system use. *MIS Quarterly* 24(1): 43–79.

Urquhart, C. (1997) Exploring analyst-client communication: using grounded theory techniques to investigate interaction in informal requirements gathering. In A. S. Lee, J. Liebenau and J. I. DeGross (Eds.), *Information Systems and Qualitative Research*. London, Chapman and Hall, 149–181.

Urquhart, C. (1998) Analysts and clients in conversation: cases in early requirements gathering. In R. A. Hirschheim, M. Newman and J. I. DeGross (Eds.), *Proceedings of the International Conference in Information Systems*, Helsinki, Finland, 115–127.

Urquhart, C. (1999) Themes in early requirements gathering: the case of the analyst, the client and the student assistance scheme. *Information Technology & People* 12(1): 44–70

Urquhart, C. (2001) An encounter with grounded theory: tackling the practical and philosophical issues. In E. Trauth (Ed.), *Qualitative Research in IS: Issues and Trends*. Hershey, Idea Group Publishing, 104–140.

Urquhart, C. (2002) Regrounding grounded theory: or reinforcing old prejudices? A brief reply to Bryant. *Journal of Information Technology Theory and Application* 4(3): 43–54.

Urquhart, C. and Fernandez, W. (2006) Grounded theory method: the researcher as blank slate and other myths. In D. Straub and S. Klein (Eds.), *Proceedings of the Twenty Seventh International Conference on Information Systems*, Milwaukee, US, 457–464

Walsham, G. (1995) Interpretive case studies in IS research: nature and method. *European Journal of Information Systems* 4: 74–81.

Walsham, G. (2002) Cross-cultural software production and use. *MIS Quarterly* 26(4): 359–380.

Walsham, G. and Sahay, S. (1999) GIS for district-level administration in India: problems and opportunities. *MIS Quarterly* 23(1): 39–66.

Weber, R. (2003) Editor's comments: theoretically speaking. *MIS Quarterly* 27(3): iii–xii.

Weick, K. E. (1989). Theory construction as disciplined imagination. *Academy of Management Review* 14(4): 516–531.

Whetten, D. A. (1989) What constitutes a theoretical contribution? *Academy of Management Review* 14(4): 490–495.

Whiteley, A. M. and Garcia, J. E. (1996) The facilitator and the chauffeur in GSS: explorations in the forging of a relationship. *Group Decision and Negotiation* 5(1): 31–50.

Yoong, P. and Gallupe, B. (2001) The emergence of a theoretical framework for GSS facilitation: the dualities of E-facilitation. *Journal of Systems and Information Technology* 5(1): 59–80.

PART V

Grounded Theory in the Research Methods Context

17

Grounded Theorizing Using Situational Analysis

Adele E. Clarke and Carrie Friese

INTRODUCTION

Grounded theory has been among the leading approaches to qualitative inquiry for decades (e.g., Atkinson, Coffey, and Delamont 2003). Initially developed and elaborated by Glaser and Strauss and later by others,[1] grounded theory focuses on systematically analyzing qualitative data to elucidate the key forms of action undertaken by participants in a particular situation. Some more contemporary versions of grounded theory have deeply enhanced the constructionist tendencies of one of its originators, Strauss, opening it up to more directly address recent poststructural/postmodern concerns with difference, reflexivity, relationality, positionality, and so on (see Charmaz 2000, 2006). These emphases both sustain and enhance Strauss's own deep symbolic interactionist commitments.[2]

Some years ago, Katovich and Reese (1993: 400–405) argued that Strauss's negotiated order and related work recuperatively pulled the social around the postmodern turn through its methodological (grounded theoretical) recognition of the partial, tenuous, shifting, and unstable nature of the empirical world and of its constructedness. Strauss also particularly furthered this 'postmoderniza-tion of the social' through his social worlds and arenas framework; the often hidden infrastructures through which negotiations are organized. Instead of viewing social life as made meaningful and coherent only at the levels of the individual (micro-social) or society as a whole writ large (macro-social),

Strauss (e.g., 1978a,b, 1991b, 1993) offered an intermediate or meso-social vision.[3] For him the commitments people make to various groups and their positions, especially the commitment to action in situations where those groups are involved, organize social life. He termed such groups social worlds. [4]

Social worlds (e.g., a recreation group, an occupation, a theoretical tradition, a discipline) generate shared identities and perspectives among participants that then form the basis for individual and collective action (see Becker 1982). Social worlds are what Mead (1938/1972: 518) termed *universes of discourse*, principal affiliative mechanisms through which people communicate and organize social life. Larger arenas of concern are constituted of multiple social worlds all focused on a given issue and prepared to act in some way. In arenas, 'various issues are debated, negotiated, fought out, forced and manipulated by representatives' of the participating worlds (Strauss 1978a: 124). Society as a whole, then, can be conceptualized as consisting of layered mosaics of social worlds and arenas that are constantly in flux. The social worlds/arenas framework offers a way of understanding the *ongoing and situated organization of negotiations:* unstable, contingent, hailing how 'things can always be otherwise,' and may be so soon.

While grounded theory has many and distinctive strengths, we would also argue that it can productively be pushed further around the postmodern turn through supplemental analytic approaches that take this postmodernization of the social initiated by Strauss very seriously. Clarke (2003, 2005) has extended grounded theory through developing situational maps and analyses which draw directly upon Strauss's social worlds/arenas/negotiations framework, thus furthering postmodernization of the social. This chapter offers an overview of situational analysis with a new extended exemplar drawn from Friese's (2007) dissertation research.

The key concern that underlies negotiations, social worlds, and arenas is the *situatedness* of action and interaction (see Haraway 1991, 1997). While Glaser and Strauss did not initially emphasize context/situatedness in their grounded theory work, Strauss later did. He did so both on his own and with Corbin through their conditional matrices.[5] These are analytic devices intended to push the researcher to seriously consider the various 'contexts' of their research focus including pertinent organizational, community, national, and international conditions. The goal was to portray how the contextual elements 'condition' the action which is the central analytic focus. But, while pointing in some 'right directions,' the conditional matrix approach is inadequate to the task, because *there is no such thing as 'context'* (see Clarke 2005: 65–73; Hall 1997).

In sharp contrast, in situational analysis, the conditions *of* the situation are *in* the situation. The conditional elements of the situation need to be specified in the analysis of the situation itself as *they are constitutive of it*, not merely surrounding it or framing it or contributing to it. They *are* it (see Figure 17.1). In situational analyses, the situation *itself* is a key unit of analysis per se.[6] The fundamental question in doing situational analysis is 'How do these conditions appear—make

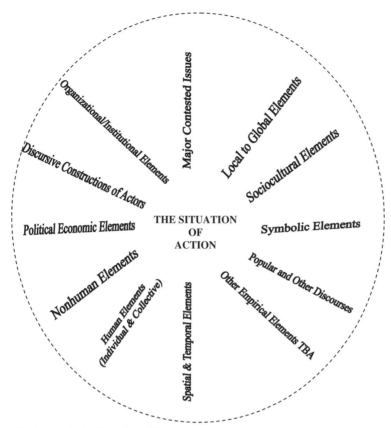

Figure 17.1 Clarke's Situational Matrix.

themselves felt as consequential—*inside* the empirical situation under examination?' Ultimately, what structures and conditions any situation is an empirical question, or set of questions. Certainly there are expectable elements of any situation that we would consider in the abstract and seek out in their specificities in the concrete in the empirical data. These are, we believe, what Strauss and Corbin (1990, 1998) were pointing toward with 'national,' 'organizational,' 'community,' and other analytic signposts.

The diagram of the Situational Matrix in Figure 17.1 frames situational analysis. In it we can see that the elements of the situation are imaged as *in* the action, as actual *parts of* the situation of action. The fundamental assumption here is that everything in the situation *both constitutes and affects* most everything else in the situation in some way(s). Everything actually in the situation or understood to be so *conditions* the possibilities of action. People and things, humans and nonhumans, fields of practice, discourses, disciplinary and other regimes/formations, symbols, controversies, organizations, and institutions, each and all can be present and mutually consequential. Here the macro/meso/micro distinctions dissolve in the face of presence/absence, while the connections among elements become more apparent.

We need to take this analytic quite a bit further, into the three modes of mapping which are situational analysis. As a part of doing systematic grounded analysis, we need maps of situations, maps that specify what is there empirically in considerable detail and from multiple angles of perception. Situational analyses also include adequate representations of the researchers and *their* position(s) on/in the maps developed. Clarke's situational analysis offers three main cartographic approaches:[7]

(1) **situational maps** which lay out the major human, nonhuman, discursive, and other elements in the research situation of concern and provoke analyses of relations among them (our focus here);
(2) **social worlds/arenas maps** which lay out the collective actors, key nonhuman elements, and the arena(s) of commitment within which they are engaged in ongoing negotiations, mesolevel interpretations of the situation; and
(3) **positional maps** which lay out the major positions taken, and *not* taken, in the data vis-à-vis particular axes of variation and difference, concern, and controversy around issues found in the situation of inquiry.

All three kinds of maps are intended as analytic exercises, fresh ways into social science data that are especially well suited to contemporary studies from solely interview-based to multi-sited research projects. Instead of centering on action (basic social processes), these maps center on elucidating the key elements and conditions that characterize the situation of concern taken up by the research project broadly conceived and move toward also making structural elements visible.

Situational maps and analyses can be used across many if not most disciplines in a wide array of research projects drawing on interview, ethnographic, historical, visual, and/or other discursive materials, including multi-site research. These methodological innovations allow researchers to draw together studies of discourses and agencies, actions and structures, images, texts and contexts, histories and the present moment, to analyze the complex *situations of inquiry* broadly conceived. In this chapter, we first briefly frame how situational analysis both relies upon and extends grounded theory. Here we include drawing grounded theory further around 'the postmodern turn' especially vis-à-vis differences, and attention to discourses. We then describe making situational maps, the initial map done in this approach. Next is the extended exemplar and discussion of actually doing situational mapping and relational analyses of the elements in the situation using such maps. In conclusion, we discuss the range of possible uses of situational analysis in research.

FROM GROUNDED THEORY TO SITUATIONAL ANALYSIS

With deep roots in symbolic interactionist sociology and pragmatist philosophy, the grounded theory method can be viewed as a theory/methods package with an interpretive, constructionist epistemology.[8] With Charmaz (2000: 510), we seek to 'reclaim these tools from their positivist underpinnings to form a revised, more open-ended practice of grounded theory that stresses its emergent, constructivist elements' and to 'use grounded theory methods as flexible, heuristic strategies.' Charmaz emphasizes that a focus on meaning-making furthers interpretive, constructivist, and we would add relativist/perspectival understandings.

In many ways, situational analysis relies on using/doing conventional grounded theory. Unique to grounded theory has been its requiring that analysis begin as soon as the researcher has data. Coding begins immediately, and theorizing based on that coding does as well, however provisionally (Glaser 1969, 1978). Second, 'sampling' is driven not necessarily (or not only) by attempts to be 'representative' of some social body or population (or its heterogeneities) but especially and explicitly by *theoretical* concerns which have emerged in the provisional analysis. Such 'theoretical sampling' focuses on finding *new data sources* (persons or things) that can best explicitly address specific theoretically interesting facets of the emergent analysis. Theoretical sampling has been integral to grounded theory from the outset, remains a fundamental strength of this analytic approach, and is also crucial for the situational analyses.[9] Other conventional aspects of grounded theory, including coding and diagramming, are done in conjunction with situational analysis as well. These should be used in situational analysis essentially as laid out in the earlier works.[10]

The problems with and critiques of grounded theory that provoked Clarke to develop situational analysis lie largely in the ways in which it did not go far enough around 'the postmodern turn.' This turn refers to an ontological/epistemological revolution that has occurred over the past several decades (and in many ways is still occurring) across the academy from the social sciences and humanities to professional schools, and throughout other sites of knowledge production such as the media, and sites of creativity in the arts, film, architecture, etc. Postmodernism consists of many things and interpretations, today essentially ubiquitous if also contested.[11] If modernism emphasized universality, generalization, simplification, permanence, stability, wholeness, rationality, regularity, homogeneity, and sufficiency, then postmodernism has shifted emphases to partialities, positionalities, complications, tenuousness, instabilities, irregularities, contradictions, heterogeneities, situatedness, and fragmentation. Most important here, postmodern scholarship involves us in 'the ontological politics of staying true to complexity' (Landstrom 2000: 475).

Research, then, is not impossible after the postmodern turn, but quite different (e.g., Bochner and Ellis 2001; Denzin and Lincoln 1994, 2000, 2005; Lather 2001, 2007; Lather and Smithies 1998). Not only have more scientistic quantitative approaches been challenged through the sociology of knowledge/science that under girds the postmodern turn, but so too have interpretive qualitative approaches to knowledge production. Qualitative research is no longer generally acceptable as serious scholarship in the absence of the kinds of reflexivities and acknowledgements of complexities that have drawn intellectual attention through the postmodern turn. Grounded theory needs to be rendered more reflexively regarding who the researchers are and the relations between researchers and participants (e.g., Bryant 2002, 2003; Charmaz 2006; Hall and Callery 2001) and so too situational analyses. To address the needs and desires for *empirical* understandings of the complex and heterogeneous worlds emerging through new world orderings, new methods are needed that are distinctly perspectival: explicit rather than tacit about their assumptions and stances. One of the key insights of the sociology of knowledge which informs the postmodern turn is that all knowledges are situated (Haraway 1999). Researchers need to make their own situatedness as individuals explicit as well as the situatedness of their research projects (e.g., funding, other sponsorship, etc.). It is these acts that are constitutive of reflexivity in practice.

Many problematics of methodology per se have been elaborated through the postmodern turn. These include an ever deepening recognition of the always already political nature of the practices of research and interpretation; the need for enhanced reflexivity; such a profound recognition of the problematics of representation that there is an ongoing 'crisis of representation'; questions of the legitimacy and authority of both research and the researcher; and de/re-positioning the researcher from 'all-knowing analyst' to 'acknowledged participant' in the production of always partial knowledges (e.g., Denzin and Lincoln 1994, 2000, 2005; Haraway 1991, 1997). In addition, methodologically the postmodern is primarily about taking situatedness, variations, differences of all kinds, and positionality/relationality very seriously in all their complexities, multiplicities, instabilities, and contradictions.[12] All of these postmodern problematics can be addressed through situational analysis.

More specifically, many if not most of the qualitative methodological moves since the postmodern turn have centered on research wherein *individual* 'voice' and its representation are at the heart of the matter, including autoethnography, interpretive ethnography, new biographies/life stories, interpretive phenomenologies, the many forms of narrative analysis, and many forms of feminist inquiry. While these are each and all crucial, the postmodern is context-driven: situation-driven. The complications, messiness, and denseness of actual *situations* in social life are central concerns. Perhaps the most innovative aspect of situational analysis is to foreground such social dimensions: the full situation of inquiry. That is, situational analysis pushes Strauss's postmodernization of the social further around the postmodern turn and grounds it in new analytic approaches that do justice to the insights of postmodern theory. Action is not enough. Our analytic focus needs to also be fully on the situation of inquiry broadly conceived.[13] The three kinds of maps do precisely this work.

Situations are complex and full of discourses of all kinds as well as people, things, and action. We dwell, in postmodern times, in 'societ[ies] of the spectacle' (Debord 1970), explosions of images, representations, and narrative discourses that constitute cultures of consumption as well as production, of politics writ a million ways, of diverse individual and collective social and cultural identities including racial, ethnic, gendered, religious, and subcultural identities, of dense histories, of old and new technologies and media from television to the Internet, and so on. Because we and the people and things we choose to study are all routinely both producing and awash in seas of discourses, analyzing only individual and collective human actors no longer suffices for many qualitative projects. Increasingly, historical, visual, narrative, and other discourse materials and nonhuman material cultural objects of all kinds must be included as elements of our research and subjected to analysis because they are increasingly understood/interpreted as both constitutive of and consequential for the phenomena we study.

It was, of course, Foucault (e.g., 1979, 1980) whose call for a focus on something other than the knowing subject has been most widely heard. And much of his own work examined discursive regimes through which knowledges come to be produced, framed, and displayed. Situational analysis draws deeply on Foucault's approach to the study of discourses and offers explicit strategies for such analyses. In situational analysis, analysis of discourses can be placed in productive conversation with Straussian contributions to the analysis of action (see Clarke 2005: 52–60). One is not forced to choose but can pursue multiple analytic strategies to grasp the situation of interest more fully.

In many ways, grounded theory was always already around the postmodern turn while in other ways it was not particularly so, and/or not clearly so. Specifically, Straussian grounded theory was always already around the postmodern turn through its explicit engagement with perspective, its materialist constructionism, and its focus on process, contingency, difference, and relationality. In contrast, grounded theory was recalcitrant against the postmodern turn in its lack of explicit reflexivity, oversimplification, singular 'basic social process,' and framing of variation as 'negative cases' (see Clarke 2005: 1–36). Situational maps and analyses pull grounded theory further around the postmodern turn. The goals of situational analysis, then, are to revise and regenerate the grounded theory method by:

- disarticulating grounded theory from its remaining positivist roots in 1950s and 1960s social science and enhancing its 'always already' present but heretofore muted postmodern capacities;
- supplementing the traditional grounded theory root metaphor of social process/action with an ecological root metaphor of social worlds/arenas/negotiations as an alternative conceptual infrastructure that allows situational analyses at the mesolevel, new social organizational/ institutional sitings;
- supplementing the traditional grounded theory analysis of a basic or key social process (action) with multiple alternatives centered on cartographic situational analyses emphasizing elements of the situation, variation and difference(s) (maps of key elements; maps of social worlds and arenas in mesolevel negotiations; and maps of issues and axes focused around difference(s) of positionality and relationality) the dense complexities of the situation of inquiry;
- generating sensitizing concepts and theoretical integration toward provocative yet provisional grounded theorizing rather than the development of substantive and formal theories as the ultimate goals; and
- framing systematic and flexible means of research design that facilitate multi-site research, including discursive textual, visual and archival historical materials and documents, as well as

ethnographic (interview and observational) transcripts and field notes to more fully take into account the complexities of postmodern life.

Situational analyses, then, are accomplished through the making of three kinds of maps and following through with analytic work and memos of various kinds. The first is **situational maps** that lay out the major human, nonhuman, discursive and other elements in the research situation of concern and provoke analyses of relations among them. These maps are intended to capture and discuss the messy complexities of the situation in their dense relations and permutations. They intentionally work *against* the usual simplifications so characteristic of scientific work (Star 1983, 1986) in particularly postmodern ways, by revealing the stunning messiness of social life.

Second, **social worlds/arenas maps** lay out all of the *collective* actors, key nonhuman elements, and the arena(s) of commitment within which they are engaged in ongoing negotiations. Such maps offer mesolevel interpretations of the situation, engaging its social organizational and institutional dimensions. They are distinctively postmodern in their assumptions: we cannot assume directionalities of influence; boundaries are open and porous; negotiations are fluid and usually ongoing. The empirical questions here are 'Who cares and what do they want to do about it?' Negotiations of many kinds from coercion to bargaining are the 'basic social processes' that stand behind and constantly destabilize the social worlds/arenas maps. Things could always be otherwise—not only individually but also collectively/organizationally/institutionally and these maps portray such postmodern possibilities.

Third and last, **positional maps** lay out the major positions taken, and *not* taken, in the data vis-à-vis particular axes of variation and difference, concern, and controversy found in the situation of concern. Perhaps most significantly, positional maps are *not* articulated with persons or groups but rather seek to represent the full range of positions on particular issues, fully allowing multiple positions and even contradictions within both individuals and collectivities to be articulated. Complexities are themselves heterogeneous and we need improved means of representing them. Now let us turn to the actual doing of a situational analysis.

MAKING SITUATIONAL MAPS

We next lay out in detail how to do just one of the three kinds of situational analyses: situational maps. There are several caveats. First, and perhaps most important, the maps produced using any or all of the strategies laid out here are not necessarily intended as forming final analytic products. While they may, of course, do so, the major use for them is 'opening up' the data and interrogating it in fresh ways. As researchers, we constantly confront the problem of 'where and how to enter.' Doing situational analyses offers three fresh paths into a full array of data sources that can lay out in various ways what you have to date.

These approaches should be considered *analytic exercises*, constituting an on-going research 'workout' of sorts, well into the research trajectory. Their most important outcome is provoking the researcher to analyze more deeply.

Second, the approaches can be used with coded data (using conventional grounded theorizing approaches to coding) or even, at least partially, with uncoded but carefully read and somewhat 'digested' data. Thus these new approaches can address the problem of 'analytic paralysis' wherein the researcher has assiduously collected data but does not know where or how to begin analysis. Analytic paralysis is, of course, not supposed to happen in a traditionally pursued grounded theory project wherein analysis, coding, and memo writing begin at the same time as data collection, and theoretical sampling then guides further data collection. But it does happen, for a wide array of reasons, especially but not only among neophytes, and usually due to fear of analysis and/or fear of making premature and/or 'erroneous' analytic commitments.

Situational maps and analyses can be used as analytic exercises simply to get the researcher moving into and then around in the data. There is nothing more important than making this happen as soon as possible in the research process. But these exercises won't work well at all unless the researcher is quite familiar with the data and can move around in/with them relatively comfortably in their own mind. Coded data (at least preliminarily and partially) are thus much better. Codes, like all other aspects of analysis, are provisional. One tries different codes on data, discards most, and then struggles to select those that fit best—and there can be and probably should be more than one. The principles of coding here remain those of constructionist grounded theory.[10] Further, coding decisions can and sometimes should be delayed. The digesting and reflecting that typically happens *after* an analysis session can be important in such decision-making.

Third, precisely *because* the goal is to stimulate your thinking, the maps should always be undertaken with the possibility for simultaneous memoing, using the precepts of basic grounded theory.[14] A pad and a tape recorder that is sound sensitive can be used so that you can speak your memos while you continue to lay out the map(s). The goal is multi-tasking in so far as you are comfortable precisely because these *relational* modes of analysis should provoke new insights into relations among the elements that need memoing promptly. Additionally, in the kinds of 'wallowing in the data' requisite to doing these maps, the researcher will notice new things already in the data that should receive analytic attention, note areas of inadequate data where further materials should be gathered, note areas of theoretical interest where particular kinds of additional data are requisite, and so on. Inadequate memoing is the major problem of almost all qualitative research projects—scribbled notes are always better than nothing and thoughtful memos on the computer are intellectual capital in the bank. And just because they are etched in silicon does not mean you cannot change your mind.

The last caveat is perhaps the most radical: the researcher should use her or his own experiences of doing the research as data for making these maps.

There is a saying in the world of qualitative inquiry that the person doing the research is the 'research instrument.' We are further asserting that that instrument is to be used more fully in doing situational analyses. Ethnographic work of multiple kinds is always ongoing in qualitative inquiry. Participant observation is part of the 'invisible work' of research, sometimes also invisible to us (Star 1991; Star and Strauss 1998). Beginning even before a research topic is decided upon, we notice and store information, impressions, images, etc., about topic areas and issues. Not only are there no tabula rasa researchers, but also we usually come with a lot of baggage. Such ideas and preconceptions become intellectual wallpaper of sorts, background tacit assumptions sometimes operating, as it were, behind our backs in the research process. Part of the process of making situational maps is to try and get such information, assumptions, etc., out on the table and, if appropriate, into the maps. There it can be addressed in terms of utility, partiality, theoretical sampling, etc. Otherwise we often do not even know such assumptions are there, though they may be doing analytically consequential work in fruitful and/or unfruitful ways.

Further, and also radical, as trained scholars in our varied fields, usually with some theoretical background, we may also suspect that certain things may be going on that have not yet explicitly appeared in our data. In seeking to be ethically accountable researchers, we need to attempt to articulate what we see as the *sites of silence* in our data. What seems present but unarticulated? What thousand-pound gorillas do we think are sitting around in our situations of concern that nobody has bothered to mention yet? Why not? How might we pursue these sites of silence and ask about the gorillas *without* putting words in the mouths of our participants? These are very very important directions for theoretical sampling.[15]

That is, the usefulness of the approach elucidated here consists in part in helping the researcher think systematically through both the design of research, especially decisions regarding future data to collect, and the vast amounts of data that one 'uploads' into one's brain and other sites during the research process. The researcher will later want to highlight particular selected parts of all the situational analyses in final products of various kinds such as presentations and publications, and/or in designing 'interventions' in education, social policy, clinical nursing or medicine, and so on. Those are downstream decisions best made long after the analysis has been basically articulated.

ABSTRACT SITUATIONAL MAPS

The locus of analysis here is the situation. *The goal is first to descriptively lay out as best one can all of the most important human and nonhuman elements in the situation of concern of the research broadly conceived.* In the Meadian sense, the questions are: Who and what are in this situation? Who and what matters in this situation? What elements 'make a difference' in this situation? Once these maps are drafted, they are used in doing relational analyses, taking each element in turn, thinking about it in relation to the other elements on the map, and specifying the nature of that relationship (described further below).

Figure 17.2 offers the Abstract Situational Map: Messy/Working Version. A situational map should include all of the analytically pertinent human and nonhuman, material and symbolic/discursive elements of a particular situation *as framed by those in it and by the analyst*. The human elements (individuals, groups, organizations, institutions, subcultures, and so on) are generally fairly easy to specify. It is likely that, over time, not all will remain of interest, but *all should be specified here*. This first abstract example is very messy, intentionally so. Hence it is very accessible and manipulable by the researcher. Some people will prefer to continue working in this fashion for some time. Make copies, date them, and keep all versions.

Nonhuman actors/actants structurally condition interactions within the situation through their specific agencies, properties, and requirements, the demands

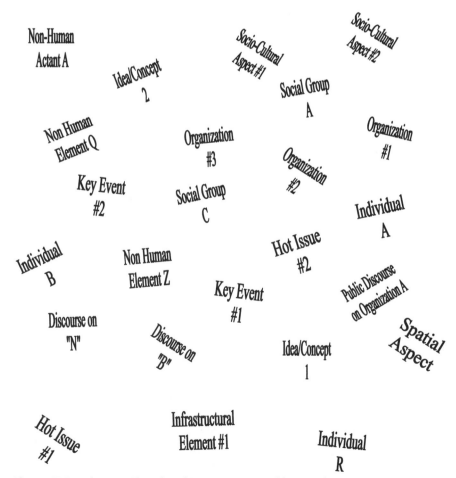

Figure 17.2   Abstract Situational Map: Messy/Working Version.

they place on humans who want to or are forced to deal with them. Their agencies and obduracies must routinely be taken into account by other actors. Some examples of nonhuman actants that should be taken into account in a situational map may be helpful. In Clarke's (1987) research on modern Western science, access to all kinds of research supplies is assumed to be available as is a certain level of physical infrastructure to do scientific work. Reliable electricity is a generally assumed, usually 'invisible,' nonhuman actor in such situations. Yet today, in many parts of the world, steady sources of power are far from common. Specifying this nonhuman actor might be important downstream. In addition, for Western medical scientists, research materials can usually be ordered today by fax or email (e.g., purebred rats, cages, food, medical, and surgical supplies, lineage forms, chemicals, cell lines, hormones, etc.). Historically, before WWI, no such research supply houses existed and just getting your research materials into the laboratory was a 'do-it-yourself' project of the first magnitude for scientists themselves, as there also were no technicians. So in a contemporary ethnographic study of a lab or other worksite, for example, ease of access to needed supplies and technologies might well be worth analytic consideration. Access certainly deserves a few moments of contemplation. What facilitates access? What hinders it? Are these represented on the map? *The key question is: what nonhuman things really 'matter' in this situation of inquiry, and to whom or what?* It is the researcher's responsibility to get these into the data, through ethnographic observations, field notes about interviews, etc., as well as through interview questions. It can be most interesting to see what is taken for granted.

We also need to ask what ideas, concepts, discourses, symbols, sites of debate, and cultural 'stuff' may 'matter' in this situation. Here we want to highlight the symbolic meanings/discursive constructions of some research materials. To many (if not most) people, there are tremendous symbolic differences between using rats and mice in research wherein they are sacrificed/killed compared to using cats and dogs, monkeys, and human stem cells. Research using pet animals historically mobilized major segments of anti-vivisection movements, unlike the use of rats and mice. The symbologies of monkeys as nonhuman primates 'close to us' triggers yet other reactions, and fetal/stem cells evoked in the USA about 150 years of debate about abortion and women's rights. The symbolic and discursive meanings of elements in situational maps may be of tremendous significance in the analysis. Again, the researcher needs to make sure they are present in the data (through careful theoretical sampling if not already present), and on the situational map. If they turn out to be of no particular importance, they will drop away in later stages of the research process.

Figure 17.3 offers the second Abstract Situational Map: Ordered/Working Version. This map is made using the messy one as data. These categories are framed both from Clarke's work and from Strauss's (1993: 252) several 'general orders' within his negotiated/processual ordering framework: spatial, temporal, technological, work, sentimental, moral, aesthetic, and so on. In terms of laying out the major elements in situations, these categories seem basic. Using your

**INDIVIDUAL HUMAN
ELEMENTS/ACTORS**

e.g., key individuals and
  significant (unorganized)
  people in the situation

**COLLECTIVE HUMAN
ELEMENTS/ACTORS**

e.g., particular groups,
  specific organizations

**DISCURSIVE CONSTRUCTIONS
OF INDIVIDUAL AND/OR
COLLECTIVE HUMAN ACTORS**

As found in the situation

**POLITICAL/ECONOMIC
ELEMENTS**

e.g., the state; particular
  industry/ies; local/regional/global
  orders; political parties; NGOs;
  politicized issues

TEMPORAL ELEMENTS

e.g., historical, seasonal, crisis,
  and/or trajectory aspects

**MAJOR ISSUES/DEBATES
(USUALLY CONTESTED)**

As found in the situation; and
  see positional map

OTHER KINDS OF ELEMENTS

As found in the situation

**NONHUMAN ELEMENTS
ACTORS/ACTANTS**

e.g., technologies, material
  infrastructures, specialized
  information and/or
  knowledges, material 'things'

**IMPLICATED/SILENT
ACTORS/ACTANTS**

As found in the situation

**DISCURSIVE CONSTRUCTION
OF NONHUMAN ACTANTS**

As found in the situation

**SOCIOCULTURAL/SYMBOLIC
ELEMENTS**

e.g., religion, race, sexuality,
  gender, ethnicity, nationality,
  logos, icons, other visual and/or
  aural symbols

SPATIAL ELEMENTS

e.g., spaces in the situation;
  geographical aspects; local,
  regional, national, global issues

**RELATED DISCOURSES
(HISTORICAL, NARRATIVE
AND/OR VISUAL)**

e.g., normative expectations of
  actors, actants, and/or other
  specified elements; moral/ethical
  elements; mass media and other
  popular cultural discourses;
  situation-specific discourses

Figure 17.3   Abstract Situational Map: Ordered/Working Version.

own messy map to build this one allows for new and different categories and/or modifications of these. *There is no absolute need to have all of these categories in any given analysis.* You may also have other categories. What appears in *your* situational map is based on *your* situation of inquiry: your project. The goal here is *not* to fill in the blanks but to really examine *your* situation of inquiry thoroughly. Some people may not even want to do the ordered working version. That's fine. It isn't necessary.

The situational map will not, of course, have absolutely everything in the situation on it, but it should at least start out erring on the side of inclusivity. Having a big piece of paper with most everything that you can figure out is important in the research situation written on it in some way can be extraordinarily powerful and empowering of the analyst. It allows you to 'get a grip' on your research which, in turn, allows analysis to proceed. Simply staring at the situational map, revising it via collapsing and expanding categories/items, adding and deleting, is analytically very provocative. This is a moment when the art of research is often strong, as one versus another form of representation of something will usually seem 'right or wrong' or at least 'better or worse.' One makes some analytic commitments (however provisional) and moves on. Memoing at the end of a mapping session about that session can be very important as well, noting new insights, signaling shifts of emphasis or direction, detailing further directions for theoretical sampling. (We assume that researchers use some version of a running research journal or audit trail, some means of chronicling changes of direction, rationales, analytic turning points, etc.)

Despite their appearance of fixity, these maps are not static in the way that street maps represent fixed entities in a more or less constant relationship with each other and are unlikely to change very much. (Of course, this is also an incorrect assumption about street maps.) In sharp contrast, there can be considerable fluidity through negotiations, repositionings, etc., in the relations portrayed in these maps, including the addition and deletion of actors and actants, and so on over time. Finally, while represented here two-dimensionally, multi-dimensional maps are also possible. Be sure to date each version of your situational maps and make a couple of photocopies so that you can tinker with them later and still file at least one clean copy of the earlier versions.

Once the basic situational map is done, the next step is to start asking questions based on it and memoing your answers. Relations among the various elements are key. One might not think to ask oneself about certain relations, but if you do what we think of as quick and dirty **relational analyses with the situational map** they can be revealing. The procedure here is to take each element in turn and think about it in relation to each other element on the map— as if you were drawing lines between them and had to *specify the nature of the relationship by describing the nature of that line*. One does this systematically from every element on the map to every other. This is the major work one does with the situational map. Sometimes it is tedious or silly, but at other times it can trigger breakthrough thinking, and this is, after all, the main analytic goal. This is one of the ways in which being very systematic in consideration of the data can flip over into the exciting and creative moments of intellectual work.

It can thus be useful to make a bunch of photocopies of the messy situational map and then write/draw these relations on the copies, in different colors perhaps, to highlight particular perspectives. For example, the perspectives of Organization #1 might be very important and hold considerable power in the situation. One could go through that organization's perspectives on all of the other actors (in a bright highlighter) to see which actors are attended to *and which are not*, as well as the actual contents of the organization's perspectives on its 'others.' Silences can thus be made to speak.

Each map in turn should lead to a memo about the relations diagrammed. At early stages of analysis, such memos should be partial and tentative, full of questions to be answered about the nature and range of particular sets of social relations, rather than answers themselves. Such memos thus help plan theoretical sampling. They can also act as analytic 'place holders' to remind the analyst to return to these relational questions later in the research process and to then 'complete' the memos if it seems worthwhile. One would answer the questions that remained both unanswered and interesting. Relational analyses are not particularly exotic, but rather provide a systematic, coherent, and potentially provocative way to enter and memo the complexities of a project laid out in a situational map.

EXEMPLAR SITUATIONAL MAPS: SITUATING THE CLONING OF ENDANGERED SPECIES

This section is based on Friese's dissertation research and I use the first person pronoun in this section to more vividly show the process of doing situational analysis. My dissertation explores contemporary meanings of cloning in the USA by studying some of the situations wherein nuclear transfer has been taken up since the birth of Dolly the Sheep, the first mammal born using nuclear transfer with an already differentiated cell (rather than a pluripotent stem cell) from an already existing animal. The cell used with Dolly was from an ewe's udder (hence Dolly).

Most of the scholarly and popular discussions about nuclear transfer have focused almost exclusively on the potential meanings and consequences of this technique if used on humans, which has largely been considered by projecting the imagined implications of this technology onto the normative structures and logics that under gird social institutions such as the family, the individual, or biomedicine. By asking how this technique may be congruent with or disruptive of these institutional sites of social practice, the implications of cloning are produced. In these discourses, the normative features of social institutions and potential threats of change are the units of analysis.

The project of my dissertation is to alternatively consider the various meanings of cloning by exploring how nuclear transfer technology has been taken up *in* specific situations and tracing the kinds of implications this has had *for* the various elements in these specific situations as well as for other situations. This redirects my attention from the imagined practice of human cloning to the real and widespread endeavors in cloning animals. I do not examine social structures as self-evident categories, but instead explore how social structures among other elements are evoked, impinged upon, and remade within the situations of cloning both discursively and in concrete practice/action. The unit of analysis in my project is thus the situation itself.

The practices of cloning animals are multiply situated, including: transgenic animals for pharmaceutical production, productive livestock in agriculture, competitive individuals in the animal racing industry, hunted animals in the sporting industry, deceased pets in the companion animal industry, model animals in the life sciences, and endangered species in zoological parks. Because the discourses about cloning animals of endangered species are rich in controversy and contestation (analytically rich sites for science and technology studies; Nelkin 1995), I decided to focus specifically on these endeavors. I then compared how nuclear transfer has been taken up with endangered animals to the situations of cloning livestock, companion animals, and laboratory animals. Making comparisons of varying situations was pivotal to my research design, deeply informed my analytic process, and is a classic aspect of grounded theory, which is known as the constant comparative method (Clarke 2005). Comparisons are very analytically productive in terms of grasping differences. Through making these comparisons I elucidated upon the ways in which the meanings of cloning are produced in and part of the concrete empirical situations wherein this technique is being used.

I began by asking a number of questions about the uptake of nuclear transfer to clone animals of endangered species. What kinds of practices and discourses are involved in cloning such animals? How do such projects relate to other cloning endeavors? How are relationships being forged between different sites, institutions, and scientific and other communities in order to enact these projects? What kinds of contestations are underway over this particular utilization of the nuclear transfer technology? How are varying understandings of, and interests in, cloning endangered animals negotiated across social worlds? What kinds of meanings, practices, and logics are being forged and/or reworked in taking up nuclear transfer with these animals? How is cloning constitutive of various humans, nonhumans, and human-animal relations? In addressing these questions, I have interviewed people directly involved or implicated in the practice of cloning animals of endangered species. I have also analyzed how this practice has been discussed in the popular media, scientific journals, position statements of organizations, and on websites. I have used situational analysis and grounded theory in designing this project, conducting research, and analyzing data.

Throughout the research process, I used situational and relational maps to develop an understanding of the varying situations wherein animals of endangered species are cloned and to consider the relationships *between* these situations. Working with these maps has been an iterative process; the maps continued to change and develop as my dissertation research moved along. Here, I am limiting my discussion to the situational and relational maps I created to understand two inter-related situations wherein nuclear transfer was used to clone endangered animals. There are other situations in my dissertation that could have been used as exemplars and there are other stories that could have been told about the situations that will be discussed. I tell this particular story because it shows how I came to appreciate the complexities of a particular situation through the analytic work of making and comparing maps to address my questions about the kinds of practices, discourses, and social worlds that are coming together in certain ways to clone animals of endangered species.

This particular exemplar also illustrates how creating situational and relational maps forced me to rethink my own assumptions about the situation itself.

Figure 17.4 is my 'messy map' of the endeavors to clone a gaur and a banteng. Both the gaur and banteng are endangered or threatened species of cattle that originate in Southeast Asia. In the messy map, I laid out all of the elements involved in these projects. I positioned the projects together in the situation because these two undertakings in cloning endangered animals occurred consecutively and, generally speaking, involved the same organizations. The initial project to clone a gaur was an integral part of the situation in which cloning the banteng was done. In this particular messy map, I used all data sources to list the elements involved. I actually included these data sources in the

Figure 17.4 Friese's messy situational map of cloning a gaur and a banteng.

messy map in order to reflect upon their role in the situation itself.[16] Here, the situation is the unit of analysis. Mass media reporting, journal articles, and many of the individuals I interviewed were all part of this situation and therefore were included in the maps.

Figure 17.5 shows the organization of the messy map into a neat map, where each element was defined. Many of the definitions used to categorize the elements were taken from Clarke (2005), while some were added because of their

Organizational/Institutional Elements
Zoos
Biotechnology industry
Laboratories
Farms
Endangered species
Advanced Cell Technology
Trans Ova Genetics
San Diego Zoological Society
San Diego Zoological Park
Center for Research of
  Endangered Species, San
  Diego Zoological Society
Frozen Zoo, San Diego
  Zoological Society
Gaur Specie Survival Plan and
  Studbook
Banteng Specie Survival Plan
  and Studbook
Ungulates Taxonomic Advisory
  Group
American Zoological and
  Aquarium Association (AZA)
International Embryo Transfer
  Society
Reproductive Science Advisory
  Group, AZA
Slaughter houses
Mass media
Science journals

Discursive Constructions of Human Actors
Cloners moving too quickly
Scientists building "brave new
  worlds"

Political Economic Elements
Endangered species
Wild/captive populations
Public relations
Endangered Species Acts
Tourism industry

Nonhuman Elements
Cloned gaur
Cloned banteng
Domestic cow ova
Domestic cow surrogates
Frozen fibroblast cells from gaur
  that had died

Frozen fibroblast cells from
  banteng that had died
MtDna

Human Elements (Individual & Collective)
Kurt Benirschke
Oliver Ryder
Philip Damiani
Robert Lanza
Geneticists
Reproductive scientists
Specie Survival Plan
  Coordinators
Zoo community
Biotechnology industry
Advanced Cell Technology
Trans Ova Genetics
San Diego Zoological Society
San Diego Zoological Park
Center for Research of
  Endangered Species, San
  Diego Zoological Society
Ungulates Taxonomic Advisory
  Group
American Zoological and
  Aquarium Association (AZA)
Reproductive Science Advisory
  Group, AZA

Spatial & Temporal Elements
Endangered species
Wild/captive populations
Zoos
Farms
Labs
Biobanks

Popular & Other Discourses
Biodiversity
Specie Conservation
Endangered species
"Good" captive breeders
Cloning is bad
Extinction
Jurassic Park
Genetic value
Hybrids
Chimeras
Purity
Stem cell controversies
Dolly the sheep

Human/animal distinction

Symbolic Elements
Live births as success
Specie Conservation
Extinction
Panda
Wooly mammoth
Zoos
Farms
Labs
Dolly the sheep

Sociocultural Elements
Specie Conservation
Wild/captive populations
Livestock
Zoo animals
Extinction

Practices as Elements
Biodiversity preservation
Specie Conservation
Assisted reproductive
  technologies
Nuclear transfer
Cryopreservation
Karyotyping
Captive breeding
Public relations
Developing techniques
Researching
Research materials exchanges
Captive breeding
Assessing/producing genetic
  diversity
Wild/captive populations

Logical Frameworks
Hierarchical logic in using
  assisted reproductive
  technologies
Venn diagrams

Major Contested Issues
Nuclear transfer is/not ready for
  use with zoo animals
Live births do/not constitute
  success
Mitochondrial DNA and hybrids
Health of offspring

Figure 17.5   Friese's ordered situational map of cloning a gaur and a banteng.

importance in the project itself. For instance, defining elements as 'logical frameworks' or 'practices' resulted from my own creation of the neat map. Notice that many elements are multiply defined. Endangered species are positioned as organizational/institutional elements because they now represent the institutionalization of certain practices. Endangered species are also positioned as symbolic elements: think of the kinds of emotional capital that the giant panda holds.

Looking at the messy map, one notices that there are a large number of organizational/institutional elements as well as practices involved in the situation. This is linked to my use of the social worlds/arenas framework in this project. Strauss (1993: 212) defined social worlds as groups with shared commitments to activities, resources, and ideologies about enactment (see also Clarke 1991). An important facet of the social worlds framework is that the boundaries between worlds are fluid and individuals often occupy multiple spaces. The questions I ask about the kinds of relations between social groups, discourses, and practices in cloning animals of endangered species shows how the social worlds/arenas framework informs my own questioning of cloning. Rather than asking how cloning impacts 'society,' I asked how cloning entered into certain social worlds and then considered the implications this entry has had not only for the social worlds involved but also for meaning-making processes around cloning itself. For instance, biotechnology companies are committed to producing capital-intensive, biological-based products and procedures for biomedical and agricultural applications among others. Zoological societies are committed to sustaining both wild and captive populations of endangered wildlife. Biotechnology companies and zoological societies intersect in their mutual utilization of assisted reproductive technologies to achieve their goals. However, these practices are quite differentially embedded in the material, political, economic, historical, logical, and symbolic elements that inform these different organizational uptakes.

A gaur was the first cloned animal of an endangered species. The project to clone a gaur was enacted through agreements made between Kurt Benirschke, the then-President of the Zoological Society of San Diego with Robert Lanza and Philip Damiani of Advanced Cell Technology (ACT), a well-known biotechnology company based in Massachusetts. Kurt Benirschke (1986) became involved in the project because he strongly believes that cloning may be an important tool for creating genetic diversity among captive animal populations of endangered species and thereby help sustain captive populations. In addition, he believes that using assisted reproductive technologies with endangered species can help produce basic knowledge about the reproductive physiologies of species that are generally under or not-at-all studied. ACT became involved in this project for public relations purposes and to prove possible the principle of interspecies nuclear transfer. Cloning animals of endangered species has largely been configured as a good application of this problematic technique in the popular press. By cloning an endangered animal, the company sought to improve public perceptions of cloning. In addition, while it was considered unethical to experiment in order to find out if cow ova would 'reprogram' human nuclei, the company rightly believed that a mass-mediated, public critique would not be raised against using cow ova to reprogram endangered cattle nuclei.

The project to clone the gaur was considered experimental research and was enacted somewhat informally through networks of professional friendship. Kurt Benirschke asked that the Frozen Zoo at the Center for Research of Endangered Species, Zoological Society of San Diego, send frozen cells taken from a gaur to ACT. Scientists at ACT then did the nuclear transfer procedure using nuclei taken from the gaur cells and enucleated ova from domestic cows. Some scientists at the company were happily surprised at the number of viable embryos that resulted. These embryos were then sent to Trans Ova Genetics, where they were implanted into domestic cow surrogates. One gaur was eventually birthed. Trans Ova Genetics is a biotechnology company located in Iowa that uses advanced reproductive technologies to meet the breeding needs and desires of ranchers in the livestock industry.

Unfortunately, the one resulting cloned gaur died 2 days after birth. As is common in the biotechnology industry, exchange relations between these individual and organizational actors were short-term and lasted for the duration of this project alone. (See the discussion of networks and assemblages below.) After the death of the gaur, broader questions arose in the Zoological Society of San Diego as to whether or not another project of cloning an animal of an endangered species should be pursued. More formal discussions and debates were conducted regarding the use of nuclear transfer and included a larger number of individuals and perspectives. People questioned whether the organization should be involved in another attempt at cloning, if a gaur should be cloned, and if the collaboration should again be forged with ACT. In light of these discussions, the Board of the Zoological Society of San Diego decided that nuclear transfer should again be attempted with ACT and Trans Ova Genetics, but that the technique should be used to clone a banteng instead of a gaur. Similar exchanges in materials resulted and two bantengs were born. Sadly, one banteng was born with enlarged calf syndrome, weighing twice what a normal banteng should, and was euthanized. The other banteng is still alive and is currently on display at the San Diego Zoological Park.

The successful birth of a surviving offspring brought another set of organizational actors into the situation of cloning endangered animals: organizations responsible for managing the reproduction of zoo species to ensure that the captive population remains 'viable' or genetically diverse. These organizations are the Specie Survival Plan (SSP) and the Studbook that represents the ungulates Taxonomic Advisory Group (TAG), all coordinated through the American Zoo and Aquarium Association. After the birth of the banteng, the ungulates Taxonomic Advisory Group had their scientific meetings where scientists described how nuclear transfer worked and how they envisioned the applicability of this technique in the zoo field. Following the presentation, the advisory group decided to continue the experiment and see if the banteng is capable of reproducing healthy offspring. For this group, the question of whether or not nuclear transfer can be a tool for conservation will begin to be addressed if and when the cloned banteng reproduces. This kind of experimentation comes with the hope that the banteng SSP will reach its goals of genetic diversity in the captive population more rapidly than previously thought possible. But it is also pursued with the knowledge that future offspring may not be possible or may have health problems associated with the nuclear transfer process.

In mapping the situations wherein the gaur and banteng were cloned, important distinctions became readily visible. I had originally mapped these two endeavors together because the same organizations were present and the gaur project provided the basis for cloning the banteng. However, the analytic process itself indicated that these organizational elements were involved differently when the two projects were compared. Whereas the project to clone a gaur was informally initiated by individuals, the Zoological Society of San Diego initiated the project to clone the banteng. Whereas the decision to clone a gaur was made by only a few individuals, the decision to clone a banteng was brought about through broader organizational efforts that included the commitment to action of many more individuals within the Zoological Society of San Diego itself.

Given these differences, I asked: What would happen analytically if I explored the situation to clone the gaur and the banteng as *both* inter-related and distinct? To do so, I then used relational maps in order to better understand the relationships and discontinuities in the gaur and banteng situations. By comparing the relations between the elements in the endeavors to clone the gaur and the banteng I was able to better understand the situations per se. Through this 'thick analysis' (Fosket 2002), I came to better understand the social processes that work to make cloning meaningful in very particular and local ways.

Figures 17.6 and 17.7 show my relational maps for the gaur and the banteng projects respectively. One important difference in the relationships between the elements in these two situations is the varying logical frameworks used to address the question of what individual, from which species, should be cloned. While the gaur project used a hierarchical logic, the decision to clone a banteng was made through the use of a Venn diagram.[17] These different logics for decision-making are situated by different social worlds. In turn, the gaur and the banteng stories illustrate the extent to which the meanings of cloning animals of endangered species are still being negotiated.

The gaur was originally chosen as the right specie to clone because there were previous successes in using interspecies *embryo* transfer wherein gaur embryos were implanted into domestic cows as surrogates. The logic that underpins this decision was connected with the notion of a hierarchy of assisted reproductive technologies, from least to most invasive, that is frequently used in the reproductive sciences when discussing issues related to the applicability of techniques. In general, the hierarchy assumes that artificial insemination is the least complicated, most useful, and most likely to be successful technique. In vivo and in vitro fertilization and embryo transfer are more complicated and less often

Figure 17.6   Friese's relational map of cloning the gaur.

successful/useful, while nuclear transfer is the most complicated and least successful/ useful technique. Following this logic, it is often argued that techniques should be pursued in a hierarchical progression within a particular species, up the ladder from least to most complicated going only one rung at a time. Because of the previous success in using interspecies embryo transfer with the gaur, it was decided that the gaur was the best animal of an endangered species to try to clone.

Following the birth and death of the cloned gaur, there were several criticisms regarding both the use of this species and of the individual cloned. In terms of the population, it was argued that the gaur is easily bred in captivity and nuclear transfer is unnecessary. In terms of the cloned individual, it was argued that this

Figure 17.7 Friese's relational map of cloning the banteng.

genome was already well represented in the captive population. Through these critiques, some people within and beyond the Zoological Society of San Diego contended that simply cloning an animal of an endangered species does not constitute a project in conservation. It was also argued that nuclear transfer should not be used with animals of endangered species simply because it is possible. Rather, critics stated that cloning would need to be used to manage gene pools efficiently for it to be a tool of conservation. Nuclear transfer remains highly inefficient in nearly all species and this remains an enduring criticism of the technique in zoo and conservation worlds. However, with the banteng project the Zoological Society of San Diego approached the issue of how nuclear transfer could be rationalized into a productive and useful technique of specie preservation.

In the midst of debates within the Zoological Society of San Diego regarding whether or not cloning should once again be attempted, the head of the Genetics Division at the Center for Research of Endangered Species, Oliver Ryder, was asked to write a white paper on the topic: a paper engaging the potential use of nuclear transfer in light of the Society's policies. In the white paper, Ryder replaced the use of a hierarchical logic in making reproductive decisions with a Venn diagram. The first factor in the Venn diagram was available technology, which Ryder defined broadly to include knowledge about the reproductive biology of the particular specie, the availability of surrogate ova, the availability of gestational surrogates, knowledge about neo-natal husbandry, and the ability of zoo staff to successfully maintain the resulting animal. The second factor was the existence of a gene pool management program for the specie, specifically a Specie Survival Plan that manages captive breeding. The third factor was the availability of saved fibroblast cells, something that the Zoological Society of San Diego has specialized in since the 1970s with the Frozen Zoo. With these three factors, Ryder created a Venn diagram made up of three overlapping circles that worked to limit the scope of cloning to a small space of intersection between all factors. Based on working using the diagram, it was decided that the gaur was not the best animal to clone. Rather, a genetically under-represented banteng who had died in puberty before reproducing was chosen. Through applying the Venn diagram, Ryder rationalized cloning to make it a potential tool of specie preservation that is premised upon managing genetic diversity and also incorporated the corresponding organizations and practices that are already capably conducting this work with captive populations. Some believe that the use of this Venn diagram was instrumental in convincing the ungulates Taxonomic Advisory Group to incorporate the cloned banteng into its captive breeding program on an experimental basis.

In comparing the relational maps of the gaur and banteng projects in Figures 17.6 and 17. 7, we see that the differing logics that informed decision-making in each instance are situated by different kinds of institutional and organizational commitments to action. The hierarchical logic is associated with commitments to developing new technologies and thereby using techniques and research materials that are likely to work. However, the hierarchical logic failed to convince many involved in the social worlds of specie conservation, which included other reproductive scientists, that cloning was a useful technique to develop for endangered species. While the hierarchical logic was associated with a definition of success based on live births of cloned individuals, the Venn diagram was associated with a definition of success based on the ability of a cloned individual to reproduce healthy offspring. Both the hierarchical logic and the Venn diagram are parts of an experimental process, but the objective of each of these experiments differs. While the hierarchical logic was associated with the production of cloned live offspring, the Venn diagram is associated with the production of healthy offspring by the clone. As such, negotiations are occurring over what constitutes success in using nuclear transfer, how this technology is to be delivered, and what it means to conserve endangered species.

REFLECTIONS ON USING SITUATIONAL MAPS

Through the use of both the situational and relational maps, I was able to see how the very meanings of cloning are constituted through negotiations over the relationships between the elements, all of which are part of the situation itself but differently constellated under different conditions. As part of the scholarly domain known as science and technology studies, my dissertation is predicated against a technologically deterministic framework, wherein meanings are understood to be inherent to the technology rather than socially mediated. Instead I examine the specific ways in which cloning is made possible and meaningful in and through its socio-technical organizations and rationalizations. As such, technologies like cloning have many inter-related meanings. Situational analysis provides a 'theories-methods package' that is especially well-suited for this kind of analysis. Clarke (2005) positions situations as a theoretical concept vis-à-vis pragmatist and interactionist threads of sociology, feminism, and post-structuralism. Drawing on Clarke's conceptualization of situations, I understand the situations themselves that cloning is becoming part of through commitments and activities as producing the very meanings of this technology. Situational and relational maps provided the methodological tools necessary to conducting this kind of analysis and representing key differences as well.

I have been working with messy and neat situational maps since the earliest design phase of this research project. These maps have been my entry point in conceptualizing the situations of cloning animals of endangered species and their relations to one another. Drawing on the methodological insight of grounded theory that data collection and analysis should occur simultaneously, working on messy and neat maps has accompanied every phase of my research endeavor. When I would analyze new interviews or articles, I would go back to my messy and neat maps and ask if there were new elements brought to light through this data source or if my thoughts about the significance or definitions of elements had changed. The maps would then generate new kinds of questions and point me in new directions, providing a basis for my theoretical sampling.

Making messy maps was a useful and user-friendly way of plunging into data. The messiness of the maps embodied the tentativeness of the analytic steps I was making in a representational format. These tentative analytic moves could then be further discussed in a memo written afterwards. The co-constitutive processes of map making and memo writing helped to generate new ideas about the data. Whenever I felt stumped or overwhelmed, I would turn to the messy maps. In turn, this process provided a window into my own changing understanding of the situations of cloning endangered animals as it developed over the research endeavor, a useful reference point at later stages in the analytic process.

Neat maps were often important reminders that the elements in the situations were not self-evident, unified categories. Going through the messy maps and defining the elements was often a surprising challenge. For instance, I had thought of endangered species as an institutionalized human-animal relationship when initiating this project. In creating the neat map, I realized that endangered species are also symbols, political economic elements, populations, embodied individuals, management practices, and popular and professional discourses. It is hard work, but grasping the contingent and multiple definitions of elements is precisely the point of situational analysis. Neat maps make the complexities of situations more readily visible. By rendering complexities, I was able to analyze their productivity within the situation itself.

One difficulty that arose while using the situational and relational maps was the assumptions of the social worlds/arenas framework that were built into this 'theory/methods package' as well as my own research design. While endeavors to clone animals of endangered species intersect with social worlds and arenas, the practice of cloning these animals is not itself an arena. Current endeavors to clone animals of endangered species are sporadic and fragmented. There are no organizations that are solely devoted to developing nuclear transfer with endangered species; nor are there any social worlds largely committed to using nuclear transfer with such animals. Moreover, this practice today remains highly contested with quite unclear futures.

The tenuous and uncertain status of the practice of cloning endangered animals is thus not necessarily best grasped with a social worlds/arenas framework, which is more attuned to processes of stabilization (e.g., Clarke 1998) where the drag of history is palpable (Clarke 2005). In my project, individuals *could not* be considered spokespersons for a social world given that the endeavor was so contentious within many of the social worlds and arenas. While some individuals are strongly in favor of and others oppose cloning animals of endangered species, many are still undecided about the utility of this experimental prospect. For example, the Zoological Society of San Diego does not currently have a position statement on cloning despite its active involvement.

However, I found the concept of the situation to be fully flexible enough to allow for the analysis of these kinds of tenuous and uncertain contemporary situations. Citing Morrione, Clarke positions the situation as 'both an object confronted and an ongoing process subsequent to that confrontation ... Situations have a career-like quality and are linked in various ways ... to other situations' (2005: 21). Situations are thus objects of inquiry that can be analyzed and also productive forces to be understood as such. My dissertation traces, among other things, the kinds of productivities the gaur and banteng situations have had in order to question the kinds of implications cloning may have, for whom, and in what ways. I thereby understand situations as having historical drag at varying temporal moments, but not necessarily in the more enduring organizational and institutional terms that are associated with social worlds and arenas. Making relational maps pointed me to the limitations of a social worlds/arenas framework for conceptualizing this particular situation.

Through the methodological tool of analyzing the situation per se, I questioned how an individual was related to a social world, how tools associated with social worlds were deployed elsewhere, and what kinds of negotiations occur when varying social worlds, ideologies, and tools intersect in a particular temporary situation. Situational analysis thereby allowed me to continue the work of analyzing social processes through grounded theorizing and to analyze social worlds and arenas as they are implicated in and by situated cloning practices. Whether the cloning of endangered species will become, over time, an established social world or subworld remains an open (empirical) question.

FINAL COMMENTS ON SITUATIONAL MAPS

Returning now to more general consideration of situational maps, the key question arises: What is a good enough situational map and how do you know when you have one? The key word here is saturation: from classical grounded theory.[18] You have worked with your map many times, tinkered, added, deleted, reorganized. You can talk at some length about every entry, and about its relations to (many if not most) other entries if there are any relations that 'matter.' It has been quite a while since you felt the need to make any major changes. You don't think you have missed much of anything. You think these are the most important elements. (Of course there are many others but they don't seem to 'make a difference' to the stories you would tell about the situation— your project.) The final test is this: If some disaster wiped out your computer files and your notes, and all you had left was this piece of paper, could you work your way back into all of the major stories you want to be able to tell about this situation?

As the research proceeds, returning to these maps can be analytically useful. In some cases, you may want to produce simplified situational maps to include only those elements you intend to address in the final products of the research. These often become project maps: maps that display various aspects of your particular project. This is fine, but don't throw away earlier more complicated even if very messy versions. Often one wants to go back because something was there that was important but now you are unable to remember.

The relational maps done using the situational map may help the analyst to decide which stories to tell. This is especially helpful in the early stages of research when we tend to feel a bit mystified about what to memo. A session doing relational analyses should produce several relational maps. The maps can diagram particularly interesting relations by circling (and boxing, triangling, etc.) certain elements and connecting them. The same element can, of course, be 'related' to multiple others. That is why a bunch of photocopies makes such work easier, and they can be attached to the memos as well.

Friese's exemplar is especially exciting because it opens up situational analysis for further uses by taking on situations where the actions/activities have nowhere near yet congealed into an established social world set in arena(s) with other related world(s). By taking the situation itself as the for-the-moment *final* unit of analysis, the question of temporality ('temporaryness') is foregrounded analytically. This links to an intriguing concept that has been circulating for some years: assemblages (e.g., Deleuze and Guattari 1987; Guattari 1992; Marcus and Saka 2006). Assemblages are temporary/contingent constellations or configurations of humans and nonhumans acting together to accomplish a specific set of goals. The under girding assumption is that 'things fall apart' unless there are sustained actions to maintain them. In grounded theory language, conditions change. The assemblage may permanently disappear, be reconstituted similarly or differently, or may even coalesce over time into a recognizable and enduring social world. Analytically, it is worthy of our attention.[19]

Friese's exemplar beautifully reveals that not every aspect of situational analysis may 'work' for a given research project. The goal of all methods is to provoke better thinking about one's project. For Friese, the very ways that the social worlds/arenas map did *not* work clarified and placed important emphasis on the highly tentative and contingent nature of cloning endangered species today. The very *absence* of an established social world devoted to it is both interesting and significant for her project.

One key task of method today is to upset the binary between modernist conceptions of knowing subjects and objects as having 'essences' and the extreme end of postmodernist conceptualization that argues that all is fragmented, unrelated, and falls into nothingness. There are intermediary relentlessly social spaces and places including social worlds and arenas and the negotiations therein. And now such spaces also include assemblages.[20]

CONCLUSIONS

In sum, situational analysis seeks to regenerate grounded theory in ways that can support researchers from the social sciences, humanities, professions, and beyond in a wide array of research endeavors. The situational maps and analyses laid out in this paper are part of the larger project. In doing situational analysis the researcher becomes not only analyst and bricouleur, but also a cartographer of sorts. These maps are useful with small or large interview-based research projects as well as ethnographic field projects. Situational analyses can also be used with historical, visual, and/or narrative discourse data, all of which have become increasingly salient to social life and deserve much more attention in sociological and related research. Because the codes and categories of a particular analysis can be both generated and applied across the full range of possible data sources, the new mapping approaches are especially useful for what is being called multi-site research (Marcus 1995; Rapp 1999). They may also be used comparatively across different data sources. Everything is situated and situational analyses map and elucidate this facet of postmodern understanding.

Bowker and Star (1999: 10) discuss 'infrastructural inversion' wherein the infrastructure of something is (unusually) revealed and even featured. An example of this would be the Pompidou Center in Paris where all of the pipes, stantions, conduits, and other building innards are instead 'outards,' exposed and attached to the exterior walls rather than hidden between the interior and exterior walls. Situational maps and analyses do a kind of 'social inversion' in making the usually invisible and inchoate social features of a situation more visible: all of the key elements in the situation and their interrelations; the social worlds and arenas (or assemblages) in which the phenomena of interest are embedded; and the positions taken and not taken by actors (human and nonhuman) on key issues. This is the postmodernization of the social in a grounded theory approach grounded in symbolic interactionism extending what Strauss initiated. Situational maps and analyses resituate grounded theory after the postmodern turn in a wide variety of ways which enable us to better grasp the discursive as well as action-centered complexities of social life.

NOTES

1 See Glaser and Strauss (1967); Glaser (1978, 1992, 2002; Glaser with Holton 2004); Strauss (1987, 1991, 1993, 1995); and Strauss and Corbin (1990, 1994, 1997, 1998). It has been further elucidated especially by Charmaz (e.g., 1983, 1995, 2000, 2002, 2005, 2006); Locke (1996, 2001); see also Bartlett and Payne (1997); Clarke (1991, 2003, 2006a,b); Clarke and Montini (1993); Corbin (1997, 1998); Dey (1999); Flick (1998); Olesen (Chapter 19); and Soulliere, Britt and Maines (2001).

2 These commitments were especially vivid during the last decade of his life as manifest in both the content and venues of his final publications. Strauss's publications are listed both chronologically and by topic on his website: www.ucsf.edu/anselmstrauss/. See also the Festschrift in his honor edited by Maines (1991), and Clarke and Star (1998).

3 Meso level or 'middle range' analytics have a long history in symbolic interactionism (e.g., Hall 1987; Hall and McGinty 2002; Maines 1995, 2001), and have become very much of interest recently within other traditions including, for example, actor-network theory (e.g., Latour 1987, 2005; Law and Hassard 1999) and assemblages (e.g., Deleuze and Guattari 1987; Guattari 1992; Marcus and Saka 2006). In quite differing ways, the works of Foucault also 'might be called a postmodern version of middle range theory' (Simon 1996: 319). Alternatively, it can also be argued that these analytics inherently refute micro/macro assumptions, a position that Strauss himself took, among others (Baszanger 1998). Clarke plans to write a paper comparing these analytics in terms of 'things organizational,' updating her earlier work (Clarke 1991).

4 Strauss developed his social worlds/arenas/negotiations framework along side but separately from his grounded theory work. See Strauss et al. (1964); Strauss (1978a,b, 1979, 1982a,b, 1984, 1988, 1991a,c, 1993).

5 See Strauss (1991, 1993; Strauss and Corbin 1990, 1991, 1994, 1998). For the actual matrices, see Strauss (1991: 457), Strauss and Corbin (1990: 163; 1998: 184), and Corbin (1991: 37).

6 On the concept of the situation, see Clarke (2005: 21–23, 52–60; In review).

7 For Clarke's work on social worlds/arenas, see Clarke (1990a,b, 1991, 1998, 2006a). For Clarke's initial articulation of the analytic importance of the situation, see Clarke and Fujimura (1992). See also Clarke and Star (2003, 2007).

8 On theory/methods packages, see Star and Griesemer (1989) and Fujimura (1992). Symbolic interactionism provides the ontological grounding. See Charmaz (2000, 2006) for excellent discussions of the range of epistemologies associated with grounded theory past and present.

9 See, on theoretical sampling, Glaser and Strauss (1967: 45–77); Glaser (1978: 36–54); Strauss (1987: 38–39); Strauss and Corbin (1998: 201–215); and Charmaz (2006: 96–122).

10 On coding, see especially Glaser and Strauss (1967: 21–43, see also Chapters 3 and 5); Glaser (1978: 55–82); Strauss (1987: 22–109); Strauss and Corbin (1998: 55–181); and Charmaz (2006: 42–72). On diagramming, see especially Strauss (1987: 130–230) and Strauss and Corbin (1990: 195–224; 1998: 217–242). For examples of diagrams, see e.g., Miller (1996) and Kearney et al. (1995).

11 On the ways in which grounded theory and/or symbolic interactionism are always already around the postmodern turn see Clarke (2003, 2005: Chapter 1).

12 Maines (1996, 2001) has eloquently argued that all this can be accomplished through pragmatism. While he may well be right (see Clarke 2005: Chapter 1), it by and large has not been. The historical provocation of the postmodern turn seems to have been requisite.

13 Charmaz (personal communication, December 10, 2006) asks 'Is there any blurring between the situation of action and the situation of inquiry? Might they not occasionally differ?' I would argue that the situation(s) of action are *inside* the situation of inquiry which is (or should be) quite broadly conceived. That is, there well may be several sites of action within any given situation of inquiry.

14 On memoing, see especially Glaser and Strauss (1967: 105–113); Glaser (1978: 83–92); Strauss (1987: 109–130, 184–214); Strauss and Corbin (1998: 217–242); and Charmaz (2006: 72–95).

15 On silences, see Poland (1998); Charmaz (2002); Star (1991); and Zerubavel (2006).

16 I have not included myself in the situation at this point in time, but recognize that I likely will do so at some point. I do not yet know if or how I have influenced the situation by entering it. However, I have told those whom I interviewed that I will share my dissertation and any articles that are derived from this project. This will likely shape the situation itself, quite probably in ways I cannot predict.

17 Venn diagrams were developed in mathematics and are illustrations of overlapping circles used to show relationships between different groups.

18 On saturation, see Glaser and Strauss (1967: 61–71, 111–112); Glaser (1978: 91–108, 124–127); Strauss (1987); Strauss and Corbin (1990: 192–193; 1998: 136–161, 212, 292–293); Charmaz (2006: 96–123).

19 In fact, situations per se can be viewed as assemblages of sorts: people, things, and actions brought together at a particular time and place under particular conditions.

20 One could also consider actor-network theory here (e.g., Latour 1987, 2005; Law and Hassard 1999). A current comparison of meso level analytics would be useful and Clarke plans to do this.

REFERENCES

Atkinson, Paul, Amanda Coffey and Sara Delamont. 2003. Key Themes in Qualitative Research: Continuities and Change. Walnut Creek, CA: Alta Mira Press/Rowman and Littlefield.

Bartlett, Dean and Payne, Sheila. 1997. Grounded Theory—Its Basis, Rationale and Procedures, pp. 173–195 in McKenzie, George, Powell, Jackie and Usher, Robin (Eds.) Understanding Social Research: Perspectives on Methodology & Practice. London/Washington DC: The Falmer Press.

Baszanger, Isabelle. 1998. The Work Sites of an American Interactionist: Anselm L. Strauss, 1917–1996. Symbolic Interaction 21(4): 353–78.

Becker, Howard S. 1982. Art Worlds. Berkeley: University of California Press.

Benirschke, K. (Ed.) 1986. Primates: The Road to Self-Sustaining Populations. New York: Springer-Verlag.

Bochner, Arthur P. and Carolyn Ellis (Eds.) 2001. Ethnographically Speaking: Autoethnography, Literature, and Aesthetics. Walnut Creek, CA: AltaMira Press.

Bowker, Geoffrey and Susan Leigh Star. 1999. Sorting Things Out: Classification and its Consequences. Cambridge, MA: MIT Press.

Bryant, Antony. 2002. Re-grounding Grounded Theory. Journal of Information Technology Theory and Application 4(1): 25–42.

Bryant, Antony. 2003. A Constructive/ist Response to Glaser. FQS: Forum for Qualitative Social Research 4(1): www.qualitative-research.net/fqs/

Charmaz, Kathy. 1983. The Grounded Theory Method: An Explication and Interpretation, pp. 109–126 in Robert M. Emerson (Ed.) Contemporary Field Research. Boston: Little Brown.

Charmaz, Kathy. 1995. Between Positivism and Postmodernism: Implications for Methods. Studies in Symbolic Interaction 17: 43–72.

Charmaz, Kathy. 2000. Grounded Theory: Objectivist and Constructivist Methods, pp. 509–536 in Norman Denzin and Yvonna Lincoln (Eds.) Handbook of Qualitative Research, 2nd ed. Thousand Oaks, CA: SAGE.

Charmaz, Kathy. 2002. Stories and Silences: Disclosures and Self in Chronic Illness. Qualitative Inquiry 8(3): 302–328.

Charmaz, Kathy. 2005. Grounded Theory in the 21st Century: A Qualitative Method for Advancing Social Justice Research. In Norman Denzin and Yvonna Lincoln (Eds.) Handbook of Qualitative Research, 3rd ed. Thousand Oaks, CA: SAGE.

Charmaz, Kathy. 2006. Constructing Grounded Theory. London: SAGE.

Clarke, Adele E. 1987/1995. Research Materials and Reproductive Science in the United States, 1910–1940, pp. 323–350 in G.L. Geison (Ed.) Physiology in the American Context, 1850–1940. Bethesda: American Physiological Society. Reprinted pp. 183–219 in S. Leigh Star (Ed.) Ecologies of Knowledge: New Directions in Sociology of Science and Technology. Albany, NY: SUNY Press, 1995.

Clarke, Adele E. 1990a. A Social Worlds Research Adventure. The Case of Reproductive Science, pp. 15–42 in Susan Cozzens and Thomas Gieryn (Eds.) Theories of Science in Society. Bloomington: Indiana University Press.

Clarke, Adele E. 1990b. Controversy and the Development of American Reproductive Sciences. Social Problems 37(1): 18–37. Reprinted in Andrea Tone (Ed.) Controlling Reproduction: An American History. Wilmington, DE: Scholarly Resources Inc., 1997.

Clarke, Adele E. 1991. Social Worlds Theory as Organization Theory, pp. 119–158 in David Maines (Ed.) Social Organization and Social Process: Essays in Honor of Anselm Strauss. Hawthorne, NY: Aldine de Gruyter.

Clarke, Adele E. 1998. Disciplining Reproduction: Modernity, American Life Sciences and the 'Problem of Sex.' Berkeley: University of California Press.

Clarke, Adele E. 2003. Situational Analyses: Grounded Theory Mapping After The Postmodern Turn. Symbolic Interaction 26(4): 553–576.

Clarke, Adele E. 2005. Situational Analysis: Grounded Theory After the Postmodern Turn. Thousand Oaks, CA: SAGE.

Clarke, Adele E. 2006a. Social Worlds. The Blackwell Encyclopedia of Sociology. Malden MA: Blackwell.

Clarke, Adele E. 2006b. Feminism, Grounded Theory and Situational Analysis, pp. 345–370 in Sharlene Hesse-Biber (Ed.) The Handbook of Feminist Research: Theory and Praxis. Thousand Oaks, CA: SAGE.

Clarke, Adele E. In review. Situational Analysis: A Haraway-Inspired Feminist Approach to Research. Sharon Ghamari-Tabrizi (Ed.) Thinking with Donna Haraway.

Clarke, Adele E. and Joan Fujimura. 1992. Introduction: What Tools? Which Jobs? Why Right?, pp. 3–46 in Adele E. Clarke and Joan Fujimura (Eds.) The Right Tools for the Job: At Work in Twentieth Century Life Sciences. Princeton: Princeton University Press.

Clarke, Adele and Theresa Montini. 1993. The Many Faces of RU486: Tales of Situated Knowledges and Technological Contestations. Science, Technology and Human Values 18(1): 42–78.

Clarke, Adele E. and Susan Leigh Star. 1998. On Coming Home and Intellectual Generosity. Introduction to Special Issue: New Work in the Tradition of Anselm L. Strauss. Symbolic Interaction 21(4): 341–349.

Clarke, Adele E. and Susan Leigh Star. 2003. Symbolic Interactionist Studies of Science, Technology and Medicine, pp. 539–574 in Larry Reynolds and Nancy Herman (Eds.) Handbook of Symbolic Interactionism. Walnut Creek, CA: Alta Mira Press.

Clarke, Adele E. and Susan Leigh Star. 2007. The Social Worlds/Arenas/Discourse Framework as a Theory-Methods Package. In Michael Lynch, Olga Amsterdamska and Ed Hackett (Eds.) The New Handbook of Science and Technology Studies. Cambridge, MA: MIT Press.

Corbin, Juliet. 1991. Anselm Strauss: An Intellectual Biography, pp. 17–42 in David Maines (Ed.) Social Organization and Social Process: Essays in Honor of Anselm Strauss. Hawthorne, NY: Aldine de Gruyter.

Corbin, Juliet M. 1997. Anselm L. Strauss, December 18, 1916–September 5, 1996. Qualitative Health Research 7(1): 150-153.

Corbin, Juliet. 1998. Comment: Alternative Interpretations—Valid or Not? Theory and Psychology 8(1): 121–128.

Debord, Guy. 1970. Society of the Spectacle. Detroit: Black and Red.

Deleuze, Gilles and Felix Guattari. 1987. A Thousand Plateaus: Capitalism and Schizophrenia. Minneapolis: University of Minnesota Press.

Denzin, Norman. 1997. Interpretive Ethnography: Ethnographic Practices for the 21st Century. Thousand Oaks, CA: SAGE.

Denzin, Norman and Yvonna Lincoln (Eds.) 1994. Handbook of Qualitative Research. Thousand Oaks, CA: SAGE.

Denzin, Norman and Yvonna Lincoln (Eds.) 2000. Handbook of Qualitative Research, 2nd ed. Thousand Oaks, CA: SAGE.

Denzin, Norman and Yvonna Lincoln (Eds.) 2005. Handbook of Qualitative Research, 3rd ed. Thousand Oaks, CA: SAGE.

Dey, Ian. 1999. Grounding Grounded Theory: Guidelines for Qualitative Inquiry. San Diego, CA: Academic Press.

Flick, Uwe. 1998. An Introduction to Qualitative Research. London: SAGE.

Fosket, Jennifer Ruth. 2002. Breast Cancer Risk and the Politics of Prevention: Analysis of a Clinical Trial. PhD dissertation in sociology, Department of Social and Behavioral Sciences, University of California, San Francisco.

Foucault, Michel. 1979. Discipline and Punish. New York: Vintage.

Foucault, Michel. 1980. Power/Knowledge: Selected Interviews and Other Writings 1972–1977. New York: Pantheon Books.

Franklin, S. 1997. Dolly: a New Form of Transgenic Breedwealth. Environmental Values 6: 427–437.

Friese, Carrie. 2007. Enacting Conservation in Biomedicine: Cloning Animals of Endangered Species in the US. PhD dissertation in sociology, Department of Social and Behavioral Sciences, University of California, San Francisco.

Fujimura, Joan. 1992. Crafting Science: Standardized Packages, Boundary Objects and 'Translation,' pp. 168–214 in Andrew Pickering (Ed.) Science as Practice and Culture. Chicago: University of Chicago Press.

Glaser, Barney G. 1969. The Constant Comparative Method of Qualitative Analysis, pp. 216–228 in G.J. McCall and J.L. Simmons (Eds.) Issues in Participant Observation. Reading, MA: Addison-Wesley.

Glaser, Barney G. 1978. Theoretical Sensitivity: Advances in the Methodology of Grounded Theory. Mill Valley, CA: The Sociology Press.

Glaser, Barney G. 1992. Emergence Versus Forcing: Basics of Grounded Theory Analysis. Mill Valley, CA: The Sociology Press.

Glaser, Barney G. 2002. Constructivist Grounded Theory? FQS Forum: Qualitative Social Research 3(3). Accessed 4/9/07 at http://www.qualitative-research.net/fqs/

Glaser, Barney G. and Anselm L. Strauss. 1967. The Discovery of Grounded Theory: Strategies for Qualitative Research. Chicago: Aldine; London: Weidenfeld and Nicolson.

Glaser, Barney G. with Judith Holton. 2004. Remodeling Grounded Theory. Forum for Qualitative Social Research 5(2). Accessed 4/9/07 at www.qualitative-research.net/fqs-texte/2-04

Guattari, Felix. 1992. Regimes, Pathways, Subjects, pp. 16–35 in Jonathan Crary and Sanford Kwinter (Eds.) Incorporations. New York: Zone.

Hall, Peter M. 1987. Interactionism and the Study of Social Organization. The Sociological Quarterly 28(1): 1–22.

Hall, Peter. 1997. Meta-Power, Social Organization, and the Shaping of Social Action. Symbolic Interaction 20(4): 397–418.

Hall, Peter M. and Patrick J.W. McGinty. 2002. Social Organization Across Space and Time: The Policy Process, Mesodomain Analysis, and Breadth of Perspective, pp. 303–322 in Sing C. Chew and David Knottnerus (Eds.) Structure, Culture and History: Recent Issues in Social Theory. Lanham MD: Rowman and Littlefield Publishers.

Hall, Wendy A. and Peter Callery. 2001. Enhancing the Rigor of Grounded Theory: Incorporating Reflexivity and Relationality. Qualitative Health Research 11(2): 257–272.

Haraway, Donna. 1991. Situated Knowledges: The Science Question in Feminism and the Privilege of Partial Perspective, pp. 183–202 in her Simians, Cyborgs, and Women: The Reinvention of Nature. New York: Routledge.

Haraway, Donna J. 1997. Modest_Witness@Second_Millennium.FemaleMan©_Meets_Oncomouse™: Feminism and Technoscience. New York: Routledge.

Haraway, Donna J. 1999. The Virtual Speculum in the New World Order, pp. 49–96 in Adele E. Clarke and Virginia L. Olesen (Eds.) Revisioning Women, Health, and Healing: Feminist, Cultural, and Technoscience Perspectives. New York: Routledge.

Katovich, Michael A. and William A. Reese. 1993. Postmodern Thought in Symbolic Interaction: Reconstructing Social Inquiry in Light of Late-Modern Concerns. The Sociological Quarterly 34(3): 391–411.

Kearney, M.H., S. Murphy, K. Irwin and M. Rosenbaum. (1995) Salvaging Self: A Grounded Theory of Pregnancy on Crack Cocaine. Nursing Research 44(4): 208–213.

Landstrom, Catharina. 2000. The Ontological Politics of Staying True to Complexity. Social Studies of Science 30(3): 475–480.

Lather, Patti. 2001. Postmodernism, Post-structuralism, and Post(Critical) Ethnography: Of Ruins, Aporias, and Angels, pp. 477–492 in Paul Atkinson, Amanda Coffey, Sara Delamont, John Lofland and Lyn Lofland (Eds.) Handbook of Ethnography. London: SAGE.

Lather, Patti. 2007. Getting Lost: Feminist Efforts Toward a Double(d) Science. Albany NY: State University of New York Press.

Lather, Patti and Chris Smithies. 1998. Troubling the Angels: Women Living with HIV/AIDS. Boulder: Westview.

Latour, Bruno. 1987. Science in Action. Cambridge: Harvard University Press.

Latour, Bruno. 2005. Reassembling the Social: An Introduction to Actor-network-theory. Oxford and New York: Oxford University Press.

Law, John and John Hassard (Eds.) 1999. Actor Network Theory and After. Malden, MA: Blackwell Publishers.

Locke, Karen. 1996. Rewriting the Discovery of Grounded Theory After 25 Years? Journal of Management Inquiry 5(1): 239–245.

Locke, Karen. 2001. Grounded Theory in Management Research. Thousand Oaks, CA: SAGE.

Maines, David R. (Ed.) 1991. Social Organization and Social Process: Essays in Honor of Anselm Strauss. New York: Aldine De Gruyter.

Maines, David R. 1995. In Search of Mesostructure: Studies in the Negotiated Order, pp. 277–286 in Nancy J. Herman and Larry J. Reynolds (Eds.) Symbolic Interaction: An Introduction to Social Psychology. New York: General Hall, Inc.

Maines, David R. 1996. On Postmodernism, Pragmatism and Plasterers: Some Interactionist Thoughts and Queries. Symbolic Interaction 19(4): 323–340.

Maines, David R. 2001. The Faultline of Consciousness: A View of Interactionism in Sociology. New York: Aldine de Gruyter.

Marcus, George. 1995. Ethnography in/of the World System: The Emergence of Multi-Sited Ethnography. Annual Review of Anthropology 24: 95–117.

Marcus, George E. and Erkan Saka. 2006. Assemblage. Theory, Culture and Society 23(2–3): 101–109.

Mead, George Herbert. 1938 [1972]. The Philosophy of the Act. Chicago: University of Chicago Press.

Miller, Suellen. 1996. Questioning, Resisting, Acquiescing, Balancing: New Mothers' Career Reentry Strategies. Health Care for Women International 17: 109–131.

Nelkin, Dorothy. 1995. Scientific Controversies, pp. 444–456 in S. Jasanoff (Ed.) Handbook of Science & Technology Studies. Thousand Oaks, CA: SAGE.

Poland, B. 1998. Reading Between the Lines: Interpreting Silences in Qualitative Research. Qualitative Inquiry 4(2): 293–312.

Rapp, Rayna. 1999. Testing Women/Testing the Fetus: The Social Impact of Amniocentesis in America. New York: Routledge.

Simon, Jonathan. 1996. Discipline and Punish: The Birth of a Middle-Range Research Strategy. Contemporary Sociology 25(3): 316–319.

Soulliere, Danielle, David W. Britt and David R. Maines. 2001. Conceptual Modeling as a Toolbox for Grounded Theorists. Sociological Quarterly 42(2): 253–269.

Star, Susan Leigh. 1983. Simplification in Scientific Work: An Example from Neuroscience Research. Social Studies of Science 13: 208–226.

Star, Susan Leigh. 1986. Triangulating Clinical and Basic Research: British Localizationists, 1870–1906. History of Science XXIV: 29–48.

Star, Susan Leigh. 1991. The Sociology of the Invisible: The Primacy of Work in the Writings of Anselm Strauss, pp. 265–283 in David R. Maines (Ed.) Social Organization and Social Process: Essays in Honor of Anselm Strauss. Hawthorne, NY: Aldine de Gruyter.

Star, Susan Leigh and James Griesemer. 1989. Institutional Ecology, 'Translations' and Boundary Objects: Amateurs and Professionals in Berkeley's Museum of Vertebrate Zoology, 1907–1939. Social Studies of Science 19: 387–420. Reprinted as pp. 505–524 in Mario Biagioli (Ed.) The Science Studies Reader. London: Routledge.

Star, Susan Leigh and Anselm L. Strauss. 1998. Layers of Silence, Arenas of Voice: The Ecology of Visible and Invisible Work. Computer Supported Cooperative Work: The Journal of Collaborative Computing 8: 9–30.

Strauss, Anselm L. 1978a. A Social Worlds Perspective. Studies in Symbolic Interaction 1: 119–128.

Strauss, Anselm L. 1978b. Negotiations: Varieties, Contexts, Processes and Social Order. San Francisco: Jossey Bass.

Strauss, Anselm L. 1982a. Interorganizational Negotiation. Urban Life 11(3): 350–367.

Strauss, Anselm L. 1982b. Social Worlds and Legitimation Processes. In Norman Denzin (Ed.) Studies in Symbolic Interaction 4: 171–190. Greenwich, CT: JAI Press.

Strauss, Anselm L. 1984. Social Worlds and Their Segmentation Processes. In Norman Denzin (Ed.) Studies in Symbolic Interaction 5: 123–139. Greenwich, CT: Jai Press.

Strauss, Anselm L. 1987. Qualitative Analysis for Social Scientists. Cambridge: Cambridge University Press.

Strauss, Anselm L. 1988. The Articulation of Project Work: An Organizational Process. The Sociological Quarterly 29:163–178.

Strauss, Anselm L. 1991a. Creating Sociological Awareness: Collective Images and Symbolic Representation. New Brunswick, NJ: Transaction Publishers.

Strauss, Anselm L. 1991b. Social Worlds and Spatial Processes: An Analytic Perspective. In A Person-Environment Theory Series/The Center for Environmental Design Research Working Paper Series, ed. W. Russell Ellis. Berkeley, CA: Department of Architecture, University of California.

Strauss, Anselm L. 1993. Continual Permutation of Action. New York: Aldine de Gruyter.

Strauss, Anselm L. 1995. Notes on the Nature and Development of General Theories. Qualitative Inquiry 1(1): 7–18.

Strauss, Anselm L. and Juliet Corbin. 1990. The Basics of Qualitative Analysis: Grounded Theory Procedures and Techniques. Thousand Oaks, CA: SAGE.

Strauss, Anselm L. and Juliet Corbin. 1991. Tracing Lines of Conditional Influence: Matrix and Paths, pp. 455–464 in Anselm L. Strauss (Ed.) Creating Sociological Awareness: Collective Images and Symbolic Representation. New Brunswick, NJ: Transaction Publishers.

Strauss, Anselm L. and Juliet Corbin. 1994. Grounded Theory Methodology: An Overview, pp. 273–285 in Norman Denzin and Yvonna Lincoln (Eds.) Handbook of Qualitative Research. Newbury Park, CA: SAGE.

Strauss, Anselm L. and Juliet Corbin (Eds.) 1997. Grounded Theory in Practice. CA: SAGE.

Strauss, Anselm L. and Juliet Corbin. 1998. The Basics of Qualitative Analysis: Grounded Theory Procedures and Techniques, 2nd ed. Thousand Oaks, CA: SAGE.

Strauss, Anselm, Leonard Schatzman, Rue Bucher, Danuta Ehrlich and Melvin Sabshin. 1964. Psychiatric Ideologies and Institutions. Glencoe, IL: The Free Press of Glencoe.

Zerubavel, Eviatar. 2006. The Elephant in the Room: Silence and Denial in Everyday Life. New York: Oxford University Press.

18

What Can Grounded Theorists and Action Researchers Learn from Each Other?

Bob Dick

INTRODUCTION

Grounded theory and action research are not usually regarded as similar approaches to research. Indeed, there are important differences. However, both develop theory grounded in specific evidence. Both are capable of being used flexibly and responsively. Their differences suggest ways in which each might be enhanced. Grounded theory is more explicit about how theory is built from evidence. Action research might well emulate this. Action research is more explicit about how understanding informs action, and sometimes collects and interprets information more efficiently. There may be useful lessons there for grounded theory. This chapter explores some of the mutual benefit for grounded theorists and action researchers in better understanding and perhaps utilizing each other's approach. I conclude with a proposal for an approach which combines much of the best of both grounded theory and action research. As its name implies, grounded theory builds theory grounded in data. The resulting theory then has a good fit to the phenomena being researched. Action research shares the purpose of building theory from experience. It may be that grounded theorists and action researchers have something to learn from each other. That is my purpose in writing this chapter.

This section begins with a brief overview of action research. The similarities and differences between action research and grounded theory are then explored. Following this I identify some learning opportunities arising from the comparison. To anticipate what follows, I suggest that action researchers can learn from grounded theorists by being more explicit about the actual theory they develop and how they do so. Grounded theorists can learn how to involve their informants more directly in the research process, how to collect and interpret data more economically, and how to involve themselves more directly in action if they wish.

I draw on the seminal work of Barney Glaser and Anselm Strauss (1967) and Glaser's subsequent elaborations (especially 1978, 1992, 1998, 2003). Important are grounded theory's flexibility, responsiveness to the research situation, treatment of literature as data, sampling techniques, and the distinction between substantive and formal theory. Studying grounded theory has enhanced my understanding of action research. The books by Karen Locke (2001) and Kathy Charmaz (2006) have been useful in addressing more succinctly many of the key features of Glaser's approach. Glaser's insights are scattered over several books, many not indexed. I could extend the comparison of action research and grounded theory to Strauss and Corbin (1998). However, for me the strongly data-driven processes of Glaser's approach align more closely with my conception of action research, which I now describe.

ACTION RESEARCH

The origins of action research are usually traced to John Collier (1945) and Kurt Lewin (1946). For Lewin, action research was 'a spiral of steps, each of which is composed of a circle of planning, action and fact-finding about the result of the action' (1946: 38). Action research was a way of engaging directly with real social problems while developing theoretical understanding. As Robin McTaggart (1991: 6) says, their practices were 'children of the times.' John Dewey (1916) had earlier argued for the importance of knowledge derived from action. Many contemporaries of Lewin and Collier used and wrote about action research. The aim was to achieve change while developing theoretical understanding. It still is. Action research is integrated action *and* research. Each turn of the action research spiral includes both research and action. The research facilitates the action, which in turn facilitates the research.

Most varieties of action research are variations on the theme of integrated research and action within a cyclic and participative process. Such varieties include participatory action research (Whyte, 1991), cooperative inquiry (Reason, 2003), and community based participatory research (Israel et al., 2005) among others.

Soft systems methodology (Checkland and Holwell, 1998), action science (Argyris, Putnam and Smith, 1985) and appreciative inquiry (Egan and Lancaster, 2005) share key features with mainstream action research while also displaying more substantial differences. Soft systems methodology, for example, uses explicit systems-based analysis to develop action plans, and is less explicitly cyclic. Action science has a strong emphasis on challenging the defensive behavior which undermines relationships and interpersonal understanding. Appreciative inquiry labels most action research as 'deficit oriented' (Whitney, 1998: 314) and limits its attention to what is positive about the organization or client group.

All action research shares a commitment to both theory development and actual change. So does action learning (for example Marquardt, 2004), using collaborative project teams to plan and implement change. Despite their different histories, action learning and action research are similar in practice. Indeed action learning is more similar to mainstream action research than are some of the more marginal action research varieties. Many action researchers such as David Coghlan (Coghlan et al., 2004) and Ortrun Zuber-Skerritt (2005) routinely use action learning. Many varieties of action research are displayed in *Handbook of Action Research* edited by Peter Reason and Hilary Bradbury (2001), currently under revision. Some key action research papers, early and more recent, have been collected in the four volume Sage publication *Fundamentals of Action Research* (Cooke and Cox, 2005). These two works reveal the extent of the action research family. Different writers emphasize different aspects with some contention about what is obligatory. For the most part, though, action research exhibits the following characteristics.

Above all, action research is *action oriented*, intended to achieve change. The change occurs as understanding develops, not as a separate and later application of the understanding. Action research is *responsive* to the situation. The understanding and the change are initially local, though the understanding can be extended through multiple studies. Accordingly, action research is *emergent*. At the beginning of a study, not enough is known either to develop good theory or to design the research methods in detail. Action research builds its theory and fine tunes its methods and develops its plans of action gradually as it proceeds. As understanding increases, methods and plans of action are improved. Because it emphasizes change, action research is usually *participative*. In many studies, the people in the research situation are directly involved from beginning to end. They choose the goal or problem, diagnose it, and plan and implement the action.

Action research theorizing is *abductive*, in the sense in which C.S. Peirce (1940) used the term. Something unexpected is observed. A plausible hypothesis is developed to explain the observation. Inductive and deductive reasoning may both be drawn upon for this purpose. The hypothesis guides the next plan, which is then immediately tested in action. Much action research occurs in *small groups*. People meet together to analyze a local issue and plan a response. They then implement and monitor their plans and meet again to plan the next step. Most varieties follow Lewin's original description in being explicitly *cyclic* or spiral. Action alternates with critical reflection. During critical reflection, theory emerges in the form of an understanding of what happened, and how. The understanding helps in planning the next action. The combination of action and reflection within each cycle allows action and research to be integrated. The cycle is often described as *plan → act and observe → reflect* (Kemmis and McTaggart, 1988). Action research is often used directly to *improve practice* (for example Marshall, 2004), ranging from individual development to the large-scale whole-industry research common in Scandinavia. Scandinavian action research described by Bjørn Gustavsen (2005) has involved multiple organizations within a national industry coming together in facilitated forums.

My approach is eclectic, borrowed from any version that suits. Like many other action researchers, I supplement action research with methods and processes from elsewhere, including facilitation (Heron, 1999) and organization development (French and Bell, 1999). I'll have more to say about this in 'Action research' below. A facilitator guides people through processes which help them to analyze their own situation, set their own goals, and develop and implement action plans. Organization development is a set of processes and techniques that a facilitator or consultant can use to assist in participative organizational change. Grounded theory and action research are not usually regarded as part of the same research family. As the above description of action research reveals, there are some differences and also some important parallels.

DIFFERENCES AND PARALLELS

Some differences are obvious. Action research pursues action. Those who do the research implement its results. Grounded theories may convert easily into action. The researchers, however, are seldom the actors. Action research is usually participative. Though sometimes less than its adherents claim (Webb, 1996), it nevertheless usually involves participants to some extent except when individuals research their individual practice. Grounded theory participants are usually involved only as informants. Indeed, Glaser (2003) discourages their further involvement, as does Janice Morse (1998) for qualitative research generally. (I address these concerns in 'Learning from action research.') In grounded theory, it is the researcher who builds the theory.

Some differences between grounded theory and action research are different emphases or arise because of different terminology. Features explicit in one are left implicit in the other. Action research is more explicitly cyclic. Grounded theory, however, has implicit cycles in the recurring process of data collection, coding, and memoing. The grounded theory literature is explicit about how to develop theory, and in what form. In this respect in particular, action researchers have much to learn from grounded theorists, as I argue in the following section.

LEARNING FROM GROUNDED THEORY

Much of the grounded theory literature is about how to convert information and experience into theory. Beginning with *The Discovery of Grounded Theory*

(Glaser and Strauss, 1967) the 'constant comparative method' of coding and theorizing continues to be the core of a grounded theory approach. In Kathy Charmaz's recent (2006) book the description of theory development is one of the themes which add to the book's coherence and usefulness. Writers about grounded theory as different as Ian Dey (1999) and Karen Locke (2001) give attention to theory construction. Though Cathy Urquhart (2001) complains that even here some detail is lacking, the grounded theory literature is more detailed than most.

Chris Huxham (2003: 243) probably speaks for many other action researchers when she says that theory building 'is probably the most challenging aspect of action research.' And, she adds, for which 'there can be no predefined methodology.' Other writers such as Chris Argyris (Argyris, Putnam and Smith, 1985) and Colin Eden and Chris Huxham (2002) deplore the lack of explicit theorizing in much action research. To be fair, others including David Partington (2000) have criticized the lack of explicit and relevant theory in qualitative research generally, grounded theory excepted.

Many of the 45 chapters in *Handbook of Action Research* (Reason and Bradbury, 2001) talk about the importance of integrating theory and practice. Few say how to do it. Victor Friedman (2001), who uses action science, gives the most substantial mention of theory building in the handbook. In other work, theory building is a strong feature of soft systems methodology (Checkland and Holwell, 1998). There it takes the form of concept maps: graphic representations of the researched situation that build a 'rich picture' typically in the form of symbols and their links. As mentioned earlier, action science and soft systems methodology are distinct and less mainstream forms of action research.

I've known several thesis candidates who chose grounded theory for data analysis within an action research thesis. Asked why, they responded that action research literature didn't explain how to analyze data: grounded theory literature did. They followed Strauss and Corbin (1998), possibly because of the detailed explanations of coding and theory building, possibly because of that book's easier availability. Glaser's form of grounded theory may have been more suitable. Being more explicitly emergent (Glaser, 1992) and less constrained it suits an action research study.

In the action research literature, theory is mentioned, though seldom in practical detail. So is the virtue of theory-practice integration. (By theory I mean an explicit model or set of statements which illuminate a situation by abstracting its key features. I say more in 'The form of theory' below.) More often than not 'theory' is mentioned. 'A theory' isn't developed. Action research theorizing is associated with reflection. Reflecting on what happened, the action researcher forms assumptions about what occurred and why, and then tests the assumptions by acting on them (Greenwood, 2002). Ernie Stringer (1999) for example explicitly equates such assumptions with theory. For the most part no process is given for doing this. One acts, and reflects on the action. From the reflection, theory somehow arises.

Anastasia White's recent (2004) paper titled 'Lewin's action research model as a tool for theory building' is revealing. Certainly, the paper reports an explicit theory of conflict. I can imagine using it to inform my own conflict management practice. How the theory was built is not described except in the most general terms. It's also telling, I think, that White chooses the Kolb learning cycle (Kolb, 1984) as the process to guide her reflection. The cycle consists of active experimentation, concrete experience, reflective observation, and *abstract conceptualization*. In much of the action research literature the theory-building step isn't as evident. In other respects, action research and experiential learning cycles are similar. There are hints in the literature of something more. Richard Winter (1998) writes about the way in which he integrates prior understanding when he plans a present action, though without an easily definable process of theory generation. McKay and Marshall (2005) use cognitive mapping for theory building, implying that action research isn't otherwise up to the task. Cognitive maps are a graphic way 'of representing the way in which an individual or group define and conceptualize a situation' (McKay and Marshall, 2005: 5). Cognitive maps can serve their purpose well. Because they are developed participatively they are likely to be acted on. The action again provides a test of the cognitive map.

Chris Huxham (2003) offers one of the few detailed descriptions of theory building I was able to find in the mainstream action research literature, illustrated by a specific case study. At some risk of oversimplification her process can be summarized as follows:

(1) identify items in the data relevant to the study's purpose;
(2) with colleagues, agree on the items to include, cluster the items, label the clusters;
(3) create a conceptual framework from the clusters;
(4) review data from other studies and refine the framework;
(5) seek comment widely, revising the framework and the arguments for it.

This is more substantial, and suits the small group and action oriented nature of action research. It bears some similarity to an approach I describe later. The puzzle is that so little action research provides similar explanations. It is not surprising, then, that some writers have turned to grounded theory to remedy the perceived shortcomings of action research. Grounded theory data analysis is often included within an action research study. The action research is chosen for its support of action. The grounded theory is assumed to provide rigor. Action research is often viewed (mistakenly, I would argue) as lacking rigor, as McKay and Marshall (2001) explain.

The combination can be very effective. The theory and the theory-building process are made evident and therefore more open to challenge. The apparent rigor of the research is enhanced in the eyes of some critics. In the section 'Other advantages of grounded theory' I offer some further comments on this. First, I wish to provide some examples of the combined use of action research and grounded theory.

There are examples in the information systems literature, including Henfridsson and Lindgren (2005), Kock (2004), and Wastell (2001).

Baskerville and Pries-Heje (1999: 1) talk of 'grounded action research,' which features grounded theory inserted into action research cycles. The intention is 'to add rigor and reliability to the theory formulation process.' Yoong and Pauleen (2004; Pauleen and Yoong, 2004) use 'grounded action learning' (in effect grounded action research) in their studies of group decision systems. As in the earlier studies cited, action research guides the intervention process. Grounded theory is used for data analysis and theory building.

The community health literature also contains examples. The motivation often appears to be to improve the perceived low status of action research (Regehr, 2000). Gerald Mohatt and colleagues (2004a, b) chose participatory action research for their study of sobriety in Alaska because it allowed sensitivity in their contact with participants. Grounded theory again provided the theory development. The sensitivity of the topic of child sexual abuse was part of the motivation for Schachter et al. (2004; Teram et al., 2005) to use action research, again complemented by grounded theory. Paul Greenall (2006) reported that he used grounded theory within an action learning study of non-compliance with prescribed medical treatment, though without details of the actual procedures.

I've been able to identify a few studies combining action research and grounded theory in other literatures. Based on his doctoral research, Richard Hale (2000) described the use of grounded theory and participatory action research to develop tools to aid mentoring. Su Wild River (2005) investigated and improved the sustainability efforts of local government. Taylor, Schauder, and Johanson (2005) studied Australian attitudes to civil society.

In almost all of the studies cited above, the research appears to have been conceived initially as action research. Grounded theory was added to make the theory building more systematic or rigorous. One of the few exceptions is Teram et al. (2005). In their view, neither grounded theory nor action research alone provided them with the combination of rigor and appropriate relationships. I have not been able to find studies where the grounded theory was foundational and action research was added, except perhaps Schachter et al. (2004). Grounded theory and action research were used for different phases of their study. Theoretical understanding was initially developed using grounded theory. Plans developed from the theory were implemented using action research. The combinations of action research and grounded theory reported above have worked well. Grounded theory complements action research by addressing those research aspects in which action research is seen as weakest. However, the coding which grounded theory requires has almost certainly slowed down the process. I therefore offer, later, a less laborious alternative.

OTHER ADVANTAGES OF GROUNDED THEORY

As far as I can tell, there has been less use made of other advantages which grounded theory might offer. In particular, action researchers might make use of explicit theoretical frameworks (Glaser, 1978: Chapter 4), literature treated as data (Glaser, 2001: Chapter 11), and the distinction between substantive and formal theory (Glaser, 1978: Chapter 9; Glaser and Strauss, 1967: Chapter 4). The third of these can be addressed to some extent in a number of ways. Multiple case studies offer one possibility, as in the study by Gwyer et al. (2004). Just as grounded theory develops substantive theory into formal theory by extended sampling, multiple cases allow the local theory resulting from action research to be generalized more confidently. Literature can also be used as data (see below in this section) and action research might make wider use of the purposeful sampling that Glaser and Strauss (1967) regarded as a central part of a grounded theory methodology.

To avoid having the literature color the data analysis, Glaser and Strauss (1967; Glaser, 2001) advocate consulting the relevant literature *after* data analysis. This is contentious in grounded theory circles, as Charmaz (2006) summarizes. Dey (1999: 245) voices the common complaint: preconceptions are not so easily put aside. There is a more compelling reason to postpone a literature review in grounded theory or action research. Initially it can be hard to know which literature is relevant. At the beginning of a change program (for it is at change work that action research excels), the researcher knows very little about the situation. The other participants know more, but not enough to improve the situation or they would already have done so. As a study proceeds, assumptions are developed and tried out in action. Understanding grows. The relevant literature becomes more easily identified. In any event, very applied work tends to span disciplinary boundaries. Applied research situations do not structure themselves in the same way as academic disciplines do.

Further, literature can later be treated as data which tests or refines the emergent theory. This also counters the criticism that action research findings don't generalize. (It's an unwarranted criticism, as Richard Baskerville and Allen Lee, 1999, explain. If it were true, practitioners would not learn from experience.) The literature can help to define the extent to which the emergent theory can be generalized. I accept that, of course, we take our preconceptions into the research situation. This, too, is less a problem than is sometimes claimed. To protect against preconceptions a researcher can vigorously seek out disconfirming evidence. In 'Theory building' (below) I describe a theory building approach which encourages this.

As I have shown, there is little clarity in action research about how theory is developed. Despite Urquhart's (2001) misgivings, grounded theory deals well, and in detail, with the theory-building process. Grounded theorists may see some virtue in the combinations of grounded theory and action research described in 'Learning from grounded theory' above. Beyond that, they are unlikely to borrow from action research unless they can preserve grounded theory's ability to derive theory grounded in evidence and to use repeatable processes to do so. That said, I think there is some useful learning to be gained by grounded theorists from the action research literature.

LEARNING FROM ACTION RESEARCH

Many of the features of action research are intended to support action. It is common for action researchers to involve participants extensively in a study so that the planned actions have the commitment of those participants. Many, such as Peter Reason and Hilary Bradbury (2001), believe democratic participation is obligatory. So do most of the other authors in *Handbook of Action Research*. When participants are involved in data analysis, transcripts and coding are less suitable than structured or unstructured discussion processes. Processes that participants can understand allow greater participation. But can (or even should) participants be involved in helping to interpret data? Janice Morse (1998) clearly believes they shouldn't. She points out, correctly in my view, that participant views are emic (local) rather than etic (generalized). As she also says, the theory emerging from a study is unlikely to be 'a perfect fit to the particular experience of a single participant' (1998: 443). Kathy Charmaz (2005) agrees that participation can raise some potential problems.

Reasonably enough, Morse objects to participants in effect vetoing the theorizing of the researcher. But that isn't necessary. A key feature of action research is that researchers and informants are regarded as equals in the research endeavor: different and equal. Researcher and informant can reconcile their differences. In this process of mutual education each of them will find their understanding deepened. I return to this below in the discussion of dialectic processes.

In action research, the researcher works with participants in a group, or several groups. The opportunities for mutual education are thus strengthened. Informant learns from informant as well as from the researcher. The researcher learns from multiple informants. As in some other qualitative research a maximum variation sample may be chosen to increase the diversity of informants. That allows more perspectives to be taken into account (Creswell, 1998: 120). Involving participants in analyzing the information they provide further capitalizes on the variety. It also offers researchers further protection against their own preconceptions. Admittedly the achievement of both rigor and participation requires certain communication and facilitation skills. The required skill level is not beyond the reach of many grounded theorists. Many such researchers carry out in-depth interviews requiring effective communication skills. Many facilitate focus groups, a demanding task, as Claudia Puchta and Jonathan Potter (2003) make evident. Although Holly Edmunds (1999) suggests using professional moderators to facilitate focus groups, many qualitative researchers facilitate their own focus groups successfully. A qualitative researcher who can facilitate a focus group can facilitate other groups.

Issues related to participation are understandably mostly ignored in the grounded theory literature. However, practitioners in the fields of community and organizational change deal with them daily. Grounded theorists' existing skills can be supplemented with processes and techniques from other literatures.

For example, Chris Argyris (2004) has provided useful interpersonal strategies for management researchers. In particular he explains the advantage of testing assumptions before acting on them. For those who find Argyris's approach difficult, Roger Schwarz (2002) has applied it to group facilitation in systematic and easily learnable ways. Viviane Robinson (Robinson and Lai, 2006) has translated Argyris's ideas into practices more easily used. Bernard Guerin (2005) has described in some detail common evidence-based intervention processes and the skills they depend on. A typical intervention for resolving conflicts (much abbreviated here) will illustrate his style (2005: 166):

> Find out the full stories of what happened ...
>
> ...
>
> Find novel solutions and problem-solve.
>
> ...
>
> Get a resolution that will commit them to the future.

In addition there is a substantial literature in fields such as community development (Mikkelsen, 2005), community psychology (Nelson and Prilleltensky, 2004), public participation (Creighton, 2005), deliberative democracy (Gastil and Levine, 2005), and organization development (Axelrod, 2002), among many others. The relevant skills and processes are not difficult to find and apply. If necessary, suitably skilled practitioners can be added to the research team.

I can think of few participant groups who would respond enthusiastically to the thought of coding the record of a group discussion. They would be more likely to favor a process which generated action plans and theories in the course of discussion. The practitioner literature offers many suggestions for generating action plans. That literature also describes processes for making sense of information (that is, for theory building) in addition to useful forms of theory.

THE FORM OF THEORY

It is not only the process for theory building that is given surprisingly little attention in the action research literature. The *form* of that theory is also often neglected. To lead to action, however, a theory is likely to take the form 'do this to achieve that.' Or, more formally: 'to achieve consequences C, carry out actions A.' Argyris and Schön (1974: 29) again have something useful to offer. Their 'theory of action' takes the form:

> In situation S, if you intend consequences C, do A, given assumptions $a_1 \ldots a_n$.

I elicit theories from participants in this form by guiding the participants through the following three pairs of questions in turn. We strive to reach consensus on each before proceeding, using conflict resolution processes if necessary:

1a What are the important features of the situation?
1b Why do we think those are the important features?
2a If we're right about the situation, what outcomes [that is, consequences] are desirable and feasible?
2b Why do we think those outcomes are desirable and feasible in that situation?
3a What actions do we think will give those outcomes in that situation?
3b Why do we think those actions will give us those outcomes in that situation?

Answers to the 'a' questions provide in turn the situation, the consequences and the actions. Answers to the 'b' questions surface assumptions. Together the answers provide a basis for theory building, which I turn to in the next section. We then carry out our planned actions and compare the results to the expected outcomes. In doing so we test (Greenwood, 2002) the adequacy of the actions and to some extent of the assumptions which underpin the actions. As Ned Kock and his colleagues (1997) point out, by including action, the iterative cycle of action research enhances rigor. Bob Williams and Bill Harris (2001) have further developed the six questions above to create a structured journal to aid reflection and understanding.

THEORY BUILDING

A grounded theory emerges from the process of constant comparison. This can also be done in structured discussion, without the onerous task of coding. I've described elsewhere (Dick, 1990, 1999) a process for doing this in both individual interview and small group settings. For ease of explanation I'll describe an individual interview process, 'convergent interviewing,' which has now been tested and critiqued by a number of other researchers. The 'engine' which drives the process can be viewed as a set of decision rules:

(1) Compare a data set (perhaps a set of interview notes) to another data set, or (after early interviews) to the emergent theory.
(2) Note overlaps between interviews (or between interview and emergent theory). Overlaps will consist of agreements or disagreements. An agreement is where both sets mention a topic and do so compatibly, for example that 'teamwork needs improvement.' A disagreement occurs when both mention the same topic but incompatibly. One may identify teamwork as needing improvement, and the other as a strength of the team.
(3) Where there is agreement probe for exceptions (in the same interview, in subsequent interviews, or both). The exceptions, when found, then constitute a disagreement.
(4) Where there is disagreement probe for explanations. 'Some say teamwork is good. Others say it requires attention. Help me to understand how this difference arises.'

The process can be viewed as a dialectic which uses apparent disagreement to generate agreement at a deeper level. It is summarized in Figure 18.1.

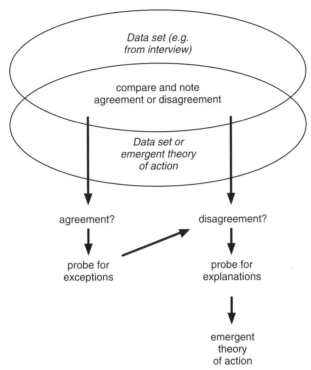

Figure 18.1   The 'data engine,' a form of constant comparison (amended from Dick, 2002).

Although I use the logic of Figure 18.1 widely in my own work, I know of relatively few published studies applying it to processes other than interviewing. One exception is the study reported by Satish Mehra and Anthony Inman (2004). They used a similar process to analyze focus group data. Terry Gatfield (2005) called on two experts to build theory from data using a combination of this process and Delphi. There are now in excess of 100 interviewing studies (including conference papers) using convergent interviewing. Most offer no critique. Those who do usually report favorably. Thompson, Donohue, and Waters-Marsh (1992) found that convergent interviewing complemented quantitative research into manager perceptions. Using convergent interviewing for market research, Sally Rao and Chad Perry (2003) reported efficient data collection with quick convergence on key issues. Wil Williams and Duncan Lewis (2005) favored the method's efficiency and recommended its use for strategic management research. These studies confirm my own experience.

Extending the method to health research, Michelle Driedger and her colleagues (Driedger et al., 2006) reported that the dialectic process of convergent inter-viewing helped a multi-disciplinary and multinational research team arrive at a shared ontology and epistemology. With a growing trend towards the multidisciplinary research advocated by Benjamin Crabtree (Crabtree, Miller and Stange, 2001) and the 'integrative research' championed by Gabriele Bammer (2005) the usefulness of dialectic processes may increase. Fernald and Duclos (2005) believe there is a growing need to manage multidisciplinary research teams but little advice on how to do so.

The logic of the analytic and theory building process above isn't limited to interviews. It can be extended to any data set. In unpublished studies, I've used it within and between focus groups or group feedback analysis groups, among other applications. In short, I propose an addition to the repertoire of both action researchers and grounded theorists: Argyris and Schön's theory of action framed as a set of reflective questions combined with the 'data engine' of Figure 18.1 for theory building. The data engine provides enough guidance for researchers, as the cited publications on convergent interviewing attest. A 'theory of action' approach supports the integration of theory and action which action researchers value. The flexibility of grounded theory and action research is maintained. The process remains strongly data-driven in the style of Glaserian grounded theory. A vigorous pursuit of disconfirmation helps to protect researchers and participants from their preconceptions. The comparatively greater efficiency of this approach may appeal to grounded theorists in some circumstances. In addition, action research may provide grounded theorists with a meta-methodology with which they can improve their use of grounded theory.

ACTION RESEARCH AS META-METHODOLOGY

Action research is frequently used by practitioners who wish to research and improve their practice; a suitable application, as Dawn Freshwater (2005) has argued. Researchers are practitioners of research. Action research can be a meta-methodology to research the practice of research. I'm not aware of grounded theorists who have used action research for this purpose, though some may have done so. Outside the grounded theory literature there are a few instances. For example Burgess, Shaw, and de Mattos (2005) used action research as a methodology to develop a methodology. Waterman et al. (2005) met regularly as an action research group to critique and refine a study of nursing practice.

As Janice Morse (2002) has advocated, the multidisciplinary trend mentioned earlier is often accompanied by the use of multiple methods. Here, too, meta-methodological action research may help to achieve a 'coherent pluralism,' in Michael Jackson's (1999: 12) apt phrase. Where several methodologies are combined, action research can provide an overarching and monitoring framework.

THE PLACE OF EMERGENT METHODOLOGIES

I believe that the case made in *The Discovery of Grounded Theory* (Glaser and Strauss, 1967) still holds. Emergent data-driven methodologies like grounded theory and action research can complement the more common theory-driven methodologies. Conceived too narrowly, the currently fashionable 'evidence based practice' can underestimate or overlook how complex and therefore unpredictable people are, individually and collectively. (In its narrower forms evidence based practice is the practice of basing all intervention on the evidence from scientific research.) Unless complemented by other approaches, it can lead too easily to theory driving evidence, and evidence in turn driving practice: *theory → evidence → practice*. Emergent methodologies can provide a balance by allowing this sequence also to be reversed in the form of practice-based evidence (Fox, 2003). Evidence gathered in practitioner settings can be an additional source of theory generation: *practice → evidence → theory*. This is not inconsistent with Jane Gilgun's (2005) thoughtful analysis of evidence-based practice in several disciplines. Tom Bourner and Penny Simpson (2005) present a similar argument for using action learning in PhD studies. Grounded theory and action research bring overlapping but different strengths to research. Grounded theorists and action researchers can expand their repertoire and their relevance to practice and theory by borrowing each other's methods, techniques, and skills.

REFERENCES

Argyris, Chris (2004). *Reasons and rationalizations: the limits to organizational knowledge*. Oxford: Oxford University Press.

Argyris, Chris, Putnam, Robert and Smith, Diana McLain (1985). *Action science: concepts, methods and skills for research and intervention*. San Francisco, CA: Jossey-Bass.

Argyris, Chris and Schön, Donald A. (1974). *Theory in practice: increasing professional effectiveness*. San Francisco, CA: Jossey-Bass.

Axelrod, Richard H. (2002). *Terms of engagement: changing the way we change organizations*. San Francisco: Berrett-Koehler.

Bammer, Gabriele (2005). Integration and implementation sciences: building a new specialization. *Ecology and Society*, 10(2), article 6. Retrieved March 1, 2006, from http://www.ecologyandsociety.org/vol10/iss2/art6/

Baskerville, Richard L. and Lee, Allen S. (1999). Distinctions among different types of generalizing in information systems research. In Introna, Ngwenyama L., Myers, M. and DeGross, J.I. (Eds.) *New information technologies in organizational processes: field studies and theoretical reflections on the future of work*, 49–65. New York: Kluwer.

Baskerville, Richard L. and Pries-Heje, Jan (1999). Grounded action research: a method for understanding IT in practice. *Accounting, Management and Information Technologies*, 9(1), 1–23.

Bourner, Tom and Simpson, Penny (2005). Practitioner-centred research and the PhD. *Action Learning: Research and Practice*, 2(2), 133–151.

Burgess, Thomas F., Shaw, Nicky E. and de Mattos, Claudio (2005). Organizational self-assessment and the adoption of managerial innovations. *International Journal of Productivity and Performance Management*, 54(2), 98–112.

Charmaz, Kathy (2005). Grounded theory in the 21st century: applications for advancing social justice studies. In Denzin, Norman K. and Lincoln, Yvonna S. (Eds.) *The Sage handbook of qualitative research*, third edition, 507–535. Thousand Oaks, CA: SAGE.

Charmaz, Kathy (2006). *Constructing grounded theory: a practical guide through qualitative analysis*. Thousand Oaks, CA: SAGE.

Checkland, Peter and Holwell, Sue (1998). *Information, systems, and information systems: making sense of the field*. Chichester: Wiley.

Coghlan, David, Dromgoole, Tony, Joynt, Pat and Sorensen, Peter (Eds.) (2004). *Managers learning in action*. London: Routledge.

Collier, John (1945). United States Indian Administration as a laboratory of ethnic relations. *Social Research*, 12(3), 265–303.

Cooke, Bill and Cox, Julie Wolfram (Eds.) (2005). *Fundamentals of action research*, 4 volumes. London: SAGE.

Crabtree, Benjamin F., Miller, William L. and Stange, Kurt C. (2001). Understanding practice from the ground up. *Journal of Family Practice*, 50(10), 881–887.

Creighton, James L. (2005). *The public participation handbook: making better decisions through citizen involvement*. San Francisco, CA: Jossey-Bass.

Creswell, John W. (1998). *Qualitative inquiry and research design: choosing among five traditions*. Thousand Oaks, CA: SAGE.

Dewey, John (1916). *Democracy and education*. New York: Macmillan.

Dey, Ian (1999). *Grounding grounded theory: guidelines for qualitative inquiry*. San Diego: Academic Press.

Dick, Bob (1990). *Convergent interviewing*, version 3. Chapel Hill, Qld: Interchange.

Dick, Bob (1999). *Rigour without numbers: the potential of dialectical processes as qualitative research tools*, 3rd edn. Chapel Hill, Qld: Interchange.

Dick, Bob (2002). Grounded theory: a thumbnail sketch. Retrieved March 19, 2007, from http://www.scu.edu.au/schools/gcm/ar/arp/grounded.html

Driedger, S. Michelle, Gallois, Cindy, Sanders, Carrie and Santesso, Nancy (2006). Finding common ground in team-based qualitative research using the convergent interviewing method. *Qualitative Health Research*, 16(8), 1145–1157.

Eden, Colin and Huxham, Chris (2002). Action research. In Partington, David (Ed.) *Essential skills for management research*, 254–272. London: SAGE.

Edmunds, Holly (1999). *The focus group: research handbook*. Chicago, IL: NTC Business Books.

Egan, Toby Marshall and Lancaster, Cynthia M. (2005). Comparing appreciative inquiry to action research: OD practitioner perspectives. *Organization Development Journal*, 23(2), 29–49.

Fernald, Douglas H. and Duclos, Christine W. (2005). Enhance your team-based qualitative research. *Annals of Family Medicine*, 3(3), 360–364.

Fox, Nick J. (2003). Practice-based evidence: towards collaborative and transgressive research. *Sociology*, 37(1), 81–102.

French, Wendell and Bell, Cecil H. (1999). *Organization development: behavioral science interventions for organizational improvement*, 6th edn. Englewood Cliffs, NJ: Prentice-Hall.

Freshwater, Dawn (2005). Action research for changing and improving practice. In Holloway, Immy (Ed.) *Qualitative research in health care*, 210–228. Maidenhead: Open University Press.

Friedman, Victor J. (2001). Action science: creating communities of inquiry in communities of practice. In Reason, Peter and Bradbury, Hilary (Eds.) *Handbook of action research: participative inquiry and practice*, 159–170. London: SAGE.

Gastil, John and Levine, Peter (Eds.) (2005). *The deliberative democracy handbook: strategies for effective civic engagement in the twenty-first century*. San Francisco, CA: Jossey-Bass.

Gatfield, Terry (2005). An investigation into PhD supervisory management styles: development of a dynamic conceptual model and its managerial implications. *Journal of Higher Education Policy and Management*, 27(3), 311–325.

Gilgun, Jane F. (2005). The four cornerstones of evidence-based practice in social work. *Research on Social Work Practice*, 15(1), 52–61.

Glaser, Barney G. (1978). *Theoretical sensitivity: advances in the methodology of grounded theory*. Mill Valley, CA: Sociology Press.

Glaser, Barney G. (1992). *Basics of grounded theory analysis: emergence vs. forcing*. Mill Valley, CA: Sociology Press.

Glaser, Barney G. (1998). *Doing grounded theory: issues and discussions*. Mill Valley, CA: Sociology Press.

Glaser, Barney G. (2001). *The grounded theory perspective: conceptualization contrasted with description*. Mill Valley, CA: Sociology Press.

Glaser, Barney G. (2003). *The grounded theory perspective II: description's remodeling of grounded theory methodology*. Mill Valley, CA: Sociology Press.

Glaser, Barney G. and Strauss, Anselm L. (1967). *The discovery of grounded theory: strategies for qualitative research*. Chicago: Aldine.

Greenall, Paul (2006). The barriers to patient-driven treatment in mental health: why patients may choose to follow their own path. *Leadership in Health Services*, 19(1), 11–25.

Greenwood, Davydd J. (2002). Action research: unfulfilled promises and unmet challenges. *Concepts and Transformation*, 7(2), 117–139.

Guerin, Bernard (2005). *Handbook of interventions for changing people and communities*. Reno, NV: Context Press.

Gustavsen, Bjørn (2005). Innovation and action research. *International Journal of Action Research*, 1(3), 267–289.

Gwyer, Jan, Jensen, Gail, Hack, Laurita and Shepard, Katherine (2004). Using a multiple case study research design to develop an understanding of clinical expertise in physical therapy. In Hammell, Karen Whalley and Carpenter, Christine (Eds.) *Qualitative research in evidence-based practice*, 103–115. Edinburgh: Churchill Livingstone.

Hale, Richard (2000). To match or mis-match? The dynamics of mentoring as a route to personal and organizational learning. *Career Development International*, 5(4–5), 223–234.

Henfridsson, Ola and Lindgren, Rickard (2005). Multi-contextuality in ubiquitous computing: investigating the car case through action research. *Information and Organization*, 15(2), 95–124.

Heron, John (1999). *The complete facilitators' handbook*. London: Kogan Page.

Huxham, Chris (2003). Action research as a methodology for theory development. *Policy and Politics*, 31(2), 239–248.

Israel, Barbara A., Eng, Eugenia, Schulz, Amy J. and Parker, Edith A. (2005). Introduction to methods in community-based participatory research for health. In Israel, Barbara A., Eng, Eugenia, Schulz, Amy J. and Parker, Edith A. (Eds.) *Methods in community based research for health*, 3–26. San Francisco, CA: Jossey-Bass.

Jackson, Michael C. (1999). Towards coherent pluralism in management science. *Journal of the Operational Research Society*, 50(1), 12–22.

Kemmis, Stephen and McTaggart, Robin (1988). *The action research planner*, 3rd edn. Victoria: Deakin University.

Kock, Ned (2004). The three threats of action research: a discussion of methodological antidotes in the context of an information systems study. *Decision Support Systems*, 37(2), 265–286.

Kock, Nereu F., Jr. ('Ned'), McQueen, Robert J. and Scott, John L. (1997). Can action research be made more rigorous in a positivist sense? The contribution of an iterative approach. *Journal of Systems and Information Technology*, 1(1), 1–24.

Kolb, David A. (1984). *Experiential learning: experience as the source of learning and development*. Englewood Cliffs, NJ: Prentice-Hall.

Lewin, Kurt (1946). Action research and minority problems. *Journal of Social Issues*, 2(4), 34–46.

Locke, Karen (2001). *Grounded theory in management research*. London: SAGE.

Marquardt, Michael J. (2004). *Optimizing the power of action learning: solving problems and building leaders in real time*. Palo Alto, CA: Davies-Black.

Marshall, Judi (2004). Living systemic thinking. *Action Research*, 2(3), 305–325.

McKay, Judy and Marshall, Peter (2001). The dual imperatives of action research. *Information Technology and People*, 14(1), 46–59.

McKay, Judy and Marshall, Peter (2005). Reflecting on the efficacy of SODA and cognitive mapping for problem analysis in information requirements determination. Presentation at the Fifth Annual SIG IS Cognitive Research Exchange Workshop, Las Vegas. Retrieved January 22, 2006, from http://www.ou.edu/is-core/Papers/McKay-Marshall.pdf

McTaggart, Robin (1991). *Action research: a short modern history*. Geelong, Vic: Deakin University.

Mehra, Satish and Inman, R. Anthony (2004). Purchasing management and business competitiveness in the coming decade. *Production Planning and Control*, 15(7), 710–718.

Mikkelsen, Britha Helene (2005). *Methods for development work and research: a new guide for practitioners*, 2nd edn. New Delhi: SAGE.

Mohatt, Gerald V., Kelly, L. Hazel, Allen, James, Stachelrodt, Mary, Helsel, Chase and Fath, Robert (2004a). Unheard Alaska: culturally anchored participatory action research on sobriety with Alaska Natives. *American Journal of Community Psychology*, 33(3/4), 263–273.

Mohatt, Gerald V., Rasmus, S. Michelle, Thomas, Lisa, Allen, James, Hazel, Kelly and Hensel, Chase (2004b). 'Tied together like a woven hat': Protective pathways to Alaska native sobriety. *Harm Reduction Journal*, 1, article 10. Retrieved November 15, 2005, from http://www.harmreductionjournal.com/content/1/1/10

Morse, Janice M. (1998). Validity by committee. *Qualitative Health Research*, 8(4), 443–445.

Morse, Janice M. (2002). Qualitative health research: challenges for the 21st century. *Qualitative Health Research*, 12(1), 116–129.

Nelson, Geoffrey and Prilleltensky, Isaac (2004). *Community psychology: in pursuit of liberation and well-being*. Basingstoke: Palgrave Macmillan.

Partington, David (2000). Building grounded theories of management action. *British Journal of Management*, 11(2), 91–102.

Pauleen, David J. and Yoong, Pak (2004). Studying human-centered IT innovation using a grounded action learning approach. *The Qualitative Report*, 9(1), 137–160. Retrieved October 20, 2005, from http://www.nova.edu/ssss/QR/QR9-1/pauleen.pdf

Peirce, Charles Sanders (1940). *Philosophical writings of Peirce*. New York: Dover Publications.

Puchta, Claudia and Potter, Jonathan (2003). *Focus group practice*. Thousand Oaks, CA: SAGE.

Rao, Sally and Perry, Chad (2003). Convergent interviewing to build a theory in under-researched areas: principles and an example investigation of Internet usage in inter-firm relationships. *Qualitative Market Research*, 6(4), 236–247.

Reason, Peter (2003). Cooperative inquiry. In Smith, Jonathan A. (Ed.) *Qualitative psychology: a practical guide to research methods*, 205–231. London: SAGE.

Reason, Peter and Bradbury, Hilary (2001). *Handbook of action research: participative inquiry and practice*. London: SAGE.

Regehr, Cheryl (2000). Action research: underlining or undermining the cause? *Social Work and Social Sciences Review*, 8(3), 194–206.

Robinson, Viviane and Lai, Mei Kuin (2006). *Practitioner research for educators: a guide to improving classrooms and schools*. Thousand Oaks, CA: Corwin.

Schachter, Candice, Teram, Eli and Stalker, Carol (2004). Integrating grounded theory and action research to develop guidelines for sensitive practice with childhood sexual abuse survivors. In Hammell, Karen Whalley and Carpenter, Christine (Eds.) *Qualitative research in evidence-based practice*, 77–88. Edinburgh: Churchill Livingstone.

Schwarz, Roger M. (2002). *The skilled facilitator: a comprehensive resource for consultants, facilitators, managers, trainers, and coaches*. San Francisco, CA: Jossey-Bass.

Strauss, Anselm and Corbin, Juliet (1998). *Basics of qualitative research: techniques and procedures for developing grounded theory*, 2nd edn. Newbury Park, CA: SAGE.

Stringer, Ernie (1999). *Action research*, 2nd edn. Thousand Oaks, CA: SAGE.

Taylor, Wallace, Schauder, Don and Johanson, Graeme (2005). The emerging role of civil society in the information society: Australian civil society engagement in the WSIS process. *Proceedings of the International Conference 'UNESCO between two Phases of the World Summit on the Information Society.'* St Petersburg, Russia, 17–19 May. Retrieved 22 March 2007 from http://confifap.cpic.ru/upload/conf2005/reports/dokladEn_382.pdf

Teram, Eli, Schachter, Candice L. and Stalker, Carol A. (2005). The case for integrating grounded theory and participatory action research: empowering clients to inform professional practice. *Qualitative Health Research,* 15(8), 1129–1140.

Thompson, Briony M., Donohue, K.J. and Waters-Marsh, T.F. (1992). Qualitative and quantitative approaches to understanding managers' perceptions of organizational environments. Paper presented at the 27th Australian Psychological Society Annual Conference, Armidale, September.

Urquhart, Cathy (2001). An encounter with grounded theory: tackling the practical and philosophical issues. In Trauth, Eileen M. (Ed.) *Qualitative research in IS: issues and trends,* 104–140. Hershey, PA: Idea Group.

Wastell, David G. (2001). Barriers to effective knowledge management: action research meets grounded theory. *Journal of Systems and Information Technology*, 5(2), 21–35.

Waterman, Heather, Harker, Rona, MacDonald, Heather, McLaughlan, Rita and Waterman, Christine (2005). Advancing ophthalmic nursing practice through action research. *Journal of Advanced Nursing,* 52(3), 281–290.

Webb, Graham (1996). *Understanding staff development.* Milton Keynes: SRHE/Open University Press.

White, Anastasia M. (2004). Lewin's action research model as a tool for theory building: a case study from South Africa. *Action Research,* 2(2), 127–144.

Whitney, Diana (1998). Let's change the subject and change our organization: an appreciative inquiry approach to organization change. *Career Development International,* 3(7), 314–319.

Whyte, William Foote (Ed.) (1991). *Participatory action research.* Newbury Park, CA: SAGE.

Wild River, Su (2005). Enhancing the sustainability efforts of local governments. *International Journal of Innovation and Sustainable Development,* 1(1/2), 46–64.

Williams, Bob and Harris, Bill (2001). Learning logs: structured journals that work for busy people. In Sankaran, Shankar, Dick, Bob, Passfield, Ron and Swepson, Pam (Eds.) *Effective change management using action learning and action research: concepts, frameworks, processes, applications,* 97–119. Lismore, NSW: Southern Cross University Press.

Williams, Wil and Lewis, Duncan (2005). Convergent interviewing: a tool for strategic investigation. *Strategic Change,* 14(4), 219–229.

Winter, Richard (1998). Managers, spectators and citizens: where does 'theory' come from in action research? *Educational Action Research,* 6(3), 361–376.

Yoong, Pak and Pauleen, David J. (2004). Generating and analysing data for applied research on emerging technologies: a grounded action learning approach. *Information Research,* 9(4), paper 195. Retrieved January 23, 2005, from http://InformationR.net/ir/9-4/paper195.html

Zuber-Skerritt, Ortrun (2005). A model of values and actions for personal knowledge management. *Journal of Workplace Learning,* 17(1–2), 49–64.

19

Feminist Qualitative Research and Grounded Theory: Complexities, Criticisms, and Opportunities

Virginia L. Olesen

Feminist qualitative research in its many methodological styles (Olesen, 2005) and grounded theory in its several iterations (Charmaz, 2000) emerged in mid-twentieth century as countervailing approaches to the over-riding positivism of Western social science which had long saturated social science disciplines, anthropology being an important exception (Steinmetz, 2005a). As the result of intellectual forces shaping qualitative research generally (Denzin and Lincoln, 2005a), both flourished and continue to diversify. Grounded theory, an analytic approach, and feminist qualitative research, multiple methods based on different epistemologies, are dynamic, complex sets of ideas that scholars have both altered and fractured since their beginnings and continue to do so. Thus, we must be aware of *which* feminism (Fonow and Cook, 2005; Laslett and Brenner, 2001; Lather, 2006: 73–76; Olesen, 1994, 2000, 2005) and *what* phase of grounded theory (Benoliel, 1996; Walker and Myrick, 2006) we are discussing.

Mindful of these two points, I will briefly recount a history of grounded theory from an historical stance and from my biographical perspective as a qualitative feminist researcher.[1] I will look briefly at the development of feminist qualitative research. I then turn to feminist criticisms of grounded theory and feminist uses of grounded theory. I will also examine feminist research influences on grounded theory. I also discuss structural and intellectual pressures which continue to alter both feminist qualitative research and grounded theory. This chapter will *not* focus on how to do grounded theory. Many classical sources provide this (Glaser, 1978; Glaser and Strauss, 1967), as do early iterations (Strauss, 1987; Strauss and Corbin, 1990, 1994), neo-classic formulations (Glaser, 1992, 1998, 2001, 2003), and constructivist and postmodernist formulations (Charmaz, 2006; Clarke, 2005; Dey, 1999).

GROUNDED THEORY BRIEFLY REVIEWED

The Discovery of Grounded Theory was published in 1967. I well remember the excitement the book's publication brought: a challenge to orthodox positivism, entrenched functionalism, and an invitation to a different research future, which I doubt anyone then visualized, that being a pre-postmodern era. Since publication, social scientists and scholars in many disciplines have done innumerable grounded theory research projects, making it the most widely used interpretive framework in the social sciences (Denzin, 1994: 508), an observation which Adele Clarke's extensive 2005–2006 bibliographic search (2006: 362, fn. 2) amply supports. GT also made its way into professional fields, most notably nursing (Benoliel, 1996), management (Locke, 1996, 2001), and education (Creswell, 2002). The dissemination was also international: German, British, and French scholars undertook GT work. A Japanese translation of Strauss and Corbin entered nursing research.

Why such widespread dissemination? This short essay permits only limited reflections, so I speculate briefly that some reasons are found in the histories of sociological and nursing research. Some claim that GT addressed the lack of rigor in Chicago School qualitative approaches (Alvesson and Skoldberg, 2000), a point also made by Strauss and Corbin (1994: 275). Strauss and Corbin note that it took two decades before researchers finally appreciated GT. They attribute growing appreciation to increasing numbers of books and papers based on the method (p. 275) and worry that GT would become fashionable. However, why did the numbers of books and papers increase? The major GT center, the Graduate Program in Sociology at UCSF, was and is a very small graduate program, hence only a handful, albeit a highly talented and significant handful, were socialized there. Perhaps, it was seen as a do-able approach (Alvesson and Skoldberg, 2000) that opened a range of research spaces rather than a single one (Pidgeon and Henwood, 2004: 627).

Other interpretations can be found in arguments which examine symbolic interactionism, Straussian GT's theoretical base, such as an analysis of the rise, fall, and reemergence of symbolic interactionism (Fine, 1993), or the claim of a 'faultline of consciousness' where sociologists utilize but do not acknowledge symbolic interactionism (Maines, 2001: 228), or the observation that symbolic interactionism 'is a resource that others draw on, transform and use to pursue their own interests and goals' (Joas, 2006: 601). These arguments suggest that scholars not fully alive to interactionism, but nevertheless willing to entertain its concepts, might have been hospitable to utilizing GT or that they may have held parallel concepts. The very term, grounded theory, attracted some.[2] Others use grounded theory, but are largely unaware of it.[3] Certain scholars may have welcomed the chance to support 'creative theory building in observational work compared to the dire abstracted empiricism present in the most wooden statistical studies' (Silverman, 1993: 47).

Speculation aside, inquiry into the widespread adoption of grounded theory, an intriguing question in the sociology of sociological research, awaits the scholar willing to interview methodologists, examine methods syllabi, and undertake exhaustive review of published research accounts. Far from an idle exercise, this query points to the labile characteristics of qualitative research and the shape of that research in ever increasing social, material, and international complexities; themes which I will examine in conclusion.

Nurse researchers' adoption and dissemination of GT paralleled the diffusion of GT within the social sciences. In a well-documented essay, Jeanne Quint Benoliel, a colleague and student of Strauss at UCSF and herself a leading grounded theorist, demonstrates widespread dissemination of GT in nursing research from 1967 through 1990 (Benoliel, 1996). (My own bibliographic search shows that this continues.) Why was GT so widely adopted in nursing research? In the years following publication of the 1967 book, nursing higher education expanded dramatically. Numerous new doctoral programs offered positions to those prepared to teach research skills to graduate students. When the UCSF School of Nursing started a doctoral nursing program in 1968, Strauss, Glaser, and their colleagues offered extensive qualitative research preparation to a growing cadre of nurse researchers who would take positions in the new doctoral programs. The combination of an expanding educational market and increasing preparation of nurse researchers oriented to GT methods enabled spread of the method within nursing. Some UCSF doctorally prepared nurses would later actively participate in the debates around the emergent divisions within GT, an issue to be discussed shortly in Alterations in GT (Stern, 1994).

The continuing, wide adoption of GT has produced a large body of work which varies greatly in the degree to which researchers have utilized GT strategies fully or selectively. Some more clearly reflect GT orientations and interpretations than others. Thus, an intriguing issue in cultural borrowing arose that can only be explored briefly here. It may be an instance of what, in social movement theory, has been called 'the paradox of diffusion and defusion' (Reed, 2006: 23). Radical ideas get diffused, but are defused as they spread, as for example, the idea of social capital (Portes, 1998). Benoliel notes that many GT studies are descriptive rather than discovery focused, selectively rather than theoretically sampled, and are not lodged in an interpretive inquiry (1996). Others claim that researchers have borrowed bits of GT (Becker, 1993) and that rarely are grounded theory strategies fully realized. Instead, researchers give lip service to the method (Bryman and Burgess, 1994: 6). Strauss and Corbin themselves commented that many users do not understand important aspects of grounded theory (1994: 277). This point reflects the observation that some GT researchers overlook 'the principled relationships between data and analysis in a grounded theory manner' (Atkinson and Delamont, 2005: 833).

ALTERATIONS WITHIN GROUNDED THEORY

As grounded theory spread, Strauss and Corbin (1990, 1994, 1998) elaborated more formalized rule-like coding procedures which gave their version of GT a 'further positivist cast' (Charmaz, 2000: 524). Strauss and Corbin then amplified and elaborated coding procedures in two main ways, elaborating axial coding and the conditional matrix. They hinted at, but did not develop, the researcher's involvement in data gathering and analysis.

Glaser claimed that Strauss and Corbin's procedures changed the character of grounded theory work (1992, 1998, 2001, 2003) from discovery of theory to 'full conceptual description' and risked forcing the data. Glaser continues to view GT as a discovery process, utilizing the techniques of constant comparison, negative cases, and theoretical sampling. He also retains a clearly objectivist view of social reality. Others have thoroughly rehearsed these disagreements and differences elsewhere (Annells, 1996; Atkinson, Coffey and Delamont, 2003: 148–152; Bryant, 2002, 2003; Charmaz, 2000, 2006; Clarke, 2005; Hall and Callery, 2001; Locke, 2001; Melia, 1996; Pidgeon and Henwood, 2004; Stern, 1994; Walker and Myrick, 2006; Wuest, 1995). Hence, only aspects of these differing approaches that significantly bear on feminist views of and utilization of grounded theory are reviewed here.

If these developments were not enough to convince readers that one must attend to *which* version of grounded theory is being discussed, there are even further complexities. Several GT scholars, *contra* a positivist view of an objective reality, have recognized the social involvement of the researcher and their participants in the research process of co-constructing 'knowledge.' They have taken grounded theory in the direction of social constructionism (Bryant, 2002, 2003; Charmaz, 2000, 2006) and postmodernism (Clarke, 2005), moves also criticized by Glaser (2002). I will return to these advances in the discussion of grounded theory and feminist qualitative research. On the way I will not slip into the warm treacle of overly adulatory praise in some accounts of 'classical' GT nor the cold bile of bitter criticism in essays on new developments, but rather focus on what feminist qualitative research and grounded theory can offer one another.

FEMINIST QUALITATIVE RESEARCH BRIEFLY REVIEWED

There are multiple feminisms with implications for different research approaches. These approaches are not static, but change as new intellectual currents shift feminist thinking, for instance, the fading of interest in class analysis in favor of inquiries into culture and identity (Acker, 2006). Following along with such developments, feminist epistemologies and research approaches have grown increasingly complex (Fonow and Cook, 2005; Olesen, 2005), generating controversies among adherents of different views and frameworks, as well as within given frameworks. Changes in and revision of standpoint theory (Olesen, 2005: 243–246) reveal such complexity and controversy and resulted in both moves away from a single feminist standpoint to a collective feminist subjectivity (Weeks, 1998: 3–11, 102) and pleas for recognition of the multiplicity of perspectives created by researchers and participants in dynamic environments (Naples, 2003: 197–198). Thus, feminist theory moved from the original assumption that all women shared a woman's standpoint to an appreciation of the ways in which class and race complicate and produce many standpoints (Collins, 1990), and to a much deeper elaboration of intersectionality theory delineating how multiple, simultaneous identities are co-constitutive, producing even further 'standpoints' (Schulz and Mullins, 2006).[4]

Though the question 'What is *feminist* qualitative research?' evokes multiple answers, various approaches share a common theme. Feminists should not merely describe women's situations, but consider how race, class, gender, sexual orientation, age, and material circumstances in multiple contexts render the taken for granted problematic in ways that move toward social justice (Olesen, 2005: 236; Roman, 1992). One of feminist researchers' earliest and most enduring positions, this powerful theme continues, though some worry that deconstructive and postmodernist views dilute the possibility of realizing this position (Maynard, 1998: 134; Olesen, 2005: 247). But it offers intriguing leads, potentially very productive for feminist research. Patricia Hill Collins has noted that, 'By focusing on marginalized, excluded and silenced dimensions of social life, postmodernism destabilizes what has been deemed natural, normal, normative, and true' (Collins, 1998: 124). However, she also comments, '… it fails to offer direction for considering alternatives' (1998: 125). This point necessitates incisive, creative maneuvers if the approach is to be used. Recent developments have begun to attempt to integrate the insights of postmodernism with research agendas that center around the many, varied, and challenging issues that fall under the rubric of 'social justice' (Denzin and Lincoln, 2005a, b; Lather, 2006; Clarke, Under Review).[5] And, as this chapter was being written, feminist scholars were preparing a volume on the potential of poststructural analysis for reconstructing policy in higher education (Allen, Iverson and Ropers-Huilman, In Preparation).

The way in which research is conducted suggests whether it is feminist work: It does *not* depict women as powerless, abnormal, or without agency. It reveals micropolitics of the research process. It explicates difference carefully, and avoids replicating oppression, also known as 'blaming the victim' (Bhavnani, 1994: 30; Cancian, 1992). Further, reflecting complex alterations in feminist qualitative work (Olesen, 2005: 239–240), it stresses ethical dimensions, the inter-relatedness of researcher and participant, and multiple ways of knowing (Dankoski, 2000).

These latter points surged into feminist qualitative research because of the substantial impact of work by women of color, gay/lesbian/transsexual/queer theorists, postcolonial and globalization theorists, disabled women, standpoint theorists, and those persuaded by postmodern and deconstructive perspectives (Olesen, 2005: 248). Among many other issues, these writings transformed ideas about women as research participants and, most critically, perspectives on feminist researchers themselves as both implicated and participatory in the production of data. Barriers between researcher and participant became seen as penetrable and fluid, hence taken-for-granted ideals of objectivity began to crumble, creating implications for research relationships, ethical issues, representation issues, and queries regarding the trustworthiness of the account. Some feminists, of course, still embrace the old, positivist views.

The issue of the relationship between the researcher and participants as co-producers of data is central to some feminist criticisms of grounded theory to which I now turn: (1) Positivist elements, (2) Reflexivity, (3) Ethical issues. (For discussion of additional criticisms, see Clarke, 2005: 11–18; 2006, Under Review; Charmaz, 2000, 2006: 9.)

FEMINIST CRITICISMS OF GROUNDED THEORY

Since publication of *The Discovery of Grounded Theory* in 1967 and into the era of *The Handbook of Grounded Theory*, feminists have been critical of grounded theory, even though feminist researchers have used it extensively, a point to which I will return in Grounded Theory and Feminist Research. These criticisms largely focus on early formulations by Glaser and Strauss and the initial Strauss–Corbin frameworks noted above, but they also bear on Glaser's recent iterations, also noted above.

Positivist elements
Chief among these critiques is that some versions of GT are essentially a type of inductive positivism which, despite inductive analytic strategies, relies, tacitly, if not explicitly, on an objective stance. Here the researcher is gazing upon the social worlds of their participants, but is distanced from and in no way a part of them (Charmaz, 2006: 10; Dey, 1999: 232; Hall and Callery, 2001; Henwood and Pidgeon, 1995; Pidgeon and Henwood, 2004; Roman, 1992: 571; Sprague, 2005: 130; Stanley and Wise, 1993: 161). Early and subsequent formulations of GT—with the exception of very recent advances which emphasize social constructionism (Charmaz, 2006) and postmodernism (Clarke, 2005)—fail to recognize the embeddedness of the researcher and thus obscure the researcher's considerable agency in data construction and interpretation, as well as the framing of accounts. Additionally, Dorothy Smith argues that GT 'methods of transposing

the researcher's impressions or intuitions into concepts that have the formal property of universality combines to displace diverging perspectives and to subdue the social organization that generates difference to a monologic interpretive scheme' (2005: 160). This is an apt criticism of which both grounded theorists and feminists should be aware.

This criticism speaks also to the early GT position that researchers start the inquiry with a mental blank slate, disavowing any knowledge about the topic at hand or any acquaintance with prior relevant theory or research (Woods, 1992). This approach advocated by Glaser and Strauss in fact clashes with both of their research experiences. Locke insightfully observes they were not merely passive observers; they knew something about those clinical settings where they did their basic work (Locke, 2001: xi) and perhaps had a point of view about these settings. These points lead directly to concerns about reflexivity.

Reflexivity

Feminist researchers (Clarke, 2005: 12–15; Cook and Fonow, 1986; Fine, 1992; Hertz, 1997; Holland and Ramazanagolu, 1994; Mauthner and Doucet, 1998; Maynard 1998, 2004) have long raised questions about reflexivity: the manner and extent to which the researchers present themselves as imbedded in the research situation and process. Foregrounding self differentiates reflexivity from mere reflection, which characterizes some grounded theory and some feminist research. (For discussion of reflexivity and reflection see Neill, 2006: 255.) Reflexivity takes several forms: (1) Full explanation of how analytic and practical issues were handled; (2) Examination of the researcher's own background and its influences on the research; and (3) Reflections on the researcher's own emotions, worries, feelings. Apropos of the first point, Strauss and Corbin (1990: 258; 1998: 269) do urge giving details of the research process, but did not develop this stance. Glaser's later writing (2001) disavows reflexivity as useful to grounded theory (Neill, 2006: 253, 258). However, Neill's examination of the potential contribution of reflexivity to Glaserian grounded theory argues that it has a critical place in theoretical sampling (2006: 258–259; see also Carr, 2006; Gardner, 2006).

Like grounded theorists in general, some feminists who have used grounded theory are not always clear about how they should use it. They rely too frequently on a ritualistic recitation of various steps, a point which echoes Benoliel's comments noted earlier. Detailed accounts of usage are scarce or, where offered, are glossed. Reports do not go much beyond first order reporting of descriptive findings, excellent though they are. The lift to theory is usually absent. Tied in with the general failure to explicate data gathering and analytic moves is a common lack of a reflexive account. Noting the critical importance of reflexivity, Mauthner and Doucet plead:

> The best we can do then is to trace and document our data analysis processes, and the choices and decisions we make, so that other researchers and interested parties can see for themselves what has been and some of what has been gained. We need to document these

reflexive processes, not just in general terms such as our class, gender and ethnic background, but in a more concrete and nitty-gritty way in terms of where, how and why particular decisions are made at particular stages (1998: 138).

They also signal the importance of reporting the researcher's attributes and subjectivities:

… the interplay between our multiple social locations and how these intersect with the particularities of our personal biographies needs to be considered, as far as possible, *at the time of* analysing data [italics in original] (Mauthner and Doucet, 2003: 419).

Nevertheless, some feminist researchers have aimed for reflexivity. Hamberg and Johansson disclose their reactions to the interview and research process. They reread coded interviews 'to scrutinize parts featuring tension, contradiction or conflicting codes …' (Hamberg and Johansson, 1989: 458). Reflexive analysis of an interview (which they include in text) leads them to conclude in part:

As researchers we were ashamed when we read this quotation (from the interview): 'When conducting the interview Kej (interviewer) was aware of the confused dialogue and tried to handle that by keeping to what she perceived as the topic at hand, rehabilitation and work. The intention was to follow up on Sally (the interviewee)'s experiences. However, by doing this Kej neglected the repeated hints that Sally made about her own experiences and points of view. Was it possible at all for Sally to describe her reality when she was silenced in this way?' (Hamberg and Johansson, 1989: 459).

Mauthner and Doucet (2003) used the voice-centered method of relational analysis to present details (too lengthy for inclusion here) on how and where they overlooked their own subjectivity in their analyses. (Voice-centered relational analysis involves multiple readings of an interview text to see the researcher in the text and how she responds emotionally and intellectually; Brown and Gilligan, 1992.) See also Hood's struggles with constant comparative analysis (1983); Finch and Mason's classical account of theoretical sampling (1990); and Jones's discussion of social class issues (1997).

Presenting a reflexive research account which fully reveals researcher moves and moods as well as respecting and incorporating the voices of the participants is not an easy task (Finlay, 2002a, b: 541–542). It requires close attention to issues of situated knowledges and partial perspectives so compellingly analyzed in Haraway's classic reflections on those issues (1991). To do it well also requires skilled, thoughtful writing (Speer, 2002).

Moreover, as Kathy Charmaz has commented in a personal communication (June 8, 2006) journal and even book editors restrict space in which to fully discuss research methods. One solution might be to present the reflexive account as fully as possible within the journal/book page limits and offer, as well, a more detailed on-line account accessible via email, or on the author's web page. Another would be to integrate reflective observations into the presentation of findings, rather than as a separate section. This strategy again requires very sophisticated writing skills and, as some have pointed out, risks privileging the researcher's experience over those of the participants (Finlay, 2002b: 541; Hall and Callery, 2001).

Even with these or other considerations, reflexivity probably can never be fully obtained (Maynard, 2004: 140). While recognizing this difficulty, GT and feminist researchers, both those using GT and other qualitative methods, would do well to strive for it. Reflexivity is a means to realize 'strong objectivity' (Harding, 1993: 71), which rejects reliance on value-free objectivity and foregrounds instead the relationship of researcher and participant in which the participant is seen as gazing back at the researcher. Trustworthiness of the research and the account are at issue here.

Ethical issues

Grounded theory is an approach or set of approaches to the analysis of data. As such, the classic works did not address other aspects of the research process. It should come as no surprise therefore that these formulations are singularly silent on ethical issues in the conduct of the research (privacy, consent, confidentiality, deceit, deception, harm). However, the classic works are also silent about ethical issues inherent in the analytic processes in GT (unwittingly or not manipulating coding or theoretical sampling processes; writing the account). This criticism should not be taken to imply that GT is a-ethical or unethical. Rather, the absence of comment is probably related to the lack of reflexivity just discussed, but these are inter-related, since standards for evaluating quality, such as presenting a transparent account, are intertwined with ethical issues (Lincoln, 1995: 287).

This absence in written GT accounts may also reflect historical differences in awareness of ethical questions. In the early GT decades, although debates occurred about ethical issues, e.g. hidden or covert research, scholars commonly and tacitly took for granted that researchers' accounts would reflect ethical conduct. Researchers rather less frequently provided particularities about structuring and sustaining ethics in the context (Olesen and Whittaker, 1968: 33–36).

In the later more difficult era of IRBs, disjunctures can emerge between the requisite, appropriate declarations in IRB protocols to assure privacy, confidentiality, and to avoid harm and events on site. Neither these disjunctures, nor the dynamic interactions in the research site which can and do create uncomfortable unanticipated ethical surprises in data gathering and analysis (Whittaker, 1981), are commonly discussed. One exception is Monica Casper's anguished and candid account of such difficulties that arose in her research on the sensitive and controversial procedure of fetal surgery (1997). A former patient, irritated at what she deemed criticism of the surgical team, sent an unpublished paper of Casper's to the surgical team. This woman's action exposed a key team member as an informant, who felt Casper had inadequately masked her identity. Casper subsequently repaired this damage, but access to the site was compromised (1997: 248–249). In contrast, some feminists have raised and explored a wide range of ethical issues, revealing the frequently uncomfortable contexts in which researchers find themselves as they gather data, analyze, and publish their findings (Olesen, 2005: 254–256). These accounts generally are highly self-reflexive, indicating researchers' worries, concerns, and resolutions.

FEMINIST GROUNDED THEORY RESEARCH

It is near impossible to cite, never mind discuss, the range and variety of contexts and topics on which feminist researchers have used grounded theory, some version of it, or some portion of it. Feminist researchers with many different concerns have utilized it in a wide range of academic and professional fields: the social, behavioral, and cultural sciences, nursing, medicine, social work, business, science, and technology studies, and education. Though some studies veer toward 'woman centered' research (Clarke, 2006), most problematize gender, its production, enactment, and performance along with race, class, and sexual orientation in material, historical, and cultural contexts (Lorber, 1996). This approach is particularly the case where feminist researchers regard gender as socially constructed in complex ways and not as a face sheet variable (Glaser, 2002).

To indicate the use of GT in many feminist contexts, I note some selected studies which point to the range of substantive topics and conceptual issues addressed. Regrettably, space does not allow citing many equally excellent projects. A long discussion can be found in Olesen (2005: 236–238); Clarke (2006) offers a richly detailed review which covers many fine projects not cited here. Not surprisingly, feminists look at issues of *socially located identity and subjectivity* including: the social construction of battering and structural issues in battered women's experiences (Lempert, 1994); women's articulation of rules in cosmetic surgery (Ancheta, 2002); agency among breast cancer patients (Kasper, 1994); and women cocaine users' strategies to protect children and preserve a sense of self (Kearney, Murphy and Rosenbaum, 1994). Feminist researchers have also examined how women experience and interpret *the influence of cultural and economic factors* such as the entrapment of battered African American women in illegal activities (Richie, 1996); staff nurses' emotional responses to work pressures in rationalizing health care systems (Bone, 2002); lesbians' creative interpretations and use of reproductive technologies (Mamo, 2006); and differential constructions of race, class, and gender by people of color with cardiovascular disease and epidemiology (Shim, 2002).

The feminist GT reach to societal and global issues is also noteworthy including: the impact of male-oriented therapies (Viagra) on the construction of male and female sexual dysfunction (Fishman, 2004); physicians' deflection of attempts by breast cancer activists to provide information to women with cancer (Montini, 1997); globalization issues in the export of Filipino migrant workers (Guevarra, 2006); and reconceptualizing social indicators to challenge traditional economic theory (Austin, Jefferson and Thein, 2003). These studies in particular suggest the utility of grounded theory in addressing policy issues of concern to feminists. Though qualitative research can be useful in policy analysis (Finch, 1986), feminist researchers have not fully developed the possibilities of grounded theory for policy research, an avenue feminist scholars outlined long ago (Estes and Edmonds, 1981). Charmaz' insights on grounded theory and advancing social justice studies offer promising leads (2005), as do advances such as Clarke's situational analysis (2005, 2006, Under Review).[6]

MEETING THE CHALLENGES: GROUNDED THEORY AND FEMINIST RESEARCH

Both grounded theorists and feminist qualitative researchers face substantial challenges as complex technical, social, cultural, and economic changes surge through societies worldwide: rising new economic powers, declining once powerful economic states; emergent nuclear states; growing unease around migrated and migrating populations, among migrants themselves, and within host societies; resurgent or revived conservatisms and fundamentalisms; unremitting advances in and spread of electronic technologies which dissolve old social forms and create new ones; growing social inequities which threaten health, well being, and social stability. These tectonic shifts produce an abundance of critical issues on which grounded theorists and feminist researchers are well positioned to do acute, incisive work, wherever they are located, particularly in light of GT's distinctive capacities to analyze process and change. However, to do so they will need every bit of extra analytic acuity they can summon to create a cutting edge with which to uncover, dissect, and understand the issues. The earlier points in this essay signal those extra bits of analytical acuity.

The work of grounded theorists will be enhanced with a return to the recognition, so deeply rooted in the symbolic interactionist bones of GT, that researcher and participant are mutually imbedded in the social context of the research and that data are co-created. Such recognition moves the analyst away from objectivist renderings of 'reality' to interpretive ones. However, the result should not lead to an account which would read like a French *nouveau-roman* wherein readers knew not who was speaking or what was being spoken about. Rather, it should produce a reflexive account, which can more easily accommodate and present the complexities of research processes, progressive ebbs and flows in the substantive area being analyzed, be it domestic violence, nursing work in hospitals, or impact of biotechnical issues. Consider Luff's reflections on her feminist research with anti-feminist women where she presents part of her research diary about an interview in which the interviewee's dress and home confounded her expectations:

> Often I was unaware of my assumptions until I was confronted by them. For example, I was surprised after a series of interviews, when I was beginning to feel comfortable about the likely lifestyles, houses and even dress sense of these women, to have these assumptions challenged.

> This interview brought me face to face with my stereotypes about links between chosen appearance and attitudes more clearly than supervision discussions about what *I* should wear and how to present *myself* ... The unspoken assumption, however, in my considerations was what any impact would have on *them from me* [italics in original] (Luff, 1999: 694).

Grounded theorists have much to learn from reflexive feminist research accounts. The reflexive account also provides a way for readers to assess the researcher in action and accord trustworthiness and credibility, a move away from the positivist concerns with objectivity as a hallmark of validity. The reflexive account also enables exploration of ethical matters encountered in grounded theory research and analysis, topics on which feminists have been more thoughtful in presenting accounts of difficult, ethically strained research projects.

Feminists, conversely, have much to learn from the newer formulations of grounded theory. The constructivist and postmodernist positions enhance feminist capacities to meaningfully analyze large scale processes, once thought (incorrectly) to lie outside the ken of grounded theory and to move beyond taken for granted issues in race, class, gender, sexual orientation, and age. Concerning large scale processes, feminists utilizing postmodernist advances are well positioned, for instance, to undertake critical inquiry into complex facets of globalization, the dominance of states, and economic factors which influence and create female subjectivities, identities, oppression, and opportunity and women's resistance. Postmodernist grounded theory can also be useful in feminist analysis of race, class, gender, sexual orientation, and age; areas where constructivist grounded theory would also facilitate a critical examination of these issues and how they are intertwined and play out in women's and men's lives (Schwalbe et al., 2000). In sum, there are mutually beneficial aspects for grounded theorists wishing to sharpen their work and feminist researchers seeking to expand their inquiries.

WHITHER GROUNDED THEORY AND FEMINIST QUALITATIVE RESEARCH?

Though positivism in the human sciences, particularly sociology, is no longer taken for granted as the only way good research is done, it is still well ingrained in institutional socialization, reinforced by funding structures, and sustained by demands for knowledge in positivist forms (Steinmetz, 2005b). These factors limit the extent to which qualitative feminist research and grounded theory in its constructivist and postmodern versions can challenge positivistic orthodoxy, sustaining the observation that antipositivist thinking has not penetrated sociology as much as some other human sciences (Steinmetz, 2005b). Feminist qualitative research and grounded theory, particularly in its constructivist and postmodern iterations, continually struggle for research funding.

However, both feminist qualitative work and GT in various forms are much more widely and deeply institutionalized than they were in the mid-1960s and in ways which facilitate critical intervention. In the mid-1960s, very few journals in English or any other language were sympathetic to or published qualitative or feminist work. (The major exceptions included *Sociology*, *Social Problems*, and *The Sociological Quarterly*.) By the new century such journals had proliferated impressively, representing diversities within feminist and grounded theory work (*Signs, Gender and Society, Feminist Studies, Feminist Inquiry, Qualitative Research, Qualitative Inquiry, Qualitative Sociology, Qualitative Health Research, Feminism and Psychology, Sociology of Health And Illness, Health, Symbolic Interaction*, and new journals in Eastern Europe and Australia). In addition to numerous sessions at professional meetings, regional, national, and international conferences in Europe and North America (three alone in 2006) focus on qualitative work and likely even more on feminist research. Specialized training workshops on qualitative analysis, including GT, are springing up (e.g. www.ResearchTalk.com). Finally, feminist and qualitative research web sites abound: www.situationalanalysis.com; www.qualitative-research.net/fqs/fqs-eng.htm; www.groundedtheory.com; and www.uofaweb.ualberta.ca/ iiqm/thinking.cfm.

The abundance of these publications, conferences, and websites, as well as the growth of publishers willing to publish feminist and qualitative work, gives feminist and GT researchers opportunities to gain research citations in peer reviewed journals so essential to academic careers. Equally important, these outlets make their work public and provide groundwork and occasion for intervention on critical issues. There are multiple sites where scholars and critics will utilize, debate, criticize, affirm, and/or alter now current forms of feminist and GT work in light of new intellectual currents and social conditions. How these dynamic systems of thought will alter or settle can only be vaguely surmised at this writing. What is critical is that both feminist qualitative research and grounded theory are vitally useful to scrutinize and intervene in crucial social and cultural issues, particularly when the points of mutual enrichment noted in this chapter, are considered.

ACKNOWLEDGMENTS

Over many years, productive and stimulating conversations with Kathy Charmaz, Anne Murcott, Elvi Whittaker, and Adele Clarke have enriched and expanded my thinking. In a typically generous gesture, Adele Clarke shared the results of her extensive exploration of grounded theory and feminist citations, a treasure trove which eased my preparation enormously. Her incisive criticisms of this chapter greatly improved it. Anselm Strauss, who recruited me to UCSF in 1960, was a wonderfully sensitive, flexible, and inspiring mentor and colleague.

NOTES

1 My involvement with and views on grounded theory and qualitative research began at UCSF during the early and mid-1960s when Strauss, Glaser, and Jeanne Quint Benoliel were doing research on death and dying while Elvi Whittaker, Fred Davis, and I were conducting an ethnographic study of student nurse socialization. My orientation to feminist perspectives had emerged during graduate school, but blossomed in the early 1970s when I began to work on women, health, and healing. Recalling early grounded theory days, I do not recall discussions with Glaser and Strauss about grounded theory. We (Whittaker, Davis, and myself) did not use grounded theory, as it was still emerging. We were also pushing to conclude our own inductive ethnographic analysis (Olesen and Whittaker, 1968). *Contra* early grounded theory, Whittaker and I emphasized the intertwining of researcher and participants in the co-production of data and provided a reflexive account re: ourselves as researchers (Olesen and Whittaker, 1968: 37), thus anticipating the later feminist emphasis on reflexivity. Absent, however, were details of our struggles with analysis. In my later work (Olesen, 1990, 1992; Olesen et al., 1992) I used what I thought were the most useful parts of grounded theory, particularly constant comparisons and theoretical sampling. I thought the search for the 'negative case,' rightly criticized later as a positivistic element, could, with care, be transformed to a thought-provoking strategy to uncover new insights which might or might not alter, clarify, or expand interpretations. To sum, I could not claim to be a 'grounded theorist,' but a socialist feminist borrower oriented to social constructionism and postmodernism's most useful elements. For a fuller biographical account of my feminist orientation, see Olesen (1994: 169, fn. 1; 2005: 259–260). In 26 years (1974–2000) teaching field research to graduate students in sociology, anthropology, and nursing, I assigned grounded theory texts and research reports, but also believed students should be aware of other analytical styles, among them strip analysis (Agar, 1986), domain analysis (Spradley, 1979), and analytic fieldwork (Katz, 1983). I also asked students to keep diaries of their involvements, analytic decision-making, and emotions, something quite foreign (at that time) to basic grounded theory approaches. I found it increasingly difficult to teach what I called the Strauss and Corbin 'cook book' analytic modes. Students (and I) would get bogged down in minutiae with little or no lift off to concepts, never mind theory (perhaps I did not understand Strauss and Corbin well, but …). The increasingly sharp differences between Glaser and Strauss and Corbin had not yet fully emerged while I was still teaching fieldwork. Were I still teaching, I would find other creative, new paths as outlined in Charmaz (2006) and Clarke (2005) useful in connection with other analytic modes.

2 Adele Clarke has observed that the word 'grounded' in GT is deeply seductive to qualitative researchers who seek to capture 'basics' of social life—or of daily life, life as experienced. Many have little or no grasp of 'the social.' Groundedness contrasts so vividly with the testing of variables in survey research.

3 Kathy Charmaz, personal communication, June 8, 2006.

4 Adele Clarke, personal communication, October 2, 2006.

5 Adele Clarke, personal communication, October 2, 2006.

6 Situational analysis involves: (1) mapping and analyzing major elements in the situation (human, nonhuman, discursive, etc.) to grasp the complexities; (2) mapping the social worlds/arenas of the actors, both human and nonhuman to show the labile and interconnected relationality of these worlds; and (3) articulating positional maps which show the range of discursive positions both taken and not taken. Situational analysis discovers, recognizes, and examines complexities that inhere in, play upon, and emerge from contexts of interest and concern to feminist researchers.

REFERENCES

Acker, J. (2006). *Class Questions: Feminist Answers*. Lanham, MD: Rowan and Littlefield.

Agar, M. H. (1986). *Speaking of Ethnography*. Beverly Hills, CA: SAGE.

Allen, E., Iverson, S. and Ropers-Huilman, B. (In Preparation). *Reconstructing Policy in Higher Education: Perspectives from Feminist Poststructural Analysis*.

Alvesson, M. and Skoldberg, K. (2000). Data-oriented methods, Empiricist techniques and procedures. In M. Alvesson and K. Skoldberg (Eds.), *Reflexive Methodology, New Vistas for Qualitative Research* (pp. 12–51). Thousand Oaks, CA: SAGE.

Ancheta, R. W. (2002). Discourse of rules: Women talk about cosmetic surgery. In K. S. Ratcliff (Ed.), *Women and Health: Power, Technology, Inequality and Conflict in a Gendered World* (pp. 143–149). Boston, MA: Allyn and Bacon.

Annells, M. (1996). Grounded theory method: Philosophical perspectives, paradigm of inquiry, and postmodernism. *Qualitative Health Research*, 6(3), 379–383.

Atkinson, P., Coffey, A. and Delamont, S. (2003). *Key Themes in Qualitative Research. Continuities and Change*. Walnut Creek, CA: Alta Mira.

Atkinson, P. and Delamont, S. (2005). Analytic perspectives. In N. K. Denzin and Y. S. Lincoln (Eds.), *The Sage Handbook of Qualitative Research* (3rd ed., pp. 821–840). Thousand Oaks, CA: SAGE.

Austin, S., Jefferson, T. and Thein, V. (2003) Gendered social indicators and grounded theory. *Feminist Economics*, 9(1), 1–18.

Becker, P. H. (1993). Common pitfalls in published grounded theory research. *Qualitative Health Research*, 3(2), 254–250.

Benoliel, J. Q. (1996). Grounded theory and nursing knowledge. *Qualitative Health Research*, 6(3), 406–428.

Bhavnani, K. K. (1994). Tracing the contours: Feminist research and feminist objectivity. In H. Afhsar and M. Maynard (Eds.), *The Dynamics of 'Race' And Gender: Some Feminist Interpretations* (pp. 26–40). London: Taylor and Francis.

Bone, D. (2002). Dilemmas of emotion work in nursing under market driven health care. *International Journal of Public Sector Management*, 15(2), 140–150.

Brown, L. M. and Gilligan, C. (1992). *Meeting at the Crossroads: Women's Psychology and Girls' Development*. Cambridge, MA: Harvard University Press.

Bryant, A. (2002). Re-grounding grounded theory. *Journal of Information Technology Theory and Application*, 4(1), 25–42.

Bryant, A. (2003). A constructivist response to Glaser. *FQS: Forum For Qualitative Research* 4(1). Retrieved November 10, 2005 from www.qualitative-research.net/fqs-eng.htm

Bryman, A. and Burgess, R. G. (1994). *Analyzing Qualitative Data*. New York: Routledge.

Cancian, F. (1992). Feminist science: methodologies that change inequality. *Gender and Society*, 6, 623–642.

Carr, E. C. J. (2006). Reflexivity: A challenge for the nurse researcher? Review. *Journal of Research in Nursing*, 11(2), 158–159.

Casper, M. J. (1997). Feminist politics and fetal surgery: Adventures of a research cowgirl on the reproductive frontier. *Feminist Studies*, 23, 233–262.

Charmaz, K. (2000). Grounded theory. Objectivist and constructionist methods. In N. K. Denzin and Y. S. Lincoln (Eds.), *Handbook of Qualitative Research* (2nd ed., pp. 509–535). Thousand Oaks, CA: SAGE.

Charmaz, K. (2005). Grounded theory in the 21st century: Applications for advancing social justice studies. In N. K. Denzin and Y. S. Lincoln (Eds.), *The Sage Handbook Qualitative Research* (3rd ed., pp. 507–536). Thousand Oaks, CA: SAGE.

Charmaz, K. (2006). *Constructing Grounded Theory. A Practical Guide Through Qualitative Analysis*. Thousand Oaks, CA: SAGE.

Clarke, A. (2005). *Situational Analysis, Grounded Theory After the Postmodern Turn*. Thousand Oaks, CA: SAGE.

Clarke, A. (2006). Feminisms, grounded theory and situational analysis. In S. Hesse-Biber (Ed.), *Handbook of Feminist Research, Theory and Praxis* (pp. 345–370). Thousand Oaks, CA: SAGE.

Clarke, A. (Under Review). Situational analysis: A Haraway-inspired feminist approach to research. In S. Ghamari-Tabrizi (Ed.), *Thinking with Donna Haraway*.

Collins, P. H. (1990). *Black Feminist Thought: Knowledge, Consciousness and the Politics of Empowerment*. Boston: Unwin Hyman.

Collins, P. H. (1998). *Fighting Words. Black Women & the Search for Justice*. Minneapolis, MN: University of Minnesota Press.

Cook, J. A. and Fonow, M. M. (1986). Knowledge and women's interests: Issues of epistemology and methodology in feminist sociological research. *Sociological Inquiry*, 56, 2–29.

Creswell, J. S. (2002). *Educational Research: Planning, Conducting, and Evaluating Quantitative and Qualitative Research*. Upper Saddle River, NJ: Merrill-Prentice Hall.

Dankoski, M. E. (2000). What makes research feminist? *Journal of Family Therapy*, 2(1), 3–19.

Denzin, N. K. (1994). The art and politics of interpretation. In N. K. Denzin and Y. S. Lincoln (Eds.), *Handbook of Qualitative Research* (pp. 500–516). Thousand Oaks, CA: SAGE.

Denzin, N. K. and Lincoln, Y. S. (2005a). Introduction. The discipline and practice of qualitative research. In N. K. Denzin and Y.S. Lincoln (Eds.), *The Sage Handbook of Qualitative Research* (3rd ed., pp. 1–32). Thousand Oaks, CA: SAGE.

Denzin, N. K. and Lincoln, Y. S. (2005b). Epilogue. The eighth and ninth moments—Qualitative research in/and the fractured future. In N. K. Denzin and Y. S. Lincoln (Eds.), *The Sage Handbook of Qualitative Research* (3rd ed., pp. 1115–1126). Thousand Oaks, CA: SAGE.

Dey, I. (1999). *Grounding Grounded Theory. Guidelines for Qualitative Inquiry*. San Diego, CA: Academic Press.

Estes, C. L. and Edmonds, B. C. (1981). Symbolic interaction and social policy analysis. *Symbolic Interaction*, 4, 75–86.

Finch, J. (1986). *Research and Policy: The Uses of Qualitative Research in Social and Educational Research*. London: Falmer.

Finch, J. and Mason, J. (1990). Decision taking in the fieldwork process: Theoretical sampling and collaborative working. In R. G. Burgess (Ed.), *Studies in Qualitative Methodology: Vol. 2, Reflections on Field Experience* (pp. 25–50). Greenwich, CT: JAI.

Fine, G. A. (1993). The sad demise, the mysterious disappearance and glorious triumph of symbolic interactionism. *Annual Review of Sociology*, 19, 61–87.

Fine, M. (Ed.) (1992). *Disruptive Voices*. Ann Arbor, MI: University of Michigan Press.

Finlay, L. (2002a). Negotiating the swamp: The opportunity and challenge of reflexivity in research practice. *Qualitative Research*, 2(2), 202–230.

Finlay, L. (2002b). 'Outing' the researcher: The provenance, process and practice of reflexivity. *Qualitative Health Research*, 12(4), 531–545.

Fishman, J. (2004). Manufacturing desire: The commodification of female sexual dysfunction. *Social Studies of Science*, 34(2), 187–218.

Fonow, M. M. and Cook, J. A. (2005). Feminist methodology: New applications in the academy and public policy. *Signs*, 30(4), 2211–2237.

Gardner, L. (2006). Grounded theory sampling. The contribution of reflexivity. Review. *Journal of Research in Nursing*, 11(3), 261–262.

Glaser, B. G. (1978). *Theoretical Sensitivity*. Mill Valley, CA: The Sociology Press.

Glaser, B. G. (1992). *Basics of Grounded Theory Analysis*. Mill Valley: CA: The Sociology Press.

Glaser, B. G. (1998). *Doing Grounded Theory: Issues and Discussion*. Mill Valley, CA: The Sociology Press.

Glaser, B. G. (2001) *The Grounded Theory Perspective: Conceptualization contrasted with Description*. Mill Valley, CA: The Sociology Press.

Glaser, B. G. (2002). Grounded theory and gender relevance. *Health Care for Women International*, 23, 786–793.

Glaser, B. G. (2003) *Conceptualization Contrasted with Description*. Mill Valley, CA: The Sociology Press.

Glaser, B. G. and Strauss, A. L. (1967) *The Discovery of Grounded Theory: Strategies for Qualitative Research*. Chicago, IL: Aldine.

Guevarra, A. (2006). Managing 'vulnerabilities' and 'empowering' migrant Filipino Workers: The Philippines' overseas employment program. *Social Identities: Journal for the Study of Race, Nation and Culture*, 12(5), 523–541.

Hall, W. A. and Callery, P. (2001). Enhancing the rigor of grounded theory: Incorporating reflexivity and rationality. *Qualitative Health Research*, 11(2), 257–272.

Hamberg, K. and Johansson, E. V. (1989). Practitioner, researcher, and gender conflict in a qualitative study. *Qualitative Health Research*, 9(4), 455–467.

Haraway, D. J. (1991). Situated knowledges: The science question in feminism and the privilege of partial perspectives. In D. J. Haraway (Ed.), *Simians, Cyborgs, and Women: The Reinvention of Nature* (pp. 183–201). New York: Routledge.

Harding, S. (1993) Rethinking standpoint epistemology. What is 'strong objectivity?' In L. Alcoff and L. Porter (Eds.), *Feminist Epistemologies* (pp. 49–52). New York: Routledge.

Henwood, K. and Pidgeon, N. (1995). Remaking the link: Qualitative research and feminist standpoint theory. *Feminism and Psychology*, 5(1), 7–30.

Hertz, R. (1997). *Reflexivity and Voice*. Thousand Oaks, CA: SAGE.

Holland, J. and Ramazanagolu, C. (1994). Coming to conclusions. Power and interpretation in researching young women's sexuality. In M. Maynard and J. Purvis (Eds.), *Researching Women's Lives From a Feminist Perspective* (pp. 125–148). London: Taylor and Francis.

Hood, J. C. (1983) *Becoming a Two-Job Family*. New York: Praeger.

Joas, H. (2006). Book Review Forum. *Symbolic Interaction*, 28 (4), 597–602. (Review of *Handbook of Symbolic Interactionism*, edited by L. T. Reynolds and N. H. Kinney, Walnut Creek, CA: Alta Mira Press, 2003.)

Jones, S. J. (1997). Reflexivity and feminist practice: Ethical dilemmas in negotiating meaning. *Feminism and Psychology*, 7(3), 348–353.

Kasper, A. (1994). A feminist qualitative methodology: A study of women with breast cancer. *Qualitative Sociology*, 17, 263–281.

Katz, J. (1983). A theory of qualitative methodology: The social system of analytic fieldwork. In R. Emerson (Ed.), *Contemporary Field Research* (pp. 127–148). Boston: Little Brown.

Kearney, M. H., Murphy, S. and Rosenbaum, M. (1994). Mothering on crack cocaine: A grounded theory analysis. *Social Science and Medicine*, 38(2), 351–361.

Laslett, B. S. and Brenner, J. (2001). Twenty-first century academic feminism in the United States: Utopian visions and practical actions. *Signs*, 25, 1231–1236.

Lather, P. (2006). *Getting Lost: Feminist Efforts Toward a Double(d) Science*. Albany, NY: SUNY Press.

Lempert, L. B. (1994) Narrative analysis of abuse: Connecting the personal, the rhetorical and the structural. *Journal of Contemporary Ethnography*, 22, 411–441.

Lincoln, Y. S. (1995). Emerging criteria for quality in qualitative and interpretive research. *Qualitative Inquiry*, 1, 275–289.

Locke, K. (1996). Rewriting the discovery of grounded theory after 25 years? *Journal of Management Inquiry*, 5(1), 239–245.

Locke, K. (2001). *Grounded Theory in Management Research*. Thousand Oaks, CA: SAGE.

Lorber, J. (1996). Beyond the binaries: Depolarizing the categories of sex, sexuality and gender. *Sociological Inquiry*, 66(2), 143–159.

Luff, D. (1999). Dialogue across the divides: 'Moments of rapport' and power in feminist research with anti-feminist women. *Sociology*, 33(4), 687–703.

Maines, D. R. (2001). *The Faultline of Consciousness: A View of Interactionism in Sociology*. New York: Aldine de Gruyter.

Mamo, L. (2006). *Queering Reproduction: Achieving Pregnancy in the Age of Technoscience*. Durham, NC: Duke University Press.

Mauthner, N. and Doucet, A. (1998). Reflections on a voice-centered relational method. Analyzing maternal and domestic voices. In J. Ribbens and R. Edwards (Eds.), *Feminist Dilemmas in Qualitative Research. Public Knowledge and Private Lives* (pp. 119–146). Thousand Oaks, CA: SAGE.

Mauthner, N. S. and Doucet, A. (2003). Reflexive accounts and accounts of reflexivity in qualitative data analysis. *Sociology*, 37(3), 413–431.

Maynard, M. (1998). Feminists' knowledge and the knowledge of feminisms: Epistemology, theory, methodology and method. In T. May and M. Williams (Eds.), *Knowing the Social World* (pp. 129–137). Philadelphia, PA: Open University Press.

Maynard, M. (2004). Feminist issues in data analysis. In M. Hardy and A. Bryman (Eds.), *Handbook of Data Analysis* (pp. 131–146). Thousand Oaks, CA: SAGE.

Melia, K. M. (1996). Rediscovering Glaser. *Qualitative Health Research*, 6(3), 368–378.

Montini, T. (1997). Resist and redirect: Physicians respond to breast cancer informed consent legislation. *Women and Health*, 12, 85–105.

Naples, N. A. (2003). *Feminism and Method, Ethnography, Discourse Analysis and Activist Research*. New York: Routledge.

Neill, S. J. (2006). Grounded theory sampling. The contribution of reflexivity. *Journal of Research in Nursing*, 11(3), 253–260.

Olesen, V. L. (1990). Immersed, amorphous and episodic fieldwork: Theory and policy in three contrasting contexts. In R. G. Burgess (Ed.), *Reflections on Field Experiences* (pp. 205–232). Greenwich, CT: JAI Press.

Olesen, V. L. (1992). The extraordinary experience and the mundane complaint: the contextual dialectics of the embodied self. In C. Ellis and M. Flaherty (Eds.), *Research on Lived Experience* (pp. 30–45). Newbury Park, CA: SAGE.

Olesen, V. L. (1994). Feminisms and models of qualitative research. In N. K. Denzin and Y. S. Lincoln (Eds.), *Handbook of Qualitative Research* (pp. 158–174). Thousand Oaks, CA: SAGE.

Olesen, V. L. (2000). Feminisms and qualitative research at and into the millennium. In N. K. Denzin and Y. S. Lincoln (Eds.), *Handbook of Qualitative Research* (2nd ed., pp. 215–256). Thousand Oaks, CA: SAGE.

Olesen, V. L. (2005). Early millennial feminist qualitative research: Challenges and contours. In N. K. Denzin and Y. S. Lincoln (Eds.), *The Sage Handbook of Qualitative Research* (3rd ed., pp. 235–279). Thousand Oaks, CA: SAGE.

Olesen, V. L., Droes, N., Hatton, D., Chico, N. and Schatzman, L. (1992). Analyzing together: Recollections of a team process. In R. G. Burgess and A. Bryman (Eds.), *Analyzing Qualitative Data* (pp. 25–40). London: Routledge.

Olesen, V. L. and Whittaker, E. W. (1968). *The Silent Dialogue: A Study in The Social Psychology of Professional Socialization*. San Francisco, CA: Jossey-Bass, Inc.

Pidgeon, N. and Henwood, K. (2004). Grounded theory. In M. Hardy and A. Bryman (Eds.), *Handbook of Data Analysis* (pp. 625–648). Thousand Oaks, CA: SAGE.

Portes, A. (1998). Social capital: Its origins and applications in modern sociology. *Annual Review of Sociology*, 24(1), 1–24.

Reed, T. V. (2006). *The Chronicle of Higher Education*, January 6, 2006, p. 23.

Richie, B. E. (1996). *Compelled to Crime: The Gender Entrapment of Battered Black Women*. New York: Routledge.

Roman, L. G. (1992). The political significance of other ways of narrating ethnography. A feminist materialist approach. In M. D. LeCompte, W. L. Millroy and J. Preissle (Eds.), *The Handbook of Qualitative Research in Education* (pp. 555–594). San Diego: Academic Press.

Schulz, A. J. and Mullings, L. (Eds.) (2006). *Race, Class, Gender and Health. Intersectional Approaches*. San Francisco, CA: Jossey-Bass.

Schwalbe, M. S., Goodwin, S., Holden, D., Schrock, D., Thompson, S., and Wolkomir, M. (2000). Group processes in the reproduction of inequality: An interactionist analysis. *Social Forces*, 79, 419–452.

Shim, J. (2002). Understanding the routinized inclusion of race, socioeconomic status and sex in epidemiology: The utility of concepts from technoscience studies. *Sociology of Health and Illness*, 24, 129–150.

Silverman, D. (1993). *Interpreting Qualitative Data, Methods for Analyzing Talk, Text and Interaction*. Thousand Oaks, CA: SAGE.

Smith, D. E. (2005). *Institutional Ethnography: A Sociology for People*. Latham, DE: Rowan and Littlefield.

Speer, S. A. (2002). What can conversational analysis contribute to feminist methodology? Putting reflexivity into practice. *Discourse and Society*, 13, 783–803.

Spradley, J. (1979). *The Ethnographic Interview*. New York: Holt, Rinehart and Winston.

Sprague, J. (2005). *Feminist Methodologies for Critical Researchers*. Walnut Creek, CA: Alta Mira.

Stanley, L. and Wise, S. (1993). *Breaking Out Again: Feminist Ontology and Epistemology*. London: Routledge.

Steinmetz, G. (2005a) Introduction. Positivism and its others in the social sciences. In G. Steinmetiz (Ed.), *The Politics of Method in the Human Sciences. Positivism and its Epistemological Others* (pp. 1–56). Durham, NC: Duke University Press.

Steinmetz, G. (2005b). Scientific authority and the transition to post-Fordism: The Plausibility of positivism in US sociology since 1945. In G. Steinmetz (Ed.), *The Politics of Method in the Human Sciences. Positivism and its Epistemological Others* (pp. 275–326). Durham, NC: Duke University Press.

Stern, P. N. (1994). Eroding grounded theory. In J. Morse (Ed.), *Critical Issues in Qualitative Research Methods* (pp. 212–223). Thousand Oaks, CA: SAGE.

Strauss, A. L. (1987). *Qualitative Analysis for Social Scientists*. New York: Cambridge University Press.

Strauss, A. L. and Corbin, J. (1990). *Basics of Qualitative Research: Grounded Theory Procedures and Techniques*. Thousand Oaks, CA: SAGE.

Strauss, A. L. and Corbin, J. (1994). Grounded theory methodology. An overview. In N. K. Denzin and Y. S. Lincoln (Eds.), *Handbook of Qualitative Research* (pp. 273–285). Thousand Oaks, CA: SAGE.

Strauss, A. L. and Corbin, J. (1998). *Basics of Qualitative Research: Grounded Theory Procedures and Techniques* (2nd ed.). Thousand Oaks, CA: Sage.

Walker, D. and Myrick, F. (2006). Grounded theory: An exploration of process and procedure. *Qualitative Health Research*, 16(4), 547–559.

Weeks, K. (1998). *Constituting Feminist Subjects*. Ithaca: Cornell University Press.

Whittaker, E. (1981). Anthropological ethics, fieldwork and epistemological disjunctures. *Philosophy of the Social Sciences*, 11(4), 437–451.

Woods, P. (1992). Symbolic interactionism: Theory and method. In M. D. LeCompte, W. L. Millroy and J. Preissle (Eds.), *The Handbook of Qualitative Research in Education* (pp. 341–404). San Diego: Academic Press.

Wuest, J. (1995). Feminist grounded theory: An exploration of the congruency and tensions between two traditions in knowledge discovery. *Qualitative Health Research*, 5(1), 125–137.

20

Accommodating Critical Theory

Barry Gibson

Critical theory includes a very broad range of theories from the Marxist and feminist traditions through to postmodern and poststructuralist critiques of society. These perspectives do not provide a coherent or a unified whole. Each approach has a range of sources, all of which lend emphasis to different aspects of the study of social and psychological worlds. Given that there is such a broad range of 'critical' traditions, it is unlikely that there will be a single solution to reaching an accommodation. Indeed, it is likely that there will be as many solutions as there are critical theories. It is therefore important from the outset to be clear that this chapter does not aim to provide a single solution to the problem but rather to set a compass for the sorts of issues that ought to be considered as the task of accommodation progresses. The main task for this chapter is to document how the productive tension between the twin goals of emancipation and the production of a comprehensive social theory will become central to any accommodation of critical theory with grounded theory. This tension is best encapsulated by comparing and contrasting the work of two well-known critical theorists: Theodor Adorno and Pierre Bourdieu.

Adorno is perhaps the quintessential critical theorist. He was a founding father of the Frankfurt school and, in many ways, represents the point of critical theory that is furthest away from grounded theory. The choice of Adorno is significant because historically he worked with Paul F. Lazarsfeld, who was a crucial influence on grounded theory (Glaser 1978; Glaser and Strauss 1967). Adorno's relationship with Lazarsfeld is widely recognized for their disagreements, especially in relation to Adorno's objections towards Lazarsfeld's positivism (Morrison 1978). It is likely that, if there is any positivism in grounded theory, this might prove to be the point where there is most disagreement with the critical theory of Adorno. Bourdieu, as we shall see, provides a useful countermand to Adorno because his reflexive sociology opposes any approach that risks falling victim to scholasticism.

The chapter commences by juxtaposing the work of these two writers with that of grounded theory. In doing so, a number of significant (and possibly irresolute) problems will emerge that will subsequently be considered over the course of the chapter. It may well be that an accommodation with some forms of critical theory might remain out of reach. However, we hope at the very least to be able to clarify the extent of the problem at hand before moving on to discuss the challenges that we face when trying to integrate various forms of critical theory. Throughout this chapter, when referring to grounded theory, this author is referring to grounded theory in its classical form. It is my firm belief that there is nothing to fear in the production of further blends (Stern 1994) of grounded theory so long as the origins of the method are clearly recognized and a healthy respect for the classical version is maintained. It follows that the preservation and clarification of classical grounded theory is as important as the production of future blends of the method. It is with this initial nod towards Glaser that we will begin.

THE CRITICAL THEORY OF ADORNO AND BOURDIEU: SOME PRODUCTIVE TENSIONS?

From the outset, grounded theory was borne out of a critique of the grand traditions of sociological theory. For Glaser and Strauss, there was an embarrassing gap between the theoretical and empirical traditions in sociology. Grounded theory was proposed as one solution to ameliorate this gap. Glaser and Strauss's (1967) central proposal was that sociological theory could be developed in the process of doing empirical research. It might not seem so controversial any more but their proposal did meet with a certain degree of skepticism.

Adorno, Bourdieu, and the Glaser and Strauss of classical grounded theory contrast very specifically in the way in which each approach one of the central problems of sociology. Simply stated, the problem is how to study society when sociologists remain firmly rooted within that society. Grounded theory in its classical form carries with it convictions about the role of theory from American pragmatism and Merton's 'middle range' approach, the basic argument is that the best position from which to view society is from the perspectives of people themselves. Additionally, sociology which focuses on the question of society becomes too general and abstract. It therefore makes good sense to focus on intermediate social phenomena. Grounded theory therefore focuses on building concepts and theory around the concerns of people who in turn become the object of study. The central goal of this process becomes securing suitable conceptualizations to account for variations in these concerns.

For Adorno, sociology was as much a product of society as capital, labor, or domination. The risk was that it might well serve to replicate patterns of domination inherent in that society (Jameson 1990). Theory became the only way to conceive of society in a different light (Jameson 1990; Karakayali 2004). In Adorno's perspective, grounded theory, because it did not go beyond the immediate appearances of society, would be nothing more than a bourgeois sociology reinforcing the domination inherent in society. This problem warrants further scrutiny.

The primary form of grounded theory is the relation between the researcher and the researched. In this relationship, the process of generating theory produces concepts. It is through the production of concepts that the subjects of a grounded theory study are transformed into theoretical objects. The basic process of grounded theory in the perspective of Adorno is therefore 'reifying,' that is it treats human phenomena as things and unifies these things into concepts. By attempting to fasten a strong link between subjects (people and their problems) and the theoretical object (the emergent theory), grounded theory is inherently ideological. In Adorno's perspective it is precisely in this relationship that grounded theory would serve to replicate the dominance inherent in the social relations of capitalism.

It is worth briefly tracing the details of this point since it is one of the key challenges directed at grounded theory from a critical theoretical perspective. In the schema of Adorno and classical Marxism, the primordial social relation is the exchange relation. The example is given of the relationship between steaks and cars. We can buy a car through the exchange of many steaks but the consumption of a steak is in no way similar to a drive in the country (Jameson 1990). What the exchange relation does then is to capture two very different consumption experiences and bring them together under the concept of exchange. This is the first relation of capitalism and it has an effect on all other relations. Likewise, in grounded theory the basic operation (the constant comparative method) compares incident with incident in the generation of concepts. What are incidents? They are the primordial ground of grounded theory and, as we shall see, they can be conceived as data, experience, or even as communications (Gibson et al. 2005). Conceptualization therefore generates objects called concepts in order to build theory and, from the perspective of Adorno, this process replicates the primordial exchange processes of capitalism. Grounded theory therefore becomes nothing more than a bourgeois sociology replicating the domination of capitalist society. What Adorno was focused on however was how to conceive of an alternative society (Jameson 1990). From a grounded theory perspective, a consequence of this concern would be to constantly force questions from his general theoretical perspective onto the data. This would amount to nothing more than a fictional exercise to be avoided at all costs, and any combination with such an approach would amount to nothing more than a significant break from grounded theory.

Classically, grounded theory warns against forcing in favor of emergence (Glaser 1992). Forcing refers to a kind of 'doctrinaire' reading of data where an already existent theory drives the interpretation of the data (Dey 1999). Awareness of the problem of emergence demands that the grounded theorist reflects on how their values can lead to bias in favoring of certain codes for coding observations over others. Since the method is basically an integrated set of observational practices, any bias in coding can quickly become a bias in sampling. This is not to say that the conduct of grounded theory can be free from values. It would be naïve to assume that the codes that eventually combine to generate a grounded theory emerge purely from reading data. Wuest (2000) provides a clear indication of the dilemmas of emergence and the careful balance between being sensitive to the range of possible ways that the emerging theory could be organized and being open to the idea that it can also be organized differently. This is the surprise of discovery but it is also a principal condition of theoretical sensitivity. In many respects, Glaser and Strauss would have had some sympathy for Bourdieu who eventually damned Marxists like Althusser for scholasticism in producing a theory about peasants without so much as speaking to a peasant.

Bourdieu's approach contrasts very neatly with that of Adorno. He starts with sociologists and their familiarity with the social world. In his work this is seen as the most difficult of obstacles. Sociologists, just like anyone else, have internalized a spontaneous knowledge of the everyday world. In his early work this 'spontaneous knowledge' was considered to be the opposite of 'scientific knowledge.' Following Bachelard, Bourdieu argued that science began with a series of epistemological breaks from familiar conceptions of this everyday world (Bourdieu et al. 1991; Karakayali 2004).

There is however a constant danger that this process would never truly be able to break from everyday discourse. The objectification process can fall prey to the pre-notions of everyday speech. Often '... metaphorical schemes are common to naïve utterances and erudite discourse, and indeed they derive their pseudo-explanatory force from this double life' (Bourdieu et al. 1991: 23). This is a crucial challenge for sociologists who need to become more familiar with the latent structure of their own sociology. Bourdieu was concerned with clearing sociology of the categories associated with spontaneous knowledge and at the same time warning about the dangers of imposing sociological categories onto the object of study. His reflexive sociology became almost totally associated with the latter problem (Karakayali 2004).

In Bourdieu, the main conflict experienced when doing research is between a familiar sociology of the everyday world and a sociology that is meant to reach beyond this. It is important to note that Bourdieu was focused on how the sociologist should do sociology. This, of course, is very similar to the focus in grounded theory on providing more and more advice on how to do it to ensure that the theoretical enterprise should remain 'grounded' in 'data.' The more Bourdieu turned to reflexivity the more he became entangled in giving methodological advice. The fundamental risk of his reflexive sociology was that it would eventually almost exclusively deal with the practice of the sociologist. The whole problem of reflexivity promotes a reference to the self so much so that a reference to society and history are potentially lost (Karakayali 2004).

In summary, with Adorno we have a critical theory that is concerned with emancipation at the expense of being grounded in everyday perspectives. This critical theory contrasts with Bourdieu's reflexive sociology which threatens to become preoccupied with procedure and eventually to lose its reference to the purpose of critical sociology to engage with some idea of society. Maintaining a focus on the nature of society enables the sociologist to focus on various program for emancipation. Without this focus it is claimed that critical theory loses its ability to be critical. A grounded theory therefore that seeks to accommodate critical theory without reflecting on society would lose its ability to be critical. In the next section, one possible solution to this problem will be introduced through a summary of the main thrust of the work of Bohman (1999). We will then move onto two further points of discussion relevant to the accommodation of critical theory.

CENTRAL FEATURES OF CRITICAL THEORY

Critical theory for its part has a distinctive purpose and overarching structure. There is a desire, for example, to construct social theories that link explanation and criticism. Critical theory is explanatory in that it aims to provide, no matter how diverse, a comprehensive perspective of society. Critical theories that are critical therefore are concerned with the problem of emancipation from 'the things that enslave' (Bohman 1999). Bohman (1999) aims to analyze what makes critical theory 'critical' by highlighting the practical and political consequences of critical theory rather than emphasizing the theoretical. In Bohman's perspective, critical theorists have always attempted to maintain a distance between themselves and their subjects. This was achieved by integrating existing theory into large theoretical edifices that attempted to establish the superiority of the theorist because of the degree of comprehensiveness of the theory. An unfortunate side effect of this strategy was that the underlying pluralism of their approach was inevitably undermined by an eventual reversion to a final normative interpretation. For example, in Marxist critical theory the historical materialist perspective is eventually 'forced' into the debate.

Before continuing, it is worth stopping to compare and contrast this version of the critical tradition with grounded theory. The term theoretical sensitivity in grounded theory reflects awareness that there is a multiplicity of theoretical accounts available in sociology and beyond. It recognizes that these are equally legitimate for the purpose of researching what exists. The difference between grounded theory and critical theory is that rather than try and integrate many of these theoretical accounts into one large theoretical superstructure, grounded theory aims to use the most appropriate method of observing for the purposes of generating a theory and reporting it. Rather than attempting to achieve the superiority of the critic, grounded theory promotes sensitivity and fit. This is grounded theory's pragmatism. This pragmatism provides great potential for accommodating critical theory.

The pluralism underpinning critical theory reflects one of the basic facts of sociology: that there is a multiplicity of accounts about society all of which explain different aspects of this complex phenomenon. The problem resulting from such a radical pluralism is often an inability to suggest how things could be different. The solution to this problem for Bohman (1999) lies in pushing critical thinkers like Habermas towards the pragmatic tradition and away from the project of building a comprehensive social theory (Bohman 1994, 1999). The idea here is that pluralism enhances and improves social inquiry. Given that grounded theory is a form of social inquiry, it is argued that there might be some merits for inspecting this approach in a little detail.

The problems associated with democracy are often cast as epistemic and moral disagreements. With the pragmatic turn, rather than seeing such disagreements as virtually impregnable they are recast as productive tensions around which social inquiry can begin (Bohman 1999). In pragmatism, Dewey talked of three modes of inquiry and subsequent relationships that involved control, strategic action, and those needed for co-operation. In democracy, co-operation is deemed essential. Social science, it is argued, provides a way to reflect on and examine social life and at the same time to scrutinize the norms associated with co-operation itself. What is suggested then is a social science that avoids technical mastery of the world that focuses on a reflective participation in social inquiry and in turn that seeks to give inquirer and agent equal standing in the inquiry process (Bohman 1999).

The implications of this for the project of accommodating critical theory are that such an accommodation would be possible so long as we inspect and reflect on the degree of co-operation during inquiry. The recommendation might be to inspect the process of doing grounded theory to see how much co-operation has been and indeed can be envisaged. By promoting this reflection it is argued that the solutions to these practices could only come from participants themselves. This point is crucial, to what extent is it possible to generate a theory on a core problem that might not be shared by participants and then to have the solution to that problem based on the consensus of the participants as part of the study? The next section seeks to develop the problem of the researcher and the participants a stage further by looking at the relationship of research as an objectifying relation worthy of some consideration.

THE OBJECTIFYING RELATION OF RESEARCH

One of the central debates in critical theory is the nature of the research relationship. Traditionally this has been interpreted as an objectifying relationship.

What this means is that the relationship between the researcher and researched is a relation where the researcher has considerable power to (*mis*)represent the researched by turning them into an object. By this we mean that participants in research are human subjects and that they become represented by the categories of the research. Bourdieu et al. (1991) argues that sociologists are objectifying subjects who ought to turn their objectifying gaze on themselves. His critical sociology engages with the objectifying relation of research in opposition to a sociology that collapses into theoreticism. In this respect, Bourdieu was referring to the kind of sociology discussed by Bohman (1999) that sought to produce a comprehensive theoretical account in order to establish the superiority of the critic for the sociologist. For Bourdieu, social scientists who become guilty of scholasticism risk losing their connection to practical consciousness. Bourdieu was critical of the scholastic break and the goal of his critical theory was to negate this (Karakayali 2004).

Naïve grounded theory, of which there are many examples, often unwittingly generates theory from what seems to be an objectifying relation that separates the knower (the grounded theorist) from the known (the participants and their problems). This is despite the call in classical grounded theory to produce a theory that 'works' and 'fits.' Grounded theory that accommodates critical theory would carry with it the added sensitivity that it is through the technologies of the method itself that important political relations can be hidden in the research process (Henwood and Pidgeon 1995; McLennan 1995). The argument of this chapter is that the pragmatics of inquiry coupled with an appreciation of Bourdieu's reflexive sociology go some way to suggesting how such objectification processes can be observed. The chapter suggests therefore that accommodating critical theory is not simply about keeping sight of the goals of emancipation, but *also* realizing emancipation in the process of social inquiry. These ideas have been recognized to some degree in critical grounded theory.

There are several good examples of a concern with the research relationship in the research process in grounded theory. In the work of Pursley-Crotteau (2001), Ford-Gilboe et al. (2005), and Wuest et al. (2003), participants are asked to give their suggestions for modifying the categories in the resulting theory. Involvement in the writing of the theory is not the only part of the process. Merritt-Gray and Wuest (1995) reflect carefully on how categories drawn from their theory on limiting intrusion could in fact be used to further marginalize women. Each of these papers provides some evidence that, for critical grounded theory, the process of generating theory is not value neutral. The implication is that in the relationship between the researcher and the researched, the researcher's values are not allowed to dominate those being researched. There is a need for some clarification at this point.

To many it will seem that the research relationship of a classical grounded theory study is based on the researchers constantly checking their interpretations with the 'data.' For them the question will be what then is being added in this chapter? The answer to this is that the classical tradition owes a lot to pragmatism.

Therefore it is not surprising to find pragmatic practices incorporated into the method and the original instruction to make sure a theory 'fits' and 'works' can be read as pragmatism in action. Making something 'fit' and 'work' however is not the same thing as including participants equally in the process of doing grounded theory. The latter exercise is political and thoroughly wedded to a pragmatism that seeks to emancipate participants. The situation is nonetheless complicated by the strategic nature of research and the interaction between the researcher and the researched.

One of the long-standing debates in critical theory is the degree to which facts and values are entangled in the generation of knowledge. In critical theory, arguments that consider claims that we should strive to separate facts from values are portrayed as a kind of 'scientism.' The goal of emancipation however involves asking questions about the good society, and such questions often involve problems associated with ideology. Ideology presents a particular problem for our project of accommodating critical theory because this often refers to action orientated belief systems such as conservatism, liberalism, and socialism. Such systems often claim a factual status for society and prescribe a normative basis for changing that society (Morrow and Brown 1994). The problem with ideology is a tendency to emphasize theoretical claims over 'facts' and the risk is that counter evidence will be ignored.

The problem of ideology is potentially the biggest test to the project of accommodating critical theory. In this sense, the degree to which grounded theory can be 'critical' depends on how well it becomes sensitive to this problem. If, for example, ideology is allowed to dominate theory development, then the method is open to accusations of 'forcing' (Glaser 1992). How then can grounded theory accommodate critical theory in this respect?

One solution to the problem has been suggested in the form of 'theoretical triangulation' (Kushner and Morrow 2003). Theoretical triangulation refers to 'a constant grounding process at the level of data gathering and analysis, coupled with internal checks (constant comparisons in the terminology of grounded theory) on theoretical arguments based on back and forth movement between questions posed within both feminist and critical theories' (Kushner and Morrow 2003: 38). The problem with this approach is: what is implied by 'triangulation.' Triangulation in the traditional sense involves the combination of different interpretations of different types of data towards a more correct representation of what is going on in the area in question. It is a technical form of mastery and in scientific discourse the claim is often made that the outcome is presumably a more objective and therefore more 'correct' position. What this actually means remains far from clear. What then does it mean to triangulate grounded theory 'data gathering and analysis' with feminist and other critical perspectives? What position lies behind such a process? The answer to this question remains somewhat unclear from the existing description. It must be noted that although the strategy has potential it remains underdeveloped.

An alternative position for accommodating critical theory is being suggested that follows the perspective of Bohman (1999). In this perspective we would be better to see grounded theory as a form of social inquiry pragmatically engaging with subjects as equal participants in the research process. It is a concern that the burden of seeking to build a comprehensive social theory would be a bridge too far for grounded theory and that a pragmatic direction would potentially be the most profitable direction to take. The chapter now turns to the problem of ideology in theory building.

BLENDS OF GROUNDED THEORY OR BLENDS OF IDEOLOGY?

Grounded theory is generated from accounts given to researchers as a result of people interacting in a substantive setting. Like it or not, when people give accounts they often use arguments that in turn present their relationship to the setting in a strategic light. How these accounts are influenced would become an important focus during the research process when attempting to accommodate a critical sensitivity. Such theory ought to echo feminist writers who see research as all too often being involved in the production of 'discourses of control' (Henwood and Pidgeon 1995). Critical grounded theory would involve asking the degree to which we are involved as researchers in producing such controlling and dominating products (Mathison 1997).

One solution to this problem would be to treat all accounts as inherently ideological and to be assured that 'data' is not neutral. The current tendency to capture 'data' in a series of semi-structured interviews without alternative supplementary methods would be considered problematic. There would be a need to approach accounts with sensitivity to the influences of the setting and mode of interviews, and the suggestion would be that grounded theory could begin to consider combining its coding practices with more openly political methods such as narrative research. For example, we know from narrative research that stories are told with a specific strategic purpose in mind (Labov 1972); when incidents of storytelling occur during the process of a grounded theory study, should they be treated differently as narrative artifacts and as having a different status to responses to various problems and questions? Such an analysis has already been achieved to some extent in the work of Mauthner (2000), who produces a complex reflexive account of her use of various research methods in her exploration of the ethical dilemmas of research into sibling friendships. The account given satisfies all of the criteria of a critical approach, and considerable depth is achieved in the analysis of the ethical problems associated with variable rates of disclosure concerning intimate relationships. The difficulty is that we are left wondering the degree to which this research utilized the grounded theory method.

A grounded theory that becomes more sensitive to the problems associated with critical theory is not discovered devoid of context but is recognized to be as subject to the vagaries of ideological influence as the accounts of participants it is based on. Such an approach would therefore reassign a role for exploring the link between context, discovery, and presentation. We could ask, for example, if there are particular disciplinary biases towards certain codes in various grounded theories. Are psychologists predisposed to basic social psychological theories or cognitive styled theories? Do sociological theorists presuppose some idea of weak social structure? Why, for example, did Glaser (1978) call one of the coding families the 'Mainline family' other than to indicate that it was a predominant form of theory at the time? Clearly the indication in classical grounded theory is that there is a plurality of options for theory building, and whatever fits and works is what should be presented as the discovery. What this author is saying is that what fits and works is by no means readily apparent. The first source of problems in this respect is that what works for one discipline might be very different for what works with another. In addition to this, further problems associated with the actual process of doing grounded theory, as we shall see, can also potentially predispose the novice to certain forms of theorizing.

Doing grounded theory is itself a process that occurs in a series of stages over time. To what extent does being 'in' the process predispose novice researchers to produce basic social psychological process theories when in fact other theoretical codes would have worked better? The problem is best described when the novice mistakes the order in which categories have been discovered for a basic social psychological process in the data, when in fact it is their own social psychological process of discovery that they have mistakenly written into the coding. As yet we have no in-depth analyses of the potential for such bias, accommodating critical theory suggests that we should recognize and explore these problems in more depth and with a certain degree of reflexive awareness. We can also go further. The theoretical coding families in grounded theory are presented largely devoid of their sociological origin (Glaser 1978). There is therefore a very real risk that grounded theory would sunder its link to the broader project of sociology. It also risks masking the potential for those codes to express ideology, especially since they would be deployed in the context of the research process.

Another very important example of ideological influences on the research process is the potential ways in which a code like 'context and conditions' in a grounded theory is deployed. Often this occurs without reflection on the nature of the relationship between the subject and the conditions that are quite often 'assumed' to shape their action. Not all of the tradition is like this but statements that grounded theory produces theory about the context and conditions under which women experience their lives are common place (Benoliel 2001; Keddy et al. 1996; Pursley-Crotteau 2001; Schreiber and Stern 2001). The positive side of these accounts is that identifying the context of experience can enable researchers to build a critical commentary on the conditions of women's experience. It is of course acceptable to include the context of everyday life as part of a critical project. Where this can become a problem is when the construction of context is used relatively unreflectively. Are we accidentally promoting a naïve social determinism?

One example taken from existing grounded theory within the critical tradition can illustrate how the problem of context and conditions is not problematized nearly enough. In a study by Leipert and Reutter (2005), an attempt is made to highlight how women develop resilience in the context of life in harsh conditions. The position that women occupy is described as one of having 'vulnerability to health risks' and their response to these risks is to 'develop resiliency.' Under 'Physical Health and Safety Risks,' we find climate and geography hazards summarized as:

> Climate and geography make travel hazardous, especially in winter. Rosie, a 59-year-old woman who lives in a remote area and who depends on travel on a river as well as a road, provides a vivid example of northern travel challenges: 'Up until 10 days ago, the river was full of open holes [of water] and it wasn't safe. Right now, you can walk on it ... So at least if we had to get out now, we could walk across the river.' Women who were geographically isolated, elderly, or physically challenged were particularly vulnerable to travel challenges. Lilac, an elderly woman in a rural area, explained, 'I will [travel] to my doctor again when the weather looks a bit better, [when it] stops snowing so much.' Because travel might need to be postponed, women might live with isolation and morbidity longer, their treatment and recovery might be more difficult, and their quality of life compromised (Leipert and Reutter 2005: 52).

Part of developing resilience is 'becoming hardy:'

> Hardiness was described as an increased feeling of confidence and the ability to carry on in spite of adversity. Elizabeth stated, '[A woman] wouldn't last very long [in the north if she wasn't hardy] or she would become a hardy breed of person. It [the north] makes or breaks you.' Becoming hardy for the women in the study involved taking a positive attitude, following spiritual beliefs, and establishing self-reliance. These attributes were important for northern women's mental and physical health (Leipert and Reutter 2005: 56).

In the first excerpt, the direct quotations from the women do not directly reflect that they experience the conditions within which they live as 'hazardous.' Rather they seem to be valorizing their lived experience in much the same way that working class people in the East End of London attempt to give positive and morally loaded accounts of their experiences of illness (Cornwell 1985). The concept of hardiness is also morally loaded and the account in the second quotation is designed to present the narrator in a positive light in much the same way as Cornwell's subjects would in public accounts of illness. The key question then is who observes the context of living in the North as hazardous, the researcher or the participants? This is a key problem for this work which appeared to need a context to condition the responses of women.

While the theory works quite well in its present form, one of the consequences of selecting context and conditions in this case was to have adopted a homeostatic model of the relationship between biological organisms interacting with their environment. In that study, women are biological organisms threatened and beset by natural and man-made hazards and, in response to this, they have developed the physical, emotional, and spiritual 'traits' of resilience. Alternative explanations of context and conditions could be given in this case. For example, it could be argued that the accounts in this study reflect that considerable value is placed on resilience in the local culture and that these values are subsequently being reflected in the women's accounts. In this account, women would be presented as primarily social beings. The message is that the context does not have to be a physical environment; it could be the culture that shapes the accounts being presented to the researcher.

The problem being discussed is the old problem of the relationship between agency and structure. The conceptualization of 'context and conditions' as part of the theoretical coding families makes this typology of observation accessible to those outside the discipline, however it can also serve to mask the complexity of the problem being confronted. The result is that if critical grounded theory is to be reflective enough, it ought to acknowledge that the project Glaser (1978) had started in *Theoretical Sensitivity* remains somewhat unfinished. Now more than ever there is a need for clarification of the formal properties of grounded theories. This means we need an analysis that presents what a grounded theory should look like and the kinds of propositions various forms of grounded theory should contain. This analysis would involve asking what a 'good' grounded theory actually is.

Existing grounded theory that has started to accommodate critical theory in many ways has begun to engage with these debates. Wuest and colleagues have consistently developed an emancipatory interest in their work on women's role in care giving (Wuest 1997a, b, 1998, 2000) and the struggle families confront when there has been a relationship breakup as a result of an abusive partner (Ford-Gilboe et al. 2005; Wuest and Merritt-Gray 2001; Wuest et al. 2003, 2004). Wuest et al.'s work highlighted for policy makers and nursing practitioners the sheer complexity and range of problems associated with care giving. The theory itself spans a decade of theoretical sampling and engagement with policymakers and practitioners. Likewise, the emerging theory of 'limiting intrusion' is a more recent example of a critical grounded theory engaging with the problems women face when they manage to separate themselves from an abusive partner. Other work has, for example, documented resilience in Northern Canada (Leipert and Reutter 2005), loneliness for female adolescents (Davidson 1995), and the problems of mothering on crack cocaine (Kearney et al. 1994; Pursley-Crotteau 2001; Sterk et al. 2000). All of this grounded theory was developed with the explicit goal of engaging with policy to varying degrees. What remains is to make a few passing comments about the problem of experience before concluding the chapter.

EXPERIENCE AS THE GROUND OF CRITICAL GROUNDED THEORY?

The argument that experience could provide the ground of critical grounded theory has become central to the existing accommodation of critical theory in grounded theory (Austen et al. 2003; Keddy et al. 1996; Ruth et al. 1996; Wuest 1995). The arguments are parallel to those put forward by Feminists (and some Marxists) who have argued that people, because of their specific experiences, are better placed than researchers as a source of a theory about their conditions (Chandler 1990). At first glance then, experience promises much for a critical grounded theory. In the same way that 'data' as the ground for classical grounded theory promised to ensure its 'scientific' credibility, experience could perhaps potentially serve to make grounded theory 'critical.'

There are however some problems with this approach. The notion of 'standpoint' in standpoint feminism was criticized for lack of clarity (Chandler 1990; Pinnick 1994). It seemed that several senses of the term were employed. In one sense, standpoint feminism was a worldview where the role of the theorist was to clarify and render the experiences of women explicit. In another sense, the feminist standpoint was said to reveal women's 'true' interests (Chandler 1990). In the literature that is supportive of the idea there is clearly a paradox between the problem of ensuring that research is more subjective and at the same time objective as a result of a broader political commitment (McLennan 1995).

The claim that experience can produce special or exclusive 'insight' is problematic because it risks entangling theory in the 'specificity' of the subject. It should be noted for example that the feminist standpoint is not a 'female' standpoint based on women's 'unreflective consciousness' but that it is theoretically articulated and 'politically' engaged with women's experiences (Chandler 1990). If experience is to become the ground of a critical grounded theory then one of the central problems is the degree to which it be portrayed as an essence, as unmediated, and therefore as relatively unproblematic. Mathison (1997) argues that there is:

> a danger of establishing 'facts' about experience without recognizing not only the situated-ness of the subject but also the tentativeness of the authorized account (Mathison 1997: 157).

Experiences are shaped by 'what people do not do as much as by what they do' (Mathison 1997), and so experiences are never unmediated but are historically located and situated. There is a tendency to generalize from a 'natural kind' experience to the properties of a group's experiences as a whole when it is well known that experience within groups can often vary dramatically (Mathison 1997). Experience demands interpretation and therefore is a rather poor foundation for an epistemology. This is especially the case since the linguistic turn, when the connection between the sign and what was being signified, became especially problematic (Ireland 2002).

The linguistic turn undermined the link between experience and knowledge and essentially doomed to failure any approach that attempted to fashion consciousness to the immediate experience of persons. One answer to this problem is to see experience as a third term between the determination of structure and agency (Thompson 1978). In other words, experience is a kind of matter against which consciousness presses, and it becomes something that circumvents ideological determination (Ireland 2002).

By now we should be aware that the appeal to experience as the ground for critical grounded theory poses a number of problems as the basis for claims about knowledge. The claims generated in such research can then be used to generalize about specific groups. An appeal to experience can have very significant and unwanted consequences. While such claims might have 'laudable' goals they can end up making historical phenomena appear natural. This risks leaving the door 'as wide open to a progressive politics of identity as to a retreat to neo-ethnic tribalism' (Ireland 2002: 87–88). The alarming thing is the political consequences that can result from this. Clough (1993) puts it well by quoting Foucault:

> The analysis of actual experience is a discourse of a mixed nature: it is directed to a specific yet ambiguous stratum, concrete enough for it to be possible to apply to it a meticulous and descriptive language, yet sufficiently removed from the positivity of things for it to be possible, from that starting-point, to escape from that naivete, to contest it and seek foundations for it. This analysis seeks to articulate the possible objectivity of a knowledge of nature upon the original experience of which the body provides an outline … It is doing no more, then, than fulfilling with greater care the hasty demands laid down when the attempt was made to make the empirical, in man, stand for the transcendental. Despite appearances to the contrary, it is evident how closely knit is the network that links thoughts of the positivist or eschatological type (Marxism being in the first rank of these) and reflections inspired by phenomenology (Foucault in Clough 1993: 172).

So there we have it. A critical grounded theory that argues for experience as its ground is still in some way related to the positive sciences. There is a kind of irony in this especially given the degree to which classical grounded theory has been attacked for being 'positivist.' The problem is that as the critical grounded theory project seeks to build knowledge grounded in experience that we would end up making claims about groups, such as women or black people. Critical grounded theory might be able to make general predictions or statements that cover all groups of people, however it would also have to remain sensitive to variable differences within groups.

Experience has largely become the ground of feminist grounded theory in the work of many different writers (Benoliel 2001; Ford-Gilboe et al. 2005; Keddy et al. 1996; Leipert and Reutter 2005; Pursley-Crotteau 2001). Some of the problems discussed have already been recognized in this work. Wuest (1997a, b; 2000) and Merritt-Gray and Wuest (1995) remain sensitive to the importance of theoretically sampling a range of experiences from various groups of women. Claims are then made that the resulting theory has a pluralistic foundation. The theory of precarious ordering for example might be pushed to a formal theory if, say, existing theoretical categories were observed in relation to the context of men's experiences as caregivers. In this respect then the theory breaks away from many of the risks associated with using purely women's experience as the ground of the theory. This does not mean that women are less likely to be caregivers.

To the contrary, it is clear that women are more likely to be caregivers. What is being suggested is that comparisons with men's experiences might expose crucial differences that might in turn reveal what it is specifically about women's experiences that can make care giving such a burden for them.

CONCLUSIONS

This chapter has attempted to critically discuss just a few of the complexities associated with the project of accommodating critical theory. The project is already underway and there are exemplary works available in the literature. The way forward appears to point towards two possible strategies. One is theoreticist and involves a back and forth movement between a comprehensive social theory and the emerging theory. The other is best summarized in Bohman's (1999) pragmatic interpretation of Habermas and involves recognizing the potential of democratic modes of inquiry for emancipation in the grounded theory research process. In some ways, the former solution has been favored by Kushner and Morrow (2003) under the proposal of 'theoretical triangulation.' I have suggested that this strategy risks hiding more than it will clarify and there remains much to be done if this approach is to prove convincing.

The chapter has suggested that the promotion of a democratic mode of inquiry would tap into pragmatism in grounded theory and circumvent the tensions associated with forcing general theoretically given values onto the emerging theory. This is of course not the favored solution by some who have interpreted such an approach as a symptom of 'worrisome accuracy' or an attempt to achieve greater validity (Glaser 2003; Morse 1998). Such criticisms miss the mark. The attempt to promote the subject's perspective is not about accuracy or validity; it is about trying to enable emancipation from the things that enslave. The goal of a critical inquiry that attempts to involve subjects is *not* to produce a more 'valid' categorization but to avoid objectifying and misrepresenting research subjects. The insight of Adorno is to warn us that to replicate an objectifying relationship in our research is to commit the ideological error of reinforcing the fundamental ideology and dominance of capitalism. Accommodating critical theory is particularly interested in avoiding the enslavement of our subjects into further misappropriated categories.

The problem of ideology, as we have seen, is not that easy to address. Adorno became focused on the problem of conceiving society in a different light, and the pragmatic solution that has been adopted here from Bohman (1999) might be accused of threatening to maintain the status quo. It is here that a consideration of Bourdieu can help us to remain sensitive to the fact that Bohman's solution is fraught with difficulties. There is no guarantee, for example, that such a project will enable the researcher and researched to fracture the binding of spontaneous sociology. There is a possibility that the program of accommodating critical theory risks becoming tied to the restrictions of the everyday discourses of subjects.

The perennial tension of generating knowledge from the specificity of the subject's perspective remains, and Bohman's (1999) pragmatic path out of the problem might turn out to be hopelessly optimistic. Being aware of the constant threat of everyday sociology in such a process, however, should enable a critically engaged grounded theory to be wary of such traps. The answer to this constant dilemma indicates that researchers need to remain ever vigilant, supporting an attitude of radical doubt that the theory could always look different. Such a pluralistic perspective was originally articulated within the tradition in the form of theoretical sensitivity. Perhaps the main message of this chapter is that we should always be trying to push this sensitivity further.

ACKNOWLEDGMENTS

I would like to acknowledge the support of Jan Hartman who made many helpful comments on early drafts of this chapter. I would also like to acknowledge the many useful, detailed, and encouraging comments I received from the anonymous reviewers and the editors. The chapter would not have taken the direction it did without your kind and supportive questions. I hope the result is not too disappointing.

REFERENCES

Austen, S., T. Jefferson et al. (2003). Gendered social indicators and grounded theory. *Feminist Economics* **9**(1): 1–18.
Benoliel, J. Q. (2001). Expanding knowledge about women through grounded theory: introduction to the collection. *Health Care for Women International* **22**(1&2): 7–9.
Bohman, J. (1994). Complexity, pluralism, and the constitutional state: on Habermas's faktizitat und geltung. *Law & Society Review* **28**(4): 897–930.
Bohman, J. (1999). Theories, practices, and pluralism: a pragmatic interpretation of critical social science. *Philosophy of the Social Sciences* **29**(4): 459–480.
Bourdieu, P., J.-C. Chamboredon et al. (1991). *The Craft of Sociology: Epistemological Preliminaries*. New York: Walter de Gruyter.
Chandler, J. (1990). Feminism and Epistemology. *Metaphilosophy* **21**(4): 367–381.
Clough, P. T. (1993). On the brink of deconstructing sociology—critical reading of Smith, Dorothy standpoint epistemology. *Sociological Quarterly* **34**(1): 169–182.
Cornwell, J. (1985). *Hard-Earned Lives: Accounts of Health and Illness from East London*. London: Routledge & Kegan Paul.
Davidson, P. (1995). The process of loneliness for female adolescents: a feminist perspective. *Health Care for Women International* **16**(1): 1–8.
Dey, I. (1999). *Grounding Grounded Theory: Guidelines for Qualitative Inquiry*. London: Academic Press.
Ford-Gilboe, M., J. Wuest et al. (2005). Strengthening capacity to limit intrusion: theorizing family health promotion in the aftermath of woman abuse. *Qualitative Health Research* **15**(4): 477–501.

Gibson, B., J. Gregory et al. (2005). The intersection between systems theory and grounded theory: the emergence of the grounded systems observer. *Qualitative Sociology Review* **1**(2): 3–21.

Glaser, B. G. (1978). *Theoretical Sensitivity: Advances in the Methodology of Grounded Theory*. Mill Valley, CA: Sociology Press.

Glaser, B. G. (1992). *Emergence versus Forcing: Basics of Grounded Theory Analysis*. Mill Valley, CA: Sociology Press.

Glaser, B. G. (2003). *The Grounded Theory Perspective, II: Description's Remodeling of Grounded Theory Methodology*. Mill Valley, CA: Sociology Press.

Glaser, B. G. and A. Strauss (1967). *The Discovery of Grounded Theory*. Chicago: Aldine.

Henwood, K. and N. Pidgeon (1995). Remaking the link: qualitative research and feminist standpoint theory. *Feminism & Psychology* **5**(1): 7–30.

Ireland, C. (2002). The appeal to experience and its consequences: variations on a persistent Thompsonian theme. *Cultural Critique* **52**(Fall): 86–107.

Jameson, F. (1990). *Late Marxism: Adorno, or, The Persistence of the Dialectic*. London: Verso.

Karakayali, N. (2004). Reading Bourdieu with Adorno: the limits of critical theory and reflexive sociology. *Sociology* **38**(2): 351–368.

Kearney, M. H., S. Murphy et al. (1994). Mothering on crack cocaine: a grounded theory analysis. *Social Science & Medicine* **38**(2): 351–361.

Keddy, B., S. L. Sims et al. (1996). Grounded theory as feminist research methodology. *Journal of Advanced Nursing* **23**(3): 448–453.

Kushner, K. E. and R. Morrow (2003). Grounded theory, feminist theory, critical theory: toward theoretical triangulation. *Advances in Nursing Science* **26**(1): 30–43.

Labov, W. (1972). *Language in the Inner City: Studies in the Black English Vernacular*. Oxford: Basil Blackwell.

Leipert, B. D. and L. Reutter (2005). Developing resilience: how women maintain their health in northern geographically isolated settings. *Qualitative Health Research* **15**(1): 49–65.

Mathison, M. A. (1997). The complicity of essentializing difference—complicity as epistemology: reinscribing the historical categories of 'woman' through standpoint feminism. *Communication Theory* **7**(2): 149–161.

Mauthner, M. (2000). Snippets and silences: ethics and reflexivity in narratives of sistering. *International Journal of Social Research Methodology: Theory & Practice* **3**(4): 287–306.

McLennan, G. (1995). Feminism, epistemology and postmodernism: reflections on current ambivalence. *Sociology: The Journal of the British Sociological Association* **29**(3): 391–409.

Merritt-Gray, M. and J. Wuest (1995). Counteracting abuse and breaking free: the process of leaving revealed through women's voices. *Health Care for Women International* **16**(5): 399–412.

Morrison, D. E. (1978). Kultur and culture: case of Adorno, Theodor, W. and Lazarsfeld, Paul, F. *Social Research* **45**(2): 331–355.

Morrow, R. and D. Brown (1994). *Critical Theory and Methodology: Contemporary Social Theory*. London: SAGE.

Morse, J. M. (1998). Validity by committee. *Qualitative Health Research* **8**(4): 443–445.

Pinnick, C. L. (1994). Feminist epistemology: implications for philosophy of science. *Philosophy of Science* **61**(4): 646–657.

Pursley-Crotteau, S. (2001). Perinatal crack users becoming temperant: the social psychological processes. *Health Care for Women International* **22**(1–2): 49–66.

Ruth, J. E., J. E. Birren et al. (1996). The projects of life reflected in autobiographies of old age. *Ageing and Society* **16**(6): 677–699.

Schreiber, R. and P. N. Stern (2001). Editorial: why grounded theory and women's health. *Health Care for Women International* **22**(1&2): 1–3.

Sterk, C. E., K. W. Elifson et al. (2000). Women and drug treatment experiences: a generational comparison of mothers and daughters. *Journal of Drug Issues* **30**(4): 839–861.

Stern, P. (1994). Eroding grounded theory. *Critical Issues in Qualitative Research Methods*. Thousand Oaks, CA: SAGE.

Thompson, E. (1978). *The Poverty of Theory & Other Essays*. London: Merlin Press.

Wuest, J. (1995). Feminist grounded theory: an exploration of the congruency and tensions between two traditions in knowledge discovery. *Qualitative Health Research* **5**(1): 125–137.

Wuest, J. (1997a). Fraying connections of caring women: an exemplar of including difference in the development of explanatory frameworks. *Canadian Journal of Nursing Research* **29**(2): 99–116.

Wuest, J. (1997b). Illuminating environmental influences on women's caring. *Journal of Advanced Nursing* **26**(1): 49–58.

Wuest, J. (1998). Setting boundaries: a strategy for precarious ordering of women's caring demands. *Research in Nursing & Health* **21**(1): 39–49.

Wuest, J. (2000). Negotiating with helping systems: an example of grounded theory evolving through emergent fit. *Qualitative Health Research* **10**(1): 51–70.

Wuest, J., M. Ford-Gilboe et al. (2003). Intrusion: the central problem for family health promotion among children and single mothers after leaving an abusive partner. *Qualitative Health Research* **13**(5): 597–622.

Wuest, J. and M. Merritt-Gray (2001). Beyond survival: reclaiming self after leaving an abusive male partner. *Canadian Journal of Nursing Research* **32**(4): 79–94.

Wuest, J., M. Merritt-Gray et al. (2004). Regenerating family: strengthening the emotional health of mothers and children in the context of intimate partner violence. *Advances in Nursing Science* **27**(4): 257–274.

21

Grounded Theory and the Politics of Interpretation

Norman K. Denzin

The writing is direct, and immediate, subversive, no big words. To wit:
The grounded theorist thinks abstractly, critically, flexibly;
Theory is the basis for social action;
Human beings create meaning through interaction;
Processes are interconnected;
Qualitative research is any type of research that produces findings not arrived at by statistical procedures or other means of quantification (Strauss and Corbin, 1998: 7, 9–11).
   The special emphasis is on how to develop theory through qualitative analysis, through codes, memos, sequences, theoretical sampling, comparative analysis, and diagrams (Strauss, 1987: iii).

Who could disagree? And subversive: there is no grand or middle or formal theory here, no formal propositions, no testable hypotheses. No wonder it is so popular. It is all grounded. It is two things at the same time, a verb, a method of inquiry, and a noun, a product of inquiry (Charmaz, 2005: 507). It is intuitive. You let the obdurate empirical world speak to you, you listen, take notes, write memos to yourself, form writing groups. No hierarchy, the social theorists are not privileged. In the world of GT anybody can be a theorist.

   Grounded theory (GT) is not a unified framework. There are, multiple versions: positivist, postpositivist, constructivist, objectivist, postmodern, situational, and computer assisted (Charmaz, 2006; Clarke, 2005). For example, traditional positivist grounded theory stresses the importance of correspondence theories of truth, of objective inquirers, and processes of discovery.

Postmodern versions, in contrast, endorse constructivist models of truth, and reject objectivist views of the inquirer, privilege Foucault over Mead, emphasize situational, discursive, social arena approaches to interpretation (Clarke, 2005: 32, 291). Yet underneath, there are commonalities: flexible guidelines for data collection and data analysis, commitments to remain close to the world being studied, and the development of integrated theoretical concepts grounded in data that show process, relationship, and social world connectedness (Charmaz, 2005: 508; Clarke, 2005: 292; Glaser and Strauss, 1967).

Now, a new generation seeks to 'reclaim the tools of the method, to form a revised, more open-ended practice … that stresses its emergent, constructivist elements' (Clarke, 2005: xxiii), 'for advancing social justice studies' (Charmaz, 2005: 507). I want to extend that project, by aligning it with Cornel West's prophetic pragmatism, Patricia Hill Collin's epistemology of empowerment, and Ron Pelias's methodology of the heart. These versions of pragmatism's GT offer interpretive leverage for those who use moral inquiry for social justice ends. This is the space I enter in this chapter (see Denzin, 2004, 2005, 2007; Denzin and Giardina, 2006; Denzin, Lincoln and Giardina, 2006); I offer a reading of the method, including its appeals, strengths, and what I perceive as its limitations. In my discussion, I emphasize the politics of interpretation, contending that nothing speaks for itself and there are only performances. Indigenous participatory theater, which nurtures a critical self-consciousness, is central to my argument (Denzin, 2005: 934). I respond to the call by indigenous scholars to develop new interpretive approaches to inquiry (Bishop, 2005).

Such approaches privilege indigenous voices. They are committed to the principles of performance, resistance, and political integrity (see below; also Smith, 2005: 89). A postcolonial, indigenous participatory theater is central to this performance discourse. Indigenous performance is a means of political representation, a form of resistance and critique, and a way of addressing issues of equity, healing, and social justice.

THE APPEAL OF GROUNDED THEORY

Grounded theory's appeals, in its constructivist, objectivist (Charmaz, 2006: 130–131), and situational (Clarke, 2005) forms are many. It provides a set of steps and procedures any researcher can follow in the construction of a theory fitted to a particular problem. For some, in its postmodern turn, it offers a situational, cartographic approach to the study of social structure, social action, and infrastructure (Clarke, 2005: xxii). GT offers guidelines for doing fieldwork, for doing interviewing, and for the analysis of qualitative materials, including ethnographic, interview, 'narrative, visual and historical discourse materials' (Clarke, 2005: xxiii). It offers a way of addressing issues of voice, discourse, texts, the materiality of power, thick analyses of complex social processes (Clarke, 2005: xxiii). Its goals clearly resonate with the postpositivist program in the human disciplines, especially the emphasis on the importance of induction and deduction, generalizability, comparisons between cases, and the systematic relating of concepts grounded in data.

At the same time its theory of action celebrates pragmatism's unique contribution to American social psychology, a linguistically based theory of mind, self, and action. This can be seen in Clarke's (2005) and Charmaz's (2005) focus on postmodern deconstructions, on interconnecting social worlds, on arenas, matrices of structure, trajectories of action, resources, hierarchies of power and influence, social policies, hierarchies of suffering, situated, and local readings of ordinary people and their lives (Charmaz, 2005: 524–528).

Grounded Theory and indigenous discourse

The Decade of the World's Indigenous Peoples (1994–2004) has ended. There is a great desire by indigenous scholars to decolonize Western epistemologies, to open up the academy to non-Western forms of wisdom, knowing, knowledge, and knowledge production (Bishop, 2005; L. Smith, 2005). Grounded theory, because of its commitment to critical, open-ended inquiry, can be a decolonizing tool for indigenous and non-indigenous scholars alike. A performance-based grounded theory using indigenous epistemologies and methodologies is one way to do this.

In proposing a conversation between critical grounded theory and indigenous discourses I am mindful of several difficulties. First, the legacy of the helping Western colonizing Other must be resisted. As Linda Smith observes (1999: 80), 'They came, They saw, They named, They Claimed.' This means, as Bishop argues (2005), that indigenous persons are excluded from discussions concerning who has control over the initiation, the methodologies, evaluations, assessments, representations, and distribution of the newly defined knowledge. The decolonization project challenges these practices.

Second, critical theory, and grounded theory, without modification, will not work within indigenous settings. The criticisms of G. Smith (2000), L. Smith (1999, 2000, 2005), Bishop (1994, 1998, 2005), and others make this very clear. There must be a commitment to transforming the institutions and practices of research. GT concerns for data, basic underlying social processes, and causal narratives may not accord with the pressing social justice concerns of indigenous persons. Critical theory's criteria for self-determination and empowerment may perpetuate neo-colonial sentiments, while turning the indigenous person into an essentialized 'other' who is spoken for (Bishop, 2005). Taking a lesson from grounded theory, critical theory must be localized, grounded in the specific meanings, traditions, customs, and community relations that operate in each indigenous setting. Localized, grounded critical theory can work if the goals of critique, resistance, struggle, and emancipation are not treated as if they have 'universal characteristics that are independent of history, context, and agency' (L. Smith, 2000: 229).

Third, there is a pressing need to decolonize and deconstruct those structures within the Western academy that privilege Western knowledge systems and their epistemologies (Mutua and Swadner, 2004: 10; Semaili and Kincheloe, 1999). Indigenous knowledge systems are too frequently turned into objects of study, treated as if they were instances of quaint folk theory held by the members of a primitive culture. The decolonizing project reverses this equation, making Western systems of knowledge the object of inquiry.

Fourth, and paraphrasing Linda Smith (2005), the spaces between decolonizing research practices and indigenous communities must be carefully and cautiously articulated. They are fraught with uncertainty. Neo-liberal and neo-conservative political economies turn knowledge about indigenous peoples into a commodity. There are conflicts between competing epistemological and ethical frameworks, including institutional human subject research regulations. Research is regulated by positivist epistemologies. Indigenous scholars and native intellectuals are pressed to produce technical knowledge that conforms to Western standards of truth and validity. Conflicts over who initiates and who benefits from such research are especially problematic (Bishop, 2005). Culturally responsive research practices must be developed. Such practices locate power within the indigenous community. What is acceptable and not acceptable research is determined and defined from within the community. Such work encourages self-determination and empowerment (Bishop, 2005).

Fifth in arguing for a dialogue between grounded, critical and indigenous theories, I recognize that I am an outsider to the indigenous colonized experience. I write as a privileged Westerner. At the same time I seek to be an 'allied other' (Kaomea, 2004: 32), a fellow-traveler, of sorts, an anti-positivist, an insider who wishes to deconstruct from within the Western academy and its positivist epistemologies.

Indigenous Grounded Theory as performance, as pedagogy

Indigenous grounded theory inquiry is performative. It connects research to struggles for liberation, to struggles which empower, which challenge the status quo, rebuild leadership, restore environments, and revitalize language, culture, and community (L. Smith, 2005: 89). 'Indigenous grounded theory research is performative research carried out by indigenous scholars, in and for indigenous communities, using the principles of indigenous grounded theory inquiry' (L. Smith, 2005: 89). This form of inquiry is collaborative and participatory and is characterized by the absence of a need to be in control, by a desire to be connected to and to be a part of a moral community where a primary goal is the compassionate understanding of another's moral position (Bishop, 1998: 203). The indigenist researcher wants to participate in a collaborative, altruistic relationship, where nothing 'is desired for the self' (Bishop, 1998: 207), where research is evaluated by participant-driven criteria, by the cultural values and practices that circulate, for example, in indigenist culture, including metaphors stressing self-determination, the sacredness of relationships, embodied understanding, and the priority of community over self.

Indigenous pedagogy

Researchers are led to develop new story lines and criteria of evaluation reflecting these understandings. These participant-driven criteria function as resources for resisting positivist and neo-conservative desires to 'establish and maintain control of the criteria for evaluating indigenous experience' (Bishop, 1998: 212). They privilege a spoken, indigenous epistemology which emphasizes indigenous knowledge, and indigenous, traditional ways of knowing. The earth is regarded as the spiritual center of the universe. There is a commitment to dismantle and resist global capitalism. Positivist forms of knowing, educating, and of doing science and research are contested (Grande, 2000; Meyer, 2003).

Indigenist pedagogy moves epistemology out of a methodological framework, into the spaces of indigenous culture. Akin to grounded theory, specific indigenist ways of knowing and being in the world are emphasized (Meyer, 2003: 187). For Meyer (2003: 193) this epistemology is organized around the themes, of spirituality, physical space, the cultural nature of the senses, relational knowing, practical knowing, language as being, and the unity of mind and body. This framework stresses the performative place of morality in knowledge production. Knowing is always moral and political. Culture restores culture. Culture is sacred. Culture is performed, culture is pedagogy. Spirituality is basic to culture. It is sensuous and embodied, involving the senses: taste, sight, smell, hearing, and touch. Knowledge is experienced and expressed in sensuous terms, in stories and critical personal narratives focusing on the importance of practice and repetition (Meyer, 2003: 185). Knowledge is a process. It is relational, it locates the person in a moral relation with the Other. This involves harmony, balance, being generous, responsible, being a good listener, and being kind.

Grounded Theory on tricky ground

Paraphrasing Linda Tuhiwai Smith (2005: 85), the ground on which grounded theory stands is tricky. It is tricky because it is 'complicated, and changeable, and it is tricky also because it can play tricks on research and on the researcher' (L. Smith, 2005: 85). Grounded theory's ground, and the spaces it encompasses, are always constructed, never bedrock solid, always nuanced, and potentially dangerous. The ground itself is a function of the researcher's shifting relationship to the world. And always 'lurking around the corners are countervailing conservative forces that seek to disrupt any agenda of social justice that may form on such tricky ground' (L. Smith, 2005: 85). These forces may seek to derail the project. They may have little tolerance for public debate, for alternative views, for grounded theory methodology, and even distain for projects espousing social justice (L. Smith, 2005: 85). Under such circumstances, interpretive grounded theory is stripped of its radical politics. It is returned 'to a positivist research paradigm that, like life in general, should be simple' (L. Smith, 2005: 85).

Interpretation is always performative, a performance event involving actors, purposes, scripts, stories, stages, and interactions. Performance is an act of intervention, a method of resistance, a form of criticism, and a way of revealing agency and presence in the world. Is this true always? Performance can certainly be routine. Performances foreground the intersection of politics, institutional sites, and embodied experience. The performative is always (or perhaps intended to be?) pedagogical, and the pedagogical is always political. A politics of representation shapes the interpretive process. The practices of interpretation involve story telling, different ways of organizing and representing the world, and different ways of making the world appear real.

Grounded theory is a performance, a set of performative and interpretive practices and ways of making the world visible. This commitment to visibility is anchored in the belief that the world, at some level, is orderly, patterned, and understandable. The world of social interaction and social experience can be theoretically sampled, saturated, located in a situational social world, arena mapped, coded, fitted into conceptual categories, diagrammed, placed in conditional and consequential matrices, and represented in narrative, visual, and historical discourses. These discourses, in turn, can be analysed in terms of social relationships, identities, and intersecting arenas and social worlds.

In contrast, the performance ethnographer is a troublemaker. The practices of ethnography are not tools for creating order out of chaos. Instead ethnographies are for creating chaos, ways of disrupting the world and its representations. Performance ethnographers see disorder in the world, reading orderliness as a dramaturgical production (Goffman, 1959; Kincheloe and McLaren, 2000). Politics of representation suggest that the world's orderliness is imposed through a political, pedagogical, and interpretive process. These pedagogies of order reinforce the belief and the appearance that the world is in fact orderly. But order is an ideological concept, a fiction, a sometimes-shameless concept that justifies the interpretive practices of science and grounded theory. Order may be partial, provisional, and temporary.

The differences here are foundational; they are about more than causing trouble. They are about how the world is represented so that social justice interventions can be produced. They are about not seeing the world in terms of disciplinary conceptual categories. Taken to its logical extension, GT is not about seeing the world in these ways either. These differences are about writing the world in this historical moment where the personal and the political intersect, in this space which is already deeply moral, critical, and interpretive. Grounded, indigenous inquiry, folded into performance, [auto]ethnography searches for ways of disrupting the smooth structures of everyday colonial and postcolonial life. Performance grounded theory sees disorder and unruliness where others see patterns, processes, and interconnections. This focus on disorder and illusion is intended to illuminate the arbitrary and unjust, the unfair practices that operate in daily life.

The ways in which the world is not a stage are not easy to specify. Today everything is already performative, staged, commodified, and dramaturgical. The dividing line between performer and actor, stage and setting, script and text, performance and reality, disappears. As this disappearance occurs, illusion and make-believe prevail. In this space, where the hyperreal appears more real than the real, pragmatists and cultural critics require apparatuses of resistance and critique, methodologies and pedagogies of truth, ways of making real realities that envision and enact pedagogies of hope.

CRITICAL PEDAGOGY, ETHICS, AND PROPHETIC PRAGMATISM

When the divisions between reality and its appearances disappear, critical indigenous grounded theory inquiry necessarily becomes disruptive, explicitly pedagogical, and radically democratic. We need a new politics of truth. We must embrace the justice of our rage. June Jordan and Patricia Hill Collins remind us (paraphrase):

> We must reclaim the neglected legacy of the
> Sixties, an unabashed moral certainty, an incredible
> outgoing energy of righteous rage. We cannot restore and
> expand the forms of justice that our lives require until and unless
> we change the language of current political and methodological
> discourse. If we do not reintroduce our concepts of Right and
> Wrong, of Truth and Evidence, then how shall we finally argue
> for our cause (Collins, 1998: 250; Jordan, 1998: 178).

I answer the call of Jordan and Collins by turning to the post-pragmatists and the social justice based grounded theorists (see Denzin, 1996, for a review; also Charmaz, 2005; Seigfried, 1996). For the post-pragmatist grounded theorist there is no neutral standpoint, no objective God's eye view of the world. The meaning of a concept, or line of action, or a representation, lies in the practical, political, moral, and social consequences it produces for an actor or collectivity. The meanings of these consequences are not objectively given. They are established through social interaction and the politics of representation. All representations are historically situated, shaped by the intersecting contingencies of power, gender, race, and class (Collins, 2000; Seigfried, 1996: 269). Representations are performance events.

Shaped by the sociological imagination, building on George Herbert Mead's discursive, performative model of the act, critical pragmatic qualitative research imagines and explores the multiple ways in which performance can be understood, including: as imitation, or *mimesis*; as *poiesis*, or construction; as *kinesis*, or movement, gendered bodies in motion (Conquergood, 1998: 31). The researcher-as-performer moves from a view of performance as imitation, or dramaturgical staging, to an emphasis on performance as liminality, construction, to a view of performance as embodied struggle, as an intervention, as breaking and remaking, as kinesis, and as a socio-political act. Viewed as struggles and interventions, performances and performance events become gendered transgressive achievements, political accomplishments which break through 'sedimented meanings and normative traditions' (Conquergood, 1998: 32). This model presumes a performative politics of resistance. Extending indigenous initiatives, this model is committed to a form of revolutionary, catalytic political theater, a project that provokes and enacts pedagogies of dissent for the new millennium. Consider the following:

> In *House Arrest and Piano* (2003), Anna Deavere Smith offers 'an epic view of slavery, sexual misconduct, and the American presidency.' Twelve actors, some in blackface, 'play across lines of race, age and gender to "become" Bill Clinton, Thomas Jefferson, Sally Hemings ... and a vast array of historical and contemporary figures' (Kondo, 2000: 81).
>
> In Native Canadian Bill Moses' play *Almighty Voice and His Wife* (1993), Native performers, wearing whiteface minstrel masks, mock such historical figures as Wild Bill Cody, Sitting Bull, and young Indian maidens called Sweet Sioux (Gilbert, 2003: 692).
>
> In Sidney, Australia aboriginal theatre groups perform statements of their indigenous rights demanding that politicians participate in these performance events 'as co-producers of meaning rather than as tacit consumers' (Magowan, 2000: 317–318).

Grounded critical theory and epistemologies of resistance

We are in the midst of global social movement of involving anticolonialist discourse. This movement is evident in the emergence and proliferation of critically grounded indigenous epistemologies and methodologies. These epistemologies are forms of critical pedagogy; they embody a critical politics of representation. They fold theory, epistemology, methodology, and praxis into strategies of resistance unique to each indigenous community. Within each indigenous pedagogy there is a commitment to an indigenism, to an indigenist outlook which, after Ward Churchill (1996), assigns the highest priority to the rights of indigenous peoples, to the traditions, bodies of knowledge and values that have 'evolved over many thousands of years by native peoples the world over' (1996: 509).

Indigenist pedagogies resist the positivist and post-positivist methodologies of Western science because these formations, for example standardized achievement tests, are too frequently used to validate colonizing knowledge about indigenous peoples. Indigenists deploy, instead, interpretive strategies and skills fitted to and grounded in the needs, language, and traditions of their respective indigenous community (Bishop, 2005). These strategies emphasize personal performance narratives, collaborative research relationships, compassionate understanding, self-determination, and the sacredness of community relationships. Researchers develop participant-driven criteria of evaluation reflecting these understandings. Grounded critical pedagogy respects indigenous epistemologies, and encourages interpretive, first person methodologies. It honors different versions of science and empirical activity, and values cultural criticism in the name of social justice. It seeks models of human subject research that are not constrained by bio-medical positivist assumptions. It turns the academy and its classrooms into sacred spaces where indigenous and non-indigenous scholars interact, share experiences, take risks, explore alternative modes of interpretation, participate in a shared agenda, and come together in a spirit of hope, love, and shared community.

Theory, method, and epistemology are aligned in this project, anchored in the moral philosophies that are taken for granted in indigenous cultures and language communities (L. Smith, 2000: 225). A pedagogy of emancipation and empowerment is endorsed, a pedagogy that encourages struggles for autonomy, cultural well-being, cooperation, and collective responsibility. This pedagogy demands that indigenous groups own the research process. It speaks the truth 'to people about the reality of their lives' (Collins, 1998: 198). It equips them with the tools to resist oppression, and it moves them to struggle, to search for justice (Collins, 1998: 198–199). This truth, sometimes unwelcome, is situated in the indigenous life-world. Some individuals or groups, for example, may not wish to affirm the oppression that researchers may define and oppose.

Indigenous research as localized critical theory

In these commitments, indigenous epistemologies overlap with critical grounded theory. Indeed, Linda Smith (2000) connects her version of indigenous inquiry, Kaupapa Maori research, with critical theory, suggesting, with G. Smith (2000), that Kaupapa Maori research is a 'local theoretical position that is the modality through which the emancipatory goal of critical theory, in a specific historical, political and social context is practised' (L. Smith, 2000: 229; also Bishop, 2005). Critical theory, like pragmatism, presumes that individuals are influenced by social and historical forces. Educational and everyday realities 'are constructed in and through people's linguistic, cultural, social, and behavioral interactions which both shape and are shaped by social, political, economic, and cultural forces' (Fishman and McLaren, 2005: 1). It is not enough to understand any given reality. There is a need to 'transform it with the goal of radically democratizing educational sites and societies' (Fishman and McLaren, 2005: 1). Critical scholars as transformative intellectuals actively shape and lead this project.

Critical pedagogy disrupts those hegemonic cultural and educational practices that reproduce the logics of neoliberal conservatism (Giroux and Giroux, 2005). Critical pedagogy subjects structures of power, knowledge, and practice to grounded theory inquiry, demanding that they be evaluated 'in terms of how they might open up or close down democratic experiences' (Giroux and Giroux, 2005: 1). Critical pedagogy holds systems of authority accountable through the critical reading of texts, the creation of radical educational practices, and the promotion of critical literacy (Giroux and Giroux, 2005: 2). Concretely, these practices help to implement the goals of critical pedagogy. In a grounded theory context, they anchor lofty goals to specific actions, patterns, arenas, and meanings.

In turn, critical pedagogy encourages resistance to the 'discourses of privatization, consumerism, the methodologies of standardization and accountability, and the new disciplinary techniques of surveillance' (Giroux and Giroux, 2005: 3). Resistance takes many interpretive forms, including calling for fair labor and non-destructive environmental practices, and endorsing organic or green consumer ideologies. Critical pedagogy provides the tools, linking discourses to practices, for understanding how cultural and educational practices contribute to the construction of neoliberal conceptions of identity, citizenship, and agency. Critical pedagogy, as critical discourse, operates in the classrooms of daily life, in the media, in schools, in offices, and in the workplace. Informed citizens model for one another alternative ways of responding to the meanings that circulate in daily life. Critical understanding is achieved when citizens understand that things are not, nor do they need to be, as they appear in the media.

Critical, pedagogical grounded theory offers the scholar a set of interpretive procedures for locating analysis in the worlds of social experience. It encourages processual thinking, requires a comparative focus, examines *how*, not *why* questions, demands intimate familiarity with a setting, values observations that challenge current ideas, draws links between the local and the institutional, and, using strategies of saturation and situational maps and analyses, suggests avenues for pursuing social justice concerns (Charmaz, 2005: 528; Clarke, 2005: 289).

Grounded theory thus merges with critical pedagogy. The local which localizes and grounds indigenous critical grounded theory is always historically specific. The local is grounded in the politics, circumstances, and economies of a particular moment, a particular time and place, and a particular set of problems, struggles, and desires. A politics of resistance and possibility (Madison, 1998; Pollock, 1998) is embedded in the local. This is a politics that confronts and breaks through local structures of resistance and oppression. This is a politics that asks 'Who writes for whom? Who is representing indigenous peoples, how, for what purposes, for which audiences, who is doing science for whom?' (L. Smith, 1999: 37).

A politics of possibility[1]

Madison shows how this politics of possibility works. In 1968, two African American women employed as cafeteria workers at the University of North Carolina led a strike. They protested for back pay, overtime pay, and better working conditions. The National Guard was mobilized. The Chapel Hill police 'circled the cafeteria with guns in hand, and classes were canceled. For the two African American women who led the strike, it was a difficult time and an unforgettable ordeal. One woman was fired; the other still works in the University cafeteria' (Madison, 1998: 279).

In 1993, the University of North Carolina was celebrating its bicentennial. Madison notes that some people 'felt it was time to honor the leaders of the (in)famous 1968 cafeteria workers strike, as well as labor culture on campus. After some time, a performance based on the personal narratives of the two leaders and other service workers was finally scheduled' (Madison, 1998: 279). On opening night the strike leaders, their partners, children, grandchildren, friends, cafeteria workers, housekeepers, brick masons, yard keepers, and mail carriers 'were the honored guests with reserved seats before an overflowing crowd' (Madison, 1998: 298). Madison observes that although the University never acknowledged the 'strike leaders' struggle or their contribution to labor equity on campus, almost thirty years later, the leaders, Mrs. Smith and Mrs. Brooks, watched themselves and their story being performed in a crowded theatre' (Madison, 1998: 279). At the end of the performance Mrs. Smith and Mrs. Brooks were introduced and 'the audience gave them a thunderous and lengthy standing ovation' (Madison, 1998: 280). Mrs. Smith said that a night like this 'made her struggle worthwhile' (Madison, 1998: 280). Her grandchildren reported that they 'now understood their grandmother's life better after seeing the performance' (Madison, 1998: 280). The next day the press reported that 'the production told a true and previously untold tale' (Madison, 1998: 280). Madison reports that, 4 years later, workers still stop her on campus and 'remember and want to talk, with pride and satisfaction, about that night four years ago when their stories were honored in performance' (Madison, 1998: 280).

The performance of these stories, grounded in the life experiences of the workers, helped these workers tell their story, empowering 'them before strangers and kin' (Madison, 1998: 280). The performance became an epiphany, a liminal event that marked a crisis in the University's history. It was an act of resistance, it made public an event that had previously been suppressed by the University administration. The performance redressed this historical breach and brought dignity and stature to those who had been dishonored by the past actions of the University. The performance allowed these women and their families to bear witness to this suppressed history. This performance did not create a revolution, but it was 'revolutionary in enlightening citizens to the possibilities that grate against injustice' (Madison, 1998: 280). This kind of indigenous political theater moves in three directions at the same time: it shapes subjects, audiences, and performers. In honoring subjects who have been mistreated, such performances contribute to a more 'Enlightened and involved citizenship' (Madison, 1998: 281). These performances interrogate and evaluate specific social, educational, economic, and political processes. This form of praxis can shape a cultural politics of change. It can help create a progressive and involved citizenship. The performance becomes the vehicle for moving persons, subjects, performers, and audience members into new, critical, political spaces. The performance gives the audience, and the performers, 'equipment for [this] journey: empathy and intellect, passion and critique' (Madison, 1998: 282).

Such performances enact a performance-centered evaluation pedagogy. Thus fusion of critical pedagogy and performance praxis uses performance as a mode of inquiry, as a method of doing evaluation ethnography, as a path to understanding, as a tool for engaging collaboratively the meanings of experience, and as a means to mobilize persons to take action in the world. This form of critical, collaborative, performance pedagogy privileges experience, the concept of voice, and the importance of turning evaluation sites into democratic public spheres. Critical performance pedagogy informs practice, which in turn supports the pedagogical conditions for an emancipatory politics.

This performance ethic seeks its external grounding in its commitment to a post-Marxism and communitarian feminism with hope but no guarantees. It seeks to understand how power and ideology operate through and across systems of discourse. It understands that moral and aesthetic criteria are always fitted to the contingencies of concrete circumstances, assessed in terms of local understandings that flow from a feminist moral ethic. This ethic calls for dialogical inquiry rooted in the concepts of care, and shared governance. How this ethic works in any specific situation cannot be predicted in advance. It has not been done before. Hence, for example, an Afrocentric feminist esthetic (and epistemology) stresses the importance of truth, knowledge, and beauty (Black is Beautiful), and a notion of wisdom that is experiential and shared. Wisdom so conceived is derived from local, lived experience, and expresses lore, folktale, and myth (Collins, 2000: 212–213). This esthetic asks that art (and ethnography) be politically committed.

A critical politics of interpretation leads the indigenous scholar to ask eight questions about any research project, including those projects guided by grounded critical theory:

(1) What research do we want done?
(2) Who is it for?
(3) What difference will it make?
(4) Who will carry it out?
(5) How do we want the research done?
(6) How will we know it is worthwhile?
(7) Who will own the research?
(8) Who will benefit?

(L. Smith, 2000: 239).

These questions are addressed to indigenous and non-indigenous scholars alike. They must be answered in the affirmative; that is indigenists must conduct, own, and benefit from any research that is done on or for them.

Criteria for Grounded Theory studies in social justice inquiry

Charmaz outlines four criteria which merge grounded theory studies with social justice inquiry. Her terms include credibility, originality, resonance, and useful-ness. Inquiry has credibility when it is anchored in the languages, values, and politics of the local. Inquiry must resonate with the local. It should be shaped by local needs. It should make a positive difference in that world. Findings should be owned by the local community. Her interpretive criteria can be read back through Smith's eight questions; that is, we want locally grounded critical inquiry that advances social justice issues for persons in indigenous communities.

These eight questions and four criteria serve to interpret critical theory through a moral lens. They shape the moral space that aligns indigenous research with grounded critical theory. Thus both formations are situated within the antipositivist debate. They both rest on antifoundational epistemologies. Each privileges performative issues of gender, race, class, equity, and social justice. Each develops its own understandings of community, critique, resistance, struggle, and emancipation (L. Smith, 2000: 228). Each understands that the outcome of a struggle can never be predicted in advance, and that struggle is always local and contingent. It is never final (L. Smith, 2000: 229).

By localizing discourses of resistance, and by connecting these discourses to performance ethnography and critical pedagogy, indigenous research enacts what grounded critical theory 'actually offers to oppressed, marginalized and silenced groups ... [that is] through emancipation groups such as the Maori would take greater control of their own lives and humanity' (L. Smith, 2000: 229). This requires that indigenous groups 'take hold of the project of emancipation and attempt to make it a reality on their own terms' (L. Smith, 2000: 229). This means that inquiry is always political and moral, grounded in principles centered on autonomy, home, family, kinship, on a collective community vision that requires that research not be a 'purchased product ... owned by the state' (L. Smith, 2000: 231). Localized critical indigenous theory, folded into grounded theory, encourages indigenists and non-indigenists to confront key challenges connected to the meanings of science, community, and democracy. In proactively framing participatory views of science, empirical research, democracy, and community, persons take control of their own fate. They refuse to be sidetracked into always responding to the attempts by the state to define their life situations (G. Smith, 2000: 210). This means that persons and communities craft their own version of science and empirical activity. They are challenged to develop a participatory model of democracy that goes beyond the 'Westminster "one person, one vote, majority rule"' (G. Smith, 2000: 212). They learn how to use grounded critical theory proactively as an agent of change. They learn how to act in ways that are accountable to the indigenous and non-indigenous community, and not just the academy and its scholarly standards.

Patricia Hill Collins (2000) offers four criteria—primacy of lived experience, dialogue, an ethics of care, an ethics of responsibility—for interpreting truth and knowledge claims. This framework privileges lived experience, emotion, empathy, and values rooted in personal expressiveness (Edwards and Mauthner, 2002: 25). The moral inquirer—whether a politician or a social scientist—builds a collaborative, reciprocal, trusting, mutually accountable relationship with those studied. This feminist ethical framework is care- and justice-based. It seeks to contextualize shared values and norms. It privileges the sacredness of life, human dignity, nonviolence, care, solidarity, love, community, empowerment, and civic transformation. It demands of any action that it positively contribute to a politics of resistance, hope, and freedom (Denzin, 2003: 258).

For the prophetic post-pragmatists there are no absolute truths, no absolute principles, no faith-based beliefs in what is true or false. At the level of politics and ideology, the post-pragmatist, following Cornel West (1989: 234; 1991: 36) acts as a critical moral agent, one whose political goal is the creation of greater individual freedom in the broader social order. Paraphrasing West (1991: 35–36), prophetic pragmatists as moral agents understand that the consequences of their interventions into the world are exclusively political, judged always in terms of their contributions to a politics of liberation, love, caring, and freedom. Following Collins (2000), Pelias (2004: 163), and Freire (1999), the moral inquirer enacts a politics of love and care, an ethic of hope and forgiveness. Love, here, to borrow from Darder and Mirón (2006):

> means to comprehend that the moral and the material are inextricably linked. And, as such, [we] must recognize love as an essential ingredient of a just society. Eagleton (2003) defines this concept of love as a political principle through which we struggle to create mutually life-enhancing opportunities for all people. It is grounded in the mutuality and interdependence of our human existence—that which we share, as much as that which we do not. This is a love nurtured by the act of relationship itself. It cultivates relationships with the freedom to be at one's best without undue fear. Such an emancipatory love allows us to realize our nature in a way that allows others to do so as well. Inherent in such a love is the understanding that we are not at liberty to be violent, authoritarian, or self-seeking (p. 150).

Materially, actions are thus judged in terms of moral consequences and the meanings people bring to them. Consequences are not self-evident. They are socially constructed through the politics of representation. The concept of truth is thus replaced with a consequential theory of meaning. Experience, folded through what Stuart Hall (1996: 473) calls the politics of representation, becomes the site of meaning and truth. Facts about the world are treated as lived experiences. The pragmatist examines the effects, or consequences, of any line of action on existing structures of domination. The pragmatist asks, what are the moral and ethical consequences of these effects for lived human experience? Do they contribute to an ethical self-consciousness that is critical and reflexive, empowering people with a language and a set of pedagogical practices that turn oppression into freedom, despair into hope, hatred into love, and doubt into trust? Do they engender a critical racial self-awareness that contributes to utopian dreams of racial equality and racial justice? If people are being oppressed, denied freedom, or dying because of these effects, then the action, of course, is morally indefensible.

I am calling for an engagement with and a promotion of a grounded theory research paradigm that imagines creative and critical responses to the feminist, indigenous, and post-pragmatic efforts outlined above. This paradigm is forthright in its belief that the personal is political, and that the political is pedagogical. It shares in experiences, problems, and hopes concerning the conduct of critical, qualitative inquiry in this time of global uncertainty. The values of progressive democracy must be at the forefront when scientific advice is used for policy-making decisions. The pragmatic consequences for a radical democracy must be taken into account when scientific recommendations for social action are implemented.

This is a gendered project, a project where feminist, postcolonial, queer, and indigenous theorists question the logic of the heterosexual ethnographic narrative. It is a moral, allegorical, and therapeutic project, one in which the researcher's own self is inscribed in the text as a prop to help men and women endure and prevail in the opening years of the twenty-first century. And it is avowed in its commitment to a project of social justice and radical progressive democracy. But there are no absolute truths, no absolute principles. The moral inquirer enacts a politics of love and care, an ethic of hope and forgiveness. As Ron Pelias suggests (2004: 162–163, 171, paraphrase):

> The heart learns that stories are truths that won't keep still. The heart learns that facts are the possibilities we pretend we trust. The heart's method of pumping, loving and forgiving encourages us to proceed with our hearts first. What matters most is that we learn how to use our rage in positive ways, to love, to struggle to forgive. We have little other choice.

Cornel West is instructive (1989: 234; 1991: 36, paraphrased):

> At the level of politics and ideology, the post-pragmatist acts as a critical moral agent, one whose political goal is the creation of greater individual freedom in the broader social order. Prophetic pragmatists as moral agents understand that the consequences of their interventions into the world are exclusively political, judged always in terms of their contributions to a politics of liberation, love, caring and freedom.

A critically grounded pragmatism embraces an ethics of truth, love, care, hope, and forgiveness. Patricia Hill Collins provides direction (2000: 251, paraphrase):

> This moral vision relies on a righteous rage to spur us on, to keep us headed in the right direction, to point the way, to move people toward justice. If it does this then it has made a very important difference in the lives of people.

We demand that history's actors use models of evidence that answer to these moral truths. An indigenous, performative, grounded theory inquiry helps us get to these truths and these spaces.

ACKNOWLEDGMENTS

I thank Kathy Charmaz and Tony Bryant for their insightful and critical comments on earlier versions of this chapter, sections of which draw from arguments in Denzin (2003, 2005), Denzin and Lincoln (2005), Denzin and Giardina (2006), and Denzin, Lincoln and Giardina (2006).

NOTES

1 This section draws from Denzin (2003: 18–20).

REFERENCES

Bishop, Russell. 1994. Initiating Empowering Research. *New Zealand Journal of Educational Studies*, 29(1): 175–188.

Bishop, Russell. 1998. Freeing Ourselves from Neo-Colonial Domination in Research: A Maori Approach to Creating Knowledge. *International Journal of Qualitative Studies in Education*, 11: 199–219.

Bishop, Russell. 2005. Freeing Ourselves from Neocolonial Domination in Research: A Kaupapa Maori Approach to Creating Knowledge. In N. K. Denzin and Y. S. Lincoln (Eds.), *Handbook of Qualitative Research*, 3/e (pp. 109–138). Thousand Oaks, CA: SAGE.

Charmaz, Kathy. 2005. Grounded Theory in the 21st century: A Qualitative Method for Advancing Social Justice Research. In N. K. Denzin and Y. S. Lincoln (Eds.), *Handbook of Qualitative Research*, 3/e (pp. 507–535). Thousand Oaks, CA: SAGE.

Charmaz, Kathy. 2006. *Constructing Grounded Theory: A Practical Guide Through Qualitative Analysis*. Thousand Oaks, CA: SAGE.

Churchill, Ward. 1996. I am an Indigenist: Notes on the Ideology of the Fourth World. In Ward Churchill (Ed.), *From a Native Son: Selected Essays in Indigenism, 1985–1995* (pp. 509–546). Boston: South End Press.

Clarke, Adele E. 2005. *Situational Analysis: Grounded Theory After the Postmodern Turn*. Thousand Oaks, CA: SAGE.

Collins, Patricia Hill. 1998. *Fighting Words: Black Women & the Search for Justice*. Minneapolis: University of Minnesota Press.

Collins, Patricia Hill. 2000. *Black Feminist Thought*, 2/e. New York: Routledge.

Conquergood, Dwight. 1998. Beyond the Text: Toward a Performative Cultural Politics. In Sheron J. Dailey (Ed.), *The Future of Performance Studies: Visions and Revisions* (pp. 25–36). Annadale, VA: National Communication Association.

Darder, A. and Mirón, L. F. 2006. Critical Pedagogy in a Time of Uncertainty: A Call to Action. In N. K. Denzin and M. D. Giardina (Eds.), *Contesting Empire/Globalizing Dissent: Cultural Studies after 9/11* (pp. 136–151). Boulder, CO: Paradigm Publishers.

Denzin, Norman K. 1996. Post-Pragmatism. *Symbolic Interaction*, 19(1): 61–75.

Denzin, Norman K. 2003. *Performance Ethnography: Critical Pedagogy and the Politics of Culture*. Thousand Oaks, CA: SAGE.

Denzin, Norman K. 2004. Remembering to Forget: Lewis and Clark and Native Americans in Yellowstone. *Communication and Critical/Cultural Studies*, 1 (September): 219–249.

Denzin, Norman K. 2005. Emancipatory Discourses and the Ethics and Politics of Interpretation. In N. K. Denzin and Y. S. Lincoln (Eds.), *Handbook of Qualitative Research*, 3/e (pp. 933–958). Thousand Oaks, CA: SAGE.

Denzin, Norman K. 2007. Sacagawea's Nickname, or the Sacagawea Problem. *Qualitative Research*, 7(1): 103–133.

Denzin, Norman K. and Michael Giardina. 2006. Introduction: Qualitative Inquiry and the Conservative Challenge. In N. K. Denzin and M. Giardina (Eds.), *Qualitative Inquiry and the Conservative Challenge* (pp. ix–xxxi). Walnut Creek, CA: Left Coast Press.

Denzin, Norman K. and Yvonna S. Lincoln. 2005. Introduction: The Discipline and Practice of Qualitative Research. In Norman K. Denzin and Yvonna S. Lincoln (Eds.), *The Handbook of Qualitative Research*, 3/e (pp. 1–32). Thousand Oaks, CA: SAGE.

Denzin, Norman K., Yvonna S. Lincoln and Michael Giardina. 2006. Disciplining Qualitative Research. *Qualitative Studies in Education*, 6: 122–144.

Edwards, Rosalind and Melanie Mauthner. 2002. Ethics and Feminist Research: Theory and Practice. In Melanie Mauthner, Maxine Birch, Julie Jessop and Tina Miller (Eds.), *Ethics in Qualitative Research* (pp. 14–31). London: SAGE.

Fishman, Gustavo E. and Peter McLaren. 2005. Rethinking Critical Pedagogy and the Gramscian Legacy: From Organic to Committed Intellectuals. *Cultural Studies— Critical Methodologies*, 5(1): 126–140.

Freire, Paulo. 1999. *Pedagogy of Hope*. Translated by Robert R. Barr. New York: Continuum. (Originally published 1992.)

Gilbert, Helen. 2003. Black and White and Re(a)d All Over Again: Indigenous Minstrelsy in Contemporary Canadian and Australian Theatre. *Theatre Journal*, 55: 679–698.

Giroux, Henry, and Susan Searls Giroux. 2005. Challenging Neoliberalism's New World Order: The Promise of Critical Pedagogy. *Cultural Studies—Critical Methodologies*, 5(1): 14–25.

Glaser, Barney G. and Anselm L. Strauss. 1967. *The Discovery of Grounded Theory: Strategies for Qualitative Research*. Chicago: Aldine.

Goffman, Erving. 1959. *The Presentation of Self in Everyday Life*. New York: Doubleday.

Grande, Sandy. 2000. American Indian Identity and Intellectualism: The Quest for a New Red Pedagogy. *Qualitative Studies in Education*, 13: 343–360.

Hall, Stuart. 1996. What is this 'Black' in Black Popular Culture? In David Morley and Kuan-Hsing Chen (Eds.), *Stuart Hall: Critical Dialogues in Cultural Studies* (pp. 465–475). London: Routledge.

Jordan, June. 1998. *Affirmative Acts*. New York: Anchor.

Kaomea, Julie. 2004. Dilemmas of an Indigenous Academic: A Native Hawaiian Story. In Kagendo Mutua and Beth Blue Swadener (Eds.), *Decolonizing Research in Cross-Cultural Contexts: Critical Personal Narratives* (pp. 27–44). Albany: SUNY Press.

Kincheloe, Joe L. and Peter McLaren. 2000. Rethinking Critical Theory and Qualitative Research. In Norman K. Denzin and Yvonna S. Lincoln (Eds.), *Handbook of Qualitative Research*, 2/e (pp. 279–314). Thousand Oaks, CA: SAGE.

Kondo, Dorine. 2000. (Re) Visions of Race: Contemporary Race Theory and the Cultural Politics of Racial Crossover in Documentary Theatre. *Theatre Journal*, 52: 81–107.

Madison, D. Soyini. 1998. Performances, Personal Narratives, and the Politics of Possibility. In Sheron J. Dailey (Ed.), *The Future of Performance Studies: Visions and Revisions* (pp. 276–286). Annadale, VA: National Communication Association.

Magowan, Fiona. 2000. Dancing with a Difference: Reconfiguring the Poetic Politics of Aboriginal Ritual as National Spectacle. *Australian Journal of Anthropology*, 11(3): 308–321.

Meyer, Manulani Aluli. 2003. *Ho'oulu: Our Time of Becoming: Hawaiian Epistemology and Early Writings*. Honolulu: 'Ai Pohaku Press Native Books.

Mutua, Kagendoo and Beth Blue Swadner, 2004. Introduction. In Kagendo Mutua and Beth Blue Swadener (Eds.), *Decolonizing Research in Cross-Cultural Contexts: Critical Personal Narratives* (pp. 1–23). Albany: SUNY Press.

Pelias, Ronald J. 2004. *A Methodology of the Heart: Evoking Academic & Daily Life*. Walnut Creek: AltaMira.

Pollock, Della. 1998. A Response to Dwight Conquergood's Essay: 'Beyond the Text: Towards a Performative Cultural Politics'. In Sheron J. Dailey (Ed.), *The Future of Performance Studies: Visions and Revisions* (pp. 37–46). Annadale, VA: National Communication Association.

Seigfried, Charlene Haddock. 1996. *Pragmatism and Feminism: Reweaving the Social Fabric*. Chicago: University of Chicago Press.

Semaili, Ladislaus, M. and Joe L. Kincheloe. 1999. Introduction: What is Indigenous Knowledge and Why should we Study it? In Ladislaus M. Semaili and Joe L. Kincheloe (Eds.), *What is Indigenous Knowledge? Voices from the Academy* (pp. 3–57). New York: Falmer Press.

Smith, Anna Deavere. 2003. *House Arrest and Piano*. New York: Anchor.

Smith, Graham. 2000. Protecting and Respecting Indigenous Knowledge. In Marie Battiste (Ed.), *Reclaiming Indigenous Voice and Vision* (pp. 209–224). Vancouver: UBC Press.

Smith, Linda Tuhiwai. 1999. *Decolonizing Methodologies: Research and Indigenous Peoples*. London: Zed Books.

Smith, Linda Tuhiwai. 2000. Kupapa Maori Research. In Marie Battiste (Ed.), *Reclaiming Indigenous Voice and Vision* (pp. 225–247). Vancouver: UBC Press.

Smith, Linda Tuhiwai. 2005. On Tricky Ground: Researching the Native in the Age of Uncertainty. In N. K. Denzin and Y. S. Lincoln (Eds.), *Handbook of Qualitative Research*, 3/e (pp. 85–108). Thousand Oaks, CA: SAGE.

Strauss, Anselm. 1987. *Qualitative Analysis for Social Scientists*. New York: Cambridge University Press.

Strauss, Anselm and Juliet Corbin. 1998. *Basics of Qualitative Research: Techniques and Procedures for Developing Grounded Theory,* 2/e. Thousand Oaks, CA: SAGE.

West, Cornel. 1989. *The American Evasion of Philosophy: A Genealogy of Pragmatism*. Madison: University of Wisconsin Press.

West, Cornel. 1991. Theory, Pragmatisms and Politics. In Jonathan Arac and Barbara Johnson (Eds.), *Consequences of Theory* (pp. 22–38). Baltimore: Johns Hopkins University Press.

22

Grounded Theory and Racial/Ethnic Diversity

Denise O'Neil Green,
John W. Creswell, Ronald J. Shope and
Vicki L. Plano Clark

INTRODUCTION

Given the increase of racial/ethnic diversity in developed countries, particularly in the USA, and ensuing social issues that accompany such global changes, grounded theory researchers have an opportunity to create new theories that explicitly integrate a diversity focus while addressing issues of process that may yield theoretical perspectives germane to diverse populations. The lack of literature which clearly articulates the methodological nuances facing the novice or seasoned researcher presents a challenge for those who wish to utilize grounded theory to explore emergent diversity phenomena and incorporate them into the research process. The purpose of this chapter is to advance a set of principles, practices, and guidelines that will help researchers incorporate a diversity focus into their grounded theory research.

Grounded theory is a qualitative approach that has been growing in appeal since it was first introduced in 1967 by Glaser and Strauss. Since that time, research designs that incorporate grounded theory's objectives and procedures have yielded three distinct designs (Creswell, 2005): constructivist (Charmaz, 2006), emergent (Glaser, 1992), and systematic (Strauss & Corbin, 1998). Each approach offers a unique perspective in conducting qualitative research that aims to develop and uncover new theories and presuppositions. Although they share similar characteristics, such as being systematic and emergent, each emphasizes particular aspects of the grounded theory tradition. Strauss and Corbin (1998) place greater emphasis on the researcher using a systematic matrix for coding; Glaser (1992) directs the researcher not to subscribe to using a matrix but to allow the emergent nature of the analysis dictate the study's direction; and Charmaz (2006) underscores that the researcher is not a separate entity but integral to the process of data collection and theory development due to the researcher's past and present experiences. While there are explicit distinctions between the three approaches, regardless of the specific design scheme, grounded theory as a qualitative approach can potentially aid social scientists and educators in understanding unique, diversity-related problems of the twenty-first century.

For example diversity-related problems, such as changing demographics (e.g. race, ethnicity, class, nationality, or place of origin, etc.) in developed countries that are impacting educational and health care systems, immigration and migration issues as well as conservative governments, foreshadow the need for different frameworks and ways of conceptualizing old problems and dysfunctional solutions. Given the increase of racial/ethnic diversity in developed countries, particularly in the USA, and ensuing social issues (i.e. greater economic inequality, environmental impacts, racism, and immigration pressures) that accompany such global changes (Law, Phillips, & Turney, 2004; RAND, 2000) grounded theory researchers have an opportunity to create new theories that explicitly integrate a racial/ethnic diversity focus while addressing issues of process that may yield theoretical perspectives germane to diverse populations.

Beginning with an assumption that the demographic imperative will profoundly impact and transform dimensions of people's experiences, outlook on life, and interactions with others, the emergent, yet a priori nature of grounded theory makes this qualitative approach the optimal methodological tool for examining new, emerging, and evolving issues pertaining to racial/ethnic diversity phenomena. Given the absence of literature that has embraced these demographic shifts and examined the byproducts of these changes, grounded theory research is able to fill that void.

Weaknesses of current social science and education research with respect to diverse populations and subsequent issues illustrate the growing need for new diversity theories based on field data. By incorporating a diversity focus, the researcher guarantees that the racial/ethnic background, experiences, and perspectives of people of color will be valued and embraced rather than marginalized or ignored. The production of knowledge that addresses the changing demographics and phenomena that accompany those changes has a high premium in a global, knowledge marketplace (Green & Trent, 2005). Grounded theory researchers can play a vital role in producing new knowledge that provides a cultural context for social science theories with respect to diverse populations. Though many grounded theory researchers take on a unicultural lens that limits acknowledgement of racial/ethnic dimensions (Barnes, 1996), cultural contexts pertinent to race and ethnicity shape research in the social and human sciences (National Research Council, 2002). As such, research questions, participants, analyses, and reported findings take on characteristics that contribute to either understanding diversity or minimizing it.

If grounded theory researchers accept the premise that these racial/ethnic demographic shifts require greater attention and a closer look, then the aim is not to reject, ignore, or remain ignorant of forces of race and ethnicity, but to engage in grounded theory research that explores how these forces permeate processes of social interactions, decision-making, etc. Nevertheless, there are tensions that exist between the emphasis placed on emergence in grounded theory research and the proposed aims of developing sensitivity to diversity issues and applying this sensitivity to grounded theory studies.

In this chapter, we advance a set of principles, practices, and guidelines that will help researchers incorporate a racial/ethnic diversity focus into their grounded theory research irrespective of the grounded theory design utilized. We articulate the methodological decisions and challenges facing novice and seasoned researchers who wish to utilize grounded theory as an emergent qualitative approach while exploring diversity phenomena. In particular, we address how a diversity perspective may be incorporated into key steps of the research process used in a grounded theory study. Lastly, we provide guidelines for researchers who are interested in advancing diversity research through the grounded theory tradition.

GROUNDED THEORY AND THE INCORPORATION OF DIVERSITY

Given the assumption that diversity should be incorporated into the research process, which phases should garner a researcher's attention? Six research phases are important for grounded theory development: (1) identifying the research problem, (2) developing research questions, (3) collecting data, (4) analyzing/interpreting data, (5) validating findings, and (6) writing the report. The researcher incorporates diversity into each step based on the level of importance assigned to the diversity phenomenon under investigation. Each step provides an opportunity for either the novice or seasoned researcher to make diversity a priority throughout the study. Conversely, these same steps simultaneously present challenges to maintain a diversity perspective throughout the inquiry. Both opportunities and challenges coupled with each step are discussed to provide the basis for a diversity focused grounded theory study or, at the least, to be attuned to latent issues pertaining to diversity as well as explicit problems.

Diversity and problem identification

Grounded theory is most suitable when the research problem entails the development of theory, explanation of a process, or the development of a general abstraction of interactions and actions of people (Creswell, 2005: 411). A researcher's first opportunity to incorporate racial/ethnic diversity into the study occurs while identifying the theory or process that needs development or modification and determining diversity's level of importance with respect to the research problem's conceptualization. There are four levels along the continuum of importance: *primary, complementary, peripheral,* or *absent*. A grounded theory study that assigns *primary* importance to diversity assumes that changing demographics and emerging interactions across race/ethnicity are central to the phenomenon under investigation. An assigned level of *primary* importance to a grounded theory study establishes a diversity orientation at the outset that influences all aspects of the research process, including conceptualization, research questions, theoretical sampling, data collection, analysis, and write up.

For example, a grounded theory study that examines the graduate school choice process of African Americans and Mexican Americans assigns a *primary* level of importance to diversity because at the outset the study aims to investigate a process phenomenon of two diverse populations without the necessity to compare findings with the majority population. An examination of these two diverse populations is sufficient within its own right. Furthermore, the study aims not only to revise prior college choice models in order to reflect the graduate school choice process found in the field data, but to generate a theory that makes visible the cultural, racial/ethnic contexts, as well as the respondents' essential experiences of the process. This particular grounded theory study is conceptualized such that it does not simply examine the experiences of diverse populations but places aspects of culture and racial/ethnic diversity at the center of the investigation (Barnes, 1996).

The *complementary* level lessens the centrality of diversity in the study but acknowledges its importance to a degree. At this level, diversity does not drive the entire research enterprise but serves to enhance the study at various points and complements its conceptualization. If diversity has a *peripheral* level of importance in a grounded theory study, it is simply a concept that functions as an add-on (Pillow, 2003) and is ascribed little to no value in the study's conceptualization, research questions, data collection, etc. When diversity is *absent* by design or oversight from a study, the outcome is the same; it has been assigned the lowest level of importance, with a guiding assumption that changing ethnic/racial demographics and interactions across racial/ethnic and cultural lines have no relevance to the study's conceptualization, theory development, process explanations, or research steps. In such *absent* studies, diversity must naturally emerge if it has any chance of becoming a central dimension of the study.

With the above diversity framework as a guide, phases of the research process are examined beginning with problem identification. Defining a problem in grounded theory is informed by the researcher's professional and personal experiences and his/her engagement with members of diverse groups, as well as his/her academic discipline and familiarity with relevant literature. At the beginning of a grounded theory study the researcher needs to make several choices with respect to conceptualizing or defining boundaries of the problem area, determining the disciplinary and/or philosophical orientation that will be used for the study, and making use of the literature (Strauss & Corbin, 1998). Making such choices functions to either integrate or remove the notion of diversity from the project. Working in concert, the problem, disciplinary orientation, and literature aid the researcher in that integration or removal process. That is, dependent on how the researcher's discipline and/or literature situate diversity, the researcher may be so inclined to follow the same thinking and assumptions. If a grounded theory researcher is not aware or conscious of the racial/ethnic order (i.e. hierarchy) that is present in the researcher's respective discipline or critical body of literature, this same order will be reflected in the process of theory development, potentially eliminating critical theoretical concepts that could enhance and strengthen the emergent or modified theory. By making the choice to simply remain in step with the discipline or conventional body of literature, the researcher determines diversity's level of significance or status (*primary*, *complementary*, *peripheral*, or *absent*eeism) by default rather than critically examine its potential contributions.

For instance, suppose the grounded theory researcher aims to understand the process of career development for African American women but the literature is lacking in its attention specifically to women of color (i.e. Richie et al., 1997). Although conceptualizing the problem strictly within the limited boundaries of the literature was an option, Richie et al. introduced concepts of sexism and racism on vocational development for White and African American-Black women into their study from the outset because it was unclear if the existing theories or models actually captured the experiences of both White women and women of color. By not remaining in step with the current literature, the authors strongly integrated diversity into the study's design and were very open to the notion that race-ethnic factors and racist and sexist environments could shape career development for women of color. The authors' major aim for this grounded theory study was 'the construction of a comprehensive theory of women's career development that truly is inclusive of the experiences of a diverse group of women' (Richie et al., 1997: 134).

The legacy of scholarship on race and ethnicity demonstrates that traditionally diverse populations and corresponding issues have not been at the forefront of the social sciences (Mertens, 2003; Pillow, 2003; Stanfield, 1994). Furthermore, historically, literature that has focused on such matters was relegated to second and third tier journals demonstrating that such areas of scholarship are typically not a part of academe's mainstream (Mertens, 2003; Pillow, 2003; Stage & Anaya, 1996; Stanfield, 1994, 1999). However, with the persistent struggle to be heard by critical race theory, multicultural, and desegregation scholars, along with demographers and others, diversity has gained more attention in academe.

Nevertheless, even with increased attention to diversity as a legitimate intellectual construct, the concept remains marginalized and is treated as an add-on in various traditions of qualitative research (Barnes, 1996), including grounded theory inquiry. Hence, the challenge to grounded theory researchers is to operate contrary to one's training to ask the question: Is diversity being neglected or overlooked yet has a legitimate place in the problem's construction? Given the nature of the inquiry, which level of importance should be ascribed? If grounded theory researchers, whether novices or seasoned, have not been properly exposed to technical or non-technical writings that have addressed diversity issues, this is the time to begin that exploration in order to develop and/or refine sensitivity to pertinent concepts and weaknesses in the literature. Although the researcher should monitor his/her balance between objectivity and sensitivity (Strauss & Corbin, 1998) to diversity as an emergent dimension or concept, the danger of too little sensitivity is more so at issue than becoming overly sensitive, especially for those whose disciplinary orientation typically overlooks its relevance.

Many fields have developed theories and models based on the dominant, elite, or majority group. In higher education, for example, prominent college student development theories, retention models, and college choice models that were formulated based on the experiences of solely white men, white students, or samples of college going students that included very few persons of color continue to be seminal works of the field. It goes without saying that these theories, models, and supporting literature are not inclusive of diverse populations and their experiences. As such, researchers who are interested in these areas need to move beyond the seminal works and introduce themselves to contemporary work and debates in the field that critique these models/theories and their limited application to populations of color. Taking these types of steps increases sensitivity to diversity concerns so that the grounded theory researcher can maintain a balance between sensitivity and objectivity. If such steps are not taken, the grounded theory researcher runs the risk of being ill-informed and biased versus objective.

Diversity and research questions in Grounded Theory

Research questions for grounded theory studies are meant to be broad and open-ended versus hypothesis driven. More importantly, guiding research questions identify the phenomenon under examination along with what the researcher aims to understand about the specified phenomenon (Strauss & Corbin, 1998). Both the phenomenon and what the researcher wants to know provide avenues for concepts of racial/ethnic diversity to enter the inquiry. As suggested above, there is a continuum of choices with which to incorporate diversity. However, introducing diversity from the start is the optimal choice.

If diversity is *absent* in the inquiry, the guiding research question(s) and subquestions do not incorporate aspects of diverse populations or relevant issues. Essentially, these types of research questions reflect a color-blind perspective that relegates race, ethnicity, and cross-cultural issues to a status of unimportance.

Grounded theory studies with research questions that place diversity on the periphery utilize diversity as an add-on concept. For example, a study may have a question such as 'How do dental phobic patients view dental anxiety and experience in dental care?' (Abrahamsson et al., 2002) or 'How do college men describe their attitudes toward body shape and composition?' (Ridgeway & Tylka, 2005). In either study, a subsequent research question may read, 'What role, if any, does the person's racial/ethnic background play in the process/phenomenon?' The subsequent question is constructed such that it places minimal value on the experiences or voices of diverse groups and, if the diversity question or component were removed, it would not drastically change the core objective of the study.

A grounded theory study that incorporates diversity from a *complementary* perspective values the experiences, voices, and issues relevant to racial/ethnic diversity. As such, the research question(s) reflects this placement by its incorporation of related concepts. Furthermore, removal of such concepts changes the study's aim and the process of theory development. For example, 'How do majority and minority students transition from high school to college?' This research question places importance on experiences of both majority and minority students. The question implies that potentially there are differences in the transition experiences of majority and minority students that must be uncovered to adequately develop a comprehensive college transition theory. Composing the question in this manner gives equal weight to majority and minority students in the study.

Diversity has a *primary* level of importance in a grounded theory study when the central research question focuses on people of color, their experiences, voices, and/or issues. When diversity is central to theory development, similar to a *complementary* approach, the removal of diversity concepts drastically changes the purpose of the study. For example, a question could read, 'How do Chinese Americans with type-2 diabetes and their families handle this disease in light of their cultural context?' (Chun & Chesla, 2004). This sample question demonstrates that a diverse population, Chinese Americans, and their cultural parameters are critical to adequately examine the phenomenon under investigation. Composing the question in this manner assigns a great deal of importance to the diverse population selected for the study. In addition, a grounded theory study of this nature potentially enhances the literature because it focuses on a population, its cultural context, experience, and voice that have received no attention in studies that examine diabetes. Lastly, the question clearly indicates that examining the experiences of a particular diverse population is necessary for theory development.

Overall, the discussion on developing research questions aims to instruct researchers to think along a continuum of racial/ethnic and cultural contexts that range from no cultural influences (level of *absence*) to explicit cultural influences (level of *primary* importance) (Barnes, 1996; Goulding, 2002). Allowing diversity to emerge as a significant dimension, construct, or property versus giving it a prominent place in the study at the outset is obviously a choice that must be made by any researcher conceptualizing a grounded theory study. However, research questions provide a lens into the researcher's thinking regarding 'conscious or unconscious theoretical perspectives that color approaches' (Strauss & Corbin, 1998: 39) to the research. The construction of research questions dictates to a large degree the remainder of the study's methods (Strauss & Corbin, 1998), including data collection, analysis, validation, and communication of the findings. Therefore, acknowledgement and incorporation of diversity at the initial stages of a grounded theory study is very important and ought not to be left to chance to emerge later (DeVault, 1995); otherwise research questions that minimize diversity's importance may eventually create a self-fulfilling prophecy.

Given this position of almost forcing the presence of diversity, the real tension with a grounded theory study that relies on following the emergent analytic and data-gathering traditions becomes very apparent at this point. If latent diversity issues become manifest because of the researcher's sensitivity to seeing them or letting them emerge, diversity is not forced. But if scrutinizing the data does not elicit these issues, to what extent can the researcher force diversity questions on the data? Although it is very possible that nothing in the data directly answers the diversity questions posed at the beginning of a study, a researcher can begin with becoming better acquainted with the cultural norms of the population under investigation by spending more time in the field. A researcher might wish to solicit the assistance of an insider (i.e. a member of that population) to review the initial guiding questions, as well as interview questions, in order to determine if the questions are culturally relevant. Reading culturally relevant literature (i.e. novels, poetry, and history) is another strategy. The assumption is that the researcher does not have sufficient experience with the participants' culture and, therefore, the researcher needs to increase his/her exposure to the culture and phenomenon to formulate appropriate questions (Barnes, 1996).

Diversity and Grounded Theory data collection

Collecting data for grounded theory studies requires interplay between the researcher and data that positions the researcher as an instrument by which data is created and constructed (Creswell, 1998; Morrow, Rakhsha, & Castaneda, 2001; Strauss & Corbin, 1998). This interplay acknowledges that subjectivity inevitably enters the research process, providing space for biases, assumptions, and experiences to influence data collection and analysis (Morrow et al., 2001). A researcher's self-awareness, knowledge of the subject under investigation, and skills to discern and be sensitive to salient but subtle aspects of the data are vital for qualitative inquiry, especially grounded theory. In light of these conditions, diversity as a property, dimension, or construct, may or may not naturally emerge due to limitations of the researcher. Since a grounded theory researcher is limited by his/her cultural perspective, which may be unicultural

(Barnes, 1996), and is shaped by systems of class, race/ethnicity, and gender (Larson, 1997), it is very plausible that important racial/ethnic diversity meanings and contextual elements will simply be missed (DeVault, 1995). However, raising the researcher's self-awareness, knowledge, skills, and sensitivity throughout the process will greatly enhance one's ability to uncover salient diversity concepts to inform the emerging theory.

Increasing opportunities for diversity to emerge, particularly in grounded theory studies which situate diversity at either a *complementary* or *primary* level of importance, requires addressing key aspects of the data collection phase. Although the data collection process for a grounded theory study may potentially include interviews, field notes from observations, journals, documents, and/or audio/video files (Strauss & Corbin, 1998), the *primary* form of data collection is face-to-face interviewing (Creswell, 1998). Based on this premise, opportunities for considering issues of diversity occur during sampling (specifically theoretical sampling), through the researcher's positionality, and by racial/ethnic matching between the researcher and participant. Below, each opportunity is described to demonstrate how grounded theory practice can take diversity into account.

Sampling for Grounded Theory interviews

In a *complementary* diversity study, the researcher initially aims for an equal number of participants from each racial/ethnic group represented in the study at the outset (Cannon, Higginbotham, & Leung, 1988). When this sampling strategy is coupled with the researcher's ability to speak, hear, and sense the racial/ethnic nuances of language and meaning of the participants' experiences, it provides an optimal condition for uncovering racial/ethnic influences. Otherwise, this strategy of having an equal sample size for each group may come to naught. However, if an equal number of each racial/ethnic group represented is not possible, the researcher can adjust the sample by at least maintaining an equal number of majority and minority participants. During theoretical sampling, which is a cumulative process (Strauss & Corbin, 1998), the researcher is also mindful of maintaining this balance, even when discriminate sampling is needed for the purposes of saturation. This strategy protects against allowing the experiences and voices of the majority to overshadow experiences and voices of diverse others.

Unfortunately, to strike even an equal balance between minority and majority voices can be challenging due to difficulty in identifying diverse communities, securing access to racially and ethnically diverse populations, and allaying any skepticism about the researcher's intentions, competency, and eventual portrayals of the diverse community (Cannon, Higginbotham, & Leung, 1988; DeVault, 1995; Vincent & Warren, 2001). The researcher's limited exposure, familiarity, and connectedness to diverse communities can also limit the ability to preserve this balance. In this situation, a researcher needs to develop alternative sampling approaches, such as snowball sampling or redefining the sample's parameters to be more inclusive of diverse populations that do not quite fit the typical profile of the majority (Andersen, 1993; DeVault, 1995; Rhoads, 1997). The researcher could also employ other researchers who would be welcome in the diverse community and/or who know the language.

For a *primary* diversity study, the sample reflects that the diverse population is more than *complementary* but the prime objective of the study, such that the number of minority participants total more than the European American/white participants. For a *primary* study, the researcher's sample is essentially comprised of participants from diverse communities or groups (i.e. African Americans, Arab Americans, Asian Americans, Native Americans, Mexican Americans) who represent one culture or multiple cultures. This sampling rule supports the logic of grounded theory studies with a *primary* diversity focus in which the aim is to investigate phenomena pertaining to one or more ethnic/racial groups.

In studies where diversity has a *peripheral* role or is completely *absent*, the researcher does not seek to maintain an equal balance between minority and majority participants. Majority participants represent the largest share or percentage of the sample whether diversity is *peripheral* to (an add-on) or *absent* from the study. Under these conditions, it is likely that the experiences and voices of the majority of European American participants will overshadow the voices and experiences of diverse others.

Theoretical sampling in grounded theory complements the emergent principle of this qualitative approach. As such, when does the researcher decide to conduct a *primary/complementary* versus a *peripheral/absent* diversity study? If the decision is driven by the type of sampling that must be conducted due to the difficulties and challenges that can arise from collecting interview or observation data from among diverse populations, the decision should be made at the outset in order to garner the appropriate resources (i.e. incentives) and assistance of fellow researchers (Cannon, Higginbotham, & Leung, 1988) to sufficiently work through all of the emergent phases of theoretical and discriminate sampling. Nevertheless, a decision to change the study's focus from *peripheral* to *complementary* or from *complementary* to *primary* may also be driven by the emerging analysis, in which case, the researcher must be prepared to change the sampling strategy.

Positionality during the interview process

Sampling plays a key role in dictating the importance and subsequent emergence of relevant diversity phenomena that are essential for theory development. Along with sampling, another feature of the data collection process, interviewing, has implications for retarding or enhancing the emergence of cultural, racial/ethnic concepts in a grounded theory study. In particular, issues of positionality and matching in the interview process should be reflected upon and addressed to ensure ample opportunities for diversity-related (i.e. racial/ethnic) concepts to surface:

> Positionality refers to the social position of the knower, i.e. the class, race, gender, sexual orientation, etc. of the knower ... The point of discussing ... 'positionality' is that everyone brings their own histories, social standing, and cultural background with them to all endeavors—including the process of researching ... (Rhoads, 1997: 480).

Acknowledgement and self-reflection of one's positionality is critical for both the grounded theory researcher and research process (Barnes, 1996; Charmaz, 2006; Clarke, 2005; Strauss & Corbin, 1998). Due to the researcher's positionality along various dimensions of race, class, ethnicity, etc., the researcher is certainly prone to a type of cultural bias that guides: (1) how the interview is conducted, (2) what type of questions are asked, (3) how the interview is recorded, and (4) what observations are ultimately made (Barnes, 1996). Likewise, the social positions of respondents also influence how their responses are framed and how they conduct themselves in the interview (Barnes, 1996). Given this dynamic between the researcher and respondent, 'understanding and acknowledging differences in racial/ethnic positioning' between the researcher and respondent aids in constructing 'a more productive basis for interviewing across racial/ethnic groups than ... asserting a disingenuous claim to commonality' (DeVault, 1995: 614).

Since the researcher's positionality may limit his/her ability to adequately understand the respondent's value system, indigenous perspective worldview, or experiences (Barnes, 1996; Morrow et al., 2001), a baseline or adequate level of competency must be developed to hear and understand the nuances of 'meanings located in social contexts where race and ethnicity ... [often] matter' (DeVault, 1995: 613). The danger in not elevating one's level of competency is that it leads to missing or misunderstanding the respondent's meaning, either in part or entirely.

Improving one's cultural competency with respect to race and ethnicity involves: (1) attending to the researcher's *awareness* of his/her own assumptions, values, and biases with respect to diverse populations or issues relevant to the study; (2) increasing the researcher's *knowledge* and understanding of the respondents' worldviews, where a worldview is 'composed of our attitudes, values, opinions, and concepts ... [that] may affect how we think, define events, make decisions, and behave' (Sue & Sue, 2003: 268); and (3) developing interview *skills* (i.e. word choice strategies, use of nonverbal signals/gestures, non threatening dress, and extent of self disclosure) to generate appropriate interview styles or approaches based on the researcher-respondent interaction (Andersen, 1993; Barnes, 1996; Morrow et al., 2001; Rhoads, 1997; Stewart & Cash, 2006; Sue & Sue, 2003).

If the grounded theory researcher concludes that an adequate level of competency is lacking and must be reached before engaging in data collection (typically interviewing),the researcher can begin to increase his/her levels of awareness, knowledge, and skills through the process of immersion (Morrow et al., 2001). By establishing a foundation of immersion experiences that consist of living and/or working with or in the culture of the respondents (Andersen, 1993; Barnes, 1996; Goulding, 2002), the grounded theory researcher increases sensitivity to the 'language and folkways ... tacit knowledge, social relationships, and patterns of respect' (Morrow et al., 2001: 595). Ultimately, incorporation of an immersion experience during data collection enriches the data collection process for the grounded theory researcher (Barnes, 1996; Charmaz, 2006; DeVault, 1995; Goulding, 2002).

Matching between interviewer and respondent
In addition to positionality, matching between researcher/interviewer and respondent along the dimensions of race, ethnicity, gender, class, age, etc., is certainly an option grounded theory researchers can utilize to address challenges of interracial, inter-ethnic interviewing (Andersen, 1993; Gunaratnam, 2003; Vincent & Warren, 2001). Some have argued that racial/ethnic matching has resolved distance or asymmetry problems of interracial interviewing (Gunaratnam, 2003). Some suggest that matching provides a fast track to access, trust, and rapport between researchers and respondents who have different cultural backgrounds; however, matching does not ensure that symmetry will be achieved in order to facilitate a connection between the respondent and researcher (Gunaratnam, 2003; Vincent & Warren, 2001). Conversely, 'closer researcher-respondent relationships may develop despite a lack of obvious symmetry' (Vincent & Warren, 2001: 43) based on racial/ethnic, class, or gender dimensions but along others (i.e. political position). These contradictions reveal that matching is not a cure all, but can serve as a possible option for researchers who wish to address racial and ethnic differences that could potentially hinder aspects of the respondent-researcher relationship.

Diversity, analysis/interpretation, and validation

Similar to the data collection process, the researcher's level of exposure, experience, awareness, knowledge, and skills in the realm of racial and ethnic diversity continue to have a role in the data analysis/interpretation and validation processes. During these processes, cultural biases, values, priorities, and beliefs of the researcher have ample opportunities to shape the codes generated, theoretical interpretations, and theory validation (Barnes, 1996; Vincent & Warren, 2001) to render diversity *absent, peripheral, complementary*, or *primary*. If the diversity focus is *absent* or *peripheral*, not much attention, if any, is given to exposing those cultural biases. For those who subscribe to either the *complementary* or *primary* level, the researcher should consider their cultural filters during analysis/interpretation and validation to increase the likelihood of unearthing diversity's relevance that might otherwise go unnoticed, especially by the novice researcher.

In addition to acknowledging and attending to one's cultural biases with respect to race and ethnicity, there are several strategies that the grounded theory researcher can utilize during both analysis/interpretation and validation processes to protect against missing or misunderstanding the respondent's meaning, either in part or entirely, where race and ethnicity are relevant. For example, while conducting open coding and axial coding, the researcher ought to direct careful attention to the respondent's narrative in order to analyze it for cultural clues, statements that clarify racial/ethnic and cultural contexts and omitted statements that allude to the invisibility of race/ethnicity (DeVault, 1995; Gunaratnam, 2003; Stanfield, 1999). In some cases, respondents will discuss aspects of their racial/ethnic or cultural identity, bouts with racism, and experiences of immigration and settlement, making the analysis of such phenomena more accessible (Gunaratnam, 2003). For example, in Richie et al.'s (1997) grounded theory study of the career development of highly achieving African American-Black and White women, most of the African American-Black participants spoke in a very transparent way regarding sociocultural issues of racism and sexism. One participant stated:

> Now to be a minority means you gotta [sic] be super good because you gotta keep the door open for someone else. And the other lesson you learn is you reach back and you help other people come through ... women have to help women and minorities have to help minorities, because otherwise we don't get through that door very often (Richie et al., 1997: 141).

It is clear that this participant revealed dimensions of her career development experience that have racial dimensions. However, this level of clarity will not occur in all cases, and respondents will likely share experiences that seem to minimize racial identity; this includes both racialized minorities and majority respondents (Stanfield, 1999). To illustrate, DeVault (1995) shares an excerpt of an interview she conducted with an African American women. The respondent reveals her excitement of the possibility of working in an African American community:

> ... And I got really excited about that, because I wanted to work-in a, sort of like an inner-city kind of thing. That's where I'm from [Eastern City], and I wanted to work with people who were like me, in a sense. So I went on an interview at the [Westside] clinic, in [the city]. And—it was nice, you know, and everyone knew each other there, and knew their patients. And I was just so excited ... (p. 617).

DeVault underscores that this respondent talks around race. Wording such as 'I wanted to work with people who were like me' and 'I wanted to work-in a, sort of like an inner-city kind of thing' imply a racial dimension without explicitly stating it outright. DeVault (1995) indicates a possible source of the respondent's hesitation is that the interviewer is 'a relatively unknown white woman, and a professional ...' (p. 618). Hence, within the first 5 minutes of the interview, instead of stating directly that she was excited with the prospect of working with other African Americans, she talks around that topic.

For the majority of respondents, the influence of race is there but there is little acknowledgement. Returning to Richie et al.'s (1997) grounded theory study, the White participants 'exhibited a general lack of awareness of racism or racial issues, which is perhaps not surprising given the privilege associated with being a part of a majority culture' (p. 140). Hence while a discussion of race was not a part of the White participants' responses, the silence communicated that their majority racial status benefited their career development.

Another example of participants' racialized identity being minimized is in Komives, Owen, Longerbeam, Mainella, and Osteen's (2005) grounded theory study of leadership identity development for college students. Although students of color identified race as a critical factor to their leadership development, the White students' majority status:

> was largely taken for granted ... most of the White students did not identify race until asked about it. Donald, a white male, reflected what many White men in the study shared that: 'Race and gender does sort of make it easier ... People sort of expect you to take on a leadership role.' Angela did not think about how being White and heterosexual helped her, although in reflection, said that it probably did (Komives et al., 2005: 600).

Therefore, in addition to attending to direct statements, terminology that circles around race, and omitted statements that allude to the invisible status of race (DeVault, 1995; Gunaratnam, 2003; Stanfield, 1999); researchers can simply ask participants questions that inquire about racial/ethnic dimensions following their answers or during follow up sessions, including member checking.

To further address analysis/interpretation and validation concerns outlined above, an independent analysis of each group is useful in preventing the natural inclination to contrast members from different cultural groups (Petersen, 2000). Furthermore, a team of diverse researchers can enhance the open and axial coding process by coding a sample of each group separately to facilitate the emergence of cultural contexts and meanings that were overlooked by other members.

The grounded theory researcher can solicit feedback from respondents by having them review and respond to transcripts. Research team members can serve as peer debriefers; team members who are from diverse backgrounds with respect to race, ethnicity, gender, academic discipline, understanding of participants' worldviews, etc., simply increases the opportunities for understanding participants' voices. Because research teams can often be homogeneous or take on the perspective of the lead researcher(s), shoring up one's research team with members from diverse backgrounds with equal status and authority to impact these processes (analysis, interpretation, validation) increases the team's attentiveness to racial/ethnic diversity constructions. Another form of peer review could also constitute inviting diverse colleagues to provide feedback at various points, especially on the evolving theory and interpretations of the data (Komives et al., 2005).

Beyond confirming the accuracy of codes, categories, and the overall theory developed by the grounded theory researcher through the solicitation of respondent feedback (member checking), respondents can potentially have more of a participatory role in both the data analysis and interpretation phases (Charmaz, 2006; Dodson & Schmalzbauer, 2005; Mertens, 2003). Participatory member checking strategies can take the form of either interviews or focus groups. First, the researcher returns to respondents and shares the emerging theory and interpretation by providing written and/or verbal overviews. After sharing, the researcher may use this interaction to confirm, check, refine, or generate new categories/interpretations; conversely the researcher can also aim to uncover what has been overlooked or understated (Charmaz, 2006). To engage respondents in this type of discussion, the researcher should strive to facilitate an exchange where the participants believe that the researcher is open to their knowledge and critique versus simply wanting a rubber stamp because the researcher is not truly open to a collaborative analysis (Dodson & Schmalzbauer, 2005). When there are potentially researcher-respondent racial or ethnic mismatches that can prevent such an optimal interaction, a strong demonstration of openness to collaboration is critical.

Unfortunately, conducting member checking with all respondents, irrespective of their racial/ethnic background, often is not a realistic option due to time constraints, limited resources, the researcher's inability to locate/contact respondents, etc. However, if member checking is conducted, the researcher should attend to who is called upon for feedback. Whenever possible, the researcher should attempt to include feedback from participants of each racial/ethnic group, irrespective of the group's proportional representation in the sample to insure their experiences and voices are not missed or minimized. To solicit feedback from one group and ignore others obviously biases the member checking process. Furthermore, if the researcher has little to no exposure to particular racial and/or ethnic populations represented in the sample, special efforts should be made to include these respondents in member checking to guarantee that the researcher's cultural filter does not overpower the interpretation and overshadow aspects of the respondents' culture, worldview, values, etc., that have a valid place in the analysis/interpretation. Additionally, when the researcher is unable to secure feedback from the original participants, solicitation of feedback from individuals with a similar profile can aid in the validation process, providing another means of debriefing.

In concert with the above strategies (diversifying the research team, calling upon diverse colleagues for feedback, ensuring feedback is solicited from diverse respondents, or inviting a new diverse sample of participants to confirm the interpretation and emerging theory), the literature has several functions throughout the grounded theory research process (Strauss & Corbin, 1998). It serves as means to confirm, validate, extend, or refine findings, essentially adding another voice(s) to the analysis/interpretation and validation processes. When the grounded theory researcher engages in this process one must use care and caution to avoid certain traps with respect to examining diverse populations.

First, the researcher should be careful not to limit the search to publications that fall within the established top-tier of the discipline. Although top-tier journals may publish on topics related to diverse populations, seminal writings on diverse populations are not consistently found in these publications (Stage & Anaya, 1996). Given the likelihood of this occurrence, the researcher should venture out and examine second and third-tier journals, dissertations, and non-technical writings. 'A small but significant body of work [may] ... exist but, in the academic marketplace of salience and citation, many of these works are undervalued' (Stage & Anaya, 1996: xiii).

Second, the researcher should make a concerted effort to include research conducted by diverse scholars. This approach parallels the strategy to invite diverse scholars to provide feedback in peer debriefings. By making a conscious effort to include literature from racially and ethnically diverse scholars and to incorporate scholarship from the respondent's culture (Barnes, 1996), the grounded theory researcher continues to invite additional voices to the interpretation and validation processes while potentially increasing theoretical sensitivity (Strauss & Corbin, 1998).

Last, grounded theory researchers should be aware of cultural deficit orientations and theoretical frameworks that have so often shaped social research on racial/ethnic populations and consequently blame those same populations for their deficiency or deviancy (Mertens, 2003; Stanfield, 1999), while ignoring their voices and experiences. Ultimately, the researcher should be circumspect when adopting literature with deficit model interpretations because such an orientation can potentially steer the researcher away from legitimate concepts that reflect the respondents' experiences while promoting cultural deficit perspectives that distort reality (Cannon, Higginbotham, & Leung, 1988).

Diversity and the written Grounded Theory report

After the grounded theory researcher has worked through the data analysis/interpretation and validation phases, writing up the findings poses another set of options and challenges which revolve around how much the researcher is willing to disclose about the methods undertaken to conduct the study. According to Barnes (1996), if cultural elements such as race and ethnicity are not made explicit, there is the danger of these cultural elements becoming invisible. Studies where diversity is *absent* or *peripheral* are likely to overlook those important cultural elements. Conversely, grounded theory studies with a *complementary* or *primary* emphasis on racial/ethnic diversity report those critical dimensions that inevitably shaped the study. What are those critical dimensions? They are the ones discussed above: orientation to diversity, research questions, data collection, data analysis/interpretation, and validation. Emphasizing rather than de-emphasizing 'the collection, recording, and analysis of data in the context in which it was collected, including the space, actors, time, and feelings of the context' (Barnes, 1996: 439), exposes the cultural conditions under which the data was created and makes the written report an honest record of the research process. For example, researchers could report the race/ethnicity and gender of both researchers and respondents in the study; indicate strategies that were used to make the sample more inclusive or heterogeneous; and record if matching was done between researchers and respondents (Cannon, Higginbotham, & Leung, 1988; Komives et al., 2005).

After sufficiently reporting the methods utilized, how will the study portray the respondents? Although the emphasis is on the emerging theory in a grounded theory study, the findings are grounded in respondents' experiences, worldviews, and perspectives. 'Presenting respondents' voices involves a process of "translation," but much can get lost or corrupted in that process' (Vincent & Warren, 2001: 49). In order to accurately engage in this process of translation, the grounded theory researcher must recognize that the objective form of writing has the danger of losing the respondents' voices. The narrative style should again try to strike a complex balance, incorporating not only academic language, but also interview texts, the researcher's comments on the research process, and contextual information (e.g. history, politics of the day, etc.). An approach of this nature departs from conventional narratives that privilege the expert authority of the researcher and disrupts traditional expectations that also give deference to the researcher (Lather, 1997; Vincent & Warren, 2001).

CONCLUSION

In summary, the changing demographics and corresponding social issues of developed countries provide grounded theory researchers with opportunities to explore diversity phenomena that pertain to new and emerging dynamics within these countries. Although there are contrasting approaches to grounded theory, systematic, emergent, and constructivist, any of the approaches may incorporate diversity in the research process based on four levels of importance: *primary*, *complementary*, *peripheral*, and *absent*. The level of importance is reflected in the research problem and corresponding questions. Aspects of data collection methods, including sampling, positionality of the interviewer, and matching between interviewer and respondent, also provide ways of exploring diversity to a greater degree. The analysis/interpretation and validation research processes allow for several ways to explore diversity, such as independent coding of groups, participatory member checking, utilization of relevant literature that is written by diverse scholars, or diverse colleagues providing feedback. Finally, the written report is said to articulate the theory and interpretation of data while capturing the participants' experiences.

Guidelines for incorporating diversity into Grounded Theory

How does grounded theory need to be improved given a diversity perspective? Here are several guidelines to improve the diversity focus of a grounded theory study for researchers who wish to incorporate diversity. When determining the research problem, the researcher should investigate any legitimate connections the problem has with diversity at the very outset. In turn, the problem will indicate if a *primary*, *complementary*, *peripheral*, or *absent* level of importance is warranted. After a *complementary* or *primary* diversity emphasis is determined, the researcher should construct questions that reflect the extent to which diversity is integral to the study versus constructing questions that avoid the racial/ethnic or cultural context of the study. Before collecting data (i.e. interviews, participant observations) from diverse populations, the researcher is encouraged to take inventory of his/her positionality, a step not often done with grounded theory researchers, but a necessary step to protect against the researcher's biases from overshadowing the respondents' voices. The grounded theory researcher, when selecting respondents for initial and subsequent sampling, should strive to strike a balance between racial/ethnic groups to give voice to all groups. Because the researcher's biases may undermine or de-emphasize diversity during coding, interpretation, or validation processes, the grounded theory researcher can minimize these cultural biases by having a diverse research team involved in the coding process and a diverse group of colleagues for peer debriefings to assist with development of the interpretive narrative. When developing the written grounded theory report, the researcher should strive for a narrative style that presents the respondents' voices and exposes the cultural conditions under which the data was created. These guidelines simply underscore the many opportunities grounded theory researchers have to incorporate diversity into their studies while remaining true to the fundamental aim of the grounded theory approach, which is to develop theory based on field data.

Authors' positionality and future research

The authors' positionality directly informed the writing of this chapter. All four authors are from the USA. The lead author is an African American female and the remaining three authors are European Americans, two male and one female. Living in Midwestern America and working at a doctoral granting university affords the authors an opportunity to be a part of an environment that is said to value racial/ethnic diversity but often enforces policies and practices that contradict these values. This region of the country is experiencing dramatic demographic shifts and the authors recognize that change is taking place; while these shifts seem slow and gradual to some, others see a need for actions that either embrace or shun such changes. In writing this chapter, the goal is to demonstrate how qualitative researchers, like us, can embrace these new demographic shifts and incorporate them into our own work. Furthermore, one of the deficits in our formal educational training is that there was little to no attention paid to how one conducted qualitative studies with racial/ethnic minorities or diverse populations in order to capture their experiences versus objectifying the findings and presenting the researcher as an expert. Although the expectation to bring their voices to the forefront was always there, very little direction in terms of methods was ever given. Philosophical writings have consistently provided a solid foundation for qualitative researchers in their work exploring phenomena linked to racially/ethnically diverse populations. In response, the authors' view is that more discussion is needed regarding methods to make this type of work more accessible to researchers like ourselves, especially in light of demographic trends in the USA, along with phenomena in other countries that are greatly influenced by social issues of race/ethnicity and culture.

Future research on diversity and qualitative methods is needed to explore the usefulness of the principles and practices discussed in this chapter. Since key aspects of the research process were emphasized in this discussion, using grounded theory to illustrate steps of that process, future research using phenomenology, case study, and narrative traditions are needed to expand the application of this diversity framework. Doing so will aid in demonstrating and articulating how diversity can be incorporated into methods that are tradition-specific.

REFERENCES

Abrahamsson, K. H., Berggren, U., Hallberg, L., & Carlsson, S. G. (2002). Dental phobic patients' view of dental anxiety and experiences in dental care: A qualitative study. *Scandinavian Journal of Caring Sciences*, 16, 188–196.

Andersen, M. (1993). Studying across difference: Race, class, and gender in qualitative research. In John H. Stanfield II and Rutledge M. Dennis (Eds.), *Race and ethnicity in research methods*. Newbury Park, CA: SAGE, pp. 39–52.

Barnes, D. M. (1996). An analysis of the grounded theory method and the concept of culture. *Qualitative Health Research*, 6 (3), 429–441.

Cannon, L. W., Higginbotham, E., & Leung, M. L. A. (1988). Race and class bias in qualitative research on women. *Gender & Society*, 2 (4), 449–462.

Charmaz, K. (2006). *Constructing grounded theory: A practical guide through qualitative analysis*. London: SAGE.

Chun, K. M., & Chesla, C. A. (2004). Cultural issues in disease management for Chinese Americans with type 2 diabetes. *Psychology and Health*, 19, 767–785.

Clarke, A. E. (2005). *Situational analysis: Grounded theory after the postmodern turn*. Thousand Oaks, CA: SAGE.

Creswell, J. W. (1998). *Qualitative inquiry and research design: Choosing among five traditions*. Thousand Oaks, CA: SAGE.

Creswell, J. W. (2005). *Educational research: Planning, conducting, and evaluating quantitative and qualitative research*, 2nd edition. Upper Saddle River, NJ: Pearson Merrill Prentice Hall.

DeVault, M. (1995). Ethnicity and expertise: Racial-ethnic knowledge in sociological research. *Gender and Society*, 9 (5), 612–631.

Dodson, L., & Schmalzbauer, L. (2005). Poor mothers and habits of hiding: Participatory methods in poverty research. *Journal of Marriage and Family*, 67, 949–959.

Glaser, B. G. (1992). *Basics of grounded theory analysis: Emergence vs. forcing*. Mill Valley, CA: The Sociology Press.

Glaser, B. G., & Strauss, A. L. (1967). *The discovery of grounded theory: Strategies for qualitative research.* Chicago: Aldine Publishing Company.

Goulding, C. (2002). *Grounded theory: A practical guide for management, business and market researchers.* Thousand Oaks, CA: SAGE.

Green, D. O., & Trent, W. (2005). The public good and a racially diverse democracy. In A. Kezar, T. Chambers, & J. Burkhardt (Eds.), *Higher education for the public good: Emerging voices from a national movement.* San Francisco, CA: Jossey-Bass, pp. 102–123.

Gunaratnam, Y. (2003). *Researching 'race' and ethnicity: Methods, knowledge and power.* London: SAGE.

Komives, S., Owen, J. E., Longerbeam, S. D., Mainella, F. C., & Osteen, L. (2005). Developing a leadership identity: A grounded theory. *Journal of College Student Development,* 46 (6), 593–611.

Larson, C. (1997). Re-presenting the subject: Problems in personal narrative inquiry. *Qualitative Studies in Education,* 10 (4), 455–469.

Lather, P. (1997). Drawing the lines at angles: Working the ruins of feminist ethnography. *Qualitative Studies in Education,* 10 (3), 285–304.

Law, I., Phillips, D., & Turney, L. (Eds.) (2004). *Institutional racism in higher education.* Stoke on Trent: Trentham Books.

Mertens, D. M. (2003). Mixed methods and the politics of human research: The transformative-emancipatory perspective. In A. Tashakkori and C. Teddlie (Eds.), *Handbook of mixed methods in social & behavioral research.* Thousand Oaks, CA: SAGE, pp. 135–164.

Morrow, S. L., Rakhsha, G., & Castaneda, C. L. (2001). Qualitative research methods for multicultural counseling. In J. G. Ponterotto, J. M. Casas, L. A. Suzuki, & C. M. Alexander (Eds.), *Handbook of multicultural counseling,* 2nd edition. Thousand Oaks, CA: SAGE, pp. 575–603.

National Research Council. (2002). *Scientific research in education.* Committee on Scientific Principles for Education Research (R. J. Shavelson & L. Towne, Eds.). Center for Education. Division of Behavioral and Social Sciences and Education. Washington, DC: National Academy Press.

Petersen, S. (2000). Multicultural perspective on middle-class women's identity development. *Journal of Counseling & Development,* 78, 63–71.

Pillow, W. (2003). Race-based methodologies multicultural methods or epistemological shifts? In G. R. Lopez and L. Parker (Eds.), *Interrogating racism in qualitative research methodology.* New York: Peter Lang, pp. 181–202.

RAND. (2000). *Global shifts in population.* (Research Brief No. 5044). Santa Monica, CA: Author. Retrieved May 2, 2006, from http://www.rand.org/pubs/research_briefs/RB5044/index1.html

Rhoads, R. (1997). Crossing sexual orientation borders: Collaborative strategies for dealing with issues of positionality and representation. *International Journal of Qualitative Studies in Education,* 10 (1), 7–23.

Richie, B. S., Fassinger, R. E., Linn, S. G., Johnson, J., Prosser, J., & Robinson, S. (1997). Persistence, connection, and passion: A qualitative study of the career development of highly achieving African American-black and white women. *Journal of Counselling Psychology,* 44 (2), 133–148.

Ridgeway, R. T., & Tylka, T. L. (2005). College men's perceptions of ideal body composition and shape. *Psychology of Men & Masculinity,* 6, 209–220.

Stage, F., & Anaya, G. (1996). Transformational view of college student research. In B. A. Jones (ASHE Reader Series Ed.) and F. Stage, G. Anaya, J. Bean, D. Hossler, & G. Kuh (Vol. Eds.), *College students: The evolving nature of research.* Needham Heights, MA: Simon & Schuster Custom Publishing, pp. xi–xxii.

Stanfield, J. H. II. (1994). Ethnic modeling in qualitative research. In N. Denzin and Y. Lincoln (Eds.), *Handbook of qualitative research methods*. Thousand Oaks, CA: SAGE, pp. 175–188.

Stanfield, J. H. II. (1999). Slipping through the front door: Relevant social scientific evaluation in the people of color century. *American Journal of Evaluation*, 20 (3), 415–432.

Stewart, C. J., & Cash, W. B. (2006). *Interviewing: Principles and practices,* 11th edition. New York: McGraw-Hill.

Strauss, A., & Corbin, J. (1998). *Basics of qualitative research: Techniques and procedures for developing grounded theory*, 2nd edition. Thousand Oaks, CA: SAGE.

Sue, D. W., & Sue, D. (2003). *Counseling the culturally diverse: Theory and practice*, 4th edition. New York: John Wiley & Sons.

Vincent, C., & Warren, S. (2001). 'This won't take long …': interviewing, ethics and diversity. *Qualitative Studies in Education*, 14 (1), 39–53.

23

Advancing Ethnographic Research through Grounded Theory Practice

Stefan Timmermans and Iddo Tavory

In its 40 years of influence, grounded theory has shed its origins in ethnography to turn into a versatile method of qualitative analysis. Grounded theory originally emerged out of Glaser and Strauss's death and dying ethnographic study in the San Francisco Bay area. Their main publication *Awareness of Dying* (Glaser and Strauss 1965) was a tremendously successful book:[1] it foreshadowed the emergence of the influential labeling theory, produced a collection of concepts that became part of the sociological canon, influenced a crystallization of late modern unease with the medicalization of the dying process, prompted change in how terminal patients were informed about the prognosis of their disease, and constituted a prime example of the application of a systematic ethnographic methodology. These methodological principles were further explicated in the polemical *Discovery of Grounded Theory* (Glaser and Strauss 1967) with the aim of legitimizing fieldwork in service of theory construction by articulating and formalizing its scientific principles ('rigorous' was the codeword of the desired methodological quality), while simultaneously taking a shot at the weakening role of ethnography in American sociology.

In the 1960s, Glaser and Strauss proposed that sociologists build theory from the ground up through systematic conceptualization and constant comparisons with similar and distinct research areas. Theories grounded in substantive areas could then lead, through further abstraction, to formal theories of social life.

They addressed the threats of three kinds of marginalization of qualitative and sociological research: theoretical marginalization with grand theorists spinning theories and looking for straightforward empirical verification, methodological marginalization with qualitative research delegated to producing hypotheses to be tested by statistical quantitative methodologies, and finally marginalization from within referring to well-known qualitative researchers who conducted (in the opinion of Glaser and Strauss) unsystematic, non-theoretical research. *Discovery of Grounded Theory* was part epistemology, part political manifesto, part methodology, part symbolic interactionist theory. In the heydays of Parsonian and Mertonian functionalist theorizing, the boom in social survey research, and C. Wright Mills's alleged empirically unfounded writings, the book became a research standard in the traditional sense of a powerful rallying point for an alternative social science. Moreover, while most of the examples were drawn from ethnographic studies, the book was more ambitious; it asserted a way of practicing sociology for all social scientists, both qualitative and quantitative.

A keyword search in databases of sociological publications suggests that grounded theory did not become the dominant qualitative methodology until the late 1980s when Strauss published *Qualitative Analysis for Social Scientists* (Strauss 1987) and Strauss and Corbin issued the user-friendly *Basics of Qualitative Research* (Strauss and Corbin 1990). As the titles suggest, both books were foremost methodology books. They pushed the formalization of qualitative methods hinted at in the *Discovery of Grounded Theory* to new levels with research paradigms, analytical matrices, different levels of coding, and systematic memo writing. Key methodological ideas such as theoretical sampling and theoretical saturation also gained prominence. Previously, grounded theory methodological practice was largely spread through apprenticeship and workshops in San Francisco but these books made it possible for researchers not trained by Glaser or Strauss to practice grounded theory. The methods also diffused through their incorporation in data analysis software programs, especially ATLAS.ti which was explicitly modeled after a grounded theory analysis but including other programs such as NVivo, Transana, and MaxQDA which also facilitate and speed up the different steps of coding and memo writing (Coffey, Holbrook, and Atkinson 1996; Dey 1999). In contrast, alternative approaches to qualitative data analysis such as analytic induction and the extended case method do not lend themselves to easy computerization. Consequently, grounded theory has turned into a normative methodological standard in the sense of a paradigmatic set of scientific assumptions proclaiming how qualitative analysis should be done. It forms the model of normal science to be improved and updated by new generations of researchers (Charmaz 2006; Clarke 2005; Devault 1995; Snow, Morrill, and Anderson 2003) or to be contested and dismissed by others (Burawoy 1998; Wacquant 2002). Over time, the link with ethnography has been considerably loosened: grounded theory is now first and foremost a systematic qualitative data analysis approach. In its most diluted form, mentioning grounded theory in a methods section functions as a placeholder for a systematic approach of a thematic qualitative analysis, glossing over opposing aims of various versions of grounded theory (Dey 1999).

Grounded theory has weathered and changed tremendously since the 1960s. Where grounded theory once constituted a positivistic model of qualitative science moored in a symbolic interactionist sensitivity to the world, it is now often utilized as a flexible and versatile data analysis technique. While its origins were ethnographic, many leading practitioners and advocates of grounded theory no longer conduct ethnographies but conduct archival research, in-depth interviews, or focus groups. This trend raises the question of grounded theory's continued relevance for ethnography.

We distinguish three tensions between ethnography and grounded theory in its current methodological incorporation. First, what is the 'ground' in ethnography? In-depth interviews, focus groups, and archival materials offer ready-made materials but ethnography puts a great premium on writing down one's own observations. The data input surely impacts the analytical output, however Glaser and Strauss and many of their followers remain quiet about the raw material of ethnography. Addressing the issue of 'ground' in ethnography means to revitalize the pragmatic and symbolic interactionist theoretical underpinnings of grounded theory. Second, what is the place of 'theory' in ethnography? Inductively creating theory that fits one's data and at the same time contributing to the corpus of sociological theorizing has long been a source of misunderstanding among grounded theorists. Many are sent into the field with little theoretical baggage and often return with little to show. If the role of theory in ethnographic work is taken to be an important one, as indeed it was for Glaser and Strauss, an appropriate balance between grounding theory and the theoretical literature remains to be articulated. Third, does grounded theory lead to better ethnographies? Here, we use the criteria researchers have suggested to evaluate ethnographies in the aftermath of the reflexive turn in ethnographic writing to understand whether a grounded theory influenced ethnography enhances the research quality. While sympathetic to grounded theory, our approach is ultimately pragmatic. As Glaser and Strauss emphasized, methodologies should be evaluated for whether they 'work' for researchers. Our aim is not to distill an essential grounded theory approach but to evaluate the usefulness of grounded theory to conduct the best ethnographies possible.

SHIFTING GROUNDS

Glaser and Strauss obfuscated the ethnographic origins of their methodology to produce a generic sociological, and later qualitative, methodology. In this and the next sections, we will retrieve some of the key advantages of grounded theory's ethnographic past for contemporary ethnographers. Glaser and Strauss paid little attention to the process of gathering ethnographic material or the quality of ethnographic data. In grounded theory, as in much of the early Chicago School sociology, there was nothing special that distinguished fieldwork from other research. Yet, the origins in fieldwork and the centrality of social interaction have made it a good methodological and theoretical fit for an ethnographic research engagement.

In essence, grounded theory presents an analytical choreography with a deep immersion in data and then a transcendence of this data to reach higher levels of abstraction. If performed well, the resulting dance emerges from lived experiences, actions, observations, and conversations while simultaneously engaging in a conceptually dense and theoretically abstract writing. Grounded theory methodology contains pointers on where to find data, how to sharpen one's observational sensibilities, and how to gradually make the step from the pages of jotted notes to the final manuscript. Grounded theory's greatest benefit may well be that it forces researchers to become acquainted with their own data in order to decide which of the many painstakingly gathered materials can be safely put aside. Even with the recent rush of computer programs, there is no shortcut for really getting to know one's data inside out. Thirteen months into a 3-year study, the discipline imposed by coding word-by-word, line-by-line, paragraph-by-paragraph, even observation-by-observation, pays analytical dividends. The tedious process of asking 'what is this really about?' may generate an almost intuitive sense of observational relevance, as new observations tweak or upset the emerging analytical scheme.[2]

Grounded theory allows researchers to distinguish with confidence between the noise and music in one's data. But how does grounded theory help with deciding what kind of data to gather in the first place? Here exists a distinction between ethnographic observations based on participation in a setting and focus group and in-depth interview data. Viewed on a continuum of the role of the researcher in generating data, the latter are closer to traditional 'data' (things that are given) while the former resembles what was called 'capta' (things that are seized; Rock 2001: 31). Interviewing, whether structured or unstructured, is an almost foolproof strategy to obtain useable empirical materials. If researchers interview 30 to 50 people about something these respondents care about, they are basically guaranteed to find analytically captivating narratives. Certainly, one or two interviews will be useless, interviewing fits certain topics better than others, and asking pertinent questions and developing a sense of conversation seems to come more easily to some people than to others (Weiss 1994) but interviewing is generally an easily taught skill, especially when probing and handling difficult questions is practiced and reviewed in video taped training sessions. Once the interview is transcribed, the text neatly captures experience in the respondent's own words (see Atkinson and Silverman, 1997, for a critique of the 'interview society'). Interviewing also allows the researcher to build in 'demographic controls' in the research design and sits well with funding organizations.

Ethnography is more challenging. More than in interviewing, ethnography requires a personal transformation from the researcher to view the world as capta to be obtained. Compared to the clean auditory quality of an interview, observations are steeped in sensory overload (Anspach 1993). They are messy and often tripped up by the vagaries of personal relationships. Ethnography is not about establishing rapport but about living rapport where every step one takes may preclude others, sometimes with disastrous results for the research project (Casper 1998; Goode 2002). Indeed, quite a few ethnographies fail and others remain marginal studies.

Why, then, do ethnography? The short answer is that it is a methodology ideally suited to understand interaction and interaction is at the heart of most social science research (Collins 2005). The choice for a methodology is often presented as the proverbial hammer making everything look like nails, but, at the same time, every hammer also selects for particular nails. Every methodology implies a range of phenomena of interest in social life and a range of potential explanations.

Ethnography selects for interaction and the interpretation of such interactions in their naturalistic unfolding, it aims to learn about how and why people behave, think, and make meaning as they do in the daily unfolding of life. Common to the many variations of ethnography in sociology and anthropology is the commitment to reconstruct the actor's own world-view faithful to the everyday life of research subjects (Hammersley and Atkinson 1983). When observing how actions evolve over time and change situations or when experiencing the corporeal sense of acting in the world, ethnographers have an opportunity to explain the collective patterning of social life. In contrast to researchers searching for Durkheimian social facts that pattern collective behavior but remain out of the cognitive reach of individuals, ethnographers tend to give credence to the practical knowledge that people use to guide their own actions, though they may transcend this local knowledge and reach conclusions surprising to the community they study. More than any other research method, ethnography allows entering the lifeworld of others and observing how they make sense of the world around them.

Grounded theory offers not only a methodological but also a theoretical fit between ethnography and interaction. Adele Clarke refers to grounded theory/symbolic interactionism as a methods/theory package (Clarke 2005). Anselm Strauss has noted that 'grounded theory methodology ... evolved out of ... the complexity of *interaction and interactional forms* that we were studying as played out in the care of dying patients' (Strauss 1993: 5). Indeed, embedded in the methodology are pragmatist and symbolic interactionist assumptions about social life. As Strauss confirmed in *Continual Permutations of Action* (1993), underlying the various substantive research projects he undertook over his career was a pragmatist-influenced theory of interaction. This theory rested on the assumption that actions are necessarily embodied. When interacting, people enact who they are; they reflexively and purposefully develop identities over time linking past, present, and imaginary future. Their actions carry meanings that may implicate other people not immediately present, or broader social ares not immediately apparent. The social world in all its cultural and structural diversity is thus created and re-created through interaction voiding the distinctions between internal and external worlds, or micro and macro levels of analysis. Important for ethnography, symbolic interactionism embraces the Meadian notion that especially in problematic interactions people take the perspective of others in order to make sense of the world (Berger and Luckmann 1966; Mead 1938; Snow 2001). By studying people doing things together, we can thus discern how they, often on a taken-for-granted level, act on the perceptions of others to order the social world. These basic assumptions allow interactionists to study how identities develop in various work settings, how order is achieved in settings from face-to-face interactions to social arenas, and how bodies, language and emotions permeate behavior and shape biographies.

Being present as interactions unfold and observe or experience first-hand how meanings evolve and are adjusted to shifting situations, the 'hard-won personal experiences' of ethnography (Glaser and Strauss 1967: 255) provide better empirical material than asking respondents to retrospectively reflect on past events or questioning them about their general attitudes. Indeed, grounded theorists are convinced that sociological concepts risk losing their relevance to research subjects if they are not embedded in people's lived experience and are not continuously tested in the world. In spite of offering an alternative scientific method to verification, Glaser and Strauss developed a methodology of verifying-while-you-go-along throughout the research process. Concepts and theoretical insights are perpetual works in progress, demanding further modification and elaboration in new research projects. Building a theoretical understanding of the world constitutes the work practices of a living community of researchers looking for new comparisons and novel research sites. Consequently, long-time everyday immersion in a research site is a necessary condition for the development of grounded theories. Researchers gain the ability to theorize through participation as social actors in the settings they work in. They learn through missteps when others correct them, or when they self-consciously reflect on smooth interactional accomplishments.

Grounded theory attempts to capture the open-ended, creative, situated, and selective character of ethnographic research while orienting researchers with methodological pointers toward interaction. As Strauss and Corbin put it:

> Grounded theory is an *action/interactional oriented method of theory building*. Whether one is studying individuals, groups, or collectives, there is action/interaction, which is directed at managing, handling, carrying out, responding to a phenomenon as it exists in context or under a specific set of perceived conditions. The interactional component refers to self as well as other interaction (Strauss and Corbin 1990: 104, italics in original).

Strauss and Corbin recommend that researchers pay attention to the processual character of actions, their purpose, and intervening conditions. They encourage researchers to document successful and failed interactions and explore how both lead to interactional consequences, providing the conditions for further change. They admonish researchers to explore conditions of interaction at various levels to delineate causality and contextual factors. Processes emerge when snapshots of action and interaction are linked together.

Grounded theory's iterative movement between gathering and analysing fits the gradual socialization process typical of an ethnography much better than any other research method. Ironically, much of ethnography utilizing grounded theorizing does not lead to 'new' theories but to conceptual variations of well-established interpretive sociology themes. Over the last decades, social psychological research on selves and identities has lost some momentum (but see Charmaz 1991) and research on emotions and embodiment has gained importance. Other concepts such as careers and trajectories seem to have an enduring saliency (Mamo 1999; Timmermans 1994). Nevertheless, grounded theory and ethnography meet around the concern of interaction with grounded theory providing not just a methodology to analyze interaction but also suggesting orienting theoretical principles to draw out interactional processes.

HOW ABOUT THEORY?

Grounded theory methods leave the novice ethnographer in confused awe. Students are often encouraged to enter the field site with little theoretical preparation or predetermined theoretical notions. Some are told that, in ethnography, the only ground that counts is the empirical realities of the field. Students are then advised to build up theory from observations, looking for salient themes, analyzing while they go along without being sidetracked with what others have written. At first sight, the grounded theory books seem to support this well-intentioned but ultimately misguided advice:

> In our approach we collect the data in the field first. Then start analysing it and generating theory. When the theory seems sufficiently grounded and developed, *then* we review the literature in the field and relate the theory to it through integration of ideas (Glaser 1978: 31).

It is exactly such stereotypical interpretation of the role of induction in grounded theory that allows Wacquant to dismiss the approach as an 'epistemological fairy tale' (Wacquant 2002: 1481) and offers Michael Burawoy the straw-man argument to propose the extended case method as alternative to grounded theory. Instead of induction, Burawoy suggests that 'We begin with our favorite theory but seek not confirmations but refutations that inspire us to deepen that theory' (Burawoy 1998: 16). In Burawoy's reading, grounded theory (and the entire Chicago School inspired tradition of ethnography) is hopelessly positivistic and misses the 'real' historical social forces and structuration of capitalism, the endless struggle between haves and have-nots in new configurations in a global economy (Burawoy 2000). Curiously, while Burawoy recommends extending theories through verification and refutation, these underlying social forces are often 'outside the realm of investigation' (Burawoy 1998) and thus unperceivable to the people studied. Only the neo-Marxist ethnographer has the vision to impose these preconceived notions on the data. Taken to its logical conclusion, the extended case researcher does not need to bother with research since empirical verification is subservient to the veracity of a theory long ago established by Marx and elaborated by Gramsci.

A careful reading of grounded theory methods actually provides a middle way between using data to illustrate 'your favorite theory' and adhering to the naïve assumption of entering the field completely devoid of theory. Historically, Glaser and Strauss's focus on induction reflects their historical commitment of battling the greater problem of a social science that was geared only toward verifying or falsifying grand (functionalist and Marxist) theories. This trend within social science, exemplified by the work of Robert Merton, delegated empirical research to a secondary position in sociological analysis. In line with the Vienna circle and Popper's philosophy of science, the role of empirical research was construed as either coming up with a 'verification' of an extant theory or else trying to disprove pre-given theories according to the principle of external falsification. Positing themselves against the sentiment that delegated fieldwork to a secondary place in theory building, Glaser and Strauss did not stress the role of pre-existing theory. Reading grounded theory carefully, however, the premise of the ideal researcher as Locke's tabula rasa is shattered. In fact, Glaser and Strauss noted in the opening pages of their original grounded theory book that theoretical study is inevitable and essential for conducting any form of research (Glaser and Strauss 1967: 3). Indeed, they recognized that it would be impossible to contribute to sociological scholarship without having an in-depth familiarity with this literature. Researchers inevitably move between immersion in an empirical world and a conceptual world full of abstractions and theories.

What, then, is the difference between reaching the field to test one's theory and the project of grounded theory? One answer takes us back to the Popperian idea of falsification, though through a more sophisticated route. According to Popper (1963), the gold standard of verification is untenable in science. A scientist might perhaps show that a theory yielded the foreseen results in a given field, but to reach out from the specific result to a general truth is an infinitely long project in which one can always imagine one more variation. The search for universal truths is thus impossible. Instead, Popper posited refutation as the hallmark of science. According to this view, theories cannot even be modified with further research, as is usually proposed within a framework of a 'conventionalist twist,' adding more caveats and modifications if the theory does not account for its dismal failure to predict the social future (Popper 1963). However, falsification can be obtained in two different ways. First, falsification can be achieved by comparing a pre-conceived theory with a series of empirical findings, recognizing that one will never attain the actual gold standard of verification, and actively trying to debunk the theory the researcher or other have created. According to this scheme, it is enough to have one finding which is not in line with the theory to reject the theory in general. This 'external refutation' would be congruous with the way the grand theorists of the 1950s and 1960s have viewed fieldwork as a site for hypothesis testing where no new theory is generated.

A second way to use the Popperian principle of falsification is much closer to the way grounded theory proceeds. Here, falsification works as a continual and internal method aiding discovery and theory building. According to such a method, the scientist constantly comes up with micro-theories arising from empirical materials. However, instead of being content with the formation of these theories, the researcher then attempts to actively look for cases that might not fit the theory, an instance of falsification adopted by grounded theory in the format of 'theoretical sampling.'[3] Both grounded theory and analytic induction thus aim for a theory of causality through continuous internal falsification, but unlike the external falsification method, the theory is not rejected as a whole but results in a streamlining of both the phenomenon studied and the social theory posited, or put differently, in a continuous process of creating a fit between explanans and explanandum.

The difference between these two versions of falsification may look marginal, yet it critically changes the way analysis proceeds. Historian Carlo Ginzburg views methodology as an opening sequence in a chess game.[4] When one begins a game, the first and seemingly insignificant moves on the board constrain later actions. Although these opening moves may seem a mere prelude to the serious chess contest, and although many different game plays can be derived from a single opening, there is an internal constraint (a direction) that the openings make possible. Ginzburg transposes the metaphor of the chess opening to the historical method: different research decisions taken almost without thought can bring about a very different telling of the same story, a different history. Much as the chess opening of historical method constrains the histories produced by researchers, different methodologies of qualitative analysis point the ethnographer in very different trajectories of research, producing different accounts.

These different trajectories do not necessarily follow conscious epistemological and ontological standpoints. Rather, the differences in the end product result from the different openings and systems of interpretation balancing the empirical and the theoretical. Where a deductive theory starts with one's 'favorite theory' and proceeds to modify or falsify it, the grounded theory inevitably starts with an arsenal of stock sociological notions of identity, community, order, and change, but, and this is crucial, grounds the precise meaning and conceptual relevance of these terms in the research. We provide two examples of the different theoretical yields of grounded theory: a study of adolescence in high risk neighborhoods conducted by Linda M. Burton (Burton 1997) and Richard Mitchell's study of survivalism (Charmaz and Mitchell 2001; Mitchell 2001).

Burton starts her grounded theory study of adolescents in high-risk neighborhoods with the observation that these neighborhoods have 'high crime and poverty rates, environmental hazards, geographic isolation, residential instability, inadequate housing, low-quality schooling, and scarce social services and economic resources' (Burton 1997: 209). Each of these descriptors stands in for a library of sociological scholarship and theorizing. Should a grounded theorist enter the field with even a rudimentary presumption of a high-risk neighborhood? If Burton took these neighborhood statistics and sociological constructs at face value, she risked forcing other people's ideas in her study. However, rather than reifying these descriptors, Burton left the causal ties between the high-risk neighborhood and adolescent social practice open for analysis. There are few analytical assumptions tied to the notion that in some neighborhoods adolescents face different odds than in other neighborhoods; this is an observable phenomenon, not a causal and deterministic pre-conception. The important empirical question is how these differences express themselves and can be explained. Similarly, Burton's decision to focus on adolescents is tacitly based on an extensive social science literature of the liminality of adolescence in Western culture; this age group faces similar challenges about school, work, sexuality, relationships, and gaining independence. From a grounded theory perspective, this limitation by age risks reifying 'adolescence' as a homogeneous analytic category and, indeed, Burton, spent much time articulating the meaning of adolescence in her study.

Burton's analytical project consists of investigating the social processes by which neighborhood characteristics lead to higher risks. She spent 5 years of participant observation in the field, conducted 186 in-depth interviews with adolescents and other social agents in the field, ran several focus groups, and provided a content analysis of documents (Burton 1995). Burton does not interpret risk a priori in any fixed urban sociological sense but instead closely observes adolescents' actions and interpretations. After coding, she highlights three central experiences that distinguish adolescence in high-risk neighborhoods: an accelerated life course, diffuse age hierarchies, and inconsistent role expectations between families and other social institutions (Burton 1997: 210). The traditional view of adolescence as a period of liminality pervaded the school setting. At home, however, adolescents were expected to carry out general 'adult responsibilities,' and are not expected to live in an Eriksonian psychological moratorium in which responsibilities are suspended. Similarly, the boundaries between adolescence and adulthood largely evaporated: old age, as one interviewee put it, meant 'stressed, sick, broke and broken hearted' (Burton 1997: 213).

This use of grounded theory allowed Burton to formulate a mid-range theory accounting for different choices and actions taken by adolescents in high-risk neighborhoods, not through a constant referral to the literature, but primarily through the issues and actions of agents in the field. To return to the issue of the starting point in ethnographic studies, it might seem that both of the ways of research, starting from one's favorite theory and grounded theory, could yield similar results. But this is not the case. While Burton was aware of and ultimately contributes to the extant theories in the field, these external verifications and refutations were only secondary to her study. Had she opened her 'chess game' with the aim of theory refutation, her field of vision may have been unduly narrowed and she may have missed the different formulations of adolescence in different social institutions such as the family and the school.

A very different use of grounded theory emerged from Mitchell's study of the survivalist movement in the USA. In his book *Dancing at Armageddon*, Mitchell tried to unravel the meaning of survivalism as it is lived by the members of the movement rather than imagined by the critics of the movement. Withholding judgement on the meaning of survivalism, Mitchell demystified the movement and simultaneously constructed an alternative theoretical explanation for belonging to survivalism as a means for empowerment while drawing from the surrounding culture. Thus, instead of psychologizing the unmet and troubled mental needs of survivalists (as other academics have done), Mitchell explored how members construct meaning in their everyday 'survivalist' lives.

As in most books, Mitchell was not very explicit about his use of the grounded theory (but see Charmaz and Mitchell 2001). Still, his book exemplified the analytical pay-off of relying on a grounded theory. Much of survivalist scholarship had focused on the content of survivalist literature and emphasized the elaborate violent and racist imagery. Mitchell showed, however, that such a priori assumptions about the use of text are misplaced among survivalists. As Mitchell described the pamphlets, 'They offered plentiful opportunities for theorizing, "reading," and textual analysis. They were also quite misleading' (Mitchell 2001: 57). Instead, Mitchell shows how these texts are artfully used by survivalists as resources in the fabrication of culture, empowering otherwise marginal social actors to produce culture, rather than passively accepting wide social definitions of culture and future.

The conclusions of an ethnographic study thus depend upon the opening stances of the theorist. Whether describing adolescents in high-risk neighborhoods or survivalists in contemporary USA, the basic theoretical agnosticism (but not atheism, see Henwood and Pidgeon 2003) of grounded theorists sensitizes the research to a fine tuning and breaking of the common explanations of social phenomena, which posit the theory before entering the field. It would have been much harder to underplay the place of the text or deconstruct the unified meaning of adolescence if their meanings were posited beforehand, instead of reached at through coding of the relevant categories in the field. Both Burton and Mitchell are well versed in theory, positing their conclusions against and in relation to other theories of the field. However, knowledge of theory does not necessarily imply its primordial use, sociology is not a uni-paradigmatic science, and competing theories and depictions proliferate in the literature. Grounded theorists read and learn these theories before, while, and after their work in the field. However, they do not subscribe to any of them a priori (but may during or after their study guided by their empirical findings), sensitive not only to the different positions, but also to the cracks between the theories, the spaces in literature, as well as in the field itself where the taken for granted categories of sociology are broken, and where theory indeed does emerge from the ground up.

DOES GROUNDED THEORY LEAD TO BETTER ETHNOGRAPHY?

The question whether grounded theory results in better ethnographies is surprisingly difficult to answer, in part because so few ethnographers explicitly align with grounded theory and those few who do vary tremendously in their commitment to grounded theory. Although many ethnographers cite Glaser and Strauss as methodological inspirations, few scholars explicitly side with practicing the grounded theory method. In methodological appendices, the work of sifting through notes and developing concepts is not as exciting as recounting how one gained the trust of gang members or made missteps while navigating the intricate professional relationships in a newborn intensive care unit. While researchers have paid attention in ethnomethodological fashion to the everyday political, pragmatic, ethical, and etiquette decisions that influence ethnographic research in the field, they tend to stop short at the intertwining of methodology and analysis (Anspach 1993). Methodological appendices tend to be defensive, elaborate generic research problems, or remain confessional (Van Maanen 1988). In addition, we suspect that few ethnographers see the usefulness of diligently coding and writing analytical memos over several years. Grounded theory may work better to get a first analytical grip on one's research rather than for extensively analyzing long-term data. Consequently, many ethnographic studies traveling under the grounded theory flag offer preciously little analytical density. The principle of theoretical sampling is also difficult to achieve in a time of stringent IRB (Institutional Review Board) and HIPAA (Health Insurance Portability and Accountability Act) regulations where every change in a research protocol requires an addendum to the originally approved application. Theoretical saturation, another one of grounded theory's key methodological notions, also remains in the eye of the beholder. Some researchers claim to experience repetition after talking to a handful of respondents. Therefore, many researchers vaguely note working in the grounded theory 'tradition' rather than signing on to all the tenets of the methodology in ethnography.

Nonetheless, grounded theory ethnographies purport to be different from generic qualitative studies. As Kathy Charmaz summarizes, 'Grounded theory ethnography gives priority to the studied *phenomenon* or *process*—rather than to a description of a setting. Thus, from the beginnings of their fieldwork, grounded theory ethnographers study what is happening in the setting and make a *conceptual* rendering of these actions' (Charmaz 2006: 22, italics in original). In contrast to other ethnographies, grounded theory ethnographies tend to be more analytical than descriptive, engaged in middle-ground conceptualizations rather than grand theorizing, and take a processual rather than structural approach.

An additional problem to answering the question of whether grounded theory leads to better ethnographies is that the criteria of good ethnographies remain controversial. For researchers working in the extended case method tradition, a good ethnography constitutes a political intervention into the world it seeks to comprehend and should thus be evaluated on its potential for social change.

Auto-ethnographers and researchers writing experimental ethnographic texts influenced by postmodern thinking evaluate ethnographic texts, among many other criteria, with their potential to substantively contribute to the understanding of social life, aesthetic merit, reflexivity, impact, and verisimilitude (Denzin 2003; Richardson 2000). Like most researchers, realist ethnographers tend to evaluate qualitative research on its ability to make a substantive contribution to empirical knowledge and/or advancement of theory (Ambert, Adler, Adler, and Detzner 1995). By design, ethnographies score low on measures of external validity; generalizability is typically sacrificed for the depth of a singular study, but internal validity can be enhanced with transparency of methods and triangulation of perspectives and data sources (Murphy and Dingwall 2003). Despite a long search for alternative criteria, credibility in ethnography foremost rests on the authority of having been in a field for long periods of time. Ethnographic authority consists of knowing what one talks about, and such knowledge reflects having been there when events unfolded. As Goffman explains, observation as a way of life leads to personal transformation, a virtual embodiment of the other; '[As a good ethnographer], you should feel you could settle down and forget about being a sociologist. The members of the opposite sex should become attractive to you. You should be able to engage in the same body rhythms, rate of movement, tapping of the feet, that sort of thing, as the people around you' (Goffman 1989: 129).

Does grounded theory, then, contribute to better theories and substantive contributions? We believe that because of the emphasis on thinking conceptually and working towards theory building, grounded theory can indeed enhance ethnographic work. Grounded theory was created in reaction against feeble qualitative work that excelled at description but made few substantive theoretical points. Ethnographic grounded theory may be able to invoke the lifeworld of others while also achieving a level of conceptual abstraction that provides sociological significance beyond the substantive area of study. An excellent example of a grounded-theory oriented ethnography is Daniel Chambliss's study of ethical problems in nursing (Chambliss 1996). Chambliss argues that moral problems are structurally part of the unique division of labor and power differences in hospitals. Nurses experience opposing demands to care for patients and perform highly technical tasks. Their specific orientation often conflicts with the priorities of others such as hospital administrators or physicians. Some of these recurring professional conflicts will be considered 'ethical.' Designating a problem as ethical serves to decontextualize the organizational production of conflicts and shifts the conflict to ethically sanctioned values such as patient autonomy. The inevitable objectification of patients and the fact that people routinely die in hospitals form repetitive battlegrounds for clashes with institutional priorities and demands. Chambliss works in the deep conceptual tradition of grounded theory. His first chapter on the routine nature of nursing work, for example, can be mapped concept by concept. Working from Everett Hughes's distinction between routine and emergency work and the Chicago tradition of professional work, Chambliss explores the consequences and interactions of working in a place where people routinely suffer and die. At the same time, Chambliss's study also works as an ethnography. His research was not only based on years of observations and interviews, but the resulting book provides an in-depth understanding of how nurses juggle different tasks and how they can sometimes avoid and resolve such conflicts. This is grounded theory at its strongest with conceptualizations enhancing the ethnographic methodology: Chambliss is able to both capture experiences and analyze them. In light of our earlier discussion, note also that Chambliss expands the key themes of Chicago School sociology of work: his study is thus a methodological and theoretical fit with grounded theory.

Unfortunately, grounded theory has given rise to a different kind of excess in ethnographic writing: the overly conceptual text that sacrifices the ethnographic 'ground' or the singularity of the field site in order to achieve theoretical generalization. Some of this excess can be found in the Strauss et al. study of work in hospitals, where the main analytical strategy seems to consist of adding the noun 'work' to salient tasks such as sentimental work, biographical work, machine work, safety work, articulation work, and comfort work (Strauss, Fagerhaugh, Suczek, and Wiener 1985). While this study is based on 4 years of interviews and observations, preciously few observational instances remain. The actual people whose work is discussed appear mainly as illustrations of long lists of concepts, their variations, and properties. Rather than ethnography enriched by grounded theory, Strauss et al. produced a grounded theory with tenuous ties to the lived experience of ethnographic research (which may be due in part to the fact that theirs was a group's ethnography). If a reader wants conceptual inspiration to understand the management of patients in hospitals, this book offers lots of pointers (see Susan Leigh Star's elaboration of articulation work, Star 1991). However as ethnography of a hospital, it falls short.

The broader danger of relying upon grounded theory in ethnographic research is a mindless formalization of coding and memo writing, losing track of the overall goal of ethnographic research. An example is the story of the physics student at a Midwestern university who wanted to do a qualitative grounded theory study. He read the grounded theory books and took the advice of doing word-by-word open coding literally. After he spent nearly an entire year coding in this fashion, his worried advisor contacted the sociology department to ask whether this was really the way one conducts this research.[5] More generally, the heuristic techniques of grounded theory aiming to sharpen the conceptual sensibilities of researchers may become the goal of the research process. Such researchers often develop concepts but lose track of an overarching research question or of what is truly captivating in their site. Rather than a comprehensive process-based grounded theory, weak grounded theory studies often suggest one or two disjointed concepts and have trouble locating their relevance in the empirical material. Such a goal displacement is supported by grounded theory's lukewarm attitude towards narrative texts. The emphasis on conceptual development as a writing style risks obliterating the in-depth, first-hand knowledge ethnography provides. Indeed, ethnography thrives on what Katz has called 'luminous description' as a form of causal explanation (Katz 2001, 2002). Grounded theory is a data analysis technique and may suggest specific strategies to gather empirical material but the process of gathering rich material itself cannot be shortchanged or masked with long lists of concepts.

It is worth noting that many of the award-winning ethnographies of the last years are not even remotely wedded to the grounded theory program, in fact they may be considered antithetical to grounded theory tenets. For example, Carol Heimer and Lisa Staffen's exemplary study of neonatal intensive care units is resolutely situated within extensive bodies of various social science theories (Heimer and Staffen 1998). Their work does not aim to discover new theory from the ground up but uses existing theory to carve out a niche for a new sociological approach: the sociology of responsibility. This book addresses the question of how institutions instill responsibility in people and uses the ethnography of neonatal intensive care units as one case study. Heimer and Staffen greatly contribute to theorizing because their work is steeped in a comprehensive in-depth familiarity of a broad range of theories and gains mileage from theoretical cross-fertilizations. At the same time, the book works also as an ethnography with densely textured descriptions. Very differently, Mitchell Duneier's book *Sidewalk* is first and foremost an ethnography of street vendors in New York with poignant descriptions of the daily life of vendors trying to make it on the street corners of New York (Duneier 1999). While the book contributes to urban sociology, it does so in a theoretically understated fashion, relying more on theoretical demonstration than conceptual assertion. Instead of grounded theorizing, the study depends on more conventional strategies for successful writing such as narrative plotting, character development, collaboration with a photographer, rich descriptions, and using real names for real people. From a different angle, Katherine Newman's successful group ethnography of working class poor people is not driven by either conceptualization or theories but by important policy questions about welfare reform, family leave, immigration policy, and health insurance (Newman 1999). What all good ethnographies have in common is that first and foremost they cover their 'ground,' they are interesting as ethnographic accounts of sites, communities, and organizations. The empirical material is rich and luscious, thickly and luminously described. Then, good ethnographies also contribute to a sociological understanding of life. Much of the work of good ethnography is to be able to figure out a site substantively and theoretically, grounded theory can help draw out conceptual themes but may also risk a reification of its methods.

For ethnographers, practicing grounded theory is thus not a guarantee for success but everything depends on how grounded theory is configured in an ethnographic project. Grounded theory should never be used to mask shortcomings of gathering empirical materials or to cover a lack of familiarity with a broad theoretical literature. Soon such deficiencies become apparent in the writing.

In order to grasp interactional nuances, understand a full temporal cycle of the phenomena under study, notice repetitions, acquire inside expertise, and observe variations, an ethnographer will almost always need to spend a lengthy period of time in the field: years rather than months or weeks. Grounded theory can help structure this time by suggesting which areas of the field merit more attention, the process of internal falsification discussed earlier. Conducting a grounded theory analysis while working a field site may shed light on which literatures to read: sociological, substantive, or otherwise. To some extent, grounded theory forms also a quality check on evolving field notes by pointing out that more interactional detail is required. Grounded theory thus forces ethnographers to organize empirical materials in a written format and, in this sense, writing is a form of understanding and analysis, not just a prerequisite for analysis (Emerson, Fretz, and Shaw 1995). In essence, grounded theory reminds ethnographers that they are experiencing the field as social scientists. To be successful, they need to stay betwixt-and-between for long periods. Such a long time immersion in a field, as many ethnographers have commented (Adler and Adler 1987; Hammersley and Atkinson 1983), can have a disorienting pull on researchers. Conceptualizing then offers a sociological purpose to the process.

In addition, grounded theory has an unsurpassed prominent place in the education of ethnographers. In spite of decades of methodological writing, novices remain baffled when they attempt to 'do' ethnography armed with methodology textbooks and examples of successful studies. Even if one is able to navigate the vagaries of access and trust during the actual fieldwork experience, how do you find out what is sociologically interesting in a setting; what do you write down; what do you do with the growing pile of notes; what happens if your research focus changes? Such questions tend to emerge and re-emerge during ethnographic research. Grounded theory's formalization of discrete analytical steps offers students a structure for working with their observations and interviews.

A grounded theory data analysis course where a small group of students (6–12) alternate their class time discussing methodological readings with analyzing their own materials may not only offer insight in qualitative data analysis but also constitute a socialization experience of doing ethnography. Anselm Strauss has provided transcripts of class sections in one such course (Strauss 1987). In an adaptation, we have offered a sequence of two graduate methods classes drawing largely on the grounded theory methodology. As soon as students conduct the first in-depth interviews or collect the first observations, the class conducts an open coding session of 1–2 pages of notes or transcripts. The student who conducted the research is asked to remain quiet during the analysis period (if allowed to talk, they tend to over explain) while the other students either go line-by-line through the text or jump to striking phrases. The instructor encourages open coding with questions about the sociological relevance of the empirical materials and writes preliminary ideas on a white board. Usually, the board quickly fills with possibilities for further research and analysis. In a second round, students conduct axial coding, picking a theme across various observations. In the third round of analysis, students present memos of their observations to their peers. The maps and concepts written on the board are only one accomplishment of the course. Often, the group dynamic works, budding ethnographers are encouraged with what others saw in their observations and interviews. Students' data analysis is preceded by either heuristic methodological texts (Abbott 2004; Becker 1998; Clarke 2005) or examples of classic or outstanding ethnographies.

Few students use the group coding as the final framework for their course papers but they often gain confidence from working on other people's materials and from the enthusiasm of others working on their own project. Seeing others apply a coding paradigm to carefully written down field notes usually stimulates the ethnographer's own thinking, especially if the ethnographer becomes convinced that others missed the point of the data. In class, grounded theory suggests a discipline for analyzing data by reminding students that similar to the maxim that the field events that were not written down may as well not have happened, the data that remains unanalyzed may as well not have been recorded. In addition, to hear a group discuss one's research aloud for an hour offers reassurance, familiarity, and insight as well as a reminder that more work remains to be done (Wellin and Fine 2001). In this sense, grounded theory is indeed a 'normal science' (Kuhn 1962), where normal is not a derogatory term but refers to the skills and commitment needed to conduct solid ethnographic work.

CONCLUSION

Grounded theory defines a common problem in ethnography (thin descriptions and disconnected conceptualizations), and offers a solution consisting of a methodological perspective to combine data gathering and data analysis with the aid of various coding and memo-writing heuristics that draw attention to relationships between concepts and emphasize social processes. As such, grounded theory highlights the sociological contributions of ethnography and aims for fresh, novel conceptualizations. When used with care and common sense, grounded theory may help focus ethnographic research, instill deep familiarity and awareness of one's data, and connect field research with broader sociological literatures. Unfortunately, the emphasis on formalization and methodological mechanics has created new problems where grounded theory ethnographies skip the in-depth experiential participation required for good research and are satisfied with 'hit and run' studies leading to quick, obvious conceptual schemes. Grounded theory always prided itself on its pragmatic flexibility: ultimately, as any grounded theory book states, the method should work for the researcher. Flexibility allowed grounded theory to become a qualitative research standard because everyone could find something they liked and ignore the rest. For ethnographers, ethnography and not grounded theory should come first. Grounded theory has proven useful in orienting and sensitizing several generations of ethnographers, but, as John Cleese observed, there are seven ways to skin an ocelot.[6] Inspiration may come from the many qualitative methodology books available but it should preferably also come from the exemplars of successful ethnographies.

NOTES

1 Glaser and Strauss wrote several substantive books based on their study: *Time for Dying* (1968) and *Anguish* (1970), however *Awareness of Dying* (1965) was the most successful.
2 Computer programs facilitating coding with Boolean operators may thus offset some of grounded theory's strengths: a researcher may have generated a long list of codes but lost the in-depth familiarity of data.
3 We offer here a narrow view of theoretical sampling. Usually, this concept is used as a means to add variation and analytical depth to a study.
4 C. Ginzburg, personal communication, February 15, 2006.
5 S. Leigh Star, personal communication, March 17, 1994.
6 http://www.playbill.com/news/article/97589.html

REFERENCES

Abbott, Andrew. 2004. *Methods of Discovery: Heuristics of the Social Sciences.* New York: Norton.
Adler, Patricia A. and Peter Adler. 1987. *Membership Roles in Field Research.* Newbury Park, CA: SAGE.
Ambert, Anne-Marie, Patricia A. Adler, Peter Adler, and Daniel F. Detzner. 1995. Understanding and Evaluating Qualitative Research. *Journal of Marriage and the Family* 57: 879–893.
Anspach, Renee. 1993. *Deciding Who Lives: Fateful Choices in the Intensive Care Nursery.* Berkeley, CA: University of California Press.
Atkinson, Paul and David Silverman. 1997. Kundera's Immortality: The Interview Society and the Invention of the Self. *Qualitative Inquiry* 3: 304–325.
Becker, Howard S. 1998. *Tricks of the Trade: How to think about your research while you're doing it.* Chicago: University of Chicago Press.
Berger, Peter L. and Thomas Luckmann. 1966. *The Social Construction of Reality: A Treatise in the Sociology of Knowledge.* New York: Anchor Books.
Burawoy, Michael. 1998. The Extended Case Method. *Sociological Theory* 16: 4–34.
Burawoy, Michael. 2000. *Global Ethnography: Forces, Connections and Imaginations in a Postmodern World.* Berkeley, CA: University of California Press.
Burton, Linda M. 1995. Intergenerational Patterns of Providing Care in African-American Families with Teenage Childbearers: Emergent Patterns in an Ethnographic Study. In *Intergenerational Issues in Aging,* edited by W. K. Schaie, V. L. Bengston, and L. M. Burton, pp. 79–96. New York: Springer Publishing.
Burton, Linda M. 1997. Ethnography and the Meaning of Adolescence in High Risk Neighborhoods. *Ethnos* 25: 208–217.
Casper, Monica. 1998. *The Making of the Unborn Patient.* New Brunswick, NJ: Rutgers University Press.
Chambliss, Daniel F. 1996. *Beyond Caring: Hospitals, Nurses, and the Social Organization of Ethics.* Chicago: University of Chicago Press.

Charmaz, Kathy. 1991. *Good Days, Bad Days: The Self in Chronic Illness and Time*. Brunswick, NJ: Rutgers University Press.

Charmaz, Kathy. 2006. *Constructing Grounded Theory: A Practical Guide Through Qualitative Analysis*. Thousand Oaks, CA: SAGE.

Charmaz, Kathy and Richard G. Mitchell. 2001. Grounded Theory in Ethnography. In *Handbook of Ethnography,* edited by P. Atkinson, A. Coffey, S. Delamont, J. Lofland, and L. Lofland. Thousand Oaks, CA: SAGE.

Clarke, Adele. 2005. *Situational Analysis: Grounded Theory after the Postmodern Turn*. Thousand Oaks, CA: SAGE.

Coffey, Amanda, Beverley Holbrook, and Paul Atkinson. 1996. Qualitative Data Analysis: Technologies and Representations. *Sociological Research Online,* 1, <http://www.socresonline.org.uk/socresonline/1/1/4.html>

Collins, Randall. 2005. *Interaction Ritual Chains*. Princeton: Princeton University Press.

Denzin, Norman K. 2003. Reading and Writing Performance. *Qualitative Research* 3: 243–268.

Devault, Marjorie. 1995. Ethnicity and Expertise: Racial-Ethnic Knowledge in Sociological Research. *Gender and Society* 9: 612–631.

Dey, Ian. 1999. *Grounding Grounded Theory*. San Diego: Academic Press.

Duneier, Mitchell. 1999. *Sidewalk*. New York: Farar, Straus, and Giroux.

Emerson, Robert M., Rachel I. Fretz, and Linda L. Shaw. 1995. *Writing Ethnographic Fieldnotes*. Chicago: University of Chicago Press.

Glaser, Barney G. 1978. *Theoretical Sensitivity: Advances in the Methodology of Grounded Theory*. Mill Valley, CA: The Sociology Press.

Glaser, Barney and Anselm Strauss. 1965. *Awareness of Dying*. Chicago: Aldine Publishing Company.

Glaser, Barney and Anselm Strauss. 1967. *The Discovery of Grounded Theory*. New York: Aldine Publishing Company.

Glaser, Barney G. and Anselm L. Strauss. 1968. *Time for Dying*. Chicago: Aldine Publishing Company.

Goffman, Erving. 1989. On Fieldwork. *Journal of Contemporary Ethnography* 18: 123–132.

Goode, Erich. 2002. Sexual Involvement and Social Research in a Fat Civil Rights Organization. *Qualitative Sociology* 25: 501–534.

Hammersley, Martyn and Paul Atkinson. 1983. *Ethnography: Principles in Practice*. London: Tavistock Publications Ltd.

Heimer, Carol A. and Lisa R. Staffen. 1998. *For the Sake of the Children: The Social Organization of Responsibility in the Hospital and the Home*. Chicago: University of Chicago Press.

Henwood, Karen L. and Nick Pidgeon. 2003. Grounded Theory in Psychology. In *Qualitative Research in Psychology: Expanding Perspectives in Methodology and Design,* edited by P. M. Camic, J. E. Rhodes, and L. Yardley. Washington, DC: American Psychological Association.

Katz, Jack. 2001. From How to Why: On Luminous Description and Causal Inference in Ethnography (Part 1). *Ethnography* 2: 443–473.

Katz, Jack. 2002. From How to Why: On Luminous Description and Causal Inference in Ethnography. *Ethnography* 3: 63–90.

Kuhn, Thomas. 1962. *The Structure of Scientific Revolutions*. Chicago: University of Chicago Press.

Mamo, Laura. 1999. Death and Dying: Confluences of Emotion and Awareness. *Sociology of Health and Illness* 21: 13–36.

Mead, George Herbert. 1938. *The Philosophy of the Act*. Chicago: University of Chicago Press.

Mitchell, Richard G. 2001. *Dancing At Armageddon: Survivalism and Chaos in Modern Times.* Chicago: University of Chicago Press.

Murphy, Elizabeth and Robert Dingwall. 2003. *Qualitative Methods and Health Policy Research.* New York: Aldine de Gruyter.

Newman, Katherine S. 1999. *No Shame in my Game.* New York: Vintage Books/Russell Sage Foundation Books.

Popper, Karl. 1963. *Conjectures and Refutations: The Growth of Scientific Knowledge.* London: Routledge.

Richardson, Laurel. 2000. Evaluating Ethnography. *Qualitative Inquiry* 6: 253–255.

Rock, Paul. 2001. Symbolic Interactionism and Ethnography. In *Handbook of Ethnography,* edited by P. Atkinson, A. Coffey, S. Delamont, J. Lofland, and L. Lofland, pp. 79–96. Thousand Oaks, CA: SAGE.

Snow, David A. 2001. Extending and Broadening Blumer's Conceptualization of Symbolic Interactionism. *Symbolic Interaction* 24: 367–377.

Snow, David A., Calvin Morrill, and Leon Anderson. 2003. Elaborating Analytic Ethnography: Linking Fieldwork and Theory. *Ethnography* 4: 181–200.

Star, S. Leigh. 1991. Power, Technologies, and the Phenomenology of Conventions: On Being Allergic to Onions. In *A Sociology of Monsters: Essays on Power, Technology and Domination,* edited by J. Law, pp. 26–56. London: Routledge.

Strauss, Anselm. 1987. *Qualitative Analysis for Social Scientists.* Cambridge: Cambridge University Press.

Strauss, Anselm. 1993. *Continual Permutations of Action.* New York: Aldine de Gruyter.

Strauss, Anselm and Juliet Corbin. 1990. *Basics of Qualitative Research.* Newbury Park, CA: SAGE.

Strauss, Anselm, S. Fagerhaugh, B. Suczek, and C. Wiener. 1985. *The Social Organization of Medical Work.* Chicago: University of Chicago Press.

Strauss, Anselm and Barney Glaser. 1970. *Anguish.* San Francisco: Sociology Press.

Timmermans, Stefan. 1994. Dying of Awareness: The Theory of Awareness Contexts Revisited. *Sociology of Health and Illness* 16: 322–339.

Van Maanen, John. 1988. *Tales of the Field: On Writing Ethnography.* Chicago: The University of Chicago Press.

Wacquant, Loic. 2002. Scrutinizing the Street: Poverty, Morality, and the Pitfalls of Urban Ethnography. *American Journal of Sociology* 107: 1468–1532.

Weiss, Robert S. 1994. *Learning from Strangers: The Art and Method of Qualitative Interview Studies.* New York: The Free Press.

Wellin, Christopher and Gary Alan Fine. 2001. Ethnography as Work: Career Socialization, Settings and Problems. In *Handbook of Ethnography,* edited by P. Atkinson, A. Coffey, S. Delamont, J. Lofland, and L. Lofland. Thousand Oaks, CA: SAGE.

PART VI

Grounded Theory in the Context of the Social Sciences

24

Grounded Theory and Reflexivity

Katja Mruck and Günter Mey

CONCERNING MULTIPLE GROUNDED THEORY METHODOLOGIES ...

Over the past few years, qualitative research has been increasingly acknowledged for its contributions in a growing field of academic research and teaching. This is evident in the widespread and significant discussions of methods in the literature, and has resulted in numerous books, journals, and academic conferences throughout the world. Also the number of Internet tools (list servers, wikis and blogs, link collections) dedicated to qualitative research and available for an international community, is continuously increasing. At the same time, funding organizations are encouraging the use of mixed methods, and qualitative methods are also employed in non-academic contexts (community services, market research, politics' consultancies, etc.).

In the social sciences, the Grounded Theory Methodology (GTM)[1] became a particular focus of interest.[2] In times of social change and globalization, the limitations of quantitative methods are evident since, by definition, they are primarily useful with regard to theories or hypotheses derived from existing and established theories. But if such theories are missing or outdated, methodologies are crucial which help to develop novel theories from empirical data.

It has been the genius of Barney Glaser and Anselm Strauss to shed light on the processes of developing theory, and to offer a methodological framework for conducting empirical research. The 'discovery of grounded theory from the data, systematically obtained and analyzed in social research,' is exactly the promise of GTM as stated in their first (and only shared) methods book (1967). But this book fulfilled primarily a programmatic purpose rather than an instructional one.[3] The methodical elaboration was done later by Glaser (1978) and Strauss (1987) separately, and increasingly incompatibly in the course of time (see also Strauss and Corbin, 1990; Corbin, 1998; Glaser with the assistance of Holton, 2004). This development meant that in part, GTM, once offered as a strategy of (self) empowerment for the 'scientific proletariat' against the 'theoretical capitalists,' then became a source of uncertainty especially for many novices trying to use the method for their research. More correctly: trying to use one of the many GTMs, since, in addition to Glaser's and Strauss's (and Corbin's) elaborations, there are a growing number of local interpretations and adaptations in different countries and disciplines. According to Charmaz (2006: 177), 'the term grounded theory has been packed with multiple meanings, but also fraught by numerous misunderstandings, and complicated by competing versions.' Not only is the term GTM used inconsistently, but so too are some core concepts of the method itself, sometimes even within one publication.

While the idea of 'misunderstandings' or 'misconceptions' (Suddaby, 2006) implies that a possible future elaboration of core concepts and a possible standardization *may* lead to a more consensual use of GTM, this view appears to us as rather optimistic, due to the great heterogeneity of qualitative and GTM research(ers): Any attempt to provide 'restrictive rules by which to manufacture qualitative research remains an arena of heated debate' (Bolam, Gleeson, and Murphy, 2003: 10); consensus is difficult to achieve when what one researcher or methods writer regards as a 'core element' is considered by others to be an unpardonable misunderstanding, especially with regard to different epistemological positions.

Moreover, like qualitative research generally, practitioners of GTM typically use methodological terms that are close to everyday language and which have not been subjected to the formalizations that characterize the apparently more rigorous terms used in quantitative methodologies. So researchers have first to interpret and then define their concepts with respect to their cited literatures and in conformity with the specific terms of their scientific locale (national, [sub-] disciplinary) and academic socialization. This is because scientific precision requires researchers to make transparent which of the 'multiple GTMs' they might deploy, to justify their choice, and to specify their concepts and uses if they are to ensure that other researchers have at least a chance to understand their procedures and results.

... AND MULTIPLE REFLEXIVITIES

That research and its results depend on time, place, and the context a researcher belongs to is a central issue in contemporary discussions on (self) reflexivity.

Historically speaking, the way (scientific) communities or individuals reflect on their knowledge and actions has a long pedigree, but became especially prominent with the 'Enlightenment idea of self-knowledge … attained through philosophical introspection, an inward-looking, sometimes confessional and self-critical examination of one's own beliefs and assumptions' (Lynch, 2000: 29). The Enlightenment idea implied the hope that such a critical examination would lead to 'deeper foundations of certainty,' to *correct* representations of *the one* reality, and to a growing corpus of positive scientific knowledge.

More recently, a critical appraisal of scientific presumption was undertaken and elaborated during the so called 'crisis of representation' debates (Clifford, 1988; Clifford and Marcus, 1986; Geertz, 1988; Rosaldo, 1987; Tedlock, 2000) and in part resulted in the subsequent call for a reflexive stance towards culturally co-constructed academic discourses and writings. In these debates, one finds that 'reflexivity' has been interpreted in a number of ways as researchers have sought to provide a variety of inventories, typologies, and programs to explain 'multiple reflexivities.' Lynch (2000), for example, differentiated between 'mechanical,' 'substantive,' 'meta-theoretical,' 'interpretative,' 'ethnomethodological,' and 'methodological' conceptions of reflexivity, and sub-divided each of these in turn. His 'methodological reflexivity' (p. 29) contained four sub-variants, including 'methodological self-consciousness' and a 'canonical feature of participant-observation,' in Lynch's opinion typical for qualitative research, whereby students were advised 'to take account of their own relations to the groups they study' (see also Ashmore, 1989; Marcus, 1998; Wilkinson, 1988; Woolgar, 1988; or Finlay and Gough, 2003, for other inventories and differentiations).

What these variations share is the idea of a recursive 'turning back on one's own experience' (Steier, 1991: 2), but how and why this should be done almost always differs and depends on the epistemological, theoretical, and disciplinary background[4] and on the issues addressed and methods applied. In some approaches, reflexivity is regarded as 'an essential human capacity, in others it is a system property, and in still others it is a critical, or self-critical, act. Reflexivity, or being reflexive, is often claimed as a methodological virtue and source of superior insight, perspicacity or awareness … Some research programs treat reflexivity as a methodological basis for enhancing objectivity, whereas others treat it as a critical weapon to undermine objectivism' (Lynch, 2000: 26). The difficulties of achieving a disciplinary consensus is evident in variations in definitions appearing in the three dictionaries published by Sage in recent years, the *Dictionary of Qualitative Inquiry* (Schwandt, 2001), *The Sage Dictionary of Social Research Methods* (Jupp, 2006), and *Keywords in Qualitative Methods* (Bloor and Wood, 2006): they each rely on completely different bodies of cited core literatures.

In GTM, reflexivity became an explicit topic of concern only recently (Breuer, 2000; Glaser, 2001, 2002; Hall and Callery, 2001; Neill, 2006; see Cutcliffe, 2000, for a short review of 'creativity and reflexivity in grounded theory'), and especially within a constructivist framework (see Bryant, 2003; Charmaz, 2000, 2006;

Mills, Bonner, and Francis, 2006a, b). Bearing in mind the theoretical founda-tions of GTM in symbolic interactionism (see Neill, 2006), one would expect reflection on the interaction between researchers and research participants to be a constitutive element of doing GTM research. But at least in the Glaserian tradition, the concept of 'emergence' of theory from the data led to a strong rejection of 'forcing GTM' (Glaser, 1992), and in a way acknowledging the impact of the researcher in this perspective means 'forcing.' So Glaser explicitly rejects reflexivity as 'paralyzing' and 'self-destructive' (see Neill, 2006, for a short summary) or, in a more modest way: 'from a GT point of view … researcher impact on data is just one more variable to consider whenever it emerges as relevant' (Glaser, 2002: 47). Strauss and Corbin, far more than Glaser, acknowledge that researchers need to build on professional and personal life experiences: 'we know that our perspectives and belief systems influence how we view and work with data. We want our readers to understand why it is important to look at experiences, feelings, action/interaction, to denote the structure or context in which these are located' (Corbin in Cisneros-Puebla, 2004: 21).[5]

In addition, some of the 'post-positivist' GTM researchers accepted the need to reflect on the research process while nonetheless 'maintaining the positivist adherence to objectivity and rigour' (Kennedy and Lingard, 2006: 102). For example Chiovitti and Piran, following Beck's (1993) schema for ensuring credibility, auditability and fittingness, underlined that GTM researchers need to explain their inquiry process because the theory development depends on the participants involved, because 'qualitative methods are not uniformly agreed upon … [and because in] grounded theory, there is more than one version of how researchers can go about implementing procedures' (Chiovitti and Piran, 2003: 428). Similarly, Cutcliffe (2000: 1479) stresses the 'need for the grounded theory researcher to acknowledge his/her prior knowledge and tacit knowledge, to bring such knowledge into the open, to discuss how it has affected the theory development' for ensuring methodological rigor and for improving the quality of the findings. Within constructivist GTM approaches a 'reflexive stance' is explicitly recommended, informing 'how the researcher conducts his or her research, relates to the research participants, and represents them in written reports' (Charmaz, 2006: 189).

RESEARCH AS AN ITERATIVE DECISION PROCESS, REQUIRING CONTINUAL REFLECTION

In the following section, we will draw a picture of research occurring in complex interactions between the researchers and the research participants within their personal and professional backgrounds, between the affordances of the scientific culture the researchers belong to or would like to belong to, and the respective field of research or practice. By engaging in this endeavor, we do not intend to convince (post-)positivist GTM researchers to give up realist or objec-tivist ideals nor to bring 'bricoleur-researchers' back to the path of ensuring scientific rigor in traditional ways. We also do not aim to provide prescriptive rules on 'how to do' reflexivity, but wish to sensitize readers to the decisions, choices, alternatives, and limitations of the research process. We will undertake this by highlighting how the researchers, their interaction with the research participants, and the contexts both belong to may influence the research process from an initial, pre-research stage over data collection and analyzing up to questions of writing and publishing. In doing this we understand reflexivity as a chance for researchers to rethink, ground, or justify their own decisions and to communicate the process of theory development to their co-researchers as well as to research participants.

Initial stage: Posing a research question and deciding for the design of a study

Research starts with a researcher who is interested in learning something new about a topic and developing a theory, or verifying or falsifying existing theoret-ical knowledge or hypotheses, depending on the paradigm, epistemology, and methodology one is relying on. As a potentially unlimited number of research questions and ways to work on them exist, preferences for theories and methods as well as the researcher's interests, competences, skills, and sensibilities, acquired during (professional) socialization within specific academic contexts and 'schools,' play a crucial role within this initial process. If psychological stud-ies, for example, are interested in research on cognition, this already implies an idea of cognition 'existing' separable from other 'functions' (emotion, action). If micro-sociological studies raise the question if schizophrenia resulted from a shared construction of the schizophrenic person and their socio-cultural context, this already implies an idea about a phenomenon, called 'schizophrenia,' and about the procedures of its 'construction.'

Not only the stock of accessible knowledge determines which terms and concepts should be used,[6] but also personal characteristics and experiences may influence the decision for a research topic. So some researchers tend to prefer topics which refer to their own biographical challenges: in the case of psychological research for example experiences with suicide or chronic illness; in sociological research gender, migration, or subcultural issues. To be involved personally is not a problem per se: personal experiences may lead to precious insights and perspectives, hardly accessible for researchers unfamiliar with such topics. Problems arise if the researcher's involvement is hidden, because he/she is afraid of negative feedback or evaluation. Here, disclosure for sure is no 'must,' especially if the costs for making an invisible 'disability' explicit would be too high. Nevertheless, in cases of a strong personal involvement or possible taboos, supervision may offer insight into the otherwise determining individual experiences and pre-assumptions to the extent of precluding new insights: what has been 'known' already in the very beginning would play a crucial role also in the theory presented at the end (e.g. that family is [not] responsible for mental illness, alcohol addiction, etc.).[7]

The choice of a research question depends also on the context of application, the sources of funding, if researchers work alone or in a research team, and how this team might be structured. As far as the context of application is concerned, studies in the field of applied market research, to mention one example, are often exposed to strict time and financial restrictions, leading to the usage of more standardized methods or to 'ad hoc-standardizations.' Standardization is also enforced for individual researchers as they often need more or less structured methods, but are overwhelmed by the vagueness of methodical concepts in qualitative research: they end up searching for 'recipes' or use methods as if such 'secure recipes' exist. Research teams often settle on 'pet methods' or accommodate the methods of those evaluating their work. Funding institutions and their reviewers often expect and even specify one or another body of methods and prescribe the kind and amount of data to collect, sampling strategies, and data analysis: they assert internal methodological requirements but additionally prescribe time- and place-sensitive standards of research (evaluation).

The impact of person, discipline, location, and time of choice is only visible if one tries to look beyond the local routines and methods preferences and national or (sub) disciplinary boundaries.[8] To decide on 'narrative interviews' (Schütze, 1983) to inquire into adolescent identity depends (besides methodological implications) on whether researchers beyond German biographical research contexts are familiar with this rather sophisticated interview variant, only recently available for non-German researchers through the work of Rosenthal (1993) or Wengraf (2001). Conversely, within Germany, GTM reception (besides Glaser and Strauss, 1967 book) for some decades has been more or less limited to the frameworks presented by Strauss (and Corbin), as their books are available in the German language, without recognizing sufficiently that other GTM versions exist.[9]

On a more finely-grained, perceptual level, research is limited by proximity: experience, thinking, and acting. Conceptually, the paradigms, epistemologies, and methodologies researchers prefer limit which kinds of reflexive analysis are accepted or rejected: those following psychoanalytical or ethnomethodological approaches, to mention just two, view the world quite differently.[10] Undeniably, all sorts of insights arrive within such methodological limitations and choices of research questions.

One remedy is to offer researchers a series of prompts to enable them to at least partially bring their presumptions and limitations to the surface. For example, we encourage introspection following the recommendations of Finlay and Gough (2003), including questions as: 'What understanding am I aiming for?' 'What kind of knowledge can I possibly gain?' 'How do I understand the role of the researcher?' 'Why this research?' or 'Why is this my passion?' We also suggest using reflexive interviews, recommended for instance by Bolam et al., in their discussion of qualitative health research, whereby the researchers turn the tables and become interviewees, enabling them to examine their roles 'as both lay person and health expert, insider and outsider' (2003: 30). In our own work, we ask our team members to interview each other as a starting point for research projects, to report their emotions and (theoretical) pre-assumptions, to reflect on the topic they decided for and its possible personal importance, and in this way try to help them to get a first overview and first insights in sometimes overwhelming differences of experiences and perspectives (Mey, 2007; Mruck and Mey, 1998). Our aim in doing this is to encourage reflection on (implicit) theories, assumptions, fantasies, fears, etc., as an important pre-condition for the discovery of presumptions in choice of a research topic. We think it helpful to create environments whereby teams, colleagues, and external supervisors can reflect on their own involvements, especially for research in sensitive and challenging areas.

Sampling/data collection

With respect to sampling strategies, GTM could be of special interest, as 'theoretical sampling' is an elaborated strategy to include data in the course of research, depending on the current development of theory. However, many studies explicitly claiming to apply GTM in our view neglect theoretical sampling or fall short of recognizing its potency (also in terms of avoiding unnecessary time and financial efforts). The iterative conceptualization of the research process in GTM, involving a continuous process of moving back and forth from data collection to analyzing and theory development, places considerable demands on novice researchers, who often tend to save all data as soon as possible and delay the vaguely anticipated 'hardship' of analyzing (even if the data collected and the interviews transcribed are of only limited interest in the context of the research question). We also observe how funding organizations and their reviewers respond partly negatively to such approaches as the representatives of these organizations typically demand exact time and work schedules and detailed specifications of how money is being disbursed. These demands hinder GTM methodologies as they require what is not possible to deliver in the very beginning: specification of exactly which and how many cases should be included in the research and at what time, such that researchers may be led to eliminate theoretical sampling from their proposals or report it in partly distorted ways. The consequences for theorizing of unsystematically included data is at the same time often not sufficiently acknowledged (see Strauss and Corbin, 1990; Cutcliffe, 2000, on the importance of a transparent use of theoretical sampling).

The concrete process of data collection (here summarized for interviews[11]) is from the first getting into contact to the interview itself and to writing a post-script exposed to complex interactions of those participating, and addressing the contexts and concepts, relevant and meaningful for them. Already the first encounter means anticipating and recognizing the respective other, his/her interests, motives, etc., and influences the interviewee's (un-)willingness to participate. During the interview, especially novices tend to work through their often-extensive interview schedules in a rather 'bureaucratic' and mechanistic manner. Some interviewers may be sensitive to some topics the interviewees offer, and ignore or avoid others, partly because, besides those directly involved in an interview, 'invisible others' are present and influential in the results derived; on the side of the interviewers those who will hear the interview tapes, read the transcripts, or evaluate the work, and who may play a crucial role in the choice of questions, the way they are asked, and account for aspects that the interviews do not mention.

From the interviewees' perspective, subjects suffering for example from chronic illness some times use interviewers as a 'megaphone' to communicate, at least tacitly, expectations of what doctors should know or acknowledge. If adult researchers interested in youth cultures interview adolescents they may remind the latter of former experiences with social workers, and their stories will probably be 'designed' accordingly: they will mention those aspects they think to be appropriate for social workers; their story would be completely different if told to a friend or in a peer group.

That both researchers and research participants provide a unique 'stimulus' for each other, determining what is mentioned and what not, is the central topic the French ethno-psychoanalyst Georges Devereux has been concerned with in his important book 'From anxiety to method in the behavioral sciences;' according to Devereux, the researcher:

> should not ignore the interaction between the object and the observer, hoping, that in time this interaction would fade away, if [s]he for a sufficiently long time continued to act as if such an interaction did not take place ... Researchers should stop exclusively underlining treatment and manipulation of the object. Instead, they should simultaneously and some times exclusively reflect and understand their role as observers (1967: 19, our translation).

Devereux recommended reflexive analysis in a period dominated by epistemologies and methodologies which tried to eliminate the subjectivity of researchers. Close to Devereux's point of view (but about 40 years later), Gardner (2006: 261) for example emphasizes that 'each encounter or interview, even if it is concerned with the same topic and conducted with the same participants, will produce different data, since it is a product of the unique circumstances operating at the time.' Nowadays, to examine the impact of researchers and participants on each other, and on the research, is far more accepted within qualitative research (see Denzin, 2001; Finlay, 2002; Fontana and Frey, 1994; Hammersley and Atkinson, 1995; or Gubrium and Holstein, 2002), though the way this reflexive analysis is done depends (as mentioned in the previous Section) on the epistemological and methodological background one is referring to.

For many GTM researchers 'the *inevitability of bias* in any research' (Freshwater, 2005: 311), still seems to be especially challenging.[12] Often the researcher is still regarded as a 'witness' who should try to 'fix' the world (views) of the research participants. For others, reflection is seen as partly limited for example to visible criteria like adequate dressing or to prescriptions like 'researchers need to be strangers' to avoid possible biases and problems of validity, as in the case of Neill (2006), who provided an example of reflecting on 'process, context and self' during sampling within a 'Glaserian grounded theory methodology.' From Devereux we learn that not only what is evident at a first glance (the way a researcher is dressed) influences the interview, but so also do the more subtle psychological interactions between the persons involved. Similarly, both being familiar and being a stranger influences data collection (and data analysis): the more researchers and participants belong to similar cultures, the more interviewers may pre-suppose concepts and values as shared, and therefore fail to attend to elaboration during the interview, so that even central topics will be obscured or lost. Conversely, intimate knowledge will hardly be given to strangers, so familiarity will provide other insights than in the case of a researcher unfamiliar with a person or issue. ('Other' in this case means not better but complementary perspectives, each of them helpful to understand different facets of the phenomenon addressed.)

There are some methods recommended for reflecting on the co-constructive character of research settings. Within a constructivist GTM framework and concerned with establishing a 'more non-hierarchical relationship,' Mills et al. (2006b: 10) suggested the use of 'conscious-raising questions' and several other strategies, such as:

> scheduling interviews at a time and location of the participant's choice, using a relatively flexible and unstructured approach to questioning so that participants assume more power over the direction of the conversation, sharing the researcher's understanding of the key issues arising and assuming an open stance towards the participant, as well as sharing personal details and answering questions asked both during the interview and afterward.

In an excellent article written from a post-positivist epistemology, Chiovitti and Piran (2003) describe 'tools' they 'used to limit the influence of pre-existing constructions on participants' including: a postcomment interview sheet, already suggested by Miles and Huberman (1984) as a 'self-monitoring tool'; a personal journal, helping the researchers to become aware of their own concepts, and 'monitoring how the literature review was used … to limit the influence of previous theoretical constructions on the theory developed' (p. 432). Also, Arber (2006) underlines the importance of personal journals to 'fix' the interviewer's emotional involvement and possible consequences for the ongoing theory development. During her ethnography in a hospice, she used methods of reflexive accounting to 'enhance the credibility' of her research, but also to help herself manage the difficult 'boundary between closeness and distance' in a setting she approached both as researcher and as practitioner. Besides journals and research diaries documenting her thoughts and feelings, she especially acknowledges the importance of 'good support' by colleagues and a peer group to help her during 'emotional labor to fit into the research setting, manage relationships and deal

THE SAGE HANDBOOK OF GROUNDED THEORY

with untoward situations' but also 'self-care strategies as "time out" relaxation techniques, debriefing and counselling strategies should be … carefully considered before, during and after fieldwork experiences' (p. 156). Similarly, Rager (2005), on the basis of her research on self-directed learning and breast cancer, stresses the importance of self-care strategies such as counseling, peer debriefing, and journal writing.

Wright and Cochrane (2000) emphasize the importance of support mechanisms and research training for supervisors. Additionally, video-taped interview training and role play may be useful for both students and experienced researchers to become aware of their specific ways of perceiving, anticipating, acting, and talking. In the case of sensitive topics, for example sexual delinquency, it may be difficult for some researchers to approach interviewees in an open and respectful manner; in such cases, supervised by experienced researchers, the use of reflexive methods like analysis of (counter)transferences, dream analysis, or analysis of fantasies may make sense (see Brown, 2006, for reflexivity and psychoanalysis, and Marks and Mönnich-Marks, 2004, for an example of using the analysis of counter-transference in interviews with persons who supported German National Socialism).

Data analysis

Data sets derived from complex interactions and then later transformed (in the case of interviews this would usually be by transcribing the audiotapes) are best seen as bound up in a process that is 'in principle interactive, social, sub/cultural, situated, and contextual constructed by all persons involved' (Mruck and Breuer, 2003: 9). However, while the co-constructive character of (generating) data is always present (though not necessarily reflected) during interviewing or while staying in the field, many researchers try to ignore it during the subsequent analysis. That a concrete research participant told a specific story to an individual researcher at a specific point of time and a specific place is lost in an approach to analysis, solely trying to lean on the (transcribed) 'responses' of interviewees without acknowledging the process which has resulted in this research 'input' being available for analysis.

Besides the ongoing impact of ideas of 'unbiased research,' one reason for this ignorance is that researchers differ in regard to their ability to tolerate lack of structure: some tend to avoid a feeling of being flooded through data and methods by looking for 'authorities' and searching for 'recipes' and by hiding away their own involvement in the analyzing process. Novices in particular are often fearful of making mistakes and of possible negative consequences for the evaluation of their work or, more generally, of damaging their reputation in the community. But experienced researchers may also resort to these actions when preparing research for submission and publication.

During the supervision of PhD students and workshops that we offer several times a year for colleagues from different disciplines and academic status groups and also for non-academic participants, we are continuously confronted with a range of uncertainties: the 'multiple GTMs' cause discomfort. As far as coding procedures are concerned, the suggestion of different approaches and the use of the different terms found in the scientific literature tend to confuse researchers (see Hentz Becker, 1993, on a fragmented use of GTM; Baker, Wuest, and Stern, 1992 on 'method slurring'; and Glaser with the assistance of Holton, 2004 on 'remodeling grounded theory'[13]). During the coding process, the varying capacities for abstraction (from data to code to category to theory) become evident. Novices especially often stick to description as they are afraid of 'unscientific' interpretations. The role of pre-existing theory in GTM is a source of confusion: researchers are asked to avoid reading too much in the substantive area. According to Glaser with the assistance of Holton (2004: 46) to 'undertake an extensive review of literature before the emergence of a core category violates the basic premise of GT' (this might be seen to contradict his 'all is data' maxim). Conversely, key instruments of GTM (Glaser's 'coding families' or Strauss and Corbin's 'paradigm model') rely explicitly on pre-existing sociological theories and require, depending on the (disciplinary) context within which GTM is used, reflection.[14]

Even the aim of applying GTM (generating theory) may be asking too much of PhD students in most cases, particularly given the differences in the accounts offered by Glaser and Strauss (and Corbin). According to Strauss, theoretical coding, theoretical sampling, and constant comparison are central issues if one wishes to do GTM research, but conversely he also advises adjusting the method to different context and purposes (Strauss in Legewie and Schervier-Legewie, 2004: 58 or Track 7 of the English tape); similarly, Strauss and Corbin (1990) stressed the 'smorgasbord table' character of GTM. Against this Glaser clearly stated that what 'is important is to use the *complete* package of GT procedures as an integrated methodological whole' (Glaser with the assistance of Holton, 2004: 41, see p. 43 onwards for the essential elements of GTM, according to Glaser).

Additional to the specific GTM version researchers use are their 'pet concepts' and preferences for specific codes and categories. These result from their respective academic socialization and background, and will necessarily gain influence during the data analysis. It is this impact, Kuhn (1962, 1977) referred to as the psychology or sociology of research in contrast to the 'logic of research' (Popper, 1934). Kuhn, in his work learned from a still rather neglected microbiologist, Ludwik Fleck, who, using research on syphilis as an example, demonstrated in detail the 'genesis and development of a scientific fact' (Fleck, 1935a) and its historical and socio-psychological grounding in so called 'thought collectives.'[15] According to Fleck, analyzing data, and more fundamentally scientific observation and understanding, is not best understood in terms of the fit between a fact and a theory which should be tested (or in the case of GTM: a theory-neutral constant comparison of data/incident-code, code-code, code-category, etc., leading to an emerging theory), but instead is better understood in terms of 'style-locked re-interpretations' within preferred epistemologies and 'thought systems' (including accessible concepts, routines, sanctions, etc.). He writes: 'There is no isolated researcher, no ahistoric, no style-free observation possible at all,' and within the respective style the 'mental past and presence of the thought collective's ... real and mental fathers' (1935b: 81, our translation) have an essential impact. For Fleck, this affiliation is unavoidable and it leads not to *one* truth, but relative, style-locked *truths*, dependent on their respective systems of reference.

Researchers, conducting data analysis alone or in a research team they have been socialized in, are hardly able to reflect on their own implicitness without the intervention of 'outsiders' who do not share these commonalities. Nevertheless recommendations like those of Chiovitti and Piran (2003) to consistently ask 'standard questions' to establish a 'consistent format of coding' may at least be helpful to structure the awareness of a researcher during the process of data analysis and in this way may enhance the auditability of GTM research. The sorts of questions the authors suggest, leaning on Glaser (1978), Strauss (1987), and Strauss and Corbin (1990), are: 'What is happening in the data?' 'What does the action in the data represent?' 'Is the conceptual label or code, part of the participant's vocabulary?' 'In what context is the code/action used?' 'Is the code related to another code?' 'Is the code encompassed by a broader code?' or 'Are there codes that reflect similar patterns?' (Chiovitti and Piran, 2003: 429).[16]

In our work, we have sought a broader heuristic framework and supportive atmosphere to sustain self-reflection. This is based on the observation that reflexive analysis at the level of a researcher's empirical work is not sufficient: following Brown, it may be necessary to conduct reflexive analysis 'in relation to the academic context in which most research and learning takes place' (Brown, 2006: 181). While Brown's example is in the realm of psychoanalytic frameworks, Hall et al. (2005) describe strategies for working with multidisciplinary qualitative research teams while relying on a GTM example, focusing beside other things on the development of reflexivity and theoretical sensitivity in the team and the shared use of data analysis. According to them, sharing 'information, articulating project goals and elements, acknowledging variation in individual goals, and engaging in reciprocity and respectful collaboration are key elements of mutual adjustment' (p. 257). Similarly, Finlay and Gough (2003) suggest 'mutual collaboration' as one variant of reflexive analysis, involving participants in a reflexive dialogue during data analysis, evaluation, and/or writing. Our 'Projektwerkstatt Qualitativen Arbeitens' (Mruck and Mey, 1998)[17] was in part based on Strauss's emphasis on using research groups in GTM (see Legewie and Schervier-Legewie's interview with Anselm Strauss, 2004) and featured the application of the concept of 'Theme-centred interaction' (TCI; Cohn, 1991). This involves using TCI as a heuristic framework to clarify and discuss factors, influencing the research process, and to establish a supportive atmosphere essential to reflect on personal involvement with the research questions.[18]

Support for this approach is to be found in the work of a number of scholars. The acceptance of multiple voices and perspectives plays a crucial role within social constructionism (Gergen, 1999; Gergen and Gergen, 1991) and also in co-operative inquiry, which treats participants as co-researchers and researchers as co-participants: both engaged in cycles of shared reflection and practice (see Reason and Bradbury, 2001, on action research; Reason and Heron, 1995, on co-operative inquiry; Arvay, 2003, for a collaborative, narrative approach). Leaning on participatory action research and regarding 'theory generation as a collective process that did not privilege any one voice,' Roth and colleagues developed forms of 'coteaching' (Roth, Lawless, and Tobin, 2000) and of 'cogenerative dialoguing and metaloguing' (Roth and Tobin, 2004). Originating in collegial debriefing, 'collective remembering' and 'collective theorizing' are used while different participants get together to describe and explain shared encounters.

Writing and publishing

The influence of anticipated audiences and publishing has also been shown to be a significant factor in shaping research. Many researchers experience twofold 'mental scissors' while writing down their theory: 'Will the research participants accept my results?' and 'Will my research be evaluated positively by my supervisor, funding organization, reference community, and the journal I submitted my article to?' Both types of question already influence the data analysis, as some interpretations may be avoided or are shaded with the respective recipients in mind.[19] They lead researchers to eliminate possible pointers to the communicative and contextual character of their research, and to report 'facts' generated independently from the various interactions between the persons involved and the impact of the everyday and scientific cultures they belong to. Thus, even in some empirical GTM studies, explicitly referring to a constructionist framework, 'the researcher—inter-acting, choosing, pre-supposing, sympathetic—becomes invisible in favor of mirroring "the other," the object, the phenomenon' (Mruck and Breuer, 2003: 9).

An often-applied strategy of being invisible and gaining reputation is to rely on traditional ways of structuring and presenting results: first the state of research is reported, afterwards methods, followed by empirical findings, and the theory developed. While such narrative structures, based on the hypothetico-deductive model, assuredly make sense in the case of quantitative research reports, for studies using GTM it is almost dysfunctional. This problem has been discussed in a recent article by Suddaby, leaning on his experience with peer reviewing articles submitted to the *Academy of Management Journal* (AMJ): Suddaby (2006: 637) argues that even 'though grounded theory research is conducted iteratively, by analyzing and collecting data simultaneously, it is usually presented sequentially ... Doing so has the unfortunate consequence of creating the impression of methodological slurring, even when the constant comparative method has been used. For those unfamiliar with grounded theory techniques, the mode of presentation may also create the unfortunate impression that grounded theory methods can be mixed with a positivist research agenda.'[20] Relying on Strauss and Corbin, Suddaby also stresses the involvement of the researchers in their own analysis and presentation. As GTM research usually means a 'close and longstanding' relationship between the researcher and research participants, 'the personality, experience, and character of a researcher become important components of the research process and should be made an explicit part of the analysis' (Suddaby, 2006: 640).

There are several authors who already 'have worked to rehabilitate the *infected* writing of the researcher, into the usually sanitized research report/thesis etc.' (Freshwater, 2005: 314). Such efforts often differentiate 'confessional tales' from endeavors of 'textual radicalism.' Confessional tales explicitly deal with ethical and methodological dilemmas experienced during research, with stories of 'infiltration, fables of fieldwork rapport, mini-melodramas of hardships endured (and overcome), and accounts of what fieldwork did to the fieldworker' (Van Maanen, 1988: 73). As they intend to provide a kind of natural (though highly subjective) history of research, the confessional has been criticized as 'a strategy for gaining authority rather than giving it away, and involves no departure from realist assumptions ... [but] constitutes a claim to authenticity' (Seale, 1999: 161). Textual radicalism therefore implies a rejection of realism and of objectivist ideals, of pure representational and monologic ways of writing. It challenges the researcher's privileged position, stressing that there is 'not one "voice" but polyvocality; not one story but many tales, dramas, pieces of fiction ...' (Lincoln and Denzin, 1994: 584; see also Hammersley and Atkinson, 1995, on the growing awareness of possible audiences, writing styles, and genres, and on ethical issues of authority and responsibility in ethnographic writing.) Current prominent examples come from autoethnography (Ellis and Bochner, 2000; Holman Jones, 2005; see also Ellis, 2003; or Humphreys, 2005, for autoethnographic vignettes) and from the 'performative' social science' approaches (Denzin, 2001; see Jones, 2006, on the use of 'arts-based [re]presentations'), employing a variety of 'postmodern' presentation and writing strategies 'including conversations between the authors, between author and reviewers, between author, other authors, reviewers, and research participants' (Roth, 2002: 31).[21] More modest attempts to explore 'what is going on' in the research process, are provided by Hand (2003) or Probert (2006), who describe the 'journey of a novice researcher' during the process of deciding upon a methodological approach. More generally, Jasper (2005) discusses 'reflective writing' as an effort to monitor research, a research method and a product of research (see also Richardson, 2000, on writing as a method of inquiry).[22] In her view, reflective writing in the first person, such as in journals and research logs, helps develop understanding and the movement of thought beyond isolated events and towards 'making connections and facilitating creativity.'

In GTM, most empirical reports still are presented in traditional, representational ways, and only very little of 'the literature and the seminal grounded
theory texts ... explicitly addresses the question of the researcher's voice in the
text' (Mills et al., 2006b: 11). Besides the ongoing post-positivist orientation of
many GTM researchers, this may partly be due to the fact that the genuine GTM
'technique initially requires the researcher to fracture the data through open
coding and then put it back together again in a more abstract and conceptual
theoretical form' (Mills et al., 2006b: 12). This does not necessarily mean that
GTM research must follow the 'myth of silent authorship' (Charmaz and
Mitchell, 1996). In 'Constructing grounding theory,' Charmaz (2006) dedicates
a complete chapter to questions of writing, stressing that GTM writings 'need
not be voiceless, objective recordings. We can weave our points of view into the
text and portray a sense of wonder, imagery, and drama' (p. 174).[23] That she
limits her concrete recommendations to technical 'how-to-do' advice[24] like
'making your mark,' 'drafting discoveries,' 'pulling the pieces together,'
'constructing arguments,' and 'scrutinizing categories' may be an indicator of the
difficult path for GTM between polyvocality and the unmasking potencies
towards hidden agendas, ascribed to (self)reflexivity (Richardson, 2000), and the
lack of tolerance of reflective research even within qualitative circles
(Freshwater, 2005; Rolfe and Gardner, 2005).

SUMMARY

As mentioned at the start, we neither intended to convince (post)positivist GTM
researchers of a relativist approach to reflexive analysis nor to force researchers
relying on postmodern or constructionist frameworks to engage in reflexive analysis
as a means for ensuring rigor. We have tried to show how using GTM (independently from the specific variant used and from the epistemology one is relying on),
from posing a question and choosing the concrete design, to sampling, collecting,
and analyzing data, to its final integration in a grounded theory and the writing and
publishing of the research results, is exposed to complex and unavoidable interactions. We tried to give at least an idea of how the concrete individuals involved
(Devereux), the 'thought style' (Fleck), and routines of the scientific community a
researcher or a team belongs to, may influence the numerous decisions taking
place during the course of research. We have also tried to summarize possible and
potential reflexive methods that might be useful during this process. As single
researchers and research teams are only partly able to reflect on their own biographical and professional pre-assumptions, on 'thought style' oriented implicitness
and on the consequences which arise for the research results and the theory generated, we additionally sought ways to help perspectives, concepts, and interpretations become visible through external supervising procedures.

Thinking about methods and reflexivity is a difficult task. Even a few minutes
(interview) conversation appears far too complex for modest interpretative

(and reflexive) procedures to be fully apprehended. Having this in mind, the old scientific dream to represent and interpret 'what has been' or 'what has been *truly* important' is doomed to failure or deficiency. To be aware of this and to try time and again to 'fix' a small, yet hopefully important, facet is for us as researchers, for our research participants/co-researchers, and for our readers, both an aspiration and a deception at the same time.

ACKNOWLEDGMENTS

We would like to sincerely thank Antony Bryant and Kathy Charmaz for their kind support and recommendations.

NOTES

1 We use the term GTM to distinguish the methodology from the result of research, grounded theory (GT).

2 For many decades, generating theories has been assigned a subordinate status, banished to the realm of pre-scientific knowledge, perhaps most notably asserted in Reichenbach's (1938) distinction between the 'context of discovery' and the 'context of justification.'

3 In these early days, Glaser and Strauss started to elaborate GTM as a methodological approach by generalizing from the achievements of their earlier empirical research (Glaser and Strauss, 1965). According to Strauss, in the beginning there had been three main purposes: to justify qualitative research; to 'attack' functionalists like Parsons and Merton and their grand theories; and to stress the importance of theories developed from (grounded in) data, as opposed to pure qualitative description (Strauss in Legewie and Schervier-Legewie, 2004: 52 or Track 7 of the English tape).

4 Besides long-lasting debates on reflexivity in sociology, communications, ethnography, and nursing (see Stocking, 1983; Ball, 1990; Buckledee and McMahon, 1994; Denzin, 1994, 1997; Hammersley and Atkinson, 1995; Denzin and Lincoln, 1998; Davies, 1999; Roberts and Sanders, 2005; Freshwater provided a commentary 'Writing, rigor and reflexivity in nursing research' on a number of articles, published in 2005 in the *Journal of Research in Nursing*), see also, for example, accounts on reflexivity in human geography (Rose, 1997) or in organizational research and 'reflexive public administration' (Cunliffe, 2003; Cunliffe and Jong, 2005).

5 See Mills et al. (2006a: 3–4) on the 'mixture of language' in Strauss and Corbin, 'with a reliance on terms such as recognizing bias and maintaining objectivity when describing the position the researcher should assume in relation to the participants and the data. Nevertheless, they mix these ideas with observations such as "we emphasize that it is not possible to be completely free of bias" ... This has led some researchers to remark that "people can find support in it for any ontology that they wish."' Bryant (2003) provides a critique of the 'positivist stance of a neutral observer' in GTM.

6 The difficulty to overcome taken-for-granted experiences, routines, and concepts is obvious while trying to imagine radical shifts in time or place. So living (and doing research) 200 years ago meant using completely different terminologies as well as completely different accesses to and ideas about 'reality' and its adequate 'representation.' See, for example, Schivelbusch, who provided an impressive description of the 'industrialization of place and time in the 19th century,' on the impact of railway traveling on human awareness, and in the long term it needed that traveling by train became an everyday experience (at least within some cultures). From an early 'witness' of this socialization process: 'The idea not to recognize things outside from a train window is superstitious: For sure, an uninterested viewer is only able to see some hedges and pylons. But after three years of training I am able to paint landscapes, flowers, and farmhouses from inside the train' (Strindberg, in Schivelbusch, 1979: 51).

7 In some cases it may be necessary to decide at an early stage if clinical involvement will be necessary.

8 *The Sage Handbook of Qualitative Research* (Denzin and Lincoln, 2005) is a valuable resource for qualitative researchers all over the world, but still rather biased towards North American sociology, communications, etc. Alternative overviews can be found in 'The State of the Art of Qualitative Research in Europe' (Knoblauch, Flick, and Maeder, 2005); for Iberoamerica, see Cisneros Puebla et al. (2006); for a critical comment see 'About qualitative research centers and peripheries' (Mruck, Cisneros Puebla, and Faux, 2005); for a short cartography see Mey and Mruck (2007).

9 In 2004, Böhm (274) wrote in *A Companion to Qualitative Research*, based on a German handbook: 'While Barney Glaser withdrew from active research in the 1980s, Strauss developed the approach further!'

10 In ethnomethodology, reflexivity is regarded as a constitutive element of *all* human behavior (Lynch, 2000; Ten Have, 2002).

11 Due to space restrictions we limit ourselves to interviews, and we also do not differentiate between different kinds of interviews. It should at least be mentioned that in many cases group discussions or participant observation could also be applied, to mention just two examples. For the latter we have often observed that researchers are rather aware of their active structuring and subjective influences when describing and preparing protocols. This is the reason why they then avoid—sometimes despite a constructivist orientation—field notes and observation protocols as 'contaminated' and less valid and reliable.

12 See Mantzoukas (2005) on how the concept of bias developed within the history of science, and on its continuing impact on positivist and post-positivist research. According to him, the 'inclusion of bias' is a 'necessary prerequisite for securing validity': studies 'are valid only if the researcher's bias is fully incorporated and becomes transparent throughout the study' (2005: 279), while Freshwater (2005: 311) insisted that a 'researcher's bias can never be fully known, what is conscious and in awareness can be articulated, but this will always be both complete and incomplete and as such presents a partial view.'

13 Ideas of 'method slurring' or 'remodeling' imply that there is a single correct use of the method, and often, as in the case of Glaser, one's own work is regarded as a part of an evolving method, while someone else's methodological development is merely 'remodeling.'

14 To acquire intimate theoretical knowledge at a very early stage is a necessary pre-condition for decisions of whether to use GTM at all. Methodologically GTM especially makes sense if an appropriate theory has not yet been developed, so researchers should know what already exists and what does not. In the case of external funding, reports on the state of the art of research within a certain domain are an unavoidable requirement; see for a short summary of the 'disputed literature review' Charmaz, 2006: 165; Cutcliffe, 2000: 1480.

15 See also http://www.ludwikfleck.ethz.ch/

16 Such questions work within a specific framework and need to be adjusted for others. Chiovitti and Piran for example used the paradigm model of Strauss and Corbin (1990), while Glaserian GTM, but also Charmaz (2000) within her constructivist approach, regard axial coding and the use of the paradigm model as possible constraints on theory development. But Mills et al. (2006a) offer a constructivist position distinct from that of Charmaz, underlining that both axial coding and the paradigm model are 'tools for reconstructing a grounded theory that is both dense and significantly analytical,' and stressing Strauss and Corbin's 'constructivist intent.'

17 Since 2000 we have additionally established the 'NetzWerkstatt Qualitativen Arbeitens' (http://www.methodenbegleitung.de/). As many PhD students work alone and receive only peripheral support in their local contexts, the NetzWerkstatt is organized mainly through the use of online tools. Each group consists of 8–10 PhD researchers, with their own mailing lists, 'virtual rooms,' and fixed chat meetings. (Peer) Supervision usually is provided during the complete research process (see Mey, Ottmar, and Mruck, 2006).

18 In a research project on interdisciplinary teamwork, for example a code 'being proud of the results of work' was derived from interviews with team members and included in a category 'consequences of successful co-operation,' which became an essential element of a theory on 'trustful co-operation: phases of interdisciplinary work.' While discussing some peculiarities in group interaction during the coding process (and already in the interview situation) we recognized that the research group puts a special focus on resources instead of, for example, stressors, and that

additionally the data (and later codes) come from interviews with members of interdisciplinary teams, interested to report 'success stories,' partly due to a kind of hidden rivalry between interviewees and interviewers. Additional cases up from the 'hidden rivalry' experience in the immediate interview interaction and in the group interaction were included in the evolving theory.

19 Often researchers have 'a secret audience' who need to be convinced, proved wrong, etc. For persons not involved in the research process this sometimes only becomes apparent later on in the process of writing and arguing, if at all.

20 The *AMJ* editor in a short preface explicitly mentioned that the main intention of Suddaby's article was to allow '*AMJ* and other journals to continue to increase the quality of insights provided by rich qualitative studies of individual, organizational, and institutional phenomena.' So the more GTM is accepted as a regular research practice, the more researchers, familiar with GTM, are also reviewing for journals not explicitly dedicated to qualitative research. Taken together this should result in acceptance of the presentation of GTM research in a more appropriate manner than the hypothetico-deductive scheme.

21 See for further examples 'Part V: The art and practices of interpretation, evaluation and presentation' in Denzin and Lincoln, 2005; and the two *FQS* issues, dedicated to 'Subjectivity and reflexivity in qualitative research' (Mruck, Roth, and Breuer, 2002; Roth, Mruck, and Breuer, 2003).

22 Jasper (2005: 253) differentiates between two kinds of reflective writing, first 'the use of the products of reflective writing, such as autobiographies, journals and logs, critical incident analyses, reflective reviews, etc. as primary data' and second 'the reflective writing of researchers themselves ... providing a commentary on both the primary data of the study and being integral to the research processes.'

23 This is, however, not an easy option, since Charmaz also encourages 'writing apart from typical scientific format without transforming it into fiction, drama, or poetry' (p. 172).

24 Advice from Charmaz is offered as part of her intention to help readers to put together a concise, cogent manuscript for journal submission etc. Nevertheless Suddaby's observations show how most GTM reports are far removed from forms giving insight to the style and full potency of GTM research. Studies applying GTM would need at least an extensive description of the way methods had been used to help other researchers and readers to understand the (reasons for the) methodological decisions throughout the research process, and this is often not done according to external criteria: limited space in the case of print journals and book chapters; publishers' demands to avoid detailed method descriptions in the case of monographs. Besides possible future changes, indicated by positions like those of *AMJ*, important innovations may come from Internet publication without severe space restrictions, and the opportunity to provide data collections even in multimedia formats, etc.

REFERENCES

Arber, Anne (2006) Reflexivity. A challenge for the researcher as practitioner? *Journal of Research in Nursing*, 11(2): 147–157.

Arvay, Marla (2003) Doing reflexivity: a collaborative, narrative approach. In Linda Finlay and Brendan Gough (eds), *Reflexivity: A Practical Guide for Researchers in Health and Social Sciences*. Oxford: Blackwell Science. pp. 163–175.

Ashmore, Malcolm (1989) *The Reflexive Thesis: Writing the Sociology of Scientific Knowledge*. Chicago: University of Chicago Press.

Baker, Cynthia, Wuest, Judith and Stern, Phyllis (1992) Method slurring: The grounded theory/phenomenology example. *Journal of Advanced Nursing*, 17: 1355–1360.

Ball, Sandra J. (1990) Self-doubt and soft data: Social and technical trajectories in ethnographic fieldwork. *Qualitative Studies in Education*, 3(2): 157–171.

Beck, Cheryl T. (1993) Qualitative research: the evaluation of its credibility, fittingness, and auditability. *Western Journal of Nursing Research*, 15: 263–266.

Bloor, Michael and Wood, Fiona (2006) *Keywords in Qualitative Methods. A Vocabulary of Research Concepts*. London: SAGE.

Böhm, Andreas (2004) Theoretical coding. Text analysis in grounded theory. In Uwe Flick, Ernst v. Kardorff and Ines Steinke (eds), *A Companion to Qualitative Research*. London: SAGE. pp. 270–275.

Bolam, Bruce, Gleeson, Kate and Murphy, Simon (2003) 'Lay person' or 'health expert'? Exploring theoretical and practical aspects of reflexivity in qualitative health research. *Forum Qualitative Sozialforschung/Forum: Qualitative Social Research*, 4(2): Art. 26. Retrieved April 2, 2007 from http://www.qualitative-research.net/fqs-texte/2-03/2-03bolametal-e.htm

Breuer, Franz (2000) Qualitative methods in the study of biographies, interactions and everyday life contexts: The development of a research style. *Forum Qualitative Sozialforschung/Forum: Qualitative Social Research*, 1(2): Art. 3. Retrieved April 2, 2007 from http://www.qualitative-research.net/fqs-texte/2-00/2-00breuer-e.htm

Brown, Joanne (2006) Reflexivity in the research process: Psychoanalytic observations. *International Journal of Social Research Methodology*, 9(3): 181–197

Bryant, Antony (2003) A constructive/ist response to Glaser. *Forum Qualitative Sozialforschung/Forum: Qualitative Social Research*, 4(1): Art. 15. Retrieved April 2, 2007 from http://www.qualitative-research.net/fqs-texte/1-03/1-03bryant-e.htm

Buckledee, Jill and McMahon, Richard (eds) (1994) *The Research Experience in Nursing*. London: Chapman & Hall.

Charmaz, Kathy (2000) Grounded theory: objectivist and constructivist methods. In Norman K. Denzin and Yvonna S. Lincoln (eds), *Handbook of Qualitative Research* (2nd edn). London: SAGE. pp. 509–536.

Charmaz, Kathy (2006) *Constructing Grounded Theory. A Practical Guide through Qualitative Analysis*. London: SAGE.

Charmaz, Kathy and Mitchell, Richard G. (1996) The myth of silent authorship: Self, substance, and style in ethnographic writing. *Symbolic Interaction*, 19: 285–302.

Chiovitti, Rosalina F. and Piran, Niva (2003) Rigour and grounded theory research. *Journal of Advanced Nursing*, 44(4): 427–435

Cisneros-Puebla, César A. (2004) 'To Learn to Think Conceptually.' Juliet Corbin in Conversation With César A. Cisneros-Puebla. *Forum Qualitative Sozialforschung/Forum: Qualitative Social Research*, 5(3): Art. 32. Retrieved April 2, 2007 from http://www.qualitative-research.net/fqs-texte/3-04/04-3-32-e.htm

Cisneros Puebla, César A., Domínguez Figaredo, Daniel; Faux, Robert; Kölbl, Carlos and Packer, Martin (eds) (2006) Qualitative research in Ibero America. *Forum Qualitative Sozialforschung/Forum: Qualitative Social Research*, 7(4). Retrieved April 2, 2007 from http://www.qualitative-research.net/fqs/fqs-e/inhalt4-06-e.htm

Clifford, James (1988) *The Predicament of Culture*. Cambridge, MA: Harvard University Press.

Clifford, James and Marcus, George E. (1986) *Writing Culture. The Poetics and Politics of Ethnography*. Berkeley: University of California Press.

Cohn, Ruth C. (1991) *Von der Psychoanalyse zur themenzentrierten Interaktion. Von der Behandlung einzelner zu einer Pädagogik für alle* (10th edn). Stuttgart: Klett-Cotta.

Corbin, Juliet M. (1998) Alternative interpretations: Valid or not? *Theory & Psychology*, 8(1): 121–128.

Cunliffe, Ann L. (2003) Reflexive inquiry in organizational research: Questions and possibilities. *Human Relations*, 56(8): 983–1003.

Cunliffe, Ann L. and Jun, Jong S. (2005) The need for reflexivity in public administration. *Administration and Society*, 37(2): 225–242.

Cutcliffe, John R. (2000) Methodological issues in grounded theory. *Journal of Advanced Nursing*, 31: 1476–1484.

Davies, Charlotte A. (1999) *Reflexive Ethnography: A guide to researching selves and others*. London: Routledge.

Denzin, Norman K. (1994) The art and politics of interpretation. In Norman K. Denzin and Yvonna S. Lincoln (eds), *Handbook of Qualitative Research*. Thousand Oaks, CA: SAGE. pp. 500–515.

Denzin, Norman K. (1997) *Interpretive Ethnography: Ethnographic practices for the 21st century*. Thousand Oaks, CA: SAGE.

Denzin, Norman K. (2001) The reflexive interview and a performative social science. *Qualitative Research*, 1(1): 23–45.

Denzin, Norman K. and Lincoln, Yvonna S. (1998) Introduction: Entering the field of qualitative research. In Norman K. Denzin and Yvonna S. Lincoln (eds), *The Landscape of Qualitative Research. Theories and issues*. Thousand Oaks, CA: SAGE. pp. 1–35.

Denzin, Norman K. and Lincoln, Yvonna S. (eds) (2005) *The Sage Handbook of Qualitative Research* (3rd edn). Thousand Oaks, CA: SAGE [1st edn 1994].

Devereux, Georges (1967/1992) *Angst und Methode in den Verhaltenswissenschaften* [From Anxiety to Method in the Behavioral Sciences]. Frankfurt: Suhrkamp.

Ellis, Carolyn (2003) Grave tending: With mom at the cemetery. *Forum Qualitative Sozialforschung/Forum: Qualitative Social Research*, 4(2): Art. 28. Retrieved April 2, 2007 from http://www.qualitative-research.net/fqs-texte/2-03/2-03ellis-e.htm

Ellis, Carolyn and Bochner, Art (2000) Autoethnography, personal narratives, reflexivity: Researcher as subject. In Norman K. Denzin and Yvonna S. Lincoln (eds), *Handbook of Qualitative Research* (2nd edn). Thousand Oaks, CA: SAGE. pp. 733–768.

Finlay, Linda (2002) Pearls, pith, and provocation. 'Outing' the researcher: the provenance, process, and practice of reflexivity. *Qualitative Health Research,* 12(4): 531–545.

Finlay, Linda and Gough, Brendan (eds) (2003) *Reflexivity: A Practical Guide for Researchers in Health and Social Sciences*. Oxford: Blackwell Science.

Fleck, Ludwik (1935a/1994) *Entstehung und Entwicklung einer wissenschaftlichen Tatsache. Einführung in die Lehre vom Denkstil und Denkkollektiv* (edited by L. Schäfer and T. Schnelle). Frankfurt: Suhrkamp.

Fleck, Ludwik (1935b/1983) Über die wissenschaftliche Beobachtung und die Wahrnehmung im allgemeinen. In *Erfahrung und Tatsache. Gesammelte Aufsätze* (edited by L. Schäfer and T. Schnelle). Frankfurt: Suhrkamp. pp. 59–83.

Fontana, Andrea and Frey, James H. (1994) Interviewing: The art of science. In Norman K. Denzin and Yvonna S. Lincoln (eds), *Handbook of Qualitative Research*. Thousand Oaks, CA: SAGE. pp. 361–376.

Freshwater, Dawn (2005) Commentary: Writing, rigour and reflexivity in nursing research. *Journal of Research in Nursing*, 10(3): 311–315.

Gardner, Lyn (2006) Review: Grounded theory sampling. The contribution of reflexivity. *Journal of Research in Nursing*, 11(3): 261–262.

Geertz, Clifford (1988) *Works and Lives: The Anthropologist as Author*. Stanford, CA: Stanford University Press.

Gergen, Ken J. (1999) *An Invitation to Social Construction*. London: SAGE.

Gergen, Ken J. and Gergen, Mary (1991) Towards reflexive methodologies. In Frederick Steier (ed), *Research and Reflexivity*. London: SAGE. pp. 21–38

Glaser, Barney G. (1978) *Theoretical Sensitivity*. Mill Valley, CA: The Sociology Press.

Glaser, Barney G. (1992) *Emergence vs Forcing. Basics of Grounded Theory Analysis*. Mill Valley, CA: Sociology Press.

Glaser, Barney G. (2001) *The Grounded Theory Perspective: Conceptualization Contrasted with Description*. Mill Valley, CA: Sociology Press.

Glaser, Barney G. (2002) Constructivist grounded theory? *Forum Qualitative Sozialforschung/Forum: Qualitative Social Research*, 3(3): Art. 12. Retrieved April 2, 2007 from http://www.qualitative-research.net/fqs-texte/3-02/3-02glaser-e.htm

Glaser, Barney G. with the assistance of Judith Holton (2004) Remodeling grounded theory. *Forum Qualitative Sozialforschung/Forum: Qualitative Social Research*, 5(2): Art. 4. Retrieved April 2, 2007 from http://www.qualitative-research.net/fqs-texte/2-04/2-04glaser-e.htm

Glaser, Barney G. and Strauss, Anselm L. (1965) *Awareness of Dying*. Chicago: Aldine.

Glaser, Barney G. and Strauss, Anselm L. (1967) *The Discovery of Grounded Theory. Strategies for Qualitative Research*. New York: Aldine de Gruyter.

Gubrium, Jaber F. and Holstein, James A. (eds) (2002) *Handbook of Interview Research: Context & Method*. Thousand Oaks, CA: SAGE.

Hall, Wendy A. and Callery, Peter (2001) Pearls, pith, and provocation. Enhancing the rigor of grounded theory: incorporating reflexivity and relationality. *Qualitative Health Research*, 11(2), 257–272.

Hall, Wendy A., Long, Bonita, Bermbach, Nicole, Jordan, Sharalyn and Patterson, Kathryn (2005) Qualitative teamwork issues and strategies: coordination through mutual adjustment. *Qualitative Health Research*, 15(3): 394–410.

Hammersley, Martyn and Atkinson, Paul (1995) *Ethnography: Principles in Practice* (2nd edn). London: Routledge.

Hand, Helen (2003) The mentor's tale: a reflexive account of semi-structured interviews. *Nurse Researcher*, 10(3): 15–27.

Hentz Becker, Patricia (1993) Common pitfalls in published grounded theory research. *Qualitative Health Research*, 3: 254–260.

Holman Jones, Stacy (2005) Autoethnography: making the personal political. In Norman K. Denzin and Yvonna S. Lincoln (eds), *The SAGE Handbook of Qualitative Research* (3rd edn). Thousand Oaks, CA: SAGE. pp. 763–792.

Humphreys, Michael (2005) Getting personal: Reflexivity and autoethnographic vignettes. *Qualitative Inquiry*, 11(6): 840–860.

Jasper, Melanie A. (2005) Using reflective writing within research. *Journal of Research in Nursing*, 10(3), 247–260.

Jones, Kip (2006) A biographic researcher in pursuit of an aesthetic: The use of arts-based (re)presentations in 'performative' dissemination of life stories. *Qualitative Sociology Review*. Retrieved April 2, 2007 from http://www.qualitativesociologyreview.org/ENG/Volume3/QSR_2_1_Jones.pdf

Jupp, Victor (ed) (2006) *The SAGE Dictionary of Social Research Methods*. London: SAGE.

Kennedy, Tara J. and Lingard, Lorelei A (2006) Making sense of grounded theory in medical education. *Medical Education*, 40(2): 101–108.

Knoblauch, Hubert, Flick, Uwe and Maeder, Christoph in cooperation with Iain Lang (eds) (2005) The State of the Art of Qualitative Research in Europe. *Forum Qualitative Sozialforschung/Forum: Qualitative Social Research*, 6(3). Retrieved April 2, 2007 from http://www.qualitative-research.net/fqs/fqs-e/inhalt3-05-e.htm

Kuhn, Thomas S. (1962/1973) *Die Struktur wissenschaftlicher Revolutionen*. Frankfurt: Suhrkamp.

Kuhn, Thomas S. (1977/1992) *Die Entstehung des Neuen. Studien zur Struktur der Wissenschaftsgeschichte* (edited by L. Krüger). Frankfurt: Suhrkamp.

Legewie, Heiner and Schervier-Legewie, Barbara (2004) 'Research is hard work, it's always a bit suffering. Therefore, on the other side research should be fun.' Anselm Strauss in conversation with Heiner Legewie and Barbara Schervier-Legewie. *Forum Qualitative Sozialforschung/Forum: Qualitative Social Research*, 5(3): Art. 22. Retrieved April 2, 2007 from http://www.qualitative-research.net/fqs-texte/3-04/04-3-22-d.htm

Lincoln, Yvonna S. and Denzin, Norman K. (1994) The fifth moment. In Norman K. Denzin and Yvonna S. (eds.), *Handbook of Qualitative Research*. London: SAGE. pp. 575–586.

Lynch, Michael (2000) Against reflexivity as an academic virtue and source of privileged knowledge. *Theory, Culture & Society*, 17(3): 26–54.

Mantzoukas, Stefanos (2005) The inclusion of bias in reflective and reflexive research. A necessary prerequisite for securing validity. *Journal of Research in Nursing*, 10(3): 279–295.

Marcus, George E. (1998) What comes (just) after 'post'? In Norman K. Denzin and Yvonna S. Lincoln (eds), *The Landscape of Qualitative Research. Theories and Issues.* Thousand Oaks, CA: SAGE. pp. 383–403.

Marks, Stephan and Mönnich-Marks, Heidi (2003) The Analysis of Counter-Transference Reactions Is a Means to Discern Latent Interview-Contents. *Forum Qualitative Sozialforschung/Forum: Qualitative Social Research*, 4(2): 36. Retrieved April 2, 2007 from http://www.qualitative-research.net/fqs-texte/2-03/2-03marks-e.htm

Mey, Günter (2007) Qualitative research on 'adolescence, identity, narration': Programmatic and empirical examples. In Aristi Born and Meike Watzlawik (eds), *Capturing Identity: Quantitative and Qualitative Methods.* Lanham, MD: University Press of America. pp. 53–69.

Mey, Günter and Mruck, Katja (2007) Qualitative research in Germany: A short cartography. *International Sociology Review of Books*, 22(2): 138–154.

Mey, Günter, Ottmar, Kariin and Mruck, Katja (2006) *NetzWerkstatt*—Pilotprojekt zur Internetbasierten Beratung und Begleitung qualitativer Forschungsarbeiten in den Sozialwissenschaften. In Karl-Siegbert Rehberg (eds), *Soziale Ungleichheit—Kulturelle Unterschiede. Verhandlungen des 32. Kongresses der Deutschen Gesellschaft für Soziologie in München 2004.* Frankfurt: Campus. [CD-Rom Version]

Miles, Matthew B. and Huberman, Michael (1984) *Qualitative Data Analysis: A sourcebook for new methods.* Beverly Hills, CA: SAGE.

Mills, Jane, Bonner, Ann and Francis, Karen (2006a) The development of constructivist grounded theory. *International Journal of Qualitative Methods*, 5(1): Retrieved April 2, 2007 from http://www.ualberta.ca/~iiqm/backissues/5_1/HTML/mills.htm

Mills, Jane, Bonner, Ann and Francis, Karen (2006b) Adopting a constructivist approach to grounded theory: Implications for research design. *International Journal of Nursing Practice*, 12: 8–13.

Mruck, Katja and Breuer, Franz (2003) Subjectivity and reflexivity in qualitative research—The FQS issues. *Forum Qualitative Sozialforschung/Forum: Qualitative Social Research*, 4(2): Art. 23. Retrieved April 2, 2007 from http://www.qualitative-research.net/fqs-texte/2-03/2-03intro-1-e.htm

Mruck, Katja and Mey, Günter (1998) Selbstreflexivität und Subjektivität im Auswertungsprozeß biographischer Materialien—zum Konzept einer 'Projektwerkstatt qualitativen Arbeitens' zwischen Colloquium, Supervision und Interpretationsgemeinschaft [Self-reflexivity and subjectivity in the process of analyzing biographical materials—The concept of a 'Project workshop for qualitative work,' bridging colloquium, supervision, and interpretation groups]. In Gerd Jüttemann and Hans Thomae (eds), *Biographische Methoden in den Humanwissenschaften.* Weinheim: Beltz/PVU. pp. 284–306.

Mruck, Katja, Cisneros Puebla, César A. and Faux, Robert (2005) Editorial: About qualitative research centers and peripheries. *Forum Qualitative Sozialforschung/Forum: Qualitative Social Research*, 6(3): Art. 49. Retrieved April 2, 2007 from http://www.qualitative-research.net/fqs-texte/3-06/06-3-49-e.htm

Mruck, Katja, Roth, Wolff-Michael and Breuer, Franz (eds) (2002) Subjectivity and reflexivity in qualitative research I. *Forum Qualitative Sozialforschung/Forum: Qualitative Social Research*, 3(3). Retrieved April 2, 2007 from http://www.qualitative-research.net/fqs/fqs-e/inhalt3-02-e.htm

Neill, Sarah J. (2006) Grounded theory sampling. The contribution of reflexivity. *Journal of Research in Nursing*, 11(3): 253–260.

Popper, Karl R. (1934/1984) *Logik der Forschung*. Tübingen: Mohr.

Probert, Anne (2006) Searching for an appropriate research design: A personal journey. *Journal of Research Practice*, 2(1): D3. Retrieved April 2, 2007 from http://jrp.icaap.org/content/v2.1/probert.html

Rager, Kathleen B. (2005) Compassion stress and the qualitative researcher. *Qualitative Health Research,* 15(3): 423–430.

Reason, Peter and Bradbury, Hilary (eds) (2001) *Handbook of Action Research: Participative Inquiry and Practice*. London: SAGE.

Reason, Peter and Heron, John (1995) Co-operative inquiry. In Jonathan, A. Smith, Rome Harré and Luk v. Langenhove (eds), *Rethinking Methods in Psychology*. London: SAGE. pp. 122–142.

Reichenbach, Hans (1938/1970) *Experience and Prediction. An Analysis of the Foundations and the Structure of Knowledge*. Chicago, London: The University of Chicago Press.

Richardson, Laurel (2000) Writing: A method of inquiry. In Norman Denzin and Yvonna S. Lincoln (eds), *Handbook of Qualitative Research*. Thousand Oaks, CA: SAGE. pp. 923–948.

Roberts, John Michael and Teela Sanders (2005) Before, during and after: realism, reflexivity and ethnography. *The Sociological Review*, 53(2): 294–313.

Rolfe, Gary and Lyn Gardner (2005) Evidence, reflexivity and the study of persons. *Journal of Research in Nursing*, 10(3), 297–310.

Rosaldo, Renato (1987) Where objectivity lies: The rhetoric of anthropology. In John S. Nelson, Allan Megill, and Donald N. McCloskey (eds), *The Rhetoric of the Human Sciences*. Madison: University of Wisconsin Press. pp. 87–110.

Rose, Gillian (1997) Situating knowledges: positionality, reflexivities and other tactics. *Progress in Human Geography*, 21(3): 305–320.

Rosenthal, Gabriele (1993) Reconstruction of life stories. Principles of selection in generating stories for narrative biographical interviews. *The Narrative Study of Lives*, 1(1): 59–91.

Roth, Wolff-Michael (2002) Grenzgänger seeks reflexive methodology. *Forum Qualitative Sozialforschung/Forum: Qualitative Social Research*, 3(3): 2. Retrieved April 2, 2007 from http://www.qualitative-research.net/fqs-texte/3-02/roth/3-02review-roth-e.htm

Roth, Wolff-Michael and Tobin, Kenneth G. (2004) Co-generative dialoguing and meta-loguing: Reflexivity of processes and genres. *Forum Qualitative Sozialforschung/Forum: Qualitative Social Research,* 5(3): Art. 7. Retrieved April 2, 2007 from http://www.qualitative-research.net/fqs-texte/3-04/04-3-7-e.htm

Roth, Wolff-Michael, Lawless, Daniel V. and Tobin, Kenneth (2000) {Coteaching I cogenerative dialoguing} as praxis of dialectic method. *Forum Qualitative Sozialforschung/Forum: Qualitative Social Research,* 1(3): Art. 32. Retrieved April 2, 2007 from http://www.qualitative-research.net/fqs-texte/3-00/3-00rothetal-e.htm

Roth, Wolff-Michael, Mruck, Katja and Breuer, Franz (eds) (2000) Subjectivity and reflexivity in qualitative research II. *Forum Qualitative Sozialforschung/Forum: Qualitative Social Research*, 4(2). Retrieved April 2, 2007 from http://www.qualitative-research.net/fqs/fqs-e/inhalt2-03-e.htm

Schivelbusch, Wolfgang (1979) *Geschichte der Eisenbahnreise. Zur Industrialisierung von Raum und Zeit im 19. Jahrhundert*. Frankfurt: Ullstein.

Schütze, Fritz (1983) Biographieforschung und narratives Interview. *Neue Praxis*, 13: 283–293.

Schwandt, Thomas A. (2001) *Dictionary of Qualitative Inquiry* (2nd edn). Thousand Oaks, CA: SAGE.

Seale, Clive (1999) *The Quality of Qualitative Research*. London: SAGE.

Steier, Frederick (1991) Introduction. Research as self-reflexivity, self-reflexivity as social process. In Frederick Steier (ed), *Research and Reflexivity*. London: SAGE. pp. 1–11.

Stocking, George W. (1983) *Observers Observed*. Madison: University of Wisconsin Press.

Strauss, Anselm L. (1987) *Qualitative Analysis for Social Scientists*. New York: Cambridge University Press.

Strauss, Anselm L. and Corbin, Juliet M. (1990) *Basics of Qualitative Research, Grounded Theory, Procedures and Techniques*. London: SAGE.

Suddaby, Roy (2006) From the editors: What grounded theory is not. *Academy of Management Journal*, 49(4), 633–642.

Tedlock, Barbara (2000) Ethnography and ethnographic representation. In Norman K. Denzin and Yvonna S. Lincoln (eds), *Handbook of Qualitative Research* (2nd edn). Thousand Oaks, CA: SAGE. pp. 455–486.

Ten Have, Paul (2002) The notion of member is the heart of the matter: On the role of membership knowledge in ethnomethodological inquiry. *Forum Qualitative Sozialforschung/Forum: Qualitative Social Research*, 3(3), Art. 21. Retrieved April 2, 2007 from http://www.qualitative-research.net/fqs-texte/3-02/3-02tenhave-e.htm

Van Maanen, John (1988) *Tales of the Field: On Writing Ethnography*. Chicago: The University of Chicago Press.

Wengraf, Tom (2001) *Qualitative Research Interviewing: Biographic Narrative and Semi-structured Method*. London: SAGE.

Wilkinson, Sue (1988) The role of reflexivity in feminist psychology. *Women's Studies International Forum*, 11: 493–502.

Woolgar, Steve (1988) Reflexivity is the ethnographer of the text. In Steve Woolgar (ed), *Knowledge and Reflexivity: New Frontiers in the Sociology of Knowledge*. Newbury Park, CA: SAGE. pp. 14–36.

Wright, Toni and Cochrane, Ray (2000) Factors influencing successful submission of PhD theses. *Studies in Higher Education*, 25(2): 181–195.

25

Mediating Structure and Interaction in Grounded Theory

Bruno Hildenbrand

INTRODUCTION

Two issues are encompassed by the title to this article: first, the theoretical question of the relationship between *structure* and *interaction* in the social sciences. Irrespective of various traditions of theory in social science, this rapport is conceived as an interaction between the structured and the structuring. The second issue relates to the consequences derived in method from the response to the first question on the relationship between structure and action. This is where we will be asking ourselves in what form the perspective of grounded theory has dealt with this interaction, and how it has developed. I will be demonstrating this development exclusively found in the works of Strauss and of Corbin and Strauss, not, however, of Glaser, by way of the methodological concepts of *conditional matrix* and *coding paradigm*. I will be discussing the criticism voiced against them from the angle of a social constructivism and a postmodern turn. In so doing, the conceptual and philosophical foundations of the grounded theory perspective will be an issue for me, in the sense of their aptitude in serving the pragmatism of research. For this reason, quite a large part of the paper is devoted to the case study described later in this chapter.

STRUCTURE AND ACTION IN SOCIOLOGICAL THEORIES

In his analysis of the Napoleonic coup d'état of December 2, 1851, Karl Marx writes: 'Men make their own history, but they do not make it as they please; they do not make it under self-selected circumstances, but under circumstances existing already, given and transmitted from the past' (Marx, 1964: 226). This study that first came out in 1852 can be viewed as the early formulation of a challenge that continues to engage sociological academia today and focuses on resolving the relation between micro- and macro-theoretical views of societies. The progression of sociological history according to Marx never fails to show a tendency towards reductionist approaches, particularly too with Marx himself. Even today, social theories can be roughly differentiated according to whether they see action as determined by structures or, vice versa, structures as dependent on action. Both positions fail to do justice to the complexities of sociological theory and methodology: in the case of structuralism as a position that gives preference to structure rather than action, there is the central risk of freezing action in the structures. In the case of interactionism that takes the opposite path, there is the risk of losing the structure in emergence.

In between these two extreme positions are theories in social science that make no difference between structure and interaction. These theories view structure and action simply as different perspectives of the same subject. The approach taken by Peter Berger and Thomas Luckmann focuses fully on the interaction between social structure and the identity of the individual: 'The social processes involved in both the formation and the maintenance of identity are determined by the social structure. Conversely, the identities produced by the interplay of organism, individual consciousness and social structure react upon the given social structure, maintaining it, modifying it, or even reshaping it' (Berger & Luckmann, 1967: 173). Pierre Bourdieu relates structure to action in the following concept: the *habitus* mediates between structure and actions, and the *strategy* denotes the practical interaction of the actor with the world, which can be such that fictions set realities (Bourdieu, 1998: 126). In this, the structure is retained; it is not merged into habitus but set in scene in relation to it.

Like Pierre Bourdieu, Anthony Giddens also works from human practices, or rather from social practices, which to him form the heart of all that is social. In these social practices, structures are produced and reproduced. They do, however, take on an independence of their own and form a framework for the actions of individuals and of society. Nevertheless, Giddens focuses on the production aspect of structures. Structures are resources of human agents in that they make action possible. As such, however, they first need to be interpreted by the actors: 'Human social activities, like some self-reproducing items in nature, are recursive. That is to say, they are not brought into being by social actors but continually recreated by them via the very means whereby they express themselves *as* actors. In and through their activities agents reproduce the conditions that make these activities possible' (Giddens, 1985: 2). The common denominator of these positions is that structures are not viewed as given, static units. Instead it is assumed that structures are generated, updated, and transformed during processes of structuring. Structure and interaction are hence inseparable. Transformations evolve, for example, when actors re-interpret structures, cause them to intersect, or shape them in settings other than the original ones (Sewell, 1992: 13).

It is one thing to theorize about an issue, but it is quite another to implement it into the methodology of social inquiry. With the grounded theory, starting with the initial conception of Barney Glaser and Anselm Strauss through to the last papers of Anselm Strauss as well as of Juliet Corbin together with Anselm Strauss, a methodology has been devised that initially devoted itself to the task of developing a method that would make it possible to generate theory from the data. Further development has not been smooth; but it is seen as controversial in the social world of grounded theory itself. A dividing line is drawn between Barney Glaser on the one hand, and Anselm Strauss and Juliet Corbin on the other. Yet the main issue at stake is that raised by Barney Glaser as to whether further developments of the grounded theory perspective, as formulated by Corbin and Strauss, actually do justice to the central aspect of *emergence*. The coding paradigm and the conditional matrix in particular (Strauss, 1987; Strauss & Corbin, 1990) have drawn his criticism. Recently discussion has also focused on assimilating the existing constructivist (Bryant, 2003; Charmaz, 2006) and postmodern (Clarke, 2005) theories into the perspective of the grounded theory. The point of this would be to give greater emphasis to the actors themselves. In this chapter, it is my intention to crystallize the assumptions on *structure* that underlie the conditional matrix and the coding paradigm, and to demonstrate how, in spite of greater orientation to the conditional matrix, i.e. in spite of a more distinct leaning towards structural modes of observation, the perspective of the actors and hence the element of emergence can stand in their own right.

FROM THE STRUCTURAL PROCESS VIA THE NEGOTIATED ORDER TO STRUCTURAL ORDERING

In *Time for Dying*, Glaser and Strauss derive conclusions of general sociological interest from their analyses of trajectories of dying at hospitals. The authors show that organizations, such as hospital wards or hospitals in general, including other types of organizations as well, all represent *structure in process* (Glaser & Strauss, 1968: 240): structures are not static in their core but are sustained by continuous transitions that evolve from interactions. Consequently there are no stable structures, since these are created and reshaped through a continuous process of change. During this process, that which is novel (the change of structures) and that which is old (the existing structures) clearly relate dialectically. In the words of Strauss: 'The action is shaped by conditions but in turn is shaped by active actors' (Strauss, 1993: 47). This follows up on George Herbert Mead, who writes: 'The emergent when it appears is always found to follow from the past, but before it appears it does not, by definition, follow from the past' (Mead, 1959: 2). Common to both of these formulations is that, depending on the time perspective taken, past and present are conceived to appear different: looking ahead, they seem to be quite separate, whereas a retrospective glance shows them to be bound up, one with the other. And in the same way actors too seem to differ: looking ahead, they appear to be engaged at their own initiative, whereas regarded retrospectively, they seem to be formed by the past. Hence the new is viewed in its relation to the old: 'The novel can only be conceived of in relation to the old, as the latter is likely to enter after debate into the former in complex ways, and perhaps in ways invisible to the actors themselves' (Strauss, 1993: 44).

Negotiated order is a term derived from a study of a psychiatric hospital, but only spelled out at a later date (Strauss et al., 1963). Here the authors were able to demonstrate that in respect of structures, *negotiation processes* actually determine everyday life of organizations, whereas, formal structures set limits to negotiatory factors. Reacting to the accusation that symbolic interactionism features an 'astructural bias' (Farberman, 1991: 481), Strauss replaces the term *negotiated order* with a new one: *processual ordering*. Strauss justifies his switch in terminology as follows: *negotiated order* not only refers to *negotiatory* processes, but also 'to the lack of fixity of social order, its temporal, mobile, and unstable character, and the flexibility of interactants faced with the need to act through interactional processes in specific localized situations where although rules and regulations exist nevertheless these are not necessarily precisely prescriptive or peremptorily constraining' (Strauss, 1993: 255).

Strauss summarizes his thoughts on the relation between structure and interaction as follows:

> 'Order refers to relatively predictable events'.
> 'Disorder is created by events that are either unpredictable or not predicted'.
> 'Ordering is ongoing'.
>   So an interactionist theory of action 'emphasizes contingencies and the inevitable changes brought about by them. But at the same time it cannot, must not, fail to link contingencies and action to the more slowly moving, more stable elements of the social environment created and maintained sometimes many generations ago' (Strauss, 1993: 260).

In *Qualitative Analysis for Social Scientists* (Strauss, 1987), we find a chapter on 'Coding for structural and interactional relationships' that specifically expresses another formulation for this selfsame position: 'Minimizing or leaving out structural conditions, whether more immediately contextual or "further away" (or, as some social scientists say, the *macroscopic* or *structural*) short-circuits the explanation. Doing the reverse, overemphasizing the structural conditions, does not do justice to the rich interactional data that put life and a sense of immediacy (or as some say, *reality*) into the analysis' (Strauss, 1987: 78).

In these formulations, Strauss shows himself to be an advocate of a structure/agency position, without having explicitly addressed the ongoing discussions on the issue. He is far removed from any 'a-structural bias'. There where he refers to 'reality', Strauss comes very close to Bourdieu. This latter justified his rejection of the structuralism of Lévi-Strauss by emphasizing the importance of bringing 'the practical relation to the world back into view' as opposed to supporting the scholasticism of structuralism (Bourdieu, 2002: 72). This development in the action theory of Strauss reflects a development in methodology. It is mirrored in the methodological concept of the conditional matrix. Component concepts here are: *conditional path, trajectory, social world, arena* (Strauss, 1993: 52; Strauss & Corbin, 1990: Chapter 10). We are now going to take a closer look at these concepts. On the basis of a case study, their efficacy will be demonstrated in the following section.

Conditional matrix. The work co-authored with Juliet Corbin, Basics of Qualitative Research (Strauss & Corbin, 1990), explains the significance of the conditional matrix for the process of research in the style of grounded theory:[1]

(1) It helps you to be **theoretically sensitive to the range of conditions** that might bear upon the phenomenon under study.
(2) It enables you to be theoretically sensitive to the **range of potential consequences** that results from action/interaction.
(3) It assists you to **systematically relate conditions, actions/interaction, and consequences to a phenomenon** (Strauss & Corbin, 1990: 161, emphasized as in the original).

Conditional matrix denotes a context of social frames, within which social interactions evolve. The main purpose of the conditional matrix is 'to help researchers to think beyond micro social structures and immediate interactions to larger social conditions and consequences' (Charmaz, 2006: 118).

Conditional path denotes the reconstruction of the course taken by an event (*cf. event or incident*) through the various levels of the conditional matrix. As a result, the coherence of the event with these levels is tapped, as well as the interindividual connection of the levels themselves.

Event or incident: If society largely means interaction, i.e. if it evolves through interaction, then events within which social interactions are manifested are the core of sociological analysis. Human agency in its ability not only to reproduce structures, but also to transform them (Sewell, 1992), can only be identified in events themselves.

Trajectory: Strauss uses this term in dual fashion: first, he means the development of a phenomenon in time, and second, the interactions contributing to this development (Strauss, 1993: 53). The trajectory is shaped during the course of this period of time: there is the 'potentiality for consequences of interaction to become, in their turn, conditions that affect further interaction, which then produces further consequences' (Strauss, 1993: 56).

Social Worlds: Adele Clarke, to whom Strauss makes reference when he explains his concept of the social world, puts it this way: 'Groups with shared commitments to certain activities, sharing resources of many kinds to achieve their goals, and building shared ideologies about how to go about this business' (Clarke, 1991: 131; in Strauss, 1993: 212). Gerson (1978) views society in all as a 'mosaic of social worlds that both touch and interpenetrate' (from Clarke, 1991: 131).

Social worlds are made up of arenas, activities, organizations, and technologies. They overlap with other social worlds, tend towards segmentation, and need legitimation. *Social worlds* have a history and they change.

Social Arenas arise from conflicts about major issues 'as whirlpools of argumentative action, they lie at the very heart of permanence and change of each social world' (Strauss, 1993: 227). These conflicts can develop within and between social worlds. It is out of these crises that *social order* and *social change* evolve: both developing from the same origin in interactionist terms, as shown by the concepts of *structural process, negotiated order*, and *structural ordering*.

These concepts interrelate as follows: the central location for commencing sociological analysis is the *social world*. The production of *social order* and *social change* takes place in *events* in *arenas* that take shape within and between social worlds. The conditional matrix localizes the respectively analyzed *social world(s)* in terms of its connection with other (relevant) *social worlds*; in this manner, it should be possible to overcome any micro- macro-dichotomy in the formation of sociological theories (Strauss, 1993: 64). The *conditional path* relates the contexts of conditions, one with the other, of a structuring process that is ongoing in the form of an *arena* within or between *social worlds*.

This overall image makes it clear that the one concept cannot be had without the other. In their association one with the other, these concepts provide an appropriate methodological framework for analyzing social processes of change. An analysis that is conducted on the basis of these concepts neither reduces interaction to structure, nor does it reduce structure to interaction. Instead it does justice to the need for placing 'processual ordering' or 'structuration' centerstage of sociological analysis.

A case study: The development of child and youth welfare in Germany after reunification of East and West Germany

We will now investigate the efficiency of the conditional matrix in the process of research, initially by way of a case study, before engaging in critical in-depth discussion. This case study has been taken from an investigation we have been conducting since 2001 for the *Collaborative Research Centre 580: Social Developments after Structural Change—Discontinuity, Tradition and Structure Formation* at the Friedrich Schiller University in Jena and the Martin Luther University in Halle-Wittenberg. Our project at this Collaborative Research Centre is part of the research efforts concentrated on actors and institutions in the social sector and addresses the restructuring of child and youth welfare since 1990 in the east and west of Germany. (Other projects relate to elite research and research on the labor market.)

The subject of this research is as follows: the acculturation process that has taken place in child welfare in Germany (both in East and West Germany) since 1990 is that an old system of child welfare has been replaced by a new system.

The replacement has been accompanied by a change in paradigm. Before 1990, the logic of child welfare was paternalistic both in East and West Germany. Persons responsible for clients were not working *with* them, but working *for* them. In West Germany, persons responsible for child welfare acted as professionals, whereas, in East Germany, professional expertise was not required explicitly. The reason for this was that problems in child welfare were treated as problems caused by capitalism. In the long run, it was assumed, socialism by its mere existence would lead to a situation where child welfare problems would simply disappear. The result of this thinking was that child welfare developed within a niche. Consequently, child welfare professionals both in East and West Germany were faced with changes in 1990, but they acted under completely different conditions when they had to cope with changes.

During the first years of the transformational process after the collapse of communism it was assumed that simply transforming the institutions would suffice to manage necessary changes. Institutions were thought to automatically gain meaning by acting. This assumption was not only shared by politicians but also by social scientists, and soon it turned out to be a naïve idea. Naïve in two respects: first theoretically, since it derived actions from structures and failed to treat structures under the aspect of structuration. And second, at a life practice level, because even without sociological analysis, it was obvious that in many places institutional transfer was simply not working. In the field of child and youth welfare, another factor was that both East and West German experts together had to learn new practices: how to promote the autonomy of clients which was demanded by law? In this process, experts from West Germany were at an advantage as far as technical knowledge and handling non-state-run institutions of child and youth welfare were concerned. Moreover during the 1970s, child and juvenile welfare in West Germany had become subjected to gradual professionalization, whereas in the GDR youth welfare had largely been conducted on an honorary footing.

The change in child and youth welfare in East and in West Germany constitutes a natural experiment worthy of long-term monitoring to sociologists who are interested in analyzing the evolution of the novel. For the purposes of this chapter, namely to investigate how the mediation between structure and interaction can be covered in the process of sociological analysis, this change provides a suitable testing ground for the methodology.

The focus of our analysis lies in the institution of the General Social Services Department, a division of the Youth Welfare Office, of a rural district. The assignments of the General Social Services Department also involve protecting children from danger and advising and supporting parents as they bring up their children. Where necessary, the General Social Services Department also approves further educational assistance or acts as mediator between other responsible agencies. The assignments and competences of those working in the General Social Services Department are governed by the Child and Juvenile Welfare Act.

Before coming to the example of analyzing material from this research project, we will first describe the practical mode of procedure in such an analysis, as proposed by Strauss or by Corbin and Strauss. As to application of the conditional matrix in the process of research, Strauss gives the following instructions (Strauss, 1993: 60):

- Each study should include all levels of the conditional matrix.
- At each level, the specific characteristics of relevance to the study should be duly incorporated; this serves the generalizability of the study.
- In so doing, factors of location and time are to be considered.
- All levels of the conditional matrix interrelate in reciprocity of conditions.

Strauss then defines eight qualities of the conditional matrix that are concentrically arranged. We will number these concentric circles in order to refer to them later on. These eight qualities combine to give a general outline for orientation; for each study they need to be adjusted as required.[2]

- The outer circle (8) denotes the international level with the political socioeconomic conditions (Strauss & Corbin, 1990), i.e. the politics, values, philosophies and international problems (Strauss, 1993).
- Next comes the national level (7) with the national policies, regulations, culture and history, values, economic factors, issues and problems.
- Level (6) relates to the level of community and its unique demographic characteristics.
- The level of organizations and institutions (5) reflects the structures, the rules, problems and their respective history.
- Level (4) has to do with the specific divisions of the organizations under study.
- Then comes the level of collective groups, groupings and individuals (3). Light is thrown on the biographies, philosophies, knowledge and the experience of the various actors.
- At level (2), focus is on the interactions.
- At the center of the conditional matrix (1) are the actual strategic and routine actions, or more generally, *work*, as understood by Strauss in his use of the term.

In the next step, *conditional paths* are reconstructed. The mode of procedure is as follows: 'Begin with an event or incident, then attempt to determine *why* this occurred, what conditions were operating, how the conditions manifested themselves, and with what consequences' (Strauss, 1993: 62). Together, these questions form the *coding paradigm* (Strauss, 1987: 27) that constitutes a habitual mode of access to the sociological material in question; 'in a short time this paradigm quite literally becomes part and parcel of the analyst's thought processes' (Strauss, 1987: 27). Subsequently the following questions need to be put (Strauss, 1993: 62): 'What levels of the conditional matrix were passed through? With what effects?' (Strauss, 1993: 62).

By way of an example (Strauss, 1993: 63), Strauss makes it clear that selection here should particularly concentrate on events that imply a disorder in action. Such events break through the continuity of routine action and may even become the initiating events for the generation of something new. When anything is novel, debate and possibly conflict is the outcome. In the social world under investigation, *arenas* take shape. And in these arenas *social order* is established and changed.

It is up to the astuteness of the researcher to uncover such arenas. Now to the analysis of the material.

'Begin with an event or incident'

We have established above that, in the interests of pragmatic research, it is not routine events that are to be selected in the process of research, but problematic ones. As a matter of principle, the processual ordering of a field of study is manifested in each event that is revealed in interactions. Problematic events, in other words, those that impede the routine actions of the actors and the interactions thus entailed, evoke this processual ordering most clearly (*cf.* George Herbert Mead, for whom the problematic situation constitutes the starting point for his analysis; Mead, 1972: 6–8). These events are reported to the researcher as critical or the scientist himself finds them to be critical. The example selected here was brought to the attention of the researcher by the actors in the field. The matter is the following:

In 2003, at the General Social Services Department of a Youth Welfare Office in one of the districts [Landkreis] we investigated, the position of social worker becomes vacant. The Public Officer in charge intends to advertise this vacancy not just locally but beyond the borders of the district. The reason for this is that suitably trained professionals in child and juvenile welfare are not found to be available in the rural district concerned. The staff representative council [a quasi shop steward system for public service employees—note of translator] prevents her doing so. The council members are interested in securing the jobs of as many employees as possible within the district administration body, notwithstanding the fact that there is nobody amongst the staff of the district administration body who is professionally qualified to fill the vacancy. At the outset of this conflict, the staff representative council gains the upper hand. The vacancy is initially advertised internally. A cook applies for the job. The Public Officer in charge refuses to consider the application, upon which the staff council calls for written justification. This is admittedly submitted, but does not satisfy the staff council. According to the chairwoman of the staff council, any woman who has brought up children is in a position to carry out the work of a social worker of the Youth Welfare Office. Even the local trade union that points out the law's requirement for professionalism of Youth Welfare Office employees fails to change her mind. [The data in this outline has been taken from official letters, fieldnotes, and interviews.]

'Then attempt to determine why this occurred, what conditions were operating, how the conditions manifested themselves, and with what consequences'

Here is where Strauss makes reference to the coding paradigm, in other words, the question of *conditions, consequences, interactions*, and *strategies* related to an event (Strauss, 1987: 27–28; Strauss & Corbin, 1990: 99). The individual points of the coding paradigm and its linkages are not brought over to the material from outside, but are found to exist in the material itself (Strauss, 1987: 456). We hence initially use this coding paradigm as a resource for questions about the event described above.

What has to happen for a cook to apply for the vacancy of social worker? This is the question as to *why this occurred*. One possibility would be that the cook interpreted the job profile wrongly. This would be easy to resolve and there would be an end to the matter. A second interpretation would be an exceptional state of mind, such as an overestimation of herself, as presented in a manic psychosis, for example. These two interpretations relate to personal misconceptions and lead no further. For if a position is advertised internally in a public office, in which there are no free social workers or similar professionals available, this is not primarily an issue of persons, but is indicative of a structural problem.

And this is where we come to the question of the *conditions* that make the above incident possible in the first place. The answer: this incident can only occur if professionalism is not a criterion for the staff council. The fact that this philosophy of the staff council reflects an ignorance of the law does call for explanation. If the council is not aware of the legal position, a simple memo can quickly rectify the matter. Or, however, the staff council is indeed aware of the law, yet deliberately turns a blind eye to it. This can be rooted in an attitude of provocation or, however, in a policy customarily practised by the staff council that is common to this particular district administration. In that case, however, it must be taken as assumed that this attitude of the staff council has already borne fruits in the past; in other words, this must be habitual action. Yet if it is habitual, then there must be a degree of complicity between the staff council and the district administration, or at least tolerance. A third interpretation would be that district administration is not aware that assignments of child and youth welfare are governed by law and that the law restricts the scope of action that may be taken by the staff council. A fourth interpretation would be that this is simply a power struggle between the staff council and the public officer in charge that is fought without respect for the law. All of these interpretations lead to two codes: (1) the public officer in charge of Youth Welfare is acting in an area of officialdom devoid of any reliable stability of the law; (2) she is caught up in a power struggle.

How the conditions manifested themselves. After the staff council reiterates its position in extensive correspondence and the public officer in charge gives no indication of complying with the staff council and recruiting the cook, the staff council files petition for an organizational analysis. It is to be investigated whether or not the position to be advertised is even required. In other words: the staff council is admittedly ignoring the law, yet is acting in line with bureaucratic logic. Should this analysis deduce that the position in question is to be struck off, the interests of the staff cannot be said to be well served. It is equally against such interests if the petition of the staff council causes a delay in recruitment. Consequently, in thus acting, the staff council takes leave of the level of pertinent logic. Code 3: this is a power struggle fought beyond the bounds of objectivity.

With what consequences? In interpreting this event, we now incorporate further developments. A new situation develops when a client from the suburb in which the vacancy has become available, attempts to commit suicide on the premises of the Youth Welfare Office. This endeavor is only thwarted at great effort. As a result, the public officer in charge refutes all 'professional responsibility for the youth welfare cases in the suburb' [quotation from a letter from the public officer]. In another letter, she threatens to sue the staff council if it fails to give its consent to the external advertising of the vacancy. She also points out that its purpose is to represent staff and not to plan the structure of the district administration body.

The public officer in charge of the Youth Welfare Office hence refuses to concede to the strategy of the staff council and is acting consistently within the bounds of pertinent logic. She is hence acting contrary to procedures common to this particular district administration, where the ignoring of laws is routine. In other words, she is pursuing a new course. She is dealing with assignments that ought to be managed at a higher level, namely at that of management of this particular district administration. Code 4: the power struggle seen here is fought on behalf of the district commissioner by the public officer in charge of the Youth Welfare Office. It serves to establish the structures of official actions that are anchored in law.

The fact that the public officer in charge of the Youth Welfare Office is changing course has something to do with the emergency situation that has occurred (attempted suicide that is related in causality to the staff situation at the Youth Welfare Office). Code 5: It is only when the life of the client is in danger that it is possible for the public officer in charge of the Youth Welfare Office to proceed contrary to the *customary procedure of the district administration body in ignoring the law.*

By applying the *coding paradigm*, we now summarize the codes as follows:

(1) Unreliable stability of the law in official action; (2) power struggle between the authority and the staff council, which (3) is fought outside the bounds of the objective level (4) on a lower level in deputizing mode and which is only defused (5) by a situation of danger. The primarily central code is: *routine disregarding of laws, rectified in risk situations.*

Up to now in the analysis of the case study, all levels of the conditional matrix have been implicitly traversed; yet it is relatively unimportant where, at which level, we commence. We will start at level 8.

Level 8 relates to the conformity of the practices of the Youth Welfare Office in the Federal Republic of Germany with the standards of youth welfare in the western world, of which the Federal Republic of Germany is a part. In the industrial societies of the west, such as the USA, Great Britain and Germany, the 20th century saw the onset of a massive process of professionalization in social work. By contrast, in the German Democratic Republic, as part of the eastern bloc, we see a reverse trend. The reason for this was that problems in child welfare were treated as problems caused by capitalism. In the long run, it was assumed, socialism by its mere existence would lead to a situation where child welfare problems simply disappear. The conflict between the public officer in charge and the staff council regarding the recruitment of a cook thus mirrors the conflict between two political systems, one that ceased to exist in 1990 and the other that is present-day. So that what we have here is a long-lasting *transformation problem.*

From here, we now take a look at level 7, the national level, and the matter of the legal framework, the culture and history of the social treatment of child and juvenile issues and the economic factors that form the framework for child and youth welfare. Not only the former GDR is affected by a change of system in child and youth welfare, but also western Germany. The acculturation process that has taken place in child welfare in Germany since 1990 is that of the replacement of an old system of child welfare with a new one. The replacement has been accompanied by a change in paradigm. Before 1990, the logic of child welfare was paternalistic, both in East and West Germany. Persons responsible for clients were not working *with* them, but working *for* them. The difference between the two parts of the country is that in the case of West Germany, professionalism set in at the latest during the 1970s. Yet in the event concerning the recruitment of a cook, the patterns of the GDR are clearly discernible.

At level 6 we can sketch out the local framework, in which this event takes place. This means the district and its socio-geographic and demographic features. Our approach to investigation entails the agro-social factors, which all lie in the past yet still have a considerable effect on local mentalities and hence local practices, although they actually ceased to exist in fact as from 1945 at the latest (Bohler, 1995). The district investigated in this case is situated in a low mountain range of Thuringia, in the eastern part of Germany. From the aspect of social history, it is part of two differing, yet associated socio-historical patterns that are typical for west, central and south Germany. In the valleys we find areas with mid-sized and large family-owned and run farms. Here the farms are handed down from one generation to the next, undivided. So that the siblings of the successor are forced (or free) to orient themselves outside the farm where they grew up. One strategy would be to marry a wife who is the heir of a farm, to work and save money to be able to buy a farm, or to leave agriculture altogether. This furthers the *development of mental structures of autonomy.* In the mountainous regions of the district are areas with small farms. Here the practice of handing down the farm from one generation to the other is to divide it up among the siblings. To make a living for a family, it is necessary to combine one's own share of the parent's farm with that of a woman from the same village or a neighboring village. Another strategy would be to combine part-time farming with a dependant occupation or with a non-agricultural business. Here, too, *autonomy is the mental structure, which is supported by this rural social structure.* A contrast to these two historical patterns in agriculture would be the northern part of eastern Germany and the eastern part of northwest Germany with dominant structures of latifundia economics. In latifundia economics, farm laborers, tenants etc. are mostly dependant on the latifundia owner for the planning of their lives. The challenge people face in these areas is to develop autonomy in the context of heteronomous social structures. This promotes the *development of mental structures that are dominated by a deep feeling of heteronomy in taking responsibility for one's own biography.* Areas with small farms tend to form commercial landscapes and these, in turn, challenge the development of specific skills: in Germany these are the locations particularly known for their innovative strengths in technology (glass industry, clocks and watches, electronics). The Black Forest and the Thuringia Forest where the region investigated is located are good examples. A non-professional orientation, such as found in the child and youth welfare of the GDR, and still practised in the district we investigated, manifests a significant contradiction, therefore, to local mentality structures.

At this juncture we can return to the quotation of Strauss, in which he says that an interactionist theory of action must not fail 'to link contingencies and action to the more slowly moving, more stable elements of the social environment created and maintained sometimes many generations ago' (Strauss, 1993: 261). More stable structures are found on three levels.[3] These are initially the *elementary structures* that are already given and unchangeable, even if actors can handle them strategically. An example would be the elementary structures of reciprocity (Mead); another one would refer to the incest taboo (Lévi-Strauss). At the second level we have the *regional structures that have long been of socio-historical impact within a national territory as well as the variable structures of social milieus*. We have defined them as regionally historical structures in agriculture, each of them differing in their scopes of autonomous action. The third level relates to the system of action, as played out through the specific structures of the individual case and its actors, here the youth welfare office—the district administration—staff council (Matthiesen, 1994: 103). It is here that the term *trajectory* comes into play, for at the level of the individual case, actions trigger off structuring processes that themselves shape the frame for actions in the future.

Yet even these more slowly moving elements of society cannot be simply taken as assumed in a perspective of grounded theory. We see them as a *frame*, which *can* be relevant, given this hypothesis, but *need not necessarily* be. They have the status of *hypothesis*.

In our project, for example, we assumed that in regions reflecting latifundia economics, the number of cases of child and youth welfare is larger than in the areas that further autonomy-oriented structures. A count of all cases from one year confirmed this hypothesis; in the district situated in a heteronomy-oriented region, 2.91% of the children and under-18s become clients of the child and youth welfare service. In the district discussed in our example, only 1.55% of this group become clients. Furthermore, we assumed that the forms of aid likewise follow this logic: heteronomy-related assistance, such as referral to a home or a foster family would consequently be expected in regions that mirror heteronomy and vice-versa. However, this is not so. This is due to the *trajectories* of the transformation process in child and youth welfare that have been triggered by the action strategies of the relevant actors.

At levels 5 and 4, focus is on the structures, rules and history of the respective organization and its sub-organizations. In Germany, it is the district administration body that bears responsibility for child and youth welfare. The position of a social worker, such as in our example, is embedded in the General Social Services Department (ASD, Allgemeiner Sozialer Dienst) of the Youth Welfare Office. The ASD is bound by law to carry out its assignments. This means furthering children and families, providing counseling and support for them and securing the well-being of a child, should this be threatened. Possible intervention ranges from providing counseling in difficult circumstances and for problems in bringing up children, through to the temporary protection of children and their committal to a home or foster parents. Structural paradoxes are generated from the parallelism of the help given, on the one hand, and the control exercised on the other in the relations between professionals and their clients, as well as from the right anchored in legislation of each individual to receive help and assistance, in contrast to the limited means made available for such help by the district administration. For the ASD to carry out its assignments, qualification in social work and social pedagogy is required; in Germany this is acquired through study at a university. In GDR times, the tasks carried out today by the ASD were the responsibility of youth welfare boards in the various municipalities that all engaged on a voluntary basis and were not particularly qualified in social work.

Level 3 revolves around the *biographies, philosophies, knowledge* and *experience* of the actors. The main actors in our example are the staff council chairwoman, on the one hand, and the public officer in charge of the Youth Welfare Office on the other. The philosophy of the staff council chairwoman in respect to her work, in this case child and youth welfare, is clear: just as in the days of the GDR, she considers that the work to be carried out does not require any special qualification but is something that can be mastered simply from experience of life. The fact that the law sees otherwise is of no consequence to her. By contrast, what is the position of the public officer in charge of the Youth Welfare Office? Does she differentiate between professionalism, practical life experience and the law? What is the biographical background that influences her in her approach to the tasks on hand?

Looking at biographical backgrounds, we reconstruct the family biographies of the actors over a period of three generations (Hildenbrand, 2004, 2005). In our opinion, genograms in their sequence of 'objective' data such as date of birth, day of death, occupation, place of residence, marriage etc. are the result of decisions that have to be taken by persons in situations of crisis against the background of objective possibilities. On the one hand, crisis situations relate to the crises of detachment that evolve during the course of life and, on the other, to critical events that occur unexpectedly, such as accidents, unemployment etc. In a sequential analysis, the researchers/consultants reconstruct these decisions and the successive choices step by step, and at each interface, lines of action and decision are developed theoretically and compared to the persons' decisions. This is to discover a pattern that allows a description of the degree of the practical autonomy of a family context. In a second step, this pattern can then be compared to the persons' interpretations. The public officer in our example reflects a biography, as the results of this analysis show, which corresponds to the autonomy-oriented and qualification-related habitus of the region in which the district administration is located, where she works. Yet this habitus is totally in contrast to that of the philosophy specific to the GDR. If the district administration (admittedly, however, only in 1999) decides to recruit such a woman to head the Youth Welfare Office, then it is paving the way for the transformation of child and youth welfare in this particular district.

Levels 2 and 1: actors are not playing their parts on their own or in direct interaction with each other in a face-to-face duo, but are embedded in social frames that were reconstructed in the *conditional matrix*. If the public officer in charge of the Youth Welfare Office with her attitude to the task on hand collides with the chairwoman of the staff council with her traits of persistence, then there are other dimensions in the background that influence their interaction. The interesting point in the inquiry is how could it transpire, given the presence of a clear regulation set down by the law, that at this particular Youth Welfare Office, 82% of the employees lack the necessary professional qualification. In general terms: How is it possible that in a public authority that has the right and indeed the duty to intervene in familial autonomy given certain circumstances and, if a child's well-being is jeopardized, for example, to remove that child from the family, i.e. annulling constitutionally anchored rights, the criterion of professionalism is not considered necessary, although it is dictated by law? And for what reason has the issue described developed into a critical situation? The provisional answer to this is: because the recruitment of a new public officer of professional mindset has introduced a new perspective into the arena and, as a result, throws doubt on the existing practice of not making professional qualifications a criterion for selection.

And on the basis of this finding that reveals a largely non-professional approach in a context for which professionalism is mandatory, an answer can now be given to the question that has already been posed, as to whether the lack in conformity with the law is a feature of the staff council or is typical for the practices of this particular district administration: namely these are practices customarily followed by the authority that, as the dispute shows, are now challenged: something new is going on.

In associating the coding paradigm with the conditional matrix it is possible to deliver statements that not only relate to the structures of the individual case, but structures in general. By way of the example given, particularly based on systematic comparisons, we reach conclusions about the process of transformation in eastern Germany over the past 15 years (Hildenbrand et al., 2007). However, to return to the case: during the further course of our study, we have to go one more step and ask ourselves about the *social worlds* and the *arenas*. A few keywords here will have to suffice:

In our example two *social worlds* confront each other, that of child and youth welfare and that of an authority, the district administration body. The world of child and youth welfare not only relates to the Youth Welfare Office as an authority, but also to its clients, to non-government organizations of child and youth welfare and ultimately to the youth welfare board responsible for stipulating the policies for child and youth welfare in that district. The other world is that of the district administration body and its priorities of economy and finance, order and safety and staff interests; in other words, subjects that are to an extent outside the realm of child and youth welfare.

With the dispute about the cook, we have come upon a central *arena* that is tangent to the policy of this particular district administration.

We now take another step forward and claim that by way of the example of the ultimately unsuccessful recruitment of a cook with the Social Services Department of a Youth Welfare Office, it is possible to develop elements of a theory on processes of social change. This theory makes no claim to being formal, but is substantive and, as such, retains the status of a hypothesis (Glaser & Strauss, 1967: 79–99). The theorist's 'sociological perspective is never finished, not even when he writes the last line of his monograph' (Glaser & Strauss, 1967: 256). This theory relates to the structure of processes of imposed social change in organizations and, in the current stage of the research process, is made up of the following elements:

- The decision of the investigated Youth Welfare Office following re-unification of Germany not to alter practices customary to the GDR and to ignore the organizational changes prescribed by law has the effect of establishing *a stable trajectory*.
- A change in management of the rural district leads to the recruitment of an actor (Head of the Youth Welfare Office) who is *open to change* and *willing to implement changes*.
- In a *central arena* (personnel administration/representation) the recruitment of this actor subsequently triggers conflict. At the outset, however, it is not at all clear whether this will lead to a *change in the course of the trajectory*.
- Only a coincidence (attempted suicide of a client at the Youth Welfare Office) induces the change in direction of the trajectory.
- The result: change, in the sense of an altered direction of a trajectory when change is imposed on organizations, is generated in the combination of (a) implementation of specific processes of administrative practices, (b) filling central positions with actors who are willing and prepared to implement change, (c) engaging in conflict by asserting these processes in relevant arenas, (d) occurrence of a coincidence, the mastering of which is determinant as to whether the direction of the trajectory will in fact be changed. There is no problem at all in aligning this finding against the thoughts of Strauss relating to the relation between structure and interaction (*cf.* Strauss, 1993: 260). All of the elements featured there are given: the *contingencies* as well as the *more stable structures*.
- More restrictedly, it has to be noted that these elements only relate to the management level of the organization investigated. Everyday routine of those employed there requires a study of its own.

These elements of a grounded theory of social change in organizations will now be investigated in the next stage of research by way of *theoretical sampling* (Glaser & Strauss, 1967: 45–77). A supremely contrasting case would, for example, be a Youth Welfare Office in East Germany where, in the wake of re-unification, processes of professionalization were launched with the staff.

Here we divert from the case sample[4] and return to the theoretical issue of mediating structure and action in grounded theory. This example illustrates the priority of the conditional matrix in the process of analysis:

(1) Each of the eight points of the conditional matrix reflects topics in their own right. This was not to be expected from the outset (unless one is of the opinion that everything in the world is inter-related). Moreover, its relevance is not the outcome of coercion exerted from the 'application' of the conditional matrix; in fact the conditional matrix has made it easier for the researchers to

apply their understanding of the field of child and youth welfare to the issue under investigation, or rather to the interactions evoked by the disputed recruitment of a cook. It becomes clear that level 7, i.e. the national level, which in our example relates historically to two separate countries, the GDR and the Federal Republic of Germany, re-emerges at local level. It is here that a clash evolves between two persons who hold positions within an organization, of which one is acting in the spirit of the Federal Republic of Germany after reunification and the other in the spirit of the former GDR. On the grounds of this contradiction, a power struggle is fought between two cultures. The older structures of the regional milieu are themselves directly compatible with the structures of a democratic society built on free market principles. As a result, the conflict observed acquires specific accentuation. It is our hypothesis that a long overdue development is in the throes of catching up with the times.

(2) Against this background, the coding paradigm and the conditional matrix serve as tools in formulating critical questions on the process of research itself. Not only this, the coding paradigm and the conditional matrix are implicitly perpetually active with skilled researchers, in so far as they are part of the research habitus of social scientists. On this, Strauss himself writes: 'Although especially helpful to beginning analysts, in a short time this paradigm quite literally becomes part and parcel of the analyst's thought process' (Strauss, 1987: 27).

(3) Thus the conditional matrix is part of the process of analysis in the style of grounded theory, and this process is one of discovery. The conditional matrix is updated in such processes, which themselves are organized around an event. It does not often come to light that an incident can imply crisis and also create structures. It is typical for the grounded theory that an incident has to be *discovered* as such, and in a sense in which Anselm Strauss, who with reference to John Dewey (1934), sees research in social science as an *art form*. In this, he makes reference to C. W. Mills, who has moulded the term 'sociological imagination' (Mills, 1959), and to John Dewey, who has described artistic action as a process of experience. Two moments are expressed here; they seem to be contradictory, yet viewed together they are distinctive for the artistic and the researching process: on the one hand, impartiality in viewing reality, uninfluenced by any preceding theory and, on the other, the shaping of reality, as it is conceptually addressed in the form in which it is voiced. Such processes of *discovery* take wing when researchers are intimate with their field and at the same time remain open to the novel. Social scientists who engage in their own culture, compared to those who conduct their studies in foreign cultures, are confronted by the task of rendering their subject artificially foreign to them (Cicourel, 1964: 39–72). The aforementioned 'impartiality' can only be attained if the researcher manages to dissociate himself from his everyday assumptions (as ordinary person, as scientist), at the same time (ethnographically) immersing himself in the field. There are maneuvers here that will help him, such as the procedures of microscopic analysis (Strauss, 2004) or sequential analysis (Oevermann, 1991), which work from a given text and through the channel of experimenting in thought, invent possible contexts in which the text to be interpreted makes sense.

The conditional matrix under fire: Glaser's rejection and more recent approaches for furthering the Grounded Theory perspective

Barney Glaser has been highly critical of the coding paradigm and of the conditional matrix, which in our view are two major steps forward in grounded theory. Glaser voices his objection to the coding paradigm claiming it codifies the process of research and hence inhibits *theoretical sensitivity* (Glaser, 1978). The researcher 'should simply code and analyze categories and properties with theoretical codes which emerge and generate their complex theory of a complex world' (Glaser, 1992: 71).

We do not consider Glaser's objection pertinent. Our reasons are twofold: first, we read the notes of Strauss and Corbin on the conditional matrix and coding paradigm not as instructions, but as proposals. Furthermore, the issues comprised in the coding paradigm are derived from life itself. Hence, they are unable to hamper the *emergence* of concepts from the material. Here is an example (relating only to the coding paradigm and not to the conditional matrix): imagine a group of prison guards confronted with the fact that an inmate has broken out and abducted a passer-by. They will ask themselves: How could this have happened (conditions)? Where can this lead (consequences)? What are we going to do now (interactions)? How shall we proceed (tactics)? Because the coding paradigm is open, it does not rule out further issues emerging from the situation during the course of analysis.

Glaser's further criticism is directed at the conditional matrix and the concept of the *conditional path*: 'To be used they have to be forced on the data' (Glaser, 1992: 97). Yet taking a look at his other wording and the wording of the texts that were compiled together with Juliet Corbin, one arrives at a different conclusion: conditional matrix and *conditional path* are points of orientation that are not forced upon the material. In our case study we have tried to make this clear.

Recently Kathy Charmaz (2006) and Adele Clarke (2005) have tabled proposals on how to further the grounded theory perspective. We would like to discuss their relevance for the issue at stake here: the significance of the conditional matrix in the process of research. Charmaz founds her argumentation on constructivism. She takes a moderate position and avoids the extreme positions of the '*constructionism*' of Kenneth Gergen (2001) and the '*radical constructivism*' of Heinz von Foerster (Segal, 1986).

In furthering the grounded theory, Charmaz draws a comparison between a 'constructivist grounded theory' (CGT) and an 'objectivist grounded theory' (OGT). The first is part of the tradition of interpretative social research, the latter is derived from positivism (Charmaz, 2006: 130). The central features of an OGT are the following (Charmaz, 2006: 129–132):

- Data are real and represent objective facts.
- Objective reality and the researcher are separate entities; as impartial observer who maintains distance to the subjects researched and their realities, the researcher uncovers the data and develops a theory from them.
- To do so, he/she applies suitable procedures.
- This enables the scientist to generate objective knowledge that can be verified.
- and does not require the self-reflexivity of the researching process.

Charmaz compares this with a constructivist approach. Accordingly the features of CGT are:

- Both data and analyses are social constructions reflecting their process of production.
- Each analysis embodies a specific index in terms of time, space, culture, and situation.
- The scientists' data and values are inter-linked, for which reason data are value-related.
- In constructivism, methods play a lesser role than in objectivism and the theories generated in the style of the CGT rather tend to be 'plausible accounts' (Charmaz, 2006: 132) more than theories that can claim any objective status.

- As a result, the CGT does not cling (Charmaz, 2006: 132) to the discovery of a 'basic process' (Barney Glaser) or a 'core category' (Anselm Strauss) because, as I see it, this would excessively freeze up the social reality in the researching process.
- Instead the CGT calls for 'an obdurate, yet ever-changing world but recognizes diverse local worlds and multiple realities, and addresses how people's actions affect their local and larger social worlds' (Charmaz, 2006: 132).

The meaning of the conditional matrix and the coding paradigm in the process of research is modified in line with this position by Charmaz (2006: 118–120). Charmaz rejects any formulation of precursory conditions, since she fears they would channel the view of the scientist into a specific direction during data collection and analysis. This would mean that the scientists would not do justice to the data (i.e. perspectives of the actors).

Clarke, who has developed the second approach to be treated here towards furthering the perspective of the grounded theory (Clarke, 2005) pleads for a *postmodern turn*. This is derived from the assumption in social science that the recent past has witnessed fundamental changes in the world: 'If modernism emphasized universality, generalization, simplification, permanence, stability, wholeness, rationality, regularity, homogeneity, and sufficiency, then post-modernism has shifted emphases to localities, partialities, positionalities, complications, tenuousness, instabilities, irregularities, contradictions, heterogeneities, situatedness, and fragmentation—complexities' (Clarke, 2003: 555). According to Clarke, social science should now follow this up with 'renovated' (Clarke, 2003: 555) procedures, such as that of grounded theory. The aim is the practice of research, 'wherein individual "voice" and its representation lie at the heart of the matter' (Clarke, 2003: 556). However, together with Giddens, Sewell, and particularly Strauss, we assume that structures are only relevant in *structuration processes* (Giddens) or in a *processual ordering* (Strauss): 'Agency (...) is the actor's capacity to reinterpret and mobilize an array of resources in terms of cultural schemas other than those that initially constituted the array' (Sewell, 1992: 19). For this reason, *structures* and *agency* are at the same level; both lie at the heart of the matter. 'Individual voice' is moreover only an aspect of human agency; another is the social structuredness of *human agency* (Sewell, 1992: 21). To Strauss as well, actors should rather be considered as collective.

Clarke's own position becomes clear from her criticism of the conditional matrix (Clarke, 2005: 65–81). Whereas Strauss still differentiates in *Negotiations* (Strauss, 1979) between a broader structural context and a narrower negotiatory context, Strauss and Corbin differentiate in their *Basics of Grounded Theory* (1990) between causal, intervening and contextual conditions. As a result, a duality is created that Clarke opposes by calling for the discovery of an action's frame conditions within the situation itself, in other words by *situational analysis*: 'I attempt to specify all the key elements in a given situation and understand them as co-constitutive—as in part constituting each other—assuming that origins, meanings, and change lie in relationality' (Clarke, 2005: 66). A challenge for the researcher is now posed by fact that as a rule the actors do not focus on hidden aspects of the dynamics of a particular situation, so that in interviews or ethnographic monitoring these aspects cannot be grasped. This is particularly true for phenomena of social deprivation and injustice, as for example: sexuality, ethnicity, colonialism.

This also corresponds to the criticism of the call from Glaser and Strauss to let the data speak for themselves. Situations need to be created in which the non-verbalized elements of social deprivation and injustice can be addressed.

Assessing the ability of constructivism and postmodernism to further the perspective of the Grounded Theory

The approach of Clarke specifically resonates with echoes from 'postmodern thinking'. Above all, this affects the actual focusing on situations and the negotiation processes, discourses, and mapping procedures that take place there. First of all, I am addressing the view taken by Glaser and Strauss on a postmodern turn in grounded theory. Both agree in their rejection of a postmodern approach to the grounded theory. Moreover, Glaser has expressed criticism of a constructivist perspective in grounded theory (Glaser, 2002).

Glaser writes that it cannot be the aim of grounded theory to *invent concepts*, but to *discover* them in the material; indeed he makes his point in *The Discovery of a Grounded Theory*. Concepts relate to *latent patterns,* in his view, and the process of bringing them to light is the *constant comparative method* (Glaser, 2002: 2). Bryant (2003), however, shows that Glaser's contribution is less a constructive critical view of Charmaz's proposal for furthering grounded theory than an attempt to segregate the genuine from the false representatives of a grounded theory perspective (Bryant, 2003: 24).

Strauss rejects postmodernist approaches to the formation of concepts, since they cause the disintegration of the *ordering* in communication processes with the result that the actors also disappear. In other words, he gives a clear answer to the question as to whether grounded theory needs a postmodern turn, as is proposed by Clarke (2005: 19): *it does not* (Strauss, 1993: 260f). He takes the stance that '"Social change" *is* a useful analytic concept, but only if we carefully separate the perspectival—social constructivist—issue from the one now being discussed, that is, How is change (or social change) related to (social) order and disorder?' (Strauss, 1993: 261). In defiance of the liquefaction of social reality in change, Strauss insists that change must always be related to 'the more slowly moving, more stable elements of the social environment created and maintained sometimes many generations ago' (Strauss, 1993: 261). This is a clear statement disputing the opinion that social reality is an invention of individual actors in discourse.

In order to present my own opinion on the constructivist and postmodernist furthering of the grounded theory perspective, I will commence by discussing the stand taken by Charmaz. As with all comparisons, comparing an OGT with a CGT is simplistic and, as such, problematic. Charmaz sees this as well (2006: 130).

The differences in the two positions wane all the more rapidly when the following points are considered:

- I do not see the danger that the interpretation of 'objectively'[5] given frame conditions, which have left their traces behind them in the world, can be equated with an analysis of variables. I do not see the conditional matrix as a set of independent variables and in the various works on the conditional matrix of Strauss and Corbin and of Strauss I have found no indication that permits this conclusion. The process involved in grounded theory (such as I have learned from Strauss and Corbin and apply in my own research and as we find it in other approaches to interpretative social research, such as in objective hermeneutics), differs from a variable analysis in that the objectively given frame conditions of an action, such as compiled in the conditional matrix, are not to be treated as independent variables. Instead, they constitute a space of 'objectively' given *possibilities* of action. Just *how* this space becomes relevant for the actors themselves depends: (a) on their location in their world in terms of time,[6] society, and culture; (b) on whether these 'objectively' given possibilities are of an imposed thematic relevance to the material (Schütz & Luckmann, 1974: 186); and (c) on the extent to which the actors perceive the space available to them for their own autonomy in order to shape the given frame conditions. In short: the 'objective' frame conditions of a particular action assembled in the conditional matrix and their adoption in human actions cannot be segregated; if they could, this would really be a sociology of variables. Structures take effect through actors and the resources available to them for this purpose; furthermore, the resources themselves are 'the media whereby transformative capacity is employed as power in the routine course of social interaction' (Giddens, 1979: 92, quoted according to Sewell, 1992: 9).
- For a researcher too, who assumes 'objectively' given frame conditions of an action, reality is not independent of the observer. If we apply the formula for social phenomenology: '*Something* (an excerpt from social reality) seems to be *as if* it were something (within a process of interpretation) *for* someone (for a researcher adopting a specific perspective of research)', then we take a view that links the scientist and the field of research in a specific manner. In that case, research no longer corresponds to the model of physical experimentation, implying a 'segregation of subject and researcher'. 'Objectivity' in interpretative social science is a specific objectivity. It is reinforced by the scientific observer explaining (and hence thinking about) their bond to the location and using methods that are apt to do justice to the concept of the possibilities. In terms of method, the assignment in opening up 'objective' possibilities is to work out how a given single case in a given situation to be decided *could* act, in order to then confront these 'objectively' given possibilities of action with how the *case actually did* act (for an example, see Hildenbrand, 2005: 25–64). I include here the *microscopic analysis* (Strauss, 2004) and the sequential analysis of the *objective hermeneutics*, as well as the *conversation analysis* (Bergmann, 1985). 'Objectivity' is attained by the scientist by explaining their theoretical concepts, by justifying their choice of methods, by testing their hypotheses developed from the material by way of contrasting, and ultimately by way of an open mindset in the course of the process of research: if the field coerces him into new perspectives, then he will have to alter his procedures or expand them. With this switch of perspective, the researcher turns into a subject for reflection, the data foundation of which is a 'natural history' of their own process of research.
- Research results that are worded, for example, in the shape of *core categories* do not determine an ultimate view of social reality that holds true. They relate to various periods of time for social structuring and last for a correspondingly different length of time. The category of the incest taboo, for example, that reflects a universal social ruling, has long existed, not to say universally existed inasmuch as it is constitutive for the development of human societies (Lévi-Strauss, 1981: 15), whereas the developments of categories or terms relating to historical processes continuously need to be revised. For this, Max Weber uses the term of the 'eternal youthfulness' of terminology in the social sciences (Weber, 1988: 206).

Further criticism voiced of grounded theory from the perspective of social constructivism has been worded as follows by Charmaz: 'The grounded theorist's analysis tells a story about people, social processes, and situations. The researcher composes the story; it does not simply unfold before the eyes of an objective viewer. The story reflects the viewer as well as the viewed' (Charmaz, 2000: 522). This is where the ever-unresolved conflict between *reconstruction logic* (in terms of the grounded theory: *the logic of discovery*) on the one hand, and neoKantism on the other (Max Weber), re-ignites. Weber speaks of the 'thought rearrangement of the immediately given reality' (1988: 207), the aim of which is the creation of *ideal types*. In the perspective of *reconstruction logic* or the *logic of discovery concepts* are found to exist in the material. They are then worded in the *language of the case* (Oevermann, 1991) or treated as 'in-vivo codes' (Strauss, 1987: 30). Alfred Schütz takes a stand in between these two positions. He differentiates between *first order constructs* of everyday actors and *second order constructs* that are expressed in scientific perspectives. Nevertheless, he does not view the *second order constructs* as reconstructions of *first order constructs* (Schütz, 1962: 1–38).

I will now comment on the stand taken by Clarke in respect of the need for a 'postmodern turn' in grounded theory:

- The requirement that conditions of an action are not to be imposed, but that they should be discovered in the action itself is not, in my opinion, competitive, but rather an alternative. In my own research, it has proved helpful to place the issue of an action's possible structuring contexts, in the sense of a conditional matrix, in front of the bracket. In other words, that which is between the brackets has to confront and address that which is outside of the brackets.
- Concealed structures: non-'postmodern' scientists are dealing with the question what kind of methodological paths allow those conditions to be discovered, which remain hidden to the actors themselves. Examples of this would be the aforementioned procedure of microscopic analysis or sequential analysis. Clarke is of a different opinion. Her solution lies in calling for scientists to take leave of their scientific standpoints and openly side with the persons on which research is focused: 'I am arguing that we are ethically and morally responsible and accountable to seek out data that can speak to such areas of silence and difficulty in the situations we choose to study' (Clarke, 2005: 74).
- My problem with this position is that Clarke is proposing a turn towards moral ethics, instead of methodologically asking *how* research subjects adopt, reproduce, and change structures, how they are impeded or encouraged in doing so, and what consequences this has for unraveling their own autonomy; ultimately, this means letting the data speak for themselves. This would also be the stand taken by Howard Becker, who replied to the question as to 'whose side are we on' in the words of Hammersley: 'What is true, though, is that Becker believes that systematic and rigorous sociological research inevitably tends to have radical political implications. In addition, he adopts a form of cultural relativism, whilst holding on to a notion of objectivity that is grounded in a commitment to pragmatism' (Hammersley, 2001: 91). In this sense, for example, it is possible to develop a research design that enables investigation of the actors' resistance to given social structures. As an example: among the assumptions relating to 'objective' structures in the process of socialization is the one that socialization takes place in a triad comprising father, mother, and child, and that the imperfectness of such triads (such as in the absence of the father) implies efforts to correct the situation. Instead of accepting this assumption that does not seem unreasonable in terms of its validity, unchecked, we systematically seek triads there, where they are incomplete. If we want to examine the gender polarity (considered to be constant) in

the relationship of couples, we pose the question: how does a couple of the same gender individually address such structures? What interpretatory processes of acceptance can we observe with the actors here? So that to start with, we set the prior assumptions concerning the universality of the social triad in brackets and, by applying suitable procedures, let the data speak for themselves, so as to then confront the results with these prior assumptions.

- By having the scientists apply suitable procedures in interpreting the actors' own interpretations of social reality, the actors are given 'voice' in a conventional process of analysis in the style of grounded theory. It is asked how they adopt their own realities in their respective social worlds, by confronting the given frame conditions. These are therefore developed from the situational analysis itself. We then return to the previously reconstructed 'objective' frames, in other words to the conditional matrix, and confront it with the actors' reconstructions of the meanings they attribute to their reality.

CONCLUSION

The history of sociology can be recorded as the history of the conceptualization of the relation between structure and action. Long periods of time bore witness to the presentation of reductionist concepts: structures were reduced to action and, even more, action to structures. For some years now, given the concepts of Bourdieu, Giddens, and Strauss, i.e. concepts of *strategy, structuration,* and *processual ordering,* the approaches to mediating structure and action in forming sociological theory have become more complex. Glaser on the one hand, and Strauss and Corbin on the other have applied the formal formation of theory to develop a methodology that does justice to such a complex approach towards mediating structure and action.

With this chapter, our interest is to demonstrate by way of the research instrument of the conditional matrix, how grounded theory in its classical form mediates *structure* and *agency.* We are critical of 'postmodern' approaches to grounded theory because in them we see the danger of nurturing a new reductionism.

ACKNOWLEDGMENTS

This chapter has benefited, during its many revisions, from the careful reading and constructive criticism of the editors and of Iddo Tavory. Translated from the German by Pauline Elsenheimer.

NOTES

1 At this point we are not going to address the amendments to the second edition of *Basics of Qualitative Research* (Strauss & Corbin, 1998).

2 It is possible to blend the concept of the conditional matrix with Giddens's concept of the duality of structure that encompasses the components 'structure as medium of social action' on the

one hand and 'structure as institutional order' on the other. The distinct benefit from such a combination would lie in introducing the term of constitutive and regulative rulings: Giddens, 1979: 118–126; Giddens, 1985.

3 *cf.* Sewell (1992: 22–24).

4 At this juncture, it would be appropriate to make reference to a formal theory on the connection between structure and action. The concepts of Oevermann (1991) and Sewell (1992) would be of particular help here, as they go farther than those submitted by Bourdieu and Giddens (*cf.* Sewell's criticism of Bourdieu and Giddens, Sewell, 1992). Yet in so doing, we would be overreaching the bounds of this paper. First and foremost we are concentrating on giving emphasis to the term of structure in theoretical and methodological thinking in grounded theory, particularly in the variants presented by Strauss or by Corbin and Strauss. Except for the brief remarks in this chapter, it will have to be left to other studies to determine exactly how this term of structure can be woven into contemporary sociological debate.

5 Here I am following in the path of Max Weber, who always set the term of objectivity in inverted commas in his essay on the subject (Weber, 1988).

6 In the original version of the *conditional matrix*, the dimension of time is missing, something in turn that is above all difficult to illustrate (*cf.* Strauss, 1959).

REFERENCES

Berger, Peter L. and Luckmann, Thomas (1967) *The Social Construction of Reality. A Treatise in the Sociology of Knowledge.* New York: Doubleday.

Bergmann, Jörg R. (1985) Flüchtigkeit und methodische Fixierung von Wirklichkeit. Aufzeichnungen als Daten der interpretativen Soziologie. In: Bonß, W., Hartmann, H. (eds.) Entzauberte Wissenschaft. Sonderband 3 der Sozialen Welt. Göttingen: Verlag Otto Schwartz & Co. pp. 299–320.

Bohler, Karl Friedrich (1995) *Regionale Gesellschaftsentwicklung und Schichtungsmuster in Deutschland.* Frankfurt am Main: Peter Lang.

Bourdieu, Pierre (1998) *Praktische Vernunft. Zur Theorie des Handelns.* Frankfurt am Main: Suhrkamp.

Bourdieu, Pierre (2002) Ein *soziologischer Selbstversuch.* Frankfurt am Main: Suhrkamp.

Bryant, Antony (2003) A Constructivist Response to Glaser [25 paragraphs]. Forum: *Qualitative Social Research* [On-line Journal] 4(1). Retrieved March 29, 2007 from http://www.qualitative-research.net/fqs-texte/1-03/1-03bryant-e.htm

Charmaz, Kathy (2000) 'Grounded Theory. Objectivist and Constructivist Methods', in: Norman K. Denzin and Yvonna S. Lincoln (eds.) *Handbook of Qualitative Research* 2nd ed. Thousand Oaks, CA: SAGE. pp. 509–535.

Charmaz, Kathy (2006) *Constructing Grounded Theory. A Practical Guide Through Qualitative Analysis.* Thousand Oaks, CA: SAGE.

Cicourel, Aron V. (1964) *Method and Measurement in Sociology.* Glencoe, IL: The Free Press.

Clarke, Adele E. (1991) 'Social Worlds/Arenas Theory as Organizational Theory', in: David R. Maines (ed.) *Social Organization and Social Process. Essay in Honor of Anselm Strauss.* New York: Aldine de Gruyter. pp. 119–158.

Clarke, Adele E. (2003) Situational Analyses: 'Grounded Theory Mapping after the Postmodern Turn'. *Symbolic Interaction* 26(4): 553–576.

Clarke, Adele E. (2005) *Situational Analysis. Grounded Theory After the Postmodern Turn.* Thousand Oaks, CA: SAGE.

Dewey, John (1934) *Art as Experience.* New York: Minton, Barlach, & Co.

Farberman, Harvey A. (1991) 'Symbolic Interaction and Postmodernism: Close Encounter of a Dubious Kind'. *Symbolic Interaction* 14(4): 471–488.

Gergen, Kenneth (2001) *An Invitation to Social Construction.* London: SAGE.

Gerson, Elihu M. (1978) 'The Unit of Analysis in Symbolic Interactionism'. Paper, Tremont Research Institute, 458 29th Street, San Francisco, CA 94131.

Giddens, Anthony (1979) *New Rules of Sociological Method*. London: Hutchinson.

Giddens, Anthony (1985) *The Constitution of Society: Outline of Structuration*. Cambridge: Polity Press.

Glaser, Barney G. (1978) *Theoretical Sensitivity*. Mill Valley, CA: Sociology Press.

Glaser, Barney G. (1992) *Emergence vs. Forcing. Basics of Grounded Theory Analysis*. Mill Valley, CA: Sociology Press.

Glaser, Barney G. (2002) Constructivist Grounded Theory? *Forum Qualitative Research* 3(3): 1–13.

Glaser, Barney G. and Strauss, Anselm L. (1967) *The Discovery of Grounded Theory: Strategies for Qualitative Research*. Chicago: Aldine.

Glaser, Barney G. and Strauss, Anselm L. (1968) *Time for Dying*. Chicago: Aldine.

Hammersley, M. (2001) *What's Wrong with Ethnography?* London: Routledge.

Hildenbrand, Bruno (2004) *Fallrekonstruktive Familienforschung 2nd ed.* Wiesbaden: VS Verlag für Sozialwissenschaften.

Hildenbrand, Bruno (2005) *Einführung in die Genogrammarbeit*. Heidelberg: Carl-Auer-Systeme Verlag.

Hildenbrand, Bruno Bohler, Karl Friedrich, Engelstädter, Anna, and Funcke, Dorett. (2007) *Transformationsprozesse der Kinder- und Jugendhilfe in Ost- und Westdeutschland nach der Einführung des KJHG*. Jena: SFB 580 Mitteilungen.

Lévi-Strauss, Claude (1981) *Die elementaren Strukturen der Verwandtschaft*. Frankfurt am Main: Suhrkamp.

Marx, Karl (1964) 'Der achtzehnte Brumaire des Louis Bonaparte', in: *Ausgewählte Schriften Vol. I*. Berlin: Dietz. pp. 222–316.

Matthiesen, Ulf (1994) 'Standbein-Spielbein. Deutungsmusteranalysen im Spannungsfeld von objektiver Hermeneutik und Sozialphänomenologie', in: Detlef Garz und Klaus Kraimer (eds.) *Die Welt als Text. Theorie, Kritik und Praxis der objektiven Hermeneutik*. Frankfurt am Main: Suhrkamp. pp. 73–113.

Mead, George Herbert (1959) *The Philosophy of the Present*. La Salle, IL: The Open Court Publishing Company.

Mead, George Herbert (1972) *Philosophy of the Act,* 7th edition. Chicago: The University of Chicago Press.

Mills, C. Wright (1959) *Sociological Imagination*. New York: Pelican.

Oevermann, Ulrich (1991) 'Genetischer Strukturalismus und das sozialwissenschaftliche Problem der Erklärung der Entstehung des Neuen', in: Stefan Müller-Doohm (ed.) *Jenseits der Utopie*. Frankfurt am Main: Suhrkamp. pp. 267–336.

Schütz, Alfred (1962) *Collected Papers* Vol. I. The Hague: Nijhoff.

Schütz, Alfred, and Luckmann, Thomas (1974) *The Structures of the Life-World*. London: Heinemann.

Segal, Lynn (1986) *The Dream of Reality*. New York, London: Norton.

Sewell, William H. (1992). 'A Theory of Structure: Duality, Agency, and Transformation'. *The American Journal of Sociology* 98(1): 1–29.

Strauss, Anselm L. (1959) *Mirrors and Masks: The Search for Identity*. Glencoe, IL: The Free Press.

Strauss, Anselm L. (1979) *Negotiations: Varieties, Contexts, Processes and Social Order*. San Francisco: Jossey-Bass.

Strauss, Anselm L. (1987) *Qualitative Analysis for Social Scientists*. Cambridge: Cambridge University Press.

Strauss, Anselm L. (1993) *Continual Permutations of Action*. New York: Aldine de Gruyter.

Strauss, Anselm L. (2004) Analysis Through Microscopical Imagination. *Sozialer Sinn* 2: 169–176.

Strauss, Anselm L. and Corbin, Juliet (1990) *Basics of Qualitative Research. Grounded Theory Procedures and Techniques.* Newbury Park, CA: SAGE.

Strauss, Anselm L. and Corbin, Juliet (1998) *Basics of Qualitative Research. Grounded Theory Procedures and Techniques*, 2nd edition. Newbury Park, CA: SAGE.

Strauss, Anselm L., Schatzman, Leonard, Bucher, Rue, Ehrlich, Danuta and Sabshin, Melvin (1963) *Psychiatric Ideologies and Institutions.* New York: Free Press.

Weber, Max (1988) *Gesammelte Aufsätze zur Wissenschaftslehre 7th edition.* Tübingen: J. C. B. Mohr (Paul Siebeck).

26

Rational Control and Irrational Free-play: Dual-thinking Modes as Necessary Tension in Grounded Theorizing

Karen Locke

A central appeal of the grounded theory approach to many researchers is its implied promise that we will be able to develop theory from our engagement with the research setting, free from the dictates and constraints of prior theoretical formulations. Certainly the initial monograph's (Glaser & Strauss, 1967) encouragement for researchers to draw on our intellectual imagination and creativity to develop our own theories relative to our areas of research interest is attractive. Yet, while enthusiastic about the approach's promise for the exercise of individual intellectual autonomy, researchers new to the approach are generally unprepared for the challenges and demands of the kind of imaginative thinking work involved in such an enterprise.

Indeed, following the publication of Glaser and Strauss's original monograph (1967), many accounts have elaborated those research procedures and practices that help us to initiate, organize, and carry forward our thinking relative to our engagements with the field, for example, coding, continuous comparing, iterative sampling in light of developments in thinking, diagramming, memo writing, and so on (e.g. Charmaz, 2006; Glaser, 1978; Locke, 2001; Strauss, 1987; Strauss & Corbin, 1990, 1998; Turner, 1983). However, they have relatively little to say about the imaginative, open-ended (discovery) aspect of our thinking that those very practices are designed to elicit and provide a scaffolding for. Acknowledging this in their discussion of qualitative research in general, Lofland and Lofland over a decade ago (1995: 181) noted, 'while we do understand something of the concrete operations that facilitate analysis, the operation of the creative and open-ended dimensions is not well understood.'

This, despite the fact that qualitative research usually carries the expectation that it will result in the so-called 'inductive' generation of new theoretical frameworks.

In this chapter, I call attention to this open-ended creative dimension by focusing on the thinking processes involved in grounded theorizing; specifically I explore the embodied operation of dual modes of thinking which I characterize as the rational controlled and the irrational free-playing modes, deliberately tilting towards the latter. I understand these two forms as necessary for working through the apparently contradictory demands that grounded theorizing places on the researcher to both stay close to the data and interpret it imaginatively (Locke, 2001). First, I'll draw on Charles Sanders Peirce's notion of abduction to provide a vantage point from which we can understand the open-ended imaginative aspect of our theorizing and consider the dual modes of thinking. While its relevance for grounded theorizing has been recognized (e.g. Charmaz, 2006; Rennie, 2000), its potential for articulating the inventive dimensions of our theoretical work has yet to be realized (Locke, Golden-Biddle & Feldman, 2004). Then, drawing on an exercise in conceptualizing, I'll sketch the operation of these dual modes in the contradictions we experience as we engage grounded theory's analytic practices and work to imaginatively interpret and theorize from our engagements with the field. Finally, I'll underscore how these two modes complement and articulate with each other in the process of theorizing. The operation of these dual thinking modes requires us to accept that ambiguity and uncertainty are necessarily part of the journey we undertake to theorize imaginatively.

Before proceeding any further, I should note that my perspective on the research act is an interpretive one; from this vantage, theorizing takes place within the confines and reach of an embodied researcher. As such, we are the primary instrument for conceptualizing and generating theory from our engagement with the lives and worlds of those we study (Charmaz, 2000, 2006; Locke, 2001). Accordingly, I also choose to write in a style consistent with this positioning.

PEIRCE'S CONCEPT OF ABDUCTION

It might seem somewhat incongruous to be introducing a theoretical element up front in the context of an essay on grounded theorizing, but I do so recognizing three points. First, as I'll indicate, Peirce was a working scientist, and his epistemological formulations derive from this personal experience. Drawing on his thinking is arguably consistent with the use of previous theory grounded in systematic observation of experience (Strauss, 1970). Second, as Peirce emphasized, our perception is always habit laden; this is the case whether we are drawing on our disciplinary or mundane habits. Thus, theory is always present in our thinking; it is a matter of what spaces we deliberately open up within it and the tentativeness with which we take up any theoretical concepts relative to our developing thinking. Third, related to this, as one of the founders of the American pragmatist tradition, Peirce is an intellectual uncle to Chicago pragmatism and symbolic interactionism; these theoretical habits informed Anselm Strauss and continue to inform many practicing grounded theorists, including those whose intellectual dispositions have turned towards the postmodern (e.g. Clarke, 2005).

Peirce introduced and developed the concept of abduction in the late nineteenth century. During this time, he was not only a philosopher living in the world of ideas, he was also a practicing scientist, and he developed a philosophy that dealt with issues of science, truth, and knowledge from direct personal experience. For example, he was a trained chemist, he worked over a period of 30 years for the US Coast Survey, and he was a scholar in astronomy, mathematics, and philosophy (Nubiola, 2006). He was a full-fledged professional scientist who, over the course of his life, worked to disclose the logic of intelligent inquiry as it operated in our everyday as well as more specialized scientific endeavors. Abduction occupied a central position in that developing logic.

What is abduction? Along with the long accepted forms of inference, induction, and deduction, which provide a means for deriving generalizations from specific instances and specific instances from generalizations, respectively, Peirce proposed abduction as a third form of inference. Peirce clarifies that whereas through induction (customarily associated with theory development) we establish an expectation based on repetition of observations, through abduction we invent a way of understanding (a conceptualization) which achieves a synthesis of observations (CP 5.171–172; CP 7.218).[1] It is an imaginative effort to understand involving living beings acting and learning in a world. Stimulated by surprise or observations needing explanation, this form of inference engenders new ideas, explanatory propositions, and theories in the prosecution of science and in the course of everyday life (Delaney, 1993; Fann, 1970). For Peirce, abduction is consequential in the inquiry process as it is the 'only' operation which 'introduces any new idea' (CP 5.171) and, thereby, the way in which 'all the ideas of science come to it' (CP 5.145). Focusing on the generation of a conceptualization that 'might be,' abduction highlights the creative and inventive dimension of theorizing; yet, because it is creative and permissive in nature, it produces 'no conclusion more definite than a conjecture' (NEM 4:319). It generates possibilities.

By attending to creative conjectural activity in scientific inquiry, Peirce emphasized that it had a rightful position in any theory of science long before other scholars (e.g. Hanson, 1958, 1960) argued for its centrality in our understanding of method. Further, he would not have accepted Popper's contention that the processes involved in this moment have no place in epistemology because they involve irrational psychological (and therefore unscientific) elements which can never be reconstructed rationally (Chauvre, 2005). Unlike Popper, Peirce believed we should care about where ideas came from; he argued that if 'discoveries' are not completely random events in the lives of people who happen to be scientists, then they must be part of the work of doing science, and they should be attended to as part of the scientific process.

DUAL THINKING MODES IN ABDUCTIVE REASONING

In his account of abduction, Peirce acknowledged that it had a dual character, involving both conscious controlled thought as well as spontaneous and creative conjecture (CP 5.171–172). This is evident in this brief outline of abduction which will echo familiarly with our efforts as grounded theory researchers examining and reflecting on our data in the process of working to assign meaning:

> The inquiry begins with pondering these phenomena in all their aspects, in the search of some point of view whence the wonder shall be resolved. At length a conjecture arises that furnishes a possible explanation (CP 6.469).

In addition to depicting the general character of the process of abduction, this short excerpt also indicates that it draws on two modes of thinking or acting to figure something out. (I deliberately use thinking and acting interchangeably, consistent with pragmatism's insistence that 'modes of thinking are themselves action,' Strauss, 1993: 132.) Thus, the inquirer is presented in the process of systematically observing and deliberately pursuing understanding. In addition to this directed activity there is also apparently some other form of thinking taking place, one that involves searching for a vantage or a way of understanding and which eventually results in 'a conjecture.' Arriving at a conjecture, a guess, or a hunch, the researchers find themselves with an idea without an explicit awareness of exactly how it happened.

These dual thinking modes are more explicitly drawn in a comparison of Peirce's concept of abduction with the practice of the fictional detective, Sherlock Holmes who was famous for collecting evidence with which he produced conjectural explanations of what might have happened, though his prowess in this is typically mistakenly identified as deductive (Czarniawska, 1999; Sebeok & Sebeok, 1984). In this account, Holmes's abductive thinking is recognized as being of a dual character, described as 'the single mindedness of a foxhound on the trail of his quarry and a sort of lethargic reverie' (Sebeok & Sebeok, 1984: 25–26), and the latter is underscored by his sidekick, Watson, as being of central importance to Holmes's skill:

> In his singular character the dual nature alternatively asserted itself, and his extreme exactness and astuteness represented, as I have often thought, the reaction against the poetic and contemplative mood which occasionally predominated in him. The swing of his nature took him from extreme languor to devouring energy; and as I knew well, he was never so truly formidable as when, for days on end, he had been lounging in his armchair amid his improvisations (Sebeok & Sebeok, 1984: 26).

In the single-mindedness, we have implicated actions that are controlled, precise, directed, organized, critical, and so on; the rational controlled mode.

Reverie and languor, conversely, point to thought processes that are free roaming, indulgent, unspecified, spontaneous, and so on; the irrational free-playing mode.

IRRATIONAL FREE-PLAYING AND RATIONAL CONTROLLED MODES

The irrational free-playing mode of thought is related to associative and creative ways of thinking that are indicated by such terms as contemplation, daydreaming, brainstorming, ruminating, and musement (a term that Peirce favored, CP 6.458–459), and that operate at both conscious and preconscious levels. In this mode, we license our imaginative impulses to throw up ideas and associations, regardless of how strange or irrelevant they may seem, to generate possible vantages from which to understand. Peirce understood this mode of thinking to be fundamental to the everyday work of doing science and critical to abduction. Emphasizing the importance of imaginative thought in intelligent inquiry, he asserts:

> When a man desires ardently to know the truth, his first effort will be to imagine what that truth can be. He cannot prosecute his pursuit long without finding that imagination unbridled is sure to carry him off the track. Yet nevertheless, it remains true that there is after all nothing but imagination that can supply an inkling of the truth. He can stare stupidly at phenomena; but in the absence of imagination they will not connect themselves together in any rational way (CP 1. 46).

For Peirce, we are dependent on this imaginative free-play of thought to generate ideas, images, and associations which in the end will give rise to fragile, plausible conjectures.

Furthermore, it is a mode of thinking which permeates our everyday lives (if we will pause a moment to notice). Going about our everyday business, as our attention moves from one thing to another, we might notice in our thoughts a playing out of recollected events, ideas, sensory apprehensions, perceptions, feelings, etc. (Strauss, 1993). For example, starting up my computer one morning, I wonder if the noise it is making is different from usual, and this sets in train a whole range of associations and ideas: images of fans whirring around unevenly inside the black box, hard drives, a recent experience of a computer crash, panic, the various tasks I just had to get done today, how much behind I am, the bills buried in the stacks of paper in the kitchen that should have been in the mail yesterday, and a host of other images and connections that I cannot recall.

As indicated by the example of an ordinary indulgence in the free play of thought, this mode is permissive and irrational; any idea, image, recalled event, feeling, and so on associated with a situation to which we attend, and as well with the associations generated, may occur to us; the good, the bad, and the downright strange. However, in the imaginative free-play of thought, good associations and ideas come with the bad, and fruitful interactions may occur among the strange ones; in the end, we cannot really know which ideas will prove useful until later (Elbow, 1981).

It is a mistake, however, to equate abduction with fanciful free association, thereby romanticizing the creative dimension of thought. As Peirce notes in the passage excerpted above, this form of thinking through which we set in train various shifts of associations and meanings, though necessary, is sure to lead us astray. While Peirce celebrated the free-play of thought, he also underscored those scientists who had made important abductive discoveries arrive at those creative moments through sustained effort and preparation that is both conscious and deliberate (Burton, 2000). Irrational playful thinking takes us nowhere without the rational controlled mode to 'bridle,' direct, and scrutinize reverie and free-play.

Rational control is indicated in the focused determination we bring to our research as we try to understand a particular phenomenon or aspect of the world. Loosening our systematic rational thinking to create a space in which we can engage our imaginations and allow ideas, images, feelings, and so on that may connect with our data and our developing conceptualizations to suggest themselves is also a controlled rational act. Similarly, interrupting the free flow of associations to take up a particular idea, a particular memory, a particular feeling, or a particular image for closer inspection as a potentially enlightening or intriguing way to understand our phenomenon, involves the exercise of control in service of what we are trying to understand and explain. Without putting our thought processes into the free-playing mode to suggest connections and associations, however irrational, we are consigned to 'stare stupidly'; without the presence of rational control in our thinking, we are likely to end up nowhere. Thus, staying firmly and single-mindedly in touch with what it is we are trying to understand at the same time as we open and loosen up our thinking to roam freely defines thinking in these dual modes. They indicate a tension in ways of working that are simultaneously very rational and also very irrational that others have pointed to as being part of the experience of creative intellectual work (e.g. Mills, 1959).

DUAL THINKING MODES AND THE TENSION IN BEING BOTH GROUNDED AND IMAGINATIVE

One of the apparent contradictions experienced in the practice of grounded theorizing is the requirement that we both stay close to the data and interpret it imaginatively (Locke, 2001). If the grounded theory approach can be said to have a primary injunction, it must be that theorizing is to be stimulated through interaction with rather than in isolation from the lives and worlds we study (Dey, 2004). Recognizing that the notion of data as direct representation of the lives and worlds of those studied is problematic (see Bryant, 2002), I here take the term to refer to the lives and worlds in which we engage, and shape and textually materialize as field notes, transcripts, visual and documentary evidence, etc.

Thus qualified, data nevertheless is pushed forward to take center stage in interpretive efforts and this is underscored in a number of grounded theory's general and operational mandates. Specifically we should orient our inquiry efforts towards issues that are problematic and relevant to the people and worlds we study and we should not bring prior theoretical propositions and structures to the analytic task, particularly during the early stages. In terms of operational practices, we should perform 'microanalysis' (Strauss & Corbin, 1998) which necessarily draws us in close to our data and brings its concrete details into focus, and we may draw on the words used by those we study, 'in vivo codes,' as theoretical indicators of their experiences. Accordingly, our interpretive efforts need to advance firmly grounded in the details of our data. However, in order to be able to develop theories that offer new ways of understanding phenomena, it is important to recognize that we need to reason abductively, drawing on the thinking modes that will support the open-ended imaginative aspects of our thinking. This allows us to move beyond a descriptive cataloguing of our data to theorizing imaginatively.

I turn now to an example to clarify and demonstrate how the dual modes of thinking operate and articulate in our analytic process. Beginning with a brief excerpt from an interview transcript, I illustrate and annotate my own coding practice, highlighting the two modes of thinking and their relationship to the grounded/imaginative tension. The excerpt comes from an interview with an experienced semi-retired business executive who is part of a volunteer corps contributing programmatically to a business school's educational offerings. This is part of a study of this group broadly focusing on the identity work involved in moving from successful lengthy careers in the business world to participate in the educational life of an academic community. In this part of the interview we are talking about how this executive sees himself in the business school and the issues he faces making a contribution. He describes this as 'bringing a corporate perspective to the program':

> Challenges to that are I have probably been fortunate enough to be in a very senior position for the last 10 years of my career where part of it could be my enthusiasm and my ability to be [charismatic person] like and stand up and get really excited about something and bring people along, and the other part quite frankly, was position, too right, where you had the ability to influence and create outcomes that you wanted, and you had the respect and credibility where people said he's been right much more than he's been wrong, we'll go with it. And, you know, I'm usually right more than I'm wrong and so, here, a challenge is, I don't just get that for showing up, and I'm not sure I should. I get challenged on whether my information is statistically valid, I get challenged on, you know, you all come with a point of view which you show ...

What might this excerpt tell us about the identity work involved in crossing over from the business world into the academic? Well-schooled in the practices of grounded theorizing, our first move when confronted with such an excerpt is to begin fracturing the presented data into discrete units, composing tentative working names or categories in the margins of our data documents (or in software we might be using), and comparing the data units with each other and the composed names. This fracturing and naming occurs in relation to small data units. Whether our practice is consistent with the guidance suggested by Glaser (1978) and Turner (1981) and breaks the data up sentence by sentence to create working units of meaning or with the suggestion by Charmaz (2006) and Strauss and Corbin (1998) to fracture the data on a line by line basis, the purpose is the same, to ensure that we attend to our data in a microscopic way, staying close to it as we conceptualize, beginning the process of naming our data in a way that will relate and organize it relative to our research question.

So, bearing in mind the imperative of staying close to our data, how might we conceptualize the excerpt from the executive's interview? How might we fracture it into units? What categories do the fragments suggest? What initial names come to mind that you might jot down in the margin as potential categories? Some that come to mind for me include: 'challenges,' 'the past—knowing how to energize group,' 'the past—could draw on formal authority,' 'I don't just get that for showing up,' 'asserting present competence,' 'being challenged in language of science,' etc. Perhaps there is some, but not complete, overlap with the names that you generated.

Now, what did you do to generate these names, what were you aware of in your thought processes as you were interacting with the data? As I turn back and reflect on my own thinking in generating these potential codes, I'm aware of a few things ... zeroing in on the text, reading first by sentence and then by line, weighing where to demark meaningful data units, scrutinizing the words carefully for those which might help me identify defining elements and name what is happening. I'm also aware that some provisional names immediately jumped out at me as did 'challenges,' after all it is repeatedly used, while I had to work harder to arrive at other terms. I'm cognizant that I acted on each of the terms, selecting some, taking them, dragging them back through the excerpt to weigh their appropriateness. There were also those terms that came to mind that I selected out; for example, I pushed away the terms 'legitimate' and 'charismatic.' For readers with a disciplinary background in organizational behavior and industrial and organizational psychology, they will be recognizable as part of a theoretical framework that describes forms of power deriving from organizational position and personal characteristics, respectively. Taking them into consideration, they would likely take me down a path of comparing the forms of power the executive had available to him now as compared with the past and that did not seem very satisfying. As I reviewed my accumulating list of terms and the data units I had attached them to, looking for ways in which they were similar to and different from each other, I noticed that most of them pointed to the past, and I wondered about that. Re-reading the excerpt, I notice there is a present oriented fragment, 'and you know, I'm usually right more than I'm wrong.'

This partial description of my thought process in my coding or naming practice seems predominantly, but not completely, in the rational controlled mode as I execute the routines that have become part of my analytic repertoire: scrutinizing the words, fracturing, generating names, comparing, and then evaluating and critically acting on the provisional names. In and of itself, however, while a foundational and necessary component of our analytic process, executing these routines and engaging the data only in the rational controlled mode will take us only so far in our analytic journey. We will likely end up with a large number of category names that simply repeat and summarize the data, telling us little beyond what our data documents tell us, albeit perhaps now organized by topics (Rennie, 1998). Without also engaging our imaginations as we execute our analytic routines we run the danger of not getting much past descriptive cataloguing. For example, I might easily create a variety of 'challenge' provisional categories that are part of the larger category, 'challenges to bringing a corporate perspective to academia.'

So, where does this leave us? To do more than descriptive cataloguing, we have to move beyond our data to transcend the particular people, situations, and events they describe. To do this, we have to treat our data as indicators of some 'thing' else; some process, structure, or characterization that we have yet to apprehend and name. Having to both stay close to our data and also move away from it to create transcending conceptualizations means that we do not take our data at face value in our analysis. Rather, in order to theorize our data, we have to treat it as a sign, an indicator of something else, and we have to imagine what that something else might be. This requires us to bring to bear and indulge our imaginations to reason abductively, and if we let it operate in a permissive, fairly loose manner relative to our data, this indulgence necessarily will put us in the irrational free-playing thinking mode.

If we now return to our data excerpt and review the brief description of creating provisional categories, we'll notice indications of this mode. If names and theoretical ideas were suggesting themselves, then, certainly some other form of thinking must have been taking place to generate those suggestions. Additionally, if I experienced myself as having to 'work harder' to generate some terms, then what was the nature of the thinking work taking place? In my own analytic practice, I find putting Glaser's generative questions to data helps to activate this work and to make it more apparent. So, let's ask, 'what is the central problem faced by the person in this situation? What's happening in this excerpt' (Glaser, 1978, 1992)? What comes to mind now? I usually find that these questions tend to prompt a different kind of engagement with the excerpted text, and for me the latter question usually sets up one that is a little more challenging.

As I put the question regarding the central problem faced by our executive in our situation to the excerpt, with a little effort I am able to compose phrases such as 'discontinuity between past and present,' 'reconciling the license I had to act with demurral I now encounter,' and 'indicating disconcertion.' Taking up the question of what's happening, it seems more difficult to compose a coherent phrase ... but something like 'holding on to who I am' eventually comes to mind. I am not sure if it is entirely satisfactory, nevertheless, I decide to hold on to it.

So what can we say about our thought processes in response to these prompts? What was the nature of the work required to generate these phrases, what was happening inside us in the time it took to generate them. Aware of the individual words on the page, I also have the sense of moving through them to the situation they point to. The prompt to discern the executive's problems makes the person of the individual executive salient. I have a sense of stepping out of my body into his, and doing so I begin to imaginatively relive the situation he describes. Letting this unfold, I start having a sense of how I, living imaginatively now as him, feel in the situation. Letting those possible feelings suggest themselves and exploring them for a while, the word 'disconcertion' comes to mind. Also, as I take that word and refocus on the language of the excerpt, the phrase, 'and you know, I'm usually right more than I'm wrong,' takes on a different, more consequential quality; the words, *I am* (I'm) particularly stand out.

To the 'what's happening' question, I'm aware of initially drawing a complete blank, nothing, perhaps because it seems like such a large open question? Then, as I prompt myself to do something about the question, it seems that I begin allowing images of the situation (more pictorial images of the scenes the executive is describing come to mind) in my mind's eye is a large auditorium filled with a large group of suited people, he is standing in front of them (my engagement is here highly visual). Other images float in, for example, a person in an office being told what they need to get done. As I move from the scenes of the auditorium to meeting rooms in the University where challenges to whether information is 'statistically valid' occur, some memories start appearing. I've been present at meetings where other similar language terms, for example, 'reliability' have been used to question and oppose proposals from this executive. Also, as a qualitative researcher I've certainly experienced them. Scenes of academic conferences in which such language has been used come to mind. I recall an occasion at one conference where I was part of a panel on writing qualitative research. A tall thin-bearded gentleman, whom I recognized from prior conferences as a 'heckler' to qualitative research, was present; he got up and walked around at the back of the room and sat down several times during the presentations. This time he waits till the final presenter is finished, then his baiting begins. I lose track of the transcript excerpt and have to bring myself back to the task, refocusing on the executive's description of being challenged. The term 'language game' (Wittgenstein's idea) comes to mind. I decide not to push this away, but to keep it around, for a while at least. Perhaps I should pursue this.

In this above, I have tried to provide a re-created intimation of the workings of the irrational, free-playing mode of thought, indicating what this conjectural activity so central to abductive reasoning might look and feel like in the context of my analytic coding practice. Certainly the content is irrational and playful in that it is a jumble of associations, but they are associations generated from engagement with the data and interaction with each other as one idea leads to another. While engaging the systematic working through of our data will likely over time, in and of itself, occasion the generation of associations from a semi-conscious mind, what Glaser (1978: 24) referred to as a 'drugless trip,' that may result in the flash of an insightful abduction, I have indicated that we can deliberately bring the playful mode of thinking into our analytic routines. We can, for example, draw on questions to engender a free-ranging playful exploration of the people and situations that comprise our data (creating space and time for them to act on us) in our mind's eye. We are then free to putter around with the various feelings and attitudes evoked, the associations and memories aroused, the ideas, and the stream of images that pass through, to see how they may connect to our data and our emerging conjectures and to consider where they may lead us in our thinking. From the perspective of this mode, our data are a resource for possible connections and relationships that will help us to imagine the processes, structures, or characterizations that might be. What is the nature of the experience the executive is living in his engagement with academic faculty? What process might capture the work the executive does to be an executive in academia? We can also create a conundrum in the data to dwell and meditate on, for instance, why did the executive switch from speaking about himself in the past to the present tense? What can these ruminations help us to discern in our data that we had previously glossed over, even fracturing and attending to our data on a line-by-line basis?

At present, I do not know how the lines of this data excerpt will end up being interpreted, what category, central problem or story they will indicate. This project is in its very early stages and the outlined ways of conceptualizing what is indicated in this data will certainly develop and change as data and names will be iteratively reconfigured and recomposed through successive phases of conceptualization and data gathering in the project. The uncertainty and ambiguity that this leaves us with in relation to this data excerpt is, thus appropriate. In the process of reasoning abductively with our data to imagine what it might signify, uncertainty and ambiguity are prevailing conditions; the elegant concepts and theoretical frameworks we read in published monographs belie the hours, months, even years, of uncertainty and ambiguity that researchers lived through working with their data, piling up bad, strange and, occasionally, insightful possibilities (retrospectively understood) for understanding their phenomena. In the moment of working with our data and the ideas they engender, we simply do not know where they will take us.

ARTICULATION OF THE RATIONAL CONTROLLED AND IRRATIONAL FREE-PLAYING MODES

This chapter's project has been to perform a figure ground reversal with regard to discourse on grounded theory's research practices. Rather than focusing on the practices and the role they play in helping us develop our theoretical elements, as most methodological discussions do, I have attended to the thinking processes that the practices support and under gird. Furthermore, I upend the form of reasoning highlighted; rather than the rational controlled mode, most easily identified with research and scientific thinking, I have stressed and highlighted the irrational playful mode to emphasize the role played by abductive reasoning in grounded theorizing.

Obviously, while I presented and illustrated each mode discretely, the two modes are simultaneous and complementary. I indicated in my discussion of the rational controlled mode, intimations of imaginative associative activity. Similarly, you might have noted the presence of rational controlled activity in my description of the playful mode. I actively chose to provoke imagination through the use of questions, directed my imagination towards reliving the executive's possible experience through the details materialized in the excerpt, decided to take up and write down some possibilities, and also decided to let go of others. In this final section, then, what remains is to examine how they complement and articulate with each other.

The irrational playful mode serves our more rational and controlled thinking by making connections from our data, generating ideas, images, and associations that are possibilities for us to work with and to carry forward in our analysis. What is thrown up ranges from ideas and images that at first blush make a lot of sense to those that can seem like nonsense. For example, theoretical concepts are part of our disciplinary repertoire, and they are likely to appear as elements that connect with our data. Other associations can seem to be capricious. There is a certain irony that some of the associations thrown up in this mode are potentially productive precisely because from the vantage point of the rational mode, they can appear to be irrelevant, arbitrary, and even nonsensical. Thus, novel ways of understanding are more likely to emanate from this mode, precisely because they may, at first blush, appear to be quite distant from what we might take as sensible ways of trying to understand something. Mills observes that our professional training is likely to make us reject such loose notions and associations but he underscores that it is 'in such forms that original ideas, if any, almost always first appear' (Mills, 1959: 212). We must be willing to entertain the ridiculous and, of course, doing so is a deliberate rational act.

Two examples will illustrate. One of the more intriguing (and celebrated) connections made in the literature on organizational decision-making is with garbage cans. In this model which (appropriately for our purposes) challenged the very rational models of decision making that prevailed at the time, choices taken in organizational decisions are viewed as being like trash cans in a factory that fill up with whatever people who happen to be there need to throw away on that particular day (Cohen, March & Olsen, 1972). It is difficult to envision this connection to decision making being generated through the rational controlled mode of thinking. In another illustration, I have elsewhere indicated (Locke, 2001) how an image of a shape-shifting jigsaw puzzle piece kept entering my thinking as my colleague and I worked to conceptualize the textual construction of contribution in scholarly writing (Locke & Golden-Biddle, 1997). That image eventually found expression in the category 'intertextual coherence' which highlighted malleability in how existing works are shaped into one of three possible representations of the current state of understanding about a phenomenon.

As indicated before, while potentially fertile, the possibilities engendered by abductive reasoning are also fragile and fallible. As Peirce noted, giving reign to imaginative possibilities may lead us astray. For example, in imaginatively trying to place ourselves in others' shoes we may project and overwrite our own experiences onto those we study (Rennie, 1998). Additionally, the connections that are thrown up are usually un- or under-specified; associations do not spring into our heads fully formed. The implications and meanings of abductive suggestions need to be deliberately and rationally worked out in order for the insight to become clear; thus, it took some time from the generation of that association to both recognize the value of the insight and to work out its implications.

In another example, in a recent workshop in which a larger excerpt of the executive's transcript was used, one of the participants offered that he felt that the relationship between the executive and academics was sort of like a marriage and he asked if such an association was allowed. I replied that anything was allowed; that was the point, to allow us to entertain the various meanings, ideas, images, emotions, situations, etc., that get evoked by the data. To determine whether it was a useful association, he would need to work through the data, figuring out what made the relationship marriage-like to him. In order for the associations to be productive, we need to select, carry them forward in our analysis, and work out the ways in which they are related to our data, for example, examining and detailing the garbage can-ness of organizational decision making or the shapeshifting structure of intertexts of prior work. To do this, we need to draw on the rational controlled mode of thinking.

Conversely, the rational controlled mode serves the irrational playful in various ways. First, and most obviously, by giving it license to operate, creating a space and time in our analytic work for it to play out. Second, even before that point, however, we need to work rationally and systematically through our data, fracturing and examining it in detail so that our data can become the generative context for the abductive suggestions made in the irrational playful mode. Systematically and deliberately fracturing and naming gets our data inside us and primes the irrational and playful modes with the textually materialized details of the lives of those we study. Third, we draw on the rational systematic to provide an anchoring for the irrational playful mode in our broad research question. Keeping our developing conceptualizations in contact with our research question becomes particularly important as over time, not only our data, but also our in-process theoretical categories, and possible informing theoretical elements will occasion associations. Holding all of these concepts, ideas about concepts, and data in tension with our research question provides some mitigation against a train of thinking that will lead us astray, trusting that over time we will be able to connect our data and our in-process theoretical categories in a way that explains what we are trying to understand.

Fourth, as indicated in our prior discussion, the connections suggested by this mode are un- or under-specified. They are just vague notions until we make something relevant of them. Accordingly, we have to draw on the rational mode of working in order to specify and detail the associations in terms of data. For example, assembling data fragments in which the quality of a marriage like relationship is expressed in the data, we can examine them in detail and force ourselves to write out a formal definition of the working category that would be self explanatory to someone unacquainted with the research (cf. Turner, 1981). We can also draw on the practice of memo writing to help us to articulate and explore our ideas about this characterization further.

In summary, we draw on the controlled mode to systematically carry out our analytic practices such as the micro level naming that helps us to become intimately acquainted with our data or those that help us to articulate and specify the defining elements of a conceptualization, to critically evaluate our categories and ideas about categories as they are developing, to put into gear our playful mode, and to reign it back into our data, categories, and research question. Finally, we draw on the rational controlled mode to condition ourselves to accept the plasticity created in all of the products derived from both these thinking modes in this approach to theorizing; they can, over the course of our analytic work, develop, change, reconfigure themselves, and also fall away from our thinking. We don't know how they will shape up and arrange themselves until they have done so.

NOTES

1 Citations to Peirce follow the convention of identifying letters to indicate the published work, followed by volume number and paragraph number in which the reference appears. CP indicates Peirce, 1931–1958; NEM indicates Peirce, 1976.

REFERENCES

Bryant, A. 2002. Grounding systems research: Re-establishing grounded theory. Proceedings of the 35th Hawaii International Conference on System Sciences.

Burton, R. 2000. The problem of control in abduction. *Transactions of the Charles S. Peirce Society*, 36(1): 149–156.

Charmaz, C. 2000. Constructivist and objectivist grounded theory. In N. K. Denzin & Y. Lincoln (Eds.) *Handbook of qualitative research*, 2nd ed.: 675–694. Thousand Oaks, CA: SAGE.

Charmaz, C. 2006. *Constructing grounded theory: a practical guide through qualitative analysis*. London: SAGE.

Chauvre, C. 2005. Peirce, Popper, abduction, and the idea of a logic of discovery. *Semiotica*, 153(1/4): 209–222.

Clarke, A. 2005. *Situational analysis: Grounded theory after the postmodern turn*. Thousand Oaks, CA: SAGE.

Cohen, M., March, J. & Olsen, J. 1972. A garbage can model of organizational choice. *Administrative Science Quarterly*, 17(1): 1–25.

Czarniawska, B. 1999. *Writing management: Organization theory as a literary genre*. Oxford: Oxford University Press.

Delaney, C. F. 1993. *Science, knowledge and mind: A study in the philosophy of C. S. Peirce*. Notre Dame: University of Notre Dame Press.

Dey, I. 2004. Grounded Theory. In C. Seale, G. Gobo, J. Gubrium & D. Silverman (Eds.) *Qualitative research practice*: 80–93. London: SAGE.

Elbow, P. 1981. *Writing with power: Techniques for mastering the writing process*. New York: Oxford University Press.

Fann, K. T. 1970. *Peirce's theory of abduction*. The Hague: Martinus Nijhoff.

Glaser, B. G. 1978. *Theoretical sensitivity*. Mill Valley, CA: Sociology Press.

Glaser, B. G. 1992. *Basics of grounded theory analysis*. Mill Valley, CA: Sociology Press.

Glaser, B. G. & Strauss, A. L. (1967). *The discovery of grounded theory*. Chicago: Aldine.

Hanson, N. R. 1958. The logic of discovery. *The Journal of Philosophy*, 55(25): 1073–1089.

Hanson, N. R. 1960. More on 'the logic of discovery.' *The Journal of Philosophy*, 57(6): 182–188.

Locke, K. 2001. *Grounded theory in management research*. London: SAGE.

Locke, K. & Golden-Biddle, K. 1997. Constructing opportunities for contribution: Structuring intertextual coherence and problematizing in organization studies. *Academy of Management Journal*, 40: 1023–1062.

Locke, K., Golden-Biddle, K. & Feldman, M. 2004. Imaginative theorizing in interpretive organizational research. *Academy of Management Best Paper Proceedings*.

Lofland, J. & Lofland, L. 1995. *Analyzing social settings*. Belmont, CA: Wadsworth.

Mills, C. W. 1959. *The sociological imagination*. New York: Oxford University Press.

Nubiola, J. 2006. Abduction or the logic of surprise. *Semiotica*, 153(1/4): 117–130.

Peirce, C. S. 1931–1958. *Collected papers of Charles Sanders Peirce*. Vols. 1–8; C. Hartshorne, P. Weiss & A. Burks (Eds.). Harvard, MA: Cambridge University Press.

Peirce, C. S. 1976. *The new elements of mathematics*. Vol. 1–4; C. Eisele (Ed.). The Hague: Mouton Publishers.

Rennie, D. L. 1998. Grounded theory methodology: The pressing need for a coherent logic of justification. *Theory & Psychology*, 8: 101–120.

Rennie, D. L. 2000. Grounded theory methodology as methodical hermeneutics: reconciling realism and relativism. *Theory and Psychology*, 10: 481–502.

Sebeok, T. & Sebeok, J. 1984. You know my method: a juxtaposition of Charles S. Peirce and Sherlock Homes. In U. Eco & T. Sebeok (Eds.) *The sign of three: Dupin, Holmes, Peirce*: 10–54. Bloomington, IN: Indiana University Press.

Strauss, A. L. 1970. Discovering new theory from previous theory. In T. Shibutani (Ed.) *Human nature and collective theory*: 46–53. Englewood Cliffs, NJ: Prentice Hall.

Strauss, A. L. 1987. *Qualitative analysis for social scientists*. Cambridge: Cambridge University Press.

Strauss, A. L. 1993. *Continual permutations of action*. New York: Walter de Gruyter.

Strauss, A. L. & Corbin, J. 1990. *Basics of qualitative research: Grounded theory procedures and techniques*. Thousand Oaks, CA: SAGE.

Strauss, A. L. & Corbin, J. 1998. *Basics of qualitative research: Techniques and Procedures for Developing Grounded Theory*, 2nd ed. Thousand Oaks, CA: SAGE.

Turner, B. A. 1981. Some practical aspects of qualitative data analysis: one way of organising the cognitive processes associated with the generation of grounded theory. *Quality and Quantity*, 15: 225–247.

Turner, B. A. 1983. The use of grounded theory for the qualitative analysis of organizational behavior. *Journal of Management Studies*, 20: 333–347.

27

Research as Pragmatic Problem-solving: The Pragmatist Roots of Empirically-grounded Theorizing

Jörg Strübing

INTRODUCTION: THE STRONG BOND BETWEEN PRAGMATIST PHILOSOPHY AND STRAUSS'S METHODOLOGICAL STANCE

One of the originators of grounded theory obviously draws heavily on the pragmatist and interactionist traditions. But what traits did this legacy go on to leave in Anselm Strauss's methodological work? I will claim that there is a strong bond between the thoughts of early North American pragmatism and both the methodological and the socio-theoretical concepts at the core of grounded theory—at least as long as it is the Straussian variant of grounded theory that we are talking about.

This chapter outlines some of the key concepts of early pragmatism, such as George Herbert Mead's notion of objective reality as that of interacting perspectives, John Dewey's iterative-circular understanding of problem-solving processes, and Charles S. Peirce's concept of abduction as the long sought-after explanation for the creation of new ideas in problem-solving. With regard to grounded theory, this chapter discusses, among other notions, the processual character of theory underlying the concept of empirically grounded theorizing and the reciprocal means-ends relationship between methods and theory. It will be shown that Strauss's understanding of empirical research as grounded theorizing is part of his attempt to improve interactionism's theoretical potential by revitalizing its pragmatist legacy.

Much writing on grounded theory is concerned with the question of how to *do* it, that is, with practical matters of doing empirical research the grounded theory way. Considerably less research effort, however, has been spent on the issue of the epistemological and socio-theoretical grounding of grounded theory. True enough, looking at the genesis of grounded theory, it is the story of a systematization of those strategies and heuristics employed in practical research endeavors, specifically in the studies on illness and dying in medical hospitals conducted by Glaser and Strauss in the 1960s (Glaser and Strauss 1965, 1968; see Strauss 1987: 5). It is also true, simultaneously, that these practices were inspired and guided by those theoretical and methodological schools of thought which shaped the originators of grounded theory in their formative years. In *The Discovery of Grounded Theory*, Glaser and Strauss name the Columbia School of Lazarsfeld and Merton and the Chicago tradition of Park and, later, Blumer as main influences on their work (Glaser and Strauss 1967: vii). Nonetheless, they do so from a critical perspective, pointing to the fact that not even their own schools (at which they received their academic training) were able to surmount the 'embarrassing gap between theory and empirical research' (Glaser and Strauss 1967: vii). In the above writing, both Glaser and Strauss were wrestling with the shortcomings of mainstream sociology with regard to a sound conception for the generation of new theory based on empirical data and they had to admit that their respective traditions (Glaser a Columbia School descendant and Strauss a Chicago-style interactionist) inevitably harbored certain flaws in spite of their acclaimed merits.

Regardless of this critique, in the process of developing their own style by systematizing their empirical research practices, it became increasingly obvious how heavily these authors drew upon the conceptual frameworks of their respective schools of thought. This was especially apparent in their later and separate writings on grounded theory. In *Emergence vs. Forcing*, the book that marked Glaser's break with Strauss, the author claims the foundation of grounded theory for the Columbia School (Glaser 1992: 7). Demonstrating a similar allegiance, Strauss clearly draws on the Chicago traditions of fieldwork and the formative role of pragmatist epistemology for his conception of grounded theory in his earlier introductory book.[1] Although the split between Glaser and Strauss has become common knowledge among grounded theory researchers, the theoretical underpinnings of this split have not yet been explored to their full extent.[2]

This chapter cannot address this question. Nevertheless, the controversy between Glaser and Strauss does constitute an important point of departure for the following discussion. The most frequently cited work on grounded theory continues to be *The Discovery of Grounded Theory*, and that is a problem. Jointly conceived and written by Glaser and Strauss, this writing represents more of a mixed bag of socio-theoretical and methodological arguments in reaction to late 1960s mainstream sociology's take on empirical research than a sound, self-contained conceptual foundation for the new approach proposed by its authors. By 1992, if not before, Glaser's accusations directed at Strauss and

Corbin that they 'wrote a whole different method' in their introductory book, one which 'distorts and misconceives grounded theory' (Glaser 1992: 2), made it clear that Glaser's understanding of the methodological basis of grounded theory differs profoundly from that of Strauss.

Rather than presenting a comparative discussion of the two versions of grounded theory represented by these authors, this chapter focuses instead on a reconstruction of the socio-philosophical and epistemological foundations of the Straussian variant of grounded theory. As a general thesis underlying this endeavor, I hold that Strauss, both in his socio-theoretical and his methodological work, remains deeply rooted in the intellectual tradition of American pragmatism established by C. S. Peirce and further developed by W. James, J. Dewey, and G. H. Mead. In order to adequately understand Strauss's methodological stance, we first need to grasp the basic understanding developed by classical pragmatists in regard to the issues of reality, problem-solving, inference, and theory. Thus, it becomes equally necessary to analyze the ways in which these philosophical notions shape Strauss's approach to grounded theory.

In order to demonstrate the pragmatist legacy in its relationship to grounded theory, I will begin by elaborating on the issue of data: What is the pragmatist understanding of data? Obviously we cannot discuss this issue without at the same time asking questions about reality, since the proposed definition of data must in one way or another relate to a certain conception of reality. In grounded theory, much emphasis has been laid on the so-called concept indicator model as presenting a specific understanding of the link between data and theory. Thus, after dealing with data, 'Theory As Process' looks at the notion of theory in pragmatism. Here, the distinctive feature is the processual perspective pragmatists have developed on theory: a perspective that can be easily rediscovered in Strauss's methodology. Linking data and theory employs different procedures of inference. For grounded theory, the issue of induction is not only one that has raised a lot of criticism, it is also the source of a most profound misunderstanding of what happens when researchers try to develop new theory based on empirical data. This issue will be dealt with in 'Inference,' while 'Inquiry as Iterative-Cyclical Problem-Solving' focuses on the iterative-cyclical form of the research process as proposed by both pragmatism and grounded theory. The concluding section will then address an overall evaluation of the strong bond between epistemological and practical procedures in grounded theory. The importance of a clear relation between these two aspects for the discussion of validity issues will be especially emphasized.

DATA: 'THE MOST DIFFICULT OF ABSTRACTIONS'

The notion of 'raw data' in empirical research presents an ill-structured, albeit common, conceptualization of data's epistemological status. The critical artificial intelligence researcher Hubert Dreyfus once noted: 'Data are far from being raw' (Dreyfus 1972). The idea behind this criticism is that in order to end up with what is often seen to be pristine empirical material, a construction process must first take place. A multitude of operations, negotiations, and decisions has already transpired before an interview transcript or a set of field notes is laid out for analysis. All this is obvious, yet the question remains: what *is* data? We are used to think of data as representing reality—not in its entirety of course, but in certain parts and perspectives. But then again: what is reality?

This brings us right to the heart of pragmatist epistemology since one of its most fundamental, axiomatic arguments is that 'for rationalism reality is ready-made and complete from all eternity, while for pragmatism it is still in the making [...],' as William James puts it (James 1907/1981: 115). Reality is not 'out there' but rather continually in the making on the part of active beings. Furthermore, a predetermined endpoint to this process is not assumed. Dimitri Shalin gives us an impressive picture of the pragmatist perspective on reality:

> Pragmatist philosophy [...] conveys an image of the world brimming with indeterminacy, pregnant with possibilities, waiting to be completed and rationalized. The fact that the world out there is 'still' in the making does not augur its final completion at some future point: the state of indeterminacy endemic to reality cannot be terminated once and for all. It can be alleviated only partially, in concrete situations, and with the help of a thinking agent. The latter has the power to carve out an object, to convert an indeterminate situation into a determinate one, because he is an active being. The familiar world of color, sound and structure is his practical accomplishment, i.e. he hears because he listens to, he sees because he looks at, he discerns a pattern because he has a stake in it, and when his attention wavers, interest ceases, and action stops—the world around him sinks back into the state of indeterminacy (Shalin 1986: 10).

It should be noted, however, that this pragmatist understanding of reality entails two theoretically and methodologically significant consequences: not only is pragmatism one among a number of 'philosophies of the flux' (Dewey 1925/1958: 50) (which necessarily arrive at a notion of data as a potential representation of parts of reality *at a certain point in time*) but it also defines reality as being made by and experienced only through human activity. Concisely: reality is nowhere else but in active experience, i.e. in action. 'Reality in itself, or in its uninterpreted nakedness, is a pragmatically meaningless notion, for it is a notion [...] of the unknowable [...]' (Thayer 1973: 68). As an initial clarification: neither is it denied that a certain 'something out there' might exist independently of social actor(s), nor do pragmatists claim reality-in-action to be an idealistic concept of a reality existing, produced, and manipulated exclusively in cerebral form. For pragmatists any possible 'something out there' can rather be likened to an undefined openness, experienced as specific kinds of obduracy requiring active dealing with for the solution of practical problems. Reality *becomes* such only insofar and as long as it is part of the environment within which actors act. Through action, obduracy is transformed from its state of opaque resistance into meaningful objects: this is much more than a labeling process, more than a naming of things; it is a materially and corporeally grounded process of bringing things-as-objects about. Pragmatists stress that not only are things meaningless if they are not acted upon, but moreover that in the absence of (inter)action they cease to have an existence for us at all as things.[3]

George Herbert Mead, drawing on both evolutionary theory and Einstein's theory of relativity, repeatedly stressed the 'relativity' that characterizes the link between actor and environment. The two, as he puts it, 'determine each other,' the result of which is the 'situation' (Mead 1908: 315). In the course of the action involved in constituting reality as an interacting ensemble of meaning-imbued objects, the concepts of perspectivity and abstraction come into play. Mead positions his notion of perspectivity critically against the idealist concept of reality as lying entirely within the realm of subjective experience (Mead 1932/1959: 161). While it is true that conceptualizing objects and thereby reality as being actively 'carved out' (Mead 1938: 660) includes the possibility of different perspectives of different actors, more often than not perspectives overlap or are in many aspects identical. Mead explains this 'objective reality of perspectives' (1932/1959: 161) by drawing on the dialectical concept of the mutual shaping of actor and object as well as by postulating his idea of interaction based on the processual integration of the 'generalized other' into one's own actions. In this way, every intelligent act of 'carving out' an object is 'social to the very core' (Mead 1934: 141). Whenever humans act with reference to their social or physical environments, they reflect their doing in light of what actions these environments might evoke in other actors. 'The individual learns to do the carving' out of objects from the hitherto unstructured world 'against the background of meaningful objects shared with others' (Shalin 1986: 12).

The 'generalized other,' however, does not determine the actions of individuals, but rather shapes them. Since the practical problems requiring a solution are different, 'each individual has a world that differs in some degree from that of any other member of the same community' (Mead 1925: 259). This is what made Thomas's 'definition of the situation' such a groundbreaking statement for sociology and garnered it a central place in interactionist social theory.[4] At the same time, the objective reality of perspectives means that every perceptive act includes the process of *abstraction*. 'Our very treatment of things as definite objects involves an abstraction, that is, it requires an active selection of certain elements from among the many encompassed in our field of experience' (Shalin 1986: 11).

In thinking about the nature of data, it follows that the sheer act of selecting a piece of data is more than a mere culling, plucking, or picking out of ready-made objects, like we might pick up shells on a sandy shore. Mead states it very pointedly: 'We cut our objects out of this world' (Mead 1936: 155). It is not only that objects are constituted solely through our activity, but that this activity inevitably involves choices based on (known or unknown) preconceptions. 'But facts are not there to be picked up. They have to be dissected out, and the data are the most difficult of abstractions in any field. More particularly, their very form is dependent upon the problem within which they lie' (Mead 1938: 98).

It is this understanding of data around which Straussian grounded theory develops its procedures: the positivistic conception of objectivity is rejected, however objectivity is not denied per se. Following in the footsteps of Mead's concept of an objective reality of perspectives, grounded theory treats data as the representational material of a reality that is under construction. In the case of empirical research, this construction involves not only the actors in the field under scrutiny but also the researchers themselves: 'what a thing is in nature depends not simply on what it is in itself, but also on the observer' (Mead 1929: 428). Thus, data itself, as well as its objectivity, is to be gained through researchers' continual negotiations with their environment including both the 'problem within which they lie' and the questions they try to answer through their analysis. Data, seen in this way, is not the unhewn material that a researcher starts out with, but rather the *relation* between the field, the research issues, and the researchers established in the course of the analytical process.

THEORY AS PROCESS

As a methodological style, grounded theory emphasizes the generation of theory. This is a distinctive feature of grounded theory as compared to both the hypothetico-deductive conception of theory testing and to some more descriptively oriented approaches in qualitative and ethnographic research. Having shown how fluid and relational the concept of 'data' is in grounded theory, it becomes apparent that we need to have a look at what pragmatism and grounded theory have in mind when they use the term 'theory.' Beginning with grounded theory, in Glaser and Strauss's *The Discovery of Grounded Theory*, we come across a phrase which provides an important initial insight into the nature of theory. The authors note: 'The published word is not the final one, but only a pause in the never-ending process of generating theory' (Glaser and Strauss 1967: 40). Evidently, the presumption of the fluid and interactive character of reality results in the need for a similarly processual understanding of theory, provided, that is, that empirically meaningful theories (in contrast to mathematical theories) make up the focus of our discussion. When the theoretical subject matter lies in selected aspects of the process of reality (as it is constantly shaped by human activity), the respective theories seeking to capture this reality need to convey not just a state of being, but the process of its evolution as well. Theory as process is among the preferred topics in Strauss and, for that matter, Corbin's methodological writings.[5] In a more theoretical article on grounded theory methodology, Strauss and Corbin characterize grounded theories as follows:

> Because they [grounded theories] embrace the interaction of multiple actors, and because they emphasize temporality and process, they [...] have a striking fluidity. They call for exploration of each new situation to see *if* they fit, *how* they might fit, and how they *might not* fit. They demand an openness of the researcher, based on the 'forever' provisional character of every theory (Strauss and Corbin 1994: 279).

In the absence of ready-made reality out there, or any pre-given ontological status or properties of things prior to the interference of knowledgeable actors, theories are, seen in this perspective, nothing more than the conceptual thinking that actors bring forth in interactively producing their reality. With this understanding, we find theories on two levels: first, the common sense theories of actors solving their everyday problems by making sense of the 'world out there' and taking measures to reach their goals. And secondly, of course, there are theories of empirical social sciences, created in processes of actively understanding what people do 'in the field' as well as the motives and causes behind these actions. From a pragmatist perspective, these two types of theory are not categorically differentiated. Instead of presenting a dualistic conceptualization, theories are seen as existing in a relation of gradual difference along a continuum of knowledge. While it is true that scientific theories distinguish themselves from common sense theories in regard to the degree of systematization, logical inference, and validation invested in the course of their construction and maintenance, all of these properties are, to a certain extent, also relevant to the conceptual knowledge gained in everyday problem-solving. *Theory* in grounded theory is therefore understood as commencing from a very basic level of abstraction. The process of theorizing literally starts with the aforementioned 'carving out' of data, that is, with the active transformation of experienced aspects of the 'world out there' into conceptual objects and their interrelation. This is an issue with which beginners in grounded theory often struggle. Largely due to their academic education, their expectations regarding proper theories tend to be located on a higher level in relation to coherency and range. In contrast to the traditional prestige accorded to more abstract and formalized theories in academia, grounded theory departs from the notion that all knowledge is theoretical to its core. The purpose of grounded theory is to elaborate the abstraction level of its theoretical results to the amount needed to solve the problems defined by the respective research purpose. In both sciences and humanities, this involves the formulation of plausible propositions that must be accessible to scrutiny. This is precisely what grounded theory aims at:

> Theory consists of *plausible* relationships proposed among *concepts* and *sets of concepts*. (Though only plausible, its plausibility is to be strengthened through continued research.) Without concepts, there can be no propositions, and thus no cumulative scientific (systematically theoretical) knowledge based on these plausible but testable propositions (Strauss and Corbin 1994: 278).

Another important aspect of grounded theory's concept of theory is that it is never seen as being made 'from scratch.' However highly we may estimate the importance of both empirical data and the embeddedness of every grounded theory in data: when even data is the result of the interplay between perception and cognition, all the more so is theory. Long debates have been held over the appropriateness of utilizing previous theoretical knowledge for the analysis of data in grounded theory projects. This is also one of the central issues surrounding the Glaser and Strauss controversy (Glaser 1978: 31 passim; Kelle 2005; Strübing 2006). This question arose not only due to Glaser's heated comments on Strauss and Corbin's *Basics of Qualitative Research* (Glaser 1992; Strauss and Corbin 1990) but also because of the suggestions put forth in *The Discovery of Grounded Theory* 'literally to ignore the literature on theory and fact on the area of study in order to assure that the emergence of categories will not be contaminated' (Glaser and Strauss 1967: 37). This misleading phrase has the ring of an inductivist tabula rasa stance—all the more so in light of Glaser's later interpretations of grounded theory. However, on the third page of their book, Glaser and Strauss explicitly reject any tabula rasa approach to encountering reality and instead state that a researcher 'must have a perspective that will help him see relevant data and abstract significant categories from his scrutiny of the data' (Glaser and Strauss 1967: 3). This reference to the necessity of a perspective clearly indicates the pragmatist roots at least in Strauss's approach to grounded theory.

The primary point here is not whether previous knowledge should be used in actual data analysis; the important insight lies rather in how to make proper use of previous knowledge. This was stated not only by Glaser and Strauss but also even earlier by Blumer (1954). Blumer's rejection of 'definitive concepts' in favor of 'sensitizing concepts' makes this point crystal clear: the only problem with preknown or preheld theoretical concepts is their potential dominance over the empirical data at hand (as it is well documented for hypothetico-deductive research). What is called for instead is a certain attitude of the researcher in actively relating knowledge and data. Throughout the whole project we are confronted with taken for granted concepts, although they might become less important as the process of theorizing comes up with a more convincing set of categories and concepts. But even so, during a project we associate aspects of prior knowledge with current research issues. The attitude called for would be to let ourselves be inspired to look in directions indicated by this knowledge without assuming that this would be the only solution to our research problem.

As we have seen in the above quote from Strauss and Corbin on 'theory' as consisting of 'plausible relationships,' the authors do not simply claim theory to be the main aim of the research process but also insist on the criterion of testability of a theory's propositions. Nonetheless, for theories 'burdened' with processuality and perspectivity, the traditional mode of theory testing does not seem appropriate. Since theories and reality are not—as in analytic epistemology— seen as different entities but instead as existing in an intertwined means-ends relationship, the question arises: which criteria might be used to test a grounded theory's claims? In the following quote, Strauss and Corbin indicate a direction which they see as providing a viable testing ground for such a theory (while also emphasizing the strong ties between grounded theory and pragmatism):

> We follow closely here the American pragmatist position [...]: A theory is not the formulation of some discovered aspect of a preexisting reality 'out there'. To think otherwise is to take a positivistic position that [...] we reject, as do most other qualitative researchers. Our position is that truth is enacted [...]: Theories are interpretations made from given perspectives as adopted or researched by researchers. To say that a given theory is an interpretation—and

therefore fallible—is not at all to deny that judgments can be made about the soundness or probable usefulness of it (Strauss and Corbin 1994: 279).

Apart from the logical soundness of the formation of a theory, its real test is in its usefulness. That brings us back to the core of the pragmatist claim: the proof of every proposition lies in its practical consequences or, colloquially speaking: 'The proof of the pudding is in the eating.'

INFERENCE

Although data and theory are joint parts on a continuum of knowledge, the transformation of data into theory requires certain types of activity that we are accustomed to call 'data-analysis.' The general understanding of data-analysis in grounded theory is the 'constant comparative analysis,' which provides the researcher with general instructions on how to proceed analytically in working with data. While only roughly addressed in *The Discovery of Grounded Theory*, in *Theoretical Sensitivity*, an in-depth explanation of the practical analytical tasks of constant comparative analysis is provided. With this latter work, Glaser introduced the 'concept-indicator model' as an analytic mode 'based on constant comparing of (1) indicator to indicator, and then when a conceptual code is generated (2) also comparing indicators to the emergent concept' (Glaser 1978: 62). It is his purpose here to advocate a comparative mode which clearly recognizes data as the point of departure for any ensuing conceptual endeavor: this in contrast to other, more quantitatively-oriented, analytic approaches. Ten years later, in his introductory monograph, Strauss (1987: 25) not only adopted this model but also the repeated references to grounded theory as an analytical method predominantly driven by induction.

The strange thing about this shared emphasis on induction in the individual works of Glaser and Strauss is that their respective methodological positions, as revealed in their later writings, differ profoundly in exactly this point: though both use the rhetoric of induction, it is only Glaser who insists strictly on what Kelle terms 'naïve empiricism' (Kelle 2005: paragraph 24) as the basic logic of research in his version of grounded theory.[6] With Strauss (and Corbin) it is another matter altogether: in his introductory book, Strauss picks up on critiques of grounded theory that 'mistakenly' understood it as an 'inductive theory' (Strauss 1987: 11). Later, he and Corbin acknowledge that this 'persistent and unfortunate misunderstanding' was partly the result of a number of dubious phrasings in *The Discovery of Grounded Theory* (Strauss and Corbin 1994: 277). And although they continued to call grounded theory a theory 'that is inductively derived from the study of the phenomenon it represents' (Strauss and Corbin 1990: 23), in those passages where details of their logic of research are discussed, they name at least three types of inference involved: 'Scientific theories require first of all that they be conceived, then elaborated, and checked out [...]

the terms that we prefer are induction, deduction, and verification' (Strauss 1987: 11). Strauss's image of an iterative-cyclical process of analysis can be understood as unfolding along the lines of these three inferential modes. The possibility of arriving at meaningful hypotheses by means of only one of the three modes is ruled out by Strauss. With respect to induction he states: '[...] How can there be hypotheses without either thinking through the implications of data or through "data in the head" (whether experiential or from previous studies) [...]' (Strauss 1987: 12).

At first reading this sounds like pragmatist epistemology proper. However, there are two aspects that do not really line up: grounded theory in general, particularly the Straussian variant thereof, emphasizes the creative aspect in the generation of theory (Strauss 1987: 9f). This emphasis is, furthermore, perfectly in line with the general claim of sciences and humanities on their ability to develop innovative ideas and new knowledge.[7] It is also in keeping with the pragmatist emphasis on creativity. Nevertheless, abduction is completely ignored in Strauss and Corbin's texts. When abduction can be seen as the predominant epistemological mode of creating new ideas for practical problems, this non-emphasis in the writings of Strauss and Corbin in relation to this point becomes hard to reconcile with pragmatists' more salient treatment of creativity in theory generation.[8]

As discussed at greater length elsewhere (Haig 1995; Kelle 2005; Reichertz 2003, Chapter 10; Strübing 2004), the research process outlined especially in Strauss's later works on grounded theory methodology is necessarily of an abductive nature; or, more precisely, it relies heavily on abductive processes in its analytic mode. It was the pragmatist Charles S. Peirce who, in his early works on the logic of inference, found out that neither deductive nor inductive inference is logically capable of producing new knowledge. In order to solve this problem, he defined a third form of logical inference, which he claimed to be a viable means of achieving this purpose (Peirce 1878). He at first called this form 'hypothesis.' Later, he found that, when considered as logical inference, not even the formulation of a hypothesis would produce new knowledge and, moreover, that logical inferences are altogether incapable of resulting in or leaving room for creative acts. Pursuing this thought further, Peirce began to conceive of hypotheses or (his revised designation) 'abduction' as a certain practical habit instead of a form of logic. He found that creative processes have their point of departure in the early phase of perception, where we sometimes need to literally 'make sense' of that material which does not 'fit' into our pre-established (learned) perceptual categories. This is the moment, Peirce contends, when a non-intentional, non-forcible, spontaneous insight comes upon the actor 'like lightning' (Peirce 1931–1935/1960: CP 1.181).[9] This spontaneous insight links current perceptions with new organizing principles but in doing so it still remains based on or adapted to previous knowledge.

Similar to abduction, but different in its epistemological basis, Peirce views 'qualitative induction' as enabling the recognition of already experienced categories of perceptual material within the contents of 'current' perceptions in problem-solving situations. In this way we might infer the existence of further qualities attributable to phenomena being deciphered, based on the resemblance of certain perceived qualities to a previously known term or concept. These qualities are inferred because they are additional qualities belonging to the previously known perceptual entity.

Obviously, both of these modes of non-logical, probabilistic inference are important components of the analytical reasoning in grounded theory's constant comparative analysis. They rely heavily, at the same time, on the researcher's previous knowledge. However imprecise Strauss's notion of the induction-deduction-verification triad might be with respect to providing a grasp on the creative part of analytic reasoning, it does nonetheless have a point in its emphasis on the importance of both deductive and verificational operations within grounded theory. This is crucial to understanding grounded theory because it clarifies the widespread (though mistaken) notion that grounded theory as an inductive approach fails to encompass the full circle of the analytic process required to arrive at a relevant and sound grounded theory from an empirical research question. The Straussian variant of grounded theory definitely is a verificational method, however, this is inseparably intertwined with its method of creating theory. The next section will shed some light on both this iterative-cyclical form of the research process in grounded theory and on its roots in the pragmatist notion of problem-solving.

INQUIRY AS ITERATIVE-CYCLICAL PROBLEM-SOLVING

When John Dewey published *Logic: The Theory of Inquiry* in 1938, his aim was a critique of the then dominant view of inquiry processes as logic-based endeavors driven by general doubt and the will to abstract reasoning. His position, as well as that of other classical pragmatists, was that the process of reasoning is a means towards the end of improving one's ability to act. He begins with the key concept of pragmatist thinking: 'If inquiry begins in doubt, it terminates in the institution of conditions that remove need for doubt. The latter state of affairs may be designated by the words belief or knowledge' (Dewey 1938: 7). Routine actions are not likely to require much reasoning in order to run smoothly and successfully. It is only when our routines start failing to achieve their desired or expected end or when we are somehow hindered from acting in the way in which we are accustomed, that we become uneasy. In his social psychology, Mead termed this an 'arrest of action under inhibition' (Mead 1932/1959: 172). This is the source of practical doubt that gives rise to activities of reasoning or problem-solving.

Departing from this basic concept, Dewey develops a circular model of problem-solving processes that he terms 'inquiry.' His definition of inquiry reflects the idea of resolving a tension which arises between the states of doubt and belief: 'Inquiry is the controlled or directed transformation of an indeterminate situation into one that is so determinate in its constituent distinctions and relations as to convert the element of the original situation into a unified whole' (Dewey 1938: 104). It is important to note, however, that Dewey thought of his model as a general model, suitable for the conceptualization of both the everyday handling of smaller or larger breaks in the flow of activity as well as those more comprehensive reasoning processes employed predominantly in the sciences and humanities, that is, in research. The pragmatist argument of continuity here results in the statement that sciences, as compared to everyday life, do not hold a privileged account of truth.

Dewey distinguishes five steps in this model (see Figure 27.1) beginning with the '*indeterminate situation*' (1938: 105). Indeterminacy denotes a state of 'unique doubtfulness' of the situation that is to be distinguished from 'uncertainty at large.' In order to evoke inquiry, the situation needs to be designated as a specific situation of uncertainty 'about' something. Emphasizing the uncertainty pertaining to the situation is meant here in contrast to 'personal states of doubt [...] not relative to some existential situation' (1938: 106). It is the situation, the activity-driven relation between actors and environment, which is experienced as uncertain by actors, and not a mental state of doubt within the actors themselves.

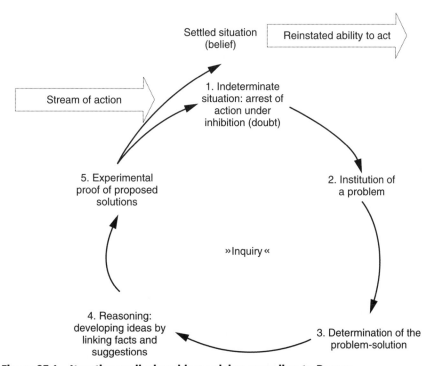

Figure 27.1   **Iterative-cyclical problem-solving according to Dewey.**

Transferring the idea of the indeterminate situation to empirical research based on grounded theory methodologies, this type of situation can be identified on various levels and in many instances throughout the research process. Entering a new field of empirical research and being stunned by the amount of difficulties one has in comprehending one's surroundings, or stumbling through the initial reading of a section in an interview transcript, without being able to make sense of the interviewee's statements are but two of a number of indeterminate situations we are commonly confronted with in research.

It is important, however, to distinguish the situation of uncertainty, the 'arrest of action under inhibition,' from a second phase of problem-solving, which Dewey labels the '*institution of a problem*' (1938: 107). The indeterminate situation is not yet problematic. Indeterminacy comes about due to 'existential causes' (1938: 107); there is nothing cognitive involved at this first stage. It is only when a situation is actively qualified as being problematic that a problem is constituted. Even though a problem, once stated as such, is still far from representing the solution, 'to mistake the problem involved is to cause subsequent inquiry to be irrelevant or to go astray' (1938: 108). In terms of empirical research, we might draw parallels relating this stage to the task of defining a research question that appropriately addresses the cause of our state of unsettledness. Thus, the problem defined has to fit the situation that we have experienced as uncertain, otherwise the answer to the ill-structured question will not contribute to settling the situation, that is, to bringing our practical concerns to rest.

This concept of problem-constitution as being existentially attached to the actor-environment relation or, for that matter, to the relation between the researchers and their empirical field sounds unspectacular; we might even have thought this anyway. However, if we compare Dewey's notion of problem-definition with Hans Reichenbach's (1938/1983) distinction between a 'context of discovery' (as merely inner-psychic processes) and a 'context of justification' as a fully rational fact-related process, the importance of Dewey's point becomes obvious: in light of the situation we are very well able to make sound judgments concerning the proper constitution of a (research) problem.

But how to proceed to its solution? According to Dewey 'first we have to recognize that no situation which is completely indeterminate can possibly be converted into a problem having definite constituents' (1938: 108). Thus in the third phase, the '*determination of the problem-solution*,' we start determining 'the constituents of a given situation which, as constituents, are settled' (1938: 108). This is where empirical observation comes into play. Through empirical investigation we come to identify 'the facts of the case,' that is, those aspects of the problem that need to be taken into account in order to reach a relevant solution. For Dewey, it is on the basis of these 'factual conditions' that 'possible solutions' are tentatively stated as *ideas*. Here we have the initial interplay between data and conceptual thinking that in grounded theory (and not only there) is called theorizing: 'Ideas are anticipated consequences (forecasts) of what will happen, when certain operations are executed under and with respect to observed conditions' (Dewey 1938: 109).

The most lucid example of how these cognitive acts proceed can be seen in those early line-by-line analyses where we try to figure out the possible consequences of certain available interpretations of the data at hand: do our tentative interpretations make sense with respect to our problem of understanding the social phenomena under scrutiny? The formation of ideas is an iterative process: because ideas at first tend to be vague, they require further refinement and logical grounding. The source of every idea for Dewey lies in *'suggestions'* which 'just spring up, flash upon us, occur to us' (Dewey 1938: 110, my italics). Dewey's characterization of suggestions here parallels Peirce's notion of how abductive inferences come to us 'like lightning.' Ideas can obviously not be induced from the facts of the case because the facts, even though they are known and thus conceptualized, do not carry the concept of a problem solution in and of themselves. Likewise, they cannot be deduced from conceptual knowledge, at least not as long as the problem determined *is* a problem to the actor/researcher.

Suggestions as derived from abductive processes in Dewey's model are far from being logically well-structured and worked out, rather they are seen as the primary conceptual material for logical ideas. The formation of ideas (Dewey terms this fourth step of his problem-solving model *'reasoning'*) consists of correlating the observed facts of the situation with suggestions. There is logic involved here. Suggestions are checked logically for their fit with perceptual material from the perspective of a possible problem-solution. The process of developing ideas is conceived of by Dewey as a rational, discursive act that aims at the progressive stabilization of ideas through the testing of their practical consequences as would-be valid solutions. We can think of reasoning as an iterative series of thought-experiments: nothing in existence is actually manipulated, but rather the practical consequences, seen as likely outcomes were the idea to be realized, are symbolically determined and used as criteria for making a decision on the appropriateness of the idea as (part of) the solution. 'In other words, the idea or meaning when developed in discourse directs the activities which, when executed, provide needed evidential material' (Dewey 1938: 112). Dewey compares this step with the elaboration of a 'hypothesis' in 'scientific reasoning.' This is not only another hint at the procedural continuity of scientific reasoning and common sense problem-solving; it is at once an indicator for the place of reasoning in grounded theory and further encourages a pendular movement between data-collection, data-analysis, and theory-building. When data-analysis, as it repeatedly does, reaches stages where a decision is required on whether a certain category or a relation between categories is sufficiently developed in order to become a settled part of the theory under construction, we return (by way of theoretical sampling) to the data in order to gather empirical evidence for the validity and appropriateness of the conceptual item under scrutiny. In those stages (that occur at various times and on different conceptual levels of the study) we build ad hoc hypotheses that basically read: if our current ideas actually hold water, then we should be able to find data supporting one or the other category within a certain domain of cases.

Consequently, in Dewey's model, the final step can be termed *experiment*. Here, existential facts and non-existential, ideational subject matter are brought together in reality. Dewey stresses, 'that both observed facts and entertained ideas, are operational' (1938: 112). Ideas are operational in that they lead to and direct further observations, while the operational character of facts consists of their organized interaction:

> When the problematic situation is such as to require extensive inquiries to effect its resolution, a series of interactions intervenes. Some observed facts point to an idea that stands for a possible solution. This idea evokes more observations. Some of the newly observed facts link up with those previously observed and are such as to rule out other observed things with respect to their evidential function. The new order of facts suggests a modified idea (or hypothesis) which occasions new observations whose result again determines a new order of facts, and so on until the existing order is both unified and complete. In the course of this serial process, the ideas that represent possible solutions are tested or 'proved' (Dewey 1938: 113).

Dewey's statement underlines once again the iterative-cyclical character of the problem-solving endeavor. It is only when a problem is settled that belief is reinstated and our activity, previously on unstable ground, can be resumed. And since our suggestions are not strictly logical inferences built upon fully known facts and rules, but rather probabilistic conclusions, they are also fallible and thus require repeated inquiry circles in order to approximate the problem-solution.

All this discussion of pragmatist problem-solving corresponds nicely with the general model of the research process employed in grounded theory. As shown in Figure 27.2, the grounded theory-oriented research process can be seen as moving in a series of loops between the empirical process under scrutiny and the stream of conceptual thinking or theorizing about it. The link between the two is enacted on the base of a general abductive attitude of researchers. They conduct repeated steps of posing questions at the empirical data (which itself is generated in this process) and interpret this material in abductive and qualitative-inductive, probabilistic inferences that, in turn, lead to provisional theoretical concepts, the validation of which is experimentally proofed by deducing expectable consequences and retesting them on the data. In this process, the conceptual level and density of the theory under construction grows—at least if all goes well. It is this repeated looping that Strauss addresses with his notion of 'induction, deduction, and verification' (Strauss 1987: 11) as signifying the analytical process in grounded theory.

CONCLUSIONS

In concluding, I shall summarize the core arguments elaborated throughout the foregoing sections. First of all, numerous traits of the pragmatist legacy can be

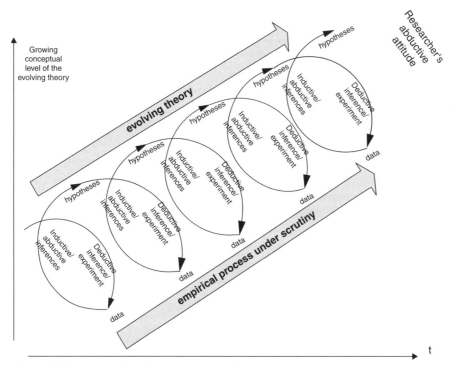

Figure 27.2   Logic of inquiry in grounded theory.

found in both the theoretical and the methodological works of Anselm Strauss, despite the fact that he and Corbin are sometimes not overly explicit in their referencing of these epistemological foundations in their methodological writing. It is mainly due to those pragmatist roots that the interpretation of the basic methodological procedures developed by Strauss and Corbin in their approach to grounded theory differs from the position adamantly held by Glaser.

The core argument with regard to methodological issues is the pragmatist claim that reality is a process enacted by intelligible organisms. In their acting, actors bring to mind the 'world out there' by 'carving out' objects in relation to their relevance for the ongoing activity. While actors act towards their environment they are also both socially and materially a part of their surroundings. The common subject-object divide—like all other dualisms established in the rationalist philosophical tradition—is rejected by pragmatist epistemology. Because reality is never a once-and-for-all completed substance existing externally and in opposition to an encapsulated individual subject, cognition, knowledge, and theory all need to be conceptualized as a dynamic process resulting from activity relating actors with environment. Theory is always oriented towards practical problems, where 'practical' instead of being confined to manual operations with physical objects, rather aims at a more all-encompassing concept of action, expanded to include processes such as understanding objects and relations between them. Moreover, theory is a gradualized concept, knowledge can be more or less theoretical, when seen as a quality that refers to the levels of abstraction and generality in the theory's propositions.

Knowledge (and that includes theoretical knowledge) results from processes of problem-solving; its proof thus lies in its potential to solve these problems. The pragmatist view is that of a tension between states of doubt and states of belief: the uneasiness resulting from an 'arrest of action,' caused by whatever obduracy blocking our pre-conscious routine activity, becomes doubt in that we become aware of the situation and experience it as such. The consequent problem-solving activity draws on previous knowledge (i.e. the 'facts of the situation'), creative (abductive and inductive) guesswork, and logical inference in order to make sense out of perceptual contents unknown to that point. These processes of reasoning result in a type of 'probationary' solutions: only if they prove capable of providing a solution for the situation are they then accepted, in an experimental step, as new knowledge and the actors experience the situation as settled. With respect to this problem-solving model of knowledge generation, no categorical difference is made between everyday problem-solving based on common sense knowledge and scientific inquiries. A researcher's 'arrest of action' lies in not having an answer to a certain empirical research problem. Doubt results from not properly understanding the empirical phenomena dealt with by the researcher. An explanatory theory on the phenomena dissipates the tension, to the extent and point that the theory stands up to continual tests of its validity, for example by successfully predicting further occurrences of the phenomena or its further development.

The pragmatist influence on grounded theory has been shown throughout the preceding sections. Though it might not be obvious in all of its techniques and heuristics, once we focus on the logic of research, the shared understanding of the research situation, the procedural components of inquiry and, finally, on the epistemic status of its proposed results, we can hardly refrain from noticing the import of pragmatist thinking in the methodological contributions of Anselm Strauss.

What has been entirely left out of the picture in this chapter is a second important legacy grounded theory draws on, which is the Chicago School of sociology with its established sociological ethnographies as well as its theoretical impact on the development of symbolic interactionism. Anselm Strauss is not only known for having profoundly contributed to the reconstruction of the Chicago school's history (see for instance Fisher and Strauss 1978). He also received his academic education at Chicago with Blumer and Burgess. Moreover, he began his professional fieldwork under the guidance of Everett C. Hughes, who had a serious influence on the development of both Strauss's theories on professional medical work and on his methodological approach. We might very well assume that the pragmatist influence on grounded theory is also largely due to the Chicago-style interactionism that Strauss picked up in his formative years.

In particular, Mead's impact on Strauss is not to be underestimated. Not only did Strauss contribute to the further development of Mead's social psychology already in the 1950s, he even reformulated the interactionist approach as inherited from Blumer, his mentor, into a proper pragmatist interactionist social theory in his later years (see Strübing 2007) by drawing on Mead's philosophical and epistemological contributions (see Strauss 1991).

With the mention of interactionist social theory, however, we might as well expand on the link between theory and methods. In the case of grounded theory, at least in the variant that Strauss and Corbin propagate, there is ample evidence for the close relation with interactionism. While it is true that with grounded theory we can develop and integrate various different theoretical approaches (as long as they are oriented towards action as the central movers of society), the relation to interactionism is a special one; we might call it a 'Wahlverwandtschaft.'[10] Both grounded theory and interactionism are based on the pragmatist conception of reality as interacting perspectives and on all of the consequences this anti-dualistic, processual understanding had for further theoretical and methodological thinking. Indeed, the most valuable extensions and developments of pragmatist-interactionist social theory in the last decades have been brought about by grounded theory-based empirical theorizing.[11] Not only is interactionism an important intellectual point of departure for the development of grounded theory, the latter, in its part, played a great role in developing interactionism proper. It is this mutual shaping of theory and method that Dewey addressed in the notion of means and ends as a dynamic interrelation of two epistemic entities.

What then is the virtue of reconstructing the epistemological underpinnings of grounded theory? Why not simply follow Glaser's emphatic advice: 'Trust grounded theory, it works! Just do it, use it, and publish' (Glaser 1998: 254)? Because we are not in church but in academia. It is as simple as that. In sciences and humanities we are not only asked to justify our claims but also the theoretical and methodological means by which we reached our conclusions. As far as empirical sciences such as sociology or psychology are concerned, we even need to spell out the epistemological grounds on which our inquiry treads. As we have seen, for instance, the pragmatist notions of reality and action exhibit a degree of singularity when compared to the respective concepts in analytic philosophy and critical rationalism. Furthermore, when it comes to evaluative criteria, we need to choose the appropriate yardstick. Conventional evaluative criteria such as representativness, validity, or objectivity are based on critical rationalism's dualistic concept of reality and subjectivity; neither the inherent qualities nor the pitfalls of processual, grounded theories are adequately accounted for in this perspective (Strübing 2002). Moreover, in thoroughly reviewing the pragmatist traits in both grounded theory and current interactionism, we can avoid the unproductive dichotomy of choosing between 'constructivist and objectivist grounded theory' (see Bryant 2003; Charmaz 2000, 2006: 131; Glaser 2002). While I would subscribe to the constructivist critique of what Charmaz terms 'objectivist,' I would nevertheless be hesitant to ascribe this position broadly to the approaches of Glaser, Strauss, and Corbin. This would fail to acknowledge the grave divide between Glaser's position, for which the label 'objectivism' is largely appropriate, and Strauss and Corbin's position, which I clearly see as being based on a pragmatist epistemology.[12]

As to the constructivist alternative offered by Charmaz and Bryant, I would say that all important notions of this approach already find themselves well established in the pragmatist position (see also Maines 1996). This is especially true for the concept of knowledge as a relation between knower and environment, where both knower and environment (the known) are not existentially separate entities but rather poles in a continuum of reality that is driven and accomplished by human activity. What is missing in the pragmatist perspective is the nominalistic undercurrent that characterizes constructivist approaches. Thus, a concise résumé of my foregoing arguments would be the following: *back to the roots*. Grounded theory can do with a more thorough explication of its philosophical and socio-theoretical foundations in order to avoid the widespread misunderstanding of its practical procedures and their epistemological grounds.

ACKNOWLEDGMENT

As a non-native speaker of English I am deeply indebted to Sarah Matthews for giving my thoughts a form that is understandable to an international audience. She is not liable, however, for any lack of consistency in my arguments.

NOTES

1 See Strauss (1987: 6) in his invitation to the researcher to study both John Dewey's and E.C. Hughes' works 'for further historical understanding of the background of grounded theory.' Similar references can be found throughout the book (e.g. 1987: 9, 110, 263).

2 First steps in this direction were undertaken by Kelle (2005), Kendall (1999), and Strübing (2007).

3 This is why Hans Joas called pragmatism a 'philosophy of action' (Joas 1987).

4 The famous quote reads: 'If men define situations as real, they are real in their consequences' (Thomas and Thomas 1928: 572).

5 Strauss himself also emphasizes this processual aspect in his socio-theoretical work with concepts such as 'processual ordering' or 'trajectory' (see Strauss 1993).

6 This is not the place to pursue this matter any further. For my very critical review of Glaser's methodological position see Strübing (2007).

7 Ian Dey (1999: 35), however, made the fine observation that, in *The Discovery of Grounded Theory*, creativity is systematically devalued in favor of a discovery metaphor that is mainly presented in a passive voice, as if the researcher were not to play an active part in the discovery process.

8 With one exception: Strauss (1987: 12) mentions Peirce's concept of abduction in a footnote. The manner in which he introduces it, however, does not indicate any familiarity with its core principles.

9 Citations to Peirce follow the convention of identifying letters to indicate the published work, followed by volume number and paragraph number in which the reference appears.

10 In science and technology studies, the term 'package' has been coined by Fujimura (1992) in order to signify sets of a theory 'bundled' with certain methods that tend to enforce each other in establishing a certain scientific claim. We might very well use this concept in order to point to the special relation between grounded theory and interactionism.

11 Like, for instance, Strauss's 'negotiated order approach' (Strauss 1978); Star and Griesemer's notion of 'boundary objects' as an interactive means of heterogeneous collaboration (Star and Griesemer 1989); the 'trajectory' concept that has proved enormously helpful in analyzing biographical processes in the life course (see Riemann and Schütze 1991); or the interactionist sociology of work that has been developed by a number of researchers around Strauss (see e.g. Gerson and Star 1986; Strauss et al. 1985).

12 True enough, *The Discovery of Grounded Theory* is a mixed bag of objectivist and pragmatist arguments with —on the whole—an objectivist bias, but even so we do find a persistent undercurrent of pragmatism throughout the book. *Basics of Qualitative Research*, might in some passages be mistaken for an objectivist approach because it fails to go to great lengths regarding methodological arguments and establishes at the same time a more instrumental and technical view of grounded theory procedures. In Strauss (1987) and in some further articles together with Corbin (especially Strauss and Corbin 1994; Corbin and Strauss 1990) they both make their pragmatist stance very clear.

REFERENCES

Blumer, Herbert (1954) What Is Wrong with Social Theory? *American Sociological Review,* 19 (1): 3–10.

Bryant, Antony (2003) A Constructive/ist Response to Glaser. *Forum Qualitative Sozialforschung/Forum: Qualitative Social Research,* 4 (1): 25 Paragraphs. Retrieved August 28, 2004, from http://www.qualitative-research.net/fqs-texte/1-03/1-03bryant-e.htm

Charmaz, Kathy (2000) Grounded Theory: Objectivist and Constructivist Methods. In Denzin, Norman K. and Lincoln, Yvonna S. (eds.) *Handbook of Qualitative Research,* 2nd Edition. Thousand Oaks, CA: SAGE, pp. 509–535.

Charmaz, Kathy (2006) *Constructing Grounded Theory a Practical Guide through Qualitative Analysis.* London: SAGE.

Corbin, Juliet and Strauss, Anselm L. (1990) Grounded Theory Research: Procedures, Canons and Evaluative Criteria. *Zeitschrift für Soziologie,* 19 (6): 418–427.

Dewey, John (1925/1958) *Experience and Nature.* New York: Dover Publications.

Dewey, John (1938) *Logic, the Theory of Inquiry.* New York: Holt, Rinehart and Winston.

Dey, Ian (1999) *Grounding Grounded Theory: Guidelines for Qualitative Inquiry.* London; Boston: Academic Press Inc.

Dreyfus, Hubert L. (1972) *What Computers Can't Do; a Critique of Artificial Reason.* New York: Harper & Row.

Fisher, Berenice and Strauss, Anselm L. (1978) The Chicago Tradition: Thomas, Park, and Their Successors. *Symbolic Interaction,* 1 (2): 5–23.

Fujimura, Joan H. (1992) Crafting Science: Standardized Packages, Boundary Objects and Translation. In Pickering, Andrew (ed.) *Science as Practice and Culture.* Chicago and London: University of Chicago Press, pp. 168–211.

Gerson, Elihu M. and Star, Susan Leigh (1986) Analyzing Due Process in the Workplace. *ACM Transactions on Office Information Systems,* 4 (3): 257–270.

Glaser, Barney G. (1978) *Theoretical Sensitivity: Advances in the Methodology of Grounded Theory.* Mill Valley, CA: Sociology Press.

Glaser, Barney G. (1992) *Emergence vs. Forcing: Basics of Grounded Theory.* Mill Valley, CA: Sociology Press.

Glaser, Barney G. (1998) *Doing Grounded Theory. Issues and Discussions.* Mill Valley, CA: Sociology Press.

Glaser, Barney G. (2002) Constructivist Grounded Theory? *Forum Qualitative Social Research,* 3 (3): 47 paragraphs. Retrieved June 23, 2003, from http://www.qualitative-research.net/fqs/fqs-eng.htm

Glaser, Barney G. and Strauss, Anselm L. (1965) *Awareness of Dying.* Chicago: Aldine.

Glaser, Barney G. and Strauss, Anselm L. (1967) *The Discovery of Grounded Theory: Strategies for Qualitative Research.* Chicago: Aldine.

Glaser, Barney G. and Strauss, Anselm L. (1968) *Time for Dying.* Chicago: Aldine.

Haig, Brian D. (1995) Grounded Theory as Scientific Method. Philosophy of Education. Retrieved August 7, 2006, from www.ed.uiuc.edu/EPS/PES-Yearbook/95_docs/haig.html

James, William (1907/1981) *Pragmatism.* Indianapolis; Cambridge: Hackett Publ.

Joas, Hans (1987) Symbolic Interactionism. In Giddens, Anthony and Turner, Jonathan H. (eds.) *Social Theory Today.* Cambridge: Polity Press, pp. 82–115.

Kelle, Udo (2005) 'Emergence' vs. 'Forcing' of Empirical Data? A Crucial Problem of 'Grounded Theory' Reconsidered. *Forum Qualitative Social Research,* 6 (2): 27 paragraphs. Retrieved December 18, 2005, from http://www.qualitative-research.net/fqs/fqs-eng.htm

Kendall, Judy (1999) Axial Coding and the Grounded Theory Controversy. *Western Journal of Nursing Research,* 21 (6): 743–757.

Maines, David (1996) On Postmodernism, Pragmatism, and Plasterers: Some Interactionist Thoughts and Queries. *Symbolic Interaction,* 19 (4): 323–340.

Mead, George Herbert (1908) The Philosophical Basis for Ethics. *International Journal of Ethics,* 18: 311–323.

Mead, George Herbert (1925) The Genesis of the Self and Social Control. *International Journal of Ethics,* 35: 251–277.

Mead, George Herbert (1929) Bishop Berkeley and his Message. *Journal of Philosophy,* 26: 421–430.

Mead, George Herbert (1932/1959) *The Philosophy of the Present.* La Salle, IL: Open Court Publishing Co.

Mead, George Herbert (1934) *Mind, Self & Society from the Standpoint of a Social Behaviorist.* Chicago, IL: The University of Chicago Press.

Mead, George Herbert (1936) *Movements of Thought in the Nineteenth Century.* Chicago: University of Chicago Press.

Mead, George Herbert (1938) *The Philosophy of the Act. Edited and with an Introduction by Charles W. Morris.* Chicago: University of Chicago Press.

Peirce, Charles S. (1878) How to Make Our Ideas Clear. *Popular Science Monthly,* 12: 286–302.

Peirce, Charles S. (1931–1935/1960) *Collected Papers of Charles Sanders Peirce.* Edited by Charles Hartshorne and Paul Weiss. Cambridge: Harvard University Press.

Reichenbach, Hans (1938/1983) *Erfahrung und Prognose. Eine Analyse der Grundlagen und der Struktur der Erkenntnis; Bd. 4.* Braunschweig; Wiesbaden: Vieweg.

Reichertz, Jo (2003) *Die Abduktion in der qualitativen Sozialforschung.* Leverkusen: Leske + Budrich.

Riemann, Gerhard and Schütze, Fritz (1991) Trajectory as a Basic Theoretical Concept for Analyzing Suffering and Disorderly Social Processes. In David R. Maines (ed.) *Social Organizations and Social Processes. Essays in Honor of Anselm Strauss.* New York: Aldine de Gruyter, pp. 333–357.

Shalin, Dmitri N. (1986) Pragmatism and Social Interactionism. *American Sociological Review,* 51: 9–29.

Star, Susan Leigh and Griesemer, James R. (1989) Institutional Ecology, 'Translations' and Boundary Objects: Amateurs and Professionals in Berkeley's Museum of Vertebrate Zoology, 1907–1939. *Social Studies of Science,* 19: 387–420.

Strauss, Anselm L. (1978) *Negotiations: Varieties, Contexts, Processes and Social Order.* San Francisco: Jossey-Bass.

Strauss, Anselm L. (1987) *Qualitative Analysis for Social Scientists.* New York: Cambridge University Press.

Strauss, Anselm L. (1991) Mead's Multiple Conceptions of Time and Evolution: Their Contexts and Their Consequences. *International Sociology,* 6: 411–426.

Strauss, Anselm L. (1993) *Continual Permutations of Action.* New York: W. de Gruyter.

Strauss, Anselm L. and Corbin, Juliet (1990) *Basics of Qualitative Research: Grounded Theory Procedures and Techniques.* Newbury Park, CA: SAGE.

Strauss, Anselm L. and Corbin, Juliet (1994) Grounded Theory Methodology: An Overview. In Denzin, Norman K. (ed.) *Handbook of Qualitative Research.* London: SAGE, pp. 273–285.

Strauss, Anselm L., Fagerhaugh, Shizuko, Suczek, Barbara and Wiener, Carolyn (1985) *Social Organization of Medical Work.* Chicago: University of Chicago Press.

Strübing, Jörg (2002) Just Do It? Zum Konzept der Herstellung und Sicherung von Qualität in Grounded Theory—basierten Forschungsarbeiten. *Kölner Zeitschrift für Soziologie und Sozialpsychologie,* 54 (2): 318–342.

Strübing, Jörg (2004) *Grounded Theory. Zur sozialtheoretischen und epistemologischen Fundierung des Verfahrens der empirisch begründeten Theoriebildung.* Wiesbaden: VS Verlag.

Strübing, Jörg (2007) Glaser vs. Strauss? Zur methodologischen und methodischen Substanz einer Unterscheidung zweier Varianten von Grounded Theory. In Mruck, Katja and Mey, Günter (eds.) HSR-Supplemente: Grounded Theory—Anmerkungen zu einem prominenten Forschungsstil. Köln: Zentrum für Historische Sozialforschung, pp. 157–173.

Strübing, Jörg (2007) Anselm Strauss. Konstanz: UVK.

Thayer, Horace S. (1973) Meaning and Action: A Study of American Pragmatism. Indianapolis: Bobbs-Merrill.

Thomas, William I. and Thomas, Dorothy Swaine (1928) *The Child in America; Behavior Problems and Programs.* New York: Alfred A. Knopf.

Discursive Glossary of Terms

The terminology used with regard to GTM can be confusing, and any effort to produce a single authoritative and definitive set of definitions is certain to be contentious and self-defeating. Different authors refer to different exemplars, and sometimes even the same author will use or imply different definitions of a single term central to GTM. Kathy Charmaz's book Constructing Grounded Theory *offers a clear and concise set of definitions, and they have been incorporated below as part of this Discursive Glossary.*

The purpose of this glossary is to illustrate how some of the contributors have characterized key GTM terms and ideas, as such it is meant to serve as an indicator and guide, prompting readers to refer to the specific chapters and to other sources. The text in italics is taken from the handbook (as are some of the headings). All non-italicized text is taken verbatim from Charmaz's book.

Abduction: a type of reasoning that begins by examining data and after scrutiny of these data, entertains all possible explanations for the observed data, and then forms hypotheses to confirm or disconfirm until the researcher arrives at the most plausible interpretation of the observed data.

A rule governed way to knowledge – Reichertz

Something unintelligible is discovered in the data, and on the basis of the mental design of a new rule the rule is discovered or invented and, at the same time, it also becomes clear what the case is. The logical form of this operation is that of abduction. Here one has decided (with whatever degree of awareness and for whatever reasons) no longer to adhere to the conventional view of things – Reichertz

Axial coding: a type of coding that treats a category as an axis around which the analyst delineates relationships and specifies the dimensions of this category. A major purpose of axial coding is to bring the data back together again into a coherent whole after the researcher has fractured them through line-by-line coding.

The coding paradigm comes into play during 'axial coding', an advanced stage of open coding. Whereas open coding starts by 'scrutinizing the fieldnote, interview, or other document very closely; line by line, or even word by word. The aim is to produce concepts that seem to fit the data' (Strauss 1987: 28), axial coding 'consists of intense analysis done around one category at time in terms of the paradigm items' (Strauss 1987: 32). This category forms the 'axis' around which further coding and category building is done and may eventually become the core category of the emerging theory – Kelle

Charmaz (2006) points to axial coding as a further type of coding introduced by Strauss in 1987 (that of relating categories to subcategories); this is a most helpful way of describing axial coding – Urquhart

open codes were grouped into categories as per the axial coding stage (following Strauss and Corbin) – Urquhart

Categorizing: the analytic step in grounded theory of selecting certain codes as having overriding significance or abstracting common themes and patterns in several codes into an analytic concept. As the researcher categorizes, he or she raises the conceptual level of the analysis from description to a more abstract, theoretical level. The researcher then tries to define the properties of the category, the conditions under which it is operative, the conditions under which it changes, and its relation to other categories. Grounded theorists make their most significant theoretical categories into the concepts of their theory.

Category

Glaser (1978) presents the meaning of categories in terms of the indicators through which they are observed. Thus the category social loss is not to be defined abstractly but in terms of particular ways in which nurses respond to patients. However, indicators are used not to substantiate a category empirically through description but rather to elaborate the category through exploring its different dimensions (Glaser 1978: 43) – Dey

Nevertheless, categories play a dual role in grounded theory which transcends the classical definition of concepts in terms of indicators. They can be both 'analytic' and 'sensitizing'. They allow us to conceptualize the key analytic features of phenomena, but also to communicate a meaningful picture of those phenomena in everyday terms. They allow us to classify phenomena, but also to construct relationships among the different elements of a theory – Dey

'A category is, simply, a range of discriminably different events that are treated "as if" equivalent' (Bruner et al. 1986: 231) – Dey

The most basic challenge in grounded category building is to reconcile the need of letting categories emerge from the material of research (instead of forcing preconceived theoretical terms on the data) with the impossibility of abandoning previous theoretical knowledge – Kelle

From the early days of grounded theory, many users of the method found it difficult to understand the notions 'category' and 'property' and to utilize them in research practice, since these terms were only vaguely defined in The Discovery of Grounded Theory – Kelle

... the crucial difference between Glaserian and Straussian category building lies in the fact that Strauss suggests the utilization of a specified theoretical framework based on a certain understanding of human action, whereas Glaser emphasizes that coding is a process of combining 'the analyst's scholarly knowledge and his research knowledge of the substantive field' (GLASER 1978: 70) and has to be realized in the ongoing coding process, which often means that it has to be conducted on the basis of a broad theoretical background knowledge which cannot be made fully explicit in the beginning of analysis – Kelle

Glaser and Strauss described categories as 'conceptual elements of a theory' (1967: 36). Categories emerge initially from a close engagement with data, but can achieve a higher level of abstraction through a process of 'constant comparison' which allows their theoretical elaboration and integration – Dey

Chicago school sociology: a tradition in sociology that arose at the University of Chicago during the early decades of the twentieth century. Pragmatist philosophy and ethnographic fieldwork formed the respective intellectual foundations and methodological principles of this tradition. Chicago school sociologists were not as homogeneous as textbooks portray them and not all members of the sociology department at the University of Chicago at that time had any affinity toward the Chicago school; however, this school spawned a rich tradition of symbolic interactionist social psychology and of ethnographic and qualitative research. Chicago school sociology assumes dynamic, reciprocal relationships between interpretation and action. Social life is interactive, emergent, and somewhat indeterminant. Chicago school ethnography fosters openness to the world and curiosity about it and symbolic interactionism fosters developing an empathetic understanding of research participants and their worlds.

Code

What is a code? A code sets up a relationship with your data, and with your respondents – Star

Codes in grounded theory are such transitional objects. They allow us to know more about the field we study, yet carry the abstraction of the new – Star

Codes capture patterns and themes and cluster them under an evocative title – Lempert

Essential relationship between data and theory is a conceptual code – Holton

Coding: the process of defining what the data is about. Unlike quantitative data which applies *preconceived* categories or codes to the data, a grounded theorist creates qualitative codes by defining what he or she sees in the data. Thus, the codes are emergent—they develop as the researcher studies his or her data. The coding process may take the researcher to unforeseen areas and research questions. Grounded theory proponents follow such leads; they do not pursue previously designed research problems that lead to dead-ends.

The most basic operations which provide the basis for category building are 'coding' and the constant comparison of data, codes and the emerging categories – Kelle

Coding is the core process in classic grounded theory methodology. It is through coding that the conceptual abstraction of data and its reintegration as theory takes place – Holton

Coding families

Given Glaser's talk of 'coding families' and the 'coding paradigm' of Strauss and Corbin it is not surprising that coding has become a central analytic procedure in grounded theory – Dey

In 1978 (more than one decade after the publication of The Discovery of Grounded Theory*), Barney Glaser tried to clarify the concept of theoretical sensitivity in his own monograph of that title. In doing so, he coined the terms 'theoretical codes', 'theoretical coding', and 'coding families' to describe a process whereby analysts have a great variety of theoretical concepts at their disposal to structure the developing categories and the emerging theory – Kelle*

The diverse coding families can obviously serve as a fund of concepts which may guide researchers in developing their ability to think about empirical observations in theoretical terms. However, their utility for the development of theoretical relations between the 'substantive codes' is limited – Kelle

It was thus usually Glaser who defined concepts such as properties, dimensions, basic social processes, or cutting points, illustrating them using data supplied by students in his seminar – Covan

Identify a basic social process that accounts for most of the observed behavior that is relevant and problematic for those involved – Wiener

Coding Paradigm

The coding paradigm fulfils the same function as a Glaserian coding family; it represents a group of abstract theoretical terms which are used to develop categories from the data and to find relations between them. Similar to Glaser's coding families, the coding paradigm takes into account that the development of categories requires either a previously defined theoretical framework or at least the possibility to draw on a selection of such frameworks if one wants to avoid being flooded by the data – Kelle

Concept

Glaser and Strauss started The Discovery of Grounded Theory *by criticizing the 'overemphasis in current sociology on the verification of theory, and a resultant de-emphasis on the prior step of discovering what concepts and hypotheses are relevant for the area that one wishes to research' (GLASER, STRAUSS 1967: 1f) – Kelle*

Often these researchers translate the instruction to let categories emerge from the data into a demand to transform every idea or concept which comes into their minds when reading the textual data into a category – Kelle

In the inductive variant by Glaser & Strauss, knowledge concepts or theories were officially and explicitly founded on induction – Reichertz

What are the boundaries and attributes of the concept? And then we sample further by seeking participants with those characteristics or experiences in situations in which humility is required. Similarly, we may also investigate what it is, or what is meant by 'losing a piece of yourself'. In this way, the project moves forward by sampling using the concepts in the interviews to guide the sampling frame – Morse

At this point, the concepts have achieved theoretical saturation and the theorist shifts attention to exploring the emergent fit of potential theoretical codes that enable the conceptual integration of the core and related concepts to produce hypotheses that account for relationships between the concepts thereby explaining the latent pattern of social behaviour that forms the basis of the emergent theory – Holton

but it is important to remember that grounded theory is about concepts that emerge from data, not the data per se – Holton

The skill of the grounded theorist is to abstract concepts by leaving the detail of the data behind, lifting the concepts above the data and integrating them into a theory that explains the latent social pattern underlying the behaviour in a substantive area (Locke, 2001) – Holton

We are now moving toward a more 'focused coding' procedure that consists of building and clarifying concepts. Focused coding employed in grounded theory starts to examine all the data in a category, by comparing each segment of data with every other segment working up to a clear definition of each concept. Such concepts are then named and become 'codes' – Hesse-Biber

researchers commonly use grounded theory method to generate concepts, as opposed to generating theory – Urquhart

It is through the production of concepts that the subjects of a grounded theory study are transformed into theoretical objects – Gibson

Concept-indicator model: a method of theory construction in which the researcher constructs concepts that account for relationships defined in the empirical data and each concept rests on empirical indications. Thus, the concept is 'grounded' in data.

Conditional/consequential matrix: a coding device to show the intersections of micro and macro conditions/consequences on actions and to clarify the connections between them.

> Conditional matrix denotes a context of social frames, within which social interactions evolve. The main purpose of the conditional matrix is 'to help researchers to think beyond micro social structures and immediate interactions to larger social conditions and consequences' (Charmaz, 2006: 118) – Hildenbrand

Constant comparative method: a method of analysis that generates successively more abstract concepts and theories through inductive processes of comparing data with data, data with category, category with category, and category to concept. Comparisons then constitute each stage of analytic development.

> The constant comparison technique is used to tease out similarities and differences and thereby refine concepts – Wiener

> Glaser and Strauss agree that comparisons can be used to establish facts and to verify theories (1967: 23–27). Indeed they explained that all general methods of data analysis including grounded theory, experimental designs and statistical analysis rely on the logic of comparison (Glaser and Strauss, 1967: 21) – Covan

> One virtue of 'constant comparison' as a method in grounded theory is that it protects against the tendency to overinterpret data and find connections where there are none. The inclination to focus on positive evidence as confirmatory can be challenged through the systematic use of constant comparison – Dey

> The most basic operations which provide the basis for category building are 'coding' and the constant comparison of data, codes and the emerging categories – Kelle

> As the twin foundations of grounded theory, the processes of constant comparison and theoretical sampling guide the development of the emergent theory – Holton

> Three types of comparison: incident to incident to generate concepts; concept to further incidents; concept to concept – Holton paraphrase

> experiential comparison that is recommended in grounded theory – Wiener

> The constant comparison technique is used to tease out similarities and differences and thereby refine concepts – Wiener

> If memos are the skeleton of the grounded theory method, use of the constant comparison is the full body – Wiener

> A grounded theory emerges from the process of constant comparison – Dick

Constructivism: a social scientific perspective that addresses how realities are made. This perspective assumes that people, including researchers, construct the realities in which they participate. Constructivist inquiry starts with the experience and asks how members construct it. To the best of their ability, constructivists enter the phenomenon, gain multiple views of it, and locate it in its web of connections and constraints. Constructivists acknowledge that their interpretation of the studied phenomenon is itself a construction.

Data

> For me, the beauty of the method lies in its everything-is-data characteristic; that is to say, everything I see, hear, smell, and feel about the target, as well as what I already know from my studies and my life experience, are data. I act as interpreter of the scene I observe, and as such I make it come to life for the reader. I grow it – Stern

flexible guidelines for data collection and data analysis, commitments to remain close to the world being studied, the development of integrated theoretical concepts grounded in data that show process, relationship, and social world connectedness – Denzin

Problem of staying too close to the data: codes simply summarize the data, and we then produce far too many codes – Locke

The assumption that data exist is common to Durkheim and Glaser & Strauss – Covan

Deduction: a type of reasoning that starts with the general or abstract concept and reasons to specific instances.

Formal theory: a theoretical rendering of a generic issue or process that cuts across several substantive areas of study. The concepts in a formal theory are abstract and general and the theory specifies the links between these concepts. Theories that deal with identity formation or loss, the construction of culture, or the development of ideologies can help us understand behavior in diverse areas such as juvenile gangs, the socialization of professionals, and the experience of immigration.

FGT's abstraction allows its application over a wide range of empirical areas virtually forever, as opposed to descriptive generalizations which are rooted in one empirical area and soon stale dated – Glaser

Formal theories exacerbate the tension between our need to create rules of thumb to get things done and our postmodern awareness that the complexity of life can never be fairly captured in any theory – Kearney

Grounded theory: a method of conducting qualitative research that focuses on creating conceptual frameworks or theories through building inductive analysis from the data. Hence, the analytic categories are directly 'grounded' in the data. The method favors analysis over description, fresh categories over preconceived ideas and extant theories, and systematically focused sequential data collection over large initial samples. This method is distinguished from others since it involves the researcher in data analysis while collecting data—we use this data analysis to inform and shape further data collection. Thus, the sharp distinction between data collection and analysis phases of traditional research is intentionally blurred in grounded theory studies.

Induction: a type of reasoning that begins with study of a range of individual cases and extrapolates patterns from them to form a conceptual category.

Memo-writing: the pivotal intermediate step in grounded theory between data collection and writing drafts of papers. When grounded theorists write memos, they stop and analyze their ideas about their codes and emerging categories in whatever way that occurs to them (see also Glaser 1998). Memo-writing is a crucial method in grounded theory because it prompts researchers to analyze their data and to develop their codes into categories early in the research process. Writing successive memos keeps researchers involved in the analysis and helps them to increase the level of abstraction of their ideas.

If data are the building blocks of the developing theory, memos are the mortar – Stern

Memos are uniquely complex research tools. They are both a methodological practice and a simultaneous exploration of processes in the social worlds of the research site. Memos are not intended to describe the social worlds of the researcher's data, instead, they conceptualize the data in narrative form. Remaining firmly grounded in the data, researchers use memos 'to create social reality' (Richardson 1998: 349) by discursively organizing and interpreting the social worlds of their respondents – Lempert

When memoing a topic analytically, the researcher generates a set of categories, contrasts, comparisons, questions, and avenues for further consideration which are more abstract than the original topic – Lempert

Objectivist grounded theory: a grounded theory approach in which the researcher takes the role of a dispassionate, neutral observer who remains separate from the research participants, analyses their world as an outside expert, and treats research relationships and representation of participants as unproblematic. Objectivist grounded theory is a form of positivist qualitative research thus subscribes to many of the assumptions and logic of the positivist tradition.

Positivism: an epistemology that subscribes to a unitary scientific method consisting of objective systematic observation and experimentation in an external world. The goal of positivistic inquiry is to discover and to establish general laws that explain the studied phenomena and from which predictions can be made. Subsequently, experimentation and prediction can lead to scientific control over the studied phenomena.

Postmodernism: a theoretical turn that challenges the foundational assumptions of the Enlightenment with its belief in human reason, belief in science, and belief in progress through science. Postmodernists range from those who wish to acknowledge intuitive forms of knowing to those who call for nihilistic rejection of modern ways of knowing and of being in the world and their foundation in Enlightenment values.

Pragmatism: an American philosophical tradition that views reality as characterized by indeterminacy and fluidity, and as open to multiple interpretations. Pragmatism assumes that people are active and creative. In pragmatist philosophy, meanings emerge through practical actions to solve problems and through actions people come to know the world. Pragmatists see facts and values as linked rather than separate and truth as relativistic and provisional.

Reflexivity: the researcher's scrutiny of his or her research experience, decisions, and interpretations in ways that bring the researcher into the process and allow readers to assess how and to what extent his or her interests, positions, and assumptions influenced the research. A reflexive stance informs how the researcher conducts his or her research, relates to the research participants, and represents them in written reports.

Serendipity

Glaser (1998) describes the 'subsequent, sequential, simultaneous, serendipitous and scheduled' (p. 15) nature of grounded theory – Holton

Reading widely opens a researcher to serendipitous discovery of new theoretical codes from other disciplines – Holton

This procedure of theoretical sampling in no way interferes with a salient aspect of qualitative research: being ready for the serendipitous opportunity – Wiener

Social constructionism: a theoretical perspective that assumes that people create social reality(ies) through individual and collective actions. Rather than seeing the world as given, constructionists ask, how is it accomplished? Thus, instead of assuming realities in an external world—including global structures and local cultures—social constructionists study what people at a particular time and place take as real, how they construct their views and actions, when different constructions arise, whose constructions become taken as definitive, and how that process ensues. Symbolic interactionism is a constructionist perspective because it assumes that meanings and obdurate realities are the product of collective processes.

Substantive theory: a theoretical interpretation or explanation of a delimited problem in a particular area, such as family relationships, formal organizations, or education.

[SGT] not only provides a stimulus to a 'good idea', but it also gives an initial direction in developing relevant categories and properties and possible modes of integration [theoretical codes] (Glaser & Strauss, 1967: 79)

By substantive theory we mean theory developed for a substantive or empirical area of sociological inquiry, such as patient care, geriatric life styles etc … By formal theory we mean theory developed for a formal or conceptual area of sociological area such as status passage, stigma, deviant behavior, etc. (Glaser & Strauss, 1971:77)

Symbolic interactionism: a theoretical perspective derived from pragmatism that assumes that people construct selves, society, and reality through interaction. Because this perspective focuses on dynamic relationships between meaning and actions, it addresses the active processes through which people create and mediate meanings. Meanings arise out of actions, and in turn influence actions. This perspective assumes that individuals are active, creative, and reflective and that social life consists of processes.

Theoretical Codes/Coding

Theoretical codes are tools for looking at a variable in an abstract rather than a substantive way – Stern

According to Charmaz (2006), 'theoretical codes specify possible relationships between categories you have developed in your focused [substantive] coding' (p. 63) – Stern

If one sets aside Glaser's inductivist rhetoric, his concepts of 'theoretical codes' and 'coding families' represent a way systematically to introduce theoretical knowledge into the coding process without 'forcing' preconceived categories on the data – Kelle

However, Glaser makes clear elsewhere that theoretical concepts do not simply arise from the data alone but require careful 'theoretical coding' (that means: the categorizing of empirical data on the basis of previous theoretical knowledge) – Kelle

Theoretical codes are terms which describe possible relations between substantive codes and thereby help to form theoretical models – Kelle

Theoretical sampling: a type of grounded theory sampling in which the researcher aims to develop the properties of his or her developing categories or theory, not to sample of randomly selected populations or to sample representative distributions of a particular population. When engaging in theoretical sampling, the researcher seeks people, events, or information to illuminate and define the boundaries and relevance of the categories. Because the purpose of theoretical sampling is to sample to develop the theoretical categories, conducting it can take the researcher across substantive areas.

Theoretical sampling is the process of data collection for generating theory whereby the analyst jointly collects, codes, and analyses his data and decides what data to collect next and where to find them, in order to develop his theory as it emerges (Glaser and Strauss, 1967: 45)

theoretical sampling; that is, directing the data search to advance the developing theory – Stern

The main principle of theoretical sampling is that the emerging categories, and the researcher's increasing understanding of the developing theory, now direct the sampling – Morse

Theoretical saturation: refers to the point at which gathering more data about a theoretical category reveals no new properties nor yields any further theoretical insights about the emerging grounded theory.

Theoretical Sensitivity

In developing categories the sociologist should employ 'theoretical sensitivity', which means the ability to 'see relevant data' and to reflect upon empirical data material with the help of theoretical terms – Kelle

Theoretical Sorting

Sorting helps the analyst integrate the theory – Stern

According to Glaser (2005) sorting is a creative activity:

Tempting one's creativity is actuated by this process. Fear that one does not have creativity stops this type of sorting and causes the fleeing to computer retrieval of data on each category, resulting in full conceptual description [Glaser's term for research that fails to reach the theoretical level]. Hand sorting releases the creativity necessary to see a TC [theoretical code] in the memos, as the analyst constantly compares and asks where each memo goes for the best fit (p. 36) – quoted by Stern

REFERENCES

Bruner, J. S., Goodnow, J. J., & Austin, George A. (1986) *A Study of Thinking*. 2nd Edition. New Brunswick, N.J.: Transaction.

Charmaz, Kathy (2006) *Constructing Grounded Theory: A Practical Guide through Qualitative Analysis*. Thousand Oaks: Sage Publications.

Glaser, B. G. (1978) *Theoretical Sensitivity: Advances in the Methodology of Grounded Theory*. Mill Valley, CA: Sociology Press.

Glasser, B. G. (1998) *Doing Grounded Theory*. Mill Valley, CA: Sociology Press.

Glaser, B. G. (2005) *The Grounded Theory Perspective: Theoretical Coding*. Mill Valley, CA: Sociology Press.

Glaser, B. G., & Strauss, A. L. (1967) *The Discovery of Grounded Theory: Strategies for Qualitative Research*. Hawthorne, NY: Aldine de Gruyter.

Glaser, B. G., & Strauss, A. L. (1971) *Status Passage*. Chicago: Aldine Atherton Inc.

Locke, K. (2001) *Grounded Theory in Management Research*. London: SAGE.

Richardson, Laurel (1998) 'Writing: A Method of Inquiry', in Norman K. Denzin and Yvonna S. Lincoln (eds.), *Collecting and Interpreting Qualitative Materials*. Thousand Oaks: Sage Publications, 345–371.

Index